D0908958

Monitoring and Operations with SAP® Solution Manager

SAP PRESS

SAP PRESS is a joint initiative of SAP and Galileo Press. The know-how offered by SAP specialists combined with the expertise of the Galileo Press publishing house offers the reader expert books in the field. SAP PRESS features first-hand information and expert advice, and provides useful skills for professional decision-making.

SAP PRESS offers a variety of books on technical and business-related topics for the SAP user. For further information, please visit our website: *www.sap-press.com*.

Sebastian Schreckenbach
SAP Administration—Practical Guide
2011, 883 pp., hardcover
ISBN 978-1-59229-383-4

Marc O. Schäfer and Matthias Melich
SAP Solution Manager (3rd Edition)
2011, 724 pp., hardcover
ISBN 978-1-59229-388-9

Frank Föse, Sigrid Hagemann, and Liane Will
SAP NetWeaver AS ABAP—System Administration (4th Edition)
2011, 747 pp., hardcover
ISBN 978-1-59229-411-4

Tony de Thomasis and Alisdair Templeton
Managing Custom Code in SAP
2012, 351 pp., hardcover
ISBN 978-1-59229-436-7

Lars Teuber, Corina Weidmann, and Liane Will

Monitoring and Operations with SAP® Solution Manager

Galileo Press

Bonn • Boston

Galileo Press is named after the Italian physicist, mathematician, and philosopher Galileo Galilei (1564–1642). He is known as one of the founders of modern science and an advocate of our contemporary, heliocentric worldview. His words *Eppur si muove* (And yet it moves) have become legendary. The Galileo Press logo depicts Jupiter orbited by the four Galilean moons, which were discovered by Galileo in 1610.

Editors Martin Angenendt, Florian Zimniak
English Edition Editor Laura Korslund
Acquisitions Editor Kelly Grace Weaver
Translation Lemoine International, Inc., Salt Lake City, UT
Copyeditor Miranda Martin
Cover Design Graham Geary
Photo Credit Fotolia/6431066/© Henri Schmit
Layout Design Vera Brauner
Production Kelly O'Callaghan
Typesetting Publishers' Design and Production Services, Inc.
Printed and bound in the United States of America, on paper from sustainable sources

ISBN 978-1-59229-884-6
© 2014 by Galileo Press Inc., Boston (MA)
1st edition 2014
1st German edition published 2013 by Galileo Press, Bonn, Germany

Library of Congress Cataloging-in-Publication Data
Weidmann, Corina.
Monitoring and operations with SAP Solution manager / Corina Weidmann, Liane Will, and Lars Teuber. — 1st edition.
pages cm
ISBN 978-1-59229-884-6 (print) — ISBN 1-59229-884-2 (print) — ISBN 978-1-59229-885-3 (e-book) —
ISBN 978-1-59229-886-0 (print and e-book) 1. Software maintenance. 2. Computer systems—Management.
3. Computer networks—Management. 4. SAP solution manager. 5. SAP ERP. I. Will, Liane. II. Teuber, Lars. III. Title.
QA76.76.S64.W44 2014
005.1'6—dc23
2013033402

Contents at a Glance

Dear Reader,

Your legs are shaking. Your palms are clammy. That's right—you're sitting at the doctor's office, and that ice-cold stethosocope is coming towards you. But monitoring your system's functions doesn't have to be that unpleasant! A wonderful team of authors has taken the time to warm the instruments up for you, and is putting you in charge.

This resource explains how to go about the job of monitoring painlessly with SAP Solution Manager, uncovering the new infrastructure and introducing you to the advanced and improved functionality in release 7.1. Go from A to Z: learn the basic concepts of monitoring, and build your knowledge until you're wielding SAP Solution Manager's many tools. You'll be effectively monitoring your system with the right tools (and with minimal fuss) in no time flat!

As always, we appreciate your business and welcome your feedback. Your comments and suggestions are the most useful tools to help us improve our books for you, the reader. We encourage you to visit our website at *www.sap-press.com* and share your feedback about *Monitoring and Operations with SAP Solution Manager*.

Laura Korslund
Editor, SAP PRESS

Galileo Press
Boston, MA

laura.korslund@galileo-press.com
www.sap-press.com

Contents

3 Implementation Projects 91

10　Job Scheduling Management 559

Foreword by the Board of Directors

The operation of SAP solutions at minimum cost and top quality is more important than ever. SAP Solution Manager forms the core element in managing a solution in all stages of its lifecycle. Also, for more than ten years, it has been an important part of SAP Service and Support. Many years of experience in SAP Service and Support and in consulting contributed to the development. SAP Solution Manager has thus matured to become a key element.

This book provides comprehensive and useful descriptions of SAP Solution Manager for your technical operations. It is based on the findings and expertise of the SAP Active Global Support and our supply partner Bautzen IT.Group GmbH & Co. KG. By the end of 2012, we successfully completed more than 5,000 installations of version 7.1 of the product. This emphasizes the capabilities of SAP Solution Manager and also the significance of and need for this central, comprehensive cockpit in an increasingly broad and complex IT world.

This first issue describes the key functionalities and possibilities for your SAP operation and shows you how to meet the typical requirements of technical operations. Hands-on examples show you how to ensure transparency and ongoing optimization of your SAP-centric solution.

I would like to thank all those involved in the creation of this book and those who have contributed their knowledge and expertise.

Gerhard Oswald
Member of the Board of SAP AG
Application Development and Support

Experience is a good teacher, but a teacher you have to pay dearly. The more important it is to learn properly the first time.
—Carl Hilty (1833–1909)

Foreword

You most certainly know these inserts you get when you purchase a new product: "Thank you for purchasing this item! You are now the owner of a high-quality product!" Since product inserts are not common with books, we would like to take the opportunity in this foreword to thank you for your interest.

This book, whether in print or electronic format, is the perfect opportunity for us to pass on our knowledge in a nice and pleasant way. With its compact form, it allows us to present topics of general interest. We believe that SAP Solution Manager is worth the effort we made to demonstrate its use in practice.

This book is something special indeed because, just as SAP Solution Manager's special strengths lie in integration, this book was developed based on the integration of the knowledge of the specialists on our team. But maybe it's our team that is so special, because we managed to integrate all our knowledge into this book to create a unified whole. We would like to sincerely thank our co-authors for this achievement! It is not something to take for granted when all members of such a large team stand with each other and collaborate without any restrictions to make an idea come true.

This project had its highs and lows, too. As always, the final phase of the project was characterized by a lack of time and too many requirements. But again, our two editors, Florian Zimniak and Martin Angenendt, did not lose confidence. And let's not forget our authors' families, who gave them their support and consideration, maybe hoping this book might be a new Harry Potter.

This book will most likely not sell quite as many copies. But we hope we wrote a recommendable book for practical monitoring and operations using SAP Solution

Manager and that it will help a great number of IT experts in their work. And who knows, maybe we'll meet on some occasion or another. We look forward to it!

Corina Weidmann
Liane Will
Lars Teuber

If you use software, you must always make sure that you're keeping the applications in operation. You can ensure the stability and security of your solutions only if you consider that software changes constantly.

1   Introduction to Technical Operations

The more distributed and complex the operations of your business processes using IT and business partners are, the more complex the requirements to the technical operations of these distributed solutions will be. At the same time, there is the pressure to keep the operating cost at least stable, if not to reduce it. The distributed, independent operation of individual systems cannot meet this requirement.

In order to effectively control a system landscape, it's therefore useful to have all separate operation information in central operations. That way, you can control all business processes and solutions at a central location and remain flexible. The *Operations Control Center* is a method developed for exactly that purpose.

This introductory chapter will introduce the concept of the Operations Control Center in detail. Apart from that, we will show you the effects the software lifecycle has on technical operations (see Section 1.2) and provide a brief overview of project management (see Section 1.4).

1.1   Operations Control Center and Run SAP Like a Factory

Figure 1.1 shows the Operations Control Center in the focus of various topics and processes of your operations. To put it simply, the Operations Control Center merges the information from the various monitoring areas and uses them to draw conclusions, which then form the basis for the permanent optimization of your technical operations. For this purpose, the Operations Control Center integrates Incident Management, Problem Management, and Change Management. Furthermore, the Operations Control Center uses central monitors, or *dashboards*, which are focused on the customer's situation, to measure and evaluate the defined Key Performance Indicators (KPIs). Their purpose is to ensure the control of your operations and solutions and to quickly detect and resolve malfunctions. The operation of solutions is thus highly standardized and automated.

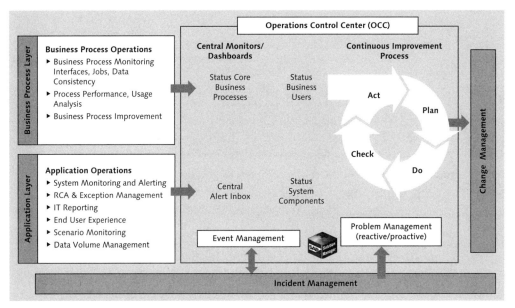

Figure 1.1 Four Perspectives of the Operations Control Center

For the processes, tools, targets, and so on in this context, SAP has coined the memorable phrase *Run SAP like a Factory*. Run SAP like a Factory pursues the following targets:

▸ **Transparency**
The aim is to create transparency, despite the distribution of technical solutions, systems, components, business processes, and teams and their expectations. This transparency is the basis for taking actions that help improve operations or prevent malfunctions.

▸ **Efficiency**
Efficiency is the key to reducing operating costs. In order to act efficiently, standardized and maximum automation of processes are required.

▸ **Optimization**
Optimization always refers to the users' expectations and needs regarding business processes. The optimization potential must be determined and analyzed,

and then the correct actions for improvement must be taken to finally increase customer satisfaction.

▶ **Proactivity**
The technical operation of business processes requires more than just waiting for incidents and reacting to them. Appropriate tools for forecasting and prospective analyses are required to allow for early actions to prevent faults. These are referred to as *proactive measures*.

▶ **Stability**
Business processes have become highly dependent on IT processes. Ensuring the stability of IT processes is therefore an important task of technical operations.

In this context, the technical operation of a solution must always be seen in connection with the processes in a solution's normal lifecycle. Therefore, there is a strong connection between technical operations and Incident and Change Management. Potential optimization in a change management process must be implemented as well.

1.2   Significance of Application Lifecycle Management for Technical Operations

The lifecycle of software is basically always the same: an accepted request is followed by the development of an adequate software solution. After that, the new software is released, tested, and applied in productive operations. Each of these phases, particularly the implementation in ongoing operations, has its challenges and involves activities for technical operations. It's important for you to be able to derive proactive and reactive decisions from the change processes. A prerequisite is that you are familiar with the lifecycle of a software product, as well as the individual software phases and their effects on operations. This is why this chapter is designed to provide an overview of the individual phases of the software lifecycle and show you how SAP Solution Manager can support you in these individual phases.

1.2.1   Application Lifecycle Management

In *Application Lifecycle Management* (ALM), all measures related to the entire lifecycle of an application are coordinated. ALM consists of multiple phases, the order of which is shown in Figure 1.2. Please note that in specialist literature, these phases are explained in varying detail. However, the order is almost always the same.

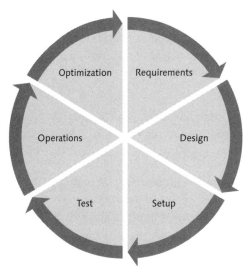

Figure 1.2 Application Lifecycle Management

At the beginning there is a requirement, which is defined as a reaction to a problem to be resolved with the help of a software application. This is followed by the software development, which is divided into the design, structure, and test phases. With the software implementation in the productive system, maintenance, which is divided into operations and optimization, comes to the fore.

In summary, ALM helps you increase the quality in your software projects and obtain a stable business application based on integrated support of your IT solutions. You are in full control of your applications, effectively implementing software projects, the success of which can be reproduced, thus increasing the transparency of your IT solutions.

Note

The term *software lifecycle* is used colloquially, as well. This book, however, mainly uses the term ALM.

1.2.2 ALM Phases

The individual ALM phases consist of individual sub-processes, as shown in Figure 1.3. We recommend defining processes for certain requirements to create standardized work flows in your business. This allows you to make software adjustments in a timely manner.

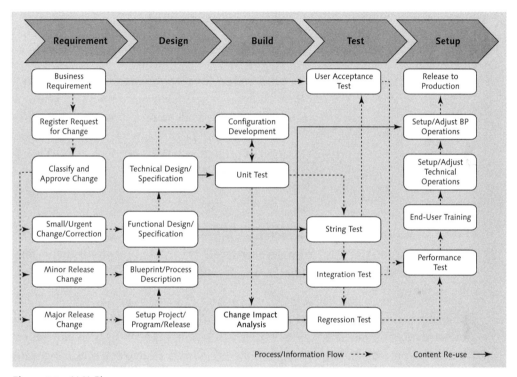

Figure 1.3 ALM Phases

Requirements

Adjusting software is a fixed part of ALM. There are a variety of possible reasons for requirements, as follows:

▶ Changing a business process

▶ Manufacturer-dependent changes that become necessary as part of maintenance

▶ Faulty applications

If a required change has been recognized and defined, it is classified based on urgency and impact. The following distinction is usually made:

- Urgent correction
- Minor change
- Major change

The classification forms the transition to the design phase.

Design

After a project is defined, a blueprint is created in preparation for implementing the requirement. This blueprint includes a process description with all relevant information, such as processes and their individual steps, a process description, process responsibilities, transaction codes, interfaces, training materials, and so on. Building on that, the specification of processes, both functional and technical, is prepared.

Structure

In the structure phase, the prerequisites for the subsequent implementation of requirements in the business process are created. The basis for this is the technical documentation.

Another activity is the so-called *Change Impact Analysis*, which examines which side effects a necessary change has on the existing solution and which following measures must be taken in this context. The result of this analysis is an illustration of objects (programs, transactions, and so on) that are affected by the change and thus are to be tested with more attention.

Testing

Testing is an essential part of ALM. Tests must be planned, test cases must be specified, and after execution, the status of a test must be evaluated. Testing ensures that the changed business processes work properly after production startup and that the daily business runs smoothly. At least, that's the theory!

Practice has shown that to many companies, testing is important, but due to a lack of time and staff resources, it is either minimized or not done at all. Basically, establishing a standardized and automated testing process within the company as far as possible is recommended; based on an effective and efficient order, such a process ensures a structured execution of software tests. For more information on this topic, see *service.sap.com/testing* and *service.sap.com/rkt-solman* • SolMan 7.1 • Test Management.

Figure 1.4 shows an example of the sequence of a testing process.

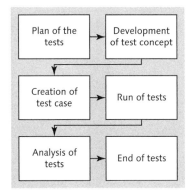

Figure 1.4 Test Procedure

Implementing and Operating

During the implementation phase, the changes are taken over into the production system. This involves end-user training, if necessary, which depends on the change level or the impact of a change on the end user. If this change has an impact on a business process, training is essential.

With the implementation of a requirement, you will need to adjust the operation of the application or business process.

After a requirement has been taken over into the production system and considered in the operation of the application or business process, the requirement has been implemented successfully.

1.2.3   ALM Processes

Each ALM phase consists of multiple processes, which are introduced in this section. You will notice that the processes can be looked at and used separately. These processes provide real added value—if they are all used—as they build up upon each other and each process uses information from the other processes.

Incident Management, Problem Management, and Request Management

The *Incident Management, Problem Management, Service Request Management,* and *Request for Change* IT service processes are part of IT Service Management.

Incident Management focuses on logging, controlling, and coordinating incidents. Incidents are logged in the form of a report and processed by first-level and second-level support. Incident Management is used to reestablish normal operation as fast as possible, which may also be done by skipping the incident center. If the result of the analysis is that the malfunction cannot be corrected immediately, a problem message is generated. Depending on the result, this turns into either a service request or a request for change.

For more information on this topic, we recommend the handbook *ITIL Pocket Guide* (Van Haren Publishing 2011).

Portfolio and Project Management

Efficient project management that's integrated into a company's processes is an important prerequisite for successful completion of a project. Projects are becoming increasingly demanding and complex, which means clear definitions of the project course, keeping deadlines and budgets in mind, are of particular importance. The integration of Portfolio and Project Management in SAP Solution Manager allows you to centrally manage your portfolio and the projects of your solution.

Solution Documentation and Implementation

The solution documentation in SAP Solution Manager allows IT-supported business process information and technical system information in SAP and non-SAP solutions to be centrally managed and updated in SAP Solution Manager. The advantage is that business processes can be uniquely allocated to a system. This creates a tight connection of IT operations and business process operations. This basic information is also necessary for implementation projects. In this context, therefore, we recommend you document all business processes for subsequent projects; this way, you can access this information for future projects or in everyday operations.

For more information, see Chapter 3.

Change, Test, and Release Management

All changes that become necessary during the life of a software program should be monitored and controlled in accordance with a standardized process, the so-called *Change Management process*. A variety of functionalities are available in SAP Solution Manager to support the Change Management process. This allows you to get an integrated and consistent overview of the implementation of changes in your heterogeneous system landscape. Part of this Change Request Management is *Quality Gate Management*, which enables you to define quality assurance milestones within the Change Management process.

Changes in the system can have a variety of causes. In many companies, a lack of planning or insufficiently tested developments are common reasons for changes to the system. Therefore, the ongoing use of Release Management and Test Management are an important prerequisite for increased stability of your IT systems.

Maintenance and Safety

Each system failure costs time and money. So, what IT service provider does not wish for minimum system downtimes in his daily operations and maintenance, and upgrade works alike? To minimize the risk of system failure, we recommend integrating IT processes and the associated tasks. This starts with the manufacturer's maintenance strategy or maintenance management and ends with a chain of processes that ensure smooth operations.

This is the interaction of individual ALM processes. These are processes from Release Management and Change Management all the way to Test Management. Tools such as the *Maintenance Optimizer* or the *Note Assistant* and methods such as *Customer Code Management*, *Landscape Transformation Management*, and *Upgrade Management* support you in ensuring a structured and documented flow of processes. A list of functionalities can be found in SAP Solution Manager, which we will explain in more detail in the next section.

1.3   Technical Operations Using SAP Solution Manager

With SAP Solution Manager, SAP offers a tool that maps all ALM phases and their processes using a centralized approach. Apart from that, SAP Solution Manager provides a basis for implementing the Operations Control Centers to monitor and control technical operations of the business process operation. This interaction between ALM and Run SAP like a Factory with SAP Solution Manager is shown in Figure 1.5.

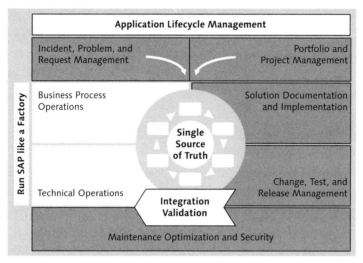

Figure 1.5 Orchestration of IT Solutions Using SAP Solution Manager

The central approach of SAP Solution Manager has the advantage that all information is provided for every phase and process via systems, servers, products, and processes and that this information is obtained from the same data source (*single source of truth*). Data sources are as follows:

▶ **System Landscape Directory and SAP Solution Manager System Landscape**
The *System Landscape Directory* (SLD) and the *SAP Solution Manager System Landscape* (SMSY) are the precursors for the data sources of technical operations. They contain all data of various applications and technologies, such as product, database, and operating system information, but also data for applications, interfaces, and so forth.

▶ **Landscape Management Database (LMDB)**
The *Landscape Management Database* (LMDB) includes all information of various applications and technologies on the entire system landscape for technical operations. The LMDB unifies the data from the SLD and the previous SMSY in SAP Solution Manager and, in this way, makes information on the entire system landscape available. The connected systems automatically send this data to the LMDB.

▶ **Solution documentation**
The solution documentation contains information on business process operations. This is data associated with processes and process steps, such as transactions, process responsibilities, and so on.

In this book, we take up the idea of *Run SAP like a Factory*. We'll show you which instruments are available in SAP Solution Manager to implement the idea of Run SAP like a Factory, and thus the Operations Control Center. Standardization and automation are important principles in this context. Monitoring important status information on business processes, critical interfaces, and the components these are based on creates transparency for the IT department and business operations. This transparency allows for quick and effective reaction to problems. In an SAP context, we differentiate between technical operations and business process operations as follows:

▶ **Technical operations**
Together with an authorization scenario, technical monitoring of system components and interfaces ensure smooth technical operations. At the creation of alerts, which can be generated manually or automatically by the system, the *IT Service Management* (ITSM) ALM process starts. Tools like *root cause analysis* and *change diagnostics* are used for error detection and handling in the event of an incident.

▶ **Business process operations**
In business process operations, it's ensured that the business process runs smoothly from the application perspective. Just as in technical operations, monitoring based on business process key figures, critical interfaces, and data consistency checks are established. If necessary, an alert is triggered and passed on to Incident Management for further processing.

SAP Solution Manager supports this very approach of an Operations Control Center. All IT-relevant and application-relevant information on all system components is displayed in a central alert inbox. Using filters, you can display exactly the information you need in a specific situation.

By applying specific tools and methods that support you in identifying and analyzing problems, you can perform the error analysis yourself. For more information on root cause analysis, see Chapter 4.

In this book, we will show you, step by step, how to integrate SAP Solution Manager into your solution operations and ALM in order to benefit from it. We will provide precise instructions that allow you to work on the system with this book at hand. The implementation of essential activities is described in detailed step-by-step instructions. Using a fictitious company named Toys Inc., we'll demonstrate how to use the tools in practice. For some key topics, we have also included a few first-hand reports from our customers.

Before we finally introduce you to Toys Inc., we will give you a brief overview of project management in the next section.

1.4 Project Management

Each change in an IT solution requires a structured implementation method. The aim is to minimize risks and not to endanger the overall process. Regardless of the extent of a change, each change should be seen as a project. Due to the permanent adjustments in IT, it's important to establish standardized processes. In a brief summary, the following section explains the significance of project management for technical operations.

1.4.1 What Is a Project?

A *project* is a plan or intent that has a specific aim, whether it is the solution to existing problems or the implementation of targets or ideas. With the help of project management, methods and tools that support the execution of the project are used.

To carry out the project in accordance with project management, the general conditions and expectations, such as contents, scope, chances of success, budget, time, staff, and so on, must be defined.

Each project is divided into several project phases. At the beginning, you should run an analysis to identify weak points that may have a significant impact on the company. Based on the requirements you have set up in the analysis phase, you create a conceptual design, in which you basically design your project, in the design phase. The next step is implementing the conceptual design, which is followed by the test phase. Throughout all the phases, the project is monitored for cost control, schedule, progress, and so on.

1.4.2 Run SAP Method

If we consider how much literature is available on project management, we understand that there is not only *one* IT project management. In addition, each project has a different structure and is dependent on various factors, such as project size, project scope, project attention in the management, funds, and, last but not least, the exact circumstances and structures of an organization.

However, with the run SAP method, SAP has developed some general guidelines designed to foster the cooperation between application areas and technical operations at an early stage when new implementations and system changes are to be made within projects. The run SAP method offers standards for the operation of solutions to unify important IT-based processes within your business and IT areas. The method accompanies you from the planning stage to the smooth operations of your IT landscape and supports you in introducing processes and adjusting existing processes to your specific requirements.

Originally, the run SAP method was developed because after going live, errors occurred within projects, requiring increased support. The reasons for this included faulty or even missing calculated hardware requirements, a lack of know-how transfer in handling the innovation on the application side, insufficient tests that could have provided information on the impact of the implementation on other areas, and so on. The main purpose of the run SAP method is to reduce faults after implementation in the productive system.

Figure 1.6 shows a roadmap with the activities that are necessary when changes are made in an IT landscape. From the planning stage to running operations, there are a number of project steps and persons involved in a project, and the success of a project can be guaranteed only if they all act as a unit.

Since this book focuses on technical operations using SAP Solution Manager, we cannot go into more detail about project management at this point. Before we take a closer look at the architecture and configuration of SAP Solution Manager in Chapter 2, we would like to introduce the fictitious company Toys Inc. We'll use this example company to demonstrate in more detail the individual tasks of technical operations using SAP Solution Manager.

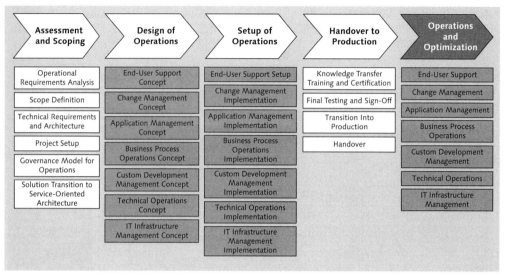

Figure 1.6 Run SAP Method: Roadmap

1.5 Toys Inc.: Initial Situation

In this section, we would like to introduce Toys Inc., which will be our example company to demonstrate how to set up SAP Solution Manager and to explain its central functionalities in more detail.

1.5.1 Company

Toys Inc., headquartered in Germany, is a medium-sized company that manufactures plastic toys. Globally, the company is active in three countries: Germany, the United States, and Singapore. At each of these locations, the company has two production sites and two distribution centers. The company's main business starts in August and ends in December. Both its suppliers (for example, of material) and its clients are all over the world.

1.5.2 System Landscape

To support the sales, production, and distribution of its products, the company uses an SAP ERP system and the SAP NetWeaver Portal. For requirements planning and production planning, it uses SAP Supply Chain Management (SCM). For stock level management, a warehouse management system is used. For evaluation of application data, SAP NetWeaver BW is used. SAP Solution Manager is the central monitoring and control unit for technical operations. The SAP NetWeaver PI system (process integration) is still in preparation. In the future, it will control the data transfer among the supplier systems, in-house warehouse management system, and SAP ERP system.

For all SAP systems, a development and testing system, as well as a production system, are available. Due to the different locations, which are also in different time zones, the systems must be available 24/7. Figure 1.7 graphically shows the system landscape of Toys Inc.

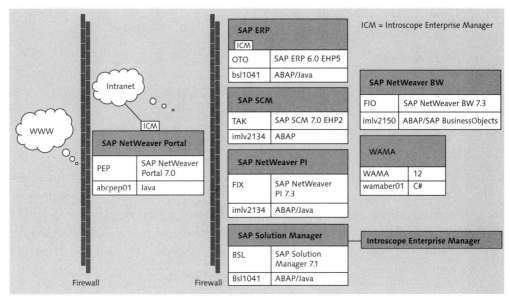

Figure 1.7 System Landscape of Toys Inc.

1.5.3 IT Operations

The systems are supported from Germany, where the entire computer technology is located. The IT system consists of four areas: system administration, Application Management, the internal IT Support, and the Operations Control Center as a virtual team. Within the first three teams mentioned, there are a few more divisions, as you can see in Figure 1.8.

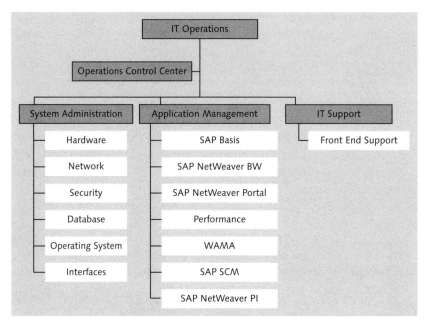

Figure 1.8 Organization of IT Operations

Operations Control Center

The Operations Control Center monitors the entire IT system landscape and business process operations and is basically the first-level support for all IT-based areas. Using monitoring tools and standardized monitoring processes, it is able to quickly recognize a fault. With the help of standardized action procedures, malfunctions that do not require expert knowledge can be corrected—for example, restarting a work process.

Of course, every error must be viewed in detail. However, by now, IT is able to differentiate among various malfunctions and put them into different categories, such as simple and critical malfunctions. The trend will continue toward standardizing and automating IT processes as far as possible.

System Administration

The system administration is responsible for hardware management. This includes procurement and maintenance of new computer technology. Another task is system support for databases and operating systems. This includes tasks such as installation and administration of the database and operating system.

Within the team, there are roles responsible for creating the data backups required for potential system recoveries. Network administrators take care of the entire network landscape. System administration is responsible for system security to protect the systems against external impacts, such as unauthorized system access. Managing user rights for databases and operating systems is part of the system administration's responsibility, as well.

> **SAP Note**
>
> Not every administrator can have all the knowledge of every area and sub-area of the IT infrastructure. Therefore, it is important to specialize in certain areas. The degree of specialization depends on the size of an organization and the complexity of its IT infrastructure.

Application Management

The Application Management team exclusively ensures smooth operations of SAP and non-SAP applications. It focuses on development and support of the applications. Activities such as ensuring good system performance are also part of this task. This also includes proper maintenance of system configurations, such as buffer settings. Interfaces such as the Core Interface (CIF) between an SAP SCM system and an SAP ERP system are checked and controlled by the system administration and the application.

With the increase of individual and IT landscapes and their rising complexity, cooperation must be created between the technical level and application areas. Without close cooperation, it will become increasingly difficult to handle the complexity of a system landscape. Just looking at a part of a landscape is no longer sufficient; to be able to correct major malfunctions, a solution must be analyzed in its entirety. Apart from that, changes always involve further measures, which can no longer be viewed only in individual aspects.

> **Example**
>
> A runtime error occurs during saving in Transaction SD01 (creating a sales order). The cause is an error in the program code. This error was caused by the import of a Support Package (SP). Why did this happen? Was the transport not imported correctly? Or, did the error get into the code by the import of the Support Package?

A possible reason is that there was not enough testing done beforehand. That could be due to inadequate coordination between the person importing the transport and the users in charge of testing on an application level. In the end, it might have been the inadequate coordination between the teams in Application Management and on the user side that caused the problem.

This example underlines the importance of communication in the organizational areas. Therefore, even the Application Management team should focus more on communication.

IT Support

IT Support supports the workstation computers or printers—essentially, all end-user devices. If, for example, a user has a problem with their PC, the team will do the troubleshooting. In order to provide quick on-site support, IT Support must be organized decentrally. The coordination of the individual IT Support teams, however, is done centrally.

Now that you know Toys Inc. a little better, we will elaborate on the architecture and configuration of SAP Solution Manager 7.1 in the following chapter.

1.6   Additional Documentation

Links

▶ *service.sap.com/testing*

▶ *service.sap.com/rkt-solman* • SOLMAN 7.1 • TEST MANAGEMENT

This chapter introduces the architecture of SAP Solution Manager in more detail. Knowing its structure forms the basis for using it and performing the initial configuration.

2   Architecture and Configuration of SAP Solution Manager 7.1

To be able to support the functions in the various applications in technical operations, you should first familiarize yourself with the architecture of SAP Solution Manager. This chapter provides an overview of the components that are installed and used in a typical system landscape. At the end of the chapter, you will understand where to find the components in your landscape, how to implement them, and how to use the tools for root cause analysis and correction in the event of an incident.

With the example of Toys Inc., we will show you how to apply SAP Solution Manager in your landscape and which configuration steps are necessary to use it in your system landscape.

2.1   Architecture of SAP Solution Manager

Within an SAP-centric system landscape, SAP Solution Manager forms a central node that is interlinked with other systems (see Figure 2.1). With the connection of the individual systems, SAP Solution Manager receives administrative access to the systems and can collect information on their use and monitoring. The connected systems are also referred to as *managed systems*. SAP Solution Manager can be accessed via end-user PCs.

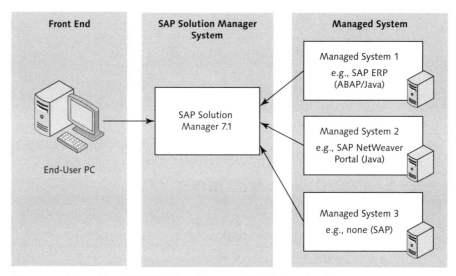

Figure 2.1 Integration of SAP Solution Manager in the System Landscape

2.1.1 User Interface

As mentioned, the end-user PC is used to access application in SAP Solution Manager. As with every SAP application, you have various options to do this:

▶ SAP GUI

▶ SAP NetWeaver Business Client

▶ Web browser (Microsoft Internet Explorer, Mozilla Firefox, etc.)

Basically, all three access possibilities are supported by the work center concept of SAP Solution Manager and can be applied by you. Regarding access via SAP GUI, however, there are a few limitations related to the Single Sign-On function (SSO). In some cases, the SSO ticket, which identifies a user and is transmitted between the various systems for authentication, cannot be passed on. This happens particularly often when SAP Solution Manager is operated using an external SAP NetWeaver Business Warehouse (BW). Therefore, we suggest starting the application either in SAP NetWeaver Business Client or directly from your browser. The browser-based access has the extra benefit that no additional work environment must be installed on the end users' PCs.

Once you decide on your work environment, you should install the following plug-ins on the end-user PCs because they are used by the SAP Solution Manager applications:

▶ **Adobe Flash Player**
Interactive graphics in the current version of SAP Solution Manager are displayed using Adobe Flash Player. Examples of such elements are graphical roadmaps in the configuration and landscape graphics of system monitoring.

▶ **Microsoft Silverlight**
Microsoft Silverlight is used for displaying information provided by CA Wily Introscope (hereafter referred to throughout the book as *Introscope*). Introscope is an application by software developer Computer Associated International. It is used to enrich performance information of non-ABAP components. Introscope can be used by all SAP customers as part of SAP Solution Manager without any additional license fees. For more information on Introscope, see Section 2.1.2.

▶ **Java Runtime Environment**
The Java runtime environment (JRE) is required to use the Introscope work environment (the Introscope workstation) and to display graphics in the end-to-end trace analysis of root cause analysis.

2.1.2   Components of the SAP Solution Manager System

The SAP Solution Manager system consists of a number of components, including an SAP NetWeaver dual-stack system, which is composed of an SAP NetWeaver Application Server (AS) ABAP and an SAP NetWeaver AS Java. As the processing unit, the AS ABAP takes over the classic processes. In the current version of SAP Solution Manager 7.1, the AS Java is used for display purposes. Apart from that, it has an important function for the communication of SAP Solution Manager with other SAP components that are Java based, such as the agents of SAP Solution Manager.

Apart from the core component, SAP NetWeaver, three additional technical components are responsible for the complete shape and structure of an SAP Solution Manager system. The components of SAP Customer Relationship Management (CRM), SAP NetWeaver BW, and Service and Support are the standard components of the system installation.

> **Note**
>
> The upgrade of SAP Solution Manager 7.0 to 7.1 includes the transition of the SAP CRM system used in SAP Solution Manager from release 5.0 to 7.0. This release involves a few functional extensions for processes, such as Change Request Management and IT Service Management (ITSM), which are based on SAP CRM.

The Service and Support component is original to SAP Solution Manager and responsible for SAP Solution Manager's release description 7.1. The SAP NetWeaver BW component can be used directly for operations and reporting or replaced with an external BW system.

Apart from the components integrated in SAP Solution Manager, one or multiple Introscope Enterprise Manager(s) is also part of SAP Solution Manager. Introscope Enterprise Manager collects high-resolution performance data, which is required especially for monitoring and root cause analysis.

2.1.3   Logical Layers

SAP Solution Manager itself can be divided into five abstraction layers, which show its functions and modes of action. In Figure 2.2, you can see the five layers building upon each other. We will explain these layers in more detail in the following subsections.

DataStores

DataStores are the locations where the data used in the SAP Solution Manager applications is stored. A distinction is made mainly between high-resolution data, which occurs in large amounts and is thus available only temporarily, and aggregated data, which is used for medium- and long-term statistical evaluations and long-term analyses. In this layer of SAP Solution Manager, Introscope and a business warehouse are used, where Introscope mainly stores non-aggregated, high-resolution data for a short period (up to three days), and the business warehouse stores the resulting data in an aggregated form.

Repositories

Repositories are storages for master and configuration data of SAP Solution Manager. This includes the environment descriptions stored in the Landscape Management Database (LMDB) and the Solution Manager System Landscape (SMSY), as well as the configuration data in the Metric, Event, & Alert Repository (MEA), which the customer can configure to store them in the Alerting Directory.

Data Retrieval (Engines and Framework)

The engines layer of SAP Solution Manager is responsible for data retrieval. For example, the extractor framework (EFWK) is used to actively collect (pull mechanism) or receive (push mechanism) data from connected systems and finally store it in the internal data warehouse of SAP Solution Manager. The configuration and change database (CCDB) stores the information based on the development and changes of components of the technical system landscape.

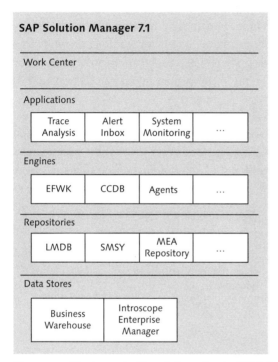

Figure 2.2 Five Layers to Show Information in SAP Solution Manager

Applications

The applications of SAP Solution Manager provide the user with the actual functions. This includes applications from all areas of SAP Solution Manager, such as the alert inbox, which allows the user to access all alerts in the monitoring infrastructure.

Work Centers

The work centers in SAP Solution Manager bundle the available applications based on the user roles common in the processes. They support the user-specific use of the applications.

For example, the TECHNICAL MONITORING work center provides access to all applications that are relevant to a system administrator in their everyday work. This comprises the alert inbox for accessing the current alerts, system monitoring to get a clear picture of the current status of a system or multiple systems, and technical reporting, which provides access to historical and aggregated data.

SAP ships the work centers in their individual versions so that they can be specifically allocated to the users. User-specific allocation is done using a role concept, which was developed specially for the various work centers in SAP Solution Manager. For information on the allocation and use of the various roles, please see Section 12.3.4.

2.1.4   Managed Systems

SAP Solution Manager can only assume its central tasks once there are systems actually connected to it. So, the connection of the systems to be managed is of special relevance.

Basically, SAP Solution Manager 7.1 can be connected with SAP systems and non-SAP systems. Depending on the type of system to be connected, various requirements must be met. As you can see in Figure 2.3, there is a variety of different agents and plug-ins, which you need to install based on the system type.

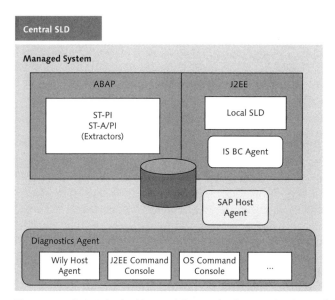

Figure 2.3 Agents in the Managed System for Communication with SAP Solution Manager

For the agents, a distinction in made between diagnostic agents and SAP host agents. Agents are independent components that, by order of an instance (in this case SAP Solution Manager), collect information of remote components and provide it to the instance. This way, the collection of information has no impact on the processes of the remote components.

Diagnostics Agent

The Diagnostics Agent mainly collects statistical data for the use of the instances that are based on Java, .NET or C++, which are non-ABAP–based systems in a broader sense.

From a purely logical perspective, the Diagnostics Agent is part of SAP Solution Manager and does not need to be managed separately. After installation of the Diagnostics Agent, all other configuration changes and software updates are performed automatically using SAP Solution Manager. The Diagnostics Agent is always run in the context of a managed component. In other words, the Diagnostics Agent is identified via the logical host name of the managed component. Therefore, it may be necessary to install multiple Diagnostics Agents on one system when multiple logical or virtual servers are operated on one physical server.

SAP Host Agent

The SAP host agent collects the statistical data to use the operating system and hardware resources.

The SAP host agent is run in the context of the physical host system and therefore must be installed only once for each physical server. In contrast to the diagnostic agent, you need to manually manage and update the SAP host agent.

Introscope Byte Code Adapter

The Introscope Byte Code Adapter is used in connection with the Introscope Enterprise Manager to collect and store performance data. This adapter is needed only for systems that are based on the AS Java (or J2EE) and .NET software. This comprises all SAP NetWeaver AS Java systems, such as SAP NetWeaver Portal, but also non-SAP systems that build on these technologies—for example, Microsoft SharePoint or IBM WebSphere.

Plug-Ins

In addition to the agents, two plug-ins are relevant: the Solution Tools Plug-In (ST-PI) and the Service Tools for Applications Plug-In (ST-A/PI), which must be installed for ABAP-based systems. In this context, it's important which products and product releases are installed on the managed system. For example, for an SAP CRM 7.0 system (which is based on SAP NetWeaver 7.0), you need to install ST-PI in version ST-PI 2008 700 and ST-A/PI in version ST-A/PI 01N CRM700. This is necessary to ensure that certain functionalities, such as data extraction of ITSM, are supported. SAP Solution Manager seeks to be state of the art in terms of technology and development. To use this progress in the collection of information in the remote systems, the plug-ins are independent of the release status of the remote system and can be updated at any time, without creating a dependency in the system stack to other components.

System Landscape Directory

The last important component of SAP Solution Manager is the landscape management component (System Landscape Directory, SLD), which you can also find in Figure 2.3. The SLD is the central infrastructure component, in which the information on the system landscape is collected and managed. This information comprises the used systems, the used resources, the status of the Support Packages, and much more.

SAP recommends creating the SLD in its own AS Java and based on the system landscape administrator's specifications. For more information on the SLD, see the online help in the SAP Service Marketplace or in the SLD installation guide.

Each system in the landscape logs into the SLD and transmits information on its technical structure, such as the host name of the servers on which it is installed or the number of installed application servers. Apart from that, it sends information on the installed products and software components. This information is transmitted directly from the SLD into the Landscape Management Database (LMDB), which is directly integrated in SAP Solution Manager.

The synchronization of the SLD to the LMDB is completely performed automatically and uses a connection between the two components so that each insert, change, and delete is directly transmitted to the LMDB and applied there. As a result, the applications in SAP Solution Manager always have current landscape information at their disposal. Figure 2.4 shows the mentioned communication of the components between SAP Solution Manager and the connected systems via the SLD.

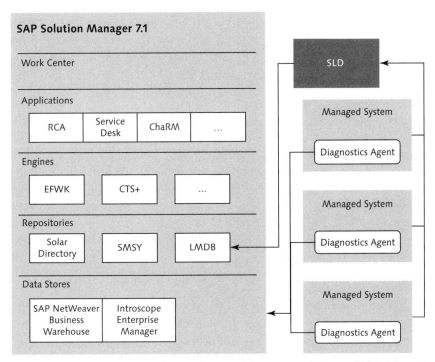

Figure 2.4 Communication and Dependencies of Components between SAP Solution Manager and the Connected (Managed) Systems

However, the Diagnostics Agents, which are installed on the managed systems and ensure the acquisition of information for SAP Solution Manager, directly connect with the SAP Solution Manager system. Also, the technical maintenance and administration of the agents is done via the direct connection to SAP Solution Manager. The configuration files and updates are provided centrally by SAP Solution Manager.

The next section describes the communication of the above infrastructure components in more detail.

2.2 Infrastructure and Communication with SAP Solution Manager

The communication with the connected systems is the core of SAP Solution Manager. To give you a basis for your decisions, SAP Solution Manager must be supplied with current information from the connected systems. There are several ways to communicate and gain information for SAP Solution Manager. This variety of possibilities we'll discuss in this section is summarized as the infrastructure of SAP Solution Manager.

In Section 2.1.2, we have already seen that the infrastructure of SAP Solution Manager has multiple components that ensure communication and the exchange of information between SAP Solution Manager and the connected components.

A typical SAP system landscape always includes essential systems and components based on ABAP. These components use the remote function call (RFC) technology to communicate with other components and exchange information with them. Diagnostics Agents communicate with non-ABAP components, such as AS Java or the operating system. These two communication types—using agents or RFCs—are the cornerstones of communication with SAP Solution Manager.

Other agents, like the agents of Introscope Enterprise Manager, are needed for the direct data exchange between SAP Solution Manager and the connected systems. These agents are used to obtain additional information on the behavior of non-ABAP components. They do not communicate directly with SAP Solution Manager but provide their information directly to Introscope Enterprise Manager, where it is then retrieved by a Diagnostics Agent and transmitted to SAP Solution Manager.

2.2.1 SAP Host Agent

The SAP host agent is used to control the operation status of the SAP components. It is also used to collect data and monitor server systems on which SAP NetWeaver components, database systems, or other components for technical mapping of core business processes are operated.

The SAP host agent thus replaces the Computing Center Management System (CCMS) agents, which previously provided the CCMS monitoring system with data. Although the CCMS can still be used for monitoring, the SAP Solution Manager 7.1 release introduces a new infrastructure that takes over the CCMS functionality: the monitoring and alerting infrastructure (MAI).

On one hand, the SAP host agent takes over the management and control of the SAP operating system information, which is still collected using the SAPOSCOL agent. On the other hand, it supports the operation of a landscape with new functions, such as the start and stop service for instances. The SAP host agent is automatically available with an installation of SAP NetWeaver components from release 7.0 EHP2, but it can also be installed manually for older SAP NetWeaver components.

Before we explain how to install the SAP host agent, we would like to familiarize you with its architecture and functioning. The SAP host agent can be applied in two different versions. Depending on which systems and components you use, it can be applied as either a host agent or an instance agent. These names refer to the role of the agent. The host agent is installed on each physical server. The instance agent, however, is installed on each SAP instance.

Host agents and instance agents complement one another and form a unity in the SAP NetWeaver components. The instance agents are implemented fully automatically, which means you need to install the only host agent. To understand what is behind these two components, let's take a more detailed look at the individual functions of the two agents.

The host agent has the following applications:

▶ **saphostcontrol**
The `saphostcontrol` application runs on the physical server and is the core application for the `sapstartsrv` service. As early as in the starting process, the role of the SAP host agent is assigned, and it is defined whether it is responsible for an instance or physical server (host). If it is responsible for a physical host, a connection to the `sapstartsrv` service is established, as shown in Figure 2.5. The host mode is recognized by the profile, which also includes the two profile parameters `SAPSystemnummer` = 99 and `SAPSystemName` = SAP.

Both applications, `saphostcontrol` and `saphostexec`, are activated with the start of the host and permanently run on it.

> **Note**
>
> For Microsoft Windows, the `saphostcontrol` service is used to ensure the automated start by using the system-specific operating system user (`<sid>adm`). On UNIX servers, the automatic start is activated using the program `sapstartsrv` and the start script `sapinit`.

The `saphostcontrol` service additionally contains the functionality of the previous CCMS agent, `SAPCCMSR`, which is the agent that monitors hosts.

▶ **saphostexec**

The `saphostexec` application forms a so-called execution level, which runs under the user `root` (UNIX) or under the local system account (Microsoft Windows). The primary job of the application is to control functions in the operating system area that requires special authorizations. Well-known examples of these functions are the operating system collector SAPOSCOL and the `sapacosprep` program (see Figure 2.5). The `saphostexec` application is locally connected with the `sapstartsrv` in the host mode, which means it is already started with the host, and a secure and fast communication is possible.

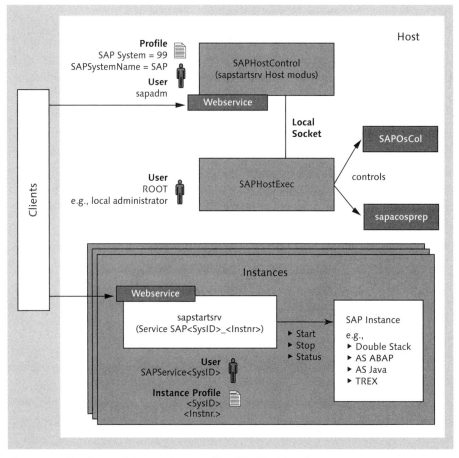

Figure 2.5 Structure and Communication of the SAP Host Agent

> **Note**
>
> Just like the `saphostcontrol` application, `saphostexec` is also ensured and started by a `saphostexec` service on Microsoft Windows servers. On UNIX servers, the executions and the automatic start are ensured by integrating the program `sapstartsrv` and the start script `sapinit`.
>
> `sapacosprep` is an executable of the Adaptive Computing Infrastructure, which executes, for example, the adding of file systems and generally the preparations on the operating-system side in order to start SAP instances.

In contrast, the instance agent includes just the `sapstartsrv` application for the instances and is allocated to the available instances and activated by the host agent. The instance agents are automatically started with the hosts and offer the possibility to query instance information via Simple Object Access Protocol (SOAP) interfaces or to control the instances via the SAP Management Console (SAP MMC).

As you can see in Figure 2.5, both host components offer both `saphostcontrol` and `sapstartsrv`, various infrastructure options that are based on web services. By now, SAP MMC is a broad application, based on interaction and web services, to control the operation status of SAP components. SAP MMC was developed in Java and is based on the Microsoft Management Console, which can be used to control services and components. Another interface is currently still partially used for the central CCMS-based monitoring of SAP systems. In the past, special CCMS agents (SAPCCM4X and SAPCCMSR) were used for the communication and data exchange between SAP Solution Manager and the managed systems. This communication has now been entirely integrated into the SAP host agent. Even if the central CCMS-based mechanisms are to be replaced, the data transmission that the shared memory provides will remain an important part of the automated monitoring solution in future releases of SAP Solution Manager.

You can also see that the host agent is responsible for controlling the operating system collector SAPOSCOL. This application is essential for a coherent and complete monitoring concept.

Installation

The installation package of the SAP host agent can be found in the SAP Service Marketplace. Go to the PATCHES navigation area and navigate to the kernel package for the corresponding server system. The package includes all required parts for the central monitoring of any host. More information can be found in the installation guide in SAP Service Marketplace under the alias *instguidesnw*. It is automatically installed with the installation of all components of SAP NetWeaver 7.0 EHP2 and later. Check in your console under Linux or in the list of running services under Microsoft Windows if the service of the SAP host agent is also active and running on each host with an SAP component.

Manual or Retroactive Installation of the SAP Host Agent

You can install the SAP host agent using the `SAPinst` program, which is the recommended method for retroactive installation in existing systems. As mentioned previously, the files required for this method can be obtained from the SAP Service Marketplace. In the area for software downloads, navigate to the server operating system configuration you use and, from the kernel component area, download the SAP HOST AGENT package. Alternatively, you can copy the SAP HOST AGENT package from one of the shipped kernel DVDs. To do this, choose the desired release in the INSTALLATION area.

The SAP HOST AGENT package contains all mentioned components of the host and of the instance, as follows:

- `saphostexec`
- `sapstartsrv`
- `sapacosprep`
- `SAPOSCOL`

Setting Up the SAP Host Agent in the System Landscape of Toys Inc.

The following describes how to set up the SAP host agent for the example of Toys Inc. In order to install the SAP host agent, you must first open a console session using the `root` user administrator. Since the agents have not yet been installed using `SAPinst`, the following steps are required for our UNIX system installation:

1. From SAP Service Marketplace, download the latest installation package for the SAP host agent. Then, in SAP SERVICE MARKETPLACE, go to the SOFTWARE PACKAGES AND PATCHES page under the following link: *http://service.sap.com/patches*. The package is available in the KERNEL section. Select the correct target operating system and then download the package for the SAP HOST AGENT from a kernel.

2. Check whether a user group named `sapsys` already exists in your operating system. This should be the case if you have already installed SAP components

on this host. If not, you first need to create a group named `sapsys` using the `groupadd` UNIX command.

3. To execute the process of the SAP host agent, the user `sapadm` is required. Check whether this user already exists on your host and whether it has already been assigned to the `sapsys` group. If the user has not been created yet, create a user named `sapadm` using the `useradd` command under Linux via the console. Then, assign the `sapsys` user group to it.

4. Now, specify a work directory for the operating system collector SAPOSCOL, which you install at a later point. In the future, SAPOSCOL will store all collected information in this directory. By default, the agent expects the work directory of the SAPOSCOL agent under */usr/sap/tmp*, but using the `DIR_PERF` profile parameter, you can assign the agent any other storage location. The profile parameter can be stored in any profile at any time. However, for SAP components, we recommend storing the parameter in the system profile of the SAP system. Add the `DIR_PERF = <path of desired work directory>` parameter.

5. Using the `SAPCAR` tool, unpack the *SAPHostAgent.SAR* package downloaded from SAP Service Marketplace. To do this, use the `SAPCAR -xvf SAP Host Agent.SAR` command.

6. The package contains the application `saphostexec`. Use the `saphostexec -install` command to perform the installation.

The SAP host agent, including the `saphostexec` control program, the system collector SAPOSCOL, and the `saphostcontrol` SAP NetWeaver agent, is not installed on the host and can be used by other components, especially SAP Solution Manager. The procedure for Microsoft Windows corresponds to the one for Linux described previously.

If you already have an SAP host agent installed and a more current version of the SAP host agent is available, you can use the `saphostexec -upgrade` command to replace the SAP host agent with that of a newly downloaded package without having to reinstall it.

2.2.2   Diagnostics Agent

The Diagnostics Agent is the most important agent applied in SAP Solution Manager. In regards to both the technical basis and functionality, it is the most extensive one. The Diagnostics Agent does the major part of communication with connected systems and, as an example, provides the information on root cause analysis or monitoring in SAP Solution Manager.

The Diagnostics Agent was initially applied in SAP Solution Manager release 4.0. Over the years, it has been constantly extended, while its basic architecture has remained the same. To give you a better understanding of the agent, the following subsections provide a brief overview of the agent, its architecture, and the technical requirements. This is followed by a few examples that show you how you can provide a Diagnostics Agent in your landscape.

Requirements and Planning

As a rule of thumb, each virtual, logical, and physical server must have a Diagnostics Agent installed by default. The Diagnostics Agent is no longer relevant only to Java systems, so you also need to assign a Diagnostics Agent to AS ABAP components. This must be considered in your planning, particularly if you operate a medium-sized to large landscape, which means that, for approximately 50 technical components to be connected, where multiple SAP systems are spread across various virtual servers.

Prior to installation of the Diagnostics Agent, some preparations are useful to facilitate the installation process. First of all, you need to select the right agent version. For SAP Solution Manager 7.1, you can generally use Diagnostics Agent 7.3 SP02. For completeness, Table 2.1 lists all other versions that are currently available on SAP Service Marketplace. The rising version numbers show you that there are newer and older solutions of Diagnostics Agents available.

SAP Solution Manager Version	Version of Connected Systems	Version of Diagnostics Agent/SAP Note
Version 7.00 (prior to EHP1)	6.40, 7.0, 7.0 EHP1 & 2, 7.1 EHP1, 7.2	7.01 SR1 SAP Note 1357812
Version 7.0 EHP1 ≥ SP18	6.40, 7.0, 7.0 EHP1 & 2, 7.1 EHP1, 7.2	7.01 SR1 SAP Note 1357812
Version 7.0 EHP1 ≥ SP20 (SP4, SP2)	6.40, 7.0, 7.0 EHP1 & 2, 7.1 EHP1, 7.2	7.20 SAP Note 1368413
Version 7.1	6.40, 7.0x, 7.1x, 7.2x, 7.3	7.3 SP02 SAP Note 1448655

Table 2.1 Overview of Currently Available Diagnostics Agent Versions

The various Diagnostics Agent versions differ mainly in their functionalities. In the last few versions, new functions were added, allowing the end user to centrally access further information. The Diagnostics Agents can now be started remotely from the Agent Administration, for example, and it's possible to evaluate various versions of profile data in one SAP Solution Manager session. To access the Agent Administration, go to the INFRASTRUCTURE view • SAP SOLUTION MANAGER ADMINISTRATION work center • FRAMEWORKS and choose AGENT FRAMEWORK. From here, you can directly access the AGENT ADMINISTRATION. Alternatively, the navigation area of the SAP SOLUTION MANAGER CONFIGURATION work center provides a link to the Agent Administration.

The Diagnostics Agents are not directly linked with the versions of SAP Solution Manager, but it is recommended that you adjust the Diagnostics Agents to the current version of SAP Solution Manager, as well, so that you can use additional functions. To download a current Diagnostics Agent version, go to SAP Service Marketplace and navigate to *http://service.sap.com/swdc* • SUPPORT PACKAGES AND PATCHES • A–Z INDEX • S • SAP SOLUTION MANAGER • SAP SOLUTION MANAGER 7.1 • ENTRY BY COMPONENT • AGENTS FOR MANAGED SYSTEMS • DIAGNOSTICS AGENT 7.3.

For our sample scenario and for other descriptions in this book, we refer to the current version at this time, which is Diagnostics Agent 7.3 SP02. Based on this version, the following section describes how to install the Diagnostics Agent in your landscape in just a few steps.

After you have selected a version of the Diagnostics Agent and downloaded it from SAP Service Marketplace, you need to make the installation package available in all locations in your landscape where you want to install it. Therefore, it is necessary to consider beforehand on which server components you wish to install the Diagnostics Agent. Please note that, for the communication between SAP Solution Manager and the connected systems, you will need a Diagnostics Agent for each physical and virtual server, as you can see in Figure 2.6.

While the SAP host agent is installed only on the physical level of the server, the Diagnostics Agent must be installed on all available instances. If you are not sure which server types are present in a landscape, you can look them up in the server detail information in the LMDB. This information is sent to the LMDB by the operating system collector.

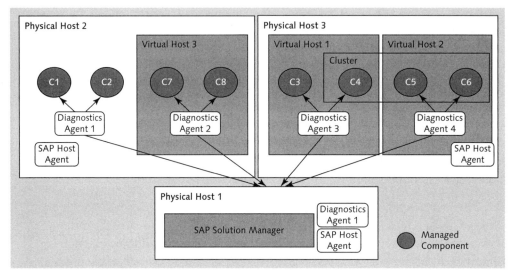

Figure 2.6 Agent Strategy in the System Landscape

Figure 2.6 shows a typical case of a system landscape, in which we allocated various virtual and physical servers to the systems clusters. Also, it is quite common that a high-availability solution is used in such cluster solutions. The classic solution and installation of Diagnostics Agents would be very complex and prone to incidents in such complex landscapes. For example, a classic Diagnostics Agent cannot see whether a cluster is no longer available or if a cluster is restarted. Without manual interference, the Diagnostics Agent remains active in such a case and tries to gather information, regardless of whether the cluster is available. For such high-availability solutions, there is a special version of the Diagnostics Agent, the *Agent Node Concept*. The concept and peculiarities of the implementation of this agent technology are described in more detail in the "Diagnostics Agent in Cluster and High-Availability Environments" subsection in this chapter.

Installation of Diagnostics Agents

Let's start with the installation of a Diagnostics Agent in the example of Toys Inc. As mentioned in the introduction, Toys Inc. has a smaller landscape, with only 19 systems to be connected. As the system to be connected, we chose the SAP ERP system OTO with a Linux system and a 64-bit Intel processor to describe the installation of a classic Diagnostics Agent. For installation in the system landscape of Toys Inc., we proceed as follows:

1. First, we must unpack the package that was downloaded from SAP Service Marketplace and save it to a location that the system to be connected can access. Open a console and go to the location where the package is. Use the SAPCAR command to unpack the package:

```
cd /<unpacking directory>/ DIAGAGT73SP02_*.SAR
SAPCAR -xvf DIAGAGT73SP02_*.SAR
```

2. Start SAPinst from the program directory. Check whether a Reflex server is active in your Linux system to ensure that the graphics can be forwarded to your client. If you do not have a so-called Reflex server, which translates graphical instructions from a Secure Shell (SSH) session to your local desktop, you can, alternatively, use the remote function of SAPinst. For this purpose, you need to re-download your Microsoft Windows system and unpack it here.

   To start a remote installation, initially activate SAPinst on the remote system using the -nogui parameter. This parameter ensures that the graphical interface of the following installation can be called on a remote desktop PC:

```
cd <unpacking directory>/SMD730_00_IM_LINUX_X86_64
./sapinst -nogui
```

   The installation process is now started on your system to be connected and stops the console at the position where the remote installation process is to continue.

3. To continue the installation process and start the graphical installation interface, go to your desktop.

4. Open the *SMD730_00_IM_WINDOWS_X86_64* folder in your installation package and start the *sapinstgui.exe* program. A new window opens (see Figure 2.7), in which you need to enter the server information to connect with the remote installation.

5. In your remote system, check which port the installation opened, and enter the port in the remote connection mask. As you can see in Figure 2.7, our example uses port 21212 for establishing the remote access.

6. Enter the server for the installation. Start the logon process of the remote agent installation.

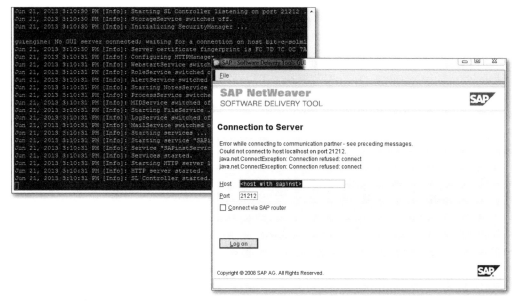

Figure 2.7 Establishing a Connection to the Remote System to Be Connected

7. Choose LOG ON to start the SAPinst program.

8. After the successful start of SAPinst, a new window opens in which you can install the Diagnostics Agent using the menu and with the help of additional information. To do this, in the SAPinst menu, navigate to the DIAGNOSTICS AGENT entry to start the agent installation using this menu path: SAP SOLUTION MANAGER DIAGNOSTICS • SAP SYSTEM • STANDALONE ENGINE • DIAGNOSTICS AGENT IN SAP SOLUTION MANAGER • DIAGNOSTICS AGENT.

9. Click NEXT to start installation of the agent on the remote system.

10. In the following phase, the parameters for installation are defined. In several steps, the installation program asks you for individual parameters. Table 2.2 is an overview of the parameters the system asks you to select during this phase. Our example of Toys Inc. shows you which details you are asked to provide in your scenario during configuration of the SAPinst program.

Requested Parameter	Entered Values in the Toys Inc. Sample Scenario
Server name	bsl1041
SAP system ID	DAA
SAP system user (operating system)	daaadm
SAP system user group (operating system)	sapsys
Instance number	90
SLD registration	No SLD registration!
Connection to SAP Solution Manager	yes, connection to SAP Solution Manager
Connection port to SAP Solution Manager	P4 port
Connection Information for Connection to SAP Solution Manager	
Server name—fully qualified server name (SAP Solution Manager)	bsl1041.wdf.sap.corp
HTTP port of SAP Central Services instance	8101
Admin user	SMD_ADMIN
SAP router connection	not available

Table 2.2 Requested Parameters

After you have entered the requested parameter values, the installation process automatically checks the requirements for the entered SID. It is possible that in your scenario, additional action is required to meet these requirements.

11. In the last step, you receive a summary of all the information you have entered. Verify your entries and continue with the next step of the agent installation.

After a few minutes, the installation process ends with a success message. If a problem occurs during installation, the installation process is interrupted, an error message is issued, and you are given the opportunity to correct the cause. Once the error has been corrected, you can continue the installation at the point where it was interrupted.

When the installation has been completed, check on the system level, or also in the agent framework, to determine whether the agent was started successfully and registered at SAP Solution Manager. To access the agent framework, go to the INFRASTRUCTURE view • SAP SOLUTION MANAGER ADMINISTRATION work center • FRAMEWORKS, and choose AGENT FRAMEWORK. The work center contents are now shown in the Agent Administration. This work area also offers you direct access to the AGENT ADMINISTRATION. Figure 2.8 shows a successfully registered Diagnostics Agent in the Agent Administration of SAP Solution Manager.

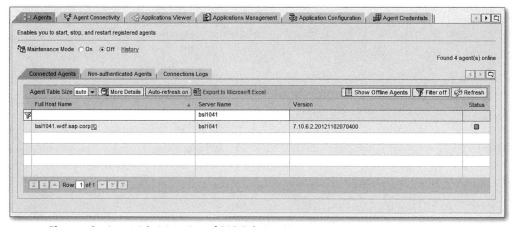

Figure 2.8 Agent Administration of SAP Solution Manager

It may take a few minutes until SAP Solution Manager shows the Diagnostics Agent with a green status because, during initial registration of the agent, SAP Solution Manager overwrites the Diagnostics Agent software version with that of SAP Solution Manager to update the agent. Also on the operating system level, you should be able to see a process with the agent instance name *SMDA90*, which is already active. In a UNIX environment, it is best to check this using the ps -ef |grep SMDA90 command.

If no such process is active, check the installation and reinstall. If the process is available, the Diagnostics Agent was successfully registered with SAP Solution Manager and is connected with it. To obtain information on the connected component in SAP Solution Manager, further configurations, which we introduce in Section 2.5.4, are necessary. The next section describes how to operate the agent in an environment that is similar to the installation introduced here. Then, we'll show you what to consider for operating a high-availability environment.

Operating Diagnostics Agents

Operating Diagnostics Agents is not complicated and consists of just integrating start and stop processes and technical updates. With a few configurations and adjustments, you can basically eliminate any manual work.

We recommend that you integrate the start and stop process of the agent in the start and stop routines of the connected SAP system. This way, it can be guaranteed that the Diagnostics Agent is always started and stopped synchronously with the connected system. For UNIX and Microsoft Windows systems, we recommend taking over the agent start and stop process into the start and stop process of the connected system. This way, you need to maintain and call up only one script.

The Diagnostics Agent, as an instrument of SAP Solution Manager, should be updated just as regularly as SAP Solution Manager itself. A fully automatic solution for this purpose, which uses SAP Solution Manager as the distributor of patches for the connected agents, is available. During logon to SAP Solution Manager, the agent checks the work version that is available there. If this work version is more up to date than the one of the Diagnostics Agent, SAP Solution Manager transfers the more up-to-date version to the agent and installs it. This process may take a few minutes, during which the Diagnostics Agent performs several logons to and logoffs from SAP Solution Manager to update and activate the individual software packages of the agent. You can obtain the current connection status in the Agent Administration, as shown in Figure 2.8. The STATUS column indicates the current connection status of the agent.

Diagnostics Agent in Cluster and High-Availability Environments

Depending on the underlying landscape, standalone installations of the Diagnostics Agent require time and resources for implementation. For initial implementation of an agent in your landscape, you should schedule up to half a day. Due to your increasing level of experience, the implementation time should decrease with each additional installation. Realistically, with sufficient experience and central access to the installation resources, an agent can be installed in less than 15 minutes.

You should make sure that sufficient hard disk and working memory is available before you start the installation in your landscape.

To support automation and minimize the manual work involved in the agent installation, you can use a Diagnostics Agent with its own instance management, the so-called *Agent-on-the-Fly Concept* (OTF), in cluster environments. The key advantage of this concept is that virtual servers automatically receive agent instances. Such agents are mainly used in cluster landscapes, which are also commonly used in high-availability environments. Such landscapes are characterized by extremely high dynamics, which means that system components can be operated in various physical environments and within very short reaction and action times. Using a single Diagnostics Agent in that situation can be very technically challenging.

The following scenario illustrates this. Let's take a medium-sized landscape with 13 productive systems, for each of which quality assurance and development systems are in place, as well. SAP Solution Manager, as well, is operated in such a three-system landscape—in other words, with its own quality assurance and development system. So, we have two additional SAP Solution Manager systems. This results in an SAP landscape of 41 systems plus further system components such as Introscope, an SLD, and various SAP BusinessObjects components.

We split up the system landscape in two network segments: one for the productive environment (PROD) and another one for development (DEV) and quality assurance (QA). For our example, we have eight mainframe servers, on which we can entirely map the clusters. The processing power of the individual mainframes on all eight server systems is equal, and the concept is that, in an emergency, all system components of the system landscape can be operated on four mainframe servers. For each of the two network segments, there are four mainframe servers available. To equally spread the load on the hardware, the clusters are distributed evenly.

Let's assume that payroll and closing accounts activities are due at the end of each month. This results in a high-workload situation at the end of every month. To avoid resource bottlenecks, all system components that are also active on this physical server, such as the productive company system (SAP ERP system), are distributed to the other physical servers 24 hours before the month-end activities begin. The SAP ERP system can, thus, fully use the resources and is not influenced by the particularly intense month-end activities

These dynamics of frequently changing system components are also joined by resource management. If there is a resource bottleneck on a mainframe server and the threshold for critical resource utilization is reached, a pre-defined group of clusters is shifted to a less utilized mainframe system. These activities are done for performance reasons, preferably for components that are not update critical and in systems of the development and quality assurance landscape.

At this point, it already becomes evident that this is a very dynamic environment; if necessary, the clusters can change between the four mainframes of our example. From installing the Diagnostics Agent, we know that the Diagnostics Agents have their own SID and their own operating system user (see Section "Installation of Diagnostics Agents"). Such a system landscape becomes really challenging when a cluster is moved to a new hardware because the individual classic Diagnostics Agent has neither any information nor influence on the move of the systems nor a fixed link to it. Using the OTF concept, the Diagnostics Agent can map these dynamics. Such Diagnostics Agents makes use of the functionality of the SAP host agent. As already described, the SAP host agent can recognize the structure and the created virtual logical servers on a physical server (see Section 2.2.1). Using the OTF concept, the Diagnostics Agent can access the list of the agents operated in the system, and with the help of a so-called agent controller, it provides a complete physical server with agent instances. This agent controller permanently monitors the physical server for changes in the cluster situation. If a system cluster is moved from one physical server to another one, the Diagnostics Agent reproduces that by ending the agent resource on the old physical server and starting a new process of the Diagnostics Agent for the system cluster on the new server.

For notes and detailed instructions on how to properly use the OTF concept in your landscape, refer to the wiki page on your technical setup of SAP Solution Manager at *http://wiki.sdn.sap.com/wiki/display/SMSETUP/Diagnostics+Agent+and+HA+Support*. This page has all the important information on necessary parameters and step-by-step instructions for successful installation and activation.

2.3 Landscape Management and Presentation in SAP Solution Manager

The majority of applications in your operations require complete documentation of the system landscape. Since the applications and tools in SAP Solution Manager require that the information of the system landscape be always up to date and complete, we don't recommend maintaining this data manually, even though it's possible. Manual maintenance is not only prone to errors with the increasing complexity of the customer landscape, but it is also unreasonably extensive. Therefore, to the greatest possible extent, SAP Solution Manager determines the landscape automatically; this also ensures completeness, consistency, and thus comparability.

To understand how to determine which data must be maintained manually, let's take a look at the available landscape modeling units. A distinction can be made between *technical systems* and the so-called *product systems*. A technical system is the installation of software on a hardware depending on whether physical hardware or virtualization solutions are used. In contrast, a product system maps the dependencies between multiple technical systems—for instance those that are necessary to operate a complete system. An example of such a product system, which is very common, are the SAP NetWeaver double-stack systems, where at least one Java stack and one ABAP stack jointly form a product system.

A product contains one product instance or multiple product instances, while a product instance consists of multiple dependent software components, which must be installed together on a technical system. The technical system is the smallest unit that can be installed separately in the product instance. In this context, a technical system can also be installed, for example, on separate host systems for databases, servers, and message servers. This means that the hardware does not have to be a physical computer.

When it comes to technical operations in SAP Solution Manager 7.1, only the technical systems and the product instances and software components installed on them are relevant. All higher modeling entities in SAP Solution Manager, such as the mentioned product systems and logical components and solutions, are not required and therefore not described in more detail.

The SLD is the infrastructure that is used for automatic data collection of the technical landscape description. Every technical system logs on to the SLD with its data supplier and regularly transmits its system data. In an SAP system based on an AS ABAP or AS Java, the data suppliers are already integrated in the system. In addition, there are generic data suppliers, which are used by third-party providers to send their data to the SLD.

In the example shown in Figure 2.9, you can see the data supplier in an AS ABAP using Transaction RZ70, which is responsible for data transmission in an ABAP system. In addition to the connection data of the SLD in the SLD BRIDGE: GATEWAY INFORMATION area, you can set the default interval for data transmission (in this example, every 720 minutes, which is every twelve hours) in the OTHER SETTINGS area. Generally, you can use the default settings of the transmission interval. If the frequency is too high for you, you can double it, but we do not recommend using a period longer than a day because important information is then transmitted into the LMDB too late. As you can see in Figure 2.9, you can also determine which data is to be collected. To do this, deactivate the programs for collection of the parameters that you do not wish to transmit, or activate them if you want them to be synchronized.

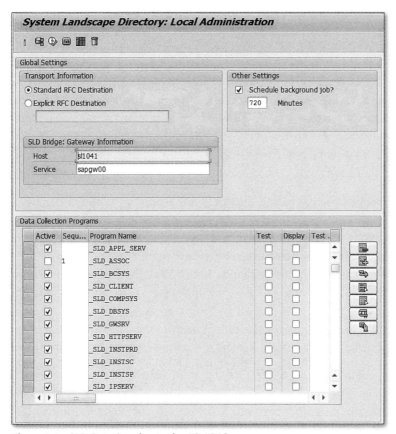

Figure 2.9 SLD Data Supplier in the AS ABAP

After the system data has been collected centrally in the SLD, it must be made available in SAP Solution Manager. This is done using the LMDB, which, as in the SLD, builds upon the SAP extension of the Common Information Model (CIM) data model of the Distributed Management Task Force (see also *www.dmtf.org*). Due to this standardization of the data model, the individual system data collected in the SLD can be synchronized in the LMDB together with the technical systems that have been modeled in CIM. This way, it is ensured that SAP Solution Manager always has current data available and that manually added or changed data is not overwritten by updates. So, be careful with manual changes in the LMDB: since automatic updating is not performed, updates concerning entries that have previously been changed manually must also be done manually.

However, the data suppliers are limited to some extent, as well. For example, only data that's available in the system can be collected and reported to the SLD. For SAP systems, this doesn't pose a major problem, but in connection with non-SAP systems, it's almost impossible to supply the same quality without complete access to the source code of the application. Therefore, SAP Solution Manager 7.1 makes it possible to not only recognize and supply data via the data suppliers from inside and as part of the system (*inside discovery*), but also to recognize and update it via the so-called *outside discovery*. Outside discovery is a mechanism that uses the installed agents of a system landscape to examine a system from outside. The data thus obtained is then sent to the LMDB in SAP Solution Manager.

An illustrative example is a separate, independent server on which a database that is to be monitored by SAP Solution Manager is installed. To allow for this, the following must be provided to SAP Solution Manager: the host, as well as the operating system, operating system version, database manufacturer, database version, and, last but not least, various installation information, such as the installation path. One possibility for providing SAP Solution Manager with this information is entering it manually, but for mentioned reasons, this method is not very useful. Outside discovery is the solution to the problem because the data is collected from outside and forwarded to SAP Solution Manager, without making manual entries necessary. The interaction between the Diagnostics Agent and the SAP host agent (see Figure 2.10) makes this possible.

In this connection, the SAP host agent offers the possibility of examining the file system of the host on which it is installed and, while doing so, discovering relevant installed software, such as databases or Microsoft-specific components. In addition, data of the operating system and the configuration of the host (for example, utilized host names, IP addresses, main memories, and processors) is obtained. Since the SAP host agent is installed only once per operating system, this data is collected and made available only once, as well. The Diagnostics Agent, which is installed in the context of the managed system, uses this data, puts it in context with the installed managed system, and then sends it to SAP Solution Manager.

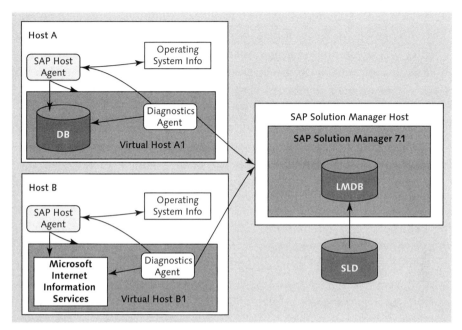

Figure 2.10 Data Flow of Outside Discovery

This way, it is possible to automatically detect not only the logical host name, but also the real host name of the server on which the system is installed, and to write it into the LMDB in SAP Solution Manager. The entire outside discovery mechanism works based on the installation of both agents and the connection of the Diagnostics Agent to an SAP Solution Manager system without further manual actions. This means that, as soon as a Diagnostics Agent and an SAP host agent are correctly installed on a host, the components installed on the host will be detected automatically. The information is transmitted directly to the LMDB, and all applications of technical operations in SAP Solution Manager can thus access the information.

As you can see, the agents also play a key role in landscape maintenance and in the complete mapping of a landscape. Make sure to include the agents early enough in your landscape planning and implementation phases.

2.4   Navigation in SAP Solution Manager 7.1: Work Center

As a central tool for navigation between various tools and applications offered by SAP Solution Manager, the work center concept was integrated in SAP Solution

Manager. From SAP Solution Manager 7.1 upwards, you can access a complete, uniform, and role-based illustration of all scenarios in SAP Solution Manager. The work center of SAP Solution Manager offers a central start to an individual work environment, which can be adjusted for each end user based on the individual roles. Depending on the tasks that need to be completed in your daily work, various work centers can be mapped. Old presentations and access options for the applications of SAP Solution Manager were almost entirely migrated into the work centers. As of release 7.1, old calls, such as the DSWP transaction, no longer work. There are still some applications that have not been migrated yet or which, due to their functionality, such as the SMSY transaction and the associated landscape management of SAP NetWeaver AS ABAP, will be gradually replaced.

A central control instrument for the presentation and structure of the work center is the authorization system with the role concept that regulates the access to the work center. For detailed information on applying authorizations for and in the work center and how to create your individual environment using work centers and authorizations, please refer to Chapter 12. This chapter focuses on the structure and handling of the work centers.

A work center was created for each work environment existing in SAP Solution Manager. The work environments are based on the tools and environments that SAP Solution Manager provides. The work centers assigned to a user can be accessed using Transaction SM_WORKCENTER. The following work centers are the ones that are, so far, the most important ones and reflect the common work environments of customers:

▶ Configuration of SAP Solution Manager

▶ Change Management

▶ Business Process Operations

▶ Root Cause Analysis

▶ Implementation/Upgrade

▶ Incident Management

▶ Test Management

▶ Job Management

▶ Assistant for Solution Documentation

▶ SAP Engagement and Service Delivery

- SAP Solution Manager Administration
- Technical Administration
- System Monitoring
- Technical Monitoring
- Data Volume Management

Figure 2.11 shows you the general structure of the work centers.

The first navigation level is the navigation bar, from which you select the work area. The navigation area is the second navigation level, from which you can select layers, functions, and cross-references for your selected work areas.

When you choose a view in the navigation area, the system updates the work area based on the authorizations assigned to you. The structure of the work area depends on the work environment you select from the navigation bar. Related objects are shown in so-called areas (trays) to allow for better and easier adjustment of the user-specific work environment.

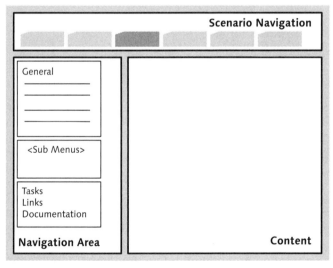

Figure 2.11 Work Center Structure in SAP Solution Manager

Depending on the selected activity in the navigation area, the object information can be presented in various ways. A number of different activities can be selected in the navigation area. Depending on the contents in the work area, the navigation area displays various contents and possible points of access. The following lists the most important elements of the navigation area:

▶ **General**
This area summarizes the most important contents of the selected work center. The displayed information is aggregated from the views and reports of the work center. Typical contents are links to filtered lists and reports. The information refers to alerts, projects, systems, solutions, etc., which are mapped to your role and your task area.

▶ **Specific views of work centers**
These views contain lists and service views that are relevant to the work center:

   ▶ Lists contain objects you can adjust as desired, and they include functions you can run from the selected view.

   ▶ Service views provide help for various tasks in the form of pictograms and explanations. In addition, you can call up related functions.

▶ **Subviews**
Here, you find related subviews of the selected work center.

▶ **Reports**
If the selected work center provides reports, they can be found here.

▶ **Typical tasks**
This area has functions that can be called up from any work center view.

▶ **Related links**
This area has links to useful information and functions with contents related to the selected work center. When you select a link, the function or information is opened in a new window. The system administrator determines which links are displayed here.

2.5   Initial Configuration of SAP Solution Manager

Now that we've looked at the architecture of the individual components in SAP Solution Manager, the next two sections show you how to set up the SAP Solution Manager system and which steps are important to successfully connect a system to SAP Solution Manager. The initial configuration for actively using SAP Solution Manager and the managed systems is done in three main phases:

1. System preparation

2. Basic configuration

3. Configuration of managed systems

The aim is to entirely prepare and set up SAP Solution Manager for your system landscape. After the second step, SAP Solution Manager already is in a basic availability mode and could, for example, be set up with ITSM. However, we recommend finishing the three mentioned phases before you continue with other scenarios or set up other applications. A large number of scenarios in SAP Solution Manager and all applications described in this book require successful completion of these three phases.

2.5.1 Configuration of SAP Solution Manager

For the configuration of SAP Solution Manager, a program is consistently used in which each setup step is explained. This configuration program was introduced with SAP Solution Manager 7.01; its interactive user guidance makes the configuration process of SAP Solution Manager considerably easier. During the ongoing development of the product, the automatic setup was extended to other applications, as well; currently, this setup program can be used for a total of ten application scenarios in SAP Solution Manager 7.1 SP05. The SAP SOLUTION MANAGER CONFIGURATION work center (Transaction SOLMAN_SETUP) offers the end user a fully documented form of the entire setup of SAP Solution Manager.

2.5.2 System Preparation

First of all, the system is prepared to allow for successful basic configuration of the SAP Solution Manager system in the next step.

Use Transaction SOLMAN_SETUP to start the program in your local web browser. It gives you an initial overview of the status of your configuration of the SAP Solution Manager system. As you can see in Figure 2.12, the view is divided into several areas. The left window pane is for navigation. Here, you can select scenarios or switch among the SYSTEM PREPARATION, BASIC CONFIGURATION, and MANAGED SYSTEMS CONFIGURATION areas. Right from the navigation area is the HELP area, where you get information on the selected scenario you want to set up. The LOG area provides information on recent changes concerning the selected activity. All steps in the program are documented, so you can use the log for analysis purposes at a later point. The view always has the same structure: the HELP area of the window provides an explanation on the activities shown in the ACTIVITIES area.

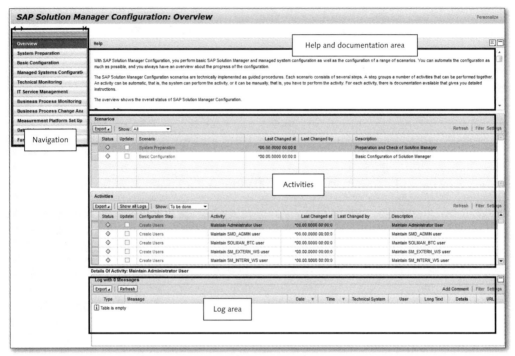

Figure 2.12 SAP Solution Manager Configuration Work Center View

In the case of new installations, the SYSTEM PREPARATION and BASIC CONFIGURA-TION entries in the SCENARIOS area have no evaluation in the STATUS column yet, and they don't have a grey diamond. This tells you that the setup has not started yet. As soon as you start your first activities in the system preparation and also in the basic configuration, this progress is displayed in the view; depending on the progress, the scenario receives a global evaluation, the so-called *status*.

Figure 2.13 shows examples of such evaluations; they are also used for the overall evaluation in the overview. Also, proactively checking mechanisms indicate, for example, that certain configuration steps need to be repeated. This can be due to a release change, adjustment of base objects, or SAP correction note. We therefore recommend regularly logging on to the SAP SOLUTION MANAGER CONFIGURATION work center. Particularly after changes to the system, you get an idea whether you need to adjust the configuration of SAP Solution Manager.

The work center navigation allows you to jump to any setup phase if individual steps need to be repeated. This way, you can directly follow the notes in a structured manner and update the changes.

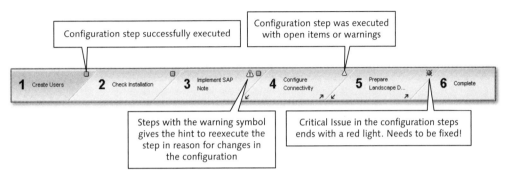

Figure 2.13 Evaluation Options in SAP Solution Manager Configuration Cockpit

The following subsections describe the steps required for successful system preparation. In the navigation bar of the configuration program, click the first area, named SYSTEM PREPARATION. In the following six steps, you prepare the technical system so that, after that, you can do the basic configuration. In Figure 2.13, we have already shown the notation and evaluation options of the status on the example of the navigation for the system preparation.

Step 1: Create Users

In the first step, we create necessary application users in SAP Solution Manager for system operations and configuration. First, you must create the user SOLMAN_ADMIN. In this first step, the administrator of SAP Solution Manager receives a full set of roles and profiles that permit the complete administration of SAP Solution Manager and the use and setup of all scenarios in SAP Solution Manager. Other users to be created are of the technical user type, as follows:

▶ SMD_ADMIN is used for communication with the agents.

▶ SOLMAN_BTC is used for background processing in SAP Solution Manager.

▶ SM_EXTERN_WS and SM_INTERN_WS are used for communication with the web services.

All four users are automatically assigned the permissions defined for their purpose.

Step 2: Check Installation

In the second step, the system is checked for various requirements as follows:

▶ The Transport Management of the SAP Solution Manager system should be active and mapped to a valid transport domain.

▶ In this step, necessary system parameters are checked for their presence and recommended values.

▶ Availability of a valid license for the product and a valid maintenance contract with SAP are checked.

▶ Depending on the basis release of SAP Solution Manager, all other components must meet the technical minimum requirements to avoid inconsistencies and ensure the functionality of all scenarios and programs.

▶ Two more checks ensure that communication with SAP Service Marketplace works smoothly. It is checked whether the parameter for automatic transmission of system data to SAP Service Marketplace is active and whether communication with SAP has been established. This communication connection is also important if you want to make use of SAP Support. The exchange of important system data, for example, allows that services, which you can request from SAP Service Marketplace, are sent to the corresponding systems. To find out which information can be sent from connected systems to SAP Service Marketplace, refer to SAP Note 993775.

Step 3: Implement SAP Note

If all requirements are met, you can go to the next step, which is implementing the composite correction note. The central composite note includes all known error corrections for the used component version of SAP Solution Manager. This means that, regardless of which components are actually in use, essentially all known corrections are implemented. This way, all functionalities are updated by default so that at a later point, you can use other scenarios without further updates. This results in a presumably high amount of corrections that are supplied with this composite note. So, make sure to allow some time for the first composite note import because object corrections, in particular, take some time.

Step 4: Configure Connectivity

After successfully importing the composite note and all included corrections, you can start setting up the options for the connection of the SAP Solution Manager system with remote components, such as managed systems. First, this step creates the basis for communication with the SAP Solution Manager system.

If you use multiple Java instances and a Web Dispatcher for communication between the instances, you can enter it in the first substep. If you do not use a Web Dispatcher, you can continue with the next substep without any changes. Next, in the second substep, you need to define the authentication options for web services, and based on that, in the third substep, create the logical ports for the web services. In the fourth and final substep, you need to define the logon procedure for Diagnostics Agents. We recommend not choosing the classic method using user name and password, but the certificate-controlled logon method instead. This facilitates maintenance of SAP Solution Manager later.

Step 5: Prepare Landscape Description

The last step of system preparation is setting up the landscape components in SAP Solution Manager. SAP Solution Manager uses components to read and prepare information. In this fifth step of system preparation, the components SLD and LMDB are set up for operations.

In contrast to releases prior to SAP Solution Manager 7.1, the SLD serves as a data supplier for the LMDB. SAP Solution Manager no longer uses the SLD as an active landscape management component, but only as a data supplier for the LMDB, as shown in Figure 2.14.

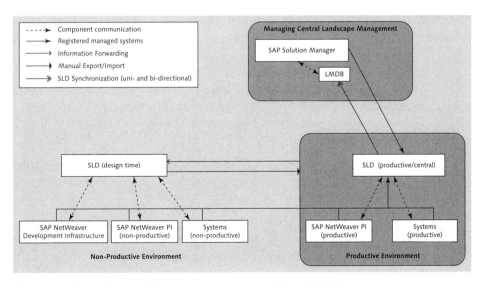

Figure 2.14 Interaction and Communication between SLD and LMDB

The interaction and structure of the SLD and LMDB are described in Section 2.3, in which we introduced the two components of SAP Solution Manager.

SAP recommends creating a central SLD as a stand-alone system component in the system of your landscape using the latest AS Java version. Normally this is not SAP Solution Manager because in SAP NetWeaver release 7.0, which is used by SAP Solution Manager, the SLD is integrated as a component. During synchronization with SAP NetWeaver releases that are higher than release 7.1, only information of the smallest release can be processed. Since SAP NetWeaver PI systems particularly contain important information in the SLD regarding information routes to be processed, a large part would not be synchronized based on a release 7.0 SLD. Therefore, we do not recommend choosing SAP Solution Manager as a host for the SLD.

SAP recommends building a dedicated SLD server that is more or less up to date in the landscape. The information from the central SLD is fully synchronized in the LMDB. As described in Section 2.3, the LMDB is the primary landscape management component. In this last step of system preparation, old data is migrated and the central SLD is connected.

Step 6: Complete

When Step 5 is complete, a summary is displayed of all activities of the system preparation phase and their statuses. Double-check that all steps have the SUCCESS-FULLY COMPLETED status and no activities need any other actions or report an error status. If a step is incomplete or has errors, you can go directly to it and repeat it. After that, the system is prepared for initial configuration of the basic tools, such as root cause analysis, SAP EarlyWatch Alert, and Maintenance Optimizer.

2.5.3   Basic Configuration

Basic configuration of the SAP Solution Manager system is based on the results of the system preparation and follows a similar guideline. Basic configuration is divided into eight substeps, which, building upon one another, prepare SAP Solution Manager for using the various applications of the application operation. At the end of the eight steps, the first basic tools are available for system administration. For example, root cause analysis, Maintenance Optimizer, or the management and presentation of landscape components can be used right after the first few systems have been connected to SAP Solution Manager. The individual steps for basic configuration are described in the following subsections.

Step 1: Specify Solution

In the first step, you can save all modifications and configurations of the system in an SAP Solution Manager project (see Chapter 3 for additional details). By creating an SAP Solution Manager project in the basic configuration, you can access the gathered information and results for another implementation project.

Therefore, create the project in this step. SAP suggests a name for the project, which you are welcome to replace. If you have a system that is based on an upgrade, it's possible that a project already exists from previous upgrades or implementations. In this case, there is no need for any action at this point, and you can select the existing project and continue with the next step.

The project is created with a new landscape. The aim is to create an independent and stand-alone landscape in which all systems relevant to the system administration and support are managed in one solution.

Step 2: Specify User & Connectivity Data

In the next step, SPECIFY USER & CONNECTIVITY DATA, all necessary technical default users, which will finally also allow for the connection of systems, are created in SAP Solution Manager. First, you can create an SAP service user (S user) for communication with SAP Support Portal. We recommend contacting SAP to apply for a dedicated user for SAP Solution Manager who is allowed to maintain all necessary systems and installations at the SAP Support Portal. This new SAP service user is, thus, independent of your personal SAP service user and can communicate with SAP Service Marketplace on behalf of SAP Solution Manager. For example, the SAP service user is used for synchronization with SAP Service Marketplace in order to update the status information on connected systems once a day. The SAP service user is also used for the automatic distribution of maintenance licenses.

When all information has been created successfully, you can continue with the next substep to use the BI data in SAP Solution Manager. Here, you decide about the future system configuration of your BI client, if you have not already done so. You can obtain the SAP NetWeaver BW resources directly from the productive client. In this case, SAP NetWeaver BW is activated directly in the productive client of your SAP Solution Manager. However, you can also decide to use a separate client or an entirely independent system. We recommend using the same client because this considerably facilitates the setup, interface communication, and maintenance of the overall system.

In the next substep, SET UP CREDENTIALS, you are requested to enter administration users, which are used for other automatic activities. We recommend using the SOLMAN_ADMIN user to ensure that the user already has all required permissions because we were able to generate this user automatically during system preparation.

> **Note**
>
> When you have set up the SAP NetWeaver Business Warehouse (BW) in a separate SAP Solution Manager client or in a separate system, you need to create an SAP NetWeaver BW administrator in the BW system or update the role profile of an existing BW administrator.

In the next substep, CREATE USERS, create more default users. You can also update authorization profiles for the default users. An update can, for example, be required due to a change in a Support Package or after importing a correction. In such cases, the user authorizations should be regenerated. The UPDATE column explicitly informs you if an update for an authorization object for a user is available.

As during the basic setup, we recommend regularly checking the overall setup status on the OVERVIEW page in the SAP SOLUTION MANAGER CONFIGURATION work center. If an update is available, this is indicated in the overall status. The users created in this step are for communication purposes and for managing systems to be connected.

In the next and final substep of SPECIFY USER & CONNECTIVITY DATA, the internal communication interfaces between the AS Java and the AS ABAP are created. The internal RFC connection WEBADMIN is set up for the direct communication and calls between the technical instances. Another communication interface, which is set up for the operations of SAP Solution Manager, provides the interaction between the SAP NetWeaver BW and SAP Solution Manager. Data collected by the systems to be connected has predefined storage locations in SAP NetWeaver BW. The interfaces obtain and address the data directly.

All required users in SAP Solution Manager have now been created.

Step 3: Specify Landscape Data

In the third step, SPECIFY LANDSCAPE DATA, the components Introscope Enterprise Manager and SAPconnect, which are used for sending email, for example, are set up. Introscope Enterprise Manager installations that are already available can already be specified in the first subset, CONFIGURE CA WILY INTROSCOPE, so that they can be connected to SAP Solution Manager.

For the first time, SAP Solution Manager 7.1 offers the possibility of creating remote installations using SAP Solution Manager. This substep provides an overview of which Introscope Enterprise Managers are already connected to SAP Solution Manager and of their current general usage situation. The usage also indicates whether you need to perform a single installation or set up a cluster solution. There are two ways to integrate Introscope Enterprise Manager in your SAP Solution Manager solution:

▶ As a single installation: there is only one instance that collects information and communicates with SAP Solution Manager.

▶ As a distributed solution: there is also one instance that communicates with SAP Solution Manager, but there are separate instances (cluster) of Enterprise Manager that collect the information of the systems to be connected.

For instance, if you have a landscape with more than a hundred systems to be connected, you should already consider a distributed solution of Introscope Enterprise Managers. An instance of Introscope Enterprise Managers is limited in processing the information of connected systems in real time. Therefore, if you have a large number of systems to be connected, it is necessary to use a distributed solution with multiple instances. Such a distributed solution of Introscope Enterprise Manager is a bit more complex in its structure because it has at least two instances in its smallest version. However, such a solution with a dynamic load distribution and the option of resource extensions, is considerably more flexible and easier to operate.

To send out email from SAP Solution Manager, it's necessary to create an interface between the SAP system and the service provider in your organization. You can set that up in the next substep, CONFIGURE SAPCONNECT. For this purpose, you are prompted to enter your provider's access point or your communication interface. SAPconnect is used to send emails and SMS messages.

Step 4: Configure Manually

This step includes a number of substeps with manual activities. Not all of these steps will be relevant to you. You decide which steps are necessary for you and then perform the steps as instructed.

The first few steps are important steps to prepare the SAP NetWeaver BW system, such as activating the BW source system, setting up the BW authorization concept, and maintaining the logical systems. In this context, you define the data structure for saving the information collected in the connected systems. You determine the logon procedure for the BW resources and set up the technical name of the BW client in the system.

In the next manual step, contents and definitions of the services in SAP Solution Manager, which SAP offers you under the maintenance contract, are updated. For example, an important service is EarlyWatch Alert; the so-called self-checks are also part of the service content. More information on these services can be found in SAP Service Marketplace under the alias *supportservices*.

Step 5: Configure Automatically

This step deals with the automatic configurations that are essential for the operations of SAP Solution Manager. These are mainly steps that relate to and ensure the internal communication of the various components, such as those of Introscope Enterprise Manager, the BW extractors, and other data collection methods.

Prior to each substep, it is checked whether the substep needs to be performed in the SAP Solution Manager system, or the activities just need to be updated, or no activity is required. This functionality assures you that the changes you made to the system—for example, activating BOMs—cannot unintentionally be overwritten with default values in the event of another execution. After all steps have been successfully completed, your SAP Solution Manager system is technically fully configured. Now, continue with the last few steps to complete the basic configuration of SAP Solution Manager.

Step 6: Configure Engagement Reports

From SAP Solution Manager 7.1 SP05 onwards, for customers with an SAP Product Support for Large Enterprises (PSLE) contract, a customer report with the same name is available. If you do not have such a maintenance contract with SAP, you will not benefit from this report because it deals with information in the context of the SAP PSLE maintenance contract. More information can be found in SAP Service Marketplace under the alias *supportservices*.

The service SAP-PSLE REPORT, which must be performed by the customer, offers you, as an SAP-PSLE customer, a comprehensive overview of all current statuses of your application, the lifecycle management of your business-critical activities, and the SAP service range. The aim is to ensure the collaboration between your IT organization and SAP in order to optimize your SAP software solutions. Apart from that, the SAP-PSLE Report is aimed at helping you solve any problems that could have a negative effect on the operations of your applications or enterprise solutions. The step CONFIGURE ENGAGEMENT REPORTS allows you to take the necessary steps to configure the report. If you are not a PSLE customer, you can skip this optional step and go to the next step, where you create the configuration users.

Step 7: Create Configuration Users

In the last step of basic configuration of your SAP Solution Manager, you create the configuration users. This step is optional for you and not a requirement for your SAP Solution Manager to function. This step allows you to create configuration users for the individual scenarios in the SAP Solution Manager system with their individual authorizations. Perform this step if you want to create a dedicated configuration user for a specific scenario, such as SAP NetWeaver BW reporting or Change Management. The users are automatically created with a complete set of all roles required for setting up a scenario.

Step 8: Complete

Finally, the overall status of the basic configuration is summarized on one page (see Figure 2.15). As you can see, all steps and substeps have a green mark in the STATUS column, which means they have been completed successfully.

As in system preparation, confirm that no steps that are important for your basic configuration are left open. Depending on your decisions, optional configurations in steps CONFIGURE MANUALLY, CONFIGURE ENGAGEMENT REPORTS, and CREATE CONFIGURATION USERS can also be grey because you skipped them. Complete all activities and exit basic configuration by closing the browser window or selecting another area in the navigation bar.

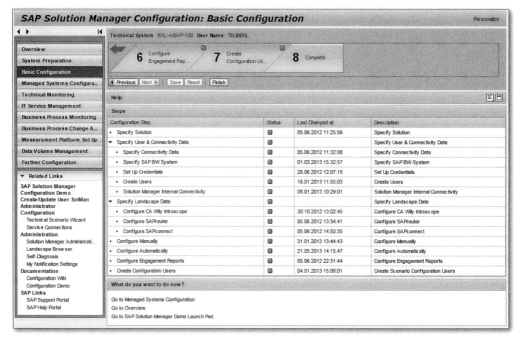

Figure 2.15 Summary and Report on Successful Completion of Basic Configuration in SAP Solution Manager 7.1

Your basic configuration is now completed, and your SAP Solution Manager system is ready for use. Now, you can set up the individual scenarios and connect systems to SAP Solution Manager.

2.5.4 Configuration of Managed Systems

After you have successfully completed all steps for system preparation and basic configuration, you can connect the systems to SAP Solution Manager. Depending on the technological basis of the systems to be connected, the setup steps are automatically adjusted by the configuration process.

SAP Solution Manager 7.1 SP05 gives you the possibility to connect not only SAP components to SAP Solution Manager, but also, for example, databases that are not used by SAP systems or server systems that don't have an SAP system installed. This allows you to get a quick overview of the status of the various components beyond SAP systems. For information on which components and systems are currently supported by your SAP Solution Manager and what you need to consider during setup, please refer to the official wiki on SAP Solution Manager. This information is available at the following URL: *http://wiki.sdn.sap.com/wiki/display/SMSETUP/Maintenance+of+Product+in+the+System+Landscape.*

In the following steps we show you which steps are necessary to set up a system connection, with the example of Toys Inc.'s SAP ERP system, which is based on SAP NetWeaver 7.0 and is named OTO. The OTO system consists of two active system cores, an SAP NetWeaver AS Java to map the staff management and auto-creation, and an SAP NetWeaver AS ABAP with the SAP ERP Central Components (ECC) to map the core business processes of Toys Inc.

1. Start the setup of the systems to be connected from the SAP SOLUTION MANAGER CONFIGURATION work center.

2. In the left-hand navigation area, choose the fourth menu item, MANAGED SYSTEMS CONFIGURATION. The right-hand action area now displays all systems that you can connect to Solution Manager. In the list, choose the system to be connected.

3. Now, start the setup of the system to be connected by selecting the desired system in the list and then choosing the SYS. CONFIG. button. A new browser window opens, in which you can find the appropriate configuration steps for your system.

Each system to be connected has a technological basis that distinguishes it from other systems. An AS Java system has different technology from an AS ABAP system. Particularly in the communication, there are differences that must be considered. Your SAP Solution Manager system can handle these differences and offers you various setup steps adjusted for your system.

The first few steps to set up the systems to be connected in SAP Solution Manager are identical regardless of mentioned different technologies.

1. In the first step, SAP Solution Manager checks whether the system component you selected is an SAP-supported format and a valid version. For our OTO system, this is equivalent to an SAP ERP system with the ECC component. As you can see in Figure 2.16, this information is obtained from the LMDB. You can adjust and extend the information in the LMDB to make sure it is displayed correctly.

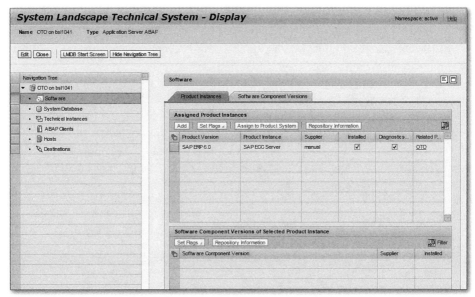

Figure 2.16 Maintenance of Product Information and Instance of the System to Be Connected

2. In the second step, the technical requirements of the system to be connected are checked. The technological system basis is checked for the minimum requirements, for example. SAP adjusts the minimum requirements regularly. For more information on version dependencies and minimum requirements for connection of systems to SAP Solution Manager, see SAP Note 1483508 (SAP Solution Manager 7.1: Prerequisites for Root Cause Analysis).

These first two substeps are necessary to ensure that no errors occur during further connection and setup.

In the third subset, the ST-PI and ST-A/PI service components are checked. The ST-PI and ST-A/PI service components should be installed on the systems to be connected in their current version to allow for current findings from SAP Support to be included during the collection of the information of systems to be connected. These two components control which information is transmitted from the systems to be connected to SAP Solution Manager. In our OTO system, all requirements are met, and both the STATUS column and the navigation bar indicate a green status, which means that we can continue with the next step.

3. In the third step, the connections are set up regardless of the selected technological basis of the system to be connected. Our AS ABAP system uses the usual RFC connections for communication among the system instances. In non-ABAP

systems, you can already connect the Diagnostics Agent in the third step, while in AS ABAP systems, this is done one step later, after the RFC connections have been created. When you connect the Diagnostics Agent, it is important to install a Diagnostics Agent on each virtual or local server. If you have a distributed system installation, you will need multiple Diagnostics Agents for connecting your system to be connected. After you have connected all technical instances with a Diagnostics Agent, you can proceed to the next step.

4. In this step, we enter all system parameters required to configure the managed system. Which parameters are to be entered depends on the type of managed system. You are requested to enter a user for your technical instance. In our example, we have to specify an administrator for the OTO system client to be connected and a valid port for the message server on which our OTO system runs.

   Maintaining the access information for the database is the same for all technical systems. After you have maintained and saved the access information, an entry for the system to be connected is created in the central database cockpit (DBA Cockpit) of SAP Solution Manager. The DBA Cockpit provides a central access point for all connected database systems to the administration and daily maintenance of database systems. You can call the DBA Cockpit using Transaction DBACOCKPIT in your SAP Solution Manager system at any time. This information and the other system parameters are used in the step for automatic configuration for setting up the system to be connected. Make sure that the user you specified has sufficient permissions on the instance to be connected to do the automatic configuration. After you have fully specified all parameters, you can proceed with the automatic configuration.

5. In the fifth step, CONFIGURE AUTOMATICALLY, extractors are created that are responsible for collecting performance information or information on changes to the technical systems. Also, communication interfaces are created, and necessary parameter changes are suggested and adjusted during a repeated setup. In the LOG below your list of ACTIVITIES, check that all substeps have been completed successfully and proceed with the manual steps.

6. In the step CONFIGURE MANUALLY, you add more parameters for the operations on the system to be connected. For AS Java instances, you also need to entirely restart the cluster of the instance once. During automatic configuration, you have already stored important parameters, which allow the Introscope tools to collect information on a non-ABAP instance, in the system to be connected. To

activate the start parameters for the Introscope Byte Code Adapters for the system to be connected and to ensure that the agent logs on to the Introscope Enterprise Manager, you must restart the instances. In our OTO system, no further manual steps are required. We therefore go to the next step before performing the final check.

7. Prior to the final check, our technical system to be connected must be assigned a LOGICAL COMPONENT that properly presents the product information and system line. For our OTO system, we create a copy of the logical component SAP ERP ECC SERVER and report that the system is a productive system. This logical component can be used by various solutions within SAP Solution Manager. You should make sure the system to be connected exists in at least one solution landscape.

8. In the step CHECK CONFIGURATION, do a final check that the system has been completed successfully.

The check completes the connection process for the systems to be connected. After that, you can use the system for scenarios such as EarlyWatch Alert, Maintenance Optimizer, the central administration, or root cause analysis. We can now use and continue configuring our OTO system for the following scenarios—for example, technical monitoring.

2.6   Customer Example: SAP Solution Manager Implemented at Munich Re

In this section, Mr. Carsten Bein, development engineer at Munich Re, tells us how SAP Solution Manager is used at Munich Re.

Munich Re

The business model of Munich Re is based on a combination of primary insurance and reinsurance under one roof. Worldwide, we cover a large variety of risks of different complexities.

Munich Re stands for extensive solution expertise, consistent risk management, financial stability, and close proximity to our customers. With premium income of over €28 billion from reinsurance alone, Munich Re is one of the world's leading reinsurers. The global and local knowledge of our roughly 11,200 staff in reinsurance is unique.

Munich Re's primary insurance operations are concentrated mainly in the ERGO Insurance Group. Worldwide, the Group is represented in more than 30 countries and concentrates on Europe and Asia. Forty-eight thousand people work for the Group, as either salaried employees or full-time, self-employed sales representatives. In 2012, Munich Re recorded a premium income of around €17 billion in the primary insurance business. Under the Munich Health brand, Munich Re combines its global healthcare knowledge in primary insurance and reinsurance with a premium income of over €6 billion.

IT Organization of Munich Re

Our consistently global corporate orientation was manifested in our internal IT organization early on. A central IT corporate center is responsible for three regional hubs. The IT hubs are divided up into AMERICAS (North and South America), EMEA (Europe, Middle East, Africa), and APAC (Asian/Pacific region). Global IT systems are operated exclusively by the EMEA hub, decentralized solutions by the local IT service centers.

In 1992, the first SAP R/3 development system was installed in Munich. The SAP HR component was implemented in 1996. The FI, CO, and MM components followed. The go-live of the so-called "GLORIA" project in 2008 marked the completion of the most extensive IT project in our corporate history to date, and SAP FS-RI was implemented. Otherwise, the so-called Global Data Warehouse, a business intelligence system for comprehensive reporting, was established. Today, SAP FS-RI and the related Global Data Warehouse system line alone comprise 22 SAP systems, including all development, test, quality assurance, and production systems. By now, our entire SAP landscape has grown to around 56 SAP systems.

Accordingly, our SAP landscape maintenance is complex. SAP Solution Manager was implemented early on. At first, for Support Package downloads and implementation, we primarily used Maintenance Optimizer. For task list management and monitoring, we used the central system administration. For system landscape monitoring, we used SAP EarlyWatch Alert, and we implemented system and business process monitoring using CCMS.

In 2011, we implemented the Change-Request Management scenario (managing change requests) for a large part of the SAP system lines. In 2012, SAP Solution

Manager was upgraded to release 7.1 SP06, which included the conversion to the new Change Request Management scenario.

Upgrade of SAP Solution Manager at Munich Re

In 2013, the CCMS-based monitoring system is planned to be replaced with technical monitoring and alerting. The new technology involves a number of infrastructural improvements, which make maintaining the monitoring solution considerably easier. For reprocessing the generated alerts, an interface for HP OpenView has been specifically developed, which means that, in the central ticketing system, incidents are automatically generated from specific alerts. Based on our experience as part of the SAP Solution Manager upgrade project, we can give other customers the following tips for a successful SAP Solution Manager upgrade project:

▶ **Include stakeholders early on**
By including stakeholders early on, we were able to consider numerous detail requirements, especially for the change-request scenario. This increased our acceptance enormously.

▶ **Prepare satellite systems in time**
For the connection of satellite systems, the components ST-PI, distributing certain technical roles, and creating technical users is necessary. Due to internal regulations, existing processes, and available resources, this task turned out to be much more time-consuming than originally planned.

▶ **Spread know-how across multiple persons**
Bundling expert knowledge of multiple SAP Solution Manager scenarios in one person can be a disadvantage. It has proven to be beneficial to be able to use multiple experts, from inside our organization and from our external partners, for the variety of scenarios.

▶ **Plan for adequate testing**
Early testing increases the quality of the configured SAP Solution Manager system already before live operations begin, which eventually has a positive effect on the end users' acceptance.

▶ **Iterative incremental method**
Applying an iterative method, we have been able to identify and minimize risks early on. The iteration extent should be manageable because, otherwise, the complexity of SAP Solution Manager cannot be handled successfully.

▶ **Choose suitable collaboration platform and media**
It is in the collaboration with external partners, in particular, where exchanging work results plays a decisive role. An effective knowledge transfer is also essential for the progress of a project and should be supported by suitable tools.

2.7   Additional Documentation

Links

▶ Wiki for technical information:
http://wiki.sdn.sap.com/wiki/display/SMSETUP/Home

▶ Installing SAP Web Dispatcher:
*http://wiki.sdn.sap.com/wiki/display/Basis/Installation+of+SAP+Web+
Dispatcher+and+SSL+Setup+%28updated+and+corrected%29*

▶ Overview of supported non-SAP components:
*http://wiki.sdn.sap.com/wiki/display/SMSETUP/Maintenance+of+
Product+in+the+System+Landscape*

▶ SAP Service Marketplace, alias *performance*

▶ SAP Service Marketplace, alias *supportservices*

SAP Notes

Table 2.3 provides a good overview of important SAP Notes concerning the architecture and configuration of SAP Solution Manager.

Contents	Note
Using the automatic update of the SAP host agent	1473974
SAP Host Agent Installation Package	1031096
Information on the data transmitted to SAP Service Marketplace	993775
SAP Solution Manager 7.1: Prerequisites for Root Cause Analysis	1483508

Table 2.3 SAP Notes on the Architecture and Configuration of SAP Solution Manager

If you have detailed documentation of your projects, you can always access information on projects and SAP systems. SAP Solution Manager supports you in creating such documentation.

3 Implementation Projects

In Chapter 1, we described Application Lifecycle Management (ALM) and project management. In this chapter, we go from theory to practice and show you how you can use SAP Solution Manager in your implementation projects.

Just like any other project, an implementation project is also executed using a project management method. Independent of the project scope, each project flow is more or less based on the same scheme. To support the project flow, you can use tools such as SAP Solution Manager, which facilitate documentation and ensure transparency during the different project phases.

The project management in SAP Solution Manager allows you to identify, add, and implement new or extended business processes and technical information. The information collected here constantly grows and is structured by the solution documentation in SAP Solution Manager in a clear and comprehensible manner.

This chapter provides an overview of how you can execute projects using SAP Solution Manager as a documentation tool, and you'll learn about the benefits of this information for the reuse of the project data after handover to operations.

3.1 Projects versus Solutions

Business processes are the basis for *projects* and *solutions*. In projects, business processes are modeled, and in solutions, these business processes are monitored. In the event of a malfunction, it's ensured that these processes work smoothly.

Due to their different tasks, projects and solutions also differ in their perspective of business processes (see Figure 3.1). The job of a project is to take a business process to productive operations, while the solution must keep the business process running in a productive environment.

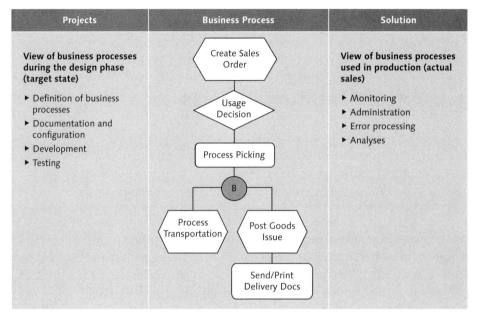

Figure 3.1 Business Processes from the Perspective of Projects and Solutions

Projects define a framework of actions within which IT requirements must be implemented. Project tasks defined in a clear project order are processed in a structured sequence. This includes developing a concept, documenting the project, implementing, and transition to operations. The purpose of project information, such as processes, process responsibilities, and process documents, is also to enhance the understanding of business processes within the company to quickly react to market changes, if necessary, and to implement them.

Solutions represent the result of a project. They contain precise information, such as documents about how your business processes are handled in your operations.

3.2 Project Types

The possibilities of implementing ALM in SAP Solution Manager are shown in Figure 3.2. Here you can see the various project types and their interactions with the solution. The next section introduces the individual project types in detail.

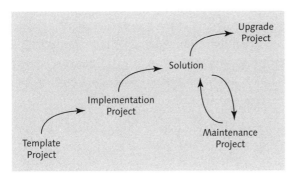

Figure 3.2 Project Types

3.2.1 Template Project

The template project is used to create and distribute templates. A template contains a defined project structure and allocated objects, such as documents, test cases, IMG objects, and developer and training material. These objects can be reused for follow-up projects, wherein their changeability can be controlled. If multiple SAP Solution Manager systems are used, templates and their contents can be transported. Template projects are useful for creating a standard process hierarchy or efficiently controlling global roll-outs.

3.2.2 Implementation Project

You use implementation projects to implement business processes in your SAP landscape. For this purpose, the structure of the business processes is mapped in a three-level hierarchy (business scenario, business process, and process step) defined by SAP Solution Manager.

To build a process structure, you can use the following sources in SAP Solution Manager:

▶ One or more template(s)

▶ Existing projects

▶ Pre-defined SAP processes from the *Business Process Repository* (BPR)

We'll introduce such an implementation project in more detail with the example of Toys Inc. in Section 3.6.

3.2.3 Maintenance Project

Maintenance projects are used to control and document changes to the production systems (solutions). These projects are supported by the use of Change Request Management.

The maintenance project receives all maintenance activities and urgent corrections of a solution. In the maintenance project, this redesign or change of information in a solution can be changed in a controlled manner.

3.2.4 Upgrade Project

An upgrade project is used to implement and document additional functions, or improve existing functions that are associated with a current solution.

3.3 Project Cycle

During a project using SAP Solution Manager, you go through several phases, as shown in Figure 3.3. The phases correspond to the ALM phases, as already described in Section 2.1.1. Building upon that, you use SAP Solution Manager as a tool for ALM. SAP Solution Manager provides a multitude of functions that support you throughout the entire project lifecycle. They allow you to process the individual project cycle phases in a structured manner and receive information on the current project status at any time.

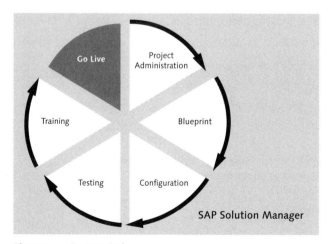

Figure 3.3 Project Cycle

In the following sections, we introduce the individual phases and functions of SAP Solution Manager.

3.3.1 Project Administration

In project administration, you create your project and define your general settings, such as the following:

▶ **System landscape**
The system landscape comprises all systems in which the business processes are defined, documented, and implemented by a project. Various system roles are represented by the *logical component*. A logical component must be assigned *logical systems* across systems and projects—for example: the main instance of the SAP Solution Manager server with release 7.1 (logical system) with the development system role for configuration.

▶ **Roadmaps**
In roadmaps, SAP provides standard procedures for projects.

▶ **Project standards**
In project standards, you define keywords and document types.

The functions for project definition and administration allow you to plan and prepare your project; for example, as a project manager. This is described in more detail in Section 3.5.

3.3.2 Blueprint

In the blueprint phase, also called *Business Blueprint*, you take the following steps:

▶ Define process structures

▶ Add documentation that describes and technically specifies business processes

▶ Add transactions that represent the process step

▶ Add structure attributes that allow for filtering the process structure

For the definition of the process structure, SAP Solution Manager specifies a three-level hierarchy of business scenario, business process, and business step (see Figure 3.4):

▶ **Business scenario (Example: sales planning)**
Business scenarios summarize the business processes and describe the tasks in a simple manner.

▶ **Business process (Example: order processing)**
The business process includes activities that are logically dependent on each another.

▶ **Process step (Example: create inquiry)**
A process step is an elementary activity for business process implementation. A process step can include various transactions.

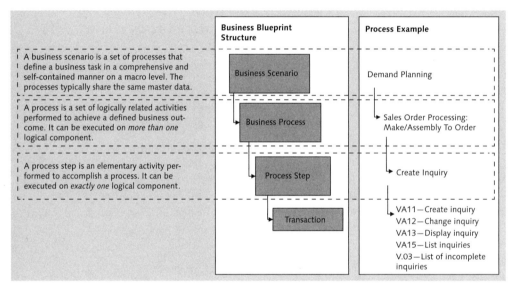

Figure 3.4 Business Blueprint Structure with Example

In Section 3.6.2, we introduce the individual activities in Business Blueprint.

3.3.3 Configuration

The configuration phase builds upon the process structure of the blueprint (design) phase and extends it: your customer-specific developments and configuration objects, test cases, and training material are documented.

These can be, for example, IMG objects, reports, function modules, or extended Computer Aided Test Tool (eCATT) test cases, an SAP-internal development for test automation, and should be added on the lowest level of the process structure, the process step.

3.3.4   Testing

Based on the test cases added to the process structure, you can create test plans. Use structure attributes or keywords to define and specify your test plans (*see Section 3.7.3*). You can reuse the process structure. In a test plan, create test packages and directly assign them to the users. The tests are also executed in SAP Solution Manager.

3.3.5   Training

In order to train your end users in new solutions and functions, you can use the training environment of the new version of SAP Solution Manager, in which you generate learning material, which is based on the existing process structure, for the various end-user tasks. For this purpose, learning material that has a clear list of content, which presents short HTML-format information on learning units and links to the learning material, is used. To improve your learning material, you should also make use of end-user feedback.

3.3.6   Go-Live

The project activities introduced so far will help you structure all necessary information and functions you need for implementing and upgrading SAP solutions. The individual functions in SAP Solution Manager always focus on the course of the project, from the evaluation of your process requirements to the go-live of your solution.

When going live, you decide which business processes and contents are handed over to the solution after completion of an implementation project. Based on this information, you can now keep your business processes up to date or use other topics, such as business process monitoring (see Chapter 11), in application management.

Now that you know the various project types and their phases, the following section describes the prerequisites for using these functions.

3.4   Prerequisites for Project Creation

In this section, we show you which configuration steps and permissions are necessary to fully use the project management functions in SAP Solution Manager.

3.4.1   General Information on Configuration

SAP Solution Manager is the central access point for your system landscape. If you want to add a new system to be managed (managed system), you must perform several basic configurations.

One of the most important configuration steps is creating remote function calls (RFCs) for communication between SAP Solution Manager and its connected system (see Section 2.5.4).

For differentiation among the individual system instances and clients in projects, logical components are defined by the basic administration. They describe on which SAP or non-SAP systems a business process is running.

3.4.2   Necessary Authorizations

Apart from the basic configuration, there are more prerequisites that are important in preparing the use of work centers for the implementation projects in SAP Solution Manager. The scope of functions for the user depends on the assigned permissions. So, depending on the tasks, a varying number of work centers can be assigned. For working with the IMPLEMENTATION/UPGRADE work center and for general activities in projects and solutions, your user needs the following authorization roles:

▶ SAP_SMWORK_BASIC

▶ SAP_SMWORK_IMPL

▶ SAP_SMWORK_SETUP

▶ SAP_SOL_PROJ_ADMIN_ALL

▶ SAP_SOLAR01_ALL

▶ SAP_SOLAR02_ALL

▶ SAP_SOL_KW_ALL

▶ SAP_SM_SOLUTION_ALL

A user's authorizations can be limited based on projects or their structures. For projects, you can use the S_PROJECT authorization object. Depending on the number of implementation projects, this authorization can be assigned to a user with access to the PROJECT_ID object.

The second option is working for a project using predefined namespaces that are defined by the project manager. The following are two examples:

▶ Namespace I_xxxx for implementation projects

▶ Namespace T_xxxx for template projects

This allows you to use the S_PROJECT authorization object in various user groups, for example:

▶ User group for implementation projects with PROJECT_ID = I*

▶ User group for template projects with PROJECT_ID = T*

For example, the S_PROJECTS and S_PROJECT authorization objects are in the SAP_SOLAR_PM authorization role, which you can copy and adjust as desired.

The extent to which a project structure can be changed by a user can be controlled in Transaction SOLAR_PROJECT_ADMIN on the PROJ. TEAM MEMBER tab, RESTRICT CHANGES TO NODES IN PROJECT TO ASSIGNED TEAM MEMBERS.

Also, for efficient and uninterrupted working in SAP Solution Manager, the user should be able to use the following transactions:

▶ SM_WORKCENTER

▶ SOLAR_PROJECT_ADMIN

▶ SOLAR_01

▶ SOLAR_02

▶ SOLAR_EVAL

▶ SOLMAN_DIRECTORY

▶ RMAUTH

▶ RMDEF

▶ RMMAIN

▶ SI80

▶ SI23

- ▶ SI24

- ▶ SPRO

- ▶ SE11

- ▶ SE16

- ▶ SE10

For more detailed information about authorizations, see Chapter 12.

3.4.3 Additional Requirements

Another requirement for the use of the full functionality in SAP Solution Manager is the implementation of *Solution Tools Implementation Content* (ST-ICO). The ST-ICO contains pre-defined contents, such as standard processes, documents, test cases, and IMG objects. This content can be used during the various phases of an implementation project.

To find the latest ST-ICO, go to *www.service.sap.com/installations* • SOFTWARE DOWNLOADS • SUPPORT PACKAGES AND PATCHES • SEARCH FOR SUPPORT PACKAGES AND PATCHES and search for ST-ICO.

3.5   Project Definition and Project Administration

Now that we have explained all important prerequisites for using the project functionality, this section describes how to proceed and create a project.

Project definition and administration allows you to initiate, plan, prepare, and execute the project. The IMPLEMENTATION/UPGRADE work center is your first and central access point for all functions around your projects; you can call it using the SM_WORKCENTER transaction. Figure 3.5 shows you the general overview of your projects.

Here, you have a clear view of the status of your projects. Apart from that, the ACTIVE QUERIES area allows you to change between the following views:

- ▶ MY PROJECTS
  Displays only projects assigned to your user.

- ▶ ALL PROJECTS
  Displays all projects for which you have permissions.

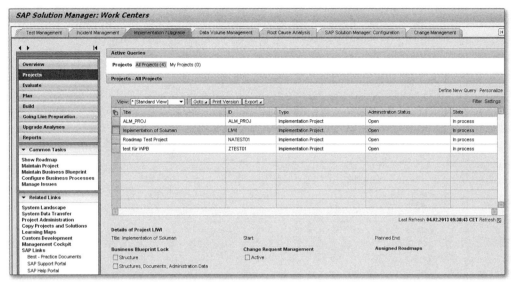

Figure 3.5 Implementation/Upgrade Work Center

The project status is indicated in the Projects–My Projects table in the Status column. A project can have the following different statuses:

▶ Current Projects

▶ Completed Projects: the entered project date is in the past.

▶ Projects Behind Schedule: the entered project date is in the past; however, the dates entered in the current end date or milestone are in the present.

If the status of a project is maintained in the SOLAR_PROJECT_ADMIN transaction, it also appears in the work center.

On the left side of the work center, the navigation area allows you to go directly to the various work areas. By clicking Maintain Project in the Common Tasks, you can start your activities in Project Administration. Alternatively, you can call the SOLAR_PROJECT_ADMIN transaction. The functionality of this transaction is described in the following section.

3.5.1   Creating a Project

To create a project, follow these steps:

1. Click the ▢ icon to create a project (see Figure 3.6).

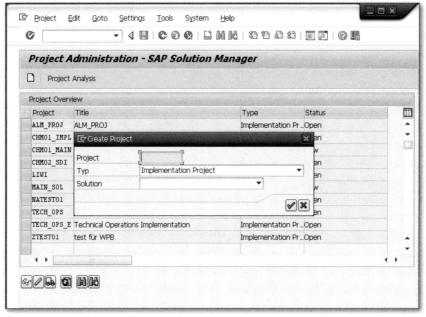

Figure 3.6 Create Project

2. In the dialog window, assign a project ID in the PROJECT field. This cannot be changed afterwards. You can enter it as a combination of letters and numbers with up to 10 characters. Also, note the information on namespaces in Section 3.4.2.

3. Select a project type in the TYPE field. For information on the individual project types, see Section 3.2. The project type cannot be changed afterwards within the same project. For example, if you have created an implementation project and then want to create templates with it at a later point, you can copy the project and change the project type in the new project.

4. If applicable, assign the project an existing solution. For more information on solutions in SAP Solution Manager, see Section 3.9.

5. Confirm your entries by clicking the ☑ icon. In the following view, you can continue maintaining your project data.

6. Assign your project a TITLE and the desired LANGUAGE. In the project language, make the language-dependent information (project documentation status information) available to all project team members, regardless of the individual

logon language. The project language cannot be changed afterwards. The project structure is built in the defined project language.

7. Save your data by clicking the SAVE icon in the menu area.

8. In the following dialog window, enter a FOLDER NAME for the folder in which you want to save the created documents in SAP Knowledge Warehouse. When projects are created, the system automatically sets up a folder in the SAP Knowledge Warehouse and saves the related documents there. The system also creates a folder group with the same name. The FOLDER group allows you to control authorizations for documents in projects, solutions, and roadmaps.

9. Click NEXT.

10. Save your project by clicking the SAVE icon in the menu area.

The project is then displayed in the project overview of SAP Solution Manager. Then, you need to define the other header data.

3.5.2 General Data for Projects

Double-click the project ID to go to PROJECT ADMINISTRATION. On the GENERAL DATA tab, you can enter not only the title and language, but also RESPONSIBILITIES, PLAN DATA, or the STATUS.

The persons responsible in the project management must be included in the user administration of the SAP system. Use the DETAILS button to display information such as the OSS user and email addresses of responsible persons.

In the GENERAL PROJECT INFORMATION area, you can add a document for project description, which, for example, explains the project in more detail.

By assigning a status, you can sort your projects in the work center at a later time. On the PROJECT STANDARDS tab, you can provide your company-specific status values.

By entering PLAN DATA, you can manually enter the dates for the planned BEGINNING and END and the DEMAND in PERSON DAYS (PD). The ACTUAL DATA is for entering the actual BEGINNING of the project.

3.5.3 Specifying the Project Scope

In the SCOPE tab, you can define the following contents for your project:

- ▶ **Solution Packages**
  Select which Solution Packages you want to apply in your project.

- ▶ **Templates**
  If you want to use a template, apply the structure of the template and the assignments for this structure in your project.

- ▶ **Roadmap**
  Select a roadmap that you want your project team members to work with.

- ▶ **Industries and countries**
  Select which countries and industries you want to consider when defining the project scope.

3.5.4 Defining Project Team Members

In the SCOPE tab, you can also create and update the team member list for your project. Each project can be assigned multiple project team members. You can assign users defined in the USER ADMINISTRATION and generic users (not created in the user administration). All team members who do not have an SAP user are highlighted in a different color in the list.

To maintain project team members, do the following:

1. Enter the name of a project team member in the PROJECT TEAM MEMBER field. If you wish to find and assign a team member defined in the user administration, you can also use the input help ([F4]).

2. In the NAME/EXPLANATION field, enter a descriptive explanation for the respective project team member. This field will be available for project-internal use in the future. If the user is known in the SAP system, the name of the project's team member is used by default.

3. To lock structure elements in the project against changes by unauthorized users, set RESTRICT CHANGES TO NODES IN PROJECT TO ASSIGNED TEAM MEMBERS. Then, team members you have not assigned to the structure element can display only the structure element and its tab in the Business Blueprint and the configuration.

4. If applicable, specify the name and details for the SAP partners who are involved in the project.

5. Use the REPLACE button to replace the newly added team member with the existing team member in the entire project structure.

3.5.5   Defining the System Landscape

To ensure that you can access the systems in the individual project phases, such as development or testing, you must first allocate the logical components to the project, as shown in Figure 3.7. To do this, open the REPLACE tab. For more information on the system landscape, see Section 3.4.1.

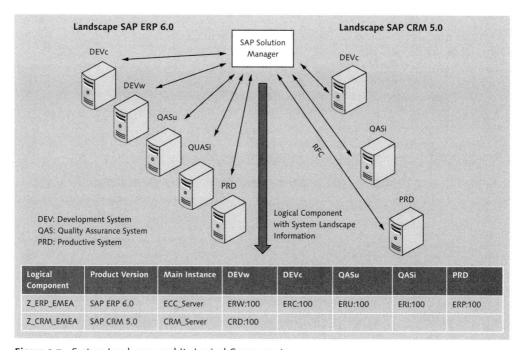

Figure 3.7   System Landscape and Its Logical Components

In the SYSTEMS sub-tab, assign your project the logical components. This allows you to define a central storage for objects, such as manual test cases, external applications, and eCATT test configurations. Apart from that, use the possibility to integrate Quality Gate Management and Change Management for your project in the CHANGE MANAGEMENT sub-tab. Integrating Quality Gate Management and Change Management allows you to have better control and documentation—for example, during project phase changes.

After you have assigned logical components to the project in the SYSTEM LANDSCAPE tab, the IMG PROJECTS tab now shows all related IMG subprojects in the managed systems related to your SAP Solution Manager projects (see Figure 3.8). Now, generate your IMG projects in the managed systems. Generation and distribution might already have taken place. This is indicated by the green and red status symbols in the VIEW column, as follows:

▶ Red (⬤): Project does not exist.

▶ Green (⬛): Project exists in the specified logical components and assigned logical systems.

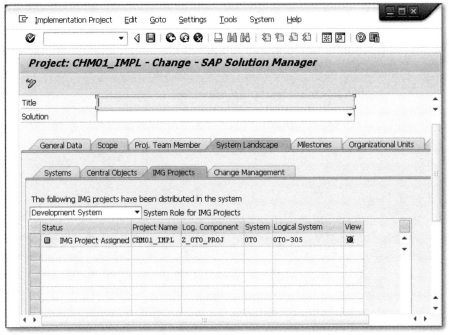

Figure 3.8 Generating and Distributing a Project

To trigger the distribution and generation of a project, do the following:

1. Select the system role for IMG projects.

   For example, if you want to generate an IMG project in the development system of a managed system, select the DEVELOPMENT SYSTEM system role for this IMG project (see Figure 3.8) from the selection menu.

2. Select the IMG project and click the CREATE IMG PROJECT button.

3. The following dialog window allows you the option of creating a transport request for the project. You can assign the transport request additional project team members.

The generation and distribution in the managed systems is started. As soon as the project exists, this is indicated by a green status symbol (⬤). The appropriate managed system issues a message once the generation has been completed.

If, in a selected managed system, there is already an IMG project you wish to assign instead of the IMG project assigned by default, proceed as follows:

1. Select the relevant IMG project.

2. Click the REPLACE button.

3. Confirm the security prompt.

4. Select an IMG project from the list and confirm your selection.

5. The following dialog window offers you the creation of a transport request. If applicable, assign further project team members a task of this request.

6. Choose NEXT to accept the entries. The PROJECT tab shows the newly assigned IMG project.

3.5.6   Creating and Changing Project Templates

The TEMPLATES tab is available only in template projects. It allows you to create, change, version, transport, and archive project templates.

While a template is being modified, it cannot be used in the entire system. By setting the VISIBILITY button to PUBLIC, you can make the template available throughout the system, and it can then be used in any project.

By activating the GLOBAL ROLLOUT FUNCTIONALITY, you can protect your templates in the Business Blueprint against changes in the local subsidiaries. This is done by using global attributes, which are assigned to a structure element by default.

Assigning structure elements to a template is possible only as long as the visibility is private. Apart from that, you can display, create, change, and delete documents and assign them to the templates.

To create a new version and archive the old version, click INCREASE VERSION COUNTER.

3.5.7 Working with Milestones in the Project

The MILESTONES tab allows you to monitor the project progress with the help of set time parameters. If you have assigned your project a roadmap, you can use its milestones. To do this, click the ROADMAP and select the desired milestones. You can make additions to milestones from the roadmap, but you cannot change them.

Apart from integrating a roadmap, you can use default milestones or your own ones.

Milestones should represent *quality gates*, which differentiate among the phases in a project. Quality gates are unique, predefined quality criteria that are decisive for approval of the next project step.

3.5.8 Working with Organizational Units in the Project

To maintain information on functions, countries, and time zones, use the ORGANIZATIONAL UNIT tab. It is exclusively for presenting information on your organizational units; the data cannot be used or evaluated in the ongoing course of the project.

3.5.9 Project Standards

The values specified in the PROJECT STANDARDS tab are used as default values in project administration, the roadmap, the Business Blueprint, and the configuration. Use the project template to define cross-project status values, keywords, and documentation types. You can access the project templates for the various project types in the project administration via GOTO and PROJECT TEMPLATE.

The PROJECT STANDARDS tab provides access to the following sub-tabs:

▶ STATUS VALUES
Status values provide information on the status of processes or projects. The status value consists of a status code and the name of the status. We recommend that you use explanatory status codes. You can filter your project structure by status values or search for them in the project analysis.

▶ KEYWORDS
Keywords serve as default values for classifying contents in the Business Blueprint, configuration, and Solution Directory. We recommend you choose concise terms for assigning keywords. You can also filter your project structure by keywords or search for them in the project analysis.

▶ DOCUMENTATION TYPES

Use documentation types to structure your project documentation. You can use the various documentation types included in the product package or create your own ones. You can distinguish whether the documentation types are to be used in a project-specific way or across projects.

▶ TABS

Here, you can define the visibility of the various tabs in the Business Blueprint or in the configuration. Apart from that, you can switch the change history log on or off. Please note that the COMPONENT VIEW and BPMN GRAPHIC exclude one another. If one of these tabs is selected, the other cannot be displayed.

In this section, we have introduced the project administration of SAP Solution Manager. You are now able to perform all administrative tasks in your projects. Based on that, the next section shows you how to create a Business Blueprint, which contains your project structure with the company-specific business scenarios. Then you can use the configuration phase to fill your documentation with the relevant configuration contents.

3.6   Project Support for Monitoring Implementation

Now that we've provided a general description of how to create a project, your next step is to fill the project with process information. With the example of Toys Inc., we will show you how to create the project with project data for technical operations. You will learn how to use SAP standard processes and roadmaps to receive a complete scenario with business processes, process steps, and other relevant project information, which you can then use as documentation for further processing.

3.6.1   Process Mapping

To map processes within a project, you have various possibilities. Apart from manually creating processes or using existing processes in SAP Solution Manager, there are a number of options. We explain these in the following subsections.

Business Process Repository

The BPR contains a multitude of business processes for all SAP core applications, such as SAP ERP, SAP CRM, SAP SRM, and SAP Solution Manager. By using the standard content offered by SAP, you can significantly accelerate an implementation. Various sources are used, and their contents are adjusted to the prerequisites and conditions in the project. These can be taken over in your created project and adjusted to your needs.

In order to map processes to your project, click PLAN in the IMPLEMENTATION/UPGRADE work center (see Figure 3.9). You can then click the DEFINE BUSINESS BLUEPRINT link to go to the blueprint (design) phase.

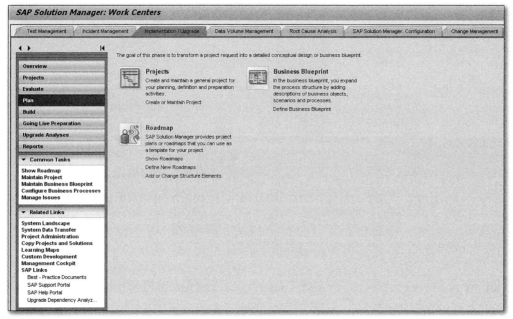

Figure 3.9 Implementation/Upgrade Work Center • Plan

This takes you to the SOLAR01 transaction, which is the access point for all work on the Business Blueprint. The screen is divided into two areas. On the left side is the navigation overview, BUSINESS BLUEPRINT STRUCTURE, which is divided into ORGANIZATIONAL UNITS, MASTER DATA, BUSINESS SCENARIOS, and INTERFACE SCENARIOS (see Figure 3.10)

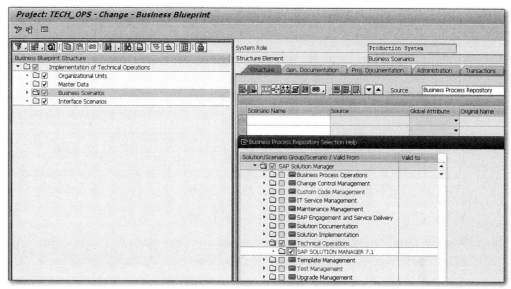

Figure 3.10 Business Process Repository

Now we'll focus on the business scenarios to map our processes there for implementation.

The right-hand side of the screen consists of various tabs. Their purpose includes creating the structure of our processes and creating documents and technical information. For more information, please see Section 3.6.2.

In order to use SAP standard processes, choose BUSINESS SCENARIOS on the left-hand side and go to the STRUCTURE tab. Under SOURCE, choose the BUSINESS PROCESS REPOSITORY, click inside an empty line in the SCENARIO NAME column, and use the input help (F4).

As shown in Figure 3.10, you get a choice of possible scenarios. Under SAP SOLUTION MANAGER, you find the TECHNICAL OPERATIONS entry. Select the entry and confirm it by clicking the ✔ icon. After you save the data, the structure is applied to the left-hand side. You can then go on and adjust the processes you just transferred (see Section 3.7.1).

Uploading Your Own Business Processes

Apart from the possibility of using SAP standard processes, you can also upload processes you have created to SAP Solution Manager using other tools, such as

Microsoft Excel or PowerPoint. This function can be found in Transaction SOLAR_ PROJECT_ADMIN. To maintain the processes, Microsoft Excel templates are used.

1. Choose your project in the SOLAR_PROJECT_ADMIN transaction.

2. In your project, choose EDIT • FILL BUSINESS BLUEPRINT • CREATE TEMPLATE FILE • STRUCTURE.

3. Save the Microsoft Excel template as a *.txt* file and open it in Microsoft Excel.

4. Fill the template file with the scenarios/processes/steps to be uploaded.

5. Resave the file in *.txt* format. The upload is also done in the project at EDIT • FILL BUSINESS BLUEPRINT • UPLOAD FILE • STRUCTURE.

6. Select your Microsoft Excel template and confirm.

A background process loads all processes into your project. As in using Business Process Repositories, uploaded processes can be further adjusted (see Section 3.7.1).

3.6.2 Business Blueprint

The Business Blueprint (Transaction SOLAR01) offers you the possibility of creating the structure of your business processes and then filling them with business-relevant information. The following example scenario of technical operations shows this in more detail. From the Business Process Repository, the following processes were taken over in our implementation project:

▶ TECHNICAL MONITORING AND ALERTING

▶ ROOT CAUSE ANALYSIS

▶ TECHNICAL ADMINISTRATION

▶ CONFIGURATION VALIDATION

▶ DATA VOLUME MANAGEMENT

▶ SERVICE LEVEL REPORT

Each of these processes is divided into further substeps; there is always a three-level hierarchy of business scenario, business process, and process step, which is explained in more detail in Section 3.3.2. You can add information in the tabs on all levels.

The tabs relevant to implementing technical operations have the following information and documents:

- STRUCTURE

  The STRUCTURE tab contains the related business processes and steps of the structure selected in the navigation. You can delete or rename structures and add new ones.

- GENERAL DOCUMENTATION

  The GENERAL DOCUMENTATION tab displays documents that were shipped by SAP or are part of a template—for example, scenario descriptions.

- ADMINISTRATION

  The ADMINISTRATION allows you to maintain the effort involved in implementing this process step or process and to enable responsible team members to search for and filter by specific business processes using keywords.

  Apart from that, the status of this process step can be maintained. This way, you can mark the implementation status of a process or process step.

- TRANSACTIONS

  The TRANSACTIONS tab includes Web Dynpro applications, programs, and transactions that are executed in the process step; extensions with customer transactions are possible. They can be called directly from the documentation and executed in the connected system.

- SERVICE MESSAGES

  If you actively use the Service Desk in SAP Solution Manager, you can save implementation-related notifications in the SERVICE MESSAGES tab. Apart from that, you can link change requests and change documents.

- COMPONENT VIEW

  The COMPONENT VIEW tab is visible only on the business process level and shows the individual steps in their logical sequence.

You can use the transactions, links, and documentations during the implementation and also at a later point during operations. The implementation object hands over all information to the solution.

To mark structures as relevant for the handover to a solution, or to define the project scope, all business scenarios, business processes, and process steps can be selected and deselected. This can be done using the check boxes directly next to the individual elements in the BUSINESS BLUEPRINT STRUCTURE navigation area. During the handover of the structures and information to a solution, you can choose whether only selected structures or all structures are to be copied (see also Section 3.9.1).

3.6.3 Maintaining Technical Contents

The following configuration phase allows you to maintain other technical objects, apart from the general documentation and transactions. From the configuration phase, you can access the Implementation/Upgrade work center. Go to the Create phase, and from there, go to Configuration • Go to Technical Configuration, or use Transaction SOLAR02.

The general interface is similar to the blueprint phase. However, it is not possible to change the structure within this phase. Apart from the tabs that are also displayed in the Business Blueprint, you can see the following tabs with a specific technical background:

▶ Configuration
In the Configuration tab, you can maintain configuration objects, such as IMG objects. On the business process level, configuration descriptions, which support you in the implementation, are available.

▶ Development
The Development tab allows you to maintain all development-relevant objects, such as function groups, BAdIs, classes, and programs. Apart from SAP objects, you can also maintain customer-specific objects.

▶ Test Cases
The Test Cases tab allows you to store test cases to accelerate the generation of test plans and test packages once development is completed, as well as allow for end-to-end–based testing.

3.6.4 Roadmap and AcceleratedSAP

Roadmaps are part of SAP Solution Manager. They include the SAP standard implementation methods, such as *AcceleratedSAP* (ASAP), and cover the key aspects and phases of an SAP implementation. By using a roadmap, you can accelerate the various project tasks. For this purpose, apart from the actual procedure, documents are available, which are also called *accelerators*. These include project plans and SAP Best Practice documents.

You can use roadmaps in connection with a project by assigning them to a specific project that follows the contained method. If you use them without a project context, they cannot be changed, but you can use the accelerators and functions they contain.

To add a roadmap to a project, follow these steps:

1. Roadmaps can be added to a project via PROJECT ADMINISTRATION. Choose your project in Transaction SOLAR_PROJECT_ADMIN.

2. Go to the SCOPE tab, and on the ROADMAP sub-tab, select the roadmap—in this example, ESRV RSLAF APPL. OPERATIONS (V*).

3. Click the SAVE icon to save your settings.

4. The roadmap can now be accessed from the PLAN menu item in the IMPLEMENTATION/UPGRADE work center.

5. There, click the SHOW ROADMAP link in the ROADMAPS area. That takes you to Transaction RMMAIN, in which all available roadmaps are displayed. To select the relevant roadmap, use the OTHER PROJECT functionality from the ROADMAP menu.

6. Select your project and confirm your selection.

Then, the ESRV RSLAF APPL. OPERATIONS (V*) roadmap is displayed (see Figure 3.11). It contains all necessary steps for successful implementation of technical operations and supports you in all further activities.

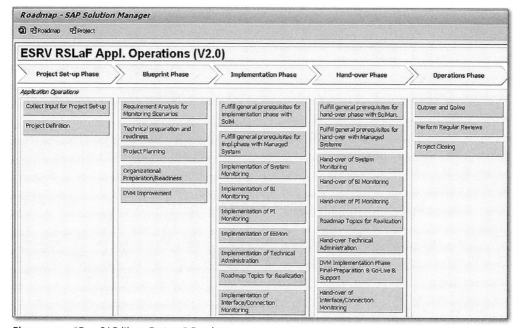

Figure 3.11 "Run SAP like a Factory" Roadmap

From this overview of the roadmap, you can access the individual phases of your project and the allocated work packages. By selecting a work package, you get into the actual structure of the roadmap. On the left-hand side, a navigation area is available, which structures the roadmap into several chapters and subchapters. Work packages are displayed as chapters. On the right-hand side, you find the following areas for all chapters:

▶ DESCRIPTIONS
The DESCRIPTIONS area provides an overview of possible input/output of this phase and a description of the activities to be performed.

▶ ACCELERATOR
The ACCELERATOR area contains documents and guides and provides help to complete the phase within a short time and with maximum quality.

▶ REFERENCES
The REFERENCES AREA provides links to other chapters/sub-chapters.

▶ STATUS/NOTICE
In the STATUS/NOTICE AREA, you can maintain the status of the activity and store comments.

▶ SERVICE MESSAGES
In the SERVICE MESSAGES area, you can create and send notifications.

▶ DOCUMENTATION
The DOCUMENTATION area allows you to use all general project documents and those document types that you allocated to your project in the Project Administration.

▶ KEYWORDS
In the KEYWORDS area, you can assign keywords, not only to structure elements and documents, but to the individual activities for further subdivision as well.

3.7   Implementation Documentation

Now that you've created the scenario of technical operations with the underlying business processes, this section describes how to adjust the scenario for your organization. You can also change business processes, upload your own documents, and add keywords to gain more clarity in your project.

3.7.1 Adjusting Business Processes

The business scenarios, business processes, and process steps added from the BPR in the previous section can be adjusted based on your needs. To do that, in the Business Blueprint (Transaction SOLAR01), call the project you've created. To extend an existing business process by a process step, proceed as follows:

1. Open the structure to the TECHNICAL MONITORING AND ALERTING business process level.

2. On the STRUCTURE tab under STEP NAME, enter the name of the new step and select the logical component in the LOGICAL COMPONENT column (see Figure 3.12).

3. Click SAVE.

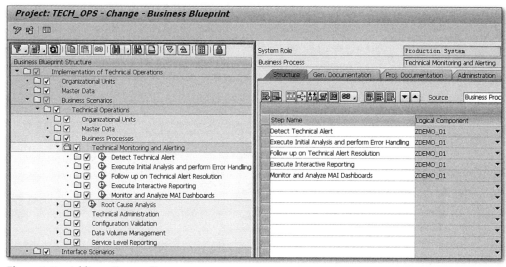

Figure 3.12 Adding a Process Step

You can also move, delete, or rename all process steps. To do this, use the menu in the STRUCTURE tab. Using the ![icon], ![icon], ![icon], and ![icon] icons, you can further individualize the business process.

3.7.2 Adding Documents and Objects

After adding the business process, you can assign customer-specific documents or objects. To assign one of your transactions to a process step, proceed as follows:

1. Select the relevant process step in the BUSINESS BLUEPRINT STRUCTURE navigation area.

2. In the TYPE column of the TRANSACTIONS tab, select TRANSACTION.

3. You can directly enter the transaction name or use the INPUT HELP (F4).

4. The system automatically inserts the name, type, and logical component.

To complete the existing documentation with new documents, first select a desired hierarchy level to which you want to assign the document. Then, go to the PROJ. DOCUMENTATION tab (see Figure 3.13).

1. Click the PLUS icon (🗎) in the menu bar.

2. As shown in Figure 3.13, define the TITLE and the DOCUMENTATION TYPE in the dialog that opens.

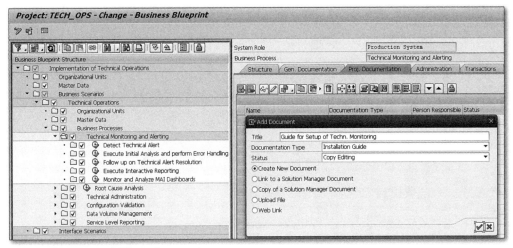

Figure 3.13 Adding a Document

3. Use the radio buttons in the lower area of the dialog to select whether you want to create a new document, link or copy a document that exists in SAP Solution Manager, upload a document from a drive, or use a web link, e.g., SharePoint.

For example, select UPLOAD FILE and confirm your selection by clicking the ✅ button. A dialog in which you can select your document opens. Finally, confirm your selection.

3.7.3   Maintaining Keywords and Attributes

To further structure your structure and the documentation in it, you can use keywords and attributes. While you can use keywords for project-internal structuring, attributes are passed on to the solution and thus allow for structuring beyond projects.

To create keywords, choose the Structure node and go to the Administration tab. Now you can assign all keywords allocated to the project as follows:

1. Click ![icon].
2. In the following pop-up window, select keywords.
3. Use the ![icon] button to accept all keywords.

After you have created keywords, you can click the Filter icon (![icon]) icon above the Business Blueprint Structure navigation area to filter by keywords in order to get a better overview of the project. The following are possible keywords:

▸ test relevant
▸ Blueprint relevant
▸ customer development

You can also attach keywords directly to a documentation to mark it for specific user groups or phases or as test-relevant.

To create an attribute, do the following:

1. Select the document and click the ![icon] button in the menu bar.
2. The Attribute Maintenance pop-up window opens. Here, you can assign SAP attributes, such as country and industry, or customer-specific attributes.
3. Use the input help (F4) in the Attribute Value column.

To search for these document keywords, attributes, and other information, use Transaction SOLAR_EVAL, as described in the next section.

3.8   Reporting

Transparency and current information on a project are necessary for the project manager and team members. To ensure a clearer picture of specific processes, documents, and transactions, various reporting features are available in SAP Solution Manager.

The REPORTS menu item in the IMPLEMENTATION/UPGRADE work center provides an overview of all available reports, as shown in Figure 3.14.

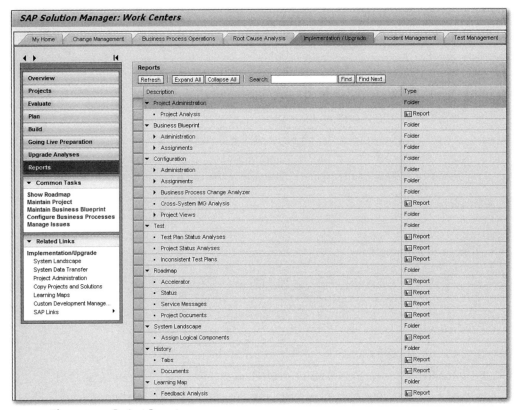

Figure 3.14 Project Reports

These reports support you in your search for information in your project. Proceed as follows:

1. Choose BUSINESS BLUEPRINT • ASSIGNMENTS • DOCUMENTATION. This takes you to the SOLAR_EVAL transaction. Here, you can select the project to be analyzed. Various filter criteria, such as team members, documentation type, and document status are available. Select the keyword previously selected to filter by all documents containing this keyword.

2. Select the corresponding criteria and press ⌨F8 to start your analysis. The result is an overview of all documents that are assigned to the project and meet the selection criteria.

3. Open the structure tree on the left-hand side.

4. Double-click the document name to go directly from Transaction SOLAR01 or SOLAR02 to the STRUCTURE node in the tab where the document is.

Use the reports to receive a quick and simple overview on open documentation, non-completed configuration objects, or the overall progress of your project at any time.

3.9 Documentation Transfer to Operations

After the technical operations scenario with the relevant IT processes has been created, the project information is provided to the application management and system administration at Toys Inc. in preparation for the implementation.

The basis for using the project information in operations is always a solution within SAP Solution Manager. To avoid losing the information from the project, all processes and objects can be transferred to a solution to serve as a documentation basis there. The next section describes how to do that.

3.9.1 Creating a New Solution

You can create a solution using the COPY PROJECT/SOLUTION function. This creates a completely new solution and fills it with all the contents from the project. You can apply this method for initial creation of a solution.

1. Go to the IMPLEMENTATION/UPGRADE work center.

2. Under RELATED LINKS, select COPY PROJECT/SOLUTION.

3. Under SELECT SOURCE in the PROJECT tab, add the implementation project (⌨F4), as shown in Figure 3.15.

4. Under SPECIFY TARGET, go to the SOLUTION tab and specify a NAME and the ROLE of the solution. The role of a solution should always be PRODUCTION SYSTEM to ensure that your production systems can be monitored later on.

5. In the DOCUMENT COPY OPTIONS area, you now need to select whether you wish to refer to or copy the documents from a project. We recommend copying documents from a project, rather than referring to them, to clearly separate between the project world and operations.

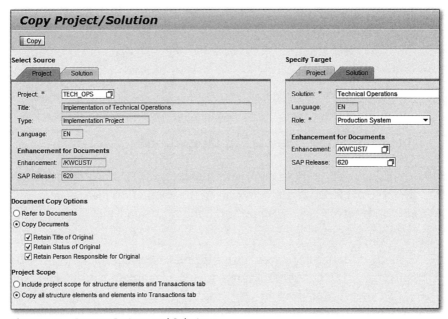

Figure 3.15 Copying Projects and Solutions

Therefore, select the COPY DOCUMENTS radio button. If you do not want to change the title, status, and person(s) responsible, select all checkboxes below the COPY DOCUMENTS radio button.

6. In the PROJECT SCOPE area, you can define whether the solution is to receive only structure elements and transactions in the focus, or if all structure elements and transactions are to be taken over into the solution (see Section 3.6.2).

7. Click the COPY button to create a new solution.

From the SAP SOLUTION MANAGER ADMINISTRATION work center or using Transaction SOLMAN_DIRECTORY, you can now access the new solution.

3.9.2 Transferring Information to an Existing Solution

If you already have a solution that is to be filled with the contents of the implementation project, this information must be copied from the project. To do this, follow these steps:

1. Go to the SAP SOLUTION MANAGER ADMINISTRATION work center and select SOLUTIONS.

2. Select the desired solution and double-click the link in the SOLUTION column.

3. The solution directory, in which you can now click the BUSINESS SCENARIO in the left-hand navigation area, opens.

4. A project should be selected as the source. Now, use the input help (F4) in the STRUCTURE tab of the SCENARIO NAME column.

5. Select the project, and all scenarios to be copied.

6. Click COPY to complete the action, and then save the process.

All processes and information included in the project are now taken over into the solution. This also applies to the logical components. This variant of information transfer can be used to transfer delta information from other projects and solutions at a later point.

You should now be able to create your own projects in SAP Solution Manager. We have shown you the different project types and which possibilities SAP offers to support you in project management. Furthermore, with the example of Toys Inc., we created the technical operations scenario with related IT processes. Now that we've established the basics, we can implement the processes of technical operations in the following chapters.

Performance problems and exception situations are just some of the daily challenges faced in IT. With root cause analysis, you can find the source of problems that occur in your SAP system landscape and keep any restrictions imposed on your system's operations to a minimum, or even eliminate them completely.

4   Root Cause Analysis

Root cause analysis is a collection of tools in SAP Solution Manager. This collection supports you in analyzing various problems that occur within a heterogeneous SAP system landscape.

Before you use root cause analysis, it's important to be familiar with the tools themselves, as well as to understand how they interact with one another. In addition, you should be familiar with the root cause analysis approach and the technologies used in the various landscape components to be analyzed. For this reason, it's useful to establish an internal support organization and involve external parties (for example, SAP Support) in the analysis process so that only essential analyses are performed when analyzing the problem, thus saving on resources, time, and money.

4.1   Root Cause Analysis in SAP Solution Manager

SAP Solution Manager provides a range of root cause analysis tools that facilitate remote and secure access to information that's contained in managed systems and the operating system. They ensure that changes cannot be made to customer systems. As a result of the central position occupied by SAP Solution Manager, analysis data is available to all other authorized users, thus making it easier to transfer the results of your analysis to other parties.

Using these tools does not pose any security risk because the analysis applications available to you primarily access landscape-based data (for example, performance data, technical change data, or error information) in read-only mode. Furthermore, the authorization concept in SAP Solution Manager rules out the possibility that users would have access to critical information stored in the production system landscape (for example, HR data).

It is for this very reason that root cause analysis tools are useful beyond their internal use within the IT organization. If a problem occurs, the entire SAP ecosystem (including SAP Support and SAP Partners) should be able to access these tools in order to support you as quickly as possible and uncover the cause of the error. This function is particularly helpful for SAP customers who, for security reasons, are not permitted to have direct access to the internal IT infrastructure.

> **Tip**
>
> If several teams are involved in the analysis process, it's often useful to document all findings and their correlations and to store this information in a central location. Ideally, you use your existing ticket system for this purpose. Alternatively, you can also store this documentation in a file on a centrally accessible file system, thus enabling others to learn from your most recent experiences.

SAP Solution Manager provides you with an infrastructure that comprises various different root cause analysis functions, such as tools that analyze different initial situations; tools that monitor technical parameters, among other things; and tools that record requirements. All these tools are available to you centrally and enable you to analyze user workstations, systems, landscape components, and the database management system, among other things. This approach is generally known as an end-to-end methodology.

Root cause analysis is divided into the following four end-to-end methodologies:

1. *Change analysis* describes the approach to analyzing a system landscape in terms of changes to individual landscape components.

2. *Workload analysis* analyzes the performance of the system landscape as well as load balancing between the landscape components.

3. *Trace analysis* involves the creation and evaluation of *traces*, which are technical recordings of the activities performed by various system landscape components.

4. *Exception analysis* is concerned with analyzing exception errors, which may be caused by background activities or end-user activities.

> **Note**
>
> Throughout this chapter on root cause analysis, we will use two terms that frequently cause some degree of confusion. Therefore, before we proceed any further, we will take a moment to highlight the difference between the following two meanings:
>
> ▸ *Tool:* The tools located under the END-TO-END ANALYSIS menu option in the ROOT CAUSE ANALYSIS work center are also known as end-to-end change analysis, end-to-end workload analysis, end-to-end trace analysis, and end-to-end exception analysis. Below, we will use this exact notation for these tools.
>
> ▸ *End-to-end methodology:* In this chapter, we will also discuss the end-to-end methodologies in which the aforementioned tools are used. Each end-to-end methodology will be handled in a separate section within root cause analysis and will be known only as "change analysis," "workload analysis," "trace analysis," and "exception analysis." If the prefix "end-to-end" occurs in connection with the above methodologies, it will occur only in the following context: "end-to-end methodology: workload analysis."

4.1.1 Prerequisites for Root Cause Analysis

If all aspects of the initial configuration described in Section 2.5 have been successfully implemented, the scenario will not require any further configuration. SAP Notes 1483508 (SAP Solution Manager 7.1: Root cause analysis pre-requisites), 1478974 (Diagnostics in SAP Solution Manager 7.1), and 1365123 (Installation of Diagnostics Agents) provide additional information and support.

If you want to specifically analyze the SAP systems within the system landscape, each of these systems must be connected to SAP Solution Manager (see Section 2.5.4). It's therefore important that the Introscope components and relevant diagnostics agents on the managed systems also work correctly so that metrics can be collected. In SAP Solution Manager, you can use *self-diagnosis* to check that these components are working properly. In the ROOT CAUSE ANALYSIS work center, self-diagnosis is available under RELATED LINKS in the ADMINISTRATION area.

If you need SAP Support to provide root cause analysis support, ensure that the relevant TCP ports are maintained in SAProuter so that SAP Support can access the tools available in SAP Solution Manager and in the managed systems or applications (for example, the Introscope components). Access to the following components is necessary:

▸ SAP Solution Manager (AS ABAP)

▸ SAP Solution Manager (AS Java)

- ▶ Introscope WebView or Workstation
- ▶ Optional: managed system (AS ABAP)
- ▶ Optional: managed system (AS Java)

Further information on the necessary TCP/IP ports is also available in the Security Guide for SAP Solution Manager, which is available on SAP Service Marketplace at *http://service.sap.com/instguides/*.

Note

If you do not wish to maintain the SAProuter table `saprouttab` manually, you can also specify SAProuter connection data in SAP Solution Manager's basic configuration under CONFIGURE SAPROUTER so that SAP Solution Manager automatically maintains these entries for you. To do this, proceed as follows:

- ▶ Start Transaction SOLMAN_SETUP.
- ▶ Navigate to BASIC CONFIGURATION and then CONFIGURE SAPROUTER.
- ▶ Enter the relevant SAProuter data here.

4.1.2 Navigation Concept

The ROOT CAUSE ANALYSIS work center in SAP Solution Manager is available to you for root cause analysis processes. For more information on the navigation concept in SAP Solution Manager, see Section 2.4.

The tools in the ROOT CAUSE ANALYSIS work center are essentially divided into the following four menu options (see Figure 4.1):

- ▶ End-to-end analysis
- ▶ System analysis
- ▶ Host analysis
- ▶ Database analysis

You generally use these four menu options to access a suitable tool for each end-to-end methodology. The more specific the application, the greater the level of detail and the more complex the analysis data. Consequently, a higher level of expertise is required when using these tools. To start the tools, proceed as follows:

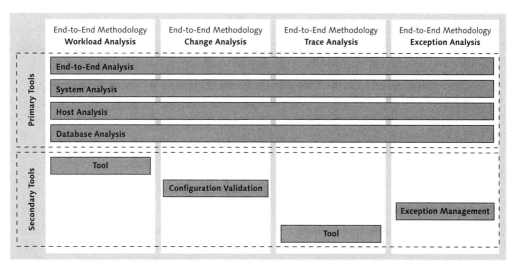

Figure 4.1 Root Cause Analysis Tools

1. Select the relevant menu option in the ROOT CAUSE ANALYSIS work center (see Figure 4.2).

2. Depending on your selection, the DETAILED SELECTION area on the right-hand side of the screen displays, in tabular form, the landscape components currently under analysis. Here, you can select precisely those elements that are relevant for your analysis. You can select one or more rows simultaneously by holding down the ⌃Ctrl key while making your selection.

3. Based on this selection, you can call the application used for the relevant end-to-end methodology, which varies depending on the problem. If you require data from SAP NetWeaver Business Warehouse, choose the link CLICK HERE TO LOAD DATA FROM BUSINESS WAREHOUSE.

In addition to the four menu options named previously, the navigation area of the work center contains additional tools, such as CONFIGURATION VALIDATION and EXCEPTION MANAGEMENT (see Figure 4.2), which will be explained in Section 4.3.6 and Section 4.6.6, respectively.

Not all root cause analysis tools are located in the work center. Some additional tools are located in managed systems or are completely standalone applications (for example, the third-party tool Introscope). Links to such tools are provided within the relevant applications or in the RELATED LINKS area (see Figure 4.2).

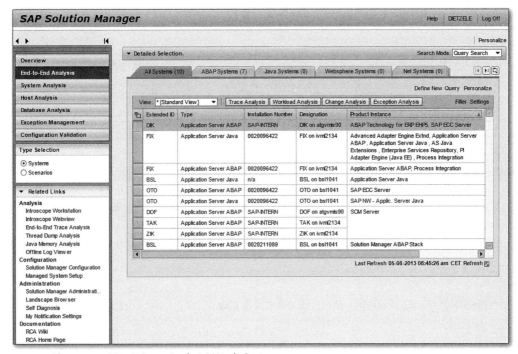

Figure 4.2 "Root Cause Analysis" Work Center

In the following sections, we will introduce you to the four most important menu options in the Root Cause Analysis work center. Each of the tools available in these areas will be presented and described in greater detail.

▶ **End-to-end analysis**

End-to-end tools are the most important functions in root cause analysis. You use them to analyze individual systems and perform cross-system analyses. These tools include the following:

  ▶ Change analysis (known as *end-to-end change analysis*; see Section 4.3.3)

  ▶ Workload analysis (known as *end-to-end workload analysis*; see Section 4.4.3)

  ▶ Trace analysis (known as *end-to-end trace analysis*; see Section 4.5.2)

  ▶ Exception analysis (known as *end-to-end exception analysis*; see Section 4.6.3)

▶ **System analysis**

System analysis provides system-specific data and enables you to visualize a system's technical status. The following tools are available at this application level:

- ▸ Introscope (see Section 4.2.3)

- ▸ Change reporting (see Section 4.3.4)

- ▸ **Expert links**
  Expert links provide technology-dependent references to other expert tools. At present, these are available only for Java systems (for example, thread dump analysis, see Section 4.4.5).

- ▸ Log viewer (see Section 4.6.4)

▸ **Host analysis**
This collection of tools is used specifically to analyze hosts. It comprises the following:

- ▸ File system browser (see Section 4.2.2)

- ▸ Introscope (see Section 4.2.3)

- ▸ Host analysis (see Section 4.4.1)

- ▸ OS command console (see Section 4.2.1)

▸ **Database analysis** (see Section 4.4.4)

4.1.3 Root Cause Analysis at Toys Inc.

In Section 4.1.2, you obtained an overview of the ROOT CAUSE ANALYSIS work center. We will now use a sample scenario at Toys Inc. to demonstrate how you can use root cause analysis tools.

An end user at Toys Inc. experiences a performance problem while maintaining his or her bank data in a portal application. In this example, which is shown in Figure 4.3, the end user calls an application on SAP NetWeaver Portal (AS Java), which communicates with the SAP ECC system (AS ABAP) in the background. Since any system or component can be the cause of the problem, an in-depth analysis is required.

The user reports the incident to the Application Management team at Toys Inc. by opening a support message in the Service Desk of SAP Solution Manager. IT Support at Toys Inc. immediately initiates root cause analysis in order to isolate, step by step, the technical components responsible for the incident.

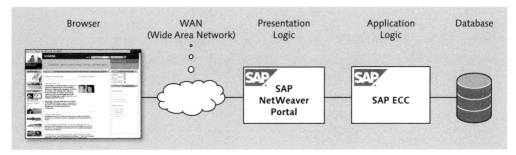

Figure 4.3 Employee Portal Application

The IT organization at Toys Inc. proceeds as follows:

1. **End-to-end analysis**
   At the start of the analysis process, all aspects of workload analysis are analyzed. The IT organization, therefore, uses end-to-end workload analysis (see Section 4.4.3) to obtain an overview of general system performance and potential cross-system interdependencies. After detecting some anomalies in the average response times on AS ABAP, the experts continue their analyses directly on the SAP ECC system.

2. **System analysis: AS ABAP**
   After evaluating the performance monitor ST03N in AS ABAP, it quickly becomes apparent that multiple users are executing a certain type of ABAP program that has an increased runtime, including our user who opened the aforementioned support message.

   IT Support then determines that database processing accounts for the largest portion of the overall runtime. When the relevant expert studies the database analysis (see Section 4.4.4), he or she does not detect any general anomalies. Therefore, the next step is to analyze the application itself.

   In order to rule out other causes of the problem, the system experts check, as a precaution, the behavior of the ABAP memory areas (also known as SAP buffers), communication performance with other systems, and hardware utilization. These areas can then be ruled out as a further cause of the problem.

3. **System analysis: Java**
   On the SAP NetWeaver Portal system, no further anomalies can be detected in relation to application performance (in end-to-end workload analysis—Java

details; see Section 4.4.3), memory consumption (through the use of Introscope; see Section 4.2.3), or data processing.

4. **End-to-end trace analysis**
   Since there is no clear indication of a general performance problem, end-to-end trace analysis is performed (see Section 4.5.2). These traces are enabled in order to take a look at a specific user transaction and isolate the landscape component causing the problem. In order to reproduce the incident as accurately as possible, one of the end users affected by the incident repeats the same activities in the system. During this time, the data on the end user's PC is recorded using *SAP Client Plug-In*, which is required for this purpose. After the recording, all the data is sent to the SAP Solution Manager system. IT Support then uses this data to start its own analysis.

   The SAP ECC server requires the longest amount of time. The trace performed as part of the analysis can be used to immediately conduct further analyses on the SAP ECC system itself without having to record the scenario again. IT Support accesses the SAP ECC system directly via end-to-end trace analysis in SAP Solution Manager. It then starts to evaluate the ABAP and SQL traces there.

5. **Trace analysis on the AS ABAP stack**
   While evaluating the ABAP trace, it becomes apparent that database queries, and not pure ABAP code, trigger the vast majority of server-side processing. IT Support uses the trace tools to identify which database calls it needs to analyze. An analysis of the long-running SQL requests, in consultation with the relevant database expert, reveals that numerous indexes are updated on individual database tables and that some of these indexes also need to be recreated.

This example has provided you with an overview of a typical approach to dealing with a performance problem. In the next section, we will introduce you to each tool in detail. Moreover, we will describe practical applications of use that will help you to make the best possible use of each of these tools.

4.2 Method-Independent Tools

Before you learn about end-to-end methodologies and their tools in great detail, we will first introduce you to the following important tools and show you how to use them:

- OS command console
- File system browser
- Introscope

These tools are used in a variety of different end-to-end methodologies. However, they can also be used completely independently of the end-to-end approach.

4.2.1 OS Command Console

The OS command console enables an employee to send different commands to an operating system within a connected server without the employee's requiring a separate user at the operating system level. Secure access is guaranteed by a pre-defined set of operating system commands that permit read access only.

Use the tool as follows:

1. In the ROOT CAUSE ANALYSIS work center, select the HOST ANALYSIS menu option.

2. In the DETAILED SELECTION area, select the host to be analyzed and then choose OS COMMAND CONSOLE to start the application. A new window opens in which you can execute all available operating system commands.

3. In the CONTEXT area, you can select which host system you want to analyze. If possible, the system-dependent operating system commands are also called.

4. In the PROMPT area, you can select the type of commands to be executed. However, you can select only those that have been pre-assigned. The commands vary depending on the operating system. To provide a better overview, the operating system commands are grouped according to topics, which you can select in the GROUP field (see Figure 4.4).

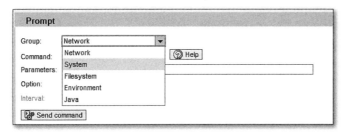

Figure 4.4 OS Command Console—Groups

The COMMAND field now enables you to select the command you require. A Help document is available for each command. Choose HELP to display these documents. The `help` command is then executed on the operating system, and the result is displayed in the RESULT area.

You can define parameters in the PARAMETERS field. In order to comply with the security standard for SAP Solution Manager, it is not possible to execute all the commands displayed in the Help. Only those parameters that display information are permitted.

5. Select the operating system command you require, specify a valid parameter, and choose SEND COMMAND to execute the command. The result associated with executing the command is displayed in Figure 4.5.

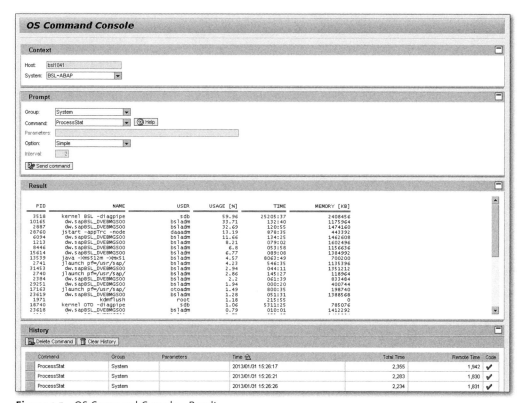

Figure 4.5 OS Command Console—Result

For some commands (for example, the PROCESSSTAT command in Figure 4.5), it is helpful to execute them several times in quick succession. Then you receive a snapshot and can also perform live tracking of the system status. The RECURRENT option in the OS command console is available to you for this purpose. You can define a *seconds* interval here. When you choose SEND COMMAND, the command is executed in the time interval defined for this command and updated in the RESULT area until you choose STOP COMMAND.

All commands and results executed once in the past are displayed in the HISTORY area.

4.2.2 File System Browser

The file system browser provides you with a central point of entry into the file system within a managed system. It is particularly suitable for evaluating log files remotely without the need for a user at the operating system level. It permits only read access to the folders associated with the managed system.

In the ROOT CAUSE ANALYSIS work center, select the HOST ANALYSIS menu option. In the DETAILED SELECTION area, select the relevant host and choose FILE SYSTEM BROWSER to start the file system browser. Just like the OS command console, the file system browser opens in a separate window (see Figure 4.6).

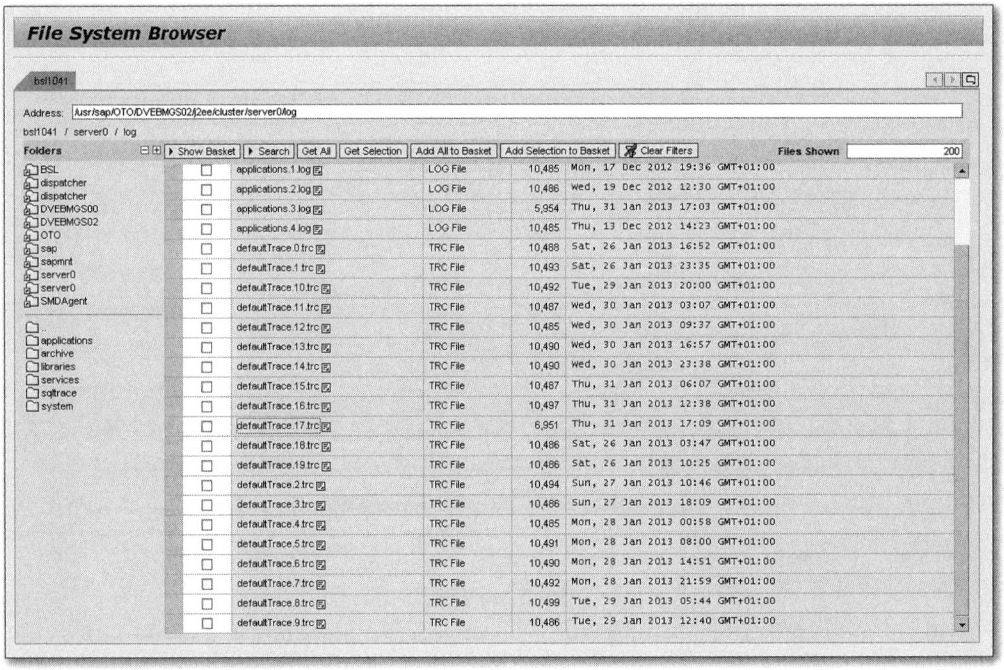

Figure 4.6 File System Browser

The file system browser is divided into three areas, as follows:

▶ **Address area**

In the upper area of the file system browser, the ADDRESS field always contains the address currently selected. If you already know your target directory (in other words, the directory that you will search for a file), you can enter this here. The address area is also directly linked to the navigation area. If you use the mouse to navigate to the target directory you require, the address area will always be updated.

▶ **Navigation area**

This area lists all important directories for an SAP system. If you select a directory, all related subdirectories are displayed below it, and all available files are displayed in the work area.

▶ **Work area**

All files available for the directory selected are listed along with their properties. Various different functions are also available to you (for example, for displaying or downloading a file).

Now, navigate to the directory that contains the file you want to analyze. Normally, you will analyze a log file or configuration file.

From here, you can download all files or only certain files to the local PC for further analysis. To download all files, choose GET ALL. For the second variant, select the relevant files in the first column and choose GET SELECTION. A small dialog box containing a link that enables you to download the files is displayed. You then receive a ZIP file, which also contains the file structure of the files you have selected.

If you want to download files from different server directories, you can also choose ADD ALL TO BASKET or ADD SELECTION TO BASKET to place them in the "basket" and later download all of them together from the BASKET dialog box. If this dialog box is not displayed, you can choose SHOW BASKET to display it.

Within the basket or display area, you can also scroll through the text file without having to download the entire file. To do this, proceed as follows: in the display area, select the file that you want to analyze or, in the basket, choose the DISPLAY icon (👓). An embedded view in which the entire file content is displayed (as shown in Figure 4.7) opens.

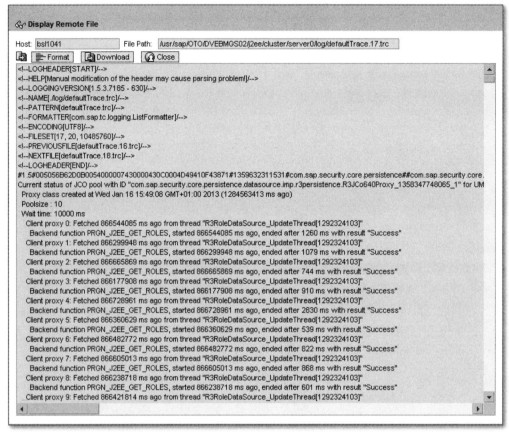

Figure 4.7   File System Browser—File Content

Here, you can download the current file (DOWNLOAD button) or choose FORMAT to display a difficult-to-read file in a more legible format, for example. In this situation, the format function converts UNIX time stamps into the standard time format.

4.2.3   Introscope

Introscope was developed to enable users to successfully manage service-oriented architectures. To this end, it provides a real-time view of critical web applications and infrastructure systems in terms of performance and availability. Since Introscope provides current and historical data in graphical form, it is used for ad-hoc analysis in relation to resource consumption, system behavior, and the general system status. It also analyzes data for different technologies in varying degrees of granularity. For this reason, Introscope is also available in most menu options within the ROOT CAUSE ANALYSIS work center.

Introscope comprises the following components (see Figure 4.8):

▶ **Introscope WebView**
The *Introscope WebView* application enables you to display Introscope data on a web-based graphical user interface. The application logic is located on the server side. The user interface is fully computed here, and an HTML page containing embedded graphics is transferred to the end user's web browser. To display the graphics correctly, you require the web browser enhancement Microsoft Silverlight (see also SAP Note 1273028).

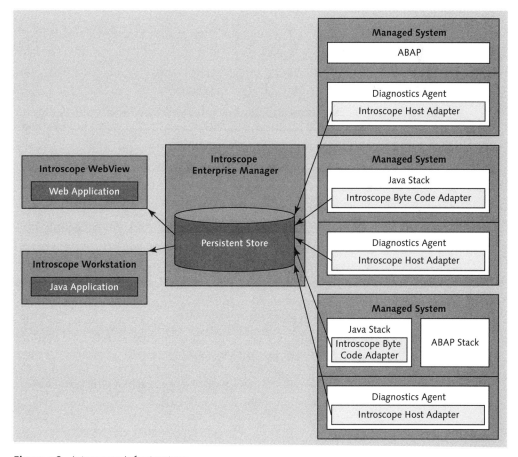

Figure 4.8 Introscope Infrastructure

▶ **Introscope Workstation**

Introscope Workstation is a Java-based user interface that is fully rendered on the end user's PC. In other words, the application logic is not executed on the server side, but on the client side. Furthermore, only the data required is transferred via the network to the end user's PC. As a prerequisite, the end user's PC must have an up-to-date Java Runtime Environment (JRE). When compared with Introscope WebView, this is the more common user interface. Furthermore, SAP recommends it to all of its customers and partners.

▶ **Agents**

The agents in the Introscope infrastructure are data providers that send the information to Introscope Enterprise Manager every 15 seconds. Two different agents are available:

  ▶ *Introscope Byte Code Adapter* is an application that runs on AS Java. When a Java program is running, it collects various pieces of data required for later analysis. When the Introscope user interface is in investigator mode, this agent is represented by the SAP NETWEAVER node.

  ▶ *Introscope Host Adapter* is an application embedded into the diagnostics agent. It collects operating system information via SAP host agents and SAPOSCOL, and it collects ABAP-specific information directly from the ABAP stack in the connected system. When the Introscope user interface is in investigator mode, this agent is also known as SAP HOSTAGENT PROCESS.

▶ **Introscope Enterprise Manager**

This is the main component of Introscope. It is responsible for collecting, storing, and displaying data. The Introscope data is placed in persistent store and retained there, by default, for a period of up to 30 days. Since Introscope Enterprise Manager records all metrics every 15 seconds, an enormous volume of data is produced in the long term. Consequently, older data stored in the Introscope Enterprise Manager memory is aggregated at regular intervals, thus limiting data growth and ensuring that, depending on the number of systems connected, the necessary memory space remains constant.

At present, there are three different modes in Introscope, each of which is available in both user interfaces (Introscope WebView and Workstation):

▶ **Console**

Predefined dashboards can be displayed in *console mode*. Dashboards are predefined graphical views of metric data. Occasionally, they use icons that provide you with a quick overview of the current landscape status. Sometimes, the dashboards are also linked to each other. If this is the case, you can easily move back and forth among the dashboards. The dashboard content always depends on the time granularity and analysis period defined by the end user.

▶ **Investigator**
Investigator mode provides a detail view for Introscope data. A tree structure enables you to select the components available in the Introscope infrastructure and navigate to the details you require. For this mode, the end user can also determine the time granularity and analysis period in which the data is displayed.

▶ **Transaction Tracer**
Transaction Tracer mode enables you to record and then evaluate individual user activities on a system's AS Java. This mode is generally used within end-to-end trace analysis.

In the case of Introscope WebView, the three modes are arranged next to each other in the upper section of the screen while, in the case of Introscope Workstation, you use the menu bar to toggle between these modes. The two user interfaces, Introscope WebView and Introscope Workstation, have a similar structure and display the same data. They differ very slightly in terms of their details and execution. We will therefore use the example of Introscope Workstation to explain how to use both user interfaces.

1. After you have started the application from the Root Cause Analysis work center, log on using a user provided for Introscope.

2. Introscope then opens in console mode. The upper screen area contains a multiple selection option in which you can select the dashboards available. The Navigation 1 dashboard (see Figure 4.9) is always the initial screen. From this dashboard, you can navigate to the main dashboards for the most important SAP products, which can be analyzed using Introscope.

The dashboards have a variety of different displays for visualizing data. Different elements of the user interface are used for this purpose:

▶ **Data viewers** are used to display data in metrics, groups of metrics, or similar, which are represented by elements (for example, alerts).

▶ **Graphics** and **text objects** are used to create a layout that helps users to search the dashboards and clarify the importance of the data in the data viewer.

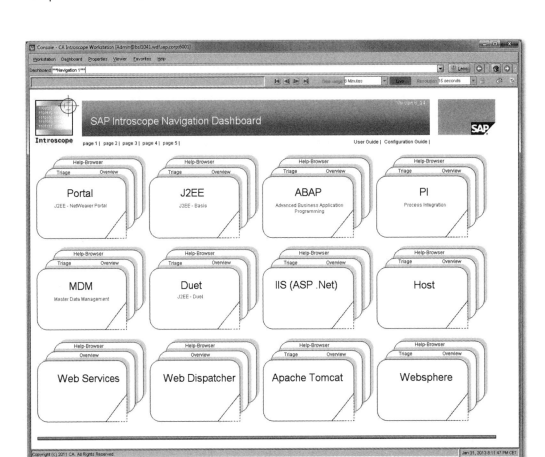

Figure 4.9 Introscope in Console Mode

3. In the upper-right area, you can select the analysis period in the Time range multiple selection option and the time-based details in the Resolution multiple selection option. Select a period that makes sense to you.

4. The upper-right area also contains the Lens function via the button ⬚ Lens. Here, you can choose which Introscope infrastructure agents are to be considered in the current view of console mode. If you call Introscope directly in the web browser, via the URL *http://<Wily IS host>:<Wily IS port/* (default port = 8081), all the agents are selected by default. If you start Introscope from the Root Cause Analysis work center, only the agents associated with the pre-selection in the Detailed Selection area (for example, the host selected) are considered.

5. Since the dashboards are interlinked, it is possible to navigate by double-clicking the various different elements in the user interface (links, status icons, and so on). You can therefore navigate from an overview dashboard to a theme-specific dashboard.

6. Charts are the smallest possible view of Introscope data. You can double-click the chart to display the HELP for the key performance indicators (KPIs) currently under analysis.

You can then perform a detailed analysis by checking individual values in investigator mode, as follows:

1. Switch from console mode to investigator mode by calling WORKSTATION • NEW INVESTIGATOR from the menu. In Introscope WebView, the investigator is located in the upper navigation area. The investigator is divided into three areas (see Figure 4.10):

   ▶ Analysis period (at the very top)

   ▶ Navigation (left)

   ▶ Work area (right)

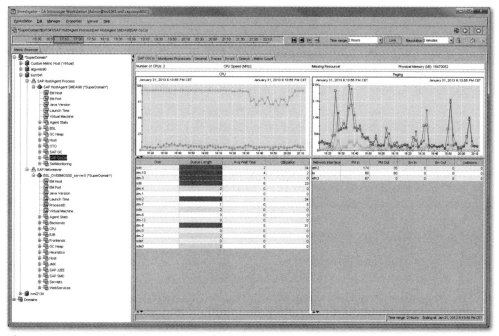

Figure 4.10 Introscope in Investigator Mode

2. In the upper area, you can once again define the analysis period in the TIME RANGE multiple selection option and the granularity in the RESOLUTION multiple selection option. This mode also contains a timeline that you can simply move back and forth using drag and drop. Changing the period automatically changes the view in the work area.

3. On the left-hand side of the screen, you can navigate within the hierarchy until you find the information you require. You can start with the host. You can then select the agents running on the host, followed by the metrics that you want to view. This is particularly helpful if you already know which metrics you want to find.

4. To some extent, you can also move back and forth by double-clicking within the mode. If, for example, you select a metric for a higher aggregation level, you will navigate directly to the relevant details. At the same time, the relevant element is selected in the navigation tree on the left-hand side.

The third mode, *Transaction Tracer*, will be described in more detail in Section 4.5.3.

Now that you have learned about the most important method-independent tools for root cause analysis, we will introduce you to some end-to-end methodologies in the following section.

4.3   End-to-End Methodology: Change Analysis

Technical changes within a system landscape can trigger both functional and performance problems. Therefore, in large distributed solutions in particular, you require effective tools that reliably monitor all changes during a particular period. This is precisely what the change analysis tools within root cause analysis do.

4.3.1   Change Analysis Tools in SAP Solution Manager

The following two tools are available to you in change analysis within SAP Solution Manager:

1. **End-to-end change analysis**
   End-to-end change analysis provides transparency in relation to changes within the entire system landscape. This type of analysis is particularly useful for quickly detecting changes that may be responsible for incidents during production operation. This tool provides you with a statistical overview of different changes

within the system landscape, which are organized into subject areas (known as *views*) (see Section 4.3.2).

These concern technical configuration data, as well as configurations for applications, content, and program code. This tool simplifies the search for changes in the system landscape that were made immediately before an incident occurred. You will learn more about how to use these tools in Section 4.3.3.

2. **Change reporting**

You can use change reporting to check the configuration for ABAP and Java systems in detail. This tool is intended for experts in SAP Basis. When you use change reporting, two functions are available to you: the display tool and the comparison tool. They enable you to practice four basic use cases for analysis purposes:

▶ Display configuration

▶ Compare two time stamps

▶ Compare two landscapes

▶ Compare multiple instances

You will learn more about how to use this tool in Section 4.3.4.

You can use the change reporting tool to compare two statuses with each other. More extensive options are provided by configuration validation, which you can use to compare several systems against each other simultaneously, on the basis of an initial configuration (see Section 4.3.6).

Before we provide a detailed introduction to each tool, we will first outline what you must consider when defining your data basis.

4.3.2 Data Extraction and Storage

In the following subsections, you'll learn about data extraction and data storage for change analysis within SAP Solution Manager. This will form the data basis for end-to-end change analysis, change reporting, and configuration validation.

Data Storage

The data required for change analysis within SAP Solution Manager is stored at two aggregation levels and, correspondingly, at two levels of data storage (see Figure 4.11):

1. **Storage in the Configuration and Change Database**
   All configuration changes (configuration parameters, values, and their history) are stored in configuration stores in the Configuration and Change Database (CCDB).

2. **Storage in SAP NetWeaver BW**
   The data in the configuration stores in the CCDB are processed, evaluated, and stored in SAP NetWeaver BW within SAP Solution Manager in aggregated form at regular intervals.

These two levels of data storage make it possible to perform both general and detailed analyses of the data. You can analyze every detail of the actual situation, as well as historical statistics in relation to changes.

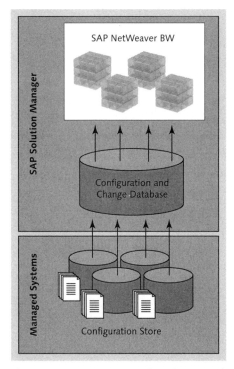

Figure 4.11 Data Storage within Change Analysis

Configuration Stores in the CCDB

The configuration stores in the CCDB are usually divided according to subject area and, therefore, provide data for a particular aspect.

In the case of ABAP systems, they cover the following areas, for example:

1. Software configuration (for example, kernel version, Support Package level, SAP Notes implemented, and transports imported into the system)

2. ABAP instance parameters (for example, active parameters in the ABAP instance and the profiles used)

3. Database configuration (in other words, all important parameters associated with the database management system)

4. Operating system configuration (for example, host, CPU, or memory parameters)

5. SAP NetWeaver BW configuration (for example, information about BW parameters and detailed configuration)

6. Configuration of RFC connections (for example, type or user)

7. Configuration of system changes (for example, client settings or global system settings)

8. Configuration of security settings (for example, standard users, valid certificates, trusted RFCs, or active web services)

9. Critical user authorizations for profiles and transactions

Thanks to a diverse range of configuration parameters, considerably more information is available for AS Java. SAP Note 1230404 provides a host of information about the configuration stores used for ABAP and Java systems.

The configuration stores have been organized into change groups (also known as *aliases*) and change categories (also known as *subaliases*). Change categories are grouped into change groups. The change category is the smallest grouping unit and can contain one or more configuration stores.

Even though the configuration data in the managed systems is usually retained and saved, this is mostly done without the use of a change time stamp and, therefore, without a history. Therefore, in the SAP Solution Manager infrastructure, a time stamp is assigned to each change as soon as it is transferred to SAP Solution Manager. Consequently, the transfer time may differ slightly from the time when the change was actually performed. The only exceptions to this are changes to SAP Notes, RFC connections, and transport requests, which are event-controlled changes and therefore, registered with a real time stamp.

> **Note**
>
> Because diagnostics agents are responsible for collecting data, they must be available on all systems under analysis (see also Section 4.1.1).

Data Extraction

The Extractor Framework (EFWK) plays a key role in data collection and processing, as well as information storage, in SAP Solution Manager. The arrows in Figure 4.11 indicate the flow direction of the change data. Data processing is described in detail in the following list:

1. Extractors start in SAP Solution Manager at regular intervals. They, in turn, start further extractors in the managed systems. Based on the type of technical system, the extractors are scheduled during the configuration of SAP Solution Manager and, depending on the technology, read the change information from the various configuration stores. In other words, only ABAP-specific configuration changes are collected for a managed system's AS ABAP (for example, ABAP parameters, SAP Notes, and so on), whereas only Java-relevant data is analyzed for AS Java (for example, JVM parameters, Java security-relevant settings, and so on).

   The first extractor run occurs immediately after a system is connected to SAP Solution Manager. During this run, the entire configuration store of the technical system is transferred into CCDB. Consequently, any subsequent extractor runs register only changes to the configuration stores in the systems, thus keeping the necessary storage capacity in the CCDB to a minimum. This makes it possible to track the entire system landscape configuration over a longer period with a minimum volume of data.

2. In the second stage of data processing, the EFWK executes an extractor on SAP Solution Manager on an hourly basis. This scans the configuration stores in the CCDB and aggregates the change details as statistical information. The results of this aggregation process are stored in InfoCubes in SAP NetWeaver Business Warehouse within SAP Solution Manager.

3. A background job scheduled on a regular basis aggregates this content further. As a result, a long-term analysis is possible even if the volume of data remains the same.

4. The BW data in SAP Solution Manager is then available to you for multi-purpose queries. End-to-end change analysis provides you with a user-friendly interface that already contains the most important views. If you have the relevant BW expertise, you can also create completely individual data analyses in the Info-Cubes in the business warehouse.

4.3.3 Using End-to-End Change Analysis

We will now show you how to use end-to-end change analysis:

1. In the ROOT CAUSE ANALYSIS work center, select the END-TO-END ANALYSIS menu option.

2. In the DETAILED SELECTION area, select the relevant technical systems. Once you have made your selection, choose CHANGE ANALYSIS to start end-to-end change analysis.

3. The changes made in each technical system are then displayed on the OVERVIEW tab page for end-to-end change analysis (see Figure 4.12).

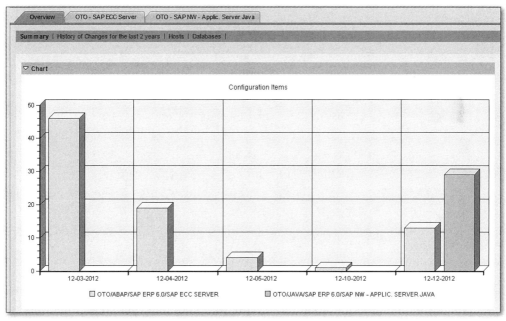

Figure 4.12 End-to-End Change Analysis—Overview

In our example involving Toys Inc., the chosen scenario comprises an AS ABAP (OTO—SAP ECC SERVER in Figure 4.12) and an AS Java (OTO—SAP NW—APPLIC. SERVER JAVA in the figure). All recorded changes are displayed on a daily basis. The lower section of the chart contains a legend that lists the technical systems represented by the various bars in the bar chart. This enables you to immediately see the period and technical system in which the changes occurred. In Figure 4.12, it is clear that a particularly large number of changes were made to the SAP ECC server on December 03, 2012.

On the OVERVIEW tab page, the changes are displayed in a table in the TABLE area below the graph (see Figure 4.13).

System ID	Maininstance Name	Change Group	ConfigStore	Calendar Day	12-10-2012	12-11-2012	Overall Result
BSL	APPLICATION SERVER JAVA	J2EE	SAP_J2EEClusterNode		9		9
			SAP_J2EEClusterNode		2		2
		J2EE-SOFTWARE	SAP_J2EEDeployedSCService		192		192
			J2EE_COMP_SPLEVEL		19		19
		JVM PARAMETERS	instance.properties		1		1
		Result			223		223
	SOLUTION MANAGER ABAP STACK	ABAP-PARAMETER	ABAP_INSTANCE_PAHI			1	1
		RFC-DESTINATIONS	RFCDES_TYPE_3		1		1
			RFCDES		1		1
			RFCDES_TYPE_3_CHECK		1		1
		SECURITY	SICF_SERVICES		2		2
		Result			5	1	6

Figure 4.13 End-to-End Change Analysis—Tabular Overview

4. For further details, use the corresponding tab page for component-specific details.

▶ **AS ABAP example**
Figure 4.14 shows the SUMMARY view on the OTO—SAP ECC SERVER tab page, which provides a summary of different views of typical changes to AS ABAP. They are color-coded and listed side by side in a legend below the chart.

The SOFTWARE MAINTENANCE view shows changes such as software component updates and their patch level, while the PARAMETER view shows changes to the ABAP instance parameters and database parameters. In the TRANSPORT REQUESTS and SAP NOTES views, changes are displayed according to the number of transports imported and the number of SAP Notes implemented. Lastly, the MISCELLANEOUS view shows other changes to the system (for example, client configurations or operating system configurations). You can use the links in the upper area to call the individual views in detail.

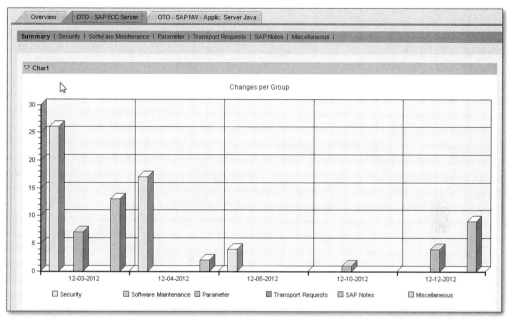

Figure 4.14   End-to-End Change Analysis—ABAP Example

▶ **AS Java example**

Figure 4.15 shows the SUMMARY view on the OTO—SAP NW—APPLIC. SERVER JAVA tab page in which typical change views for a J2EE technical system are displayed. They are organized as follows: SECURITY, DISPATCHER CONFIGURATION, SERVER CONFIGURATION, NODE TYPE INDEPENDENT CONFIGURATION, and SOFTWARE MAINTENANCE.

5. Navigate from the SUMMARY view on the tab page for component-specific details to the view containing the relevant change type.

Figure 4.16 shows, for example, the PARAMETER view, which contains all ABAP-relevant parameter changes to the SAP ECC server at Toys Inc. Depending on the type of change, they are further subdivided semantically. In the case of parameter changes, a distinction is made between instance-independent and instance-dependent parameter changes. The NO APPLICABLE DATA FOUND message in the PARAMETER CHANGES: INSTANCE INDEPENDENT area means that no changes were made in the period and area selected.

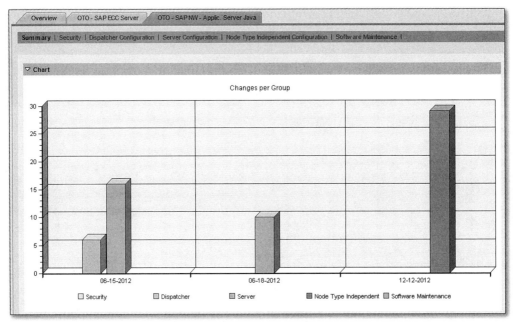

Figure 4.15 End-to-End Change Analysis—Java Example

Calendar Day	12-03-2012	12-10-2012	12-12-2012	12-17-2012	12-18-2012	12-19-2012	12-20-2012
Instance Name	Changes	Changes	Changes	Changes	Changes	Changes	Changes
Overall Result	7	1	4	3	1	1	2
▽ DVEBMGS02 (BSL1041_OTO_02)	7	1	4	3	1	1	2
▽ ABAP-PARAMETER	1	1	2	2	1		2
▽ PAHI	1	1	2	2	1		2
ABAP_INSTANCE_PAHI	1	1	2	2	1		2
▽ PROFILE	6		2	1		1	
▽ INSTANCE	6		1	1		1	
ABAP_INSTANCE_PROFILE	6		1	1		1	
▽ START			1				
ABAP_START_PROFILE			1				

Figure 4.16 End-to-End Change Analysis—ABAP Parameter Details

At Toys Inc., four different types of changes were registered on December 12, 2012. The rows `ABAP_INSTANCE_PAHI`, `ABAP_INSTANCE_PROFILE`, and `ABAP_START_PROFILE` are highlighted in green. This means that further details are available.

6. If you select a green field in a row for which you want to view further details, the system will automatically bring you to the change reporting tool. This navigation option is available for almost every change type. In the next section, we'll show you how to use the change reporting tool.

4.3.4 Using the Change Reporting Tool

You use the change reporting tool to access change details stored in the CCDB. To use this tool, proceed as follows:

1. Select the SYSTEM ANALYSIS menu option in the navigation bar of the ROOT CAUSE ANALYSIS work center.

2. In the DETAILED SELECTION area, select the technical system(s) you wish to analyze as the primary landscape component.

3. Choose CHANGE REPORTING. If you have selected more than one system, they are displayed as separate tab pages.

4. Choose between the following two functions:

   ▶ The display tool (VIEWER tab page)

   ▶ The comparison tool (COMPARE tab page)

The following procedure will differ depending on whether you want to display or compare changes.

Use Case 1: Display Configuration

1. Select the VIEWER tab to open the display tool. The navigation elements are displayed on the left-hand side of the screen, while the content elements are displayed on the right-hand side. The following areas are displayed on the left:

   ▶ **Filters**
   In the FILTERS area (see Figure 4.17), you can use different criteria (for example, STORE GROUPS FILTERS, STORE FILTERS, or STORE ELEMENTS FILTERS) to restrict the manner in which the configuration stores under analysis are displayed. This is particularly helpful if you already know which type of configuration store you wish to search for configuration details.

▶ **Search Store Elements**

In the SEARCH STORE ELEMENTS area (see Figure 4.17), you can apply further display restrictions to the configuration stores displayed. To do this, enter a search term. The system then searches the CCDB for this term. It searches through the names of configuration stores, parameters, or values. This enables you to search for terms that are part of the configuration.

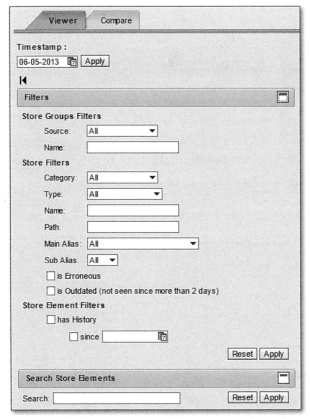

Figure 4.17 Change Reporting—Filter Function and Search Function

▶ **Navigation**

The NAVIGATION area contains a tree structure that is sorted hierarchically in a manner suited to the respective landscape (BY LANDSCAPE tab) or depending on the type of configuration store (BY ALIAS tab) (see Figure 4.18).

2. When using the filter function or search function, or when navigating directly within the tree structure, select the store type in the navigation area. The INSTANCE type was selected in our Toys Inc. example (see Figure 4.18).

Based on this selection, the STORE LIST is displayed on the right-hand side of the screen. It contains all configuration stores that belong to the type selected. In the table, the properties of the configuration stores are displayed in columns under the headings NAME, ALIAS: SUBALIAS, TYPE, STORE STATE, LOG, and MORE DETAILS. If you want to know where the data comes from or why certain information may not be contained in the CCDB, you can analyze this in greater detail here.

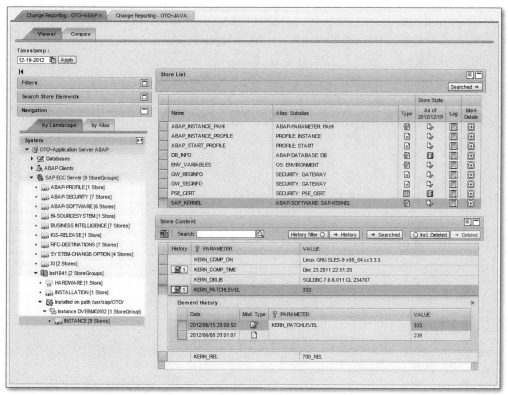

Figure 4.18 Change Reporting—Viewer

3. In the STORE LIST, select the row that corresponds to the configuration store to be analyzed. The contents of the configuration store are displayed below (in the STORE CONTENT area). Depending on the type of configuration store, these

contents are always displayed in tabular form. Figure 4.18 shows the contents of the SAP_KERNEL configuration store.

4. If a small icon (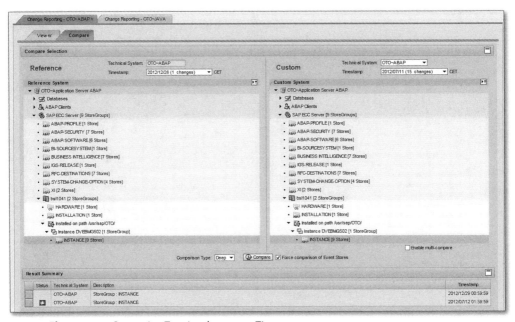 1) is displayed in the HISTORY column (see Figure 4.18), this means that the value in this row changed during the recording of the CCDB. Choose 1 to display details of these changes. Detailed information (for example, the original value, changes made in the meantime, and the current value for the relevant element) is displayed in the table in the ELEMENT HISTORY area. All entries have a corresponding time stamp. Our example in Figure 4.18 shows that Toys Inc. imported a new patch level for the SAP kernel on June 15.

Use Cases 2 and 3: Compare Two Landscapes or Times

1. Select the COMPARE tab to open the comparison tool.

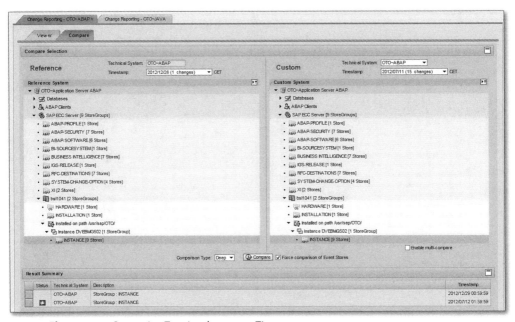

Figure 4.19 Comparing Two Landscapes or Times

2. The upper sections of the REFERENCE and CUSTOM areas (see Figure 4.19) contain the TECHNICAL SYSTEM and TIMESTAMP for the configuration status currently under analysis. When you access this screen, the reference system you previously selected in the DETAILED SELECTION area is selected in the REFERENCE area on the left. You can change the time stamp. The system previously selected in

the DETAILED SELECTION area is pre-assigned in the CUSTOM area on the right. A TIMESTAMP is also pre-assigned. However, you can change both. You can:

▶ Compare the configuration of different systems by selecting different systems in the TECHNICAL SYSTEM field and specifying the same time stamp in the TIMESTAMP field in both areas.

▶ Compare the configuration of one system at different times by specifying the same system in the TECHNICAL SYSTEM field in both areas and different time stamps in the TIMESTAMP field.

3. In the REFERENCE area on the left, select the configuration store type that you want to compare. An equivalent configuration store type is automatically selected in the CUSTOM area.

4. Once a configuration store type has been selected on both sides, the system displays the COMPARE button, which you use to start the comparison. Before you start the comparison, you can make the following selection in the COMPARISON TYPE field:

▶ FAST
When this option is selected, the comparison displays only those configuration items that have actually been changed. Unchanged or deleted configuration objects are not considered here.

▶ DEEP
When this option is selected, all configurations are compared against each other and subsequently displayed. It goes without saying that this demands much more computing time. All configuration items are displayed (in other words, unchanged, different, and deleted). When you select this option, it takes significantly longer to process the comparison operations.

Once you have selected an option, choose COMPARE to start the comparison. After a short period of computation, the RESULT SUMMARY is displayed in the lower area of the interface (see Figure 4.20).

The reference landscape is always displayed in the first row. The next row shows whether the landscape on the right-hand side (CUSTOM area) differs in terms of the reference landscape. In Figure 4.20, this is indicated by the icon ⊞ in the STATUS column, which suggests that the instance of the OTO system clearly differs from the reference system in every regard. Any unchanged configuration statuses would have been displayed with an "equals" sign (⚌).

Figure 4.20 Comparing Two Landscapes or Times—Result

5. Select a row that was assigned a "not equals" sign. The RESULT DETAILS area then displays the reference values in the REFERENCE VALUE column on the left and the comparison values in the CUSTOM VALUE column on the right. All configuration stores within the store type selected are listed. If you expand these in succession, you see only differing configurations by default. Only if you have selected the comparison type DEEP can you now select SHOW ALL in the FILTERS multiple selection option.

For some configurations, the magnifying glass is displayed in the DETAILS column on the right-hand side. You can use this if you wish to display further details. In our example (see Figure 4.20), Toys Inc. made the parameter `rdisp/wp_no_dia` smaller, thus reducing the number of work processes available. This may have been caused by a resource bottleneck, for example.

Use Case 4: Compare Multiple Instances

The option to compare multiple instances was developed so that multiple instances within a system could be homogenized. Let's imagine that you are using multiple instances, one of which differs from the others in terms of its behavior. The comparison tool enables you to detect configuration differences between instances that exhibit "good" and "bad" behavior.

A comparison of two instances is possible for both ABAP and Java instances. The only difference is that, in the case of AS ABAP, the instances are analyzed, while in the case of AS Java, the server nodes within the Java cluster are analyzed. Essentially, you use the comparison tool the same way you used it to compare two landscapes or times. Therefore, in the next section, we will focus solely on deviations from the approach outlined above:

1. On the left-hand side, select the reference object as usual, namely the reference instance for AS ABAP and the relevant server node for AS Java. To compare several instances against the reference instance simultaneously, select the ENABLE MULTI-COMPARE checkbox in the CUSTOM area (bottom right in Figure 4.21). A checkbox then appears next to the instance node or server node on the right-hand side (in the CUSTOM area). You then select the instances you wish to compare against the reference instance.

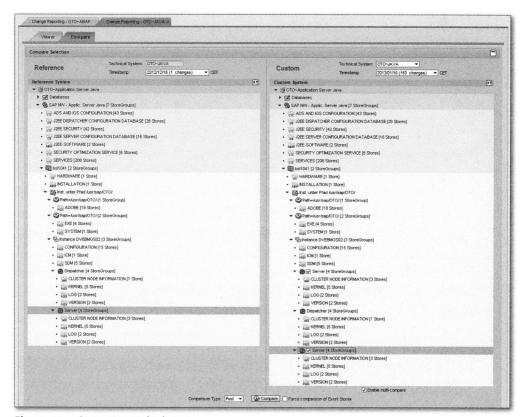

Figure 4.21 Comparing Multiple Instances

2. Choose COMPARE to start the comparison.

3. If you have selected multiple instances, you will find additional entries in the RESULT SUMMARY. Each time an instance is compared against the reference instance, a separate result is displayed with a corresponding status (see Figure 4.22).

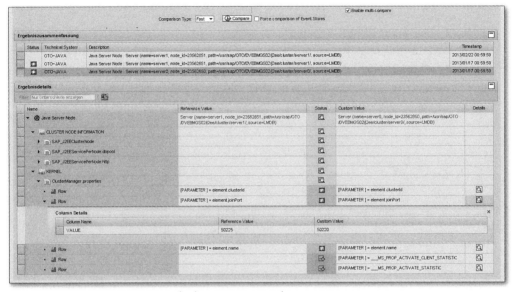

Figure 4.22 Comparing Multiple Instances—Result

4. You evaluate the comparison results the same way you evaluate the results associated with comparing two landscapes or times.

All of the tools introduced so far have given you a good idea of the current system landscape configuration. However, to unequivocally demonstrate that a problem was caused by a change to the configuration, it may be necessary to conduct further analysis. Expert knowledge may also be required. You should also check the actual data sources again in order to confirm your analysis results in SAP Solution Manager.

At this point, we wish to refer you to two additional expert tools:

▶ The enhanced Change and Transport System (CTS+) is suitable for analyzing transports. When analyzing transports, click the relevant transport request in the change reporting tool or use Transaction STMS in the transport controller responsible for the connected system. Here, you analyze both classical ABAP transports and non-ABAP objects (for example, Java objects) from the SAP NetWeaver Development infrastructure, the SAP NetWeaver Exchange infrastructure, the SAP NetWeaver Portal content, or other customer-specific objects.

▶ You can use the file system browser, which was introduced in Section 4.2.2, specifically to analyze files as a data source for configurations.

4.3.5 Approaches and Examples

In change analysis, you analyze and check the configuration of all system landscape components involved. The application examples in the following subsections are merely suggestions that may assist you in similar situations. Consequently, the methods of analysis we describe in the next subsections have only been broadly outlined to give you an idea of the situations in which these tools can be used.

There are usually three initial situations in which change analysis is used. We will outline each of these initial situations below. We will also provide you with an overview of the steps that need to be taken in each case.

Example 1: One or More Systems Exhibit Poor Performance or Cause Errors

You are investigating the possible cause of a performance or functional problem and, therefore, conduct an analysis of the system landscape. In this case, the following approach is appropriate:

1. The first step in change analysis is to use end-to-end change analysis to obtain an overview of the changes made to all landscape components involved. If possible, conduct the analysis in a time frame in which the performance problems or error messages occurred. Find the technical system that experienced the most changes. The greatest potential for errors is most likely here.

2. In end-to-end change analysis, navigate to the component details for the technical system you have identified and search for further anomalies. Here, analyze which types of changes were made. Furthermore, verify each change category and group in the time frame under analysis.

3. So far, you have analyzed only statistical information. Now you wish to know precisely what has changed and how this change manifests itself. Therefore, navigate to the change reporting tool. Here, examine the changes in detail and check them in relation to the symptom that has occurred. This enables you to identify a potential cause for the problem that has arisen.

Example 2: The Development System Behaves Differently from the Production System

If the development system behaves differently from the production system, it is useful to not only analyze the changes, but also compare two components. In this case, you usually proceed as follows:

1. At the start of the analysis process, compare the development system against the production system in end-to-end change analysis. For all change categories, check whether an almost identical number of changes were made to both systems.

> **Note**
>
> Since a large number of configurations (for example, corrections to SAP Notes) are usually transported, changes to a downstream system may also have been recorded as part of a transport, and therefore not as a separate change. Furthermore, the changes to both systems may also be displayed at different times.

2. If the number of changes to both systems differs, use the change reporting tool to perform a direct comparison of the configuration store that you identified earlier. This enables you to quickly obtain an overview of the settings potentially responsible for this different behavior.

Example 3: Certain Java Instances of the Production System Behave Differently from Other Instances

If you observe that the behavior of certain Java instances of the production system differs from the behavior of other instances, it is useful to perform a direct comparison within AS Java. You normally conduct the analysis as follows:

1. In end-to-end change analysis, analyze only the technical system on which the differences were identified. Focus on the Java component details and analyze the configuration of all server nodes.

2. Analyze the server node exhibiting the unusual behavior, along with another server node that is considered to be representative of high-performance server nodes. If you ascertain that changes were made in different ways and at different times, you should conduct a more in-depth analysis of the relevant changes (for example, using the display tool in change reporting).

3. If, however, you still don't have any concrete information that would indicate that the server nodes differ, use the comparison function within change reporting. You can use direct comparison, for example, to compare the configuration of multiple Java instances and then update them to the same level, if you wish.

Now that you are familiar with the most important root cause analysis tools in change analysis, we will introduce you to one further tool within this context: configuration validation. This tool is not only suitable for root cause analysis; it can also be integrated into the processes deployed by an IT department so that you can check the configuration of system landscapes.

4.3.6 Configuration Validation

As the name "configuration validation" suggests, this function enables you to check that your system landscape's settings or configurations are correct, thus ensuring the homogeneity of your system landscape. Several different validation options exist. For example, you can compare real systems against each other or use your own definitions of a required setting for checking real systems.

Several different parameters are also available here. For example, you can use configuration validation to check parameter settings, security settings, or changes implemented in the form of transports. Its flexible framework also allows for extensive adjustments, as well as design options for creating very individual queries.

In the following subsections, we'll describe the basic prerequisites for configuration validation, as well as the information and functions available to you when using configuration validation. We will then use some application scenarios to show you how you can benefit from using configuration validation.

Basic Prerequisites

Various prerequisites must be fulfilled before you can use configuration validation. A brief description of each is provided in the following sections. It involves verifying the necessary analysis data and ensuring access to the relevant function.

Setting Up Technical Systems

The basic principle of configuration validation is to compare data from various different managed systems. The first step in fulfilling the basic prerequisite is to check that these systems are connected properly. For more information about connecting systems to SAP Solution Manager, see Section 2.5.4.

As soon as you have ensured that those systems that will later undergo configuration validation are connected to SAP Solution Manager correctly, it should be possible to extract data from the system. In the next step, we will check whether or not this particular data extraction is successful.

Checking Data Extraction

As described in Section 4.3.2, the configuration validation data is organized into configuration stores within the CCDB in SAP Solution Manager. To check that data extraction was performed correctly, open the SAP SOLUTION MANAGER ADMINISTRATION work center. Then, select the INFRASTRUCTURE option from the menu on the left-hand side and choose the multiple selection option ADMINISTRATION • CONFIGURATION CHANGE DATABASE in the work area on the right-hand side of the screen.

You then receive an overview of the current status of data extraction. Figure 4.23 shows an example of a check that was successfully performed on data procured by the extractors.

If you want to obtain further details, you can select the TECHNICAL SYSTEMS tab. You will then see a detail view that comprises various pieces of information (for example, the number of failed extractors or the total number of extractors). You can then click any of the numeric values to display further detail views.

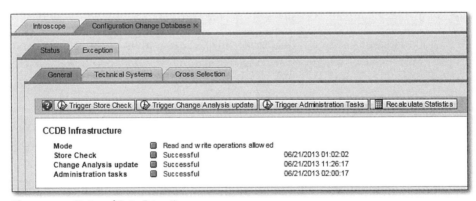

Figure 4.23 Status of Data Extraction

Status of InfoCube Filling

In the CONFIGURATION CHANGE DATABASE overview, you can also check whether the extracted data is also available in the InfoCube 0SMD_CA02, which is required for configuration validation. To do this, go to the CCDB INFRASTRUCTURE area on the STATUS • GENERAL tab page and take a look at the status next to CHANGE ANALYSIS UPDATE. If this status is green (SUCCESSFUL), the data was stored correctly.

You should also check the InfoProviders `0SMD_VCA1` and `0SMD_VCA2` in Transaction RSDIPROP for read mode parameter A (QUERY TO READ ALL DATA AT ONCE).

Authorizations

You must then ensure that your user has the necessary authorizations for configuration validation.

Two composite roles are available for configuration validation. Each composite role contains a collection of single roles, each of which is briefly outlined here:

► `SAP_CV_ADMIN_COMP` (administrator for configuration validation)

 ► `SAP_CV_ALL` (full authorization for configuration validation)

 ► `SAP_SMWORK_BASIC` (WORK CENTER: BASIC AUTHORIZATION OBJECTS)

 ► `SAP_SMWORK_CHANGE_MAN` (WORK CENTER: CHANGE REQUEST MANAGEMENT)

 ► `SAP_SYSTEM_REPOSITORY_DIS` (Solution Manager System Landscape - display authorizations)

► `SAP_CV_DISPLAY_COMP` (Master: Display User for Configuration Validation)

 ► `SAP_CV_DIS` (Display Authorization for Configuration Validation)

 ► `SAP_SMWORK_BASIC` (WORK CENTER: BASIC AUTHORIZATION OBJECTS)

 ► `SAP_SMWORK_CHANGE_MAN` (WORK CENTER: CHANGE REQUEST MANAGEMENT)

 ► `SAP_SYSTEM_REPOSITORY_DIS` (Solution Manager System Landscape - display authorizations)

Furthermore, the role `SAP_BI_E2E` should be assigned for BI reporting.

For more detailed information on the authorization concept for SAP Solution Manager, see Chapter 12.

Introduction to Functions

Configuration validation can be called via the ROOT CAUSE ANALYSIS and CHANGE MANAGEMENT work centers. The CHANGE MANAGEMENT work center contains a corresponding link in the lower-left area of the navigation menu (RELATED LINKS), while the ROOT CAUSE ANALYSIS work center contains a separate CONFIGURATION VALIDATION menu option in the navigation menu on the left-hand side.

You can also call configuration validation from the SAP Easy Access menu. To facilitate this, create a link to the Web Dynpro application `AGS_WORK_CHANGE_MAN` in the SAP Easy Access menu.

In configuration validation, one or more comparison systems, which are grouped together in a *comparison list*, are always compared against a *target system* (in other words, the initial configuration). In the following sections, we'll discuss how to maintain the target system or comparison list (sometimes also known in the system as a *system list*) and how to perform a comparison.

Maintaining Target Systems

In configuration validation, defining a target system is the starting point for subsequent validation reports. When comparing systems in configuration validation, the target system is also known as the *reference system*. A reference system represents the target configuration and, therefore, the basis against which all other systems are compared. Such a reference system can come from a real system, or it can be freely defined. A free definition is appropriate, for example, if the desired target scenario is defined in the form of configuration parameters and will later be compared against all real systems that exist.

After you call configuration validation, the screen shown in Figure 4.24 is displayed. On the first tab page (TARGET SYSTEM MAINTENANCE), you define target systems.

Figure 4.24 Maintaining a Target System

You can define your target system in the CREATE area. Three options are available to you:

▶ CREATE EMPTY

You can use the CREATE EMPTY button to define an "empty" target system without first having to define a configuration store. The source system that you can define here forms the basis for configuration stores that you can select later.

▶ TECHNICAL SYSTEM AS A TEMPLATE

If you already know which configuration stores you want to define in the target system and on which LMDB technical systems they are to be based, you can create the target system directly in the SOURCE SYSTEM area. If you select a real system in the area on the left-hand side (SELECT SOURCE SYSTEMS), the associated configuration stores are displayed on the right-hand side. You can now select those configuration stores that are important to you and then choose CREATE FROM SELECTED STORES to define a new target system.

▶ TARGET SYSTEM AS A TEMPLATE

Choose CREATE WITH TEMPLATE to select an existing target system that you will use as a template. All configuration stores defined here, as well as all validation definitions, are transferred.

Once you have created a target system, it is displayed in the EDIT area, where it can be edited further. To do this, first select the target system and then select the configuration store on the right-hand side. Figure 4.25 shows an example of a target system defined for security-relevant information.

Once you have selected a configuration store, the corresponding content and associated operators are displayed in the lower screen area. You can now make various changes here. For example, you can add or remove configuration items or adjust the operators. You can use the icon 🔳 to call examples of different operator options. A test option at the end of the rows enables you to test whether the operators are working correctly. This is illustrated by the comparison value "6" in the row selected in Figure 4.25. You can then use the 🖫 icon to save your settings.

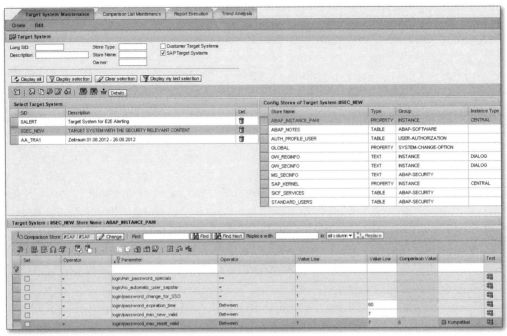

Figure 4.25 Maintaining Target Systems with Operators

Maintaining the Comparison List

On the Comparison List Maintenance tab page, you can group systems together according to the criteria selected. This is particularly useful for regular validations of specific system groups. Various different criteria are available for defining a comparison list. For example, databases, system types, or software levels can be used as the basis for a grouping. A group of ABAP systems is defined in the example shown in Figure 4.26.

After the comparison list is created, it's stored as a fixed list on the Comparison List Maintenance tab page and is available to you when you execute reports. If you select the comparison list, all the systems associated with the comparison list are automatically included in the validation. A list of comparison systems is contained in the dialog box for query variables, which is displayed before you execute the report. If you wish, you can add more systems to or remove some systems from this list.

You can also edit the comparison list retroactively. To do this, select the relevant list on the Comparison List Maintenance tab page, as shown in Figure 4.27.

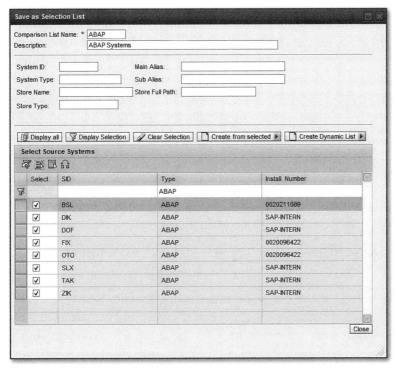

Figure 4.26 Maintaining the Comparison List

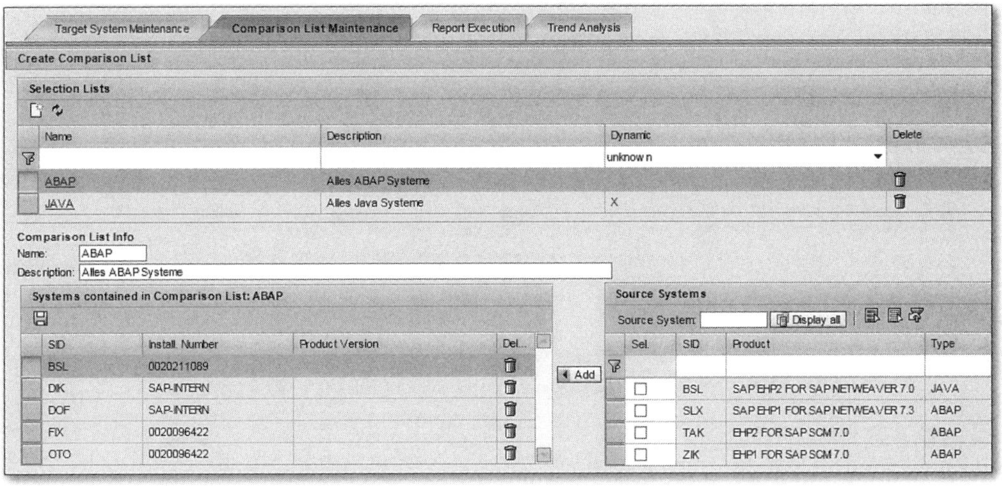

Figure 4.27 Editing Comparison Lists

You can then delete existing systems or add more source systems.

In addition to the static variant of a list, you can also create dynamic lists. In this case, the corresponding search criterion (for example, system type Java) is defined when the comparison list is created. You can choose DISPLAY SELECTION to validate the search. You can then choose CREATE DYNAMIC LIST to create a list. If you now use this comparison list when executing reports, the corresponding number of systems currently available will be determined at the same time.

Executing Reports

Once you have maintained some target systems and comparison lists, you can use the four different options available for configuration validation reports on the REPORT EXECUTION tab page. We briefly explain them here.

In the first area, REFERENCE SYSTEM AND COMPARISON SYSTEMS, you can define corresponding reference systems and comparison systems.

Here, the screen is divided into two sections: CHOOSE REFERENCE SYSTEM (left) and CHOOSE SYSTEMS FOR COMPARISON (right). Choose DISPLAY on both sides and then select the systems you require. If you do not select any systems at this stage, which is the case in Figure 4.28, then when you use the following validation reports, you will obtain an empty input template in which you can manually define systems as a reference system or comparison system.

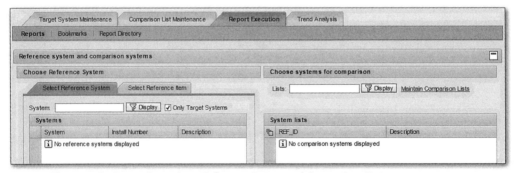

Figure 4.28 Report Execution—Reference System and Comparison System

On the SELECT REFERENCE ITEM tab page, you can define a single evaluation value instead of a system. Here, you define the configuration store and item that you want to validate.

Figure 4.29 demonstrates this using the example of the configuration store ABAP_ NOTES. In the NOTE field, you can enter a special SAP Note that can then be validated against other systems.

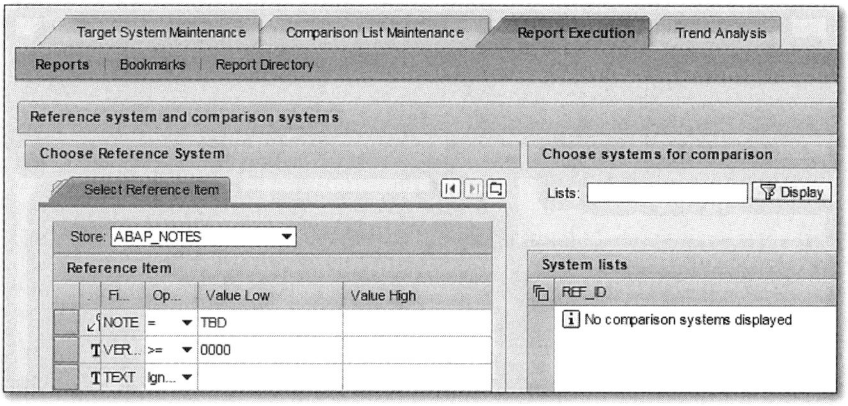

Figure 4.29 Validating a Reference Item

The CONSISTENCY VALIDATION area contains a range of analysis reports delivered by SAP (see Figure 4.30). In these reports, the configuration stores are usually pre-defined according to subject area. Therefore, all that remains is for you to define the target and reference systems.

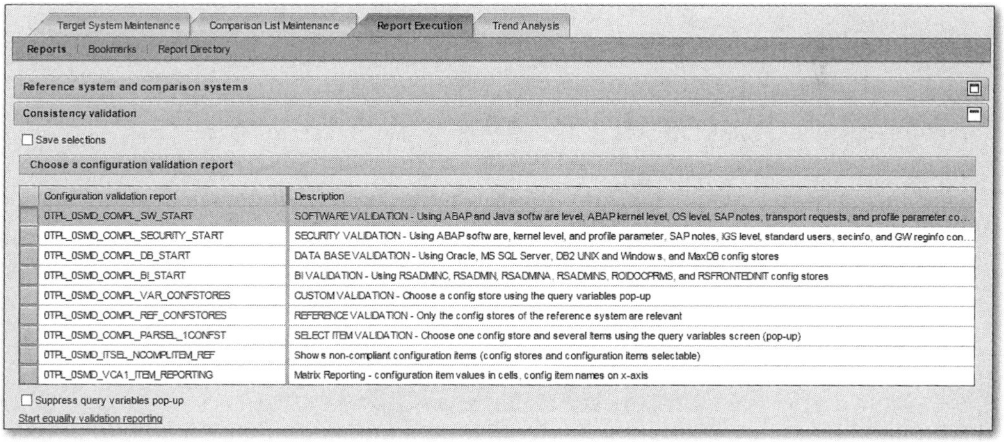

Figure 4.30 Report Execution—Consistency Validation

For example, you can use the report `OTPL_OSMD_COMPL_SECURITY_START` to query different aspects of security. Another example is the report `OTPL_OSMD_COMPL_PARSEL_1CONFST`, which you can use specifically to check individual configuration items, such as the database version or kernel version. If, for example, you want to check whether a certain transport has been imported into the target systems, you can use the report `OTPL_OSMD_COMPL_VAR_CONFSTORES` to create this query.

> **Note**
>
> We generally recommend that you use the change reporting tool (see Section 4.3.4) to validate the corresponding configuration stores in advance. This enables you to determine the correct configuration stores (in other words, the stores that contain the information you require) immediately.

After you have selected a template, you can execute the report by selecting the Start equality validation reporting link located in the lower screen area (see Figure 4.30). The result list initially provides a complete overview with the option to navigate to individual subareas (for example, the configuration validation report `OTPL_OSMD_COMPL_SW_START`), as shown in Figure 4.31.

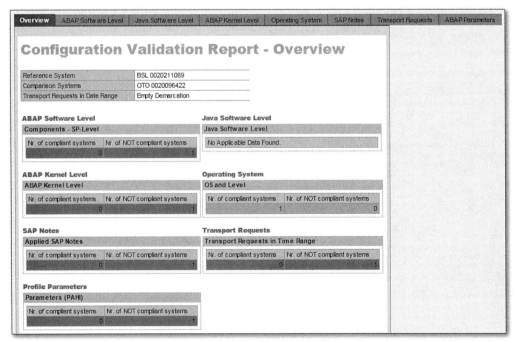

Figure 4.31 Configuration Validation Report—Result

The red and green highlighting enables you to quickly see whether the comparison system(s) correspond to the target system you selected. You can then select the relevant tab to navigate to the detail view, which contains information about the exact location of any deviation.

While the CONSISTENCY VALIDATION area performs an equality check for the reference system, the OPERATOR VALIDATION area contains additional options for querying and evaluating information. For example, you can qualify the number of elements to be compared and define their analysis in detail (exact match, exclusion criteria, value ranges, and so on). Operator validation also provides evaluation templates (see Figure 4.32) for the information displayed on screen and the configuration stores used. Individual reference systems can be defined with operators (see Figure 4.25) in order, for example, to exclude values or define value ranges that were evaluated as being either compliant or non-compliant during the validation process.

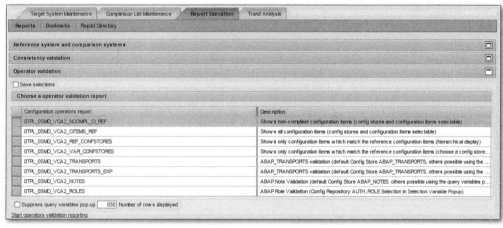

Figure 4.32 Report Execution—Operator Validation

Since the report `OTPL_OSMD_VCA2_REF_CONFSTORES` provides very few additional query options, it is particularly suitable for direct system comparisons. The report `OTPL_OSMD_VCA2_VAR_CONFSTORES`, on the other hand, makes it possible to significantly reduce the validation content and, therefore, restrict it to one particular aspect.

The report `OTPL_OSMD_VCA2_NCOMPL_CI_REF` is limited to displaying all non-compliant parameters, while the report `OTPL_OSMD_VCA2_CITEMS_REF` initially displays all data, irrespective of whether it is compliant or non-compliant.

In the case of transports, you can use the report `OTPL_OSMD_VCA2_TRANSPORTS` to create transport statistics for a real system (reference system). Here, release time stamps and import time stamps are determined in order to calculate the lead times for transports. This enables you, for example, to ascertain how long a change was available for testing in a test system before it was imported into the production system. The report `OTPL_OSMD_VCA2_TRANSPORTS_EX` creates a comparison list of transports sorted according to the objects contained in each transport.

The report `OTPL_OSMD_VCA2_NOTES` is available for SAP Notes. You can use this report to check whether the SAP Notes implemented in the reference system are also contained in the target systems. The report `OTPL_OSMD_VCA2_ROLES` is based on the same principle. In this case, the existence of authorization roles is validated.

As stated previously, you can define reference systems or target systems and their conformity rules in a flexible manner in operator validation. The use of operators was discussed earlier in the section entitled "Maintaining Target Systems." Detailed instructions for different application scenarios and possible target system configurations are provided on the wiki page *http://wiki.sdn.sap.com/wiki/display/TechOps/ConfVal_Home#ConfVal_Home-BestPractises*. This page is continuously updated and contains a large number of technical descriptions that would go beyond the scope of this chapter. Depending on which operator validation report you choose, it is possible to adjust the way the information contained in the result list is displayed. Filters and options for changing how the rows and columns are displayed make it possible to design highly individual displays. The wiki page provides some examples.

The Configuration Reporting area contains templates for reports that are solely used for reporting purposes, and, therefore, contain no validation options whatsoever.

A total of four configuration reporting templates are available. The report `OTPL_OSMD_VCA2_VAR_REP_HER` supports a hierarchical display of configuration items, while the report `OTPL_OSMD_VCA2_VAR_REP_FLAT` generates a flat list. The report `OTPL_OSMD_VCA2_VAR_REP_CELL` generates a matrix in which the configuration item values are displayed in rows, while the names are displayed in columns. The report `OTPL_OSMD_VCA2_SYS_RECOMM_NOTES` displays those SAP Notes that the SAP Solution Manager function System Recommendations (in the Change Management work center) recommends for a selected SAP product.

In the case of the report `OTPL_OSMD_VCA2_VAR_REP_FLAT`, you can select the reference system and the system(s) to be compared. You can also use further parameters (for example, system type, configuration store, configuration item, or transport requests) to restrict the selection further. Figure 4.33 shows the relevant selection screen.

Variables for Configuration Reporting - Items and values - flat list

- Reference System
- Systems — [Insert Row]
- Type of System (ABAP, JAVA, ...)
- Config Store — [Insert Row]
- Configuration Item — [Insert Row]
- Transport Requests in Date Range ... To
- Use selective Read of CIs — X

[Execute] [Check]

Figure 4.33 Variables for Configuration Reporting

Configuration Reporting - Items and values - flat list

Selection: Reference and Comparison System, Config Store and Item(s)
BSL 0020211089; OTO 0020096422; ABAP_NOTES; ABAP; Empty Demarcation; Empty Demarcation

Configuration Item	Config. Item Value	Cf. Item Value Info	System	Host Name	Instance	ConfigStore Name	Last Check (UTC)
0000187687	Version 0012 Obsolete version implemented	BAPI_PO_CREATE und Commit Work	OTO 0020096422	#	#	ABAP_NOTES	20130620180132
0000488004	Version 0004 Completely implemented	Dump mit C7135 bei Auftragsnetzterminierung	OTO 0020096422	#	#	ABAP_NOTES	20130620180132
0000574251	Version 0001 Completely implemented	Dump NOT_FOUND w/ activated BAdI ALM_ME_NOTIF_HEADER	OTO 0020096422	#	#	ABAP_NOTES	20130620180132
0000612313	Version 0001 Completely implemented	RAJABS00: AU075 bei Verwendung RAPERB2000	OTO 0020096422	#	#	ABAP_NOTES	20130620180132
0000622510	Version 0002 Completely implemented	Performance of ALM_ME_GET_MYORDERS	OTO 0020096422	#	#	ABAP_NOTES	20130620180132
0000646650	Version 0005 Incompletely implemented	DFB1 mit erlösführenden Innenaufträgen	OTO 0020096422	#	#	ABAP_NOTES	20130620180132
0000654291	Version 0005 Incompletely implemented	XSteps für Fertigungsaufträge aktivieren	OTO 0020096422	#	#	ABAP_NOTES	20130620180132
0000669081	Version 0020 Obsolete version implemented	IN39 - Creation of legal Brazilian report	OTO 0020096422	#	#	ABAP_NOTES	20130620180132
0000696023	Version 0003 Incompletely implemented	PE02: Tree editor reports syntax errors with operation NUMV	OTO 0020096422	#	#	ABAP_NOTES	20130620180132
0000755611	Version 0002 Incompletely implemented	Display of collection code in Nota Fiscal writer	OTO 0020096422	#	#	ABAP_NOTES	20130620180132
0000756037	Version 0001 Completely implemented	WHT Base Contains ICMS Complementar Amount	OTO 0020096422	#	#	ABAP_NOTES	20130620180132
0000765478	Version 0001 Incompletely implemented	Payroll function ARMP returns tax (/417) in retrocalculation	OTO 0020096422	#	#	ABAP_NOTES	20130620180132
0000766657	Version 0001 Incompletely implemented	Equipment: Problems with BTE integration	OTO 0020096422	#	#	ABAP_NOTES	20130620180132
0000773260	Version 0002 Obsolete version implemented	Synchronizer correction in Support Package 10	OTO 0020096422	#	#	ABAP_NOTES	20130620180132
0000775239	Version 0002 Obsolete version implemented	Item data in download does not contain sync key	OTO 0020096422	#	#	ABAP_NOTES	20130620180132
0000777815	Version 0002 Obsolete version implemented	Server Driven replication for SyncBOs with multiple keys	OTO 0020096422	#	#	ABAP_NOTES	20130620180132
0000779375	Version 0001 Obsolete version implemented	Referencing instance not removed for Timed 2-way SyncBO	OTO 0020096422	#	#	ABAP_NOTES	20130620180132
0000786983	Version 0002 Obsolete version implemented	Adjustment of item key handling	OTO 0020096422	#	#	ABAP_NOTES	20130620180132
0000789807	Version 0001 Incompletely implemented	CV04N: Classification Data Screen incorrect	OTO 0020096422	#	#	ABAP_NOTES	20130620180132
0000790942	Version 0002 Obsolete version implemented	Component Allocation incorrect After Upgrade	OTO 0020096422	#	#	ABAP_NOTES	20130620180132
0000797729	Version 0006 Incompletely implemented	Brazilian modelo 3 (J_1BLB03): Wrong NF reporting	OTO 0020096422	#	#	ABAP_NOTES	20130620180132
0000809474	Version 0005 Obsolete version implemented	Reset status in the DELTABO queue	OTO 0020096422	#	#	ABAP_NOTES	20130620180132
0000813666	Version 0001 Obsolete version implemented	Log Monitor does not show message text	OTO 0020096422	#	#	ABAP_NOTES	20130620180132
0000816676	Version 0002 Incompletely implemented	Nota Fiscal writer: correction of ISS functionality	OTO 0020096422	#	#	ABAP_NOTES	20130620180132
0000816985	Version 0003 Incompletely implemented	amount of wage type disappears in off-cycle workbench	OTO 0020096422	#	#	ABAP_NOTES	20130620180132
0000821403	Version 0002 Incompletely implemented	Brazilian modelo 3: Nota Fiscal search corrections	OTO 0020096422	#	#	ABAP_NOTES	20130620180132
0000821575	Version 0002 Incompletely implemented	Einzelwerberichtigung: fehlende Verteilung im Probelauf	OTO 0020096422	#	#	ABAP_NOTES	20130620180132
0000847949	Version 0002 Incompletely implemented	SCE: KB extraction for documents does not work	OTO 0020096422	#	#	ABAP_NOTES	20130620180132
0000853580	Version 0004 Incompletely implemented	Classification Screen cleared when called from CDESK	OTO 0020096422	#	#	ABAP_NOTES	20130620180132
0000861924	Version 0006 Incompletely implemented	LM07: dump in 'system guided' picking TO transaction	OTO 0020096422	#	#	ABAP_NOTES	20130620180132

Row 1 / 469

Figure 4.34 Configuration Reporting—Result List

After you have executed the report, the system displays a result list. However, you can change the way these results are displayed by changing the columns and rows, as well as the items displayed. In the example shown in Figure 4.34, the configuration store ABAP_NOTES was used to display the SAP Notes implemented in two different systems, thus making it possible to see which SAP Notes have been implemented in each system.

If you apply filters or use the options for changing how rows or columns in the result list are displayed, you can also save this modified display as a separate view and reuse it later. To do this, choose SAVE VIEW (icon ▯) on the left-hand side of the result list.

If you regularly execute reports for a particular selection, you can also save the URL that you call (including the execution parameters) as a bookmark in the web browser and, therefore, retrieve it quickly on subsequent occasions. To do this, right-click in the result display to open the context menu for the BW report and choose BOOKMARK. Copy the URL to the browser window that opens and then, in configuration validation, choose BOOKMARKS on the REPORT EXECUTION tab page. Create a new bookmark here and insert the previously copied URL into the BOOK-MARK URL field (see Figure 4.35).

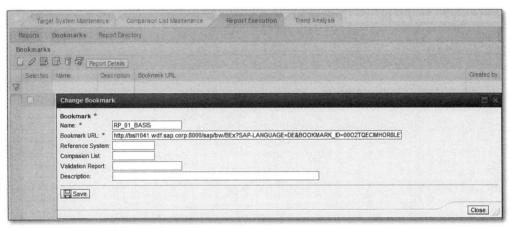

Figure 4.35 Adding a Bookmark

On the left-hand side of the screen, choose SAVE to save your settings. In the future, the execution parameters for the report will be available to you as a direct link.

On the REPORT EXECUTION tab page, you can store previously generated reports in the REPORT DIRECTORY area so that they can be quickly generated again. In addition to customized reports, SAP reports provided by default are also available here. Figure 4.36 shows the selection screen for a report and any related details.

Optional settings are available to adjust report execution or the analysis period at any time.

The SAP reports include a report that checks the Support Packages currently available, as well as a report that checks recommended SAP Notes for the relevant target systems.

The advantage of having reports available in the report directory is swift implementation without necessarily having to define a target system. The various different aspects checked by these reports help to ensure that you have an extremely stable, high-quality solution.

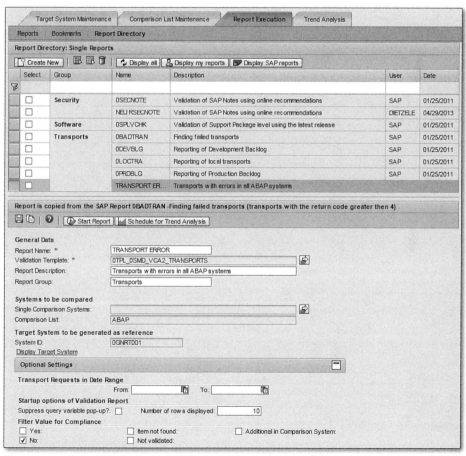

Figure 4.36 Report Directory

Trend Analysis

The last tab page, TREND ANALYSIS, contains a new configuration validation function. Since SP05, you can save analysis results and analyze them over a period of time.

Reports made available in this way come from the REPORT DIRECTORY. If you want to use an SAP standard report, choose COPY to create a copy of this report in the report directory. You can then use this new report for trend analysis. In the report directory, you also have the option to immediately schedule a report for trend analysis (see Figure 4.37).

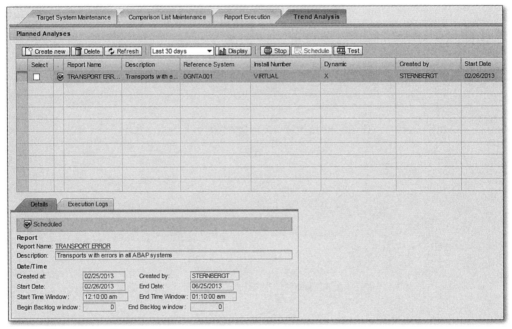

Figure 4.37 Trend Analysis

After you have selected an entry in the list, you can check the EXECUTION LOGS tab page to see whether the report was executed correctly. Then, after you have selected a report, you can choose DISPLAY to navigate to the corresponding period-based analysis.

We have now explained the basic functions of configuration validation. In the next section, we will introduce you to some typical application scenarios for configuration validation.

Application Scenarios

In the following subsections, we will introduce you to some typical use cases for reports. These will show you when it may be useful to use certain reports.

Transport Analysis

Transport analysis is always useful if you are looking for answers to the following questions:

1. **Have all transports been imported into a target system?**
   If some transports were not transported into the target system as intended, this may jeopardize data consistency.

2. **How long did it take to import the transports into a target system?**
   The answer to this question allows conclusions to be drawn in relation to the quality of testing. If the transports are quickly transported into the target system, testing will also be concluded quickly. If, on the other hand, it takes a very long time to import the transports, this may indicate that there are problems with the test plans because it seems that some objects were not tested in a timely manner.

3. **Did some transports have a return code greater than 4?**
   If a return code higher than 4 occurs when importing transports, these error messages are serious and indicate that imports were not fully executed. These errors must always be carefully analyzed because they could easily cause inconsistencies.

4. **How many open transports are there in the development system?**
   The number of open transports in the development system allows conclusions to be drawn in relation to change activities, as well as the time and effort required to perform tests and imports in quality assurance and production systems.

5. **Were local transports created in a system?**
   Local transport requests always mean local changes that are not transported. This will invariably result in differences between the changed system and the systems downstream from the transport view. Consequently, local change requests harbor a special risk.

Analyzing Authorizations or Security Settings

Configuration validation can also be used to check different aspects of security. The following questions are the main focus here:

6. **Do some users have the authorization profile SAP_ALL, and so on?**
   Such users have unrestricted authorizations or system-critical or business-critical authorizations in the system and therefore represent a potential risk.

7. **Are there RFC connections with registered users or RFC connections to critical systems?**
   Users can use such connections to log on to another system and, thus, bypass security restrictions.

8. **Which parameter settings were made for the systems (for example, settings for expiring passwords, login attempts, and so on)?**
   This is helpful when checking security settings.

9. **Do certain users have the same authorizations in managed systems?**
   This question is posed if users with identical tasks in the systems observe a different access behavior.

10. **Are some users permitted to execute security-critical transactions, such as those associated with configuring RFC connections (Transaction SM59) or using ABAP Editor (Transaction SE38)?**
    Certain transactions, if used incorrectly or maliciously, may endanger the systems. You should, therefore, carefully check which users may be able to execute security-relevant transactions and on which system.

11. **Which relevant SAP Notes and, in particular, which security-relevant notes were implemented on the basis of system recommendations (Change Management work center) and online recommendations (*http://service.sap.com/ secnotes*)?**
    SAP delivers new security notes at regular intervals. If key SAP Notes are not implemented, potential security gaps may occur. Therefore, make sure you have implemented, or at least verified, the SAP Notes relevant for your system.

12. **Do all the systems in a system landscape have the software level required in accordance with customer specifications?**
    Check the software level and the relevant SAP Notes in the system landscape.

Individual or Complete Validation of Systems

Complete system validation is necessary in order to prepare for a change of release, for example. In the target systems, you can check whether the settings correspond to the requirements. For example, you can check whether the system has the correct software level (Support Package, kernel version, and so on) and parameter settings, and whether it contains all required SAP Notes or transports.

These application scenarios should provide you with some ideas and demonstrate the wide range of potential uses for configuration validation. In time, you will think of many other areas in which you can use configuration validation to its full potential.

4.4   End-to-End Methodology: Workload Analysis

Workload analysis is used if the performance of IT-supported business processes is unsatisfactory. In this case, the challenge is to analyze in which process step, or in which system involved in a process distributed across multiple systems, time is actually lost.

Workload analysis provides you with the necessary utilization information for the entire system landscape so that you can identify performance problems. You generally start by evaluating response times. These help you to ascertain which area you need to search in order to identify the cause of performance problems.

The workload analysis tools comprise different monitors and analysis tools, which you can also call in the ROOT CAUSE ANALYSIS work center. You can use these tools to conduct both general and extremely detailed analyses.

4.4.1   Workload Analysis Tools in SAP Solution Manager

In SAP Solution Manager, the most important tools for workload analysis are as follows:

▸ **End-to-end workload analysis**
End-to-end workload analysis enables you to achieve unified access to the workload statistics in the entire system landscape. This tool delivers KPIs, such as the response times of different technical components in a single view. Here, the information is integrated across different technologies and can be displayed in separate product-specific views. We will describe end-to-end analysis in greater detail in Section 4.4.3.

▸ **Introscope**
Introscope was developed primarily to analyze the performance and availability of web applications and infrastructure systems. Nowadays, Introscope also collects KPIs for many other technologies, including technologies for ABAP and

Java systems. You learned about the tools available within Introscope, both in terms of their functionality and use in Section 4.2.3.

▶ **Thread dump analysis**
Thread dump analysis can be used to create a snapshot of threads currently being processed. This snapshot is created in a Java Virtual Machine (JVM) and is known as a *thread dump*. Thread dumps can be analyzed online or offline. The thread dump is evaluated in order to classify the threads and to identify those that are blocked or in another such critical state. For more information about thread dump analysis, see Section 4.4.5.

▶ **Database analysis**
Database analysis enables you to analyze the behavior of the database within a freely definable period. Statistical information about various KPIs in the database is provided here. Depending on the maker of the database, the information may differ in individual cases, both in terms of its volume and the level of detail. You will obtain further information about database analysis in Section 4.4.4.

▶ **DBA Cockpit**
The DBA Cockpit in SAP Solution Manager provides centralized access to databases in managed systems. To ensure that users cannot damage this function, they should be granted read-only authorizations to the DBA Cockpit. The standard root cause analysis authorizations contained in the role SAP_DBA_DISP provide a suitable template. To use the DBA Cockpit, you require a certain level of knowledge in terms of the database management system used.

▶ **Host analysis**
Host analysis provides a statistical display of different host-specific metrics for a freely definable time frame.

4.4.2   Data Extraction and Storage

Workload analysis in SAP Solution Manager provides you with an overview of product-specific data for a selected period if the necessary data was previously collected from managed systems.

Therefore, the EFWK plays an important role here. Figure 4.38 shows a schematic diagram of how workload data is extracted and stored.

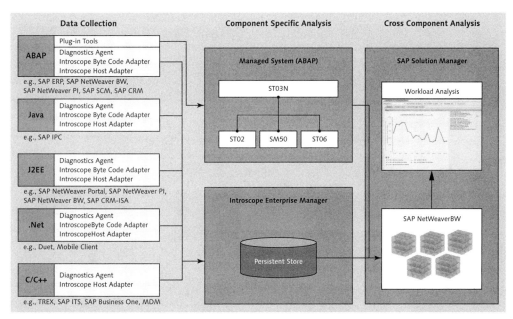

Figure 4.38 Extracting and Storing Workload Data

In general, different agents or the software component ST-PI are used to collect data on managed systems:

▶ For AS ABAP, the data is collected mainly using reports associated with the component ST-PI and stored on the managed system itself. Data such as the performance data in the workload monitor (Transaction ST03N) is aggregated at regular intervals. This aggregation contributes to the fact that the required data volume on the managed system increases only up to a certain level and then remains constant. Other relevant information for an ABAP system (for example, work process activities, gateway behavior, RFC activities, or host data) is also collected using diagnostics agents or the Introscope Host Adapter located on the system and then stored in the memory of Introscope Enterprise Manager.

▶ In the Java stack of the managed system, JVM performance data (response times) is collected using the Introscope Byte Code Adapter and sent to Introscope Enterprise Manager every 15 seconds. In turn, the performance data for the host on which the Java stack is installed is collected by the Introscope Host Adapter and also sent to Introscope Enterprise Manager every 15 seconds.

▶ For all other technologies associated with managed systems (for example, Java, .Net, or C/C++), data is collected and stored in the same way as it is for Java technology.

In the next step, extractors in SAP Solution Manager load the workload data from the managed ABAP systems on an hourly basis via an RFC connection. In the case of all other technologies, workload data is loaded from Introscope Enterprise Manager. This data is processed immediately and then stored in product-specific InfoCubes in BW within SAP Solution Manager.

A background job for regular data cleansing is automatically activated during the basic configuration of SAP Solution Manager. This aggregates the data by periodically copying the information into highly aggregated InfoCubes (for example, from an InfoCube with hourly granularity to an InfoCube with daily granularity). The data is then deleted from the original InfoCube after a certain period of time, which you can configure individually for each InfoCube, thus making it possible to significantly reduce data growth.

The end user can use complex and diverse queries to subsequently display and evaluate the data in SAP NetWeaver BW within SAP Solution Manager. End-to-end workload analysis provides predefined information views for this purpose. In the next section, we will describe end-to-end workload analysis in greater detail.

4.4.3 Using End-to-End Workload Analysis

To call end-to-end workload analysis, select the END-TO-END ANALYSIS menu option in the ROOT CAUSE ANALYSIS work center. Then, in the DETAILED SELECTION area, select the system that you want to analyze. You can select more than one system by holding down the ⌐Ctrl⌐ key while making your selection. Then, choose WORKLOAD ANALYSIS.

The overview of end-to-end workload analysis shows you a graphical overview of the KPIs in your system landscape. In the upper area of the tool, you select the relevant analysis period. The right-hand side contains the KPIs and their values sorted according to the technical systems. This overview contains only metrics for which data exists in the period currently under analysis. It is therefore possible for a chart to contain fewer metrics than shown in the legend. You use the multiple selection option above the graph to change its view. Here, you can choose the options outlined next. Figure 4.39 shows different chart types:

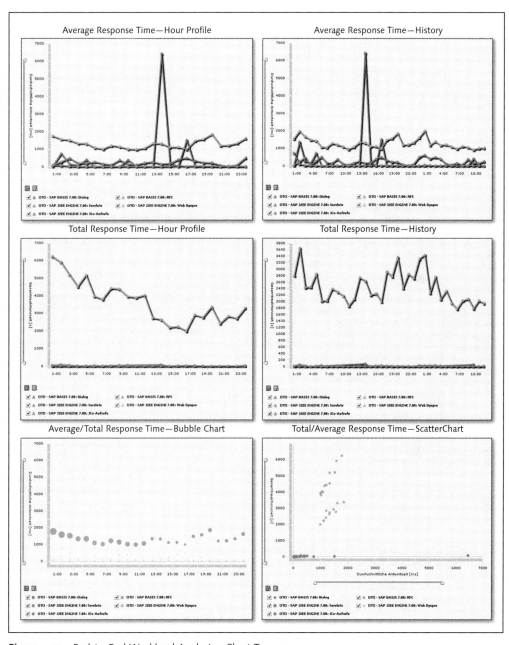

Figure 4.39 End-to-End Workload Analysis—Chart Types

▶ AVERAGE RESPONSE TIME — HOUR PROFILE

This is the standard view. It is shown at the start of end-to-end workload analysis. The summarized daily profile is displayed here, irrespective of the time frame selected. In other words, even if you change the time frame for the view, 00:00 to 23:00 is always displayed on the x-axis. The average response time is specified in milliseconds.

This chart enables you to quickly recognize peak loads directly linked to the system's typical working hours. As long as the users on the system being monitored are not global users, you should be able to observe daily patterns with peaks throughout the day and a very low load at night.

▶ AVERAGE RESPONSE TIME — HISTORY

This chart displays the same information as the hour profile. The only difference is that the times are not summarized here. Instead, they are displayed individually for each day and hour. If the period you have selected is too large, the chart shows a plethora of points next to each other and, as a result, individual values are no longer discernible. Therefore, make sure that you adjust the display in terms of its granularity.

▶ TOTAL RESPONSE TIME — HOUR PROFILE

This chart shows you an hour profile for the total response time. The response times in each analysis period are cumulated into the total response time. As a result, their relationship with the average response time is as follows: *total response time = average response time × number of executions*. In the graph, the total response time is shown in seconds.

High total response times have the greatest impact on system performance. Therefore, the first thing you should do when analyzing performance is search for high total response times. In order to achieve the greatest possible potential for optimization, they should, if possible, be associated with high average response times.

▶ TOTAL RESPONSE TIME — HISTORY

This chart also displays the total response time. In this case, however, it is for the entire display period. You can increase the readability of the values by adjusting the granularity.

▶ TOTAL/AVERAGE RESPONSE TIME — SCATTER CHART

The scatter chart displays the average response times on the x-axis and the total response time on the y-axis. As with the time profile charts, the data points are displayed as hourly average values for the selected time frame.

The scatter chart helps you to identify bottlenecks. Divide the chart into four logical quadrants (see Figure 4.40).

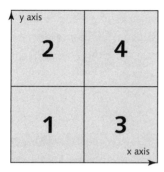

Figure 4.40   Dividing a Chart into Quadrants

The first quadrant contains low average response times and a low total response time. These values are, therefore, non-critical values. Of more interest are the values in the second quadrant with a high total response time and a low average response time. Equally interesting are the values in the third quadrant with a high average response time and a low total response time. However, the values in both of these quadrants offer only a moderate potential for optimization. The most critical quadrant for overall system performance is the fourth quadrant (top right) in which both the total response time and the average response time are high. Here, you will find the greatest potential for optimization and, proportionately, you will have to invest the least time and effort into achieving this.

▶ AVERAGE/TOTAL RESPONSE TIME – BUBBLE CHART
In the bubble chart, the average response time is shown on the y-axis and the time profile for the day is shown on the x-axis. The size of the bubbles represents the total response time. Therefore, critical situations are represented by particularly large bubbles.

If several technical systems are displayed in the charts, you can compare these against each other in order to detect any possible parallels. We will now show you what to do if you ascertain that load balancing between the components is less than optimal and it is particularly apparent that the main load is on certain systems.

Navigate to component-specific analysis by selecting one of the component tabs next to the OVERVIEW tab (see Figure 4.41). Each of these tabs contains additional tabs, depending on the component currently under analysis. In the case of the

OTO—SAP ECC SERVER tab page, these are ABAP BASIS, RFC, VMC, and HOST, for example. Below these tabs, you will find a series of links that provide workload data for the different metrics. Technically, each of these views is linked to an SAP NetWeaver BW query. When displaying graphs, end-to-end workload analysis gives you the option to adjust the time granularity to hourly or daily granularity. Daily granularity, however, is suitable only if you select at least three days in the analysis period.

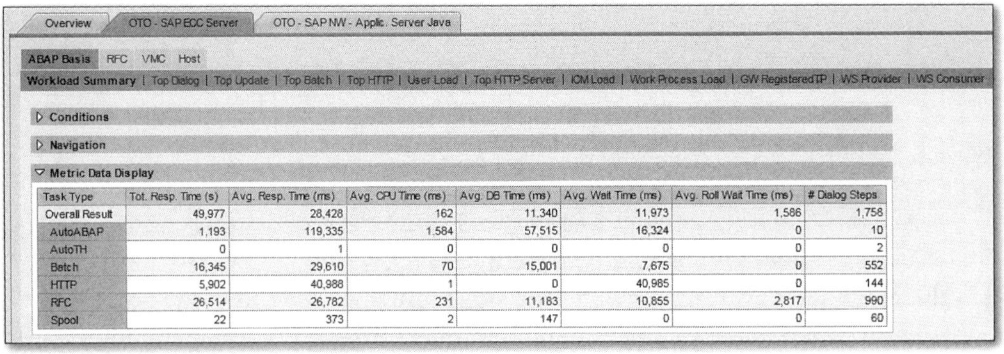
Overview
OTO - SAP ECC Server
OTO - SAP NW - Applic. Server Java
ABAP Basis
RFC
VMC
Host
Workload Summary | Top Dialog | Top Update | Top Batch | Top HTTP | User Load | Top HTTP Server | ICM Load | Work Process Load | GW RegisteredTP | WS Provider | WS Consumer
Conditions
Navigation
Metric Data Display
Task Type | Tot. Resp. Time (s) | Avg. Resp. Time (ms) | Avg. CPU Time (ms) | Avg. DB Time (ms) | Avg. Wait Time (ms) | Avg. Roll Wait Time (ms) | # Dialog Steps
Overall Result | 49,977 | 28,428 | 162 | 11,340 | 11,973 | 1,586 | 1,758
AutoABAP | 1,193 | 119,335 | 1,584 | 57,515 | 16,324 | 0 | 10
AutoTH | 0 | 1 | 0 | 0 | 0 | 0 | 2
Batch | 16,345 | 29,610 | 70 | 15,001 | 7,675 | 0 | 552
HTTP | 5,902 | 40,988 | 1 | 0 | 40,985 | 0 | 144
RFC | 26,514 | 26,782 | 231 | 11,183 | 10,855 | 2,817 | 990
Spool | 22 | 373 | 2 | 147 | 0 | 0 | 60

Figure 4.41 Workload Analysis—ABAP Overview

An explanation of each of these views is beyond the scope of this book. Furthermore, the KPIs depend heavily on the components under analysis. Therefore, if necessary, you should consult with an application expert who can correctly interpret the values for you. In most monitors, you can view different response times in relation to the components selected. When evaluating these monitors, the following rule of thumb always applies: in the utilization overview, determine which type of task or metric causes the greatest total load (highest total response time) on the system. Then, take a look at the view for the relevant metric and determine which system calls cause the greatest load.

Once you have used end-to-end workload analysis to rule out certain problems and establish the origins of the various performance problems, use other tools to perform a detailed analysis. We will start with database analysis. You use this tool if you have identified anomalies in the database area (for example, high database times).

4.4.4 Using Database Analysis

To use database analysis, proceed as follows:

1. In the ROOT CAUSE ANALYSIS work center, select the DATABASE ANALYSIS menu option.

2. In the DETAILED SELECTION area, select the database associated with the system in question and then choose DATABASE ANALYSIS.

3. On the initial screen, you immediately see the WORKLOAD associated with the database (see Figure 4.42). It may still be necessary for you to load data from SAP NetWeaver BW within SAP Solution Manager by clicking the link CLICK HERE TO LOAD DATA FROM BUSINESS WAREHOUSE.

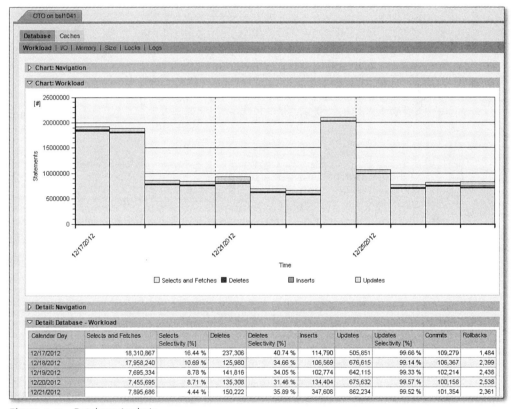

Figure 4.42 Database Analysis

The DATABASE tab page provides a good overview of the most important information in relation to database performance. This includes the following:

▸ Workload

▸ Read and write activities (I/O)

▶ Memory

▶ Size

▶ Locks

▶ Logs

Often, statistics are displayed in a table below the graphic displayed.

4. Here, you also see the CACHES tab page, which provides key information about the access quality of all SQL queries on the database. Generally, the access quality should always be above 95%. Anything below this figure indicates that, while the queries were being accessed, too much data had to be loaded directly from the memory instead of using caches. This may be due to missing indexes in database tables, time-consuming SQL queries, or caches that are too small.

In addition to an analysis at the database level, you should also be able to perform analyses at application level. In Section 4.4.1, we described some of the tools available in SAP Solution Manager. We will now take a closer look at thread dump analysis.

4.4.5 Using Thread Dump Analysis

Thread dump analysis has the same function as Transaction SM50 in an ABAP system. It is used to obtain an overview of all threads currently running within a JVM. For this purpose, a snapshot of the thread dump, which you can use to analyze the status of the Java thread activity (for example, after a JVM shutdown), is created. The following are two examples of when to use thread dump analysis:

▶ The system does not respond to requests, or its response is extremely slow. In this case, start a series of thread dumps at short intervals so that you capture the user activities.

▶ Naturally, the system hangs and after a short period of time, it no longer responds to requests. In this case, you get the system up and running again (for example, by restarting the Java instance) and use a series of thread dumps, at a greater time interval, to record the activities until another shutdown occurs. Schedule, for example, a series of dumps every 15 minutes over a period of several days.

Thread dumps contain the status for each Java thread, as well as information about the Java package currently being processed or a reference to other threads.

Start the application as follows:

1. In the ROOT CAUSE ANALYSIS work center, select the SYSTEM ANALYSIS menu option.

2. In the DETAILED SELECTION area, select the Java system that you want to analyze and choose EXPERT LINKS.

3. The THREAD DUMP ANALYSIS link for starting thread dump analysis is displayed on the next screen.

4. Now, select one or more server nodes to be analyzed and choose TRIGGER THREAD DUMP to trigger a thread dump (see Figure 4.43).

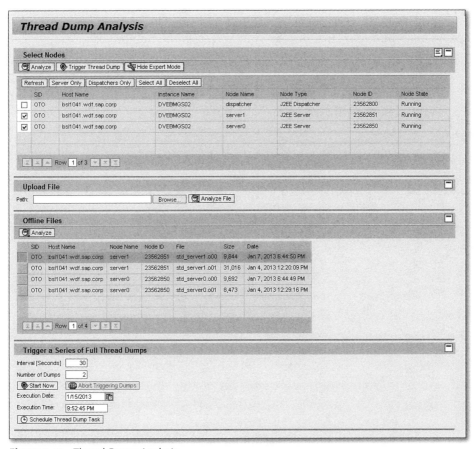

Figure 4.43 Thread Dump Analysis

> **Note**
>
> Depending on the use case, we also recommend creating a series of thread dumps in one go.
>
> To do this, choose EXPERT MODE to switch to expert mode (see Figure 4.43). When creating a series of thread dumps, you need to specify only a seconds interval and the number of thread dumps you want to create. Then, choose START NOW. The upper area of the application displays a message for every thread dump generated.

5. To start thread dump analysis, choose ANALYZE. Different tab pages are available here:

   ▶ The OVERVIEW tab page contains a summarization table. Here, a column is displayed for every server node analyzed (see Figure 4.44). Here, you also obtain information about the system restart, the number of thread dumps, and system runtime. If a dump contains a deadlock, this is displayed and marked with a red triangle. You can perform an offline analysis by choosing DOWNLOAD COMPLETE VM LOG. You can also choose TRIGGER THREAD DUMP to trigger a new thread dump.

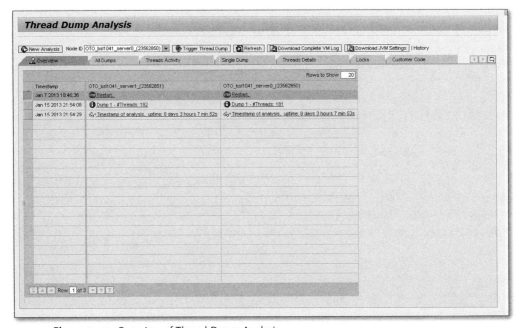

Figure 4.44 Overview of Thread Dump Analysis

▶ The ALL DUMPS tab page provides you with an overview of load balancing across all thread dumps. Here, you see one column for each thread dump, whereby all threads are grouped together. In this view, you can easily detect changes in the thread status across the thread dumps.

▶ On the THREADS ACTIVITY tab page, all threads are displayed below each other, and a color status is assigned to the right of each thread. If you are analyzing several thread dumps, this view is also suitable for detecting changes in the activities. Critical threads are assigned a red status 🔴. For further analysis, choose LOCKED BY THREAD <THREAD NAME> in the lower area. The LOCKS tab appears automatically, and the locked threads are displayed.

▶ On the SINGLE DUMP tab page, all details relating to an individual thread dump that you explicitly selected in the overview or in the upper area are displayed. All the threads recorded in this thread dump are grouped according to their status.

> **Note**
>
> In the thread dumps, you should look for threads with the status WAITING ON MONITOR ENTRY because they may point to a deadlock situation where the application is blocked and the end user no longer receives any confirmation of his or her system request.

The THREADS DETAILS tab page contains a list of detailed information for all threads recorded in a thread dump (for example, status, Java package, relationship with other threads, or the thread ID).

The LOCKS tab page, on the other hand, displays information only if there is a blocked thread or if it is in a critical state. In order to display details here, you must click one of the other aforementioned tabs. The threads shown here can have a very serious impact on system performance.

If you also process a customer-developed application on AS Java, it will be displayed on the CUSTOMER CODE tab page. This enables you to quickly respond to the program behavior of a custom development.

4.4.6 Approaches and Examples

Essentially, performance problems can be divided into system-wide and specific performance problems. Before we describe the main approach to analyzing a performance problem in greater detail, we will introduce you to the two categories involved here.

System-Wide Performance Problem

A system-wide performance problem generally manifests itself through considerably longer runtimes than usual for all activities on the system concerned. This affects not only user activities (also known as *dialog activities*), but also all other processes (for example, background processing). Therefore, if hardware resources are limited, one activity may slow down another, which may in turn negatively impact yet another activity. If this continues, a chain reaction may be set in motion, ultimately resulting in a complete system breakdown.

One or more factors may be the cause here. Often, such a problem occurs immediately after the system goes live. Possible factors include the go-live phase after system implementation, an upgrade, or other significant changes in terms of user load. In this case, inadequate hardware resources are frequently the cause. It is also possible that various basic settings (for example, memory parameters) are incorrect and, as a result, utilization of the available hardware is less than optimal. To avoid these particular problems, SAP provides various going-live check services and corresponding standard recommendations for system configuration. Further information is available on SAP Service Marketplace at *http://service.sap.com/supportofferings*.

Specific Performance Problems

A specific performance problem can take many forms, such as the following:

- A user or user group experiences a performance problem.
- Individual transactions or programs exhibit poor performance.
- A certain type of work process (for example, dialog, background, or update) has long runtimes.

The cause of a specific performance problem can be as diverse as the problem itself. Generally, however, the cause is directly linked to the situation. Therefore, at the start of the analysis process, you should consider the immediate situation from various different perspectives. In fact, it is best to demonstrate the problem so that it can be fully reproduced for you. For the most part, possible causes become evident in the meantime or when you first take a look at the relevant system monitor.

Basic Procedure

Starting with a system-wide performance problem, we will explain, by means of an example, how to proceed when conducting a workload analysis. A brief description is provided below to assist you in understanding workload analysis. We have already described in great detail how to actually use the tools.

1. To identify a general performance problem, start as usual with end-to-end workload analysis. Use this to analyze the response times of system landscape components and use various KPIs to isolate the problem. Determine whether there are dependencies between individual components and whether components behave in the same way.

2. As soon as you have identified the problematic landscape component in the overview for end-to-end workload analysis (for example, the component with the greatest load), you can continue with a component-specific analysis. To do this, use the relevant view in end-to-end workload analysis and analyze the various KPIs for SAP Basis and the application on the technical system. Depending on the technology, analyze all possible areas (for example, hardware utilization, memory consumption, system activity runtimes, and so on) and search for anomalies. Using the knowledge acquired, you should be able to deduce potential causes and isolate the problem further. This will help you ascertain which tool to use next, either in your analysis or to definitively confirm the cause of the problem.

3. In this step, focus primarily on the application level (in other words, all program activities above database level). Here, distinguish between the technology types (ABAP, Java, and so on) and, depending on the technology type, navigate directly to the managed system or open the relevant expert tool in the SAP Solution Manager landscape.

   ▶ An ABAP system contains almost all required tools. The most important monitors here are the ABAP workload monitor (Transaction ST03N) and additional resources such as the monitors for the SAP buffer (Transaction ST02), the operating system (Transaction ST06), and the work processes (Transactions SM50 and SM66).

   Start by using the various views in Transaction ST03N to evaluate the response times. These will help you ascertain whether the problem tends to concern a hardware bottleneck, an SAP buffer problem, or another problem. Then, consult one of the other monitors to obtain sufficient proof to support your suspicions.

Since this book is primarily oriented toward the tools available within the SAP Solution Manager landscape, a detailed description of ABAP tools would go beyond the scope of this book. Therefore, for more information, refer to the book *SAP Performance Optimization Guide* by Thomas Schneider (7th edition, SAP PRESS 2013).

▶ Unfortunately, analysis tools in the Java stack within an SAP NetWeaver system are not, by their very nature, as comprehensive as the analysis tools in the ABAP stack. Therefore, it is best to use the tools available within SAP Solution Manager for a Java system. One of the most important tools is Introscope, which enables you to use numerous dashboards and metrics to obtain an overview of the Java stack's general performance. In addition to different response times, Introscope also displays metrics in relation to JVM memory behavior or utilization. The integrated Introscope dashboards were provided by SAP for this purpose and give an overview of JVM's current memory situation. This area is frequently responsible for long-running user requests. The section below, JVM Memory Analysis, will provide a more in-depth insight into JVM memory analysis. In the case of such long-running requests, thread dump analysis is often used to detect deadlock situations or blocked threads, which may also cause the problem (see Section 4.4.5). Thread dump analysis provides numerous views and functions.

4. If, when analyzing the response times (landscape, certain technologies, or individual applications), it transpires that the database time constitutes the largest portion of the response time, you should also take a look at the database tools available:

▶ Database analysis is relatively independent of the type of database (see Section 4.4.4). You can use it to quickly obtain a statistical overview of all database behavior. In particular, you check the system load, log behavior, size, fill level, and database growth. The quality of the database buffer can also be an indication of time-consuming database queries if, for example, SQL statements increase the database load.

▶ If you wish to conduct a more in-depth database analysis because you have found anomalies or have a particular suspicion, you should use the DBA Cockpit. During the analysis, it may be necessary to consult with a database expert because the details of the analysis may differ depending on the type of database. The aforementioned book, *SAP Performance Optimization Guide* by

Thomas Schneider, contains further information on how to proceed during database analysis.

5. Naturally, a server containing the relevant hardware resources is located below the database and application instance. The cause of poor response times (for example, if the server's CPU resources have been used up) can also be found here. Therefore, you should always obtain an overview of the hardware resources and their utilization within the system landscape. Of course, this assumes that you have some knowledge of the server and its systems and databases or that you are, at the very least, able to obtain this information.

The host analysis in the ROOT CAUSE ANALYSIS work center provides you with a quick overview of the servers available. Here, you check CPU utilization, paging activities, and file system utilization within the period under analysis. Note that depending on the type of operating system, high operating system paging may result in a high CPU load, and therefore poor performance. Use of the network connection for the host can also be analyzed using host analysis.

To analyze a specific performance problem, you normally use trace analysis immediately (see Section 4.5). However, it is advisable to also include the workload analysis monitors in your analysis so that you do not miss out on useful information concerning the response times of user and background activities or individual transactions.

We'll now briefly discuss JVM memory analysis, which forms part of component-specific performance analysis.

JVM Memory Analysis

Memory problems within a server node of the Java cluster are one possible cause for long-running user requests for web applications. Often, these are caused by application errors. The following three monitors support you during analysis:

▶ **End-to-end workload analysis**
You can use end-to-end workload analysis to perform an initial memory analysis for a JVM. In addition to monitors with different response times, you will also find valuable KPIs for JVM memory management under the link JAVA MEMORY USAGE (see Figure 4.45). Here, you will find the most important KPIs in relation to a server node's memory behavior, which already reveal a lot of information to you, in terms of JVM behavior.

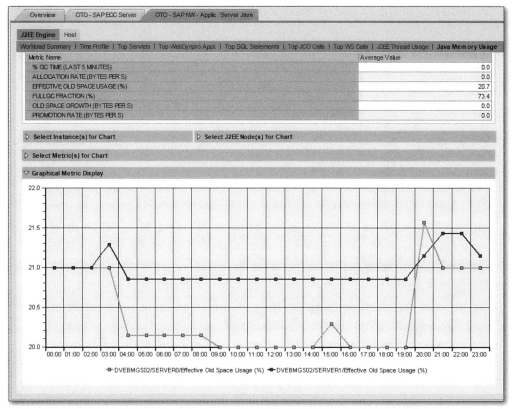

Figure 4.45 Workload Analysis—Java Memory Usage

You use Introscope (see Section 4.2.3) to perform a more in-depth analysis. In an ideal situation, the problem still exists, and you can observe it live in Introscope WebView or Introscope Workstation.

▶ **Console mode**
When you use console mode, the J2EE GC OVERVIEW dashboard opens. Once again, the most important KPIs in relation to JVM memory management are displayed here. Note that this view is much more detailed than end-to-end workload analysis.

▶ **Investigator mode**
You use investigator mode to obtain a more precise overview of the KPIs. Here, you use the relevant host and Introscope Host Adapter to navigate within the tree structure to the server node in question. Here, you find a GC HEAP area under which all KPIs can be analyzed.

Since providing an explanation and interpreting all possible KPIs in JVM memory management is beyond the scope of this book, we will discuss only the most important KPIs. You can recognize potential bottleneck situations in JVM memory management when the GC TIME (the time required for garbage collections within a specific period) or the FULLGC FRACTION (the proportion of full garbage collections compared with all garbage collections in the period under analysis) are too high over a longer period of time. Usually, the values for both KPIs are consistently below 5%. During the analysis, however, make sure to analyze different periods. Furthermore, do not rely on only one identified maximum value.

4.5 End-to-End Methodology: Trace Analysis

You can use trace analysis to analyze a specific performance problem. As mentioned in Section 4.4.6 in the subsection "Specific Performance Problems," a specific performance problem can manifest itself in many different ways.

You can use trace analysis not only to address such a problem on a single AS ABAP or AS Java, but also to analyze the entire situation (from the actions of the end user in the browser or SAP GUI through to the data written on the database).

4.5.1 Trace Analysis Tools in SAP Solution Manager

The following tools are available here:

▶ **End-to-end trace analysis**
  You use this tool to determine how the entire runtime of a user transaction is divided across all landscape components. This analysis requires performance data from all systems in the SAP landscape and on the client side. Recording such information is controlled centrally via end-to-end trace analysis in SAP Solution Manager.

  In contrast to the trace tools described next, data recording does not start immediately after the trace is enabled. Performance data is not recorded until a user query reaches a system. The advantage of this is that an unnecessary load is not generated on systems, thus making end-to-end trace analysis less critical for production systems. In Section 4.5.2, we'll discuss how to use this tool in greater detail.

▶ **ABAP trace**
The ABAP trace is an expert tool used on the managed system. It's used to conduct a performance-based analysis of programs on AS ABAP with the goal of optimizing runtimes. To this end, all ABAP activities are recorded in the background. They can then be evaluated by an expert.

▶ **ABAP SQL trace**
The ABAP SQL trace is another expert tool located on the managed system. You can use this tool to identify long-running activities while a program is running and find possible optimization solutions. To this end, the SQL queries sent to the database are recorded and prepared for a performance analysis.

▶ **Introscope Transaction Trace**
Introscope Transaction Trace is a tool for detecting application problems in the Java infrastructure. It records performance data and then presents the Java program sections in chronological order. This enables you to identify long-running program parts more quickly and introduce additional performance optimization steps in a targeted manner.

4.5.2 Using End-to-End Trace Analysis

We will now show you how to use end-to-end trace analysis. Here, we will assume that you do not know precisely which systems access the user transaction you want to analyze. For example, the end user may send a request to an SAP system that, in turn, communicates with other SAP systems in the background.

Preparing for the Trace

A plug-in is required in order to record activities on the end user's PC. This plug-in assigns a *correlation ID* to the user request you want to analyze. This ID is linked to the request for the entire duration, so that all systems called know that performance data also needs to be recorded for this query. At a later stage, end-to-end trace analysis will use the correlation ID to bring the distributed traces together again in a meaningful way in order to evaluate the user request.

Here, we distinguish between two different plug-ins:

▶ `/SDF/E2E_TRACE` is a program that runs on the managed ABAP system for SAP GUI user requests. The report is delivered as part of the software component ST-PI and is immediately available on the managed system. There are no major preparations in advance of using the program. The user executing the program just needs the necessary authorizations.

▶ *SAP Client Plug-In* is an application that is started locally on the end user's PC and uses the web browser to record user activities. You can use this plug-in to analyze web applications based on Web Dynpro ABAP, Java, or business server pages.

In contrast to the SAP GUI plug-in, this plug-in is usually not available on the end user's PC. You download it as part of SAP Note 1435190 or you download it from the OPTIONS tab in end-to-end trace analysis and make it available to the end user.

You then activate data collection on all systems in which the user request is processed. Use end-to-end analysis for this purpose:

1. In the ROOT CAUSE ANALYSIS work center, select the END-TO-END ANALYSIS menu option.

2. In the DETAILED SELECTION area, select all SAP landscape systems under analysis and choose TRACE ANALYSIS to start the tool.

3. A new window opens. Here, you navigate to the second tab entitled TRACE ENABLING.

4. The systems you have selected are displayed in rows across two columns (ABAP and Java). You could enable the trace for each individual technical system. However, since we made a selection earlier (under DETAILED SELECTION), you can choose ENABLE ALL to enable the trace for all systems. The managed systems are ready to record the data of the user activities. If you forget to disable the trace afterwards, it will automatically be disabled by default after 180 minutes.

Performing the Trace

In the next step, the user executes the system activities that are to be analyzed. Ideally, the user executes two completely identical system calls in quick succession. The purpose of the first run is to fill various buffers on the database and application servers, while the second execution, whereby the user uses the relevant plug-in to start the data collection process, is recorded.

Here, we will demonstrate this using the SAP Client Plug-In for web-based applications. You use the report /SDF/E2E_TRACE for SAP GUI queries in the same way:

1. Close all web browser windows on the end user's PC.

2. Use the previously downloaded *.exe* file to start SAP Client Plug-In. The plug-in unpacks some files and then opens the main window (see Figure 4.46). Select MICROSOFT INTERNET EXPLORER in the APPLICATION field and then choose LAUNCH.

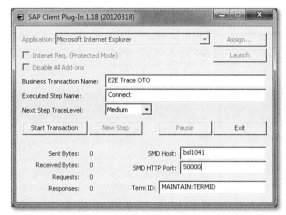

Figure 4.46 SAP Client Plug-In—Main Window

3. In the plug-in window, enter a name for your recording under BUSINESS TRANSACTION NAME so that you will recognize it again later in end-to-end trace analysis. In the lower-right area, enter the relevant connection data for the Java part of SAP Solution Manager.

4. Choose START TRANSACTION, which means that the plug-in is ready to record.

5. In the EXECUTED STEP NAME field, you see the name STEP-1 as a default value. Change this if you want to specify another name for the first dialog step executed. In Figure 4.46, we chose the name CONNECT.

6. Open Microsoft Internet Explorer and execute the required URL or activity. In the plug-in window, the numeric values in the SENT BYTES and RECEIVED BYTES fields can indicate that the plug-in on the end user's PC is collecting data. At the same time, trace data is recorded on all SAP landscape systems involved on the server side.

7. The first dialog step concludes once the web page you have called opens successfully in the web browser.

8. In the plug-in window, choose NEW STEP. A new STEP-X name is then proposed in the EXECUTED STEP NAME field. In the field, you can once again enter your own name for the next step.

9. Execute another dialog step in the web browser and wait until the screen is fully displayed.

10. For all other dialog steps, perform the last two instructions in this description until you have recorded all the activities.

> **Note**
>
> If you do not yet know precisely which of the user's dialog steps is causing the problem, you can record a range of activities, as described above, and decide, at the start of the analysis, what you want to examine in greater detail. Otherwise, it is also possible for the end user to start the plug-in and then navigate within the web browser to the site of the problem before choosing START TRANSACTION to start the trace.

11. Once all the relevant dialog steps have been recorded, the user can choose STOP TRANSACTION to stop the recording on the end user's PC.

If the connection between the end user and SAP Solution Manager is working correctly, the plug-in transfers the client's trace data to SAP Solution Manager. If you obtain an error message here, you can manually upload the data to end-to-end trace analysis. This is possible in the MANUAL UPLOAD area within end-to-end trace analysis in SAP Solution Manager (see Figure 4.47).

Post-Processing the Trace

The end user has fulfilled his or her task. The next step is to process the trace:

1. First, the trace information is collected from the landscape. To do this, start END-TO-END TRACE ANALYSIS in the ROOT CAUSE ANALYSIS work center. If the TRACE ANALYSIS tab is not already selected, select it now. The list displayed in the BUSINESS TRANSACTIONS area contains all previously performed end-to-end traces. The trace you have just performed should appear at the very top with the most recent time stamp in the DATE/TIME column and a gray status in the STATE column (see Figure 4.47). If this is not the case, go to the MANUAL UPLOAD area of end-to-end trace analysis and upload the file BUSINESSTRANSACTION.XML in the plug-in directory of the end user's PC.

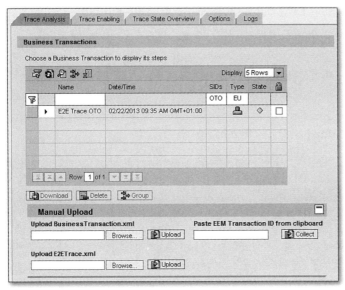

Figure 4.47 End-to-End Trace Analysis

2. Select the row. You are then asked whether you want to start data collection from the landscape components involved.

3. Choose YES to confirm this action. You then see how the individual traces are collected, in succession, within the system landscape. Wait until the list of traces is displayed. If all the data has been collected properly, your trace then has a green status in the STATE column to indicate that the data has been collected properly.

4. Once the data becomes available centrally, stop the trace preparation on the server. To do this, choose DISABLE ALL on the TRACE ENABLING tab.

Analyzing the Trace

1. On the TRACE ANALYSIS tab page, select the recording you want to analyze. In the TRANSACTION STEPS area below, you see all the dialog steps that have been recorded, including their time stamps and runtimes (see the DURATION column). Here, you can see which steps had longer runtimes.

Note

If the user does not choose NEW STEP between each dialog step being recorded, all the steps are displayed together as one step. This hampers the analysis considerably because it is no longer possible to individually filter out those steps that are performing poorly. Therefore, make sure that the user performs the recording correctly.

2. Select one of the steps for which the user has complained of poor performance. If possible, this step should have a long runtime so that it also has a high optimization potential.

3. Choose DISPLAY to call a summary of end-to-end trace analysis.

The trace summary contains various pieces of information about the user transaction (see Figure 4.48).

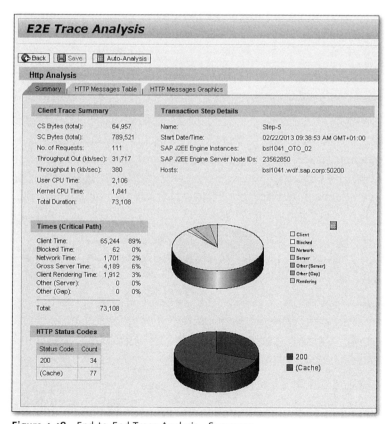

Figure 4.48 End-to-End Trace Analysis—Summary

▶ CLIENT TRACE SUMMARY
This area summarizes all necessary client information detected while recording the dialog step.

▶ TRANSACTION STEP DETAILS
This area contains the technical information for the recorded transaction. This information may be useful for trace analysis.

▶ TIMES (CRITICAL PATH)
The total response time of a dialog step is divided into different time components. In each case, the critical path for a component is always analyzed. The overview shows you how much time was spent on each individual component. On the right-hand side of the screen, a pie chart provides a visualization of how the time is distributed.

▶ HTTP STATUS CODES
An HTTP request comprises several subrequests. This area shows you all HTTP message types (for example, ERROR 404) returned to the end user's PC for the step currently under analysis. Once again, a visual representation is provided on the right-hand side.

The pie chart for TIMES (CRITICAL PATH) enables you to quickly understand which component consumed the most time:

▶ In the example involving Toys Inc. (see Figure 4.48), the most time was consumed on the client (CLIENT TIME). In this case, you would introduce additional steps for analyzing and optimizing the end user's PC. BMC AppSight is suitable for this task, but a detailed description of this tool is beyond the scope of this book. This tool is free of charge and can be used, under the SAP Solution Manager license, to analyze SAP transactions.

▶ If network-based problems occur, we recommend that you perform a network analysis (using the NIPING tool, for example). However, we will not discuss it further here.

We will assume that server processing, and not the client component, accounts for the largest part of the total response time. Choose AUTO-ANALYSIS or perform the analysis manually.

To do this, switch to the HTTP MESSAGES TABLE tab page. Choose HIDE CACHED above the table. All the individual browser subrequests that belong to the dialog step under analysis are displayed in the table.

In the sRT column (for server response time), you see the amount of time required for a subrequest to the server. Select the longest running request here. Then, in the SERVER ANALYSIS area below, a row is automatically selected in the REQUEST TREE. The SYSTEM column in this view shows you which technical system in the SAP landscape processed this substep. Further left, in the TYPE column, you see whether it concerns AS ABAP or AS Java processing. In the next area, DISTRIBUTED STATISTICS RECORD, you obtain additional information about the step you have selected.

This is the highest level of detail that you can achieve with end-to-end trace analysis. If a server response time of more than 1,000 ms (1 second) is displayed for individual subrequests, you can use other tools to conduct further analysis.

Using Expert Tools for Further Analysis

The expert tools required for further analysis are linked to the SERVER ANALYSIS section of the screen described above:

▶ INTROSCOPE TRANSACTION TRACE: analysis of the Java application

▶ J2EE SQL TRACE: analysis of database queries in AS Java

▶ ABAP TRACE: analysis of the ABAP application

▶ ABAP SQL TRACE: analysis of database queries in AS ABAP

On the right-hand side of the REQUEST TREE table, you see the icons 🔍 and 🔍 for some steps. If you move the mouse pointer over an icon, you will see a tooltip that enables you to navigate from the aforementioned applications. A summary of the relevant trace data is concealed behind each link. Each of these summaries on the DETAILS tab page contains a link, which you can use to access that actual expert tool that presents you with the data for this end-to-end trace.

In the following section, we will use the example of Introscope Transaction Trace to provide a more detailed introduction to detailed analysis. We will not discuss the other expert tools in detail here; the book *SAP Performance Optimization Guide* by Thomas Schneider provides detailed information about using trace tools and creating reports.

4.5.3 Using Introscope Transaction Trace

In this section, we will explain detailed analysis for Java applications. In contrast to the other trace tools for experts, this application is provided in Introscope Enterprise

Manager, which is located outside the managed system. You can start the recording yourself or use the recording for end-to-end trace analysis:

▶ If you have performed the Java trace manually, start Introscope Transaction Trace to open the analysis. Use WORKSTATION • QUERY HISTORICAL EVENTS to open the trace that you created recently.

▶ If you have used end-to-end trace analysis and navigated from there to Introscope Transaction Trace, the recording opens automatically.

Introscope Transaction Trace displays the existing trace(s) in the upper part of the window. All details relating to the trace you have selected are displayed in the lower part of the window, which is divided into different tab pages:

▶ SUMMARY VIEW
Internal Java program calls for all hierarchies are listed on this tab page. The following information is displayed here: the number of calls; the aggregated runtime for these calls; and the shortest, longest, and average time for these calls. Furthermore, information about the recorded user call in the Java stack is displayed above the table.

▶ TRACE VIEW
All internal processing steps are displayed here in graphical form, both in relation to each other and in a time scale. In the chart, a longer bar can be used to quickly show which component used a lot of time.

▶ TREE VIEW
In this hierarchical arrangement, all subelements and their interdependencies are displayed in a tree structure. You can expand the individual nodes specifically to search for large time portions. Focus on those elements that have been assigned a red or yellow rating.

▶ PLAIN TABLE VIEW
This tab page displays all subcalls in the Java stack in tabular form. In addition to the hierarchy level, you can also learn about the GROSS and NET times.

As is the case with other trace analyses, always concentrate on the largest time portions in the recording. Search for a high net time. These calls do not contain any other subcalls and, therefore, have the greatest potential for time-based optimization. During the analysis, use Introscope Transaction Trace to determine which

Java package causes the long runtimes. Then, forward the analysis results to the relevant development team.

4.5.4   Approaches and Examples

In the case of a trace analysis, you should ensure that it is possible to reproduce the user transaction you want to analyze. In other words, it should be recorded under the same conditions as those experienced when the problems were detected. Before you start the recording, decide which tool is most suitable for the analysis:

- If you do not yet know precisely which systems will access the user transaction, use end-to-end trace analysis in SAP Solution Manager.

- If you are already sure that a user transaction will be processed on an AS ABAP only, use one of the following expert tools:
  - ABAP trace
  - ABAP SQL trace

- For applications on AS Java, use the following expert tools:
  - Introscope Transaction Trace
  - J2EE SQL trace

The approach is almost identical for each tool and corresponds to the information provided in Section 4.5.2.

4.6   End-to-End Methodology: Exception Analysis

Exception analysis involves the analysis of functional problems in a heterogeneous landscape. It concerns error messages in online mode, which occur on the end user's PC or in the background when data is being processed on systems.

The main challenge associated with analyzing exception situations is the complex infrastructure of the IT system landscapes, which makes it difficult to identify the actual cause of a problem. The exception analysis end-to-end methodology makes error analysis easier. It helps you obtain coherent information about the entire IT landscape at a glance. Exception analysis makes error logs and log files available to you in a central overview, thus avoiding the need to perform individual searches of various data sources.

4.6.1 Exception Analysis Tools in SAP Solution Manager

The following tools in the SAP Solution Manager landscape support you in analyzing exception errors:

▶ **End-to-end exception analysis**
End-to-end exception analysis is the central entry point for handling exception errors in an SAP system landscape. It provides an overview of different categories of errors within the system landscape. Furthermore, a selection of predefined KPIs helps you quickly and effectively assess the situation. For more information about using this tool, see Section 4.6.3.

▶ **Log viewer**
The log viewer for displaying log files is already part of SAP NetWeaver and is therefore available in most managed systems. SAP Solution Manager, on the other hand, provides this function centrally so that you can perform the analysis in the ROOT CAUSE ANALYSIS work center without having to log on to a managed system or even having to log on at the operating system level.

The log viewer also provides unified access to the log files in a Java environment. Instead of having to read several files, you can also use the time stamp to bring files together and display their contents. Furthermore, the log viewer visually formats the log files in such a way that you can identify important content (for example, errors) more easily.

4.6.2 Data Extraction and Storage

Once again, the EFWK in SAP Solution Manager is used to collect data for end-to-end exception analysis. The process of collecting data for exception analysis is almost identical to that of collecting data for workload analysis (see Section 4.4.2):

▶ The data on the managed system is recorded (in database tables or logs).

▶ ST-PI reports and diagnostics agents analyze this data and send it to SAP Solution Manager.

▶ The data is processed, and all statistical information is stored centrally in SAP NetWeaver BW within SAP Solution Manager.

▶ The predefined views in end-to-end exception analysis provide the end user with easy access to statistical BW data.

4.6.3 Using End-to-End Exception Analysis

To use end-to-end exception analysis, proceed as follows:

1. In the ROOT CAUSE ANALYSIS work center, select the END-TO-END ANALYSIS menu option.

2. In the DETAILED SELECTION area, select the technical systems to be analyzed and choose EXCEPTION ANALYSIS.

3. The OVERVIEW tab page contains a graph representing all different categories of errors. Here, the number of errors is displayed on the y-axis and the time scale is shown on the x-axis. On the right-hand side of the screen, the application shows you the most important KPIs so that, at a glance, you are able to assess the situation for the period selected.

   If you see a high number of errors in one particular error category, you should try to find the source of this problem. In our example involving Toys Inc., Figure 4.49 shows that in the period between December 12, 2012 and December 17, 2012, J2EE application errors increasingly occurred on the Java side, while SysLog errors increasingly occurred on the ABAP side. J2EE system errors should not be ignored, either.

4. To obtain further information about the individual components, switch to one of the tabs next to the OVERVIEW tab. Depending on the technology and product definition for the technical system, you can use the relevant links in the upper area of the relevant tab pages to call further details:

   ▶ For AS ABAP, these are typically ABAP SYSLOG ERRORS, ABAP DUMPS, ABAP UPDATE ERRORS, or IDOC ERRORS.

   ▶ For AS Java, these are typically J2EE SYSTEM ERRORS, J2EE APPLICATION ERRORS, or J2EE DUMPS (see Figure 4.50).

   Depending on your technical system, a further tab (for example, RFC) may be displayed next to the AS ABAP and AS Java tabs.

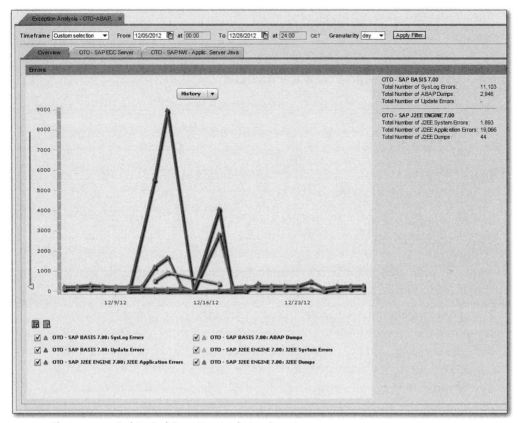

Figure 4.49 End-to-End Exception Analysis—Overview

Even though errors may occur at all these levels, they are not always critical. Pay particular attention to database errors because they can lead to inconsistencies that, if not dealt with promptly, may require a great deal of time and effort to resolve, or it may not be possible to resolve them at all. Furthermore, J2EE dumps are critical because it is very likely that a server node crashed unexpectedly (for example, as a result of a memory bottleneck). Less critical errors may also cause a serious situation, especially if they occur frequently. For example, if data is written to the logs at high frequency, this could place a heavy load on the hard disk system and trigger a performance problem. In general, the decision about which errors are classified as critical very much depends on your system. You should, therefore, include all errors in end-to-end analysis and then focus on those that are most relevant for your system.

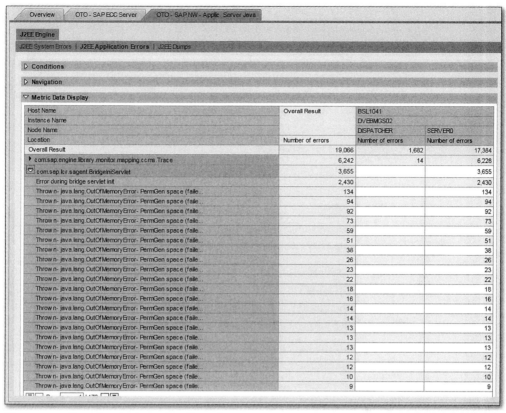

| Overview | OTO - SAP ECC Server | OTO - SAP NW - Applic Server Java | | | |

J2EE Engine
J2EE System Errors | J2EE Application Errors | J2EE Dumps

▷ Conditions

▷ Navigation

▽ Metric Data Display

Host Name	Overall Result	BSL1041	
Instance Name		DVEBMGS02	
Node Name		DISPATCHER	SERVER0
Location	Number of errors	Number of errors	Number of errors
Overall Result	19,066	1,682	17,384
▶ com.sap.engine.library.monitor.mapping.ccms.Trace	6,242	14	6,228
▢ com.sap.lcr.sagent.BridgeIniServlet	3,655		3,655
Error during bridge servlet init	2,430		2,430
Throw n- java.lang.OutOfMemoryError- PermGen space (faile...	134		134
Throw n- java.lang.OutOfMemoryError- PermGen space (faile...	94		94
Throw n- java.lang.OutOfMemoryError- PermGen space (faile...	92		92
Throw n- java.lang.OutOfMemoryError- PermGen space (faile...	73		73
Throw n- java.lang.OutOfMemoryError- PermGen space (faile...	59		59
Throw n- java.lang.OutOfMemoryError- PermGen space (faile...	51		51
Throw n- java.lang.OutOfMemoryError- PermGen space (faile...	38		38
Throw n- java.lang.OutOfMemoryError- PermGen space (faile...	26		26
Throw n- java.lang.OutOfMemoryError- PermGen space (faile...	23		23
Throw n- java.lang.OutOfMemoryError- PermGen space (faile...	22		22
Throw n- java.lang.OutOfMemoryError- PermGen space (faile...	18		18
Throw n- java.lang.OutOfMemoryError- PermGen space (faile...	16		16
Throw n- java.lang.OutOfMemoryError- PermGen space (faile...	14		14
Throw n- java.lang.OutOfMemoryError- PermGen space (faile...	14		14
Throw n- java.lang.OutOfMemoryError- PermGen space (faile...	13		13
Throw n- java.lang.OutOfMemoryError- PermGen space (faile...	13		13
Throw n- java.lang.OutOfMemoryError- PermGen space (faile...	13		13
Throw n- java.lang.OutOfMemoryError- PermGen space (faile...	12		12
Throw n- java.lang.OutOfMemoryError- PermGen space (faile...	12		12
Throw n- java.lang.OutOfMemoryError- PermGen space (faile...	10		10
Throw n- java.lang.OutOfMemoryError- PermGen space (faile...	9		9

Figure 4.50   Exception Analysis—Java Example

In Section 4.6.5, we will show you how you can apply the expertise that you have just acquired to using the relevant expert tools.

4.6.4   Using the Log Viewer

We will now show you how to use the log viewer:

1. In the ROOT CAUSE ANALYSIS work center, select the SYSTEM ANALYSIS menu option.

2. In the DETAILED SELECTION area, select a Java system whose logs you wish to analyze and then choose LOG VIEWER. A new window opens (see Figure 4.51). Here, you see whether the necessary diagnostics agent is working and which logs are currently available for the system.

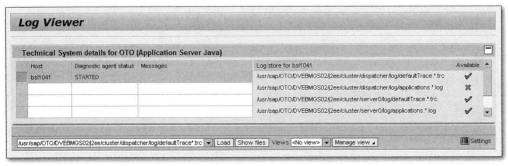

Figure 4.51 Log Viewer—Start-Up Window

3. On the left-hand side of the lower part of the window, you can select the log file you require (see Figure 4.51). If you want to display the file you have selected, choose LOAD. If you select another file, the content is automatically loaded.

4. Different logs (for example, *DefaultTrace.trc* or *applications.log*) in AS Java are sequentially written to several files of the same name. The log viewer brings these together, thus making the logs easier to read and analyze. If you want to display the exact file names in the sequence, choose SHOW FILES.

5. After the contents of the log have been loaded (as described in step 3), all entries are displayed below the log name (see Figure 4.52), along with their time stamp and other key information. The SEVERITY column contains information about the severity of the error.

> **Note**
>
> By default, Java systems do not log errors until they reach a certain level of severity, thus avoiding a high load as a result of data being frequently written to the logs. If necessary, you can adjust the log configuration in SAP NetWeaver Administrator within the system and then reset this again. This enables you to obtain more background information about the problem, which may be very helpful to you when conducting the analysis.

The LOCATION column displays the application causing the problem or, at the very least, the Java package responsible for the problem. The TEXT column provides a short description of the error, while the THREADNAME column specifies the relevant server node thread. This data gives you additional information about which parts of the system you can search.

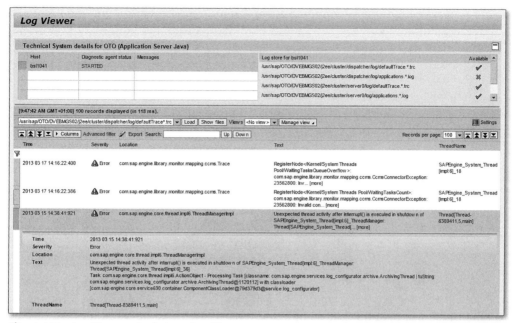

Figure 4.52 Log Viewer—Analyzing a Log File

6. If you wish to obtain additional information about the error, you can choose COLUMNS to insert more columns. However, these columns are displayed only if data is available for the errors shown.

7. If you select an entry in the log, further details are displayed below the entry (see Figure 4.52). This information is useful for a detailed analysis and needs to be interpreted or evaluated by an expert or developer with the relevant expertise.

8. If you have a particular suspicion or want to search for a keyword within an error, use the search function below the log name. To do this, enter a term in the SEARCH field and choose UP or DOWN. Depending on your selection, either the next or previous error that contains this term is displayed in the log.

9. If you want to forward the log for continuative analysis, you can select the EXPORT link to download all or part of the file.

4.6.5 Approaches and Examples

Exception analysis is fundamentally suited to two typical use cases:

- A user caused a program to terminate at a particular time and under certain conditions. Alternatively, during your daily maintenance work, you discover that a background job triggered an error at a particular time.

- You want to conduct a trend analysis for exception errors. This will analyze system behavior over a longer period of time.

  This is useful, for example, in identifying a system landscape component that causes a high number of errors. Furthermore, you can determine whether a higher number of errors occurred in the system landscape after changes were made to individual components (for example, patches, Support Packages, or configuration changes).

In such cases, you can consider using the following process for exception analysis:

1. First, use end-to-end exception analysis to obtain an overview of all problems that occurred in the landscape. Then, compare the various different technical systems in order to identify any interdependencies. If you want to analyze a particular situation, restrict the period under analysis accordingly. In the case of trend analysis, you should view information relating to a period of several weeks or even months so that you can perform a meaningful analysis.

2. If you identify a landscape component with critical errors or a noticeably large number of errors, switch to the component-specific part of end-to-end exception analysis. Then, depending on the technology involved, analyze the relevant error categories on the basis of the available statistics.

3. In this third step, use the relevant expert tools to conduct a detailed analysis of the error description for the relevant technology:

   - For ABAP, work directly on the managed system. Here, use Transaction ST22 for ABAP dump analysis, Transaction SM21 to evaluate system logs, Transaction SM13 for update errors, or Transaction SLG1 for application logs. In this book, we will not discuss the use of ABAP tools in any great detail.

   - For Java, you can use the aforementioned *file system browser* (see Section 4.2.2) to access the log files and search them for anomalies. However, this is very time consuming. Instead, use the log viewer to obtain an easy-to-read view of the system logs (see Section 4.6.4).

You have now learned about the methodologies and tools for analyzing errors in the SAP system landscape. We will now show you a tool that you can use to analyze and track individual errors, as well as analyze more complex relationships between different exceptions in heterogeneous system landscapes.

4.6.6 Exception Management

Since SAP Solution Manager 7.1 SP05, a further tool, known as *exception management*, is available to you within root cause analysis.

In contrast to end-to-end exception analysis, which you use to obtain a statistical overview of certain errors in the components involved, exception management enables you to specifically analyze and document individual exceptions and trigger follow-up activities, such as creating a support message.

Furthermore, this new function is linked to the Monitoring and Alerting Infrastructure (MAI), thus making it possible to specifically trigger alerts for certain exceptions.

One significant advantage of using exception management in SAP Solution Manager is that any correlated errors associated with an exception you have selected can also be displayed across system boundaries. Time and time again, the process of collecting all relevant error information when functional problems occur, which is a prerequisite for successful root cause analysis, represents a major challenge for the administrator. He needs to know which parts of the systems in question contain information about certain error situations and, in particular, which exceptions belong together. Exception management in SAP Solution Manager can help you answer this type of question.

The following exceptions can be collected for managed systems:

- ABAP short dumps (runtime errors)
- ABAP SysLog error messages
- ABAP aborted jobs
- ABAP application log errors
- ABAP web service errors

You can also use your own code implementations to document error messages for critical business process steps.

If you want to use exception management, you must have at least SAP Solution Manager 7.1 SP05 and ST-PI 2008_1 700 SP06 or higher. Once these prerequisites have been fulfilled, you can use the following menu path to activate exception management in the SAP SOLUTION MANAGER CONFIGURATION work center: MAN-AGED SYSTEMS CONFIGURATION • CONFIGURE MANUALLY • ENABLE EXCEPTION MANAGEMENT.

Here, you can define which exceptions are to be collected for each system. You can also set filters to restrict exceptions to certain runtime errors or special background jobs, for example.

> **Note**
>
> Fully configured root cause analysis tools are not a prerequisite for using exception management. However, SAP recommends that you be able to conduct a complete root cause analysis for a wide range of problems.

You can use exception management to analyze individual exceptions or exceptions that comprise several steps. In the next section, we will start by showing you how to proceed when analyzing an individual exception.

Analyzing Individual Exceptions

1. In the ROOT CAUSE ANALYSIS work center, select the EXCEPTION MANAGEMENT menu option.

2. In the work area on the right-hand side of the screen, choose MONITORING. You can choose whether you want exception management to be embedded in the screen or open in a new window.

3. In the table, select the category (for example, ABAP Aborted Jobs) that you want to analyze (see Figure 4.53).

The lower INSTANCE GROUP area displays individual exceptions for the category you have selected. A time stamp is also displayed in each case. Exceptions from the last two days are displayed as default values. You can choose SHOW QUICK CRITERIA MAINTENANCE to adjust the time frame accordingly.

In the AUTO REFRESH setting, you can define the time interval at which the display is automatically refreshed. Various different extractors automatically collect the error messages every ten minutes. Both the frequency with which the data is collected and the retention period are defined in the CONFIGURATION area, which we will discuss briefly in the subsection "Exception Management Configuration."

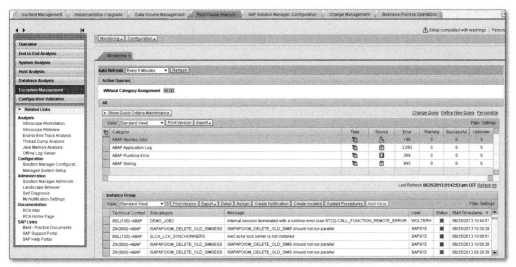

Figure 4.53 Exception Management Cockpit—Overview

You can start several follow-up activities in exception management. To this end, the following buttons are available in the INSTANCE GROUP area:

▶ PRINT VERSION
You can use the Adobe Document Service to print the list of exceptions displayed on the screen.

▶ EXPORT
You can use this function to export the list of exceptions to Microsoft Excel.

▶ DETAIL
You can use this button to access the detail view for an exception you have selected. Here, you can display information about the call list, variable assignments, or the passport used. *Passport* is the term used for information automatically assigned to each call (for example, information about the transaction ID, sender, and recipient). When you choose CORRELATED EXCEPTIONS, all errors relating to the exception you have selected are displayed, even across system boundaries. In the event of an error, this function enables you to display a complete list of all exceptions that were triggered in all systems involved, thus making it easier for you to search for the causal error message.

▶ ASSIGN
You can use this function to specify a person responsible and set a status for the exception.

▶ CREATE NOTIFICATION
For the exceptions selected, you can send an SMS message, email, or both. You can enter email addresses here or access users' email addresses or recipient lists that you defined in notification management as part of technical administration.

▶ CREATE INCIDENT
This function is integrated with IT Service Management (ITSM) in SAP Solution Manager. As a follow-up activity to the selected exception, you can create an incident (transaction type SMIN), support notification (SNWS), or test case error (SMDT), which you can then process in ITSM.

▶ GUIDED PROCEDURES
This function can be used for centralized documentation and correction handling. Since it is integrated with the guided procedure framework, exception management for certain errors can be documented centrally. Furthermore, you can search for existing documentation or ready-made solutions. You can also define your own guided procedure for managing exceptions according to predefined rules.

▶ ALERT INBOX
This function is integrated with the MAI in SAP Solution Manager. You can place certain exceptions (for example, special ABAP runtime errors or important jobs that have been aborted) in the alert inbox in the TECHNICAL MONITORING work center. An exception configured in this way would trigger an alert accordingly. You can choose ALERT INBOX to navigate directly to the alert inbox. The necessary configuration also takes place in the TECHNICAL MONITORING work center.

We'll now use an example to demonstrate how to use the relevant tools. In the system BSL at Toys Inc., it has become apparent that the background job DEMO_JOB2 has been aborted.

Therefore, in the exception management cockpit, we select the error relating to the job DEMO_JOB2 and choose DETAILS (Figure 4.53).

Then, in the detail view, we select CORRELATED EXCEPTIONS (❶ in Figure 4.54). The CORRELATED EXCEPTIONS window contains all error messages generated in those systems in which this job was aborted. (❷). You do not have to search for the systems involved; this is done automatically. In the window that opens, we select the exception associated with the runtime error. The display screen branches to the detail view for the runtime error generated by the system (❸). In the PRODUCT SYSTEM field, you can see that the runtime error was triggered in the system OTO.

If you choose EXCEPTION SOURCE (see Figure 4.54), you can navigate via the Web GUI directly to Transaction ST22 in the system OTO and view the entire dump there.

In this example, the job aborted in the system called a function module, which, in turn, tried to call another function module. Since this second function module does not exist in the system, however, the job was aborted in the system BSL. This example clearly illustrates the advantage of using this function. Namely, it would have been considerably more difficult to manually search for the systems involved and the error messages generated.

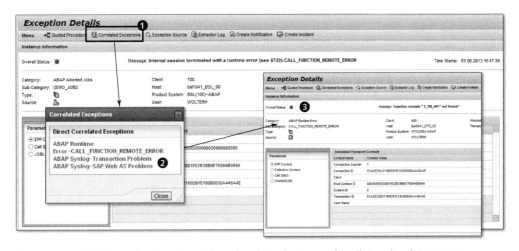

Figure 4.54 Detail View for Exception Selected and Display Screen for All Correlated Exceptions

Analyzing Multistep Exceptions

In order to make it possible to efficiently track critical business process steps across system boundaries, the SAP Exception Management Instrumentation Platform was introduced with the latest version of exception management. You can use this platform to check whether important process steps were fully executed or whether problems or errors occurred while these process steps were being executed.

To this end, you can add your own implementations, in the form of enhancements, to the classes and function modules used by the individual process steps, thus making it possible, for example, to respond to incomplete process steps with customized error messages. When the system is running, it uses an enhancement to SAP Passport technology known as the SAP Business Passport concept. SAP Passport makes it possible to exchange information about the transaction IDs in use, thus facilitating correlations within distributed statistical records, while additional information about the preceding and subsequent steps in the processes is saved in the enhanced SAP Business Passport concept.

For more information about configuring multistep exceptions, see *http://wiki.sdn. sap.com/wiki/display/TechOps/ExMan_Home*.

As is the case with individual exceptions, you can also analyze multistep exceptions in the exception management cockpit. Once again, we will use an example to demonstrate this approach.

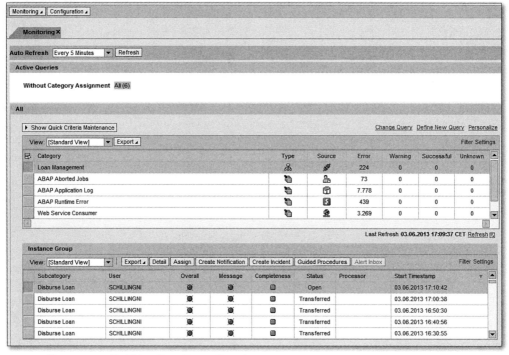

Figure 4.55 Multistep Exceptions—Overview

This overview contains all individual exceptions, as well as all exceptions relating to multistep processes (see Figure 4.55). The LOAN MANAGEMENT process is one such process. You want to analyze this multistep process here. Figure 4.55 shows that a total of 224 errors occurred in Loan Management. The remaining errors relate to individual exceptions from the following areas: ABAP Aborted Jobs, ABAP

Runtime Error, or ABAP Application Log. To conduct a more in-depth analysis of Loan Management, select this process in the cockpit. All messages relating to the process you have selected are displayed in the INSTANCE GROUP area. Here, select an entry and choose DETAIL. In the next window (Figure 4.56), you receive information about the individual steps:

▸ EXTENDED PASSPORT INFORMATION area: passport information

▸ INSTANCE INFORMATION area: information about the overall status of the complete process

▸ INSTANCE FLOW area: list of all process steps and their statuses

▸ STEP INFORMATION area: context information and the call list (call stack) for the individual steps

▸ UNIT INFORMATION area: error messages and related details

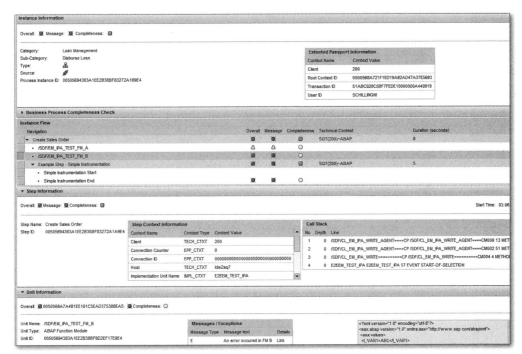

Figure 4.56 Multistep Exceptions—Details

In the detail view, we can see that the CREATE SALES ORDER step was executed. Within this step, however, there was an error in the function module /SDF/ EM_IPA_TEST_FM_B and, as a result, the following message text was issued in the MESSAGES/EXCEPTIONS area: AN ERROR OCCURRED IN FM B.

You can now continue to analyze the individual messages for the relevant substeps.

From this example, it is clear to see that you obtain very detailed information about the analysis of multistep exceptions. In other words, you know precisely what happened while the individual steps were being executed.

Configuring Exception Management

On the initial screen for exception management, you can choose CONFIGURATION to display or change configurations or Customizing settings for exception management.

The following tabs are available here, each with different analysis views:

▶ The exceptions and filters set for individual systems are displayed on the OVER-VIEW tab page. These are defined when you configure the managed systems and cannot be changed here. This view is solely for information purposes. As of SAP Solution Manager SP8, you can also change these setting here.

▶ On the INSTRUMENTATION PLATFORM tab page, you specify which detailed information is to be collected for the exceptions (for example, the call stack or additional application log information).

▶ On the HOUSEKEEPING tab page, you define the retention period for different categories of exceptions—in other words, the length of time that must pass before they are automatically deleted by the system.

▶ On the REPOSITORY tab page, you define multistep processes for which you can later implement customized exceptions.

▶ Lastly, on the SELFMONITORING tab page, you find not only the logs but also log information relating to the individual extractors responsible for collecting the various exceptions. You can also change the time interval for individual extractors here. To do this, choose CHANGE • EXPERT MODE • EXTRACTOR DETAIL • CONFIGURATION • PERIOD. The minimum value is five minutes.

4.7 Additional Documentation

Links

1. Further documentation and demos on the root cause analysis tools in SAP Solution Manager is available at *http://service.sap.com/diagnostics* and *http://wiki.sdn.sap.com/wiki/display/TechOps/RCA_Home*.

2. Further information on using configuration validation is available at *http://service.sap.com/rkt-solman* • SAP SOLUTION MANAGER 7.1 • CHANGE CONTROL MANAGEMENT • CHANGE DIAGNOSTICS&CONFIGURATION VALIDATION.

3. Technical information on change analysis and configuration validation is available at *http://wiki.sdn.sap.com/wiki/display/TechOps/Home*.

4. Online training for configuration validation for enterprise support customers is available at *http://service.sap.com/enterprisesupport*.

5. Further information on configuration validation is available on SAP Help Portal at *http://help.sap.com/solutionmanager71* • RELEASE NOTES • APPLICATIONHELP • CHANGE CONTROL MANAGEMENT • CONFIGURATION CHECK.

6. Full documentation on using and configuring the exception management tool (including multistep exceptions) is available at *http://wiki.sdn.sap.com/wiki/display/TechOps/ExMan_Home*.

SAP Notes

Table 4.1 provides an overview of important SAP Notes for root cause analysis.

Contents	SAP Note
SAP Solution Manager 7.1: Root cause analysis pre-requisites	1483508
Diagnostics in SAP Solution Manager 7.1	1478974
Installation of Diagnostics Agents	1365123
E2E CA Store Content List	1230404
SAP Client Plug-In	1435190
End-to-End Diagnostics	1010428
How to create/record an end-to-end trace for root cause analysis	1608474

Table 4.1 SAP Notes for Root Cause Analysis

Technical monitoring is a prerequisite for controlling and managing your IT system landscape. At the same time, monitoring tasks are becoming increasingly automated and new functions are making IT systems more secure.

5 Technical Monitoring

SAP Solution Manager 7.1 provides a new technical monitoring option for system landscapes. The *Monitoring and Alerting Infrastructure* (MAI) solution has new and improved workings that replace the functions and concepts from Computing Center Management System (CCMS) Monitoring and SAP Solution Manager 7.0.

In this chapter, we'll use practical examples to provide detailed insight into setting up technical monitoring. You will also learn the meaning behind the term *technical monitoring* and how the new MAI differs from its predecessor, the CCMS. Finally, we will outline the advantages of using the MAI so that you can achieve the maximum benefit from your solution.

5.1 Motivation

If you compare a typical SAP system landscape (one used by SAP customers up until a few years ago) with today's system landscapes, it becomes clear that system landscapes have become more and more complex and increasingly heterogeneous.

In order to ensure the stability of the system landscape and keep users happy, system administrators need to be very knowledgeable of new technologies and how to use not only them, but also various application components including those outside the SAP portfolio, along with a myriad of interfaces. Even in enterprises that operate a manageable system landscape comprising two or three systems, system monitoring is playing an ever greater role and becoming an integral part of the daily running of an IT department. MAI's collection of tools helps the administrator automate system landscape monitoring to the greatest possible extent. Nowadays, manual monitoring (for example, using checklists) is barely imaginable and rarely used.

Automated monitoring of the system landscape saves the administrator time, which can then be devoted to other tasks. It also provides the administrator with reliable information. If there is a malfunction that could threaten operations, an incident is automatically created in the system in order to alert the administrator in time.

In addition to implementing permanent and automated monitoring of your system landscape, SAP Solution Manager 7.1 collects all information centrally so that it can be used in reporting. Various tools in SAP Solution Manager 7.1 (for example, *root cause analysis*) also use this information (see Chapter 4). You can use the MAI monitoring tool to analyze and optimize the performance and status of systems in complex landscapes.

5.2 Overview of Technical Monitoring

Technical monitoring in SAP Solution Manager 7.1 contains a range of product-specific monitoring types and tools that consider various scenarios during central monitoring of the system landscape. SAP Solution Manager 7.1, which is currently available, provides the following monitoring scenarios:

▶ System monitoring

▶ Database monitoring

▶ Server monitoring

▶ BI monitoring

▶ PI monitoring

▶ End-user experience monitoring

▶ Interface channel monitoring

▶ Interface monitoring

▶ Self-monitoring of the SAP Solution Manager system and technical infrastructure

Additional scenarios (for example, document-based, interactive reporting and a central alert inbox) are linked to the aforementioned scenarios in SAP Solution Manager 7.1. In the following sections, you'll learn more about each scenario and the areas associated with technical monitoring in SAP Solution Manager 7.1.

5.3   Monitoring and Alerting Infrastructure

The introduction of the MAI set a new SAP standard for central monitoring and alerting. This infrastructure is based on an established architecture in SAP Solution Manager 7.0 EHP1, known as *end-to-end diagnostics*. In the new release of SAP Solution Manager 7.1, the end-to-end diagnostics components (for example, the diagnostics agents or Introscope Enterprise Manager) are no longer significant for root cause analysis alone. They are also are an important part of the MAI.

At the same time, a new TECHNICAL MONITORING work center, which contains all the aforementioned monitoring types, was introduced. Therefore, the user can query the status of a system more quickly or navigate without any problems among the individual areas. The new infrastructure also facilitates better integration with different tools in SAP Solution Manager 7.1 (for example, *work mode management* or root cause analysis).

5.3.1   MAI Architecture

A number of prerequisites must be fulfilled before you can start to set up technical monitoring. These include the following:

▶ Installation of diagnostics agents and SAP host agents on hosts on which satellite systems or components are installed and are to be monitored (see Section 2.2.1 and Section 2.2.2)

▶ Installation and configuration of Introscope Enterprise Manager (see Section 2.5.3)

▶ Registration of managed systems in the System Landscape Directory (SLD) followed by system preparation (see Section 2.5.2) and the basic configuration (see Section 2.5.3)

▶ Configuration of the relevant managed systems (see Section 2.5.4)

When setting up managed systems, other elements of the MAI infrastructure are configured:

▶ Implementation of adapters (Introscope Host Adapter and Introscope Byte Code Adapter)

▶ Scheduling of extractors in the Extractor Framework (EFWK)

▶ Execution of the DB setup

Figure 5.1 shows you which MAI components must be installed on which system components and how they communicate with each other. A functioning infrastructure will be at your disposal only once you have completed your basic configuration of SAP Solution Manager 7.1, as described in Section 2.5.3.

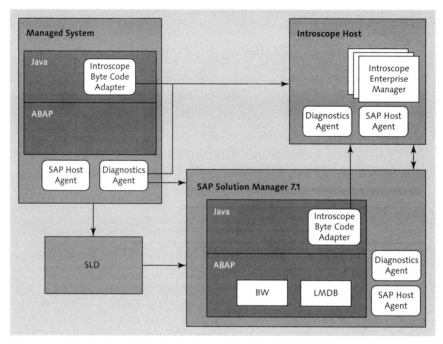

Figure 5.1 Monitoring and Alerting Infrastructure

At runtime, the MAI uses different data collection sources, known as *data providers*, to periodically send the values that have been collected to the SAP Solution Manager system. These values, also known as *metrics*, are first processed using the *Data Provider Connector*.

Essentially, the Data Provider Connector has two tasks. The first task is to store the information delivered by the data providers in the BW Store, which can be used later for reporting. The second task is to forward the metric values to the *Event Calculation Engine, which* stores the data in the Metric and Event Store as results, which are then available for monitoring. At the same time, the engine forwards these events to the *Alert Consumer Connector*. At this point, generated alerts are stored in the *Alert Store*. Furthermore, the Alert Consumer Connector is responsible for forwarding the alerts to the relevant alert consumers. We'll describe individual areas within this process in more detail in the following text.

Figure 5.2 gives you an overview of the aforementioned components and their function when the MAI is used in monitoring at runtime.

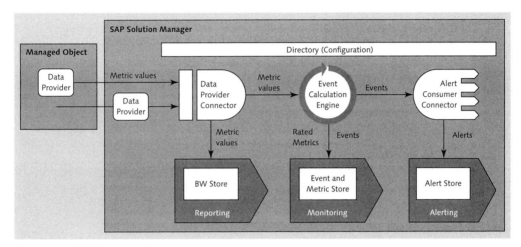

Figure 5.2 MAI Components

We have listed the individual process steps associated with technical monitoring at runtime here:

1. The data providers collect the relevant data in managed systems.

2. The Data Provider Connector receives the data from the data providers.

3. The Data Provider Connector sends the data to the Alert Store.

4. The Event Calculation Engine receives the metric values from the Data Provider Connector.

5. The Event Calculation Engine calculates alerts on the basis of the values delivered.

6. The alerts are stored in the Alert Store.

7. The Alert Consumer Connector forwards the generated alerts to the alert consumers that have been defined.

5.3.2   MAI Data Providers

Data providers are responsible for collecting information that is used to create metric values. Different data provider types exist because information must be collected for various technical components. First, data providers are differentiated on the basis of their delivery method. Then, data providers can be roughly divided into two types:

▶ **Push data providers**
Push data providers deliver data from external sources (for example, data collected by diagnostics agents or data from Introscope Enterprise Manager) and send this data to the SAP Solution Manager system.

▶ **Pull data providers**
Pull data providers deliver data directly from the SAP Solution Manager system, or this data is requested and actively transferred from external components.

Before we provide you with a broad overview of the data delivery process, we will give you a detailed introduction to the individual data providers.

RFC Pull: ST-PI

The data provider RFC Pull: ST-PI is scheduled in the SAP Solution Manager system (exactly one extractor for each satellite system). The SAP Solution Manager system then uses the RFC call to send a list of all metrics that need to be collected to the system connected. Afterward, function modules belonging to the Solution Tool Plug-In (ST-PI) collect these metrics locally on the satellite system. Within this RFC call, the SAP Solution Manager system receives the requested data, as shown in Figure 5.3.

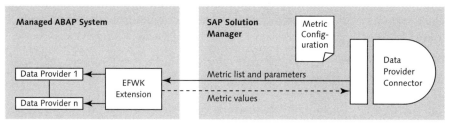

Figure 5.3   Data Provider—RFC Pull: ST-PI

This data provider collects the following data, for example:

▸ Metrics from the local CCMS in the ABAP system

▸ ABAP work process information

▸ ABAP memory information

RFC Pull: ST

As with the ST-PI data provider, the ST data provider is scheduled in the form of an extractor in the SAP Solution Manager system. The internal RFC call forces function modules to collect metrics locally, as shown in Figure 5.4.

This data provider collects the following data, for example:

▸ Data from the Configuration and Change Database (CDDB), which is acquired via end-to-end change analysis

▸ Data from the SAP EarlyWatch Alert report

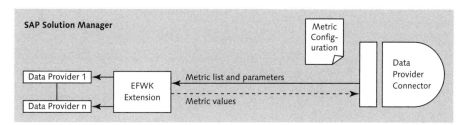

Figure 5.4 Data Provider—RFC Pull: ST

RFC Pull: ST-BW

In the case of this data provider, the SAP Solution Manager system calls the ABAP functions modules, which then pull the necessary information from an internal or external SAP NetWeaver BW system or client (see Figure 5.5). An RFC from SAP Solution Manager connected to the specified SAP NetWeaver BW clients is responsible for collecting the data from the BW InfoCubes.

This data provider collects the following data, for example:

▸ Data from the InfoCubes for end-to-end workload analysis

▸ Data from the InfoCubes for end-to-end exception analysis

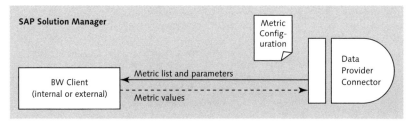

Figure 5.5 Data Provider—RFC Pull: ST-BW

RFC Pull: DBMS

This data provider is responsible for database-specific metrics. In the SAP Solution Manager system, an extractor is scheduled for each database. A function module connected to the database by means of an ABAP Database Connectivity (ADBC) connection extracts the relevant DB-specific data (see Figure 5.6).

This data provider collects the following data, for example:

▶ Backup status of the database

▶ Free database tablespaces

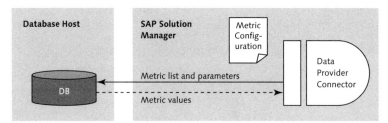

Figure 5.6 Data Provider—Pull DBMS

Push Introscope

As you can see in Figure 5.7, the metrics are collected directly in Introscope Enterprise Manager. Any metrics that are relevant for monitoring and are to be sent to the SAP Solution Manager system are stored in an XML file, which is received by the diagnostics agent installed on the Introscope Enterprise Manager host. The corresponding metrics are then forwarded via a web service to the Data Provider Connector.

This data provider collects the following data, for example:

▶ Java 2 Platform, Enterprise Edition (J2EE) metrics

▶ SAP BusinessObjects metrics

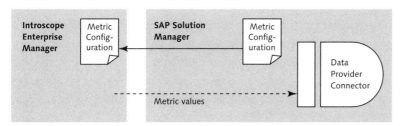

Figure 5.7   Data Provider—Push Introscope

Push Diagnostics Agent

The push diagnostics agent collects the metrics locally, on the host of the satellite system, and then uses the web service call to send the data to the SAP Solution Manager system. As with the Introscope data provider, each agent receives an XML file, as shown in Figure 5.8. This file contains a list of metrics that are to be collected.

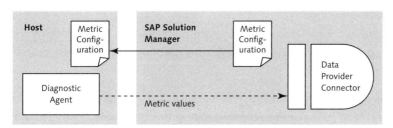

Figure 5.8   Data Provider—Push Diagnostics Agent

This data provider collects the following data, for example:

▶ OS-specific data from the operating system collector SAPOSCOL (see Section 2.2.1)

▶ HTTP URL ping/RFC ping for an ABAP instance

▶ Process status in sapstartsrv (see also Section 2.2.1)

The data delivery process comprises two steps, as follows:

1. In the first step, the metrics are collected. The decision about which metrics are collected is configured centrally in SAP Solution Manager. Here, the following criteria can be defined more precisely:

- ▶ Data provider type
- ▶ Collection interval
- ▶ Metric parameter

2. In the second step, the metrics are sent to the Data Provider Connector. If an error occurs at this point, the Data Provider Connector receives the error message from the relevant data provider via web services. There are two additional sub-steps:

   - ▶ The metrics are then checked in terms of their validity. Any metrics not known to the system in the central configuration are rejected.

   - ▶ In the next step, the Data Provider Connector decides whether the metrics received are relevant for reporting. If they are, it stores them in the BW Store. Furthermore, it checks whether the metrics are relevant for monitoring and alerting. In such cases, the data is forwarded to the Event Calculation Engine.

5.3.3 Event Calculation Engine

The Event Calculation Engine has several tasks in the MAI. Primarily, it is responsible for calculating the current status of a metric and event. The status of a metric is set using thresholds defined during configuration. In other words, a status is set (for example, green or red) depending on whether the value currently measured exceeds the threshold.

Furthermore, the Event Calculation Engine also calculates the event status, which comprises related metrics and event rules. Afterwards, the status calculated for metrics and events is written to the Metric and Event Store. In a final step, the events are made available to the Alert Consumer Connector, which then forwards the information to the relevant alert consumers.

The Event Calculation Engine comprises a report that is executed in the background every minute. This background job is scheduled as part of the basic configuration of the SAP Solution Manager system (see step 5 in Section 2.5.3).

> **Note**
>
> In earlier releases of SAP Solution Manager, this step was executed in the setup for the TECHNICAL MONITORING work center. Scheduling did not become part of the basic setup until Support Package Stack 5.

If scheduling is successful, this job should be displayed as scheduled in the background processing overview (Transaction SM37) under the name SAP_ALERT_CAL-CULATION_ENGINE. Figure 5.9 shows a list of executed alert calculation jobs in Transaction SM37.

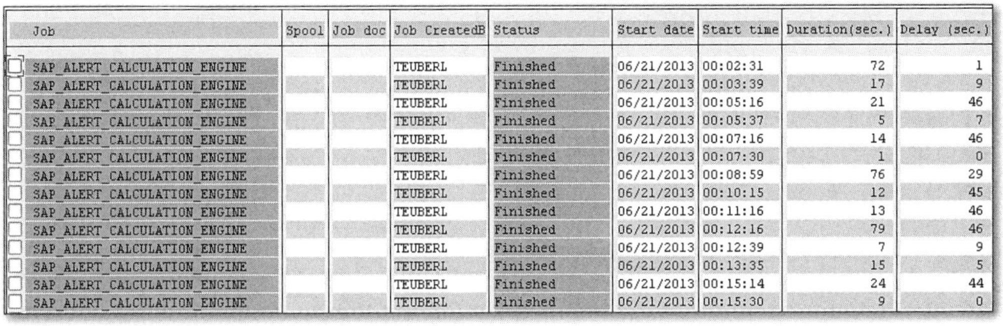

Job	Spool	Job doc	Job CreatedB	Status	Start date	Start time	Duration(sec.)	Delay (sec.)
SAP_ALERT_CALCULATION_ENGINE			TEUBERL	Finished	06/21/2013	00:02:31	72	1
SAP_ALERT_CALCULATION_ENGINE			TEUBERL	Finished	06/21/2013	00:03:39	17	9
SAP_ALERT_CALCULATION_ENGINE			TEUBERL	Finished	06/21/2013	00:05:16	21	46
SAP_ALERT_CALCULATION_ENGINE			TEUBERL	Finished	06/21/2013	00:05:37	5	7
SAP_ALERT_CALCULATION_ENGINE			TEUBERL	Finished	06/21/2013	00:07:16	14	46
SAP_ALERT_CALCULATION_ENGINE			TEUBERL	Finished	06/21/2013	00:07:30	1	0
SAP_ALERT_CALCULATION_ENGINE			TEUBERL	Finished	06/21/2013	00:08:59	76	29
SAP_ALERT_CALCULATION_ENGINE			TEUBERL	Finished	06/21/2013	00:10:15	12	45
SAP_ALERT_CALCULATION_ENGINE			TEUBERL	Finished	06/21/2013	00:11:16	13	46
SAP_ALERT_CALCULATION_ENGINE			TEUBERL	Finished	06/21/2013	00:12:16	79	46
SAP_ALERT_CALCULATION_ENGINE			TEUBERL	Finished	06/21/2013	00:12:39	7	9
SAP_ALERT_CALCULATION_ENGINE			TEUBERL	Finished	06/21/2013	00:13:35	15	5
SAP_ALERT_CALCULATION_ENGINE			TEUBERL	Finished	06/21/2013	00:15:14	24	44
SAP_ALERT_CALCULATION_ENGINE			TEUBERL	Finished	06/21/2013	00:15:30	9	0

Figure 5.9 Alert Calculation Job

If a job is not completed after a period of one minute, a second job is started in parallel. Up to four background jobs can run simultaneously.

As described in step 5 in Section 2.5.3, additional activities that are relevant for technical monitoring are executed during the basic configuration (see Figure 5.10).

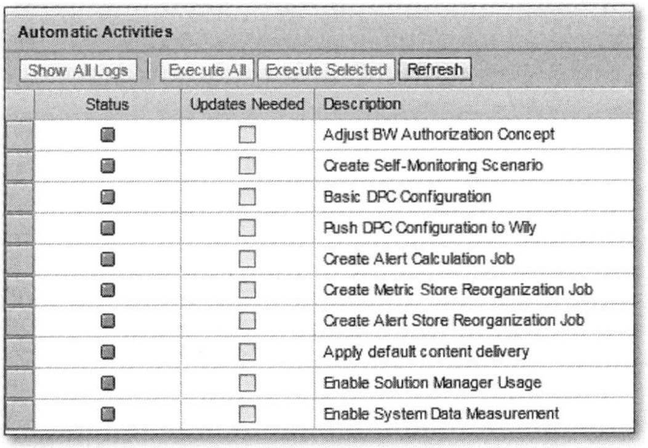

Figure 5.10 Automatic Activities—Technical Monitoring

The following steps are relevant for technical monitoring:

► CREATE SELF-MONITORING SCENARIO

► BASIC DPC CONFIGURATION

- ▶ Push DPC Configuration to Wily

- ▶ Create Alert Calculation Job

- ▶ Create Metric Store Reorganization Job

- ▶ Create Alert Store Reorganization Job

- ▶ Apply Default Content Delivery

We will now provide a detailed description of the individual elements that play a role when the Event Calculation Engine is used to calculate statuses. We will also explain how these elements relate to each other.

Metrics

A *metric* is always assigned to a category and represents measurement readings that constitute the result. For example, an availability metric contains data on the availability of instances. A metric has its own thresholds, which determine the status of the metric on the basis of the values measured. Each independent metric forms a unit that is also independent and cannot be influenced by other factors, such as additional metrics or events within its own evaluation.

Figure 5.11 shows an example of a metric for the ABAP dialog response time. In this example, the currently measured value of 2,200 milliseconds is above the defined threshold of 2,000 milliseconds and triggers the first warning. Since the threshold has been exceeded, a yellow status is calculated for this metric in the Event Calculation Engine and forwarded to the relevant alert consumers.

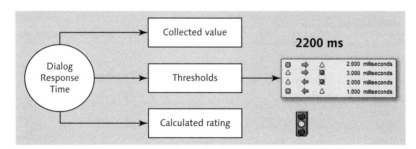

Figure 5.11 Dialog Response Time Metric

The threshold type determines which values are delivered by the metric. The numeric type is the threshold type most frequently used in technical monitoring.

Events

An *event* describes a change in status, which can have an effect on IT Service Management (ITSM). In technical monitoring, an event is triggered if the status of a managed object changes significantly. Such a change is determined using one or more metrics. An event is always assigned to a category, and the status of an event can be determined from several metrics or other events (see Figure 5.12).

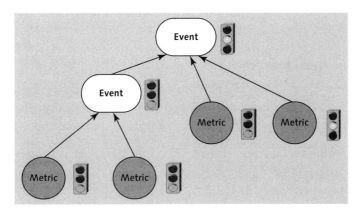

Figure 5.12 Monitoring Event

The status of an event is always calculated in accordance with an event rule. These rules are defined during configuration in the technical monitoring area. As you can see in Figure 5.13, three different event rules are available for selection. The traffic lights on the left-hand side represent values for two metrics. You can use the configuration to determine which status the event on the right-hand side should have on the basis of the values available.

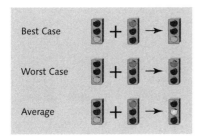

Figure 5.13 Event Rules

Alerts

An *alert* occurs as soon as the threshold is reached, something changes, or an error occurs. An alert is characterized by the following properties:

- ▸ It is an object that represents a specific situation that requires a response.
- ▸ It has several attributes (for example, status, category, description, and so on).
- ▸ It can be triggered only by an event.
- ▸ It is assigned to a category.

Metrics, Events, and the Alerts Hierarchy

Metrics, events, and alerts have a hierarchical relationship with each other. First of all, one or more metrics (depending on the defined event rule) determine the status of an event, which in turn determines whether an alert is triggered.

The ABAP instance availability example, shown in Figure 5.14), demonstrates this hierarchical dependency very well. In this example, an event comprises three metrics that deliver information about the status and availability of an instance. By default, a "worst-case" event rule is applied here. In other words, if at least one of these metrics is reported as "not available," the entire event obtains the red status. If an event has the red status, the alert ABAP INSTANCE NOT AVAILABLE appears in the alert inbox.

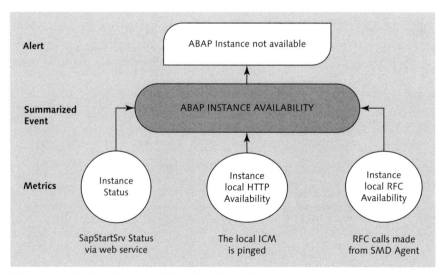

Figure 5.14 Metrics, Events, and the Alerts Hierarchy

5.3.4 Alert Consumer Connector

SAP Solution Manager release 7.1 and its infrastructure provide various alert methods. You can also contact different alert consumers.

In addition to the central alert inbox, which lists all alerts and has a real-time monitoring tool as a graphical interface, you can also set up automatic notifications via email or SMS in the standard delivery. As a result of integration with the Service Desk, incident messages can be generated automatically in the event of an alert. Furthermore, the BAdI interface can be used to transfer alerts to non-SAP alert consumers, as shown in Figure 5.15.

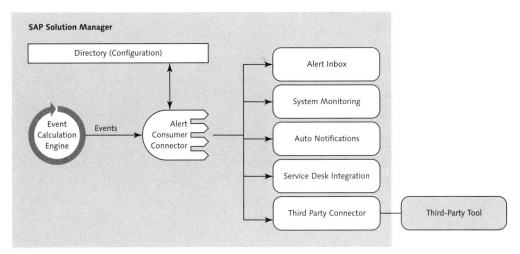

Figure 5.15 Alert Consumer

An alert consumer receives a new event from the Event Calculation Engine. Then, a decision is made about whether a new alert is to be created or an existing alert updated in the alert group (see also the "Alert Group View" subsection in Section 5.5.2). At the same time, the alert information is stored in the Alert Store.

First, the Alert Consumer Connector forwards all alerts to the alert inbox and the system monitoring UI. The current overall status of a system or the status of each individual metric is displayed there immediately. Furthermore, if additional alert consumers have been configured, the Alert Consumer Connector forwards alerts to any consumer (for example, the relevant employee) by email.

5.3.5 Template Concept for Monitoring System Components

The *template concept* is an integral part of technical monitoring. This concept makes it easy to configure monitoring. It also enables you to add a system to monitoring in just a few steps.

You may be wondering what a template is in this context. Templates are automatically delivered with the technical monitoring content. In other words, these templates in SAP Solution Manager 7.1 are already contained in the standard delivery. A template comprises SAP's best practices and standards for monitoring a system. Strictly speaking, a template is a collection of metrics that can be used for a particular product. These metrics are preconfigured, contain certain thresholds, already have an assigned data provider, belong to a certain alerts hierarchy, and so on. Consequently, they are known as *SAP standard templates*.

When you start to set up technical monitoring, you will find a range of SAP standard templates, which can be used immediately. A template always belongs to a category that maps a component (for example, a database in the system landscape). A total of four categories are available: Hosts, Databases, Instances, and Systems. Together, these categories form a technical scenario in system monitoring.

Each category contains SAP standard templates that represent a certain product, as shown in Figure 5.16. The Hosts category, for example, contains SAP standard templates for Microsoft Windows, Linux, and Solaris. As a result, the administrator can activate a scenario in just three clicks:

1. System selection
2. Automatic assignment of templates
3. Template activation

Once you have selected the relevant system, the SAP standard templates are assigned automatically. The system-specific information in the Landscape Management Database (LMDB) determines which templates are assigned. For this reason, it is important that the systems are maintained correctly in the LMDB.

The SAP standard templates are updated regularly. This occurs automatically with the Service Content Update provided by SAP. Furthermore, the option exists to transport templates (for example, from an SAP Solution Manager development system into the production system). In their original state, the SAP standard templates are not very flexible. However, they can be easily adjusted or enhanced by copying them into customer templates.

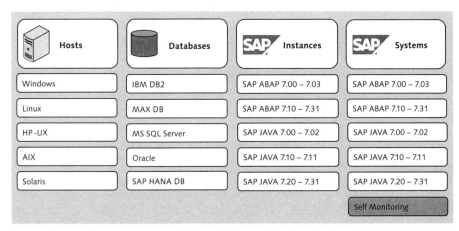

Hosts	Databases	SAP Instances	SAP Systems
Windows	IBM DB2	SAP ABAP 7.00 – 7.03	SAP ABAP 7.00 – 7.03
Linux	MAX DB	SAP ABAP 7.10 – 7.31	SAP ABAP 7.10 – 7.31
HP-UX	MS SQL Server	SAP JAVA 7.00 – 7.02	SAP JAVA 7.00 – 7.02
AIX	Oracle	SAP JAVA 7.10 – 7.11	SAP JAVA 7.10 – 7.11
Solaris	SAP HANA DB	SAP JAVA 7.20 – 7.31	SAP JAVA 7.20 – 7.31
			Self Monitoring

Figure 5.16 Categories for SAP Standard Templates

Characteristics of SAP Standard Templates

SAP standard templates are characterized by the following:

▶ They are automatically provided by SAP.

▶ They are automatically assigned to installed product releases of a managed object.

▶ They contain standard definitions for alerts, metrics, and events.

▶ They contain settings for incident management.

▶ They contain settings for automatic notifications.

Unlike a standard template, you can freely configure customer templates to your requirements. Almost all options are available to you here. These range from changing thresholds to creating your own metrics and alerts.

Characteristics of Customer Templates

Customer templates have the following characteristics:

▶ They contain changes and enhancements to SAP standard templates.

▶ They can be assigned to several managed objects.

▶ They can be used to create, activate, or deactivate alerts, metrics, and events.

▶ They can be used to change alert behavior settings (for example, automatic notifications).

▶ They can be used to change thresholds.

▶ They can be used to change text or add links for analysis purposes.

You can use template maintenance to create as many customer templates as you like. Depending on the concept you apply, you can reuse a template for several systems or assign different versions of a template to the same system (for example, the development and production system). Therefore, if the same components occur in your system landscape several times (for example, ABAP systems with the same ABAP version), you can in theory apply one template to all these systems in monitoring.

Template Hierarchy

The templates are arranged hierarchically, as shown in Figure 5.17.

SAP standard templates, which can be activated without too much time and effort, form the first hierarchy level. If you want to adjust the template according to your requirements, you must first create a customer template, which is merely a copy of the standard template. Customer templates form the second hierarchy level.

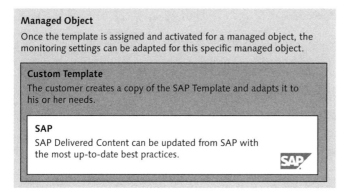

Managed Object
Once the template is assigned and activated for a managed object, the monitoring settings can be adapted for this specific managed object.

Custom Template
The customer creates a copy of the SAP Template and adapts it to his or her needs.

SAP
SAP Delivered Content can be updated from SAP with the most up-to-date best practices.

Figure 5.17 Template Hierarchy

A further option for adjusting templates is available on the third hierarchy level. Once you've assigned your customer templates to the relevant system, you can change them again before activating them. The settings you make at this third level apply only to the managed object you have selected. In other words, the original settings from the customer template are overwritten, but this is only visible for the object selected.

The configuration for an AS ABAP system in a system landscape with a development system and a production system can look as follows (see Figure 5.18):

▶ You copy an SAP standard template to a customer template.

▶ One customer template contains the configuration for development systems:

- ▶ Monitoring critical alerts and system exceptions
- ▶ Higher thresholds
- ▶ Service Desk integration deactivated

▶ A second customer template is created for production systems:

- ▶ Activation of all metrics
- ▶ Lower thresholds
- ▶ Use of Service Desk integration
- ▶ Activation of automatic notifications

The example in Figure 5.18 only broadly outlines how templates can be designed and created. In Section 5.4.4, we will explain in detail how you can design templates according to your requirements.

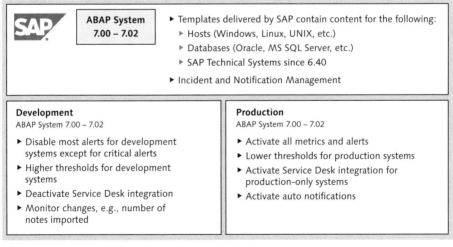

Figure 5.18 Template Concept

In addition to the template hierarchy just described, there's another three-level structure, which can be used to configure templates. Here, you can make configurations for the following special use cases:

▶ Incidents

▶ Notifications

▶ Third-party components

▶ Work modes

These use cases can be configured at the following levels:

▶ **Global settings**
Global settings are configured in Transaction SOLMAN_SETUP • TECHNICAL MONITORING WORK CENTER • SYSTEM MONITORING • CONFIGURE INFRASTRUCTURE. They are used as default values if no specific settings have been defined at the template or alert level.

▶ **Template settings**
Template settings form the second level. These settings are made directly in the template. Consequently, they overwrite the global entries.

▶ **Alert settings**
Alert settings form the third level and are available on the ALERTS tab page within a template. This procedure overwrites both global and template-specific settings. A detailed description of template maintenance is available in Section 5.4.4.

5.4   Technical Monitoring Configuration

Once you've fulfilled all the necessary prerequisites (including executing the basic configuration, connecting the relevant systems, and installing diagnostics agents), you can start to configure technical monitoring.

The starting point for the configuration is the SAP SOLUTION MANAGER CONFIGURATION work center (Transaction SOLMAN_SETUP). In the navigation area, choose TECHNICAL MONITORING. Then, choose SYSTEM MONITORING from the selection options available on the left-hand side of the screen.

5.4.1 Overview

The first step, OVERVIEW, is the initial screen for configuring system monitoring (see Figure 5.19). System monitoring involves monitoring technical systems, databases, and hosts. The status icon colors represent the monitoring infrastructure's current configuration status. You can use the links in the OVERVIEW area on the right-hand side of the screen to navigate to the next step, where you will check or change the infrastructure's configuration. Alternatively, you can use them to navigate to the initial screen for configuring system monitoring for a technical scenario (system, database, or host).

Figure 5.19 Technical Monitoring—Setup—Overview

5.4.2 Configure Infrastructure

In the next configuration section, CONFIGURE INFRASTRUCTURE, the initial basic configuration for monitoring is implemented in several steps. In the STEPS area, you obtain an overview of the individual steps associated with this configuration section (see Figure 5.20). The following steps are configured here:

▶ CHECK PREREQUISITES

▶ CONFIGURE MANUALLY

▶ DEFAULT SETTINGS

- ► REPORTING—SETTINGS

- ► HOUSEKEEPING

- ► WORKMODE SETTINGS

- ► UPDATE CONTENT

If you want to navigate to a subitem, you can select the relevant step either in the navigation bar or directly in the STEPS area. For the very first configuration, we recommend that you do not skip any steps and instead use the PREVIOUS or NEXT buttons to navigate through the configuration.

Figure 5.20 Configure Infrastructure

Check Prerequisites

In this step, the system checks whether all the prerequisites for configuring the infrastructure have been fulfilled. The steps to be executed are displayed in the AUTOMATIC ACTIVITIES area (see Figure 5.21). You can execute either all steps simultaneously or only the step that you have selected.

In order to be able to execute the required activities, you must first switch to editing mode. To do this, choose EDIT and then EXECUTE ALL. After you have completed the checks, the status is displayed in the first column.

At any time, you can view the logs for all previous configuration steps and their status (see Figure 5.21).

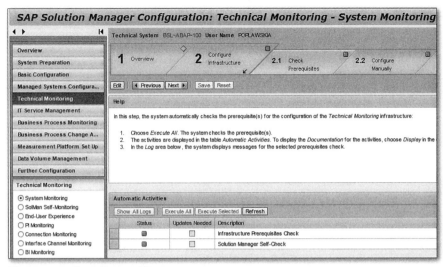

Figure 5.21 Check Prerequisites

In Figure 5.22, you see detailed information about each individual step. You can conduct analyses here if a check step does not have the green status. Once all the check results are positive and the overall status has been confirmed with the green status, continue with the next step.

Name	Value
▪ □ Specify Solution	Activity: Specify Solution from step: Specify Solution performed
▪ □ Maintain Connection	Activity: Maintain Connection from step: Specify Connectivity Data performed
▪ □ Setup BW System	Activity: Setup BW System from step: Specify SAP BW System performed
▪ □ Setup Credentials	Activity: Setup Credentials from step: Set Up Credentials performed
▪ □ Maintain SAPSUPPORT user	Activity: Maintain SAPSUPPORT user from step: Create Users performed
▪ □ Maintain BMC Appsight user	Activity: Maintain BMC Appsight user from step: Create Users performed
▪ □ Maintain SMD_RFC user	Activity: Maintain SMD_RFC user from step: Create Users performed
▪ □ Maintain SERVICE user	Activity: Maintain SERVICE user from step: Create Users performed
▪ □ Maintain BI_CALLBACK user	Activity: Maintain BI_CALLBACK user from step: Create Users performed
▪ □ Maintain EFWK user	Activity: Maintain EFWK user from step: Create Users performed
▪ □ Creates RFC connectivity (WEBADMIN)	Activity: Creates RFC connectivity (WEBADMIN) from step: Solution Manager Internal Connectivity performed

Display Message Context

Value: [   ] [Search] [Reset]

Figure 5.22 Check Prerequisites—Details

Configure Manually

In the manual setup, you decide which configuration activities and advanced configuration options are relevant for your scenario. In the Description column (see Figure 5.23), all optional steps have the word *optional* next to them in parentheses. The following manual activities are available:

- ▶ Agent Framework (optional)
- ▶ Extractor Framework (optional)
- ▶ Alerting Framework (optional)
- ▶ Content Customization

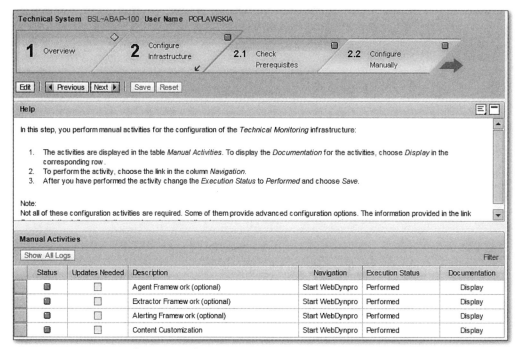

Figure 5.23 Configure Manually

The first three steps contain additional configuration options, which you can make in a separate window if you select the respective Start WebDynpro link.

Based on our experience, manual activities are generally not required here. Nevertheless, you should execute these steps to ensure that everything has been configured properly. Table 5.1 explains how these activities are used.

Configuration Step	Usage
AGENT FRAMEWORK	To display the current status of the diagnostics agents installed and, if necessary, change the assignment of roles to agents
EXTRACTOR FRAMEWORK	To manage scheduled extractors
ALERTING FRAMEWORK	To provide an overview of all Data Provider Collector extractors

Table 5.1 Technical Monitoring—Configure Manually

In the last manual step, CONTENT CUSTOMIZATION, you can configure how analysis reports, email, incident messages, and SMS messages are displayed for alerting purposes. For example, for each incident type, you can define which information modules will later be seen in the incident automatically created by the system. At the very least, you should check this step. The default settings have already been defined for these incidents. If necessary, you can adjust the first default setting in relation to how the incidents are displayed.

Choose START WEBDYNPRO to maintain the way alerting information is displayed. A new window opens. In the navigation area, you can select the relevant area whose content you want to adjust. In the same window, you can use the sample preview to see how the content of the incident message will change. Depending on the incident type, different settings can be made here. Furthermore, they can be made individually for each incident type.

Default Settings

This step deals with the settings for automatic notifications in technical monitoring. Here, you can define default settings that are valid for all monitoring templates. In this step, global settings are configured for automatic notifications or incidents, which we explained in Section 5.3.5.

This step comprises the following four tab pages: SUMMARY, INCIDENTS, NOTIFICATIONS, and THIRD-PARTY COMPONENTS. On the SUMMARY tab page, you can decide which of the available notification channels you want to use actively (see Figure 5.24). If you want to select an option, you must be in editing mode. If you select the ACTIVE option, the incident or notification is automatically created by means of an alert. If you deactivate this function, you can manually create the incident later, directly in the alert inbox.

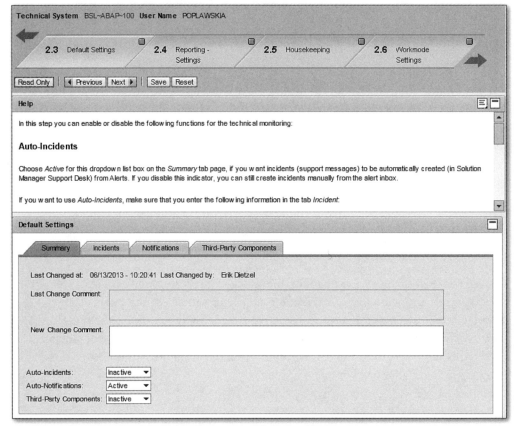

Figure 5.24 Default Settings—Summary

If you choose to use auto-incidents, you must make the necessary default settings on the INCIDENTS tab page (see Figure 5.25).

In order to make the necessary settings, select the ACTIVE option in the AUTO-INCIDENTS field, if it is not already preselected. You can then specify the support component to which you want the incident to be assigned. To do this, open the input help in the ASSIGNED SUPPORT COMPONENT field. A list of all available support components is displayed in a dialog box. You must also assign a suitable CRM TRANSACTION TYPE—for example, INCIDENT (IT SERVICE MANAGEMENT). If you also want to close the corresponding alert when closing an incident, activate the checkbox in the INCIDENT CONFIRMATION CLOSES ALERT field.

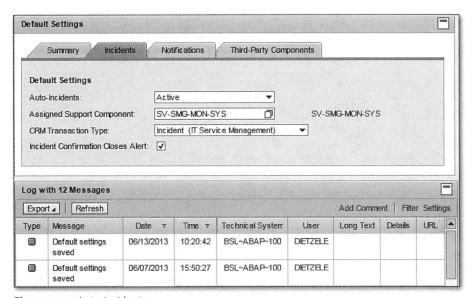

Figure 5.25 Auto-Incidents

If you want alerts to be sent in the form of emails or SMS messages, you can make the relevant notification settings on the NOTIFICATIONS tab page (see Figure 5.26). First, select the ACTIVE option in the AUTO-NOTIFICATIONS field, if it's not already preselected.

If you want to edit the recipients in notification management, they must already be available in a global recipient pool. This recipient pool contains the names of all users who can be used, among other things, for automatic notifications in technical monitoring. If you want to add a user to this recipient pool, select the link MY NOTIFICATION SETTINGS at the bottom of the screen. In the next dialog box, choose YES in response to the question asked. Your user is then added to the pool and available for selection there. If you want to see this pool of all available users, choose MAINTAIN GLOBAL RECIPIENTS. In this view, you can display or change the notification settings for the recipients. You can also add new recipients here.

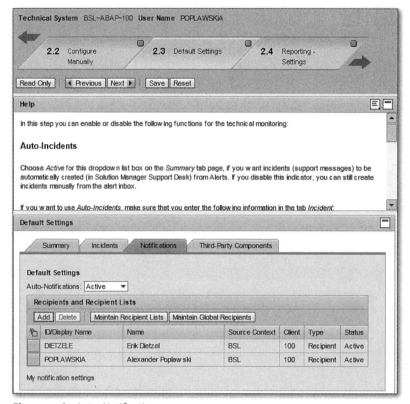

Figure 5.26 Auto-Notifications

Afterward, you can maintain notification-relevant settings for your own user, as shown on the WHEN PRESENT (ON-DUTY) tab page in Figure 5.27. In the STATUS field, you specify whether you want the user to be available as a recipient. Alternatively, you can select the FORWARD TO SUBSTITUTE option. In this case, the message is forwarded to a substitute. This is useful if, for example, the recipient is absent for a long period of time. In addition to the status, you can also select your current TIMEZONE.

Furthermore, you can decide what happens on regular workdays and standard absences, such as public holidays and weekends. Here, you can use the factory calendar and public holiday calendar to determine precisely when alerts are sent to the recipient (in other words, on which days and during which period). Conversely, you can also define days as non-working days.

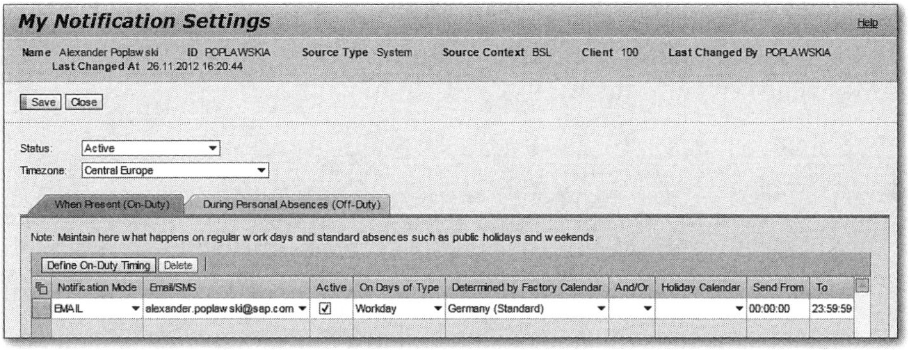

Figure 5.27 Notification Settings—On-Duty

On the second tab page, DURING PERSONAL ABSENCES (OFF-DUTY), you define what happens when a recipient is absent (for example, due to vacation leave) (see Figure 5.28). Choose CREATE ABSENCE here and specify the period for the planned absence. If necessary, you can also add a substitute who will receive notifications while the recipient is absent. To do this, choose ADD SUBSTITUTE.

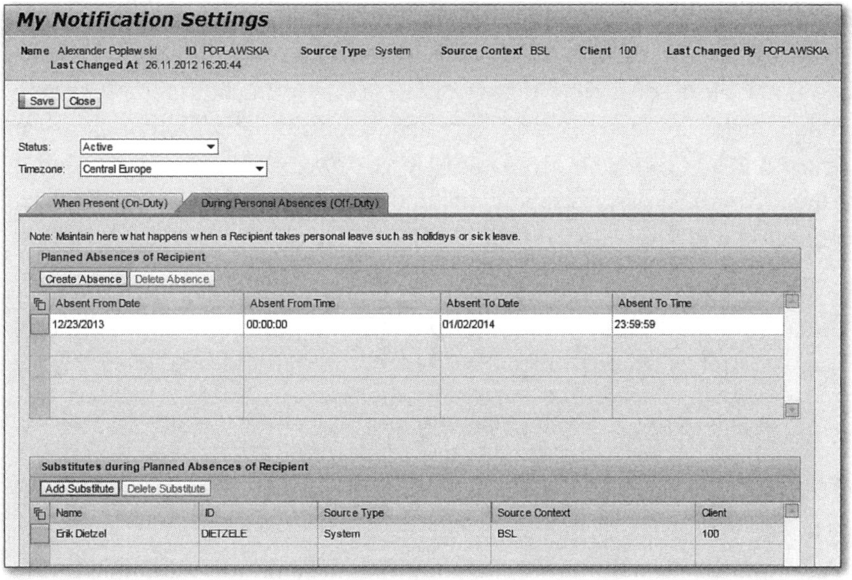

Figure 5.28 Notification Settings—Off-Duty

You also have the option to group individual recipients into a recipient list. For example, you can map teams that are responsible for entire areas or components.

Select the NOTIFICATIONS tab here and choose MAINTAIN RECIPIENT LISTS. Figure 5.29 shows an example of recipient lists that can be edited. You can also choose CREATE to add new recipient lists.

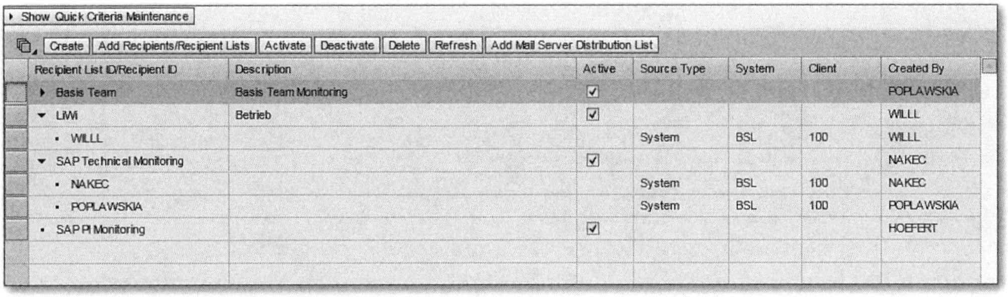

Recipient List ID/Recipient ID	Description	Active	Source Type	System	Client	Created By
▶ Basis Team	Basis Team Monitoring	☑				POPLAWSKIA
▼ LiWi	Betrieb	☑				WILLL
• WILLL			System	BSL	100	WILLL
▼ SAP Technical Monitoring		☑				NAKEC
• NAKEC			System	BSL	100	NAKEC
• POPLAWSKIA			System	BSL	100	POPLAWSKIA
• SAP PI Monitoring		☑				HOEFERT

(toolbar: Create | Add Recipients/Recipient Lists | Activate | Deactivate | Delete | Refresh | Add Mail Server Distribution List)

Figure 5.29 Recipient Lists

Finally, on the NOTIFICATIONS tab page, you can choose ADD to supplement the recipients or recipient lists created and then use them as a default setting for notifications.

In SAP Solution Manager 7.1, the BAdI interface enables you to use non-SAP products in the TECHNICAL MONITORING work center. You can therefore implement additional alert consumers that are not contained in the standard system. For example, incident messages can be created in a third-party tool, or alerts can be transferred to a console. On the THIRD-PARTY COMPONENTS tab page, you can activate the use of third-party components. In this view, you also specify the third-party connector and scope filter for the alert response that was added.

> **Note**
>
> Expert development knowledge is required in order to use the BAdI interface to implement a third-party component. Additional information is available at *http://wiki.sdn.sap.com/wiki/display/TechOps/System+Monitoring+-++Home.*

Reporting: Settings

The information collected during monitoring can also be prepared for the purpose of reporting historical values. To this end, additional configuration steps for reporting are required in SAP Solution Manager. One such step is the *health check*, which analyzes the current system status.

If you want to be able to activate BI Content for SAP NetWeaver Business Warehouse in SAP Solution Manager, you must ensure that a green STATUS is displayed for all components that undergo the health check. BI Content can be activated only if the health check does not return any errors. The results of the self-check for BI-based reporting are displayed in the REPORTING - SETTINGS step (see Figure 5.30).

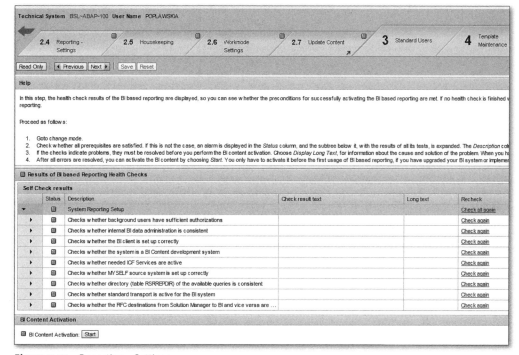

Figure 5.30 Reporting - Settings

In the lower SELF CHECK RESULTS area, each row has its own status. If problems occurred during the check, a red status icon is displayed. The areas that were checked are specified in the DESCRIPTION column. The LONG TEXT column contains further information about the cause of and solution to the problem that was reported.

Once all the checks have the green status, you can choose START to activate BI Content. Note that BI Content needs to be activated if you are performing BI-based reporting for the first time, if you have updated your BI system, or if you have implemented a new Support Package.

Housekeeping

In the next step, you determine the retention period for metrics in the SAP NetWeaver BW system and for data in the Alert Store and Event Store. This configuration step comprises two areas: LIFETIME OF DATA IN BI FOR EACH GRANULARITY and OPTIONS FOR HOUSEKEEPING, which are shown in Figure 5.31. You also have the option to retain the proposed default values for the lifetime and for housekeeping or to adjust them, if necessary.

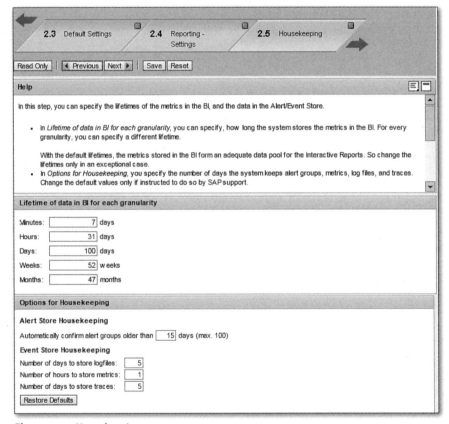

Figure 5.31 Housekeeping

In the LIFETIME OF DATA IN BI FOR EACH GRANULARITY area, a separate value can be defined for each granularity. In the example shown in Figure 5.31, the MINUTES value indicates that data is retained for seven days before being cleansed by the system. The default lifetime values are, therefore, preconfigured in such a way that the metrics saved in the SAP NetWeaver BW system can be used in an optimal manner for interactive reporting. However, you can shorten the lifetime of the selected granularity here (for example, the MINUTES value), thus enabling you to control and better restrict database growth.

In the OPTIONS FOR HOUSEKEEPING area, you can specify how long alert groups, metrics, log files, and traces are to be archived in the system. All values, including metrics, are specified in days, while you define the archiving period for metrics in hours.

Workmode Settings

In the WORKMODE SETTINGS step, you make work mode–specific settings that are relevant for monitoring. For each work mode, you can determine whether you want monitoring to be activated or deactivated. The actual work modes are maintained in the TECHNICAL ADMINISTRATION work center (see Section 7.6).

You can use work mode management to schedule and maintain work modes for the components you have selected. In the standard system, all available work modes are initially activated for monitoring and, as a result of integrating work mode management, included in technical monitoring at runtime.

The following monitoring settings for the work mode associated with monitored scenarios/systems are available for selection in technical monitoring:

- NO WORK MODE CONFIGURED
- PLANNED DOWNTIME
- PEAK BUSINESS HOURS
- NON-PEAK BUSINESS HOURS
- NON-BUSINESS HOURS
- MAINTENANCE

Configuring work modes can be an important means of reducing alerts, whereby the defined maintenance windows, core business hours, and so on are taken into account when monitoring systems. For example, you can use work mode management to prevent unnecessary alerts while planned backups or Support Package updates are being performed. Here, an alerting pause is inserted for the relevant system. You can also adjust the thresholds for work modes at the template level.

Update Content

The UPDATE CONTENT step is the final step in the CONFIGURE INFRASTRUCTURE section. Monitoring content plays an important role for all use cases in technical monitoring. After a new content version is imported, the entire content is updated for all use cases.

A separate content version exists for each Support Package. After a Support Package update in SAP Solution Manager (from example, from SP05 to SP06), the content version must also be adjusted accordingly. This activity is required in order to make changes available for the use cases (for example, new functions as well as new or updated templates). The latest content may contain minor changes, even though the content version is the same. In this case, you should download the updated content version and import it again.

In content administration, the following options are available to you (see Figure 5.32):

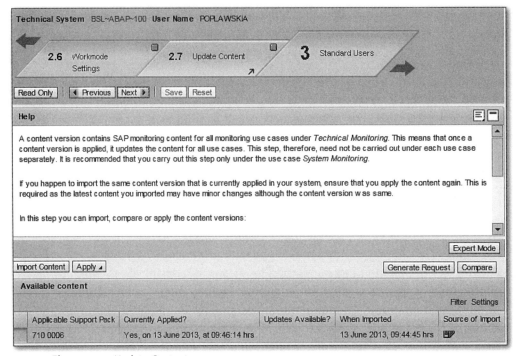

Figure 5.32 Update Content

- You can choose IMPORT CONTENT to import the content version you have selected.
- The APPLY button gives you two options:
  - If you select APPLY DIRECTLY, the downloaded content is applied without an impact analysis.
  - If you select APPLY WITH ANALYSIS, you can use an impact analysis to preview the effects associated with importing the content. You can then decide whether to apply the content.
- If you choose GENERATE REQUEST, a new tool opens. Here, you have the option to append the content to the transport request.
- If you choose COMPARE, you can compare different content versions of an SAP standard template with each other.

You can also perform a manual content update in EXPERT MODE. However, this option is not yet available in the current release of Support Package Stack 6.

5.4.3 Standard Users

The STANDARD USERS step, as shown in Figure 5.33, is an optional step in which you can create standard users for technical monitoring in SAP Solution Manager. This enables you to roll out recommended authorizations to predefined user groups. Here, users with a particular authorization profile can be created automatically.

In the ACTION field, you can choose among three options, the following two of which are relevant here:

- CREATE NEW USER
  The corresponding SAP roles are assigned to the user created. To do this, select the CREATE NEW USER option in the ACTION field. Enter the user and password, and then choose EXECUTE.
- SPECIFY EXISTING USER
  The system assigns the relevant roles. To do this, select the SPECIFY EXISTING USER option in the ACTION field. Enter the user and password, and then choose EXECUTE.

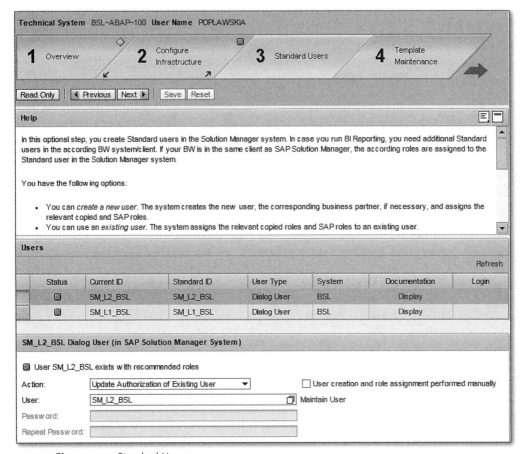

Figure 5.33 Standard Users

If your SAP NetWeaver BW client differs from the live SAP Solution Manager client or is located in a completely different system, you must assign BW-specific roles to the standard users in the respective BW client. In a standard BW scenario, this additional step is not necessary.

The following user templates can be used to create or assign a user: System Monitoring Level 1 (SM_L1_SID) and System Monitoring Level 2 (SM_L2_SID).

▶ The level 1 user is authorized to perform the following:

  ▶ Display alerts in the alert inbox (technical monitoring)

  ▶ Distribute alerts and close them at the alert type and alert group levels

- ▶ Create incidents and notifications
- ▶ Display the landscape browser
- ▶ In addition to the authorizations assigned to a level 1 user, a level 2 user is authorized to perform the following:
  - ▶ Call the TECHNICAL MONITORING and ROOT CAUSE ANALYSIS work centers
  - ▶ Display relevant alerts for SAP Solution Manager monitoring in the alert inbox
  - ▶ Perform connection monitoring and status monitoring
  - ▶ Process alerts and confirm them at the alert type and alert group levels
  - ▶ Perform root cause analysis
  - ▶ Perform problem context analysis
  - ▶ Create incidents and notifications
  - ▶ Log on to the managed system
  - ▶ Display the landscape browser

In some cases, the system may issue a warning indicating that these activities should be performed again as a result of a change within the system. To remove this warning, you must update the role assignment by selecting UPDATE AUTHORIZATION OF EXISTING USER in the ACTION field. Then, choose EXECUTE.

> **Note**
>
> If an additional copy of an SAP role exists, the system marks this role assignment as update-relevant after you have made the necessary user and role assignments, even though all roles are correctly assigned. You must therefore check the other copies of the relevant SAP role for essential updates. All users and user roles are merely templates.
>
> If your user definitions and processes deviate from the standard system, you must adjust the users, user roles, and their authorizations accordingly. Further information is available in the Security Guide at *http://service.sap.com/instguides* under INSTALLATION & UPGRADE GUIDES • SAP COMPONENTS • SAP SOLUTION MANAGER • RELEASE 7.1 • OPERATIONS.

The lower screen area contains a list of roles assigned to a user (see Figure 5.34).

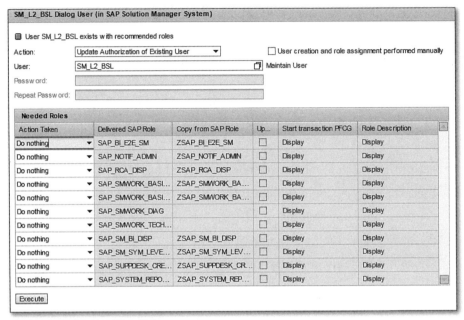

Figure 5.34 Standard User Roles

5.4.4 Template Maintenance

In Section 5.3.5, we described how system monitoring in the MAI is based on templates delivered by SAP by default. These SAP standard templates are preconfigured and can be used immediately. If you want to design templates according to your requirements, you can create customized templates.

To create or edit templates, choose CONFIGURATION EXPLORER in the TEMPLATE MAINTENANCE step. On the left-hand side of Configuration Explorer in the navigation bar, you see a list of all templates available for each managed object type (see Figure 5.35). A *managed object* represents a component (for example, a database) in your system landscape. A template exists for each product (for example, MaxDB for the "database" object type). Such templates have a standard configuration that contains metric, event, and alert values.

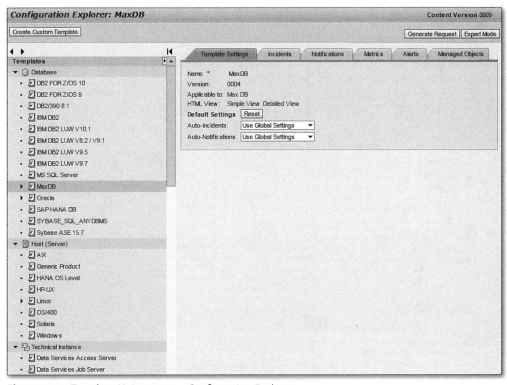

Figure 5.35 Template Maintenance—Configuration Explorer

You can also create customer templates, which are used as standard templates. To do this, select the required managed object type in the navigation bar. On the right-hand side, a list of standard templates for each product is displayed on the DEFAULT ASSIGNMENT tab page (see Figure 5.36). When you are in editing mode, you can change the default assignment by assigning your own customer template.

> **Note**
>
> If you activate monitoring for a system or scenario you have selected in the SETUP MONITORING step (see Section 5.4.6), SAP standard templates are automatically assigned by default. You can change this assignment, for example, by selecting your own templates on the DEFAULT ASSIGNMENT tab page.

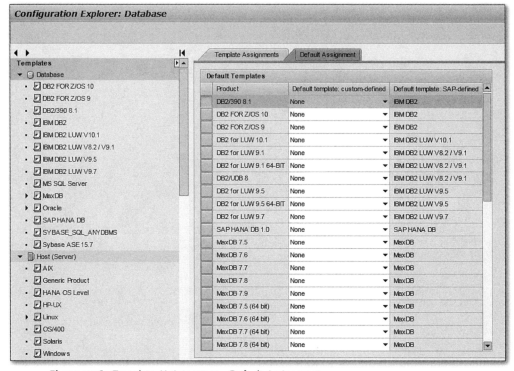

Figure 5.36 Template Maintenance—Default Assignment

Creating a Template

To create a customized template, follow these steps:

1. Go to the navigation bar and select the template you want to use as a basis for your customer template. For example, select DATABASE as a managed object and ORACLE as a product (see Figure 5.37).

2. Choose CREATE CUSTOM TEMPLATE.

3. Assign a development package to the template so that it can be stored there. This ensures that customized templates created in an SAP Solution Manager development system can later be transported to the production system. Alternatively, you can save the template in a local object. Choose SAVE to save the template. A dialog box in which you assign the template to a package (see Figure 5.38) opens. In our example, we have activated the LOCAL OBJECT checkbox. Choose OK to create the template for the product you require.

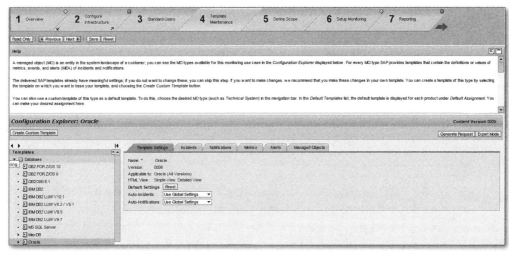

Figure 5.37 Creating a Template

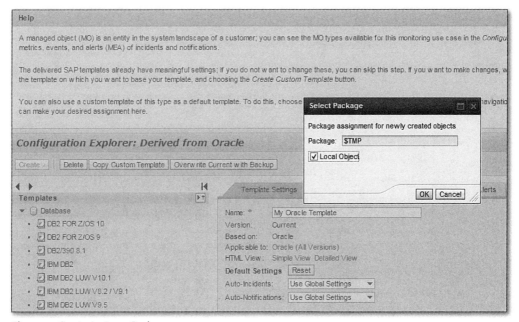

Figure 5.38 Assigning a Package

There are two modes available for editing templates, which we'll discuss in the following subsections: standard mode and expert mode. You can choose STANDARD MODE or EXPERT MODE to toggle between them.

Configuration in Standard Mode

In standard mode, you can define settings for automatic notifications, metrics, and alerts. By default, these are the settings defined in the DEFAULT SETTINGS substep within the CONFIGURE INFRASTRUCTURE step. Such settings are valid for all templates.

On the TEMPLATE SETTINGS tab page, you can see which settings are currently in use. On the other tab pages, namely INCIDENTS and NOTIFICATIONS, global settings can be overwritten with template-specific settings.

Metrics

As you can see in Figure 5.39, the METRICS tab page in Configuration Explorer contains a list of all metrics available. You can use such metrics when monitoring a managed object that you have selected.

Figure 5.39 "Metrics" Tab Page

You can also manage the metrics listed here. The MODIFIED column tells you which metrics have already been adjusted, and therefore deviate from the default settings. The original settings can be restored without any problems. To do this, select the metric you require and choose RESTORE SETTINGS. After you have selected a metric, additional tab pages become available in the lower screen area, as shown in Figure 5.40. Here, you can make detailed settings for individual metrics.

On the OVERVIEW tab page, you can add customer-specific descriptions to the standard text modules for a metric. In the description editor, you can insert symbols, URLs, or images that will enhance the text. In this area, you can, for example, create instructions for technical operations in the event that an alert is triggered. You can describe the next few steps for analyzing the incident. Alternatively, you can define responsibilities and additional information for the metric.

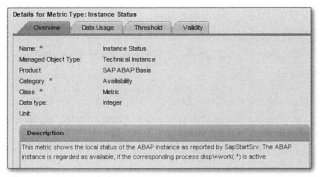

Figure 5.40 Details for Metric Type—Overview

On the second tab page, DATA USAGE, you define whether you want to send collected values to the EVENT CALCULATION ENGINE and SAP BUSINESS WAREHOUSE. Both options are selected by default.

Template Settings	Incidents	Notifications	Metrics	Alerts	Managed Objects		

Change Settings | Restore Settings

Description	Category	Active
• Instance Local Http Availability	Availability	☑
• Instance Local Logon Test	Availability	☑
• Instance Local RFC Availability	Availability	☑
• Instance Status	Availability	☑
• Frequency of Short Dumps [\min]	Exceptions	☑
• Frequency of System Log messages [/min]	Exceptions	☑
• Number of Short Dumps on instance	Exceptions	☑
• Number of Short Dumps on instance (Today)	Exceptions	☑
• Number of Short Dumps on instance (Yesterday)	Exceptions	☑
▶ Number of specific ABAP System Log Messages	Exceptions	☑

Details for Metric Type: Number of Short Dumps on instance

Overview	Data Usage	Threshold	Validity

Threshold Type : * Numeric Threshold (GtoY/YtoR/RtoY/Yto [i])
Monitored Value: Average Value
Trigger if value: exceeds threshold

▢	➡	△	5
△	➡	◉	10
△	⬅	◉	7
▢	⬅	△	3

Figure 5.41 Details for Metric Type—Threshold

Figure 5.41 shows the THRESHOLD tab page. The threshold type currently in use is displayed here. You can also change it, if necessary. If you select the information icon (🛈) next to the threshold type you have selected, a detailed description is provided. Here, you can also determine which value (for example, the average value or maximum value) is monitored and when an alert is to be triggered (for example, if the value is exceeded).

On the VALIDITY tab page, you can define whether the metric selected is to be considered for all scenarios or only in one particular case. All scenarios are considered by default.

Alerts

The ALERTS tab page in Configuration Explorer displays a list of all alerts that can be triggered for the managed object. A description of an alert is provided in Section 5.3.3. In the list of alert types available (see Figure 5.42), you can choose which settings applied to the template for incidents and notifications are to be overwritten.

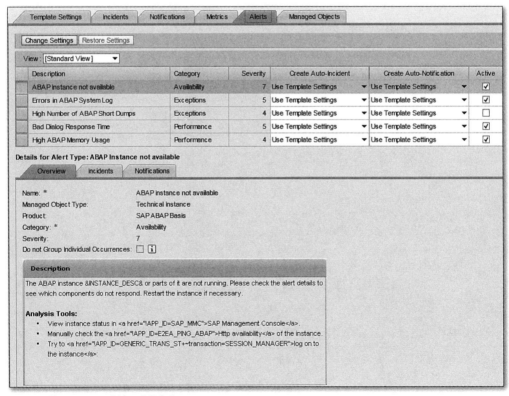

Figure 5.42 "Alerts" Tab Page

Managed Objects

On the last tab page, MANAGED OBJECTS, you see which managed objects have already been assigned to this template, along with their respective statuses. A green status in the ASSIGNMENT STATUS column indicates that the corresponding managed object was activated successfully (see Figure 5.43). If, on the other hand, a yellow status is displayed, a reconfiguration is required. Lastly, a red status indicates that the assignment is incorrect.

Figure 5.43   "Managed Objects" Tab Page

Configuration in Expert Mode

Expert mode provides you with an advanced configuration option for customer templates. In addition to the options described in standard mode, you can define different work modes on the TEMPLATE SETTINGS tab page and determine what is to happen with auto-notifications and auto-incidents.

In addition to the INCIDENTS and NOTIFICATIONS tab pages, you can change the default values or overwrite the global settings on the THIRD-PARTY COMPONENTS tab page. Additional expert settings are available to you on the METRICS tab page. On the DATA COLLECTION tab page, you can view data provider and data collector parameters for individual metrics and change them, if necessary (see Figure 5.44). The data provider determines which parameters are selected.

The use of customer templates makes it possible for you to add your own metrics (for example, a metric from the CCMS). All required settings must be made in expert mode.

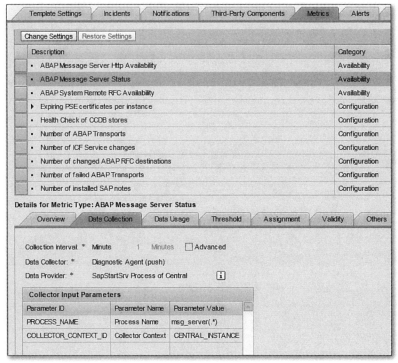

Figure 5.44 Details for Metric Type—Data Collection

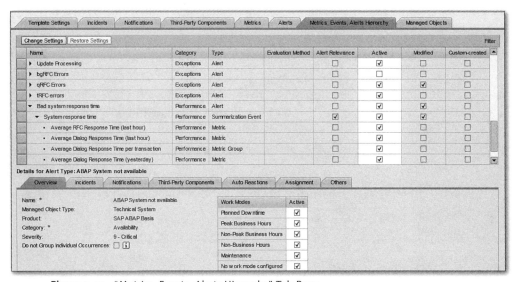

Figure 5.45 "Metrics, Events, Alerts Hierarchy" Tab Page

A further tab page, METRICS, EVENTS, ALERTS HIERARCHY, is displayed in this mode (see Figure 5.45). In this view, you see the relationship among alerts, metrics, and events (see the "Metrics, Events, and the Alerts Hierarchy" subsection in Section 5.3.3). In the EVALUATION METHOD column, you see which event rule is currently in use.

Adding Metrics and Alerts

Sometimes, the metric you want to see in technical monitoring is not contained in the SAP standard template. In the customer template, you have the option to create your own metrics or alerts. In this section, we will use the example of a CCMS metric to explain how you can map your own metric in the MAI.

Determining the MTE Class and Data Collector

Since the values for each metric are collected by a data provider, you must first determine which data provider will deliver the metric you require. In this case, we want to use the content from CCMS Monitoring. The RFC Pull collector type is responsible for this (see Section 5.3.2).

In order to map the CCMS metric in technical monitoring, you require the corresponding MTE class (Monitoring Tree Element). You can use Transaction RZ20 to see which metrics are available to you in CCMS Monitoring (see Figure 5.46). It is important that this metric (or the associated MTE class) in Transaction RZ20 is filled with data regularly.

In addition to the name of the MTE class, the following properties may play a role when creating metrics:

▶ Object name
▶ Instance
▶ Attribute name
▶ Granularity

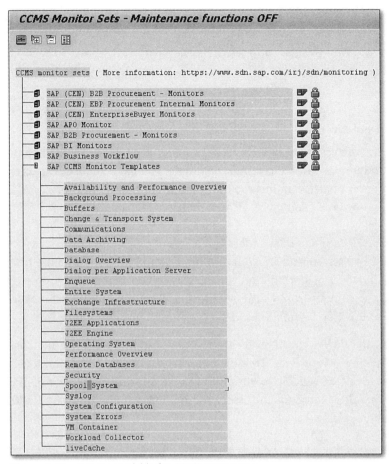

Figure 5.46 Metrics Available for CCMS Monitoring

Apart from granularity, you can find these properties of the MTE classes as follows: find the relevant MTE class, select it, and choose PROPERTIES in the upper menu bar (see Figure 5.47). In our example, we selected the MTE class QUEUE LENGTH. The MONITORING: PROPERTIES AND METHODS view opens (see Figure 5.48). The full name of the MTE you have selected is displayed in the PROPERTIES OF field. This name comprises the following:

<system ID>\<context name>\ <path element>\<object name>\<attribute name>.

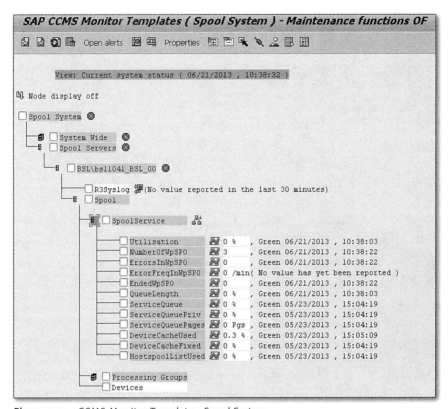

Figure 5.47 CCMS Monitor Template—Spool System

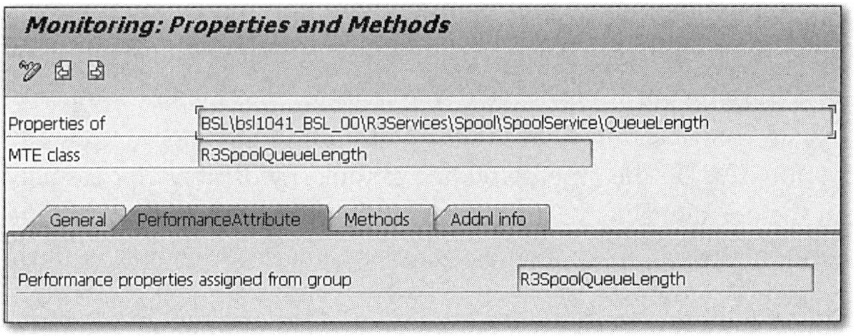

Figure 5.48 MTE Properties

Table 5.2 shows you the properties that make up our example and provides a description of each.

Element	Example	Description/Notes
<System ID>	BSL	Local system ID
<Context name>		In the case of an instance metric, the context contains the name of the instance. In the case of a system metric, it may contain something else.
<Path element>	R3Services\Spool	A CCMS metric can have one or more path elements, or none at all.
<Object name>	SpoolService	Name of the object
<Attribute name>	QueueLength	Name of the attribute

Table 5.2 MTE Properties

Note

The name of the MTE class is not contained in the structure described here. Instead, it is displayed separately in the MTE CLASS field. In our example, this is R3SPOOLQUEUELENGTH.

When implementing the metric, it is also necessary to specify the granularity of this metric. In other words, you must define the time interval during which the metrics are collected. The default value is five minutes. Setting a granularity of less than five minutes is useful only in extremely rare cases because the *DPC infrastructure* (Data Provider Connector) does not call the data providers more frequently than every five minutes. On the other hand, the granularity of an MTE class may be greater than the default value. In this case, you should adjust this value in the template. Otherwise, the status of a metric is queried unnecessarily often without a change to the object.

To ascertain whether longer times may be required for the granularity, you should check this value in CCMS Monitoring. To do this, choose DISPLAY DETAILS (⧉). In the SMOOTHED PERFORMANCE VALUES OF THE LAST 30 MINUTES table, you can now see the frequency with which these values exist (see Figure 5.49). In our example, you can see that the value is delivered only every ten minutes, which in turn signifies that the default value for our template should be adjusted.

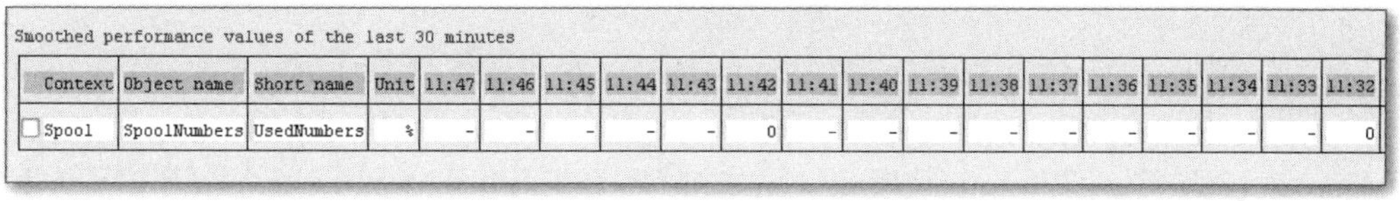

Smoothed performance values of the last 30 minutes																		
Context	Object name	Short name	Unit	11:47	11:46	11:45	11:44	11:43	11:42	11:41	11:40	11:39	11:38	11:37	11:36	11:35	11:34	11:33	11:32
☐ Spool	SpoolNumbers	UsedNumbers	%	-	-	-	-	-	0	-	-	-	-	-	-	-	-	-	0

Figure 5.49 MTE Granularity

Selecting Data Providers

In Table 5.3, you see the CCMS data providers available for the collector type RFC Pull.

Name of Data Provider	Description	Implementation of Data Provider	Parameter
CCMS Get Current Values (Pull)	Gets current values from the MTE class	/SDF/E2E_CCMS_MTE_CURRENT	CONTEXT MTE_CLASS
CCMS MTE (Pull)	Gets information from the CCMS (name of the MTE class)	/SDF/E2E_CCMS_MTE	MTE_CLASS GRANULARITY INSTANCE
CCMS MTE + Object name (Pull)	Gets information from the CCMS (name of the MTE class and object)	/SDF/E2E_CCMS_MTE	KEY_FIGURE OBJECT_NAME GRANULARITY INSTANCE
CCMS System wide MTEs (Pull)	Receives information from the CCMS (name of the MTE class and object for system-wide metrics)	/SDF/E2E_CCMS_MTE	MTE_CLASS OBJECT_NAME GRANULARITY

Table 5.3 Overview of MTE Data Providers

The data provider implementation /SDF/E2E_CCMS_MTE can be used for numeric values. This data provider always expects the following input: MTE class and granularity.

277

The second data provider type, /SDF/E2E_CCMS_MTE_CURRENT, always delivers the current MTE value. In addition to the numeric values, it can also return text values and the status of MTEs.

Creating a Metric—Defining a Parameter

Now that you have "identified" the metric you require, you can create this metric. To do this, switch to editing mode in Configuration Explorer, and then to expert mode. In the left screen area, select the customer template you want to edit. To do this, choose CREATE on the left-hand side of Configuration Explorer (see Figure 5.50). In the dropdown menu, select METRIC to create a new metric.

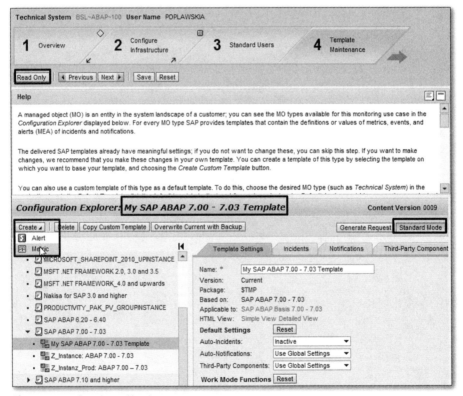

Figure 5.50 Creating a Metric

After you have made your selection, a custom metric creation wizard is displayed (see Figure 5.51). Here, you are prompted, step by step, to maintain all relevant parameters. We will use the SPOOL SERVICE QUEUE metric as an example of a CCMS metric (see Figure 5.51). The CCMS metric can exist at the instance or system level. An instance metric must be created in the *Technical Instance* template, while a system metric must be created in the *Technical System* template.

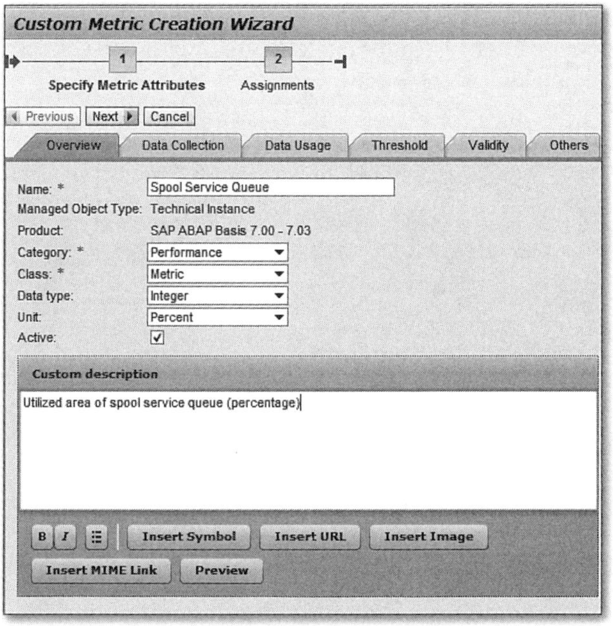

Figure 5.51 Metric Creation Wizard: Overview

For the purpose of our example, we will use the instance-specific MTE for the SPOOL SERVICE QUEUE, which is located in the MTE node for the instance name in Transaction RZ20.

On the first tab page, OVERVIEW, you must enter the following parameters (see Figure 5.51):

▸ Name of the metric

▸ Category

▸ Class

▸ Data type

▸ Unit (optional)

You can also maintain your own description for the metric in the CUSTOM DESCRIPTION area.

On the second tab page, DATA COLLECTION, you define the DATA COLLECTOR, DATA PROVIDER, and COLLECTION INTERVAL (see Figure 5.52). Here, you must find the right data collector and corresponding data provider so that the values are collected properly. For the DATA COLLECTOR input parameter, the MTE class and granularity are specified in the PARAMETER VALUE column. Since this concerns a metric at instance level, the INSTANCE parameter is automatically filled with the variable $INSTANCE_DESC$.

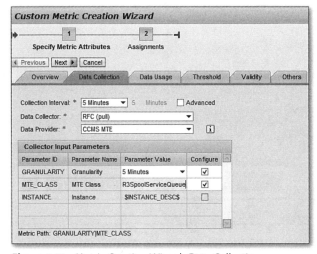

Figure 5.52 Metric Creation Wizard: Data Collection

On the next tab page, DATA USAGE, you can use two checkboxes to decide whether the new metric is to be available for monitoring (SEND VALUES TO EVENT CALCULATION ENGINE) and/or reporting (SEND VALUES TO SAP NETWEAVER BUSINESS WAREHOUSE). Both options are activated by default (see Figure 5.53).

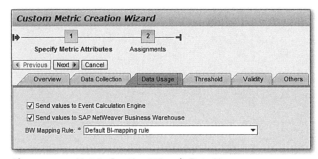

Figure 5.53 Metric Creation Wizard: Data Usage

Figure 5.54 shows the THRESHOLD tab page. It contains settings for the metric's thresholds. Since we want our metric to deliver numeric values, any numeric threshold type can be selected here.

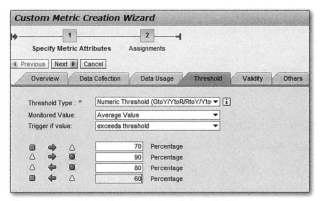

Figure 5.54 Metric Creation Wizard: Threshold

The VALIDITY tab page is shown in Figure 5.55. Here, you can specify precisely when the metric is to be taken into account. If you wish to specify additional conditions, activate the CHECK ADDITIONAL VALIDITY checkbox and select a restriction (for example, ONLY VALID FOR VIRTUAL HOSTS). In the standard delivery, the checkbox is deactivated and the metric is valid for all scenarios.

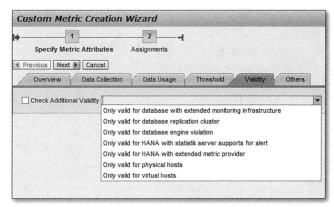

Figure 5.55 Metric Creation Wizard: Validity

On the last tab page, OTHERS, define the name of the metric in the TECHNICAL NAME field. As you can see in Figure 5.56, the name, which is saved in the customer namespace, starts with the letter Z.

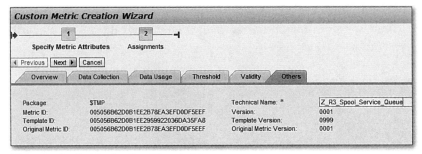

Figure 5.56 Metric Creation Wizard: Others

Then, choose NEXT to assign the metric to an alert. Since an alert has not been created yet, the list is blank. Therefore, save the changes and exit the wizard.

The metric is now visible in the template you have selected. It is also selected in the CUSTOM-CREATED column (see Figure 5.57). In the next step, we will create an alert in a similar way.

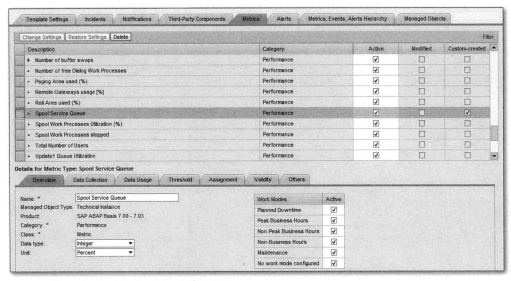

Figure 5.57 A Custom-Created Metric

Creating an Alert

Figure 5.58 shows the OVERVIEW tab page in the CUSTOM ALERT CREATION WIZARD. To call this wizard, navigate as follows: TEMPLATE MAINTENANCE • EDIT • EXPERT MODE • SELECT CUSTOMER TEMPLATE • CREATE • ALERT.

First, determine the alert's NAME and CATEGORY. When selecting the category for the alert, it's important to choose the category you specified when creating the metric. Otherwise, it won't be possible to assign the metric to the alert later because the category is the first evaluation criterion.

You can also specify the priority of the alert in the SEVERITY field and create a CUSTOM DESCRIPTION. The priority will play a role later in the alert inbox. The higher the priority, the higher the position in the list the alert occupies. When creating a description, you can use symbols and placeholders; for example, to ensure that a system's current SID is always displayed.

The next four tab pages—INCIDENTS, NOTIFICATIONS, THIRD-PARTY COMPONENTS, and AUTO REACTIONS—contain the settings for automatic notifications and incidents. You can maintain these settings now or later, on the ALERTS tab page in the template.

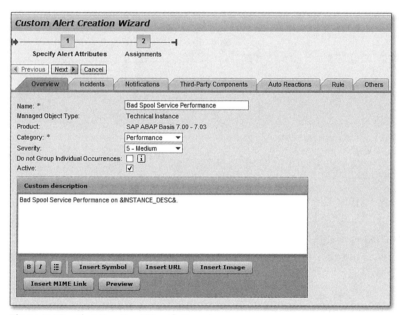

Figure 5.58 Alert Creation Wizard: Overview

The event rule is defined on the RULE tab page. In other words, you define when an alert is to be generated (see Figure 5.59). In the SAP standard templates, the "WORSTCASE RULE" is always defined in the RULE TYPE field. In this case, the worst value in the metric group determines the status of the event. Further information is available under the "Event" subsection in Section 5.3.3.

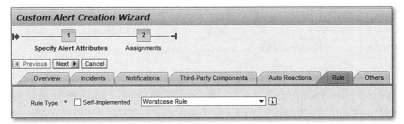

Figure 5.59 Alert Creation Wizard – Overview – Rule

On the last tab page, OTHERS, you enter the name of the alert in the ALERT NAME field. Ensure that this name is similar to the name you entered when you created the metric (see Figure 5.60).

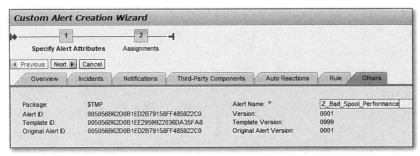

Figure 5.60 Alert Creation Wizard: Others

Finally, you have to link the metric and alert to each other.

In the final step within the wizard, ASSIGNMENTS (see Figure 5.61), you see, for example, the list of metrics to which an alert has yet to be assigned. In our example, the metric we created is automatically proposed for assignment because, at present, it's the only metric in the list. You can then choose FINISH to confirm the selection and save your changes.

Figure 5.61 Alert Creation Wizard: Assignments

In the alerts hierarchy, the alert is now displayed together with the metric (see Figure 5.62). As a final step, you should activate the templates for the required system, thus triggering the metric collection process. Further information is available below.

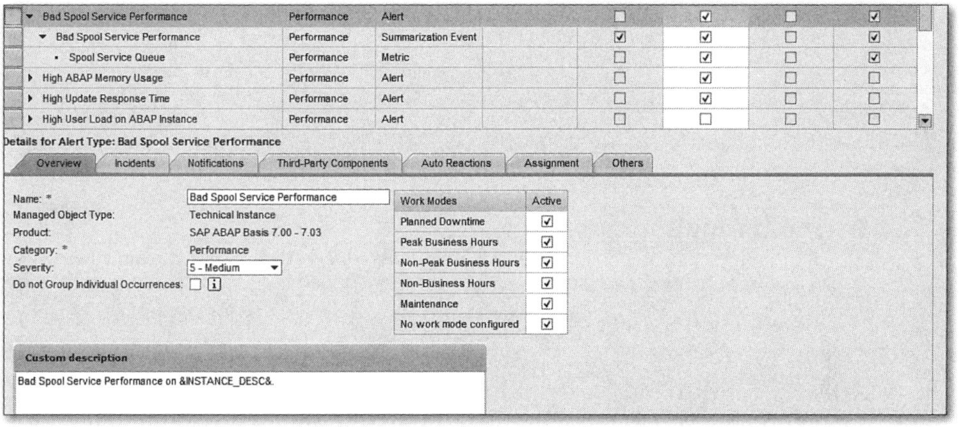

Figure 5.62 Custom-Created Alert

5.4.5 Define Scope

In the next step, we will select the objects to be managed, which will then be included in monitoring. This is done in the DEFINE SCOPE step, which is the fifth step in setting up technical monitoring (see Figure 5.63).

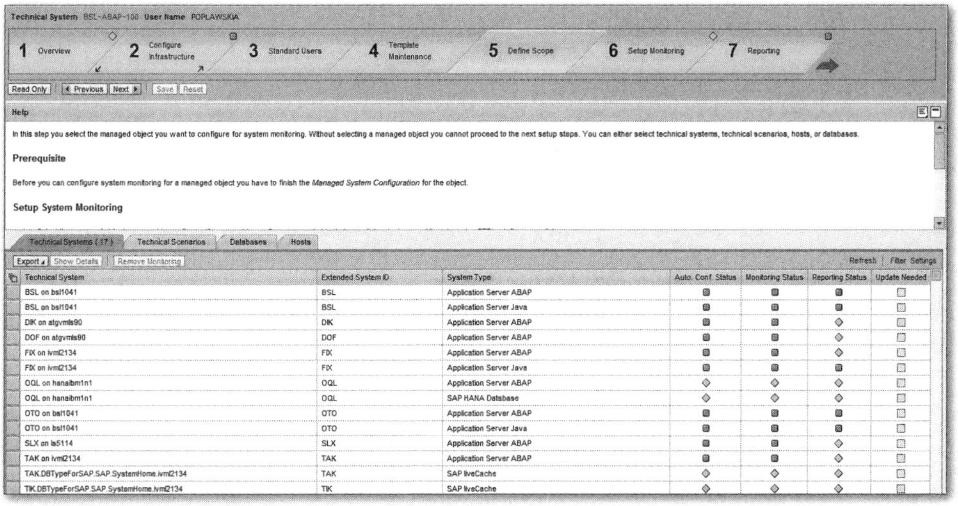

Figure 5.63 Define Scope

The screen displays a list of systems for which monitoring can be configured. It is important that the relevant system or object is fully connected to SAP Solution Manager (see Section 2.5.4). A total of four categories are available across the four tab pages: TECHNICAL SYSTEMS, TECHNICAL SCENARIOS, DATABASES, and HOSTS.

On the TECHNICAL SCENARIOS tab page, you have the option of grouping several objects together (for example, ABAP stack, Java stack, host, and database) and using all components simultaneously during activation. You access the next step only when you have selected at least one system or object. Choose NEXT to call the next step.

5.4.6 Setup Monitoring

Once you have selected the required system, you must assign a corresponding monitoring template to each component in the technical system (for example, the technical instance). By default, the template assignment is preconfigured in such a way that the SAP standard templates are automatically selected in the SETUP MONITORING step (see Figure 5.64). Choose APPLY AND ACTIVATE to confirm the template selection. Following successful activation, the data providers start to collect data for monitoring.

Figure 5.64 Setup Monitoring

In addition to purely activating monitoring, you can use the CONFIGURE MANAGED OBJECT link, which is displayed on the right-hand side of the lower half of the screen, to change the general template settings. Here, you can, among other things, deactivate a specific metric or adjust the thresholds (see Figure 5.65).

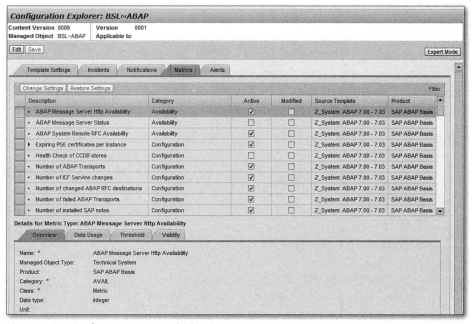

Figure 5.65 Configuring a Managed Object

In general, the settings you can maintain in template maintenance are also available to you here (see Section 5.4.4), the only difference being that the settings made here apply only to the objects selected, thus making it possible to overwrite the original values with object-specific individual values. However, the template itself remains unchanged.

5.4.7 Reporting

In the REPORTING step, you specify from which managed system the metrics are to be collected for interactive reporting. You do this by activating the checkbox next to the relevant object or system (see the first column in Figure 5.66). Then, choose ACTIVATE to apply the settings. At this point, data collection is activated for reporting only. For more information about data collection, see Chapter 8.

The REPORTING step concludes the technical configuration of the monitoring environment.

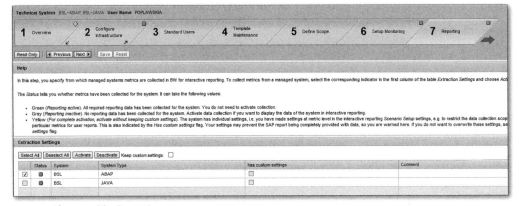

Figure 5.66 Reporting

5.4.8 Complete

In the COMPLETE step, you obtain a summary of all executed configuration steps, including their status (see Figure 5.67).

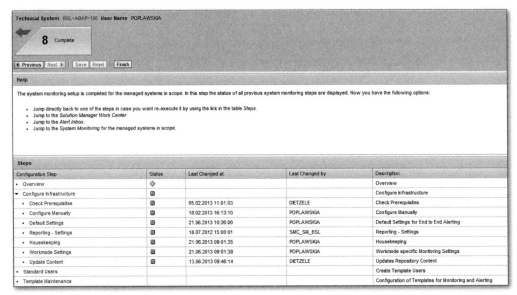

Figure 5.67 Complete

From here, you can navigate to different areas, for example:

▶ The relevant configuration step

▶ The SAP Solution Manager work center overview

▶ The alert inbox

▶ The system monitoring UI

5.5   Technical Monitoring Work Center

Now that you have configured technical monitoring, you can use the TECHNICAL MONITORING work center for all operational activities (for example, displaying the system status or analyzing alerts that have occurred).

The TECHNICAL MONITORING work center contains all areas of technical monitoring that can be used at runtime (see Figure 5.68). Here, you can, among other things, select the ALERT INBOX and SYSTEM MONITORING areas, which we will describe in greater detail below. All other areas of the TECHNICAL MONITORING work center will be explained in detail in Chapter 6.

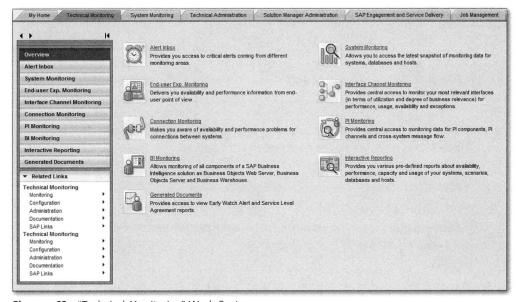

Figure 5.68   "Technical Monitoring" Work Center

5.5.1 System Monitoring—Monitoring UI

Once you have activated central system monitoring for a technical system or scenario, the current status of the managed object can be displayed in the SYSTEM MONITORING area. To do this, select the SYSTEM MONITORING link in the OVERVIEW area of the TECHNICAL MONITORING work center.

You can use the tabs displayed on the screen to select those system types you need (for example, ABAP SYSTEMS or JAVA SYSTEMS). By default, all systems are displayed (see Figure 5.69). You can also select several systems simultaneously. Furthermore, you can display the graphical interface in the same window or in a separate window. To make your selection, choose SYSTEM MONITORING. You can also choose WORKSTATION to call Introscope Enterprise Manager.

On the left-hand side of the screen, in the TYPE SELECTION area within the navigation area for the work center, you can change the system list by selecting the type you require (for example, SYSTEMS or HOSTS).

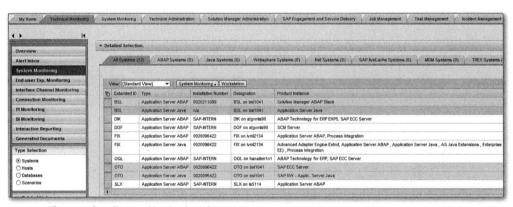

Figure 5.69 System Monitoring: Overview

System List

In the SYSTEM LIST area, the four categories we learned about earlier are displayed next to each system: AVAILABILITY, PERFORMANCE, CONFIGURATION, AND EXCEPTION (see Figure 5.70).

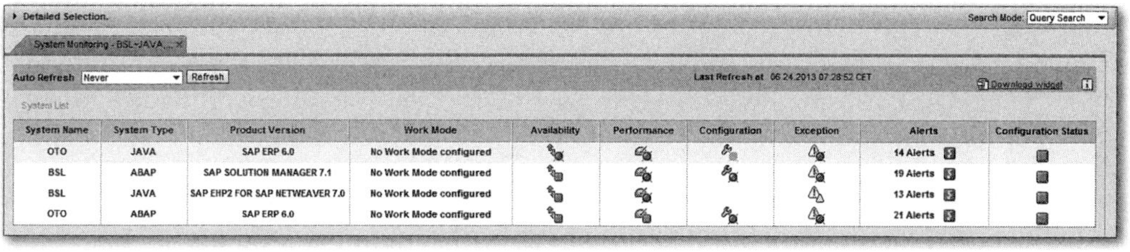

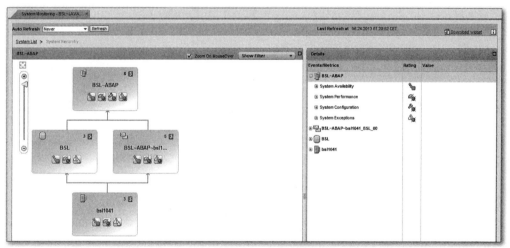

Figure 5.70 System List

The current overall status of each category is displayed in the list. This overall status represents the "critical" status recorded in each category. In addition, the ALERTS column states the number of alerts that have an open status in the alert inbox.

System Hierarchy

The next level in this graphical display is the SYSTEM HIERARCHY view. To access this view, select a system in the SYSTEM NAME column (see Figure 5.71).

Figure 5.71 System Hierarchy

On the left-hand side of this view, you see a complete overview of the current status of all components that belong to the technical system you have selected: technical system, technical instance(s), host, and database. Each box represents exactly one object. As the name of this view suggests, the hierarchical relationships among all managed objects are shown here. The uppermost level always represents the technical system, while the technical instances and the database are shown on the lower level. Finally, the hosts installed on the objects are shown on the third level. The corresponding categories and their overall status are displayed for each managed object.

The upper-right corner of the box contains the total number of alerts to be confirmed. If you choose the ALERT icon (⬛), you navigate directly to the alert inbox. We will skip this step for the moment because the functions and individual areas of the alert inbox will be discussed in the next section.

If you select the relevant category icons for system availability (🔧), performance (🔧), configuration (🔧), and exceptions (🔧), the EVENTS/METRICS view is called. Here, you see the status of the individual events and metrics that were configured in the templates.

Events/Metrics

The EVENTS/METRICS view contains detailed information about each metric (see Figure 5.72). The navigation bar is shown on the right-hand side of the screen. The events and associated status are shown for each category. When you expand the events, the individual metrics, currently reported status, and values collected are listed here.

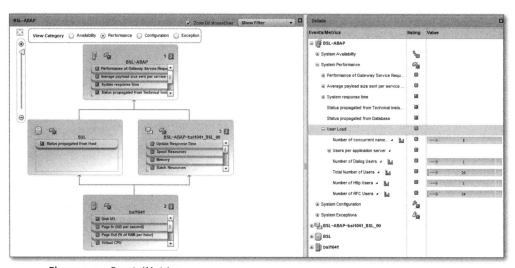

Figure 5.72 Events/Metrics

On the left-hand side, you can switch back and forth between the categories available, as well as select the required object and metric. The information displayed in the navigation bar then changes accordingly.

Metric Monitor

The metric monitor forms part of interactive reporting in technical monitoring. This tool becomes available to you as soon as you have activated monitoring and reporting in the setup for technical monitoring and stored, in SAP NetWeaver Business Warehouse, all monitoring values that have been collected. The metric monitor shows you the historical values for the selected metric. It does this in both graphical and tabular form, as shown in Figure 5.73.

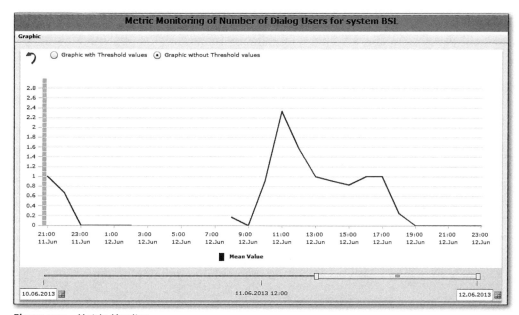

Figure 5.73 Metric Monitor

To call the tool, you can choose either INTERACTIVE REPORTING in the overview of the TECHNICAL MONITORING work center or the bar chart icon (🔊) next to the metric in the DETAILS area on the right-hand side of the screen, as shown in Figure 5.72.

This tool supports you in analyzing and evaluating historical data. By using curve graphs or the progression of values, you can promptly counteract any critical trends and risks.

5.5.2 Alert Inbox

To access the alert inbox, choose ALERT INBOX in the TECHNICAL MONITORING work center. It is the main entry point for monitoring. The alerts are stored in a structured manner within the alert inbox and sorted by category (for example, database-specific or host-specific alerts), thus enabling you to quickly obtain an overview of the current status.

The alert inbox comprises the following three levels or views, and facilitates a drilldown: *alert type view*, *alert group view*, and *detail view*.

Alert Type View

When you call the alert inbox, the first view displayed there is the alert type view in which all alerts that have occurred are listed together with their current and critical status (see Figure 5.74). In this window, you can decide how you need to proceed. Here, you can notify the relevant employees electronically or create an incident message, for example.

You can also add supplementary comments to alerts, postpone processing, and confirm and close alerts after the cause has been eliminated.

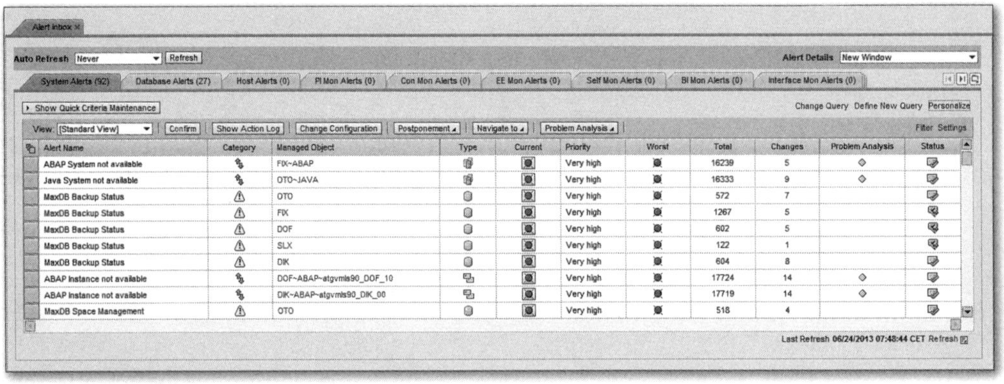

Figure 5.74 Alert Inbox: Alert Type View

Alert Group View

In order to prevent *alert flooding* (in other words, a flood of notifications and new alerts), a new mechanism has been implemented in the alert calculation process. Thanks to the concept of *alert groups*, alerts that relate to a monitoring object, come from the same event, and represent the same status are grouped together. Alerts are added up as long as, for example, a technical instance of a system in SAP Solution Manager is reported as "not available." In this case, the employee receives only one notification indicating that a technical instance is not available, even if the system determines this status every minute. If the status of an alert changes (for example, from red to yellow), a new alert group is created, and all relevant alerts are written to the new alert group as long as the status does not change again.

Therefore, in the second view (known as the *alert group view*), alerts are created only for each alert group. To call this view, select a particular alert name. Here, you can view all alert groups that exist for a specific alert (see Figure 5.75).

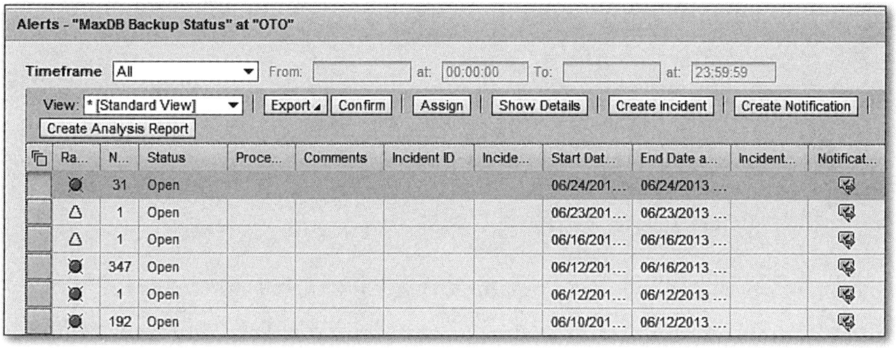

Figure 5.75 Alert Inbox: Alert Group View

Detail View

The detail view is the last view available in the drilldown menu of the alert inbox. It enables you to start a detailed analysis. To call the detail view, select the relevant group in the *alert group view* and choose SHOW DETAILS. Various analysis tools are available to you (for example, the metric monitor, the analysis report, or certain transactions on the satellite system; see Figure 5.76).

You can call the metric monitor by choosing the bar chart icon () next to the name of a metric contained in the table in the ALERT DETAILS area. The metric monitor is then started in a new window. When you select a metric, the analysis tools available (for example, E2E WORKLOAD ANALYSIS) appear in the METRIC DESCRIPTION area. Only those analysis tools available in or added to the metric description in setup monitoring are displayed for each metric. You can then choose CREATE ANALYSIS REPORT to call the analysis report.

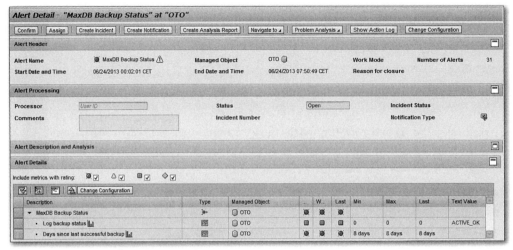

Figure 5.76 Alert Inbox: Detail View

5.6 Monitoring Concept at Toys Inc.

A *monitoring concept*, which is a document that contains all necessary monitoring information, should form the basis for all system monitoring. It includes a definition of the scope, a definition of the alerting methods, and a description of the areas of responsibility. Since implementation of system monitoring should be considered from the perspective of a project, it is important to document all steps in detail.

This section describes only key approaches that may be helpful when developing the monitoring concept. We will now use the system landscape of Toys Inc. to explain the individual areas of the monitoring concept. This book does not aim to provide the complete concept for monitoring your system landscape. Since the conceptual design differs from company to company, an individual approach is required. This, however, may depend on a number of influencing factors (for example, the use of different SAP or non-SAP components or company-specific requirements for system monitoring), which cannot be considered in this book, but nevertheless play a significant role in your system landscape.

The monitoring concept document contains all the details that are relevant for everyday use, ranging from a detailed description of the requirements for system monitoring to instructions for resolving a problem that occurs during monitoring. Since system monitoring is an ongoing process, this document should also be continuously amended to include changes or new developments in the monitoring environment. It is, therefore, important for this area to have a contact person who not only maintains changes in the document, but is also available to process change requests and decide whether such requested changes are necessary. In order to use the information from the monitoring concept as effectively as possible, the document should be stored in a central location so that all employees involved in the process can access it at all times without difficulty.

5.6.1 Requirements for System Monitoring

The requirements for system monitoring should be defined in the first section of the concept. First and foremost, all problems that occurred in the past should undergo analysis. A decision about whether these problems represent a risk to system operations in the future should be made on the basis of the analysis result. It is important to consider such points when creating the document and include them in the concept as requirements.

At Toys Inc., for example, there were times in the past when the absence of a database memory caused the systems to shut down.

5.6.2 System Landscape Documentation

The overview of the system landscape is another important part of the monitoring concept. At this point, everyone should make their own decision in terms of how detailed the system landscape description should be, as well as which form it should take. Of course, the current requirements will determine whether the entire system landscape or only one part is described. For example, at first, you may want to add only one particular production environment, which constitutes the company's core business, to monitoring. Alternatively, you may want to fully map the system landscape from the outset.

To ensure that the document remains clear, we recommend that you subdivide the system landscape into several areas, according to application component. One option is to create a separate table for each area (for example, systems, instances, databases, and hosts). Table 5.4 lists the SAP application components in use at Toys Inc.

Application Component	Product Release	SID	Installation Number	System Description
SAP ECC 6.0 EHP5	7.00	OTO	0020096422	Production system
SAP NetWeaver PI 7.3	7.31	FIX	0020096423	Production system
SAP SCM 7.0 EHP2	7.31	TAK	0020096424	Production system
SAP NetWeaver Portal 7.0	7.00	PEP	0020096422	Production system
...	...	...	...	...

Table 5.4 SAP System Landscape of Toys Inc.

Of course, you should also record any third-party products in use in your system landscape. Toys Inc. also uses non-SAP products in its landscape (see Table 5.5).

SID	Product/ Version	Maker	Server Name	Description
WAMA	WAMA/12	Outside AG	wamaber01	Warehouse Management System
XCH10	Exchange 2010	Microsoft	bslxchng06	Microsoft Exchange Server 2010

Table 5.5 Overview of Third-Party Products at Toys Inc.

In a second overview, we will group together all hardware information relating to the SAP components. Table 5.6 shows the hardware information for Toys Inc.

SID	Instance	Server Name	RAM in GB	CPU Frequency in MHz	Operating System/Version
OTO	bsl1041_OTO_02	bsl1041	10	2.300	Linux/SLES11
FIX	imlv2134_FIX_01	imlv2134	10	2.000	Linux/SLES1

Table 5.6 Overview of Hardware at Toys Inc.

SID	Instance	Server Name	RAM in GB	CPU Frequency in MHz	Operating System/Version
TAK	imlv2134_TAK_10	imlv2134	10	2.000	Linux/SLES11
PEP	abcpep01_PEP_10	abcpep01	8	1.600	Linux/SLES11
FIO	imlv2150_FIO_10	lmlv2150	10	2.000	Linux/SLES11

Table 5.6 Overview of Hardware at Toys Inc. (Cont.)

The databases used are listed next. The following information is worth mentioning here: the name and release of the databases, as well as the name of the server on which the databases are installed. Table 5.7 shows the database overview for Toys Inc.

SID	Database Server	DB System and Release
OTO	bsl1041	SAP MaxDB 7.8
FIX	imlv2134	SAP MaxDB 7.8
TAK	imlv2134	SAP MaxDB 7.8
PEP	abcpep01	SAP MaxDB 7.8
FIO	imlv2150	SAP MaxDB 7.8

Table 5.7 Overview of Databases at Toys Inc.

5.6.3 Roles and Responsibilities

As is the case for all other areas, there should also be a contact person for central monitoring. Ideally, this person should also be responsible for maintaining the monitoring concept. This contact person is available to respond to questions, suggestions, and so on, relating to the system monitoring environment.

Furthermore, the responsibilities are assigned according to particular groups or teams. In the documentation, a contact person must be specified for each monitoring area. Once again, the structure of the individual teams depends on the company structure and the size of the system landscape. Table 5.8 is a directory of contact persons and responsibilities at Toys Inc.

Team	Contact Person for	Name of CP	Telephone/Email
System Administration	Hardware	...	...
	Interfaces	...	...
	Network	...	...
	Security	...	...
	Database	...	...
	Operating system	...	...

Table 5.8 Sample Directory of Contact Persons/Responsibilities

5.6.4 Metrics

In Section 5.4.4, we introduced you to metrics within the concept of template creation. Here, we described metrics as elements. Technical monitoring within SAP Solution Manager 7.1 provides you with a range of metrics contained in SAP standard templates, for example. In general, there is no reason not to use SAP standard templates. However, experience has shown that they will provide the desired level of efficient monitoring only in extremely rare cases.

To pave the way for monitoring that supports operations, it is essential to select metrics according to your requirements. Among other things, you can use some of the points listed in the requirements catalog to determine which metrics can play a role in monitoring. Another possible indicator can be, for example, the definition of service level agreements (SLA) for system availability and system performance.

Another possible approach would be to divide metrics into categories and areas, in the way that you did for templates. At the same time, the overview can be used to prioritize metrics and define alerting methods.

Table 5.9 shows an excerpt from the overview at Toys Inc.

Category	Area	Priority
Operating system	CPU	High
	File systems	High
	Memory	High
	Availability	High
Databases	Data memory space	High
	Backup status	High
	Availability	Very high
ABAP	Instance availability	Very high
	ABAP short dumps	Medium
	Dialog resources	Medium
	Updates	Medium
	Dialog response times	Medium

Table 5.9 Metric Categories and Priorities

5.6.5 Defining Thresholds

If system monitoring is automated, thresholds determine when an alert is triggered. For this reason, each metric must contain an appropriate threshold definition. This includes, among other things, selecting the threshold type and specifying which values are taken into account (for example, smoothing values from the past 15 minutes). Table 5.10 shows a sample definition for a threshold at Toys Inc.

Monitoring Attribute	Thresholds			
	Green to Yellow	Yellow to Red	Red to Yellow	Yellow to Green
CPU utilization	90 %	95 %	92 %	87 %
Number of short dumps	5	10	7	3
Free memory space in the file system	7 %	5 %	8 %	10 %

Table 5.10 Sample Threshold Definition

5.6.6 Auto-Reaction Mechanisms

In this step, we will describe the auto-reaction methods you use when generating an alert. Toys Inc. opts for two auto-reactions that are available in SAP Solution Manager 7.1 by default, namely auto-notifications by email and automatic creation of incident messages.

Toys Inc. decides that auto-incidents will be created for alerts that have a "very high" priority (for example, INSTANCE NOT AVAILABLE). Very critical alerts require a swift response. The ITSM scenario can be used to shorten response times. It does this by assigning the incident to the corresponding component. At the same time, greater attention is paid to the problem.

Auto-notifications are generated for alerts that have a "high" or "medium" priority and are sent by email to the recipient defined previously. Auto-reactions are not to be triggered for alerts with a priority lower than "low." However, such alerts are visible in the alert inbox.

5.6.7 Instructions and Escalation Paths

Instructions are another important aspect of the monitoring concept. Clear and coherent instructions ensure that the cause of known problems and incidents can be quickly determined so that the problem can be quickly resolved.

In the case of known problems, the instructions will describe the solution or sequence of steps that must be performed. If it will take too long to solve a problem, the next support level should intervene, if possible. If no one takes care of the incident or problem after a predefined period of time, an escalation must occur. In other words, the problem must be forwarded to the next higher support level.

5.7 Customer Example: Using SAP Solution Manager 7.1 for Technical Monitoring of an SAP Landscape for an Education Service Provider

The SAP University Competence Center (UCC) is part of the SAP University Alliances program whereby SAP AG gives teaching staff and students all over the world access to SAP technologies. This program is aimed at universities and vocational institutions that want to actively integrate SAP applications into their teaching. SAP UCC currently provides SAP applications to more than 400 German and international institutions and educational centers, and therefore to approximately 80,000 students, thus making it the largest center of its kind worldwide.

In order to cater to the different needs of such a large number of institutions, SAP UCC runs more than 150 SAP systems, which account for a large part of SAP's software portfolio. At present, 15 full-time employees and a number of student or graduate assistants work at SAP UCC. To provide efficient and effective system operations, SAP UCC, together with SAP AG and Hewlett-Packard GmbH, is conducting research in the areas of adaptive computing, virtualization, and providing application service.

To ensure uninterrupted operations around the clock, a monitoring infrastructure must exist to ensure efficient and effective monitoring of the various systems. Since the legacy application was no longer able to cope with the new challenges associated with system monitoring, a decision was made to implement a completely new monitoring solution. The existing heterogeneous system landscape, the steady growth being experienced by SAP UCC, along with the need for better integration into existing service processes, placed high demands on the future monitoring solution. Table 5.11 lists those products in the system landscape that are used in production operation by customers and therefore must be monitored extensively.

System	Products		
1	SAP ERP 5.0	SAP BusinessObjects XI 3.1	SAP NetWeaver AS Java 7.01
2	SAP ERP 6.0	SAP BusinessObjects Enterprise 4	SAP NetWeaver AS Java 7.3
3	SAP ERP 6.04	SAP CRM 5.2	SAP NetWeaver CE 7.11
4	SAP ERP 6.05	SAP CRM 7.0	SAP NetWeaver PI 7.11
5	SAP NetWeaver BW 7.30	SAP CRM 7.02	SAP for Retail 6.0
6	SAP NetWeaver BW 7.31	SAP Solution Manager 7.1	SAP for Healthcare 6.0
7	SAP NetWeaver BW 7.0	SAP NetWeaver AS Java 7.0	
8	SAP SCM 7.0	SAP SRM 7.0	

Table 5.11 Products in the System Landscape

Aside from existing SAP systems, further new technologies will be added to the SAP UCC portfolio in the near future (for example, SAP HANA, Sybase Unwired Platform, and IBM DB2 10.1). Therefore, it must be possible to enhance the future monitoring solution in a flexible manner and to be able to cater to new technologies promptly in order to ensure continuous, uninterrupted, risk-free operations.

In addition to the systems themselves, the monitoring solution must also be able to monitor the resources running on the SAP systems. This includes the operating system level and HP-UX on database servers, as well as Suse Linux Enterprise Server 10 and 11 and Windows Server 2008 on SAP systems. The following three solutions must be monitored at the database level: Oracle 10.2g, IBM DB2 9.7 and Microsoft SQL Server 2008.

In addition to the regular SAP landscape, which is managed by an SAP Adaptive Computing Controller, it must also be possible to monitor the test systems (optional), which run in a VMware environment, in order to be able to assess performance parameters and errors that occur in production systems.

Availability, configuration, error, and performance metrics must be monitored at all levels. In the future, the data collected will be used to evaluate how to optimize operations from a performance and configuration perspective and how to shorten the maintenance window.

The application previously used to monitor the system landscape was operated as a standalone application without being integrated into existing service processes and structures. When the monitoring solution changes, the service processes will become further integrated, and system monitoring will be incorporated into the existing ITSM in SAP Solution Manager, which is already being used to process customer inquiries.

Due to the type and number of requests and challenges, system monitoring in SAP Solution Manager 7.1 was chosen as a monitoring solution for the system landscape. Not only are all of the systems that need to be monitored seamlessly integrated into monitoring, but new SAP technologies are also incorporated through regular updates of the monitoring content. Furthermore, alerts are forwarded to the ITSM implemented in SAP Solution Manager. Figure 5.77 shows an example of the planned monitoring landscape at UCC Magdeburg.

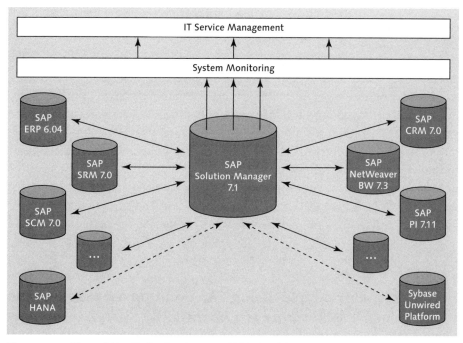

Figure 5.77 Planned Monitoring Landscape at UCC Magdeburg

If parameters measured using pre-assigned or newly created metrics exceed a defined warning threshold, an incident ticket is created and assigned the priority "low." Since the ITSM is a fixed part of the SAP UCC employee's working environment, processing occurs immediately. Not only are tickets created automatically, but auto-notifications are also implemented by email. If critical problems occur, auto-notification emails are sent to the relevant employees who are available at the time. The exact configuration depends on how critical the problem is, as well as the type and number of systems affected. For example, incidents that affect the availability of a database server for 30 SAP systems are prioritized above performance problems on test servers.

At present, the various systems in the landscape are integrated into the monitoring system within SAP Solution Manager whereby the operating systems, databases, and SAP ERP are already fully integrated, and integration of SAP NetWeaver AS Java 7.3 has commenced. Once this has been fully integrated and the employees have received training, there will be a brief period of parallel operations, after which the legacy application will be fully replaced by system monitoring in SAP Solution Manager.

Further integration of the different components offered by SAP Solution Manager is planned for the future. In the case of linked systems, connection monitoring will monitor and measure critical RFC connections among systems. Furthermore, the native reporting options available in SAP Solution Manager will contribute to optimizing operations and support services. The final phase of component integration, which is currently being planned, involves linking incident tickets with the Knowledge Base integrated into SAP Solution Manager. The desired goal of implementing system monitoring with SAP Solution Manager 7.1, including an integrated ITSM, will give SAP UCC a reliable, extensive, and efficient infrastructure that, in turn, will ensure optimum performance and availability of the systems and services rendered.

5.8 Customer Example: Using SAP Solution Manager 7.1 for Technical Monitoring at Geberit

Mr. Daniel Rothmund, senior IT application analyst for SAP software at Geberit Verwaltungs GmbH, has kindly provided us with another customer example of technical monitoring.

About Geberit

The Geberit Group is the European market leader in sanitary technology, with a large global presence. Since its establishment in 1874, the company has been a pioneer in the sector, consistently setting new trends with its comprehensive system solutions. The company's range of products is designed for use in new buildings, as well as in renovation and modernization projects. It comprises the following product lines: sanitary systems (installation systems, cisterns and mechanisms, faucets and flushing systems, waste fittings and traps, and toilets) and piping systems (building drainage systems and supply systems). Geberit is listed on the Swiss Stock Exchange and is actively represented in 41 countries, with 16 production sites in seven countries. In 2011, the Geberit Group (with more than 6,000 employees worldwide) generated sales of CHF 2.1 billion.

Initial Situation

Since 2002, we have been using SAP Solution Manager as our main SAP system monitoring tool. We started using it in release 2.1/2.2. At first, all AS ABAP systems were monitored. Then, in 2008, root cause analysis and AS Java monitoring were added in Support Package 15. SAP Solution Manger is our main tool for managing our applications, ranging from ITSM for SAP to change request management and technical monitoring.

Project Description

The use of new SAP technologies—for example, SAP BusinessObjects or SAP Business Warehouse Accelerator (BWA)—created a new set of challenges in the area of monitoring. Furthermore, the existing monitoring solution was no longer able to fully cover all our internal processes and requirements. Following the ramp-up to release 7.1, we were able to conduct initial tests on the new technical monitoring solution. These tests showed that the new technical monitoring solution would be a solid basis for monitoring our SAP systems.

Therefore, in early 2012, we started a new project for technical monitoring on the basis of SAP Solution Manager 7.1. The purpose of this project was to transfer all SAP and non-SAP systems to the new technical monitoring solution. To summarize, this involved 23 AS ABAP instances, 8 AS Java instances, and 5 third-party instances.

At the very outset of the project, it emerged that one of the most important things was system landscape maintenance. We have broadly summarized the main tasks of the project here:

► Define technical requirements for the connected systems.

► Install and assign agents.

► Create users and assign the corresponding roles (authorizations).

► Accurately maintain the system landscape data in the LMDB.

► Ensure the connection and availability of system information in the SLD.

► Define the required metrics and their thresholds in terms of triggering alerts.

► Define a checklist for connecting systems.

In terms of time and effort, accurate maintenance of the system landscape data in the LMDB was one of the most comprehensive and important aspects of our project. Technical monitoring without this foundation in Solution Manager is not recommended. Another key point was defining templates for monitoring. Here, we used the SAP standard templates as a basis for our discussion. To ensure transparent monitoring, we adopted the "keep it simple" approach when defining our templates. We now use three templates for each system type:

► Productive systems

► Test and quality systems

► Legacy systems

By using a BAdI (BADI_ALERT_REACTION), we were able to connect our internal telephone server to monitoring and, therefore, to our alerting technologies. We also use the BAdI for sending Apple push messages to smartphones and tablets.

The relevant on-call employee processes the open alerts in the alert inbox or by using the monitoring apps for smartphones or tablets. These apps are available in the relevant app store, thus making it possible for the employee to quickly process the alerts and get a clear first picture of the problem.

In particular, I wish to highlight a function that we developed together with SAP. This function enables us to connect external shell scripts or our own programs at the operating system level to monitoring. Consequently, we can now enhance technical monitoring with our own OS scripts in a flexible manner, thus enabling us to monitor metrics that are closely related to the operating system (Software Raid, system time, network bounding, and so on), as well as database-specific metrics such as Oracle Dataguard or Oracle Flashback. This new function may become available to all customers in one of the next Support Packages for SAP Solution Manager.

Challenges

The main challenges here were centralized system landscape maintenance and the definition of templates, metrics, and thresholds. The necessary support processes had already been established for the monitoring solution previously in use. Consequently, we only had to ensure its integration into the new monitoring solution, along with the requisite transfer of knowledge. The basic approaches and courses of action had been established to the greatest possible extent.

Conclusion

In summary, we were able to replace our entire existing SAP monitoring solution with the new technical monitoring solution without any difficulty. We have now also integrated our SAP-related third-party systems into monitoring, thus closing any gaps we had as a result of the lack of all the monitoring functions we needed in SAP Solution Manager 7.0.

Monitoring requirements vary depending on which tasks a system or solution needs to complete. In this chapter, we'll show you how to use SAP Solution Manager to monitor special solutions.

6   Monitoring Special Solutions

Technical monitoring, which we described in Chapter 5, does not provide adequate monitoring in the case of a heterogeneous system landscape, which is the main landscape used by enterprises today. By using our example of Toys Inc., we have already illustrated how a large number of different solutions can be implemented in a system landscape.

Often, a system landscape comprises special components and systems that require a special form of monitoring. Such system landscapes present us with challenges that require monitoring to go beyond simply observing the status of a technical component if we are to meet all the requirements of a system landscape. So far, we have discussed basic monitoring concepts and their implementation into your landscape, which form not only the basis, but also the minimum prerequisite for general technical monitoring. In this chapter, we will introduce you to other monitoring solutions that supplement general technical monitoring with special system-specific and component-specific monitoring technologies.

In the next section, we will show you how to set up and use the solutions for BI monitoring, SAP NetWeaver PI monitoring, end-user experience monitoring, connection monitoring, and self-monitoring. You will learn how to implement and use technical monitoring for the above solutions according to your requirements.

6.1   BI Monitoring with SAP Solution Manager

Typical business intelligence (BI) scenarios involve not only SAP NetWeaver BW systems (Business Warehouse), but also, more and more frequently, SAP BusinessObjects systems. In such scenarios, the SAP NetWeaver BW systems are given priority when it comes to extracting and aggregating company data from operational systems, while the SAP BusinessObjects systems essentially prepare and present the data acquired from the BW systems. Figure 6.1 shows one possible way to monitor BI scenarios, including all their technical components and related solutions.

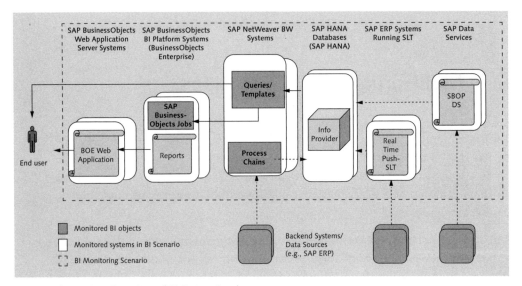

Figure 6.1 Overview of BI System Landscape

Such an architecture presents system monitoring with new challenges. It is no longer sufficient to monitor individual systems. Rather, the administrator must not only monitor individual system components, as is the case with business process monitoring, but also keep an eye on the flow of information through such a landscape. For BI scenarios, this means, for example, that BI-specific objects such as process chains, background jobs, queries, or templates must be monitored. In SAP Solution Manager 7.1, BI monitoring is available for this purpose.

BI monitoring helps administrators answer the following question: are the BI applications running without error and within the defined time window? Technically, at least, it is also possible to say that the correct data is made available to the decision makers within a company in good time.

With BI monitoring, SAP provides a central platform that provides information and facilitates monitoring via BW process chains, queries (reporting), templates, and SAP BusinessObjects jobs.

At present, it is possible to add the following system types to BI monitoring:

▶ SAP BusinessObjects systems (SAP BusinessObjects Enterprise XI 3.1 and SAP BusinessObjects BI Platform 4.0 or higher) and the associated web application server

▶ SAP NetWeaver BW systems as of release 7.0

▶ SAP Data Services (as of SAP Solution Manager 7.1 SP7)

▶ SAP System Landscape Transformation systems (SLT)

▶ SAP HANA systems

▶ ABAP source systems

Users need SAP NetWeaver BW knowledge in order to monitor BI scenarios. In particular, some experience of BI objects is necessary for configuring thresholds. Before all this, you should give some thought to which key performance indicators are characteristic of meaningful monitoring. Such empirical values can be used to define the initial thresholds. A universal recommendation cannot be made here.

6.1.1 Properties of BI Monitoring

BI monitoring is an enhancement to technical monitoring. It provides additional functions that are essential for monitoring SAP NetWeaver BW and SAP Business Objects systems. In the next section, we will provide you with a detailed introduction to the monitoring functions within BI monitoring.

Status Overview of BI System Landscape

The status overview (BI Overview Monitor) uses status icons to enable you to see the overall status of the BI system landscape at a glance.

As you can see in Figure 6.2, each system type within the landscape is displayed separately. In this case, BO Web Application Systems, BO Server Systems, and BW Systems are displayed separately. You therefore have a broad overview of the status of the entire landscape as soon as you access the status overview. Depending on which system types were configured in your BI monitoring, you may have more elements than those shown in Figure 6.2. From this broad overview, you can navigate to the system monitors for all systems assigned to a particular type. Specific system monitors exist for the aforementioned system types.

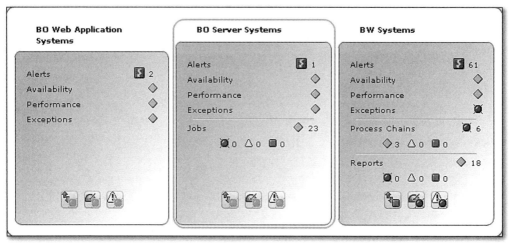

Figure 6.2 Status Overview for a Landscape Comprising an SAP BusinessObjects System and an SAP NetWeaver BW System

Monitoring BW Process Chains

BW process chains can be monitored in individual systems or across several systems. Both entire process chains and individual steps within a process chain can be monitored.

Administrators can see, at a glance, which process chains have errors or did not run during the defined time window. Figure 6.3 shows several process chains and process steps, some of which were assigned the error status at the end of the process. As is the case in the status overview, you can then choose the relevant status icon to navigate to detailed information about the process chain.

Process Chain Details

System	Process Chain	Status	Duration (mins)	Not Started on Time	Out of Time Window	Records Processed	Data Packages Processed	Alerts	
CIA~ABAP		◉	◉	◉	◉	◉	◉	14	⑤
	Z00CHAIN01	◉	0 ▦			0.000 ◉	0.000 ◉	4	⑤
	Z00CHAIN011	▦	4 ◉	254 ◉		152520.000	3.000 ◉	5	⑤
	Z00CHAIN012	▦	2 △		243 ◉	305040.000	5.000 ◉	5	⑤
RWS~ABAP		◉						2	⑤
	OSM_BPM_DELTA_P02	◉						1	⑤
	OSM_BPM_INIT_P01	◉						1	⑤

Figure 6.3 Process Chain Monitoring

Monitoring SAP BusinessObjects Jobs

Just like process chains, the jobs in the SAP BusinessObjects systems are a key element in preparing and providing data that may come from different data sources. Figure 6.4 shows SAP BusinessObjects jobs, some of which were processed with errors. Once again, you can choose the relevant status icons to obtain further detailed information about the errors that have occurred.

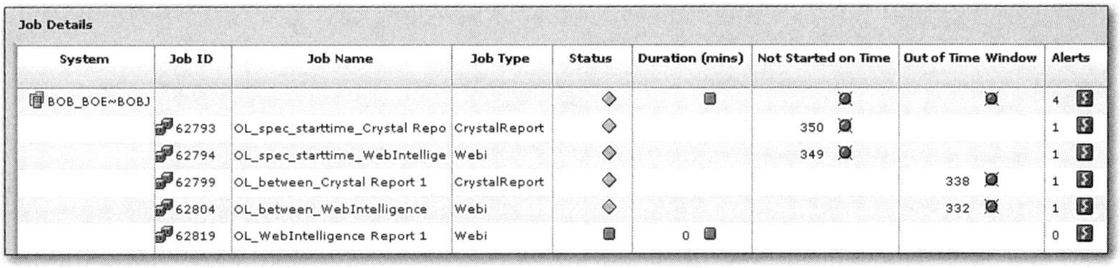

Job Details

System	Job ID	Job Name	Job Type	Status	Duration (mins)	Not Started on Time	Out of Time Window	Alerts
BOB_BOE~BOBJ				◇	▣	◉	◉	4
	62793	OL_spec_starttime_Crystal Repo	CrystalReport	◇		350 ◉		1
	62794	OL_spec_starttime_WebIntellige	Webi	◇		349 ◉		1
	62799	OL_between_Crystal Report 1	CrystalReport	◇			338 ◉	1
	62804	OL_between_WebIntelligence	Webi	◇			332 ◉	1
	62819	OL_WebIntelligence Report 1	Webi	▣	0 ▣			0

Figure 6.4 SAP BusinessObjects Job Monitor

BW Report Monitor

Queries and templates are the most commonly used analysis functions within a BW system. Data collected in a BW system can be made available in this way and tailored to different user requirements within an enterprise. In a query itself, it is no longer possible to see whether the underlying data (from process chains, for example) is correct. In the BW report monitor, the main issue is whether the reports themselves ran without error or whether their runtime was too long, as shown in Figure 6.5.

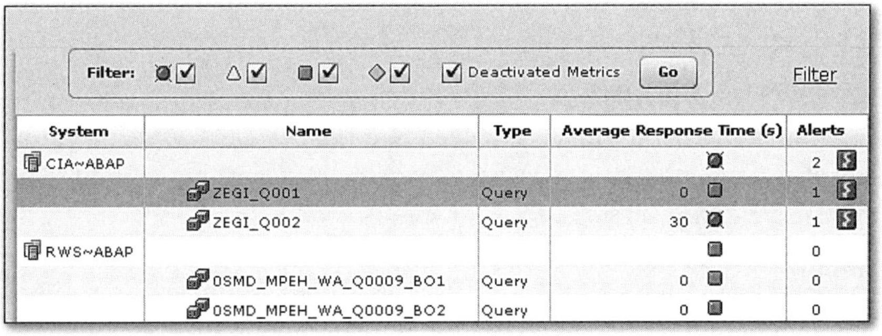

Filter: ◉☑ △☑ ▣☑ ◇☑ ☑ Deactivated Metrics [Go]				Filter

System	Name	Type	Average Response Time (s)	Alerts
CIA~ABAP			◉	2
	ZEGI_Q001	Query	0 ▣	1
	ZEGI_Q002	Query	30 ◉	1
RWS~ABAP			▣	0
	0SMD_MPEH_WA_Q0009_BO1	Query	0 ▣	0
	0SMD_MPEH_WA_Q0009_BO2	Query	0 ▣	0

Figure 6.5 BW Report Monitor

Integration into the Central Alert Inbox and the ITSM Functions

As was shown in Section 5.3, one of the aims associated with developing SAP Solution Manager 7.1 was to provide a central Monitoring and Alerting Infrastructure (MAI). Any alerts displayed in the individual views within BI monitoring come from the central alert inbox. If you select an alert icon in one of the monitors, you immediately access the alert inbox, can view the alerts in detail, and edit them there. Furthermore, you can see from the figures provided here that the ITSM functions available in SAP Solution Manager are not integrated only into the individual monitors, but also into the alert inbox.

6.1.2 Configuring BI Monitoring

The starting point for the configuration is the SAP Solution Manager Configuration work center (Transaction SOLMAN_SETUP). In the navigation area, choose Technical Monitoring. Then choose BI Monitoring from the selection options available on the left-hand side of the screen. As you already know from the other configuration scenarios, the colored status icons represent different configuration statuses.

Here, you can choose Edit to change modes within the configuration. You are then guided through the individual configuration steps.

Step 1: Overview

This configuration is based on the tried-and-tested guided procedures technology within SAP Solution Manager. In step 1, you see an overview of the configuration steps.

Step 2: Configure Infrastructure

Step 2, Configure Infrastructure, is divided into smaller substeps that are processed systematically. In the case of technical monitoring, some of these substeps need to be executed only once.

▶ Check Prerequisites
When you start a technical monitoring scenario configuration for the first time, you must check the prerequisites to ensure that the system preparation and basic configuration of SAP Solution Manager have been successful.

▶ CONFIGURE MANUALLY

Once you have successfully checked the software prerequisites, the next substep is CONFIGURE MANUALLY. We recommend that you check those steps marked as optional first. Here, for example, you can quickly see whether the extractors are active for the relevant systems and whether they are running without error and collecting data.

▶ DEFAULT SETTINGS

In the DEFAULT SETTINGS substep, you determine the information you want analysis reports, email, SMS messages, or events to contain. You therefore specify a template that will be used as the standard template in all subsequent configuration steps.

▶ WORKMODE SETTINGS

In the WORKMODE SETTINGS substep, you can activate various different modes (for example, peak load times or planned downtimes). For more information, see Section 7.6.

▶ UPDATE CONTENT

The UPDATE CONTENT substep should have been processed successfully when you set up system monitoring (see Section 5.4.2). We recommend that you update the content only in the context of system monitoring.

Step 3: Standard Users

In this optional step, you create users for BI reporting. These users are template users to whom the roles required for BI reporting are assigned. At the same time, a business partner is created for use in Support Desk messages, for example.

Step 4: Define Scope

The BI scenario is a logical view of your BI system landscape. In this view, you select logically related systems for shared monitoring. Essentially, the data flows in your BI landscape will determine which systems are considered to be related. All the technical components and systems that deliver data to the BI system should be grouped together into one logical scenario.

To create such a scenario, proceed as follows:

1. First, check whether change mode has been activated. Then, choose CREATE to create a new scenario. If you want to change existing scenarios, choose EDIT.

2. Assign a name to this scenario and enter a technical description. Then, choose NEXT to select the technical systems in the next substep.

3. You can now add the individual technical systems to the BI scenario. Make sure to select only systems that are already managed and configured (see Section 2.5.4). Figure 6.6 shows two tables with different system layers.

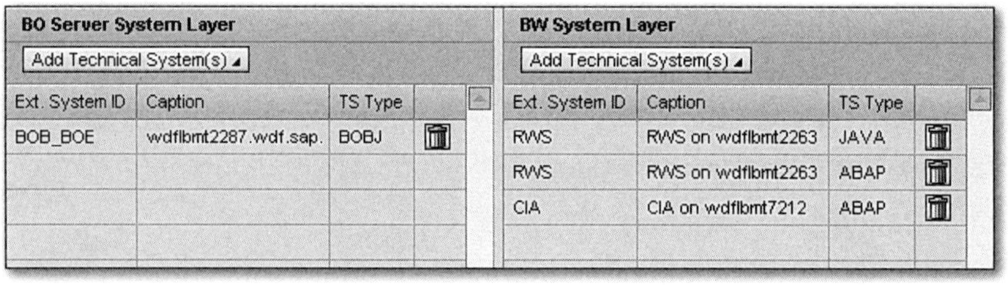

BO Server System Layer					BW System Layer				
Add Technical System(s) ◢					Add Technical System(s) ◢				
Ext. System ID	Caption	TS Type		▲	Ext. System ID	Caption	TS Type		▲
BOB_BOE	wdflbmt2287.wdf.sap.	BOBJ	🗑		RWS	RWS on wdflbmt2263	JAVA	🗑	
					RWS	RWS on wdflbmt2263	ABAP	🗑	
					CIA	CIA on wdflbmt7212	ABAP	🗑	

Figure 6.6 Selecting the BI System Layers

▶ BO: WEB SYSTEM LAYER
In the BO: WEB SYSTEM LAYER area, you select the relevant web application servers. To do this, choose ADD TECHNICAL SYSTEM(S). SAP BusinessObjects systems can work with SAP NetWeaver AS Java, Apache Tomcat, or IBM Websphere. If you wish, you can choose ADD OTHERS to add other web application servers to monitoring. However, there are no special monitoring elements for these systems.

▶ BO: SERVER SYSTEM LAYER
Here, you select the production system you created in the LMDB for the SAP BusinessObjects cluster. A cluster is considered to be the entire SAP Business Objects system, including all servers and instances.

▶ BW: SYSTEM LAYER
Here, choose ADD ABAP or ADD JAVA to select the relevant BW systems.

In the next substep, you will select additional system layers. The following system layers are available:

▶ SAP Data Services system layer

▶ SLT system layer

- ► SAP HANA system layer

- ► ABAP source system layer

4. When you have finished defining the scenario, an overview of your selection is displayed. You can check whether all the systems relevant for your scenario are listed here. Then, save the scenario.

You have now defined the content of your technical scenario and can proceed to the next step.

Step 5: Scenario Defaults

The next step in the configuration process is step 5, SCENARIO DEFAULTS. In this step, you integrate the message and notification system that you want to use with the systems to be monitored and their functions (SAP BusinessObjects jobs, SAP NetWeaver BW process chains, BW queries, and BW templates). You determine how monitoring should respond if an incident occurs. For example, (email) notifications and support messages can be sent directly to the relevant employees, while taking known work modes into account. Furthermore, alerts or notifications can be suppressed if, for example, a system shutdown is planned.

Step 6: Monitoring & Alerting

In the MONITORING & ALERTING step (see Figure 6.7), you configure the following modules in the relevant substeps:

- ► BO JOB MONITOR

- ► BW PROCESS CHAIN MONITOR

- ► BW REPORT MONITOR

- ► BO DATA SERVICES MONITOR (new in SP07)

> **Note**
>
> Prior to SAP Solution Manager SP07, the configurations for BW queries and BW templates were separate. As of Support Package 07, these two steps are grouped together in the configuration for the BW Report Monitor module.

We will now describe each of the steps associated with configuring these modules.

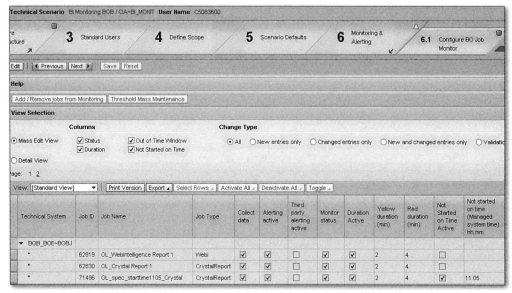

Figure 6.7   Configuration Overview

Configuring the BO Job Monitor

The following steps enable you to expand monitoring to include monitoring of important SAP BusinessObjects jobs from the relevant technical systems. Figure 6.7 shows the job selection screen for the BO job monitor.

Figure 6.8   Configuring the BO Job Monitor

1. Choose ADD/REMOVE JOBS FROM MONITORING.

2. In the window displayed, search for the job you want to monitor (see Figure 6.9).

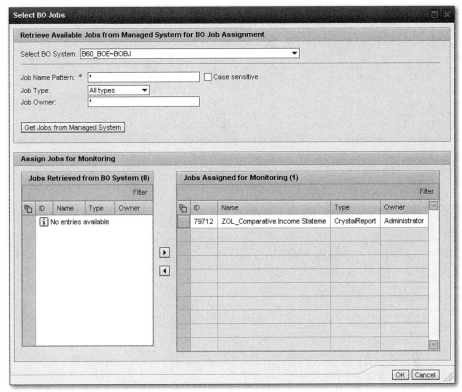

Figure 6.9 Selecting SAP BusinessObjects Jobs

First, you can select the technical SAP BusinessObjects system in the SELECT BO SYSTEM field. The JOB NAME PATTERN, JOB TYPE, and JOB OWNER filters can be used to restrict the number and type of jobs available for selection.

3. You can then choose GET JOBS FROM MANAGED SYSTEM to integrate the SAP BusinessObjects jobs into monitoring (see Figure 6.9).

4. Then, select the relevant jobs in the JOBS RETRIEVED FROM BO SYSTEM results table and select the icon ▶ to add these jobs to the JOBS ASSIGNED FOR MONITORING column.

5. Choose OK to close the window.

The jobs you have added are now displayed in the jobs table (see Figure 6.10). Now, define thresholds for monitoring the jobs that you have added, either individually or by using the THRESHOLD MASS MAINTENANCE function, if you want to maintain several jobs.

Alerting active	Third party alerting active	Monitor status	Duration Active	Yellow duration (min)	Red duration (min)	Not Started on Time Active	Not started on time (Managed system time) hh:mm	Not started on time yellow (min)	Not started on time red (min)	Out of Time Window Active	Time Window (Managed System Time) hh:mm - hh:mm	Out of time window yellow (min)	Out of time window red (min)
☑	☐	☑	☐			☑	10:34	2	4	☐			
☑	☐	☑	☐			☑	10:35	2	4	☐			
☑	☐	☑	☐			☐				☑	10:44-10:46	2	4
☑	☐	☑	☐			☐				☑	10:50-10:52	2	4

Figure 6.10 Monitoring Thresholds

The following thresholds are available:

▶ STATUS
You use the STATUS threshold to define whether you want an alert to be triggered in the event of an error. If status monitoring is active, you receive a message if the SAP BusinessObjects job could not be processed successfully.

▶ DURATION
You can use the DURATION threshold to check compliance with the expected runtime.

Example: If you define a duration of 120 minutes, an alert is triggered as soon as the runtime exceeds two hours.

▶ NOT STARTED ON TIME
You can use the NOT STARTED ON TIME threshold to check whether a job is active at the planned start time. If the job starts late, an alert is triggered. This setting is not suitable for jobs that run several times per day or whose start time is not always the same.

Example: Here you can set, for example, 14:00 as the start time, with a maximum delay of five minutes. If this time is exceeded, an alert is triggered.

▶ OUT OF TIME WINDOW
You can use the OUT OF TIME WINDOW to trigger an alert if the SAP BusinessObjects job is not processed within the specified time window. This variant

is suitable for jobs that do not have a fixed start time but are activated as a result of an event, for example. It is not suitable for jobs that run several times per day or jobs that run on several days at different times.

Example: The planned time window ranges from 04:00 to 06:00, with a threshold of ten minutes. An alert is triggered if the SAP BusinessObjects job starts before 03:50 or ends after 06:10.

The thresholds can be adjusted at any time in order to move toward ideal values. However, it would make sense to give some thought to the actual thresholds themselves before you configure suitable values. Completely unsuitable thresholds can easily open the floodgates in terms of alerts.

Setting Up Monitoring for BW Process Chains

BW process chain monitoring is configured at the same time as the BO job monitor. In other words, in this setup step, you can also integrate the relevant BW process chains from the technical system. However, two additional monitoring methods are available for monitoring the process chains or individual steps within a process chain. You can choose between the method based on data records or the one based on data packages (see Figure 6.11).

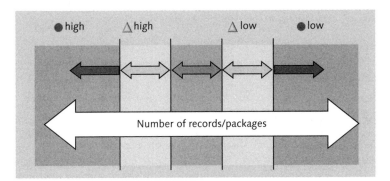

Figure 6.11 Thresholds for Processed Data Records and Data Packages

▶ DATA RECORDS PROCESSED
If you select the DATA RECORDS PROCESSED option, an alert is triggered on the basis of the number of data records processed. To this end, you must set upper limit and lower limit thresholds that meet your requirements. Use lower limits

if you want to receive alerts (yellow or red, depending on the defined threshold). Note that the lower limit for red alerts must be lower than the lower limit for yellow alerts. Typically, a check is performed to determine whether any data has been selected.

Example: Set the threshold to 1 so that an alert is triggered if the process chain processes 0 data records.

▶ DATA PACKAGES PROCESSED

If you select the DATA PACKAGES PROCESSED option, you can check whether the data packages processed in a process chain do not exceed a certain number. You can therefore find out whether the package size needs to be adjusted (because too many packages are being processed in parallel) or whether the degree of parallelization can be changed.

Setting Up the BW Query Monitor (SP06)

Choose ADD QUERY TO MONITOR to select the queries you want to monitor. Then, select the technical name and specify a pattern in the QUERY NAME PATTERN field. Once you have selected the relevant BW queries and added them to monitoring, activate the COLLECT DATA and/or ALERTING ACTIVE checkboxes.

Now, choose THRESHOLD MASS MAINTENANCE to define the relevant thresholds for the average runtime. Alternatively, select the query directly.

Once you have successfully activated data collection and alerting, you can define the average response time for a query. The previous period (60 minutes) is considered a reference value.

Setting Up the BW Template Monitor (SP06)

This step is executed in the same way as the SET UP BW QUERY MONITOR step and is used to monitor an average response time for templates.

BW Report Monitor (SP08)

Since the BW query monitor and BW template monitor configurations are very similar, as of Support Package 08, they are grouped together to form one shared substep: the BW report monitor.

BO Data Services Monitor (as of SP07)

In this step, you can analyze SAP BusinessObjects data services jobs as of Support Package 07. Choose ADD/REMOVE DATA SERVICES JOBS FROM BO SYSTEM for this purpose (see Figure 6.12).

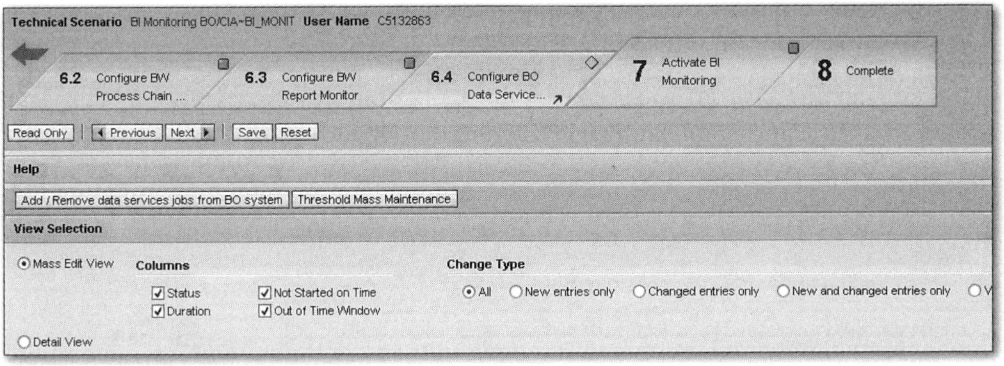

Figure 6.12 Adding Data Services Jobs

In the next window (see Figure 6.13), the following selection options are available to you:

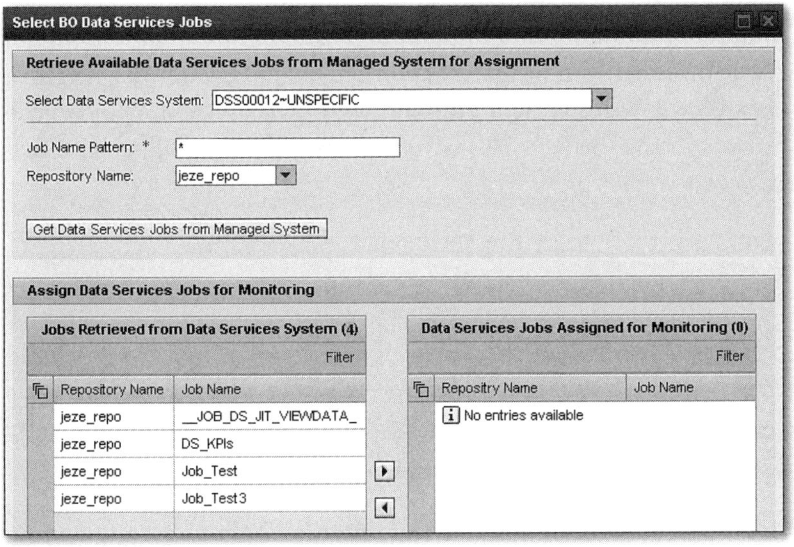

Figure 6.13 Selecting Data Services Jobs

▶ SELECT DATA SERVICES SYSTEM: Select the relevant technical system.

▶ JOB NAME PATTERN: Enter a relevant search pattern here.

▶ REPOSITORY NAME: Select the repository that you have created or select the relevant work area.

As is the case with making selections when configuring the BO job monitor, the following configuration and monitoring options are available to you when configuring the BO data services monitor: STATUS, DURATION, NOT STARTED ON TIME, and OUT OF TIME WINDOW.

In the future, you will also have the option of monitoring data flows (in other words, data records that have been written/read).

BI Activation

This step shows you an overview of all components you have integrated into BI monitoring. Here, check whether all expected technical systems, jobs/process chains, and reports have been selected. If this is the case, you can choose ACTIVATE BI MONITORING to activate monitoring. Make sure the ACTIVATE IN BACKGROUND MODE checkbox is selected.

6.1.3   Purpose of BI Monitoring

Generally, several different systems need to work together in order to generate a BI report in an SAP NetWeaver BW or SAP BusinessObjects system. The purpose of BI monitoring is to support you in answering questions that will ensure that these systems work together properly:

1. What is the overall status of my BI system landscape?

   ▶ Are all BI systems working properly, and are they technically correct?

   ▶ Are there delays or incidents in the data flow between systems?

   ▶ Are all systems performing to an acceptable level?

   ▶ Have alerts occurred in the system landscape as a result of critical statuses?

   ▶ Who must be notified if alerts occur?

2. Are the SAP BusinessObjects jobs being executed successfully?

   ▶ Have the SAP BusinessObjects jobs been executed without error?

   ▶ Have the SAP BusinessObjects jobs started within the planned time interval?

- ▶ Have the SAP BusinessObjects jobs processed the data correctly?

- ▶ Are SAP BusinessObjects jobs being executed to an acceptable performance level?

3. How are process chains being processed in the BW systems?

- ▶ Are there delays in BW process-chain processing? If so, why?

- ▶ Have the process chains collected data within the planned scope?

- ▶ Have all the steps in the process chains been successful?

4. Are additional systems (for example, SAP HANA, SLT, and the source systems) working correctly? Can the source systems be reached, and are they also delivering data?

BI monitoring in SAP Solution Manager can help you answer all these questions. In the following sections, we will show you how to proceed when answering these questions.

6.1.4 Using BI Monitoring

BI monitoring is integrated into the TECHNICAL MONITORING work center within SAP Solution Manager. Therefore, to start the application, open the work center and select the BI MONITORING link. As shown in Figure 6.14, you then access a list of previously defined scenarios. Select one of the scenarios here and choose the relevant button to start the monitoring function you require. At the start, you can choose whether you want to start the application in a new window (OPEN NEW WINDOW) or in the same window (START EMBEDDED).

In all BI monitoring applications, you can use buttons to toggle between the following rating methods:

- ▶ BI OBJECT RATINGS BASED ON: LAST RUN
  Here, only the last run concerning the relevant object is used for the overall rating.

- ▶ BI OBJECT RATINGS BASED ON: WORST CASE
  If an earlier run concerning the object has a worse rating than the last run, the status is set to the worst value.

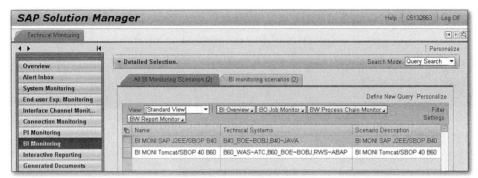

Figure 6.14 Initial Screen for the BI Monitoring Application

Entry via the BI Overview Monitor

The questions from the previous section are usually answered in the BI OVERVIEW monitor. Here, choose BI OVERVIEW to open the overview, which is divided into the areas shown in Figure 6.15.

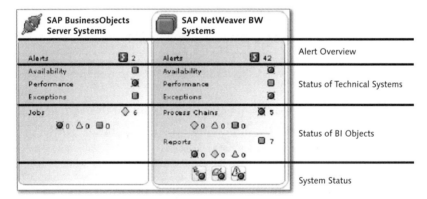

Figure 6.15 Areas of the BI Overview Monitor

▶ ALERT OVERVIEW

The alert overview displays the number of alerts in all BW systems within the scenario. It is not possible to determine the significance or relevance of the alerts here. To do this, you must switch to the alert inbox. In the example shown in Figure 6.15, no alerts are displayed, no analysis is required.

▶ STATUS OF TECHNICAL SYSTEMS

The worst status assigned to a technical system in the scenario is inherited as the status. Even if, for example, only one system had a critical status, a red status is displayed in the overview, irrespective of the status assigned to the other systems.

► STATUS OF BI OBJECTS
The aggregated status is also displayed here. Even if only one SAP BusinessObjects job or one BW process chain in the scenario ended with an error, the status in the overview is red.

► SYSTEM STATUS
The overall status of the production systems in the scenario is displayed here. The three icons in the system status stand for system availability (), performance (), and exceptions (). These three elements are monitored separately. In each case, the display indicates the worst case. Therefore, in the example provided, the BW systems in the BI scenario were always available. However, there were critical performance values and critical exceptions.

This broad overview provides the error statuses at a glance, aggregated according to system type. If you want to access the details, you can select either the relevant status icons or the system type. In both cases, you access the overview for individual systems, subdivided according to the technical instances of a system. In the case of SAP BusinessObjects server systems, each server process in SAP Solution Manager is implemented as a technical instance. Consequently, a large number of elements are displayed for this system type. For the other system types, only the technical systems are displayed (see Figure 6.16 and Figure 6.17).

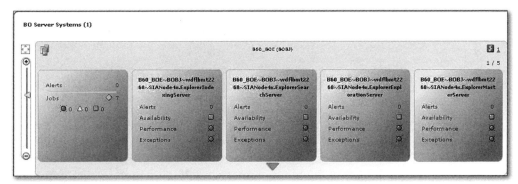

Figure 6.16 System Overview for SAP BusinessObjects Server Systems

Within this view, you can navigate to the alert inbox, the process chain monitor, and the SAP BusinessObjects jobs or system monitor by selecting the relevant system type or status icon.

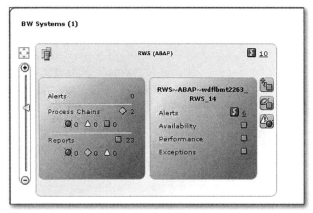

Figure 6.17 System Overview for BW Systems

You can use the system monitor to monitor individual technical instances and systems. Figure 6.18 shows the system monitor for a server process in an SAP BusinessObjects system. So in just a few clicks, you can navigate from the complete overview for your BI scenario to the technical details of a particular system. The system monitor is divided into two areas. The left-hand side of the system monitor contains an overview in which you can monitor the overall technical status and the individual system hosts, while the right-hand side of the screen displays the details that resulted in the overall status.

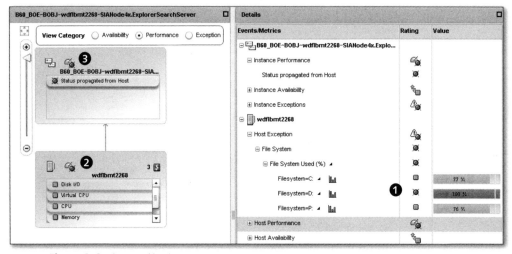

Figure 6.18 System Monitor

The example shown in Figure 6.18 represents a situation in which a host's file system (FILESYSTEM=D:) is completely full (100%) (❶). For this reason, the host `wdflbmt2268` is assigned a red status (❷). This red status for the host `wdflbmt2268` is then forwarded to the technical instance (in this case, an SAP BusinessObjects server process). Consequently, a red status (in other words, a critical status) is displayed for the technical instance (❸), which, in turn, forwards this status to the next higher level, the technical system `B60_BOE~BOBJ`. From here, the critical status is passed on to the system layer in the BI OVERVIEW monitor, which is also assigned a red status. This example shows you how BI monitoring and system monitoring are interconnected.

Monitoring BW Process Chains

Similarly, you can navigate from the BI OVERVIEW monitor to BW process chain monitoring or SAP BusinessObjects job monitoring by selecting the relevant status icon in the PROCESS CHAINS area. However, you can also start BW process chain monitoring directly from the initial view in the work center (see Figure 6.14). To do this, select a scenario and choose BW PROCESS CHAIN MONITOR.

In both cases, you access the overview for BW process chains (see Figure 6.19). This figure also displays the most important control elements on the BW process chain monitor:

▶ You can choose NAVIGATE TO to navigate to a detailed analysis of a process chain. The detailed analysis brings you directly to the analysis transaction (for example, Transaction RSPC1) in the SAP NetWeaver BW system.

▶ You can choose CREATE NOTIFICATION and CREATE INCIDENT to notify a person by email or to create an incident in the service desk.

▶ In the FILTER area, you can filter the alerts according to color. If you want to filter according to systems and process chains, you can enter a term in the first row of the relevant column. In our example, the system ST7~ABAP was filtered.

These control elements are also available in the BO job monitor, BW report monitor, and BO data services monitor.

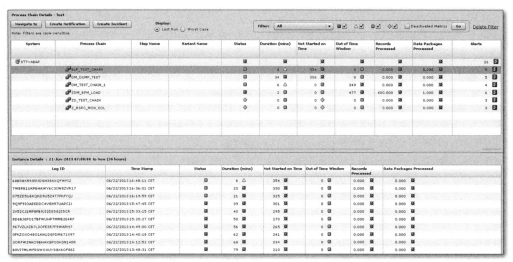

Figure 6.19 BW Process Chain Monitor

The initial view of the BW process chain monitor contains an overview, broken down according to the individual systems in the scenario, and the process chains selected for each system with status icons for the following monitor elements:

▶ STATUS
The status of a process chain, not the status of an individual step within the chain, is shown here.

▶ DURATION, NOT STARTED ON TIME, and OUT OF TIME WINDOW
These three time characteristics are important monitoring elements for a process chain. These status icons enable you to see, at a glance, whether the start time, end time, and processing duration correspond to expected values, thus enabling administrators to identify, in good time, changes that occur while processing a process chain and to respond to these changes, if necessary.

▶ RECORDS PROCESSED and DATA PACKAGES PROCESSED
The status icons in these two columns show you whether the process chain has processed the expected number of data records or data packages.

▶ ALERTS
If alerts occurred while processing a process chain, the alert icon (📶) in the ALERTS column is red, and the number of alerts are listed.

Figure 6.19 clearly shows that the status, errors that occurred, and runtime of a BW process are rated independently of each other. As a result, a process chain can have a green status even if errors or time limits have occurred. In our example, this is evident from the BW process chains DM_DUMP_TEST and DM_TEST_CHAIN_1 shown in Figure 6.19. Here, you also see that the worst status assigned to an individual BW process chain determines the status of the overall system ST7~ABAP.

You can choose NAVIGATE TO to navigate to the BW analysis tools (Transactions RSPC1 and ST13) or to BW reporting. Figure 6.20 shows the jump to the detailed analysis of a process chain in RSPC1. A BW expert can now conduct further analysis.

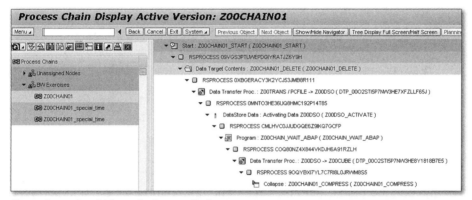

Figure 6.20 Detail View of a Process Chain

In the initial view of process chain monitoring, you can create notifications or incidents and navigate to the detailed analysis.

Monitoring SAP BusinessObjects Jobs

SAP BusinessObjects jobs are monitored in a similar way to monitoring process chains. In the initial view of BI monitoring, select the function BO JOB MONITOR. You obtain the view shown in Figure 6.21.

The status icons displayed here are the same as those displayed in the BW process chain monitor. Therefore, in addition to processing a job correctly, you can monitor runtimes and compliance with the planned time interval. You can then choose NAVIGATE TO to navigate to a detailed analysis of the SAP BusinessObjects jobs for the Central Management Console (CMC) or to BW reporting.

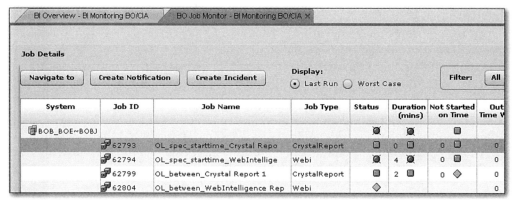

Figure 6.21 BO Job Monitor

Monitoring Reporting Activities

You use the BW report monitor (see Figure 6.22) to monitor reporting activities in SAP NetWeaver Business Warehouse.

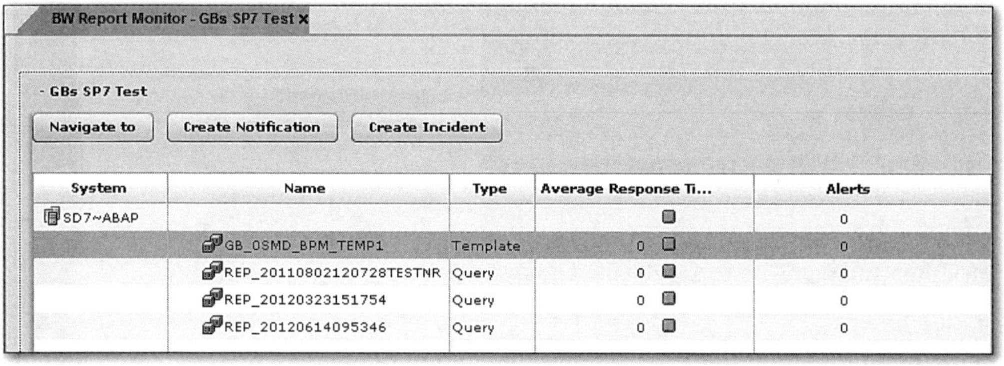

Figure 6.22 BW Report Monitor

The BW report monitor displays a list of all reports monitored, grouped according to the BW system. You can monitor the following two parameters for each report:

▶ AVERAGE RESPONSE TIME
You use the AVERAGE RESPONSE TIME parameter to monitor the average report execution time in seconds.

▶ ALERTS

You use the ALERTS parameter to monitor the number of alerts that occurred while executing the query or template.

You can then choose NAVIGATE TO to navigate, for the purpose of a detailed analysis, to the collection of BI performance tools, the load analysis in Transaction ST03, or the BW reporting tools.

Monitoring SAP Data Services Jobs

The BO data services monitor is used to analyze SAP data services jobs. In addition to the status overview, the following measurement readings are displayed with status icons:

▶ DURATION (mins)

▶ NOT STARTED ON TIME

▶ OUT OF TIME WINDOW

These status icons have the same meaning as those mentioned in the context of BW process chains.

SAP HANA and SLT Systems in BI Monitoring

Only the following technical parameters are displayed for SAP HANA and SLT systems (see Figure 6.23):

▶ Alerts

▶ Availability

▶ Performance

▶ Exceptions

Systems that do not have their own BI objects (for example, SAP HANA systems, SLT systems, or source systems) can be monitored only in the BI OVERVIEW monitor. As already shown, you access the overview of individual systems by selecting the relevant component in the system type view. From here, you can access the system monitor for the system you have selected.

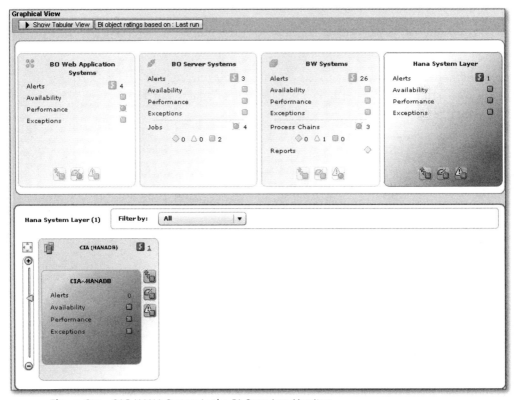

Figure 6.23 SAP HANA System in the BI Overview Monitor

6.2 Central Monitoring of SAP NetWeaver PI

IT departments are under increasing pressure to implement incident-free opera-tions while, at the same time, keeping the operating costs associated with the IT infrastructure low. In order to achieve this while responding to rapidly changing requirements, it makes sense to integrate applications from various providers. SAP NetWeaver PI facilitates such integration.

In other words, you can use SAP NetWeaver PI to integrate business processes that span different software components, departments, and organizations within a company. Incident-free operation of SAP NetWeaver PI is essential for ensuring that cross-system processes work properly and can be executed. Efficient process-ing of messages that need to be exchanged and the successful transfer of messages play a major role here.

The central monitoring platform of SAP Solution Manager provides monitors for monitoring all the PI domains connected to SAP Solution Manager. A PI domain comprises all technical SAP and non-SAP systems, also known as business systems, as well as all technical components that exchange data among each other via a PI system. Figure 6.24 shows a schematic diagram of a PI domain.

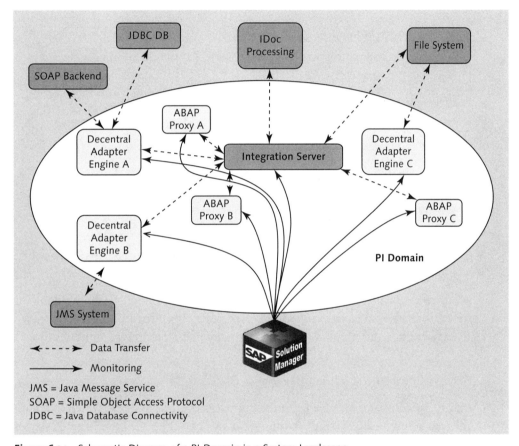

Figure 6.24 Schematic Diagram of a PI Domain in a System Landscape

In the next section, we will show you how to implement technical monitoring for PI domains. We will use our example of Toys Inc. to demonstrate how to use the PI monitoring functions in a useful manner.

6.2.1 Advantages of PI Monitoring with SAP Solution Manager

Centralized monitoring of the PI domains helps you identify problems early on and resolve them in a targeted manner. This in turn ensures high availability of the integration server, which is responsible for receiving and forwarding messages among various SAP and non-SAP systems. In addition to this general task, PI monitoring also helps to answer the following questions:

▶ What is the general status of all PI components in the productive PI domain?

▶ Which business-critical interfaces have been disrupted? In other words, which have been assigned an error status?

▶ Which PI components have experienced the most errors?

▶ Which errors have occurred most often?

▶ How many communication channels have errors?

▶ How many messages were received during the year and via which communication channel?

▶ Were the messages received from various customers processed successfully?

▶ Is there a backlog of messages? If so, is this linked to the general volume of messages received? What is the reason messages were not processed in the specified manner?

All these questions arise in the course of pure system operations and are submitted to you or the administrative support team responsible for the PI landscape. In order to answer these questions, we will next show you how to implement monitoring.

6.2.2 Configuring PI Monitoring

Before you start to set up PI monitoring, you must first check which software releases are necessary for SAP Solution Manager and the PI system. In general, you can use central monitoring in the scope described here as of SAP Solution Manager 7.1 SP05 and SAP NetWeaver PI Release 7.11 SP06. Since PI monitoring, in comparison to other monitoring options, is still relatively new, the functions have gradually been enhanced with subsequent Support Packages for SAP NetWeaver PI. For example, some additional functions and improvements were implemented with SAP NetWeaver PI 7.30. You can now perform the following tasks:

▶ Retrieve detailed information for self-testing the PI components

▶ Use enhanced log information for communication channels

▶ Use a ping function to perform an availability check on PI communication channels

▶ Use additional information about the message status, which supports root cause analysis in the event of a problem

A central, user-defined message search function is available as of SAP NetWeaver PI release 7.31 and SAP Solution Manager 7.1 SP2. Here, you can use business data attributes (known as *payload attributes*) to specifically search for messages for all or individual runtime components. Consequently, a manual check of the individual runtime components is unnecessary, thus resulting in faster analyses.

Furthermore, you can use PI message alerting as of SAP NetWeaver PI release 7.31 and SAP Solution Manager 7.1 SP05. The advantage of this enhancement is that alerts resulting from a failed message can be retrieved directly from the alert inbox.

A prerequisite for setting up PI monitoring is that the basic configuration of SAP Solution Manager has been set up along with technical monitoring for all systems within a PI domain. In this context, a PI domain represents a technical scenario. In addition to runtime components from SAP NetWeaver PI, this scenario contains SAP business systems and any non-SAP systems. It is defined in the System Landscape Directory (SLD).

A PI domain is defined by means of data suppliers. In the case of AS ABAP systems, data collection programs are executed periodically, and an RFC connection is used to send the data via a gateway and SLD bridge to the SLD. The data suppliers of J2EE-based systems use an HTTP connection to send data to the SLD. Such data suppliers are usually set up accordingly when you install AS Java.

If, in the SLD, you want to register systems that do not contain any SAP NetWeaver components, use the relevant host, sldreg. However, this requires you to have installed an SAP host agent on the host. Section 2.2.1 provided information on how to install this SAP host agent on a server. Information about using sldreg to register the host with the SLD is available via the following link: *http://help.sap. com/saphelp_nwpi71/helpdata/en/45/4a167edf6008d1e10000000a11466f/content.htm*

If the system data is in the corresponding PI-SLD, it must be transferred to the LMDB for SAP Solution Manager. This transfer is performed using the SLD connection to the LMDB, as described in step 5: Landscape Description in Section 2.5.2. As soon as the SLD is connected to the LMDB, the data is automatically synchronized in regular background processing. Depending on the infrastructure, the following three transfer options are available to you for synchronizing data from the PI-SLD for the LMDB in SAP Solution Manager:

▶ The first option involves using a central SLD. Here, the PI-SLD data is transmitted by means of unidirectional synchronization into the central SLD. The data is then transferred from the central SLD to the LMDB in SAP Solution Manager. In this option, the transfer is fully automated, and changes in the PI-SLD are synchronized directly with the LMDB. However, this option requires central SLD version 7.10 or higher.

▶ A manual data transfer using a copy program.

▶ Direct data synchronization with the LMDB.

Unfortunately, the differences among the various synchronization methods, as well as the pros and cons of each, are beyond the scope of this book. In principle, however, each of these methods is supported in monitoring within SAP Solution Manager.

In our Toys Inc. system landscape, we are using SAP Solution Manager 7.1 SP6 and SAP NetWeaver PI 7.3.

Configuring PI Monitoring

The starting point for the configuration is the SAP SOLUTION MANAGER CONFIGURATION work center (Transaction SOLMAN_SETUP). In the navigation area, choose TECHNICAL MONITORING. Then, choose PI MONITORING from the selection options available on the left-hand side of the screen.

> **Note**
>
> Note that all the systems to be managed, as well as system monitoring of such systems, which are mapped in a PI domain, must be configured beforehand.

Overview

Step 1, the configuration overview, serves as a point of entry to all other configuration steps. Here, you obtain an overview of all previously active configurations and their respective statuses, which are illustrated by a colored status icon.

Configure Infrastructure

In this step, you can check or change the infrastructure's configuration. Since we already described this step in detail in Section 5.4.2 we will focus on the CREATE STANDARD USERS substep in SAP Solution Manager here. To do this, choose EDIT.

Various standard users are available here and differentiated by the authorizations assigned to each. In the standard SAP system, we differentiate between two user types: level 1 and level 2 users. The level 1 user type works in the alert inbox within technical monitoring. Based on the authorizations assigned to this user type, its activities are limited to the responsibilities outlined below. In other words, a level 1 user can perform only the following activities:

▶ Operate the PI overview monitor

▶ Operate the component monitor

▶ Create incidents and notifications in the form of an email or SMS message

The level 2 user type has additional authorizations, which build upon the level 1 user type. This user has additional responsibilities in terms of root cause analysis and processing relevant problems. A level 2 user can perform the following activities:

▶ Call the TECHNICAL MONITORING and ROOT CAUSE ANALYSIS work centers

▶ Operate the PI overview monitor

▶ Operate the component monitor

▶ Operate the channel monitor

▶ Operate the PI message monitor

▶ Use root cause analysis

▶ Create incidents and notifications

This user is needed if you want to distribute potential alerts, as well as conduct and process error analyses. SAP also enables you to create such users with their own authorizations and user names. Furthermore, you can adjust the authorizations assigned to an existing user or use your own existing user if the operational process design requires this.

Once you have created the relevant users, you can proceed to the next step in the setup.

Define Scope

In the DEFINE SCOPE step, select the PI domains you want to monitor. PI domains comprise runtime components (for example, the central integration engine, the business process engine, centralized or decentralized adapters, or business systems). These components run on different technical systems in the system landscape and are described in PI-SLD on the basis of the Common Information Model (CIM) standard, which, in turn, is based on the object-oriented modeling approach for hardware and software elements.

If you want to define a PI domain, you must create a technical scenario that contains data from the PI infrastructure and the business systems. As already described in Section 2.3, this data is transferred from the SLD to the LMDB by means of a background job. The SCENARIO SELECTION table now contains the PI domains known from the LMDB. Choose CREATE. A dialog box in which you can define the properties of the technical scenario opens (see Figure 6.25).

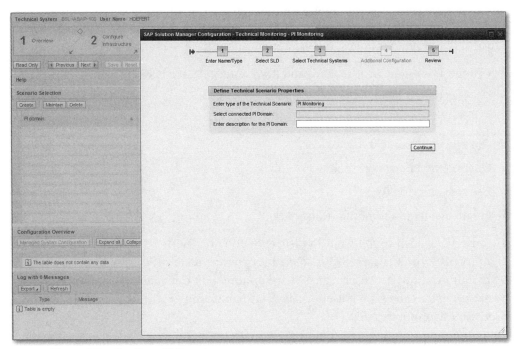

Figure 6.25 Creating a PI Domain

You are prompted to enter parameters in the input fields. Here, the necessary parameters include a description of the PI domain, associated SLD, and technical systems to be monitored. At the same time, you can hide those business systems for which monitoring is not relevant. If you have defined these parameters, the technical scenario is created successfully. To exit the substep, choose SETUP.

Editing an existing scenario is similar to creating a PI domain. To do this, select an existing PI domain and choose EDIT. A dialog box in which you can make the relevant changes opens.

Monitoring & Alerting

In the MONITORING & ALERTING step within the PI monitoring setup, you implement the setup steps associated with monitoring and/or alerting for the technical scenario you defined previously. This step is divided into several substeps, each of which is described in the next subsections.

PI Domain Overview

First, in the PI DOMAIN OVERVIEW substep, you obtain an overview of known PI domains (see Figure 6.26).

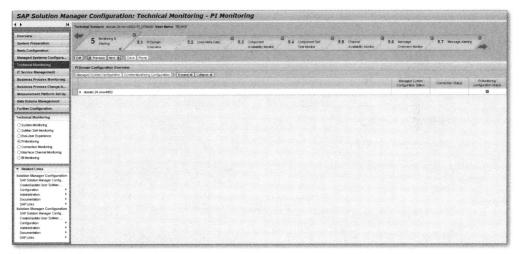

Figure 6.26 PI Domain Overview

If you now expand the nodes, you will see the business systems involved, as well as the components of the PI integration server (for example, `domain.24.vmw.4802`).

If some connections have errors, they are indicated by status icons in the PI MONITORING CONFIGURATION STATUS column. In Figure 6.26, the domain was assigned a green status icon. If, however, the domain had been assigned a yellow or red status icon and you therefore needed to make corrections to an erroneous configuration, you could choose MANAGED SYSTEM CONFIGURATION or SYSTEM MONITORING CONFIGURATION to process such corrections.

Load Meta-Data

The LOAD META-DATA substep executes a range of automatic activities. For example, the data for the relevant PI components is determined in this way. Here, the data is read again from the LMDB. Furthermore, master data texts from SAP NetWeaver PI are loaded into the BI system assigned to SAP Solution Manager because PI message monitoring needs these master data texts for the message monitor.

A data collector, scheduled to run periodically, loads channel attributes (for example, the channel name, channel status, and short log type) into SAP Solution Manager. This process is also executed automatically. Once these activities have been completed, you can navigate to the third substep.

Component Availability Monitor

In the COMPONENT AVAILABILITY MONITOR, you activate monitoring for the following components:

▶ **Central Integration Engine:** is responsible for the central services within the integration server (for example, routing and mapping)

▶ **Central Adapter Engine:** is based on the adapter framework and enables the integration engine to be connected to SAP and non-SAP systems

▶ **Adapter Engine:** facilitates a connection to an integration engine

▶ **ABAP Proxy:** is a communication interface based on the ABAP programming language

▶ **Enterprise Services Repository:** contains metadata for the services

▶ **Integration Directory:** contains the configuration data for the business processes of a particular system landscape

▶ **Mapping Runtime:** is the runtime associated with displaying items from a source catalog in a target catalog

▶ **Business Process Engine:** is the runtime engine for integration processes

For each component, you can make customer-defined settings for the availability check, which take account of special requests in terms of notifications and their content, thus enabling you to adjust the configuration to the requirements of the relevant user departments.

Here, the first step is to select the relevant component (see Figure 6.27). Therefore, choose CHANGE SAP SETTINGS to make the necessary adjustments. If you wish, you can adjust the data collection periods, alerting severity, and general data collection. Choose CHANGE SAP SETTINGS for this purpose. On the tab pages shown in Figure 6.27, you can integrate the adjustments into notification management or ITSM. To make customer-defined settings, choose the INCIDENT TICKETS and NOTIFICA-TIONS tab pages.

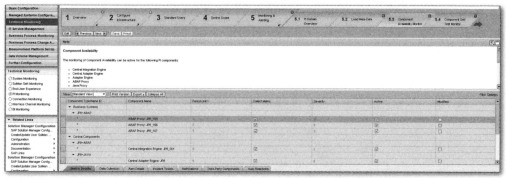

Figure 6.27 Adjusting Customer-Defined Settings for Component Availability

Component Self Test Monitor

Once the required settings have been activated, you can proceed with the substep, specifically, with the settings for the COMPONENT SELF TEST MONITOR. This test uses different component-dependent check objects to check that the components are working without error. You can perform the component self-test for the following components:

▸ Central integration engine

▸ Central adapter engine

▸ Adapter engine

▸ ABAP proxy

▸ Business process engine

▸ Enterprise services repository

▸ Integration directory

▸ Mapping runtime

The settings for the component self-test are made in the same way as configuring the component availability monitor. Their integration into notification management and ITSM occurs in exactly the same way as described in the previous step (in other words, using the same tab pages).

Channel Availability Monitor

The CHANNEL AVAILABILITY MONITOR substep enables you to activate channel status information for all centralized or decentralized adapter engines in the PI domains you have selected. The overall channel availability status is calculated from the channel that defines inbound and outbound processing for a message and from a channel's activation status.

If you want to change the settings provided by SAP, select the relevant adapter engine. As soon as you have made a change, the checkbox in the MODIFIED column is displayed as active. Select the DATA COLLECTION tab. Various parameters for controlling the channel information to be collected are available here. Table 6.1 provides an explanation of each parameter.

Parameter	Explanation
CHANNELONLYERR	This parameter means that data is not collected from channels that have the status SUCCESSFUL.
SHORTLOGCOLLECT	Short log data is collected.
SHORTLOGONLYERR	If this indicator is set, short log data is not collected for channels that have the status SUCCESSFUL. This setting is relevant if CHANNELONLYERR is not set. The number of characters to be collected for the short log (for each channel and server node). This can lie between 300 and 1,500 characters.
SHORTLOGSIZE	The number of characters to be collected for the short log (for each channel and server node). This can lie between 300 and 1,500 characters.
SHORTLOGTRIM	Stack traces are not added to the short log so that the log remains easy to read.

Table 6.1 Parameters Available for Controlling Channel Monitoring

Message Overview Monitor

In the MESSAGE OVERVIEW MONITOR substep, message status information is defined for the following PI components (see Figure 6.28):

- ► Central integration engine
- ► Central adapter engine
- ► Adapter engine
- ► ABAP proxy

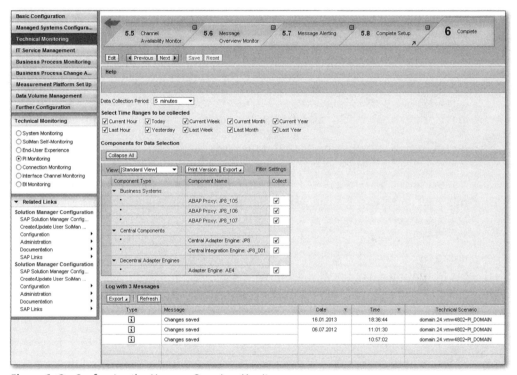

Figure 6.28 Configuring the Message Overview Monitor

To obtain message status information for a component, activate the relevant checkbox in the COLLECT column. You can also use the checkboxes in the SELECT TIME RANGES TO BE COLLECTED area to define the periods during which you want information to be collected.

Message Alerting

In the next substep, MESSAGE ALERTING, you can register SAP Solution Manager as a consumer of message alerts.

For this to happen, you must have used single sign-on (SSO) to log on to the relevant PI system. Furthermore, the configuration user must have the SAP role `SAP_XI_ALERTCONFIGURATOR_J2EE`. If you want to use rules-based alerting, you must first use the alert rule to define which alerts are to be collected in the SAP NetWeaver PI infrastructure. A detailed description for configuring alert rules is available in SAP Help. To do this, call *http://help.sap.com* and choose SAP NETWEAVER PROCESS INTEGRATION LIBRARY • FUNCTION-ORIENTED VIEW • PROCESS INTEGRATION • ADMINISTERING PROCESS INTEGRATION • COMPONENT-BASED MESSAGE ALERTING.

If you have already defined alert rules, they are displayed in the main table in the configuration area. To register SAP Solution Manager as a consumer, select the checkbox in the ACTIVE column in order to trigger data collection for the failed PI messages associated with all relevant PI runtime components for this rule.

If problems occur while processing a message in a PI system, this erroneous message is added to a queue and the definition of your alert rule is used to check whether an event needs to be set for this message. Once the conditions of the alert rule have been fulfilled, the registered consumer (in other words, SAP Solution Manager) retrieves the events and processes them within the alert engine. You can also specify whether you receive individual alerts or aggregated alerts for failed PI messages. Note that aggregated message alerts are created using a combination of the PI runtime component, name of the alert rule, name of the integration flow, and status details. They do not contain any details about the individual messages. For individual alerts, you can call the following details for failed messages:

- ▶ PI runtime component
- ▶ Name of the alert rule
- ▶ Name of the integration flow
- ▶ Status details
- ▶ Sender/receiver attributes
- ▶ Message ID
- ▶ User-Defined Search (UDS) attributes and corresponding values

> **Warning**
>
> If you activate the checkbox in the ALERTS PER PI MESSAGE column in the RULE LIST table, you obtain an individual alert for each failed PI message. Note that creating individual alerts generates an additional system load and increases the volume of data within the system. Therefore, we do not recommend creating individual alerts unless it is absolutely necessary.

Complete Setup

The COMPLETE SETUP substep activates all the settings made in the preceding steps. To do this, choose ACTIVATE MONITORING & ALERTING.

Complete

In the final step, COMPLETE, you obtain an overview of the configuration steps you executed (see Figure 6.29).

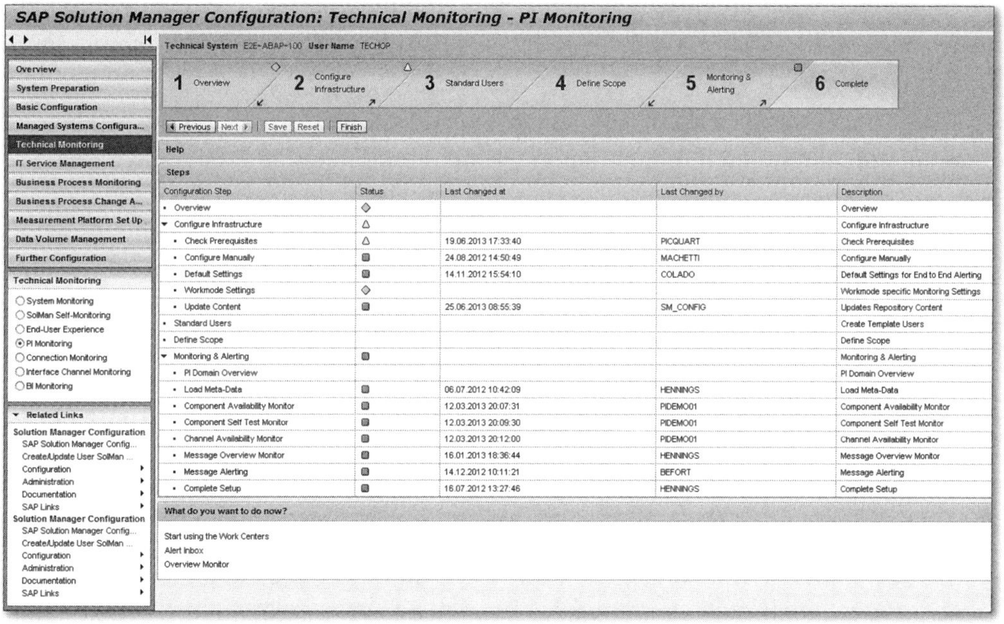

Figure 6.29 Overview of Configuration Steps Executed

Figure 6.29 shows our configuration. The status is green, which means we have successfully completed the configuration.

You can now use PI monitoring. We will demonstrate this in the next section.

6.2.3 Using PI Monitoring

You can call SAP NetWeaver PI monitoring via the TECHNICAL MONITORING work center. PI monitoring contains all PI domains connected to SAP Solution Manager. You can start the available individual monitors by selecting the relevant monitor in a new window or an embedded window, as we explained in Section 6.1.4. We will discuss the individual monitors in the following subsections. Figure 6.30 shows the starting point for PI monitoring. The individual monitors are started using the buttons of the same name.

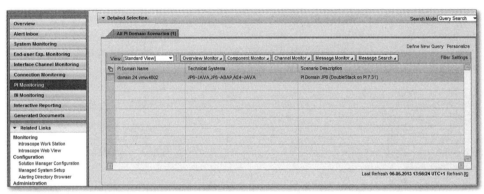

Figure 6.30 Starting Point for PI Monitoring

Overview Monitor

To call the overview monitor, choose OVERVIEW MONITOR. Here, you can obtain an overview of the overall status of a PI domain. This current overview status, which can be adjusted by restricting the period, is displayed in a table or graphic. You can display any time between the current hour and the past week. Figure 6.31 displays information about the central components, de-central adapter engines, and business systems.

The green status next to the AVAILABILITY field in Figure 6.31 indicates that the central components are available. The yellow status next to the SELF-TEST field indicates that the self-test was not completely successful. The channels have also experienced some serious problems. The self-test for the business systems also has a green status. Overall, however, three alerts occurred. Therefore, an expert should examine this situation.

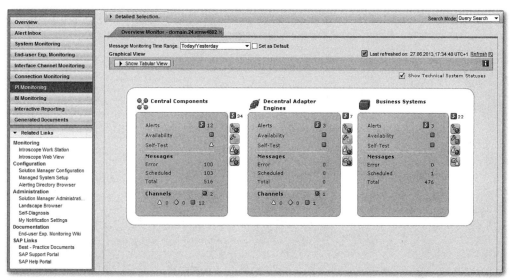

Figure 6.31 Overview Monitor

If you want to call detailed information about the individual components (for example, the integration engine and central adapter engine), you can select the individual alerts or status icons. The following categories are available here:

▶ Number of existing alerts

▶ Availability of components

▶ Self-test for applications

▶ Number of messages with an error status or in process, and the total volume of messages for the time interval selected

In the case of technical systems, the information already known from system monitoring is also displayed. The following information is taken directly from technical monitoring:

▶ Availability information

▶ Exception status

▶ Configuration status

▶ System performance status

If you wish, you can use the status icons to navigate directly to technical monitoring, where you will obtain a detailed overview of the cause of the rating.

Component Monitor

Choose COMPONENT MONITOR to open the component monitor (see Figure 6.32). The aggregated status messages relating to availability are displayed in a table here, along with the status of the self-test for individual application components. Expand the CENTRAL COMPONENTS, DECENTRAL ADAPTER ENGINES, and BUSINESS SYSTEMS nodes. You now have a detailed insight into the status of the components used.

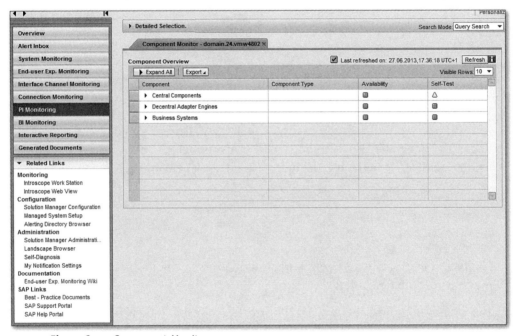

Figure 6.32 Component Monitor

If you select an individual component, a table that contains information about the self-tests performed is displayed in the lower screen area (see Figure 6.33).

The component monitor provides you with a range of analysis tools. If you want to trigger a *ping* and perform self-tests manually, you can choose MANAGE. Then, choose NAVIGATE TO. You can now use single sign-on to call the relevant analysis tools for the systems you want to manage. You can also create notifications in the form of SMS messages, email, or a support ticket and send them to specific persons. If you want to call this function, choose CREATE.

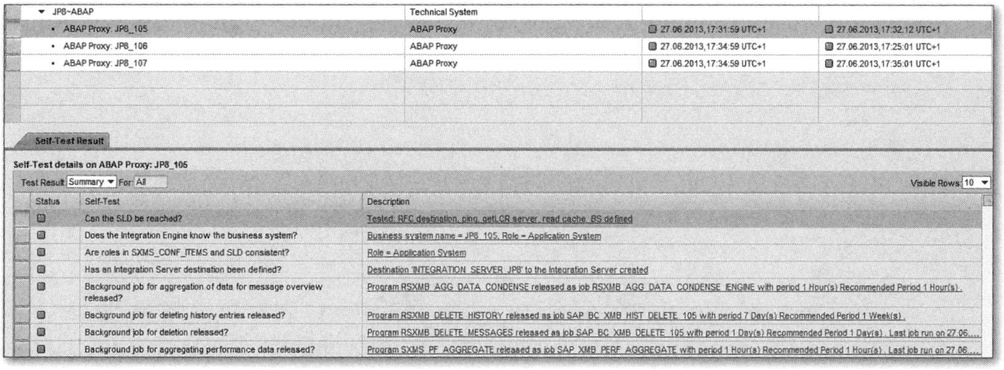

Figure 6.33 Detailed Information about Self Tests

Choose NAVIGATE TO to navigate directly to the local expert tools for the relevant components. Since many of these tools require PI-specific knowledge and expertise, we will not discuss them further here. For further information, we recommend that you read the book *Mastering SAP NetWeaver PI—Administration*, by Marcus Banner, Heinzpeter Klein, and Christian Riesener (SAP PRESS 2009).

Channel Monitor

Choose CHANNEL MONITOR to call the channel monitor. In this monitor, you can retrieve information about the adapter for specific connections (communication channels). Here, you can use the filter options in the CHANNEL FILTER area to filter according to the ADAPTER ENGINE, ADAPTER TYPE, CHANNEL NAME, and CHANNEL STATUS (see Figure 6.34).

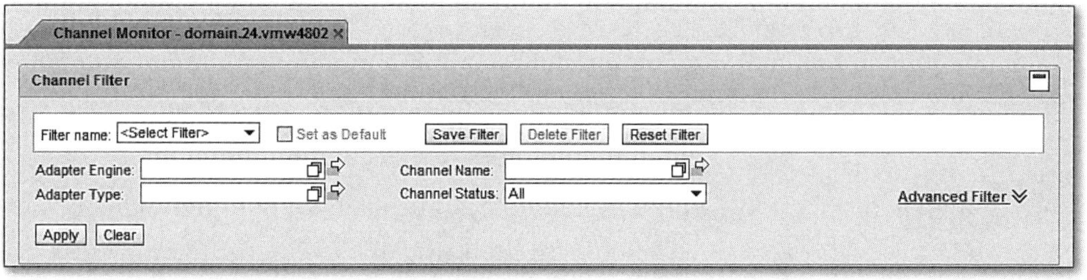

Figure 6.34 Channel Filters in the Channel Monitor

If you do not set a filter here, all the communication channels for all adapter engines are displayed and can be monitored at a glance (see Figure 6.35). In addition to the activation state and channel state, you can also display short log information in the event of an error. You can also test, start, or stop communication channels here. To do this, choose MANAGE. As already described for the component monitor, you can choose CREATE to create a notification or an incident ticket.

The situation outlined in Figure 6.35 is representative of a rather serious problem because a red status is displayed for three of the channels being monitored. Here, you can choose NAVIGATE TO to call the relevant analysis tools for starting error analysis.

If you want to obtain more detailed information about a particular error, select the relevant row so that the system displays this information on the CHANNEL DETAILS tab page. Figure 6.35 shows detailed information for channel XIDemoChannel_FileXML_.

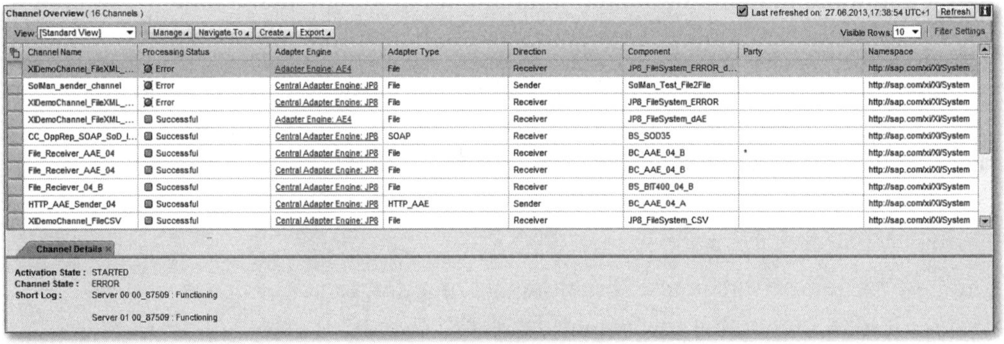

Figure 6.35 Channel Overview and Channel Details in the Channel Monitor

Message Monitor

The message monitor summarizes the information associated with message processing. To call this monitor, choose MESSAGE MONITOR. This information is displayed in graphics on the following three tab pages: ERROR MONITOR, BACKLOG MONITOR, and MESSAGE OVERVIEW MONITOR. As of Support Package 08, the MESSAGE FLOW MONITOR was renamed the MESSAGE OVERVIEW MONITOR.

Different filters are available for all monitors. You have the option to enhance and store these filters, as well as use them for a simplified and accelerated search. In the next section, we will briefly introduce you to each monitor.

354

Backlog Monitor

Figure 6.36 shows the backlog monitor. In this monitor, the information is presented in the same way as it is in the error monitor. However, only those messages that still do not have a final status and, therefore, have yet to be processed are displayed. A final status means that processing was either successful or canceled. Therefore, the backlog monitor displays messages that have the status PLANNED.

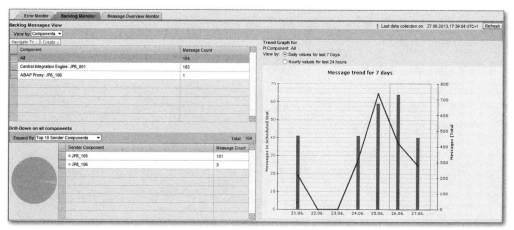

Figure 6.36 Backlog Monitor

Error Monitor

First, we will take a look at the error monitor, as shown in Figure 6.37.

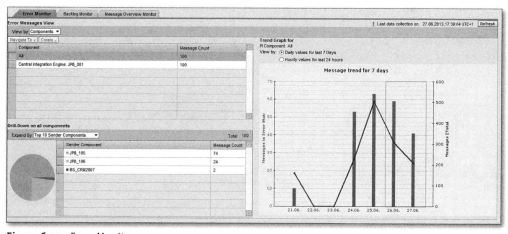

Figure 6.37 Error Monitor

Two different views are available in the error monitor. In the VIEW BY field, you can choose between the COMPONENTS view and the STATUS view. The COMPONENTS view is selected in Figure 6.37.

Depending on the runtime component, the messages assigned an error status are displayed here. In Figure 6.37, there are 100 messages in the MESSAGE COUNT column. A trend graph is shown on the right-hand side of the error monitor. You can use the radio buttons to select whether daily values from the last seven days or hourly values from the last 24 hours are to be displayed. In our example, the message trend is clearly on the rise.

In the EXPAND BY field in the lower DRILL-DOWN ON ALL COMPONENTS area, you can display different top 10 views. In our example in Figure 6.37, we selected the TOP 10 SENDER COMPONENTS option. As you can see, there are 74 messages related to JP8_105, 24 related to JP8_106, and 2 related to BS_CRM2007.

In the STATUS view, failed messages for different error status messages are listed for a specific time window. You can also call different top 10 views here.

Message Overview Monitor

The message overview monitor is the third monitor in the group of message monitors. This monitor records all messages statuses and can be used on a cross-runtime component basis. Figure 6.38 shows the FORWARDED column. This means that the message still does not have a final status, but the individual PI components were processed successfully. Here, you can choose MANAGE to restart PI messages that have been assigned an error status.

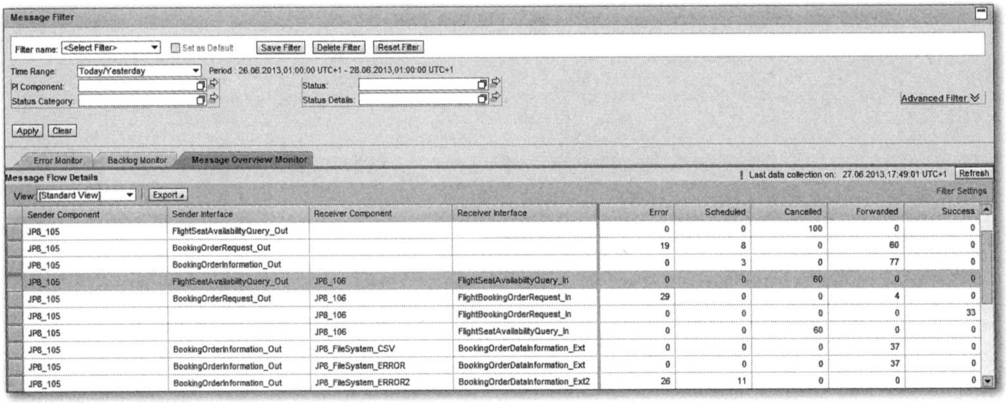

Figure 6.38 Message Overview Monitor

You can also choose SHOW TREND to display a graphic for message processing.

6.2.4   Message Search

The central message search function was made available in SAP Solution Manager 7.1 SP2 and SAP NetWeaver PI 7.3 EHP1. This practical function provides you with tools that enable you to search for messages on a content or cross-runtime component basis or within archives. To start a message search, choose MESSAGE SEARCH. You can enter selection criteria or use placeholders to display messages relating to the PI components. As with all the monitors, you can create follow-up activities here and export the results to Microsoft Excel for reporting purposes.

You have now learned about the options available within central PI monitoring. Before we show you how to configure and use end-user experience monitoring, we wish to tell you about some useful SAP notes and links that contain further information.

6.2.5   Additional Documentation

Links

- Wiki for technical information:
  http//wiki.sdn.sap.com/wiki/display/TechOps/techAdm_Home

- *http://help.sap.com/saphelp_nwpi71/helpdata/en/45/4a167edf6008d1e10000000a11466f/content.htm*

- *http://help.sap.com/saphelp_nwpi71/helpdata/en/45/4a167edf6008d1e10000000a11466f/content.htm*

- *http://wiki.sdn.sap.com/wiki/display/TechOps/PiMon_Overview*

SAP Notes

Table 6.2 provides an overview of important SAP Notes for PI monitoring, which are available on SAP Service Marketplace.

Contents	SAP Note
Configuration missing for JCO/RFC connections in the SLD	1057720
Configuring the RFC gateway for the SLD supplier	1172161
Error while using RFC to access a remote SLD	1476839
Server names in the SLD	1052122
SLD configuration for PI-SLD	1631346

Table 6.2 SAP Notes for Configuring PI Monitoring

6.3   End-User Experience Monitoring

In general, the term *end-user experience monitoring* (EEMon) describes a procedure that provides information about the availability and performance of a particular IT system from the perspective of the end user.

6.3.1   Concept of End-User Experience Monitoring

While the data for system monitoring (see Section 5.5.1) is collected close to the IT system to be monitored in order to accurately describe the actual status of an IT system at any time, the data in EEMon, on the other hand, is collected in close proximity to the end user of an IT system. This change in perspective makes it possible to not only consider the IT system to be monitored, but also to integrate into monitoring all technical components used en route from the user to the IT system.

In contrast to various other EEMon solutions, which directly monitor how the end user interacts with an IT system, SAP EEMon simulates the activities of the end user on the IT system by executing scripts on a regular basis. The advantage of this approach is that your IT systems are monitored even if no end user is working on them. In contrast to your end users, EEMon never sleeps and can therefore also identify incidents at times when your end users are not working on the IT system. This enables you to respond at an early stage and resolve incidents before your end user wants to work on the system. Another advantage to this approach is that the privacy of your end user is protected because he or she does not fear that their activities are being "monitored" by EEMon.

EEMon is not intended to replace your existing system monitoring, but to supplement it in a useful manner. It provides additional added value by extending the focus of your system monitoring toward your end users so that it can also identify incidents that your existing monitoring infrastructure cannot detect. EEMon enables you to automate monitoring of the availability and performance of your IT systems from within any enterprise location (see Figure 6.39).

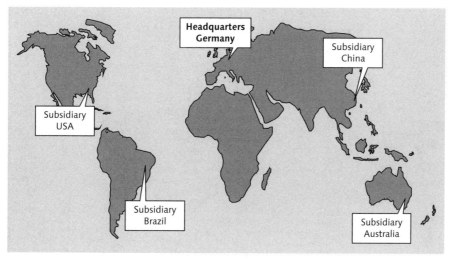

Figure 6.39 Global Monitoring of IT Systems

Furthermore, EEMon supports you in identifying the cause of an incident by being integrated into end-to-end trace analysis (see Section 4.5), which you can use to create detailed performance analyses for an IT system, if necessary. This makes it possible to quickly identify the cause of an incident and, therefore, also the IT department responsible for resolving the error, thus avoiding situations in which no one feels responsible for a particular incident while it is not classified.

Another reason for using EEMon is the option to define service level agreements (SLA) from the perspective of the end user and to monitor and document compliance with such agreements. Finally, EEMon also provides the analysis options usually available in SAP Solution Manager (for example, management dashboard, interactive reporting, and so on), which enable you to detect trends at an early stage and respond accordingly.

6.3.2 Technical Infrastructure

In order to understand how EEMon works, you should familiarize yourself with the technical infrastructure of EEMon. Figure 6.40 provides a broad overview of this technical infrastructure, which we will discuss in greater detail next.

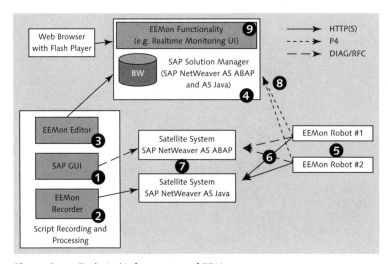

Figure 6.40 Technical Infrastructure of EEMon

EEMon scripts are the main element of EEMon. They contain all the information needed to simulate a typical end-user activity on a particular IT system. In addition to SAP GUI scripts for ABAP-based systems, which can be recorded by SAP GUI (see (❶) in Figure 6.40), there are also HTTP scripts, which are created using a special program, known as the EEMon recorder (❷). After the recording, the EEMon editor (❸) is used to edit and test the scripts. We will describe these three programs in greater detail in Section 6.3.4.

SAP Solution Manager (❹) is at the core of the technical infrastructure of the EEMon scenario. The EEMon function is configured and managed in SAP Solution Manager. Furthermore, EEMon scripts, as well as availability and performance data, are stored there. SAP Solution Manager also provides the graphical interface for analyses and various functions for collecting data and processing such data further.

The EEMon scripts are transferred to SAP Solution Manager. From here, they are distributed to the EEMon robots (❺) connected to SAP Solution Manager. From a technical perspective, an EEMon robot is simply the diagnostics agent you already know from root cause analysis and technical monitoring (see Section 2.2.2). However, while the diagnostics agent runs on the server of the IT system you want to monitor, you generally install EEMon robots on client PCs in the offices of the end users at various locations (subsidiaries, for example). Each of these EEMon robots automatically executes one or more EEMon scripts (❻) on a regular basis and collects, based on the steps outlined in the relevant script, all data concerning the availability and performance of the IT systems to be monitored (❼).

The EEMon robot then sends the data collected while executing the script to SAP Solution Manager (❽), where it is processed.

Depending on how the EEMon function is configured, it may be possible, in the event of an incident, to automatically send notifications by email or SMS or to generate an incident message (also known as an *incident*). Employees in an IT department can also use the graphical interface (real-time monitoring UI) to check, at any time, the status of all IT systems being monitored (❾).

The EEMon data is stored on a permanent basis in Business Warehouse within SAP Solution Manager. If required, different analyses can be generated on the basis of this data. The many different ways in which the EEMon scenario can be used will be described in greater detail in Section 6.3.5.

6.3.3 Configuring End-User Experience Monitoring

Before you start to set up SAP EEMon, you should develop a monitoring concept in which you define which end-user activities are to be monitored, which IT systems are involved, and the geographical location of the corresponding end users. Furthermore, you should specify which situations are to be treated as incidents and how SAP Solution Manager, as the monitoring system, is to respond to such incidents (see also Section 5.5.2).

You should also ensure that the SAP Solution Manager to be configured fulfills the following prerequisites:

► System preparation completed successfully
► Basic configuration completed successfully
► All satellite systems to be monitored via EEMon are fully connected to SAP Solution Manager (see Section 2.5.4).

▶ If you want to use service desk integration so that incident messages are automatically generated when problems occur, the ITSM scenario must also be set up.

In addition to the diagnostics agents that may already be in use for root cause analysis and technical monitoring, you should now install one or more EEMon robots on computers in the end user's network and connect them to SAP Solution Manager. Here, you should install the latest version of the diagnostics agent, which was 7.30 SP02 at the time this book went to press. If you want to check whether the EEMon robot is connected to SAP Solution Manager, you can use agent administration for this purpose. Since the EEMon robot uses SAP GUI to execute SAP GUI scripts, it is imperative that an SAP GUI is installed locally on the host of the EEMon robot, which, in turn, implies that the EEMon robot must be installed on a Microsoft Windows host. Before installation, you should also check that the new SAP GUI versions are compatible with executing your EEMon scripts.

To ensure that your EEMon works without error, you should import the latest version of the EEMon correction note. The note number varies depending on the release version of your SAP Solution Manager system.

Once you have met all prerequisites, call the SAP SOLUTION MANAGER CONFIGURATION work center (Transaction SOLMAN_SETUP). In the navigation area, choose TECHNICAL MONITORING. Then, choose END-USER EXPERIENCE from the selection options available on the left-hand side of the screen. We will now briefly introduce you to the individual steps in the EEMon configuration:

1. OVERVIEW
   This step does not contain any configuration options. Rather, it provides a brief overview of the status of the EEMon infrastructure configuration.

2. CONFIGURE INFRASTRUCTURE
   This comprehensive step contains the initial configuration of the EEMon scenario, which in turn comprises several substeps for setting up the technical infrastructure already described. They include the following substeps:

   ▶ Check the technical prerequisites for setting up EEMon.

   ▶ Define global settings (for example, with regard to internal communication between the AS ABAP and AS Java stack or with regard to storing and reorganizing collected EEMon data in business warehouse within SAP Solution Manager).

- Configure the EEMon robots.

- Set up different work modes for the EEMon scenario (see the "Workmode Settings" subsection in Section 5.4.2).

3. SCRIPT MANAGEMENT

You activate EEMon in this step. To do this, create a *technical scenario* (in other words, a group of systems needed to execute the recorded end-user activity). Then, assign the technical scenario to your EEMon script. Finally, distribute the EEMon scripts to your EEMon robots, which then start to execute the scripts immediately.

4. MONITORING

This step provides a wide range of options for achieving a highly granular configuration of the EEMon scenario or for changing this scenario, either temporarily or permanently, at different levels (for example, per EEMon script or EEMon robot). In this step, you can specify, for example, the interval during which you want to execute an EEMon script.

5. ALERTING

Here, you can activate integration into the alert inbox and define thresholds for generating alerts, which in turn form the basis for sending email or SMS messages or for generating incident messages.

6. REPORTING

This step comprises the configuration options for SLA reporting. Here, you specify the calculation method and change, if necessary, the thresholds that form the basis for the SLA reports.

7. STANDARD USERS

In this optional configuration step, you can create users for managing and using the EEMon scenario on SAP Solution Manager. The necessary authorizations are automatically assigned to these users.

8. COMPLETE

The final step does not contain any additional configuration options. Rather, it provides some navigation options (for example, to the TECHNICAL MONITORING work center from where you can, in turn, navigate to the graphical interface for EEMon, known as the *real-time monitoring UI*) (see Section 6.3.5).

6.3.4 Creating EEMon Scripts

Aside from the technical infrastructure, EEMon scripts are the most important element of the EEMon scenario. Following their initial recording with SAP GUI or the EEMon recorder, the scripts are edited in the EEMon editor and then transferred to SAP Solution Manager. When you configure the EEMon scenario (see Section 6.3.3), the scripts are distributed to the EEMon robots, which immediately start to execute the scripts on a regular basis and collect data in relation to the availability and performance of the satellite systems to be monitored.

Before you start to create the EEMon scripts, you should give some thought to which typical end-user activities you want to monitor. The following questions may help:

▶ Are certain applications occasionally unavailable for end users?

▶ Do your end users complain of performance problems when using certain applications?

▶ Do they occasionally experience problems when logging on to an IT system or executing a certain transaction or function within an IT system?

For the most part, companies that decide to implement EEMon have already identified specific application scenarios that they are unable to cover with their existing monitoring solutions. As a further preparatory measure, you should ensure that you have a user with the relevant authorizations for executing the scenario on the IT system to be monitored. To ensure stable monitoring, we recommend that you create a dedicated user for recording and executing the scrip on the same IT system, instead of "misusing" one of your end users.

The next step is to procure the relevant programs for creating and editing EEMon scripts and to familiarize yourself with how they operate. General information concerning some restrictions associated with EEMon scripts is available in SAP Note 1357045 and the EEMon wiki, which is an EEMon knowledge database provided by SAP. You can access the EEMon wiki at *http://wiki.sdn.sap.com/wiki/display/EEM/Home*.

Recording SAP GUI Scripts

You do not require any additional software in order to create an SAP GUI script. The functions needed to record the script are already part of SAP GUI. However, to activate this recording function, you must first activate the profile parameter `sapgui/user_scripting` on the SAP system that you want to use to create the script. You do this by setting the profile parameter to `true`. For more information, see SAP Note 480149.

As soon as this profile parameter is active, you can call the SAP GUI scripting dialog, which you see in Figure 6.41, under the menu path ADJUST LOCAL LAYOUT • SCRIPT RECORDING AND PLAYBACK.

Figure 6.41 SAP GUI Scripting Dialog

This auxiliary program now enables you to record every interaction between the user and the SAP system (for example, calling transactions, entering data on selection screens, choosing buttons, and so on). A new step is created in the script each time a user calls a new screen or selects a new step. Now, record the relevant activity in the SAP system. The result of this recording is a Visual Basic script, which is saved locally and can be edited further in the EEMon editor (see the subsection titled "Using the EEMon Editor to Edit Scripts"). Specific restrictions concerning the creation of SAP GUI scripts are outlined in SAP Note 587202.

Recording an HTTP Script

To record HTTP scripts, you require the EEMon recorder. This program records all communication between Microsoft Internet Explorer and the remote web server and then generates an XML file. The EEMon recorder is essentially the SAP Client Plug-In that you already know from root cause analysis (see Section 4.5.2), which has been slightly modified for the EEMon scenario. For general information about this program, as well as the browser and operating system versions supported, known problems, and how to resolve them, see SAP Note 1435190. The latest version of the EEMon recorder is attached to the note.

In order to record data traffic, the EEMon recorder must toggle between your browser and the remote web server. Therefore, close all open browser windows and start the EEMon recorder (see Figure 6.42). You can then start a new browser session. In this new browser window, execute the activity you want to record.

To give your script some structure, we recommend that you define a new script step for each step in the system (for example, each click). You can do this by choosing NEW STEP in the EEMon recorder at any time. You can also choose STOP TRANSACTION to end script recording at any time. The result of this recording is an XML file that you can edit further in the EEMon editor (see the subsection "Using the EEMon Editor to Edit Scripts").

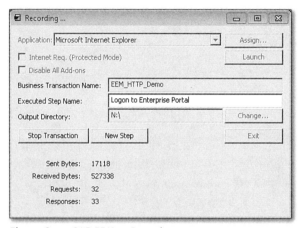

Figure 6.42 SAP EEMon Recorder

In principle, the EEMon recorder is able to record any form of HTTP(S) communication. You can therefore create HTTP scripts not only for SAP systems, but also for all other web servers. The relevant restrictions are outlined in SAP Note 1357045.

Using the EEMon Editor to Edit Scripts

The EEMon editor is a tool that SAP has specifically provided for configuring and editing EEMon scripts. It is based on the widely used Eclipse development environment and provides various functions for modifying and enhancing EEMon scripts. In step 3 of the EEMon configuration, you can download the EEMon editor directly from your SAP Solution Manager (see Section 6.3.3). However, to benefit from up-to-date functional enhancements, we recommend that you download the latest version of the EEMon editor from the EEMon wiki.

After you have started the EEMon editor, the first step is to create a project. You can then import the Visual Basic or XML files previously created using SAP GUI or the EEMon recorder into the EEMon editor. Figure 6.43 shows an example of the EEMon editor interface when editing an SAP GUI script.

To create a fully functional SAP GUI script, you must define system data for the SAP system on which you want to execute the script (DNS name or IP address, instance number, user name, and password). You do this in the script configuration for the EEMon editor under SCRIPT • SCRIPT CONFIGURATION • VARIABLES. Since this information is not recorded by the SAP GUI scripting dialog, the recorded script can also be applied to another SAP system, if necessary. HTTP scripts already contain the necessary system information in the HTTP URLs.

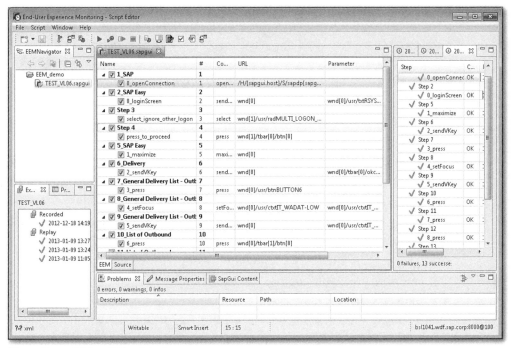

Figure 6.43 EEMon Editor Interface

As soon as this information is defined in the script, you should execute the recorded script once as a test. When executing SAP GUI scripts in the EEMon editor, you can perform live tracking of each system interaction in SAP GUI. Each time a script is executed for the first time, the initial thresholds for executing each script step are calculated from the target system's response times. These thresholds are used to categorize the performance of the IT system or the activity recorded on this IT system while the EEMon scenario is running. Of course, you can also adjust these initial thresholds in the EEMon configuration procedure at any time.

However, you can also edit your scripts further in the EEMon editor. Table 6.3 lists some of the modifications you can make in the EEMon editor.

Modification	Explanation
Rename script steps	Script steps should have meaningful names that make them easier to identify.
Parameterization (HTTP scripts)	Dynamic URL components (for example, session IDs) are replaced with variable placeholders.
Text checks	A positive/negative check can be performed to check whether certain text elements exist.
Status bar check (SAP GUI scripts)	The return values in the status bar are checked.

Table 6.3 Some Modification Options in the EEMon Editor

A detailed description of all functions in the EEMon editor is available in the handbook that forms part of the EEMon editor installation package, which should be consulted if problems occur or you have any questions about the editor.

As soon as the EEMon script meets your requirements, you can transfer it to SAP Solution Manager. To do this, configure the connection to SAP Solution Manager in the EEMon editor under FILE • EDITOR CONFIGURATION • EDITOR • SOLUTION MANAGER CONNECTION and use the context menu entry EXPORT TO EEM ADMIN REPOSITORY to transfer the EEMon script. Alternatively, you can export your EEMon script from the EEMon editor and manually import it using the upload function in step 3 of the EEMon configuration procedure (see Section 6.3.3).

6.3.5 Using End-User Experience Monitoring

As soon as the initial SAP EEMon setup is complete and, in step 4 of the EEMon configuration, you have distributed at least one script to your EEMon robots (see Section 6.3.3), you can use the various available EEMon functions. If you want to test the EEMon scenario without scripts you have created yourself, you can use the EEMon self-check script delivered by SAP by default. We will introduce you to each individual EEMon function next.

EEMon Real-Time Monitoring User Interface

The EEMon real-time monitoring user interface (UI) is the main graphical interface used with the EEMon scenario. Since the EEMon real-time monitoring UI is based on the Adobe Flash platform, you should check whether the Adobe Flash plug-in is available in your browser.

To start the application, choose END-USER EXPERIENCE MONITORING in the TECHNICAL MONITORING work center. Here, select one of your technical scenarios and choose MONITORING to call the EEMon real-time monitoring UI. You will quickly discover that the EEMon real-time monitoring UI is easy to understand and intuitive to use and provides extensive configuration options. The results associated with executing each script or script step are visualized on this interface in different views. The individual views are not static, but interactive in nature.

The following two views (Figure 6.44 and Figure 6.45) are merely examples of the visualization options available in the EEMon real-time monitoring UI.

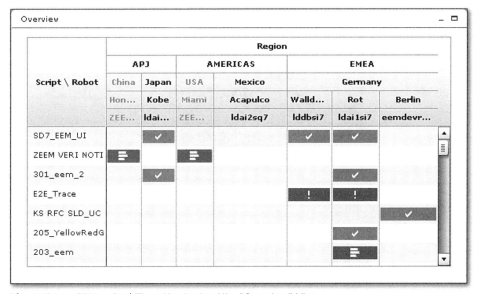

Figure 6.44 EEMon Real-Time Monitoring UI—"Overview" View

Figure 6.44 shows, for example, the OVERVIEW view. Each of the scripts shown in Figure 6.44 executes a specific activity on a specific IT system. Three of the scripts are successfully executed in the time predetermined by the thresholds. This means that, at this particular moment in time, your end users in the various regions can perform these activities on the relevant IT system as expected. However, three scripts cannot be executed at all or, at the very least, not in the predetermined time frame. Therefore, your end users cannot perform the activities at present, or they observe that system performance is poor when they try to do so. The employees in the IT department could now use the end-to-end trace analysis integrated into EEMon to determine the cause of the problem.

You can use the STATUS STATISTICS (see Figure 6.45) to quickly obtain an overview of the availability and performance of all monitored IT systems and process steps within a specific region. Note that this overview is from the perspective of the end users associated with these IT systems.

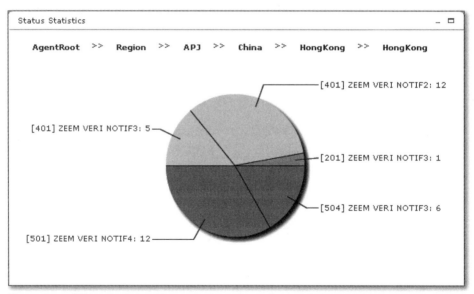

Figure 6.45 EEMon Real-time Monitoring UI—"Status Statistics" View

Integration into the Alert Inbox

As a result of integrating EEMon into the alert inbox in the MAI, you can be notified of any problems that occur in the systems being monitored. Once this alerting function has been set up, EEMon generates an alert in the alert inbox as soon as a critical situation occurs while executing a script.

For example, you could arrange to receive an alert if it takes an exceptionally long time to execute a step within a script (in other words, to execute a specific end-user activity). If the threshold defined for this script step is exceeded, SAP EEMon generates a corresponding alert in the alert inbox. Depending on the configuration, this alert can be sent as a notification by email or SMS to the relevant system administrator or forwarded to ITSM as an incident message, just like all other monitoring alerts in SAP Solution Manager. The last row in Figure 6.46 shows an EEMon alert in the alert inbox of SAP Solution Manager.

Alert Name	Category	Managed Object	Type	Current	Priority	Worst	Total	Changes	Status
Propagation from Script-Execution to Script		ZEEM VERI NOTIF4			Very high		6087	6	
EEM Script on Robot Performance Alert		EEM REDYELLOWGREEN SCRIPT_07~lddbsi7			High		1994	1989	
Propagation from Script-Execution to Script		SharedInst_SI7_CI			High		3	3	
Propagation from Script-Execution to Script		KS RFC SLD_UC			Medium		1	1	
Propagation from Script-Execution to Script		EEM Selfcheck Script			Medium		37	9	

Figure 6.46 Alert Inbox for EEMon Alerts

Integration into End-to-End Trace Analysis

In order to quickly identify the cause of a performance problem, EEMon works closely with end-to-end trace analysis, which is a root cause analysis tool (see Section 4.5). Within the EEMon real-time monitoring UI, you can activate end-to-end trace analysis for a certain script. This makes it possible to record not only the EEMon performance data for the individual scripts, but also the execution times for the script steps in the individual components of the IT system (application server, database, network, and so on). You can therefore analyze which component is the cause of the performance problem.

End-to-end trace analysis also works across system boundaries, thus making it considerably easier to analyze performance problems in complex landscapes. For example, you can monitor a portal system that in turn accesses an HR system in order to process requests in the background.

EEMon Reporting

In addition to the EEMon real-time monitoring UI, there are other ways in which to display and analyze EEMon data that has been collected. While the EEMon real-time monitoring UI is primarily used to analyze EEMon data collected over a short period of time (ranging from a few hours to a few days), SLA reporting and in particular, scenario reports, are used to analyze data over a longer period (ranging from a few days to a few years). These two reporting options are available in the END-USER EXPERIENCE MONITORING area within the TECHNICAL MONITORING work center. Select a scenario here and choose the relevant button for displaying the SLA report or scenario reports.

In the SLA report, you see, at a glance, the availability and performance of a certain scenario in the past month and the trend in comparison to the previous month. Figure 6.47 shows, for example, that the performance of a particular scenario is currently within the green area of the defined service level, but deteriorating. There is an urgent need for action here so that certain SLAs are not violated. For a particular system or scenario, this report should give the relevant person a quick overview of the system statuses from a user's perspective. You can also use this report to quickly check whether defined service level agreements have been observed and will presumably continue to be observed in the future.

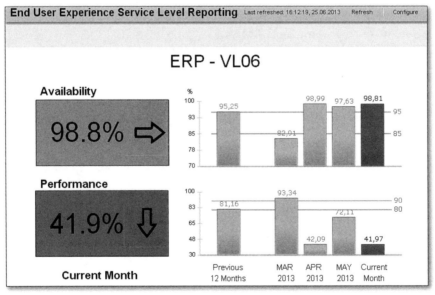

Figure 6.47 SLA Report based on EEMon Data

The SLA report is based on EEMon data stored in the business warehouse within SAP Solution Manager and on management dashboards known from other areas. You can easily configure the SLA report and show or hide certain scenarios.

Scenario reports are also based on the EEMon data stored in the business warehouse. However, they provide more detailed reporting options than the SLA report. Here, you can display detailed performance and availability data on the basis of scenarios, scripts, robots, and even script steps. You can also freely choose the period to be analyzed. Interactive reporting technology is used to visualize the data. You can use scenario reports to identify long-term trends, as well as phenomena that recur on a regular basis. Figure 6.48 shows an example of execution times for the EEMon self-check script in the context of the scenario report.

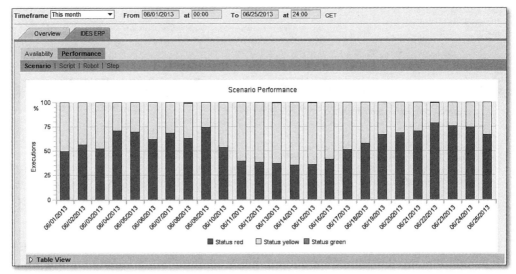

Figure 6.48 Scenario Report based on EEMon Data

As of SAP Solution Manager 7.1 SP Stack 6, you also have the option to access certain EEMon functions from your smartphone or tablet. You simply require the SAP USER EXPERIENCE MONITOR app, which you can download for free from the relevant app store for your platform (iOS or Android). Figure 6.49 shows a screenshot of this app on an Android-based tablet. For more information, see SAP Note 1786546.

Figure 6.49 SAP User Experience Monitor

6.3.6 Implementing EEMon in Toys Inc.

Now that we have considered the EEMon functions from various perspectives, we will use the example of Toys Inc. to outline the process associated with an EEMon implementation project.

Every day, Toys Inc. employees from different subsidiaries across Germany access the company's PEP system to record their working times, among other things. To the detriment of all employees, however, problems repeatedly occur when they access time recording. From time to time, the system cannot be accessed from various locations. Even when the system can be accessed, the performance of the time recording application is so poor that, after each click, the user has to wait several seconds for the next screen to be displayed. Since these two problems cannot be detected using system monitoring, disgruntled end users repeatedly contact the IT department at Toys Inc. to complain about the poor availability and performance of the application.

In addition to these specific problems, there are still some other business-critical applications that cannot be adequately controlled using the existing system monitoring. Therefore, the head of the IT department at Toys Inc. has approved the budget for a project in which end-user experience monitoring will be implemented on SAP Solution Manager in order to adequately monitor these critical applications from the perspective of the end user and to ensure their functional efficiency.

At the start of the project, a meeting is scheduled to communicate the various project goals, outline management's expectations, and introduce the parties involved (project management, IT administrations, key users, and SAP consultants). The current situation is then discussed by all parties who, at the same time, learn how EEMon works. An EEMon monitoring concept is then defined jointly on the basis of the following questions:

▶ Which applications are to be monitored?

▶ Which IT systems are involved?

▶ From which locations should monitoring occur?

▶ How should alerting work in the event of an incident?

In the first phase of the project, an IT administrator takes care of the basic configuration of SAP Solution Manager and connects the satellite systems to SAP Solution Manager. During this time, the administrator is supported by an experienced SAP consultant. The necessary EEMon robots are also installed in the subsidiaries of Toys Inc. At the same time, an SAP consultant works with some key users to create the necessary EEMon scripts and edit them in the EEMon editor until they contain the required scope of functions.

At the start of the second phase of the project, the EEMon scenario is set up on SAP Solution Manager from a technical perspective. The scripts that were created earlier are transferred to the SAP Solution Manager system and distributed to some robots. The project now enters a test phase during which any problems that occur are resolved, and the scripts that were created earlier are further optimized. The test cases prepared for this phase include the following functions, among others:

▶ EEMon real-time monitoring UI: triggering error situations

▶ Alert inbox: sending notifications by email

▶ End-to-end trace analysis: creating end-to-end traces

▶ Automatic ticket generation in ITSM within SAP Solution Manager

In addition to testing the individual EEMon functions, the thresholds that apply when you execute the individual script steps are also adjusted in this phase in such a way that not too many alerts are generated, and no error situations remain undetected, either. This process can take quite some time. At the same time, the future EEMon administrators are trained to use the new monitoring tools. As soon as the thresholds have been sufficiently adjusted and all tests have been successfully concluded, the new solution goes live with the EEMon scripts' being rolled out on all other robots. Toys Inc. is also supported by experienced SAP consultants during the go-live phase.

Since in principle some scripts may no longer work after a release upgrade of the satellite system (for example, if the names of certain screen elements change), the affected scripts are tested after each release upgrade and, if necessary, adjusted to the new release as part of the post-processing work undertaken by Toys Inc. following an upgrade.

6.3.7 Additional Documentation

Links

For more information, including information about known problems and how to resolve them, refer to the EEMon wiki at *http://wiki.sdn.sap.com/wiki/display/EEM/Home.*

If you have any questions in relation to the EEMon editor, please refer to the user handbook delivered with the EEMon editor.

SAP Notes

Table 6.4 provides an overview of important SAP Notes for EEMon, which are available on SAP Service Marketplace.

Contents	SAP Note
Central note for end user experience monitoring	1357045
Composite SAP note for SAP GUI scripting	527737
Restrictions when using SAP GUI scripting	587202
SAP GUI scripting: status and lifetime	612454

Table 6.4 Overview of SAP Notes for EEMon

Contents	SAP Note
New profile parameter for front-end user scripting	480149
SAP GUI scripting support for SAP applications	619459
Example of using SAP GUI scripting: Visual Basic recorder	592685
SAP Client Plug-In	1435190
Guide for the SAP User Experience monitor for the iPhone/iPad	1786546
Correction note for SPS03	1621836
Correction note for SPS04	1651279
Correction note for SPS05	1703150
Correction note for SPS06/SPS07	1768544

Table 6.4 Overview of SAP Notes for EEMon (Cont.)

6.4   Monitoring Technical Connections

In this context, the term "connection" stands for all RFC or HTTP-based connections between systems and technical components. With connection monitoring, SAP Solution Manager provides you with a central monitoring platform for mapping connections between the technical systems in a work center. Such connections are grouped together in the form of scenarios. The availability and connection latency of RFC and HTTP connections are checked using automatic or manual checks. Automatic checks use the ping function and are executed as a background job on an hourly or daily basis.

The process of monitoring communication and interfaces in the system landscape is an integral part of monitoring because it ensures that all communication among the technical systems runs smoothly. Connection monitoring is one part of monitoring interfaces and communications. With connection monitoring, you can activate a permanent availability check for technical RFC and HTTP connections. You can then use this availability check to determine whether a connection is working and whether the response time is acceptable.

As with all the scenarios introduced previously, connection monitoring is fully integrated into the MAI of SAP Solution Manager. You can therefore fully integrate connection monitoring into your monitoring concept and use defined work modes and alerting methods for connection monitoring. Interface channel monitoring, which monitors the availability of an interface and its functional efficiency, is another part of monitoring. In the next section, we will show you how to set up connection monitoring and describe the adjustment options available to you.

6.4.1 Configuring Connection Monitoring

The starting point for the configuration is the SAP SOLUTION MANAGER CONFIGURATION work center (Transaction SOLMAN_SETUP). In the navigation area, choose TECHNICAL MONITORING. Then, choose CONNECTION MONITORING from the selection options available on the left-hand side of the screen.

Figure 6.50 shows the initial screen for configuring connection monitoring.

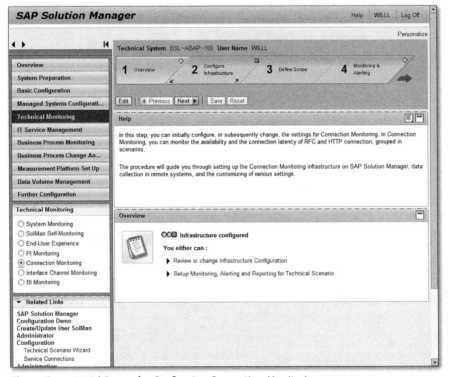

Figure 6.50 Initial Screen for Configuring Connection Monitoring

Here, you see that the structure of the configuration procedure is, once again, based on guided procedures and can therefore be managed in the same way as the configuration of other scenarios.

Each of the steps to be executed is supported by explanations in the display area. Note that you can make changes only when editing mode is active. To activate editing mode, choose EDIT. Otherwise, all the data is grayed out and write protected. To configure connection monitoring, follow the steps in the next subsections.

Overview

As you already know from configuring the other scenarios, step 1, OVERVIEW, provides you with an overview of your system landscape. In particular, you can check the infrastructure configuration again and adjust it, if necessary. In Figure 6.51, the infrastructure was configured successfully. This is indicated by the green status. Of course, this is generally not the case in a system that has not been configured.

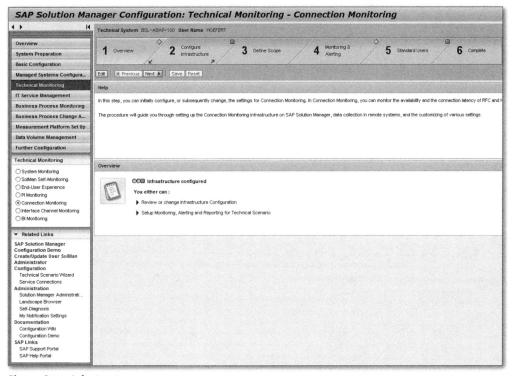

Figure 6.51 Infrastructure

Now that you have obtained an overview of your system landscape, you can choose NEXT to navigate directly to the next step.

Configure Infrastructure

This step is divided into substeps already known to you, namely CHECK PREREQUISITES, CONFIGURE MANUALLY, DEFAULT SETTINGS, WORKMODE SETTINGS, and UPDATE CONTENT. Therefore, when processing these steps, please refer to the explanations provided in Section 5.4.2.

Define Scope

In the DEFINE SCOPE step, you create a scenario that contains the technical systems to be monitored, as well as their system-relevant RFC or HTTP connections. In Figure 6.52, a scenario was created for Toys Inc.

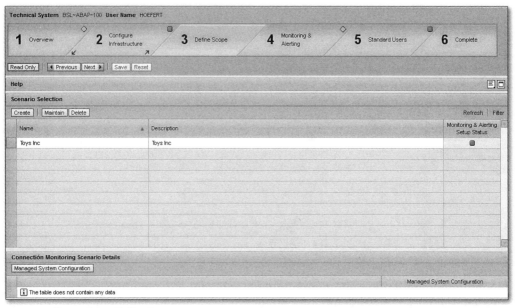

Figure 6.52 Define Scope

We will now show you how to define a new connection scenario or change an existing connection scenario:

1. Choose CREATE to create a new connection scenario. Alternatively, choose MAINTAIN to edit an existing scenario.

2. You are prompted to enter a type, name, and description for the technical scenario (see Figure 6.53). Make an entry in all three fields and choose CONTINUE.

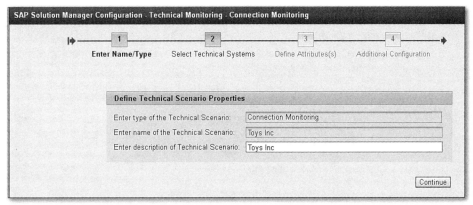

Figure 6.53 Maintaining the Relevant Scenario

3. In the next step, specify the technical systems that are relevant for monitoring. The connections already recorded in SAP Solution Manager are displayed in the NBR OF CONN. column (see Figure 6.54).

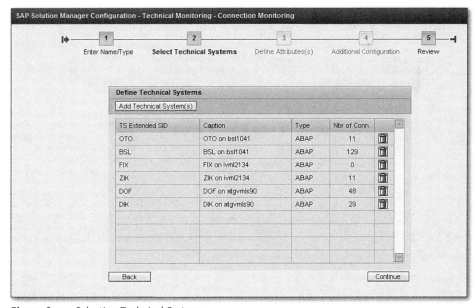

Figure 6.54 Selecting Technical Systems

Choose ADD TECHNICAL SYSTEM(S) to add a new system to the list. A list of all managed systems is displayed. From this list, you can choose the systems you require.

4. Once you have added all the systems you need, choose CONTINUE. A window in which you are reminded that data relating to all known RFC connections is collected in the background opens. Since this can take some time, you may have to check, at a later date, whether additional RFC connections have been added. Confirm this information and continue with the remaining configuration steps.

> **Warning**
>
> If you want to create additional connections at a later stage, you must repeat this step so that new connections will be detected.

5. DEFINE ATTRIBUTE(S) is the next substep in the scenario definition. The list displayed here contains all the connections that have been found and can be monitored (see Figure 6.55).

    Here, you can add new connections and delete those that you do not need to monitor. To delete connections, choose 🗑. Alternatively, to add a new connection to a target system, choose ADD CONNECTION and define the source system.

6. Then, choose CONTINUE to confirm the list of connections. This brings you to step 5.

7. You can now check the connections you have grouped together. If you want to make changes, choose BACK to repeat one of the preceding steps.

8. To complete the configuration, choose SAVE.

You have now configured the scope for connection monitoring.

Monitoring & Alerting

In the MONITORING & ALERTING step, you activate monitoring for the scope defined in step 3. In other words, you activate monitoring for the technical scenario to be monitored. Note that the configuration setting depends on the level selected. Essentially, the following three levels are available:

1. Scenario level
2. Connection level
3. Check level

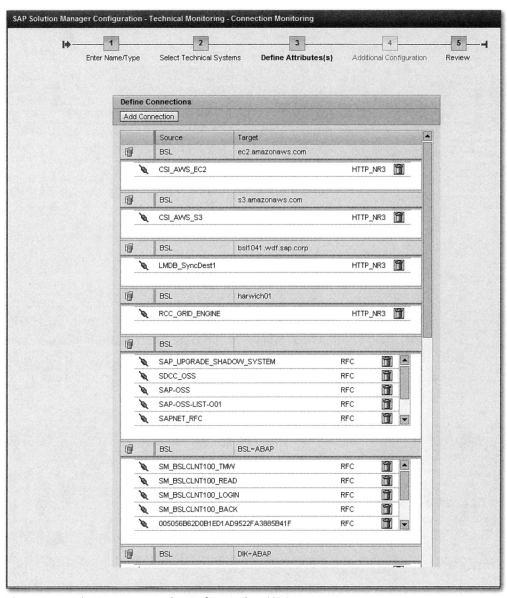

Figure 6.55 Selecting Systems in the "Define Attribute(s)" Step

As you can see in Figure 6.56, the levels are structured as follows. At the scenario level, you see a description of the technical scenario titled Toys Inc. At the connection level, which is one level lower, you see the connection `CSI_AWS_EC2`.

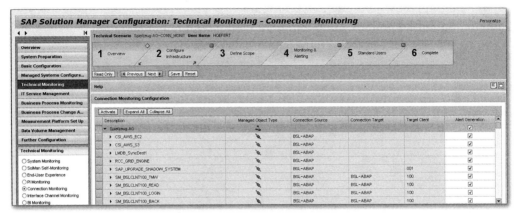

Figure 6.56 Scenario Level

In Figure 6.57, you can now see, at the check level, that the HTTP PING and HTTP LATENCY checks are available for the connection CSI_AWS_EC2.

At the scenario level, you can activate or deactivate alerting for all connections among the systems grouped together in a scenario. To do this, activate the checkbox in the ALERT GENERATION column in the table. Individual notifications and work mode–specific settings can be adjusted at the RFC connection level, while thresholds, customer-specific notification texts, and auto-reaction management are configured at the check level.

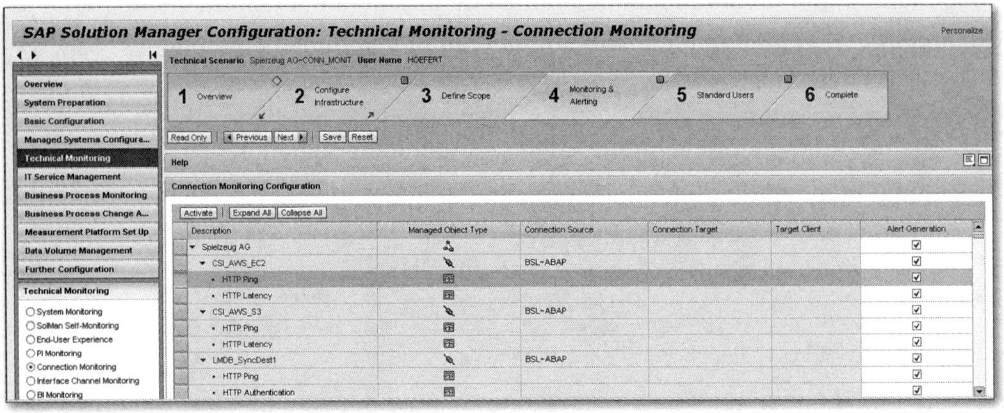

Figure 6.57 Check Level

Now we will use the connection SM_DIKCLNT001_Read, which you can see in Figure 6.58, to introduce you to the individual configuration options in detail.

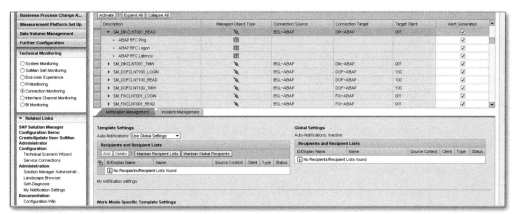

Figure 6.58 Configuring ITSM Integration

In the CONNECTION SOURCE column, you can identify the source system associated with the connection. The target system for the connection is displayed in the CONNECTION TARGET column, while the TARGET CLIENT column displays the target system client used for the connection.

Select the connection SM_DIKCLNT001_Read (DESCRIPTION column). You can now facilitate integration into notification management or IT Service Management. The NOTIFICATION MANAGEMENT and INCIDENT MANAGEMENT tab pages are available for this purpose (see Figure 6.58).

By selecting the individual check levels, namely ABAP RFC PING, ABAP RFC LOGON, and ABAP RFC LATENCY, you can define thresholds, adjust customer-defined alert descriptions, assign third-party connectors (known as *business add-ins*) for connection to non-SAP service desk tools, and activate an auto-reaction method on these tab pages.

If you have configured a work mode, you can also make these settings there. Please note the following: If modifications are made at the check level, the settings made at the higher levels, namely at the connection and scenario levels, are rejected in order to preserve the customer-defined settings. In other words, global settings are overwritten. Finally, choose ACTIVATE to activate monitoring for the connections that you have selected.

Standard Users

This substep is optional. If you want to create the standard users delivered by SAP, namely level 1 and level 2 users, choose EXECUTE. These users differ in terms of the authorizations assigned to them. For example, a level 1 user works in the alert inbox and is authorized to distribute alerts. This user is also permitted to create notifications and incidents in the ITSM environment. The level 2 user, on the other hand, has additional authorizations that enable the user to address the cause of existing problems. In the standard delivery, both users are created with the naming convention SM_L1 or SM_L2 and the corresponding SAP Solution Manager system names. You can also create users with your own choice of user name and authorizations.

Complete

In the final step, COMPLETE, you complete the configuration. In the next section, we will show you how to use connection monitoring.

6.4.2 Using Connection Monitoring

To display the results of the connection test, select the CONNECTION MONITORING link in the TECHNICAL MONITORING work center (see Figure 6.59).

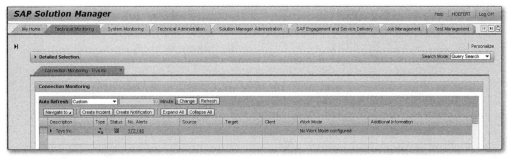

Figure 6.59 Connection Monitoring

A scenario that was created earlier, Toys Inc., is displayed in the DESCRIPTION column, while the STATUS column provides an aggregated overview of the individual status messages relating to all connections in the scenario. If one of the connections within the scenario has an error status, the scenario's overall status is also an error status.

The total number of alerts is displayed in the No. ALERTS column. Here, you can expand the node for the scenario in order to access the connection level and check level. The status message provides information about the status of a connection. If a connection has a red status, one or more errors have occurred. If a connection has a yellow status, no errors have occurred.

The relevant employee at Toys Inc. can now create service messages or notifications that will be further processed. Alternatively, the employee can choose NAVIGATE TO to navigate to the alert inbox or landscape browser. Valuable information about the underlying problem can be obtained from the ADDITIONAL INFORMATION column. Error messages and descriptions are displayed here. Figure 6.60 shows detailed information about an erroneous connection. The error message is ICM_HTTP_CON-NECTION_FAILED, and the error code is 400.

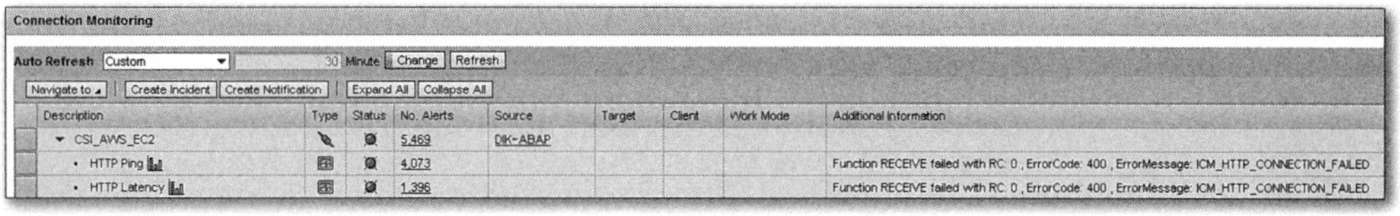

Figure 6.60 Additional Information

We will now turn our attention to interface channel monitoring. Here, we will use an example to illustrate the configuration of interface monitoring.

6.5   Interface Channel Monitoring

Interface channel monitoring is another part of monitoring within SAP Solution Manager. This monitoring function facilitates real-time monitoring of the interfaces and connections among your technical systems. An interface channel is a bundle of individual interfaces. It is assigned a particular direction. In other words, system A transmits in the direction of system B and uses a specific connection type for this purpose. Channels can also be assigned specific attributes. Such attributes are used as filter criteria in the data view.

In the next section, we will first describe how to set up interface channel monitoring in SAP Solution Manager. We will then briefly outline how to use this function.

6.5.1 Prerequisites for Interface Channel Monitoring

Since SAP Solution Manager SP05, it is possible to monitor interface channels. Before you can set up interface channel monitoring, you must connect the relevant SAP NetWeaver systems to SAP Solution Manager, as described in Section 2.5.4.

It is important to use the latest version of the interface channel monitoring UI in SAP Solution Manager. Further updated information is available in the relevant SAP Notes. In each managed system, the ST-PI release should correspond to the SAP Solution Manager version in order to ensure that performance-relevant data is collected properly. For more information, see the relevant SAP Notes.

Further information is also available at *http://wiki.sdn. sap.com/wiki/display/TechOps/ Home* INTERFACE MONITORING • INTERFACE & CONNECTION MONITORING WIKI • PREREQUISITES. Here, you will find a list of all SAP Notes that you should import before you start the configuration in SAP Solution Manager.

6.5.2 Configuring Interface Channel Monitoring

The starting point for the configuration is the SAP SOLUTION MANAGER CONFIGURATION work center (Transaction SOLMAN_SETUP). In the navigation area, choose TECHNICAL MONITORING. Then, choose INTERFACE CHANNEL MONITORING from the selection options available on the left-hand side of the screen.

Overview

Figure 6.61 shows the first configuration step: the OVERVIEW step. To access the next step, choose NEXT. Before doing so, choose EDIT to switch to change mode.

Configure Infrastructure

In the next step, CONFIGURE INFRASTRUCTURE, check the prerequisites that were put in place during the basic configuration. All actions should have already been completed. If the STEPS area contains an error status, you can make some corrections. Essentially, the overall status should be green in order to ensure that the configuration is successful.

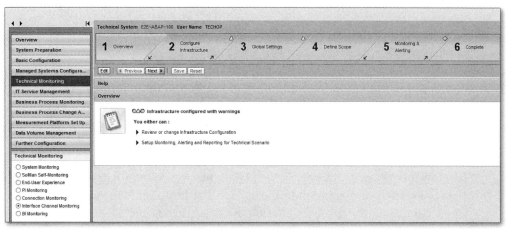

Figure 6.61 Initial Screen for Configuring Interface Channel Monitoring

Global Settings

In step 3, GLOBAL SETTINGS, the prerequisites for availability monitoring in interface channels are implemented (see Figure 6.62). As a prerequisite, the EEMon tool must be available here. In the NAVIGATION column, select the OPEN URL link to download the EEMon editor. Then, execute the relevant steps for installing the EEMon editor.

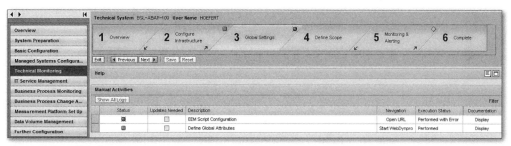

Figure 6.62 Global Settings

Then, define global attributes, which can be used later as tags for the interface channels. You can use these interface channel attributes as filters in the interface channel monitor so that the displayed data is restricted to a subset of the interface channels associated with a particular scenario. Interface channel attributes are global. In other words, they can be used by several scenarios.

To define attributes, choose START WEBDYNPRO in the NAVIGATION column.

Define Scope

Next, define the monitoring scope in the DEFINE SCOPE step. To do this, select a technical scenario of the type INTERFACE CHANNEL MONITORING. You can either use an existing scenario or create a new scenario.

To create a new scenario, choose CREATE. A new window opens. Execute the steps in sequence. When you are finished, check the status of the managed systems in the lower INTERFACE CHANNEL SCENARIO DETAILS area. If the status is not green, you can call system configuration immediately in order to remove any errors. Figure 6.63 shows a newly created scenario called THE WEB SHOP.

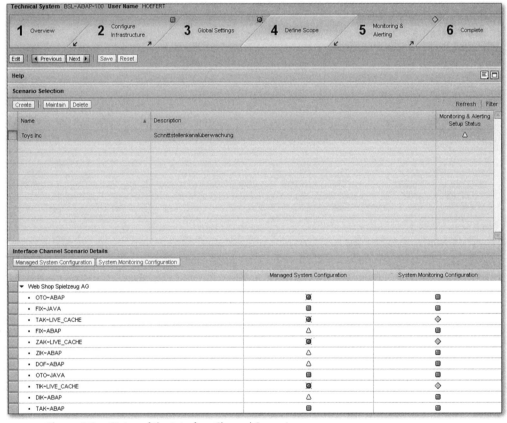

Figure 6.63 Status of the Interface Channel Scenario

Monitoring & Alerting

The MONITORING & ALERTING step contains several substeps, each of which is described here.

In the first substep, PERFORM AUTOMATIC PREREQUISITES, you schedule extractors that retrieve, on a daily basis, all available RFC connections associated with the technical systems within a scenario. The background job `SMSETUP: E2E_MAI_IF_SCOPE_EXT` is responsible for checking RFC connections and, therefore, ensuring that all RFC connections are available in the input help for subsequent configuration activities.

You perform the second substep, PERFORM MANUAL PREREQUISITES, if you have defined global attributes in the GLOBAL SETTINGS step and wish to set up performance monitoring for synchronous web service calls (see Figure 6.64).

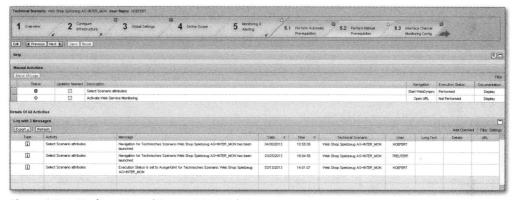

Figure 6.64 "Perform Manual Prerequisites" Substep

The global attributes can be assigned to a technical scenario. In the MANUAL ACTIVITIES area, choose START WEBDYNPRO in the NAVIGATION column. A new window opens. Activate the checkbox in the IS ASSIGNED column and choose SAVE (see Figure 6.65). You have now activated the attributes for the technical scenario.

Interface channel attributes assigned to scenario Web Shop Spielzeug AG–INTER_MON			
Save			
Is assigned	Technical name	Display name	Description
☑	BUSINESS AREA	Business Area	Business Area

Figure 6.65 Assigning Global Attributes

As a prerequisite for the calls and for performance monitoring of web services, you must activate monitoring on the systems to be managed. The attachment to SAP Note 1639329 contains the following guide: *Web Service Monitoring with ST_PI.pdf*. Once the prerequisites have been fulfilled, manually set the EXECUTION STATUS to EXECUTED.

In the third substep, INTERFACE CHANNEL MONITORING CONFIG, create different interface channels for a scenario (see Figure 6.66). At present, there are three types of interfaces for which you can create channels: remote function call (RFC), web service (WS), and SAP Process Integration (PI).

Next, we will use the example of RFC interface channels to explain this additional configuration. On the RFC INTERFACE CHANNELS tab page, choose CREATE and, in a new window, enter a name for the interface channel. Specify a source system and target system here, and save your entries.

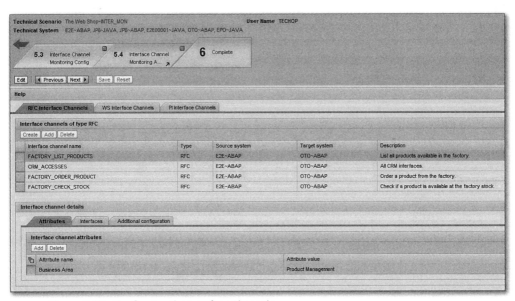

Figure 6.66 Configuring the Interface Channels

If you want to make further adjustments, you can use the additional maintenance options available on the three tab pages in the lower INTERFACE CHANNEL DETAILS area. We will briefly outline them here:

▶ ATTRIBUTES

On this tab page, assign the attributes you defined in the PERFORM MANUAL PREREQUISITES step to the interface channel.

▶ INTERFACES

On the INTERFACES tab page, define the RFC connections used in relation to the interface channel names. You can assign several RFC connections to an interface channel. When defining interfaces, you can work with placeholders.

▶ ADDITIONAL CONFIGURATION

For availability monitoring of the interface channels, select the ADDITIONAL CONFIGURATION tab. Then select an available script. A prerequisite for using availability monitoring is that you have made a script available for interface channel monitoring. For more information about creating and editing scripts, see Section 6.3. Detailed information is also available on the wiki page *http:// wiki.sdn.sap.com/wiki/display/TechOps/Home* • INTERFACE & CONNECTION MONITORING WIKI. Here, you can learn how to create ICM-specific scripts in EEMon, among other things.

The final substep, INTERFACE CHANNEL MONITORING ACTIVATION, provides an overview of the configured scenario and the metrics to be collected for the individual channels. Checkboxes in the ALERTING and MONITORING columns control whether the relevant metric can trigger an alert and whether the metric is to be displayed in the interface channel monitoring UI. You can override the default thresholds for each metric and at the interface channel level.

By using the icons in the CATEGORY, PERFORMANCE, and EXCEPTION columns, you can view the available checks at the connection level. At this level, thresholds can be adjusted on the THRESHOLDS tab page.

Here, you can adjust integration into notification management and ITSM by selecting the interface channel name. To do this, select the relevant interface channel name in the upper screen area. The NOTIFICATION MANAGEMENT and INCIDENT MANAGEMENT tab pages are then available for selection, and you can create individual notifications or incidents here.

Since you now know how to configure interface channel monitoring in SAP Solution Manager, we will now briefly outline how to use interface channel monitoring.

6.5.3   Using Interface Channel Monitoring

Interface channel monitoring is called in the TECHNICAL MONITORING work center. To do this, choose INTERFACE CHANNEL MONITORING from the selection options available in the navigation area. Now, choose the button of the same name, INTERFACE CHANNEL MONITORING, to display the interface channel topology. Figure 6.67 shows interface channel monitoring for the configured scenario THE WEB SHOP.

Select or deselect the filter attributes in the lower area of the box on the left-hand side of the screen to change the display screen for RFC connections, web services, and PI interface channels accordingly. Each group of connections is assigned a unique color, making it easier to understand the overview.

If you want more detailed information about erroneous connections, you can choose, for example, the icon 🔺 for exceptions. This detailed information is then displayed in the screen area on the right. In our example, the detailed information includes the receiver component, receiver interface, and receiver name, as well as the sender component, sender interface, and sender name (see Figure 6.67).

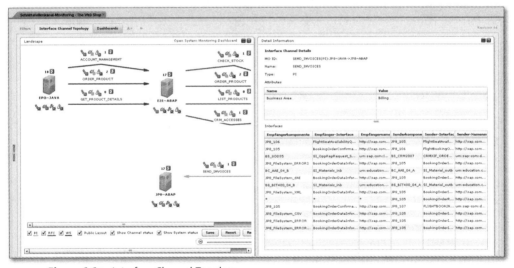

Figure 6.67   Interface Channel Topology

If you select the DASHBOARDS tab, the following system monitoring information is displayed: AVAILABILITY, EXCEPTIONS, RESPONSE TIMES, and the use of individual interface channels (see Figure 6.68). This information is displayed in time diagrams. Here, you can specify the time interval yourself.

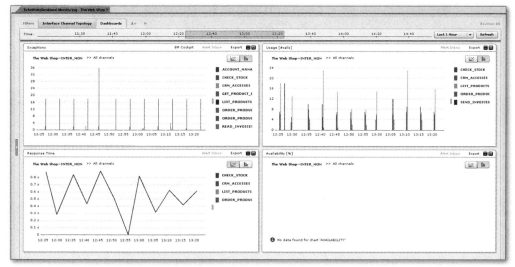

Figure 6.68 Dashboard Interface Channel Monitoring

It's possible to use filters to restrict a display screen to data for individual or all interface channels associated with a scenario. Later releases will provide an instance-specific view for RFC performance metrics and web service performance metrics.

If you select the relevant interface channel, you can use the link provided here to navigate directly to the alert inbox, where you can initiate further processing of an incident. In the case of web service and RFC exceptions, you can navigate to the *exception management cockpit,* where you can retrieve detailed information about individual exceptions.

6.5.4 Additional Documentation

Links

Further documentation is available in the Technical Operations wiki, which is available at *http://wiki.sdn.sap.com/wiki/ display/TechOps/Home* • INTERFACE & CONNECTION MONITORING WIKI.

SAP Notes

Table 6.5 provides an overview of important SAP Notes for interface channel monitoring, which are available on SAP Service Marketplace.

Description	SAP Note
Corrections for ICMON 7.1 with SP05	1713380
Corrections for ICMON 7.1 SP06	1754704
Corrections for ICMON 7.1 with SP07	1769743
Web service monitoring	1639329

Table 6.5 Important SAP Notes for Interface Channel Monitoring

6.6 Self-Monitoring in SAP Solution Manager

In the previous chapters, you learned about the extensive functions that SAP Solution Manager provides in terms of supporting the technical operations within your system landscape. However, how does a system administrator know whether the myriad of functions within SAP Solution Manager are working reliably? For example, is it possible to make a statement about the availability of all diagnostics agents? Is data collection working reliably? When alerts are sent, is this in line with expectations and in accordance with the setup? How can we ensure, for example, that the relevant employee is quickly and purposefully informed about an incident in the support infrastructure? To answer these questions, we will use the example of Toys Inc. to demonstrate how you can use self-monitoring in SAP Solution Manager.

The support infrastructures for the MAI and other central SAP Solution Manager functions are monitored using self-monitoring and self-diagnosis. Integration into notification management and IT Service Management (ITSM) ensures that problems are forwarded to and processed by the relevant employees.

In the following sections, we will show you the necessary configuration steps for setting up self-monitoring.

6.6.1 Setting Up Self-Monitoring

The starting point for the configuration is the SAP SOLUTION MANAGER CONFIGURA-TION work center (Transaction SOLMAN_SETUP). In the navigation area, choose TECHNICAL MONITORING. Then, choose SOLMAN SELF-MONITORING from the selection options available on the left-hand side of the screen.

The configuration for self-monitoring follows the principle approach described in the previous chapters. Therefore, we will not discuss the OVERVIEW and CONFIGURE INFRASTRUCTURE steps here. Instead, we will limit our discussion to those specific characteristics associated with setting up self-monitoring.

We will therefore start with step 3, in which we will set up MONITORING & ALERT-ING. The most important step here is step 3.2, which contains the actual configuration for self-monitoring. In this step, you specify the administration objects for which alert generation is to be activated. A table outlining all possible options is displayed in this step. The first column displays all possible self-monitoring options for SAP Solution Manager in a tree structure. The main components of the support infrastructure are as follows:

- Agent Framework
- Self-Diagnosis
- Introscope Enterprise Manager
- LMDB
- Monitoring and Alerting Infrastructure
- Alert Consumer Connector

Each of these components is checked in terms of the categories you have assigned. For this to happen, configure alert generation by selecting the relevant monitoring categories in the GENERATE ALERTS column. Choose SAVE to save your settings and exit the basic configuration.

You have now activated self-monitoring for the elements you have selected. As you already know from other scenarios, you can now generate standard users or define notification scenarios.

6.6.2 Using Self-Monitoring

The starting point for using self-monitoring and monitoring of the central functions in SAP Solution Manager is the SAP SOLUTION MANAGER ADMINISTRATION work center (see Figure 6.69).

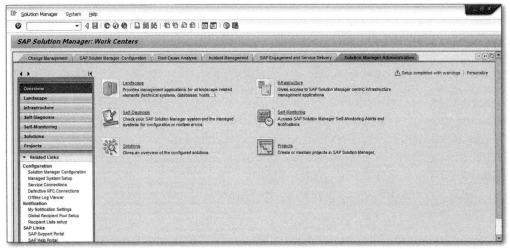

Figure 6.69 SAP Solution Manager Administration Work Center (Including Self-Diagnosis)

In the following subsections, we will reveal which functions are concealed behind the SELF-MONITORING and INFRASTRUCTURE menu options.

Self-Monitoring

First, choose the SELF-MONITORING menu option to obtain an overview of the infrastructure components and any errors. You can then choose SELF MONITORING OVERVIEW to open the overview in a new window. The SELF MONITORING ALERT INBOX enables you to navigate directly to the alert inbox.

The COMPONENT column provides an overview of the components in the support infrastructure (see Figure 6.70). The number of alerts collected for each support infrastructure component is displayed in the VALUE column. Table 6.6 lists the categories available for system monitoring values.

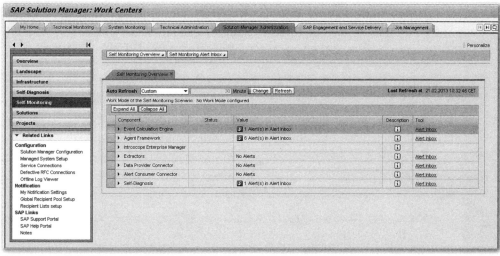

Figure 6.70 Self-Monitoring Overview

Category	Explanation
Availability	Information about the system's availability and instances.
Configuration	Information about the system's configuration status, including the check results for and changes to configuration settings.
Exception	Information about error messages in the system.
Performance	Information about the status of critical performance indicators. In addition to the current value, you can display a value history that will enable you to identify trends in the longer term or to compare the current value against long-term developments.

Table 6.6 Value Categories

If you wish to obtain detailed information, you can expand the individual nodes in the support infrastructure components. Such detailed information includes the relevant status messages. In the DESCRIPTION column, you can obtain additional facts and figures for the individual components being monitored. Explanations and instructions for error analysis are also stored here.

In Figure 6.71, you see, for example, that performance problems occurred in the EVENT CALCULATION ENGINE area at a particular time. You recognize this by the yellow warning in the STATUS column for the row CALCULATION OPERATIONS PER SECOND. Double-click the row CALCULATION OPERATIONS PER SECOND to call detailed information. Here, you can see that the Event Calculation Engine is executed with the job `SAP_ALERT_CALCULATION_ENGINE` and the report `ACE_CALCULATION_CONTROL-LER`. To analyze the problem further, the system suggests executing Transaction SLG1 with the relevant parameters in the OBJECT and SUBOBJECT fields.

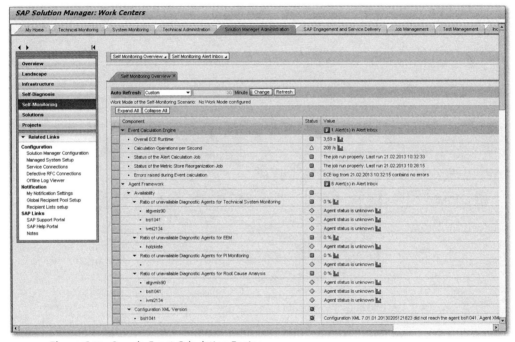

Figure 6.71 Sample Event Calculation Engine

Now, choose ECE PERFORMANCE HISTORY in the TOOL column, which denotes the Event Calculation Engine. You thus navigate directly to a graphical display of the alert calculation performance history, runtime components involved, metric counter, and arithmetic operations executed per second (see Figure 6.72). This provides you with additional hints for solving the problem.

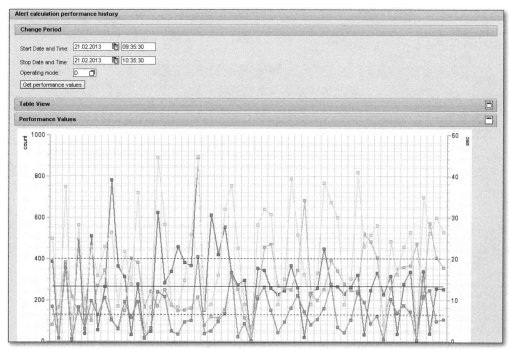

Figure 6.72 Alert Calculation Performance History

Infrastructure Monitoring

A complete, well-functioning infrastructure is a prerequisite for consistent, well-functioning system landscape monitoring. In other words, you must ensure that the components that supply the MAI in SAP Solution Manager with information are also available and ready for use. You can call infrastructure monitoring from the INFRASTRUCTURE menu option in the navigation area of the SAP SOLUTION MANAGER work center. Its primary purpose is to monitor and manage the following components, as well as analyze any problems that arise:

▸ Introscope Enterprise Manager

▸ Diagnostics Agent Framework

▸ EFWK

▸ Alerting Framework

You can select the relevant work area by choosing INTROSCOPE, OFFLINE LOG VIEWER, BW REPORTING, FRAMEWORK, and ADMINISTRATION (see Figure 6.73).

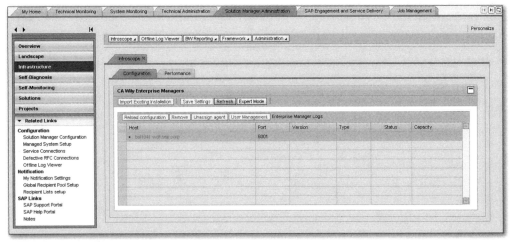

Figure 6.73 Infrastructure Monitoring

You can then select the relevant component on the INTROSCOPE, AGENT FRAMEWORK, EXTRACTOR FRAMEWORK, and ALERTING FRAMEWORK tab pages. Depending on the area you have selected, you can select further options in the underlying area.

Next we will describe the settings for the individual components in greater detail.

Introscope Enterprise Manager

Figure 6.73 shows a detailed overview of the information and settings associated with Introscope Enterprise Manager—for example, the product version used (VERSION column), percentage utilization (CAPACITY column), and communication port used (PORT column).

On the CONFIGURATION tab page within the relevant tab page for the component, you can import installed Enterprise Manager installations in order to respond to a percentage utilization that is too high or connect existing Enterprise Manager installations with SAP Solution Manager. Furthermore, you can implement *Introscope Enterprise Manager Cluster* or *Introscope Enterprise Manager of Managers*. Further information is available on SAP Service Marketplace at *service.sap.com/diagnostics*.

The PERFORMANCE tab page contains performance-relevant metric information for a freely definable period. The most important characteristics are listed below and can be displayed in a detailed graphic via the selection list, which you open by choosing DISPLAY:

▶ Number of agents connected to Enterprise Manager

▶ Number of metrics known to Enterprise Manager

▶ Total capacity, which is calculated from different metrics in order to obtain a total value for the Enterprise Manager utilization. This value is displayed as a percentage. CPU utilization, garbage collection, and utilization of the dynamic memory, among other things, form the basis for the calculation.

▶ Necessary system load analysis data from the smart store. The smart store is a data store from Introscope, in which all Introscope metrics are stored. The system load over the duration of the smart store query is displayed.

▶ The heap capacity shows utilization of the dynamic memory on which Introscope Enterprise Manager is running. The percentage EM CPU usage provides information about CPU utilization for Enterprise Manager.

▶ GC duration for analyzing the duration of the garbage collection on the virtual machine on which Introscope Enterprise Manager is processed.

The example shown in Figure 6.74 refers to the number of metrics that are to be processed. Here, you see the number of metrics processed by Enterprise Manager in 15-second time intervals.

If the number of metrics processed is fewer than the number of metrics known to Enterprise Manager, there may be performance problems in Enterprise Manager. In this case, you should look into setting up Introscope Enterprise Manager of Managers for the purposes of load balancing.

Diagnostics Agent Framework

The agent framework contains different tools and functions for central monitoring of diagnostics agents (see Figure 6.75).

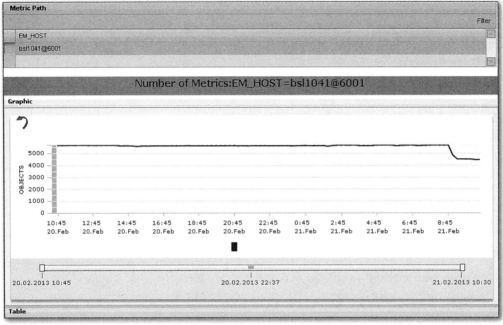

Figure 6.74 Number of Metrics Available

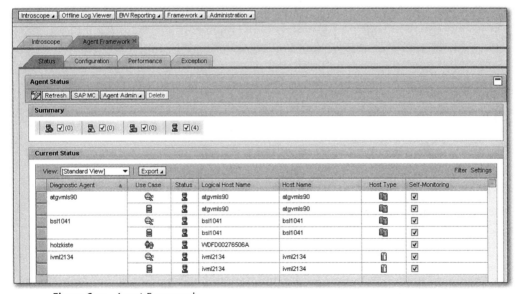

Figure 6.75 Agent Framework

You obtain an overview of all diagnostics agents registered on SAP Solution Manager and can use status icons to read statuses at a glance. In the SUMMARY area in Figure 6.75, you see that none of the diagnostics agents have a green status (⬛).

Here, you can choose AGENT ADMIN to access various functions for managing diagnostics agents. The SAP MC button starts a central administration platform known as the SAP Management Console.

The following four tab pages are also available to you:

▶ STATUS
On the STATUS tab page, you see whether the agents are connected to SAP Solution Manager.

▶ CONFIGURATION
On the CONFIGURATION tab page, you can assign a new diagnostics agent to a technical component if the diagnostics agent that was originally assigned is not available.

▶ PERFORMANCE
On the PERFORMANCE tab page, you can view the time a diagnostics data collector requires in order to collect data for a particular period.

▶ EXCEPTIONS
The EXCEPTION tab page provides information about existing problems with individual diagnostics agents. If you want to obtain further information, select the erroneous diagnostics agent.

Extractor Framework

The Extractor Framework (EFWK) in SAP Solution Manager is used as the central infrastructure for data collection and distribution. If errors occur in this framework, no alerts or only alerts of limited use are generated. Consequently, the EFWK is extremely important for monitoring the system landscape.

To obtain status information about the extractors and perform an error diagnosis, call the following tab pages in succession: EXTRACTOR FRAMEWORK • STATUS • EXTRACTOR FRAMEWORK (see Figure 6.76). Alternatively, choose FRAMEWORK and then select the EXTRACTOR FRAMEWORK option.

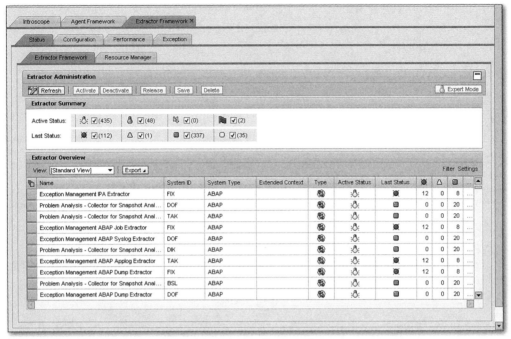

Figure 6.76 Status Overview of the Extractor Framework

The tab pages already introduced in conjunction with other frameworks are also available for the EFWK. In addition, the EFWK also has the RESOURCE MANAGER tab page on the third level.

In the following list, we will introduce you to the most important options in the EFWK and describe the tab pages on which they are located:

▶ EXTRACTOR FRAMEWORK • STATUS • EXTRACTOR FRAMEWORK tab page
Here, you see an overview of all extractors and their respective status. You can choose ACTIVATE or DEACTIVATE to activate or deactivate erroneous extractors.

▶ EXTRACTOR FRAMEWORK • STATUS • RESOURCE MANAGER tab page
On this tab page, you see the next planned run for the resource manager.

▶ EXTRACTOR FRAMEWORK • CONFIGURATION tab page
On this tab page, you can check and manage the necessary resource cap settings for the RFC connections.

▶ EXTRACTOR FRAMEWORK • PERFORMANCE • EXTRACTOR FRAMEWORK tab page
On this tab page, you retrieve performance-relevant information for the EFWK.

▶ Extractor Framework • Performance • Resource Manager tab page
On this tab page, the following fields are available:

  ▶ In the Metric Name field, you can select whether you want to analyze the runtime or throughput.

  ▶ The Resource Manager Runtime field provides information about the time needed to process the results of the extractors.

  ▶ The Resource Manager Throughput field displays, in a graphic, the percentage number of extractors started. Here, the value 1 corresponds to 100%. In general, if you find lower values here, you can assume that there is a performance problem. Further information is available at the end of this section. If you want to switch between the graphical and numerical displays for measurement readings, you can choose Graphic or Table.

▶ Extractor Framework • Exception tab page
This tab page provides information relevant for conducting an error analysis on the extractors, which you can also run by calling Transaction SLG1.

Alerting Framework

You call the Alerting Framework on the corresponding tab page. Alternatively, you can choose Framework and then select the Alerting Framework option (see Figure 6.77). You can use the functions available here to check the status, performance, configuration, and potential exception situations associated with alert generation in SAP Solution Manager.

The Alerting Framework comprises the Alert Consumer Connector, data providers, and the Event Calculation Engine. It is the centerpiece of alert generation. We have already discussed in detail how alert generation works (see Section 5.3). Therefore, we will now take a look at the individual monitoring or configuration options for the components involved.

Figure 6.77 shows the Status tab page, which contains status information on data providers. Here, you can use the View field to restrict the view to the Active Status or Last Status. In the Active Status view, you see whether the extractor is running. In the Last Status view, on the other hand, you see the result.

You can use the relevant buttons (Activate and Deactivate) to query error messages or to start or switch off the data providers. We do not recommend switching off a data provider.

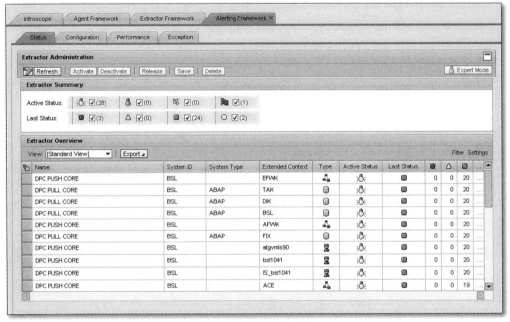

Figure 6.77 Status Overview of the Alerting Framework

On the CONFIGURATION tab page, you can adjust the data provider configuration and, for example, configure load balancing for the web services to be processed (see Figure 6.78). Here, load balancing is defined on the basis of the following two parameters: rdisp/http_check and rdisp/http_min_wait_dia_wp.

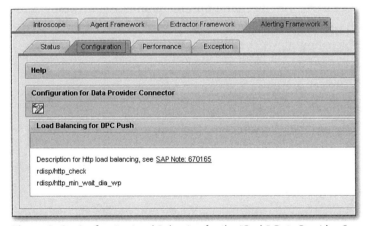

Figure 6.78 Configuring Load Balancing for the "Push" Data Provider Connector

The parameter `rdisp/http_check` defines how to execute a test that checks the availability of a sufficient number of free dialog work processes, which are needed to process the web services. You can use Transaction RZ11 to set this parameter to the value 1 and, therefore, to active. A system restart is not required here.

The parameter `rdisp/http_min_wait_dia_wp` defines the number of dialog processes available for the end user. In order to avoid performance bottlenecks, you should take the settings for these dynamic parameters into account. For more information about load balancing, see SAP Note 751873.

On the PERFORMANCE tab page, you can consider the runtime of various infrastructure components in a variety of ways.

In each case, there is a separate tab page for the Data Provider Connector (DPC), Event Calculation Engine, and Alert Consumer Connector, along with numerous performance-relevant metrics. The values associated with the data available can be used for further error analysis. A detailed description of the metrics is available at *http://help.sap.com/saphelp_sm71_sp01/helpdata/en/ba/533defc9724d47b636c5ddff 28d456/content.htm.*

Using the CCDB to Perform a Consistency Check on Landscape Components

The Change and Configuration Database (CCDB) contains configuration data for the system landscape and thus enables you to analyze, among other things, information about changes made. This is particularly useful in relation to change diagnostics analysis, reporting, and the cross-system validation of configurations. The configuration data is loaded from the relevant managed systems once per day via the EFWK. The configuration data (for example, parameters, settings, database configurations, software configurations, user authorizations, and so on) is then saved to the configuration store in the CCDB. This data is available for applications such as SAP Service sessions, change analysis, and configuration validation.

To check the status of the CCDB, choose ADMINISTRATION and then select the CONFIGURATION CHANGE DATABASE option.

You can determine a general status for the CCDB infrastructure on the following tab pages: CONFIGURATION CHANGE DATABASE • STATUS • GENERAL. Figure 6.79 shows that four critical problems occurred in the configuration store.

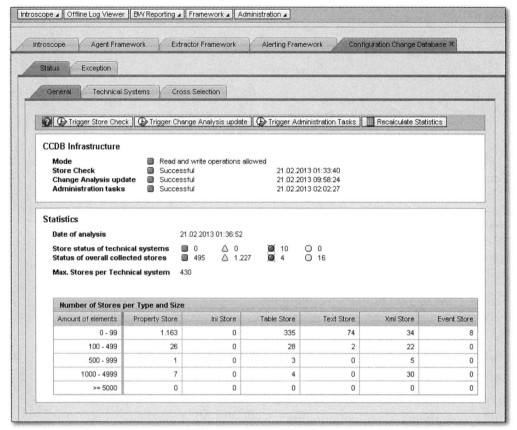

Figure 6.79 CCDB Status

You can now analyze the CCDB infrastructure and the status of the configuration stores and thus perform an additional error analysis in a targeted manner.

Call the lower-level TECHNICAL SYSTEMS tab to display the status messages relating to the technical systems in the CCDB (see Figure 6.80). The number of failed attempts at loading configuration data into the configuration store is displayed in the ERROR column.

As you can see in Figure 6.80, one error occurred while loading data into the ABAP instance of the system BSL. You can view information about failed extractors in the same way as information about the configuration store—in other words, in the FAILED EXTRACTORS column. Consequently, an extractor run failed for the ABAP instance of the system BSL. To display further information about the errors in the area below the table, select the relevant rows that contain one or more red entries. Any entries that are not considered relevant have a gray status, which indicates that these configuration stores are no longer required.

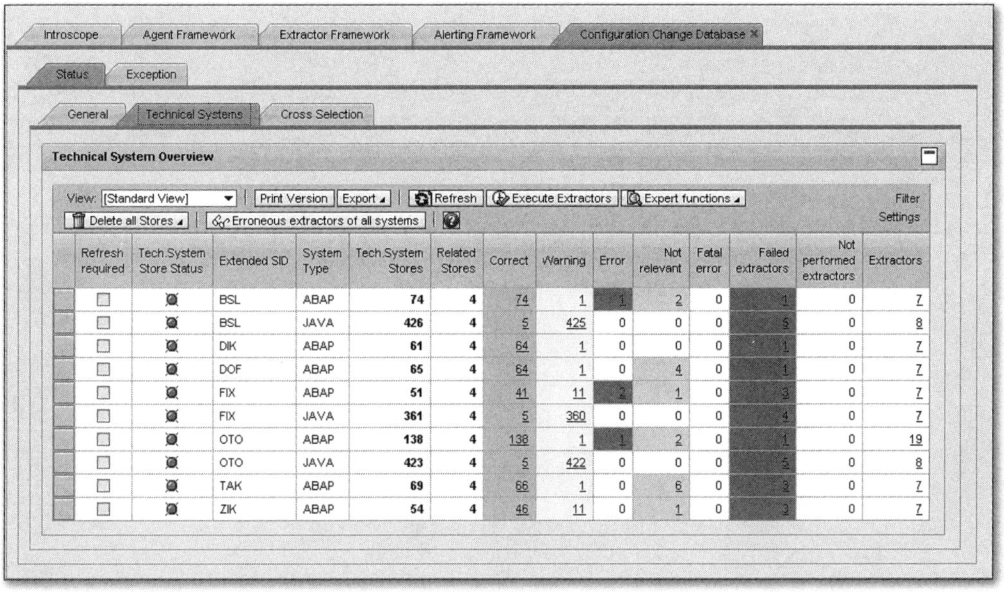

Refresh required	Tech.System Store Status	Extended SID	System Type	Tech.System Stores	Related Stores	Correct	Warning	Error	Not relevant	Fatal error	Failed extractors	Not performed extractors	Extractors
☐	⊚	BSL	ABAP	74	4	74	1	1	2	0	1	0	7
☐	⊚	BSL	JAVA	426	4	5	425	0	0	0	5	0	8
☐	⊚	DIK	ABAP	61	4	64	1	0	0	0	1	0	7
☐	⊚	DOF	ABAP	65	4	64	1	0	4	0	1	0	7
☐	⊚	FIX	ABAP	51	4	41	11	2	1	0	3	0	7
☐	⊚	FIX	JAVA	361	4	5	360	0	0	0	4	0	7
☐	⊚	OTO	ABAP	138	4	138	1	1	2	0	1	0	19
☐	⊚	OTO	JAVA	423	4	5	422	0	0	0	5	0	8
☐	⊚	TAK	ABAP	69	4	66	1	0	6	0	3	0	7
☐	⊚	ZIK	ABAP	54	4	46	11	0	1	0	3	0	7

Figure 6.80 Overview of Technical Systems

By using these examples, we have demonstrated the basic principles associated with using self-monitoring or infrastructure monitoring and, therefore, laid the foundation for performing a technical analysis of the system landscape. In Chapter 7, we will turn our attention to technical analysis and its implementation in SAP Solution Manager. Furthermore, we will use the example of Toys Inc. to explain how to set up technical administration.

6.6.3   Additional Documentation

Links

Further information about performance metrics is available at the following URLs:

▶ *http://help.sap.com/saphelp_sm71_sp01/helpdata/de/ba/533defc9724d47b636c5ddff 28d456/content.htm*

▶ *http://help.sap.com/saphelp_sm71_sp05/helpdata/de/d0/e46b2f15dd40ae-80bd0dae2981de83/content.htm*

SAP Notes

Table 6.7 provides an overview of important SAP Notes for self-monitoring in SAP Solution Manager.

Contents	SAP Note
Problem analysis during HTTP load balancing	751873
RFC and HTTP checks in the dispatcher	670165

Table 6.7 SAP Notes for Self-Monitoring

Despite automation, we still need tools that can support manual actions during system landscape monitoring. Such manual actions may also need to be repeated from time to time. We'll now introduce you to these tools.

7   Technical Administration

In addition to ongoing and preferably automated technical monitoring of the system landscape, it is also necessary to perform some manual activities in system operations, especially in exception situations but sometimes also on a regular basis. Exception situations can include, for example, regular maintenance that may require a system shutdown. Technical administration also comprises tools that enable you to execute tasks manually. This may involve tasks that cannot be automated because it would require too much time and effort, or because they cannot be implemented using SAP software. However, there are also tasks that simply have not been automated yet and, as a result, their key performance indicators (KPI) need to be monitored manually.

All technical administration tools are grouped together and made available in the TECHNICAL ADMINISTRATION work center.

Specifically, this involves the following topics, which we will introduce to you over the course of this chapter:

▶ Notification management

▶ Task Inbox

▶ Work mode management

▶ IT calendar

▶ Central tool access

7.1   Notification Management

Notifications can be used in many different ways. Their purpose is to inform all system landscape users affected by an action or event, or to initiate actions. For this to happen, the relevant users must be made known to notification management. The first basic prerequisite here is to maintain the corresponding settings in the SPECIFY LANDSCAPE DATA step under BASIC CONFIGURATION (see Section 2.5.3).

The SAPconnect interface, which you are familiar with from system administration, forms the basis for external communication by an SAP system. Further information about SAPconnect administration is available in the book entitled *SAP NetWeaver AS ABAP: System Administration* by Frank Föse, Sigrid Hagemann, and Liane Will (SAP PRESS, 2011).

At this point, we will assume that the relevant connections have been established. In other words, SAP Solution Manager can send and receive email or SMS messages.

If you intend to use notification management, you must also make sure that the relevant user data has been fully maintained (email addresses, for example).

You can then maintain the global recipient pool in notification management, both for users and business partners in SAP Solution Manager and managed systems.

In contrast to physical users, *business partners* are used to map user roles in processes such as incident and problem management or change management. Business partners can represent persons or organizations. Relationships among business partners can also be shown (for example, among employees within an organizational unit). The use of business partners makes it possible to assign notifications to specific roles.

The business partners themselves, however, are created when you implement the relevant processes. Therefore, we will not discuss this further here. Further information is available in Transaction SPRO under the menu path SAP REFERENCE IMG • SAP SOLUTION MANAGER: IMPLEMENTATION GUIDE • SAP SOLUTION MANAGER • TECHNICAL SETTINGS • BUSINESS PARTNERS. Business partners can be created automatically using Transaction BP_GEN or BP_USER_GEN, or manually using Transaction BP or SM_CRM. Once business partners have been maintained, they can be used as notification recipients.

Figure 7.1 shows how to maintain recipients in a managed system. Here, quick criteria maintenance was used to restrict the view to the system OTO and client 500.

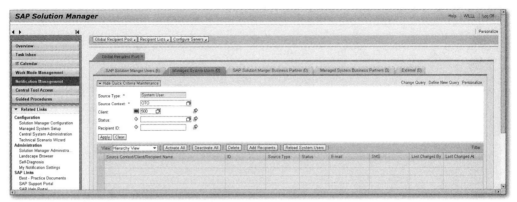

Figure 7.1 Maintaining a Notification Recipient

As the recipient, you can maintain personal attendance times during which notifications can be sent to you. To maintain your personal data, select the ADMINISTRATION • MY NOTIFICATION SETTINGS option in the RELATED LINKS area within the TECHNICAL ADMINISTRATION work center. You must maintain the following settings:

▶ **Status**
   The following statuses are permitted here: ACTIVE, INACTIVE, and FORWARD TO SUBSTITUTE.

▶ **Time zone**
   The time zone of the place of work is permitted here.

Then, choose DEFINE ON-DUTY TIMING to insert a new row in the detail table. In this row, use the factory and public holiday calendars to enter your general attendance times and periods of availability. Furthermore, select your preferred notification method (email or SMS messages) and enter the corresponding email address or telephone number.

Then, maintain your absence times and potential substitutes on the DURING PERSONAL ABSENCES (OFF-DUTY) tab page.

Warning

Currently, you must make sure that the relevant recipients are maintained without any gaps and that they are available for the entire period. A warning will not be issued if no notification recipient has been defined for a particular period.

When you have finished maintaining the notification settings, choose to exit securely through the SAVE button. In particular, notification management can be used to manage work modes and to monitor alerts (see the following information, and also Chapter 5 and Chapter 6).

7.2   Maintaining Repeatable Activities: Overview

Regular, repetitive, or similar tasks frequently need to be performed as part of the technical operations associated with SAP solutions. To live up to its claim of being a central operating tool within the solution landscape, SAP Solution Manager provides various implementation methods for this purpose, namely task management, guided procedures, and central system administration (CSA).

Tasks are scheduled activities that frequently occur on a regular basis and are directly linked to the calendar available.

Guided procedures, on the other hand, are more complex in nature. They can comprise different work steps, the execution of which is supported by customer-specific documentation. Like tasks, guided procedures are also repeatable activities. Until Support Package 8, however, they were not scheduled in a calendar. Guided procedures are triggered by exception situations and the results of root cause analyses or data consistency checks.

CSA plays a special role here because it contains a collection of common, regular tasks from the area of system administration (for example, checks relating to the system log, security audit log, spool status, locked users, or terminations during background processing). Since almost every operator of an SAP solution has to perform these tasks at one time or another, each of them has been prepared and documented in CSA. From here, you can select and schedule the tasks you need to perform.

Table 7.1 presents the three technologies side by side so that you can see the main differences among them in Support Package 6 (currently available).

	Task	Guided Procedure in SP6	Central System Administration (CSA)
Definition Method	Freely definable task with a plain-text description	Guided text-supported execution of freely definable actions	An SAP collection of standard tasks associated with running various SAP solutions, which can be supplemented with freely definable tasks and actions
Usage	Supported manual execution	Activities can be performed automatically initiated manually.	From the collection, users select what they consider to be the most important tasks for them. A user-defined repetition interval can be assigned to each task.
Calendar Integration	Can be integrated into the calendar as a one-time task	Cannot be integrated into the calendar	Cannot be integrated into the calendar
User/Organization	Can be assigned to user groups or users	The three categories of guided procedures (authorizations for exception management, database consistency checks, and technical administration) can be controlled by means of the work center role concept.	Users can be assigned by means of the role concept and integrated workflow management.

Table 7.1 Comparison of Options Available for Planned, Regular Activities in SAP Solution Manager 7.1, Support Package 6

	Task	Guided Procedure in SP6	Central System Administration (CSA)
Documentation	Task execution and results can be documented manually.	The execution times for the actions are recorded.	Manual description of task execution in the comment area of the log or task
Logging	Logging of task execution	Logging of task execution	Historical reporting function by means of the execution log and the comment area in the log

Table 7.1 Comparison of Options Available for Planned, Regular Activities in SAP Solution Manager 7.1, Support Package 6 (Cont.)

You still decide which recurring activities are implemented and in which form. Neither the classification nor the assignment is set in stone. Since Support Package 5, however, SAP prefers to use guided procedures. Even though Support Package 5 contained only the development environment in which customers can create guided procedures, similar collections of tasks, like those previously provided by CSA, are envisaged for the future. It is also envisaged that those functions that are still missing (for example, connection to the IT calendar, recurring scheduling or processor assignment, and complete reporting) will be delivered in future Feature Packages. SAP already uses guided procedures extensively (for example, during the initial configuration of SAP Solution Manager).

Therefore, in the following sections, we will only briefly outline task management and CSA and instead focus mainly on guided procedures.

7.3 Task Management

Regular tasks are a common activity within system administration. You can access task management under the TASK INBOX menu option in the TECHNICAL ADMINISTRATION work center. Figure 7.2 shows the initial screen for maintaining, executing, and analyzing tasks.

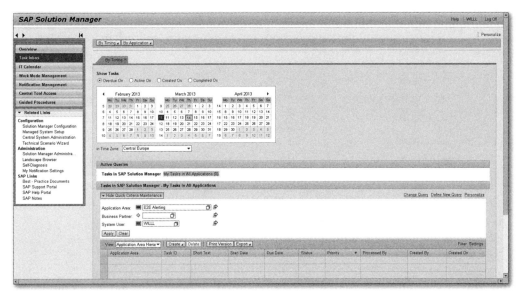

Figure 7.2 Initial Screen for Task Management

The initial screen is usually the By TIMING tab page where pending tasks are displayed in chronological order for the user who has to execute these tasks. However, it is also possible to switch to the By APPLICATION tab page where you can view the tasks by application.

Quick criteria maintenance helps you to obtain an overview of pending tasks and select the relevant tasks.

The usual application areas are already contained in the standard delivery. You can use the button APPLICATION AREA and then choose or select the application area via the field APPLICATION AREA. However, you can also create further application areas and assign tasks to these areas.

If you want to create a new task, first maintain the corresponding selection criteria and then choose APPLY. In the next step, choose CREATE and decide whether you want to create a lean or complex task.

A lean task comprises the following elements:

▶ TASK HEADER
Here, you assign a priority ("Low" to "Very High") and specify the start date and due date in the time zone you have selected.

▶ CONTEXT

Here, you specify the solution, system, logon group, and instance to which the task refers.

▶ DESCRIPTION

Here, you provide a plain-text description, as well as instructions on how to execute the task.

▶ EXECUTION

Here, you define the completion criteria and processing log. You also assign a processor here.

A complex task, on the other hand, comprises additional lean tasks, which you can assign on the additional RELATED TASKS tab page.

When you save the task, it is automatically added to the calendar and assigned to the relevant user or processor group. In other words, it is placed in the task inbox. When the display screen is refreshed, the tasks are displayed in the tabular list on the initial screen according to their preselected criteria.

Tasks that need to be executed on a regular basis are considered a fixed part of the usual administration tasks, and by contrast must be created in CSA, which we will describe in the next section.

7.4 Central System Administration (CSA)

Since CSA is based on task management, which we described in Section 7.3, tasks are handled in a similar manner here.

However, before you can use CSA, you must select and assign those tasks that are relevant for your systems and solutions from the collection of tasks delivered by SAP. To do this, open the TECHNICAL ADMINISTRATION work center and navigate to TASK INBOX. To configure CSA use the entry CENTRAL SYSTEM ADMINISTRATION in the CONFIGURATION area under RELATED LINKS. All the systems connected to SAP Solution Manager are contained in the SAP SOLUTION table entry. You then choose the SETUP CSA table entry to navigate to the detailed list of connected systems. Here, you select the systems for which you want to use CSA. Depending on which solution is associated with the system, system-specific collections of tasks are available for selection.

Figure 7.3 shows the initial screen for configuring CSA for the system OTO. The configuration steps for CSA, including the tasks, are arranged in a tree structure on the left-hand side of the display screen. If you select one of these defined steps, this step is explained in more detail in the upper-right area. In the lower-right area, known as the *execution area*, you make your selection or enter the relevant data. CSA is available in English, Chinese, Japanese, and Russian.

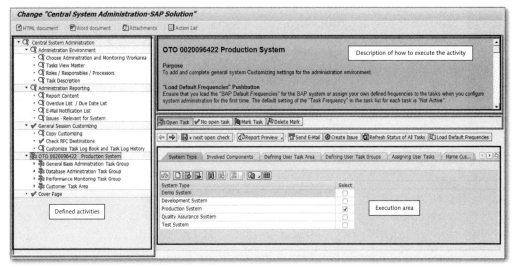

Figure 7.3 Configuring CSA for System OTO

In addition to selecting the actual tasks, you also have to maintain the organizational and administrative data associated with using CSA:

▶ In the ADMINISTRATION ENVIRONMENT area (see Figure 7.3), you define the group of CSA users to which you wish to assign tasks, for example. CSA keeps an automatic log book in which the name of the person who executed the task and the time when the task was executed are logged.

▶ In the ADMINISTRATION REPORTING area, you define the framework parameters for this form of reporting.

▶ In the GENERAL SESSION CUSTOMIZING area, you define the number of historical entries that will appear in the report (via the log book).
CSA has a warning and alarm function. You can ensure that you or another person responsible is notified by email if a task was not executed within a defined

period and is therefore overdue. You can also specify whether a warning email will be sent before a task is assigned the status "Overdue."

▶ In the Cover Page area, you can enter additional information about the city and country in which the system is located. This information will be displayed on the cover page of the report, which you can generate after you have performed the relevant checks.

▶ The actual administration tasks for each system are provided in the <SID> <INSTALLATION NUMBER> area.

We will now take a look at the administration tasks in the <SID> <INSTALLATION NUMBER> area. In our example, this is the area OTO 0020096422.

The first step is to determine which type of system it is. Is it a production, quality assurance, development, or demo system? This selection refines the list of tasks and, in particular, the frequency with which the tasks proposed by SAP are executed. If you want to accept the proposal, choose Load Default Frequencies in the lower-right execution area.

The tasks that SAP delivers by default are divided into the following categories: general Basis Administration tasks, database administration tasks, and performance tasks. You can define a group of users that will be responsible for each task area or task. If necessary, you can also adjust the execution frequency here. You do this using the various tab pages in the execution area of each task.

A *task notepad* in which you can record notes is always available for each task. If there are customer-specific instructions for executing a task, you maintain these on the Company Specific Task Description tab page for the task. On the E-Mail Text tab page, you can pre-formulate the text that will be sent in email notifications.

You can enhance CSA with additional customer-specific tasks that are to be executed on a regular basis. To do this, proceed as follows: in the required SAP solution, start CSA for the system you have selected. (In the Technical Administration work center, choose Related Links • Configuration • Central system Administration • Setup CSA and then the SAP solution and system.) A tree that specifically contains the tasks selected in the CSA for the system you had selected opens.

To integrate your own tasks into this tree, proceed as follows:

1. Select the system node for the system (<SID> <INSTALLATION NUMBER>). In the execution area of the node, various tab pages are available for each task.

2. Select the DEFINING USER TASK AREA tab page. When you enter a name for a USER TASK AREA, you generate a sub-node within CSA in the CUSTOMER TASK AREA node (see the left-hand screen area in Figure 7.3). In Figure 7.4, two user task areas, namely the German user task area AUFGABEN IM DEUTSCHSPRACHIGEN RAUM and the English task area TASK IN ENGLISH SPEAKING AREAS, were created. Save your entries.

Figure 7.4 Creating User Task Areas

3. Now, switch to the DEFINING USER TASK GROUPS tab page. A table in which you can make further entries opens.

> In the USER TASK AREA column, select the USER TASK AREA that you created earlier and now want to use. Figure 7.5 shows that a task was created for each of the created USER TASK AREAS. Here, the task is to call Transaction SM21 (system log check).

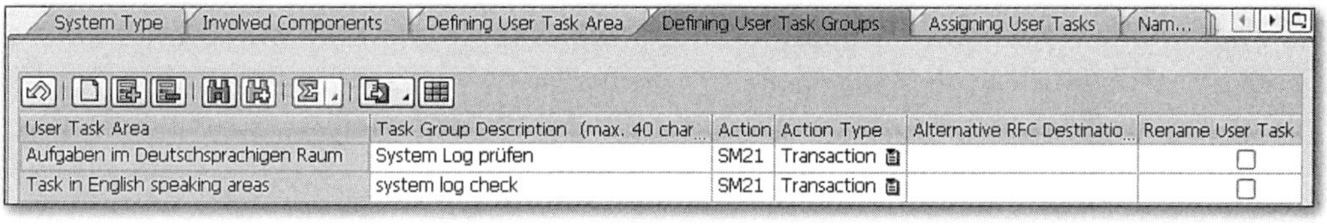

User Task Area	Task Group Description (max. 40 char	Action	Action Type	Alternative RFC Destinatio	Rename User Task
Aufgaben im Deutschsprachigen Raum	System Log prüfen	SM21	Transaction		☐
Task in English speaking areas	system log check	SM21	Transaction		☐

Figure 7.5 Maintaining Tasks

> Define a description in the TASK GROUP DESCRIPTION column. By doing so, you generate a task that bears the name you defined in the TASK GROUP DESCRIPTION column in the USER TASK AREA sub-node of the CUSTOMER TASK AREA node.

> In the ACTION TYPE and ACTION columns, determine the action associated with the task. Select a suitable action type for your action. The following action types are possible: transaction, program, URL, or an operating system command.

423

▶ In the ACTION column, maintain the associated action to be executed (for example, Transaction SM21). Save your entries.

4. In the next step, assign the tasks you have just created. To do this, switch to the ASSIGNING USER TASKS tab page and save the assignment (see Figure 7.6).

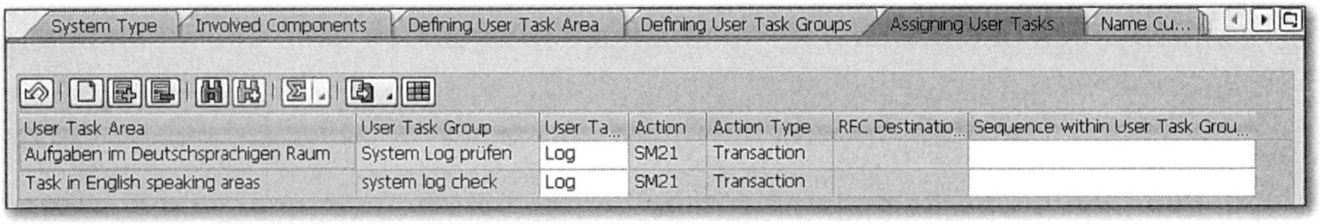

Figure 7.6 Assigning User Task Areas and Groups to a User Task

This ensures that the corresponding sub-nodes for the CUSTOMER TASK AREA node are created in the lower area of the CSA tree, as shown in Figure 7.7, for the tasks you have created.

Figure 7.7 Customer-Specific Tasks Added to the CSA Tree

5. Now, branch to the CUSTOMER TASK AREA node in the left-hand screen area and open the task you have created. You can now use the tab pages and table entries available here to define descriptions for this task (on the COMPANY SPECIFIC TASK DESCRIPTION tab page) or the repetition frequency (in the FREQUENCY field on the TASK LIST tab page) in the execution area of the display screen. In Figure 7.8, WEEKLY was selected as the repetition frequency.

Figure 7.8 Maintaining Customer-Defined Tasks

6. Save your entries as usual or choose the SAVE AND CHECK icon in the task area to automatically navigate to the next check (task) that needs to be performed.

Thanks to the CSA configuration, the tasks you have selected are placed, at an appropriate time, in the task inboxes of the persons responsible for the tasks. Alternatively, you can also start CSA directly and perform any of the individual tasks or checks in the tree. When you create a task, a button is automatically created so that you can perform the action you defined earlier (see Figure 7.8). In this case, the START SM21 button was created.

You can analyze the execution data and results associated with the tasks at any time, either directly within the CSA session or in the TECHNICAL ADMINISTRATION work center under RELATED LINKS • CONFIGURATION • CENTRAL SYSTEM ADMINISTRATION • SETUP CSA. In a final step, you can generate the log book report under ACTIVITIES.

7.5 Guided Procedures

Depending on the level of automation associated with technical monitoring, some manual activities remain and, to some extent, need to be performed on a regular basis. In such cases, you want to provide instructions and, where possible, log their execution. Another scenario here involves guided instructions for exception situations whose automation, when compared against the frequency with which such situations arise, would require a disproportionate amount of time and effort. *Guided procedures*—in other words, instructions managed in SAP Solution Manager—are suitable in such cases.

Guided procedures support a defined sequence of actions whereby a descriptive text is provided for each step. Figure 7.9 shows one possible setup for guided procedures. This particular setup comprises steps (and possibly substeps), descriptive text, assigned activities, and associated help texts.

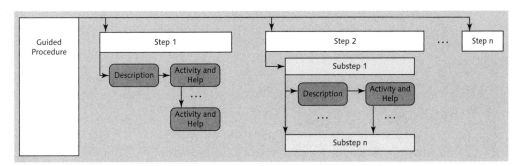

Figure 7.9 Architecture of Guided Procedures

All executed actions can be documented and their results logged. In SAP, guided procedures are also used during the basic configuration of SAP Solution Manager. Therefore, if you have the required level of expertise, you can also create similar procedures yourself. In this section, we wish to introduce you to the initial screen of the development environment for guided procedures.

7.5.1 Preparation

Before you start to create guided procedures, you and your team should agree on certain naming conventions. This will make it easier to assign, execute, and transport guided procedures later.

If you want to collect the descriptive texts in a package so that you can transport them later, define such a package before you create guided procedures. The best way to do this is using the ABAP Workbench (Transaction SE80). Choose PACKAGE and maintain as descriptive an object name as possible for the package. This name must be within the customer namespace. The BC-GP application component (Basis – Guided Procedures) must be assigned.

Text modules are managed within document maintenance (Transaction SE61). The descriptions you enter here in the context of guided procedures must be assigned to the class TX (general text). The text elements are managed irrespective of the assignments to guided procedures. Maintenance is easier if meaningful naming rules were defined as part of the naming convention.

When you create your own descriptions, this automatically brings the topic of country-specific languages to the fore. If you want to use guided procedures in different languages, you must translate the text modules in the standard translation environment (Transaction SE63) under the menu path TRANSLATION • ABAP OBJECTS • LONG TEXTS (DOCUMENTATION) • L5 F1 HELP • TX GENERAL TEXTS. Various tools provide document maintenance support. However, a description of their use is beyond the scope of this book.

7.5.2 Types of Guided Procedures

The guided procedures currently provided, namely guided procedures for business process operations, exception management within root cause analysis, and technical administration, are aligned with user roles. In accordance with this differentiation, both the maintenance and use of these guided procedures are assigned to the corresponding work centers.

In the relevant work center, you maintain and use guided procedures in the context of the following tasks:

▶ **Business process operations**
(BUSINESS PROCESS OPERATIONS work center • DATA CONSISTENCY MANAGEMENT • CROSS-DATABASE COMPARISON • SHOW LAST RESULT • GUIDED PROCEDURES)

These guided procedures are directly linked to defined comparison runs. Consequently, guided procedures cannot be defined until you have created the associated consistency check runs.

▶ **Root cause analysis**
(ROOT CAUSE ANALYSIS work center • EXCEPTION MANAGEMENT)

Here, you select one of the following categories: ABAP ABORTED JOBS, ABAP APPLICATION LOG, ABAP RUNTIME ERROR, or ABAP SYSLOG. Any messages that occurred within this category are displayed in the lower screen area. Other functions, including a button for creating or executing guided procedures, are also displayed here.

▶ **Technical administration**
(TECHNICAL ADMINISTRATION work center • GUIDED PROCEDURES)

A separate tab page is available for each technical component. If there are a large number of managed systems in SAP Solution Manager, you may find it extremely helpful to have a breakdown by technical component.

7.5.3 Maintaining Guided Procedures

Guided procedure maintenance always follows the same pattern irrespective of the type of guided procedure and the context in which it is used. First, you select the relevant reference (in other words, the technical system, the message relating to the error that has occurred, or even the consistency check run itself). Then, the GUIDED PROCEDURE button enables you to start the maintenance process in the current window or open a new maintenance window. A display screen opens in which all the guided procedures available for this component or system, as well as the options to create, change, and execute these guided procedures, are listed.

Since the number of available guided procedures can grow quickly, even for one system, quick criteria maintenance enables you to restrict the view area to only those guided procedures you require. When you display quick criteria maintenance, the following three input fields open:

▶ SYSTEM TYPE
In the SYSTEM TYPE field, you can restrict guided procedures to the technical type you require (for example, ABAP or Java).

▶ CONTEXT TYPE
In the CONTEXT TYPE field, you describe the environment associated with the guided procedure you require (for example, the technical system, technical instance, host [server] or database).

▶ PRODUCT ID
In the PRODUCT ID field, you enter the internal administration number for the guided procedure you require. The more you use this ID, the more familiar it will become to you.

However, in order to benefit from using quick criteria maintenance, you also need to maintain the relevant criteria when you create a guided procedure.

Here, you also have the option of choosing EXPORT to output individual guided procedures in a Microsoft Excel–compatible format, thus enabling you to integrate the steps and explanations defined in SAP Solution Manager for a guided procedure into other documents.

> **Warning**
>
> At present, guided procedures always refer to a technical component within a system. It is not possible to create cross-system guided procedures, but this function is expected to become available in later Feature Packages.

Creating a New Guided Procedure

In this subsection, we will use an example of a guided procedure from the technical administration area to show you how to create a new guided procedure. Preferably, you will have chosen GUIDED PROCEDURES to open guided procedure maintenance in a new window. Now, proceed as follows:

1. Choose CREATE to create a new guided procedure. On the next display screen (see Figure 7.10), you can use an existing guided procedure as a copy template

and then adjust it accordingly (Copy From option). Alternatively, you can choose the Reference From option to create a new guided procedure. In this case, you apply the steps from an existing guided procedure to a new guided procedure. You can add new steps or change the sequence of the steps contained in the guided procedure. However, you cannot change the content of any steps taken from an existing guided procedure.

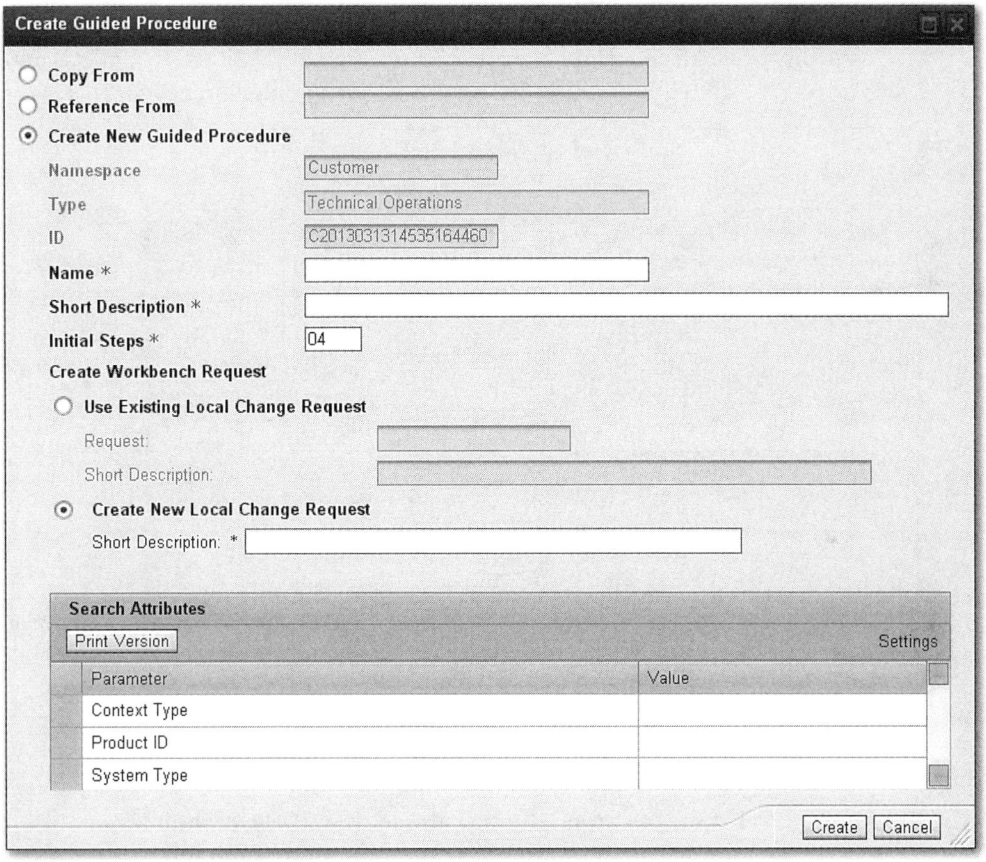

Figure 7.10 Creating the Framework for a New Guided Procedure

2. If you want to use the Create New Guided Procedure option, choose a name that is as meaningful as possible and provide a brief explanation. If you intend to create further guided procedures, it may be useful to specify a naming concept. The namespace Customer, the type Technical Operations, and an

internal identification number (ID) are assigned automatically and cannot be changed.

3. A guided procedure can comprise several tasks. The number of steps (in the INITIAL STEPS field) is 4 by default. However, you can change this entry.

4. Since guided procedures can be transported, you are asked to enter the associated transport request (CREATE WORKBENCH REQUEST area in Figure 7.10).

5. Once you have made the necessary entries, choose CREATE (see Figure 7.10).

6. You then define each step up to the total number of steps defined earlier. Figure 7.11 shows the framework generated for a guided procedure that comprises three steps.

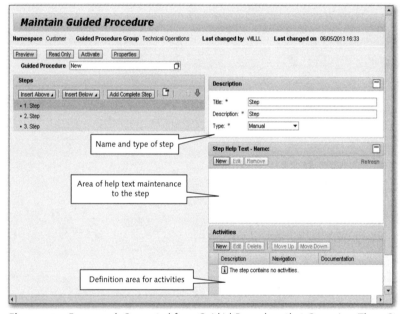

Figure 7.11 Framework Generated for a Guided Procedure that Comprises Three Steps

Before you start to define the individual steps, you should give some thought to the overall structure. It therefore makes sense to create a specific plan in relation to the structure of subsequent guided procedures. One step can comprise one or more activities, and the step itself can be divided into substeps. Existing guided procedures can also be used in a guided procedure. SAP uses guided procedures to create complex services. When performing such a service, SAP employees follow the steps defined in a guided procedure. Comprehensive guided procedures can also be developed accordingly.

Defining the Steps

The initial framework for a new guided procedure is always generated on the basis of a predefined number of simple steps. If you want to adjust this number, choose INSERT ABOVE or INSERT BELOW and use the relevant up and down arrows accordingly. These buttons enable you to insert not only a simple step before or after the step that you have selected, but also a substep in a step. If you select this substep, you can in turn use the aforementioned buttons to insert or delete substeps before or after this one. You can also use a complete step (ADD COMPLETE STEP), which displays a final text.

To define the steps in a guided procedure, proceed as follows:

1. In the initial framework you have generated for your guided procedure, select the step before or after which you want to insert a step made up of substeps. In Figure 7.12, the first step was selected.

Figure 7.12 Selecting the First Step

2. Now, choose INSERT ABOVE or INSERT BELOW.

3. Select the SUB-STEP option from the selection list that opens. If you insert a step that comprises a substep, the display screen changes accordingly (see Figure 7.13).

4. If you want to insert additional steps or substeps, proceed as follows: Select the relevant step or substep and insert additional steps before or after a step on the same level or a substep below.

Substeps, for their part, are treated as normal steps. They can also have the properties and functions associated with steps.

Figure 7.13 Step and Substep Inserted

If you want to execute another guided procedure within a guided procedure, use the Nested Guided Procedures option provided as part of the insert functions. On the right-hand side of the display screen, you can then name the guided procedure you want to execute.

Determining Activities

Various activities can be assigned to steps. The step type determines how the step is executed. You can choose among the following execution types:

▶ **Manual**
A manual step requires the user to perform an action. In other words, the user must, for example, explicitly select the action in order for it to be executed.

▶ **Automatic**
In contrast, an automatic step is executed without the user's performing an action. This may be useful if, for example, you want to conduct regular analyses and save them. For example, SAP uses automatic guided procedures when setting up SAP Solution Manager. Since creating such guided procedures requires some programming knowledge, we will only broadly outline the process here.

▶ **Custom&Auto and Custom&Manual**
These two types support both manual and automatic execution while using a customer-specific user interface (UI). To use them, you must create separate Web Dynpro components and assign them here. Due to their complexity and probable infrequent use, we will not provide a description here.

To make a user's work easier, help texts can provide support when executing individual steps.

Manual Step

Within guided procedures, manual activities are the most frequently used step type for normal operational activities, which are generally complex in nature. Guided procedures can also be used to map tasks contained in CSA. Now we'll show you how to define a manual step for executing a transaction in a managed system. After you have created a step, proceed as follows:

1. Give the step a title (for example, "Check Work Processes") and maintain a brief description for it (for example, "Check the status of work processes").

2. Now, specify "Manual" as the step type.

3. Write a help text that will support the user and provide an explanation when the step is executed later. To do this, proceed as follows:

   ▶ Choose NEW. A window in which you maintain the new document module opens (see Figure 7.14).

   ▶ Enter a name for the document. Make sure to choose a name within the customer namespace.

   ▶ Choose OK to confirm your entry.

Figure 7.14 Creating a New Document as Help Text for a Step

   ▶ Now, enter the relevant text and choose SAVE. A window opens in which you can assign the document package that you created for this purpose in Section 7.5.1 (see Figure 7.15).

   ▶ Choose OK to confirm your entry.

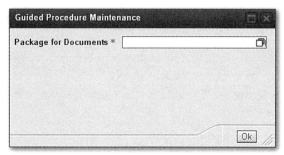

Figure 7.15 Assigning a Package for Documents

You have now entered your help text and can proceed to defining an actual activity.

4. In the area in which you define the activity, choose NEW. A new window opens in which you must enter the name of the activity (see Figure 7.16).

Figure 7.16 Creating a New Activity

- ▸ Assign a meaningful name here because activities can have multiple uses without reference to a guided procedure.

- ▸ The system automatically assigns a multi-digit ID number.

- ▸ SIMPLE is pre-assigned as the type. Alternatively, you can select the EXPERT type, which provides much more complex options. However, these require considerably more developer expertise. The SIMPLE type should suffice for normal, everyday tasks.

- ▸ Choose OK to confirm your entry.

5. Now, choose NEW to assign an action to your activity. A window in which you maintain various options for activities opens (see Figure 7.17).

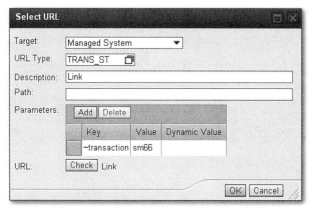

Figure 7.17 Creating an Activity for Executing a Transaction

▸ In the CONTEXTS area, select the relevant system if you want to execute the transaction on a managed system. In this case, it is the instance BSL~ABAP.

▸ In the TARGET field, determine where you want the action to be executed later. The following options are available for selection: SOLUTION MANAGER SYSTEM, MANAGED SYSTEM, and OTHERS.

▸ In the URL TYPE field, specify the type of activity you want to execute (for example, ABAP TRANSACTION, JAVAWEB DYNPRO, or JAVA SERVLET). If you want to execute a transaction in a managed system, select the URL TYPE TRANS_ST, which pre-fills the PARAMETERS table (also shown in Figure 7.17).

▸ In the VALUE field, you need to define only those transaction names that you want to execute.

▸ You can then choose CHECK to test whether your entries can be executed.

▸ Choose OK to confirm your entry. The window closes, and you can proceed to maintaining the activity.

6. In the final step, maintain the relevant help text for executing the activity. This is done in accordance with the documentation text template for a step. The package for documents must be assigned again here. You can also assign links to the text. Save the activity help text.

You can now define further activities for this step. Another possibility is to define a separate step for each activity or use steps that comprise substeps. The availability of these options once again underlines the benefits associated with your team's defining a management strategy for guided procedures before you start to use guided procedures. Figure 7.18 shows a step defined within a guided procedure called PERFORMANCE-EN.

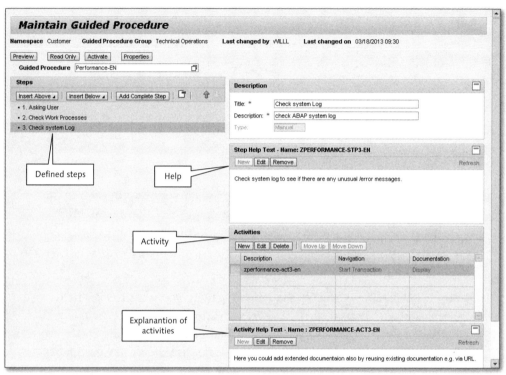

Figure 7.18   Step 2 of the Guided Procedure "Performance-EN"

Another interesting possibility associated with using guided procedures is the support provided when implementing central correction notes. Therefore, in step 5 (Explanation of the TARGET and URL TYPE fields) of the procedure described above, select OTHERS as the target and SAP_NOTE as the URL type, as shown in Figure 7.19 for SAP Note 1652693. When you choose CHECK, a link is automatically created and stored next to the CHECK button. If you select this link, it is copied into the DESCRIPTION field. In the PATH field, you enter the SAP Note you require.

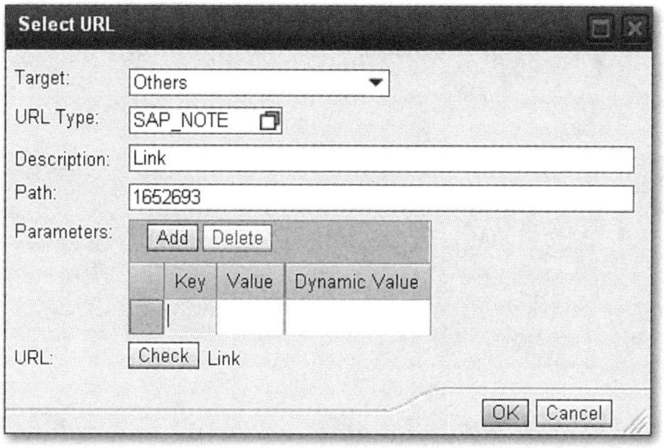

Figure 7.19 Support when Using Guided Procedures to Implement SAP Notes

After you have saved this activity, the system automatically branches to the relevant SAP Note whenever this activity is executed. From there, you can upload the corrections contained in the SAP Note.

Automatic Steps

As already mentioned, *automatic* means that the customer-specific code contained in the step is executed during a guided procedure without the user's having to do anything. Therefore, the first step is to implement the corresponding code. You use the development environment (Transaction SE80) within the SAP systems for this purpose. In this case, you use SAP Solution Manager.

SAP has already prepared the `EXECUTE_CONFIGURATION` method in the `CL_SISE_ACTIV-ITY_AUTO` class. Copy this method and pay attention to customer namespaces and any custom development agreements that may be in place within your enterprise. Then, in this method, implement the code you want the system to execute automatically. When doing so, avoid making any changes to other objects.

To create an automatic step, select the AUTOMATIC option as a property of the step. Create an activity. In the CLASS NAME field, enter a name for the method you have created.

Preview, Activate, and Execute

All entries and activities are saved immediately. You do not need to explicitly save these. If you wish, you can choose PREVIEW (see Figure 7.18) to test a newly created guided procedure in its entirety.

Once you have successfully completed the guided procedure, choose ACTIVATE (also shown in Figure 7.18) to lock the guided procedure against changes, thus making it available for transportation to a downstream system.

> **Warning**
>
> Note the following in relation to release 7.1, Support Package 6: once you have activated a guided procedure, it is locked against changes until it is transported. Therefore, only activate a guided procedure when you have finished maintaining it and want to transport it to the quality assurance system or production system.

It is possible to execute a guided procedure within a list of available guided procedures. To do this, choose EXECUTE in the relevant work center. Make sure that you have entered the correct selection criteria in quick criteria maintenance. Otherwise, your search for the guided procedure that you have created will be in vain.

When executing a guided procedure, step 2 of the guided procedure looks as shown in Figure 7.20. We have already created this step.

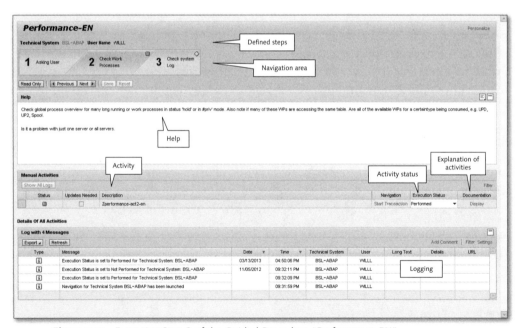

Figure 7.20 Executing Step 2 of the Guided Procedure "Performance EN"

The user can use the navigation area at the top of the display screen to move from one step to another and execute the actions that he or she has defined. Alternatively, these actions can be executed automatically. The manner in which the guided procedure is executed is documented in the lower area. You can adjust the execution mode manually. Changes are also recorded. The status of an activity shows whether the action was also executed. This helps you determine whether certain actions were performed as planned and if so, when they were executed.

Expert Mode

In addition to guided procedure maintenance (described previously), which is linked to a work center, an editor that is completely independent of the work center is also available under the following link:

http://<solution_manager_host>:<Port>/sap/bc/webdynpro/sap/ags_gpa_wda_gp_brwsr?APP_ID=AGS_GPA_BROWSER&CONSUMER=CL_GPA_BRWSR_CNSMR_TO

As the name implies, this editor is intended for experienced specialists who want to create a large number of guided procedures for various roles. The type of guided procedure is then specified manually by entering one of the following consumers:

▶ CL_GPA_BRWSR_CNSMT_TO for technical administration

▶ CL_E2EEM_GP_CNSMR for exception management

▶ CL_DSWP_CDC_GP_CNSMR for a consistency comparison

7.6   Work Mode Management

In addition to the normal operations associated with a solution, special actions are occasionally necessary as part of system maintenance (for example, performing an upgrade or implementing a Support Package). Year-end closing can also represent a special challenge for a system. Common to both are actions that essentially deviate from normal, daily operations and therefore have an effect on the monitoring process configured for normal operations, including its measurements and thresholds. Since such special actions are executed only as scheduled actions, it makes sense to map them in *work modes*.

Work mode management is available in the TECHNICAL ADMINISTRATION work center. Since a work mode always refers to a technical component or an entire system, all available technical components and systems are displayed on the initial screen for work mode management. If a very large number of systems are running in the managed landscape, the tab pages provided, depending on the type of component (for example, Java systems, WebSphere systems, or .NET systems), can be very helpful because of the preselected information they contain.

To make your selection, select the component or system you require. Then choose WORK MODE MANAGEMENT and open maintenance in the current window (embedded) or in a new window (see Figure 7.21).

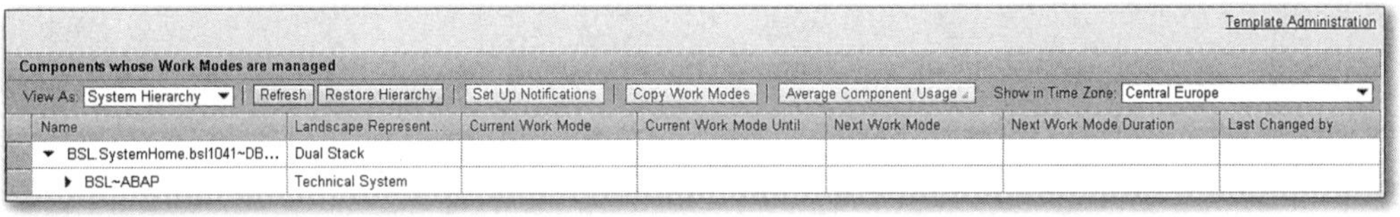

Template Administration								
Components whose Work Modes are managed								
View As: System Hierarchy ▼		Refresh	Restore Hierarchy	Set Up Notifications	Copy Work Modes	Average Component Usage ⌄	Show in Time Zone: Central Europe	▼
Name	Landscape Represent...	Current Work Mode		Current Work Mode Until	Next Work Mode		Next Work Mode Duration	Last Changed by
▼ BSL SystemHome.bsl1041~DB...	Dual Stack							
▶ BSL~ABAP	Technical System							

Figure 7.21 Initial Screen for Maintaining a Work Mode for Web AS ABAP "BSL"

When you open the maintenance screen for a component for the very first time, the overview is still empty. If, on the other hand, work modes have already been defined and executed, this will be apparent from the table displayed.

To create and assign a work mode, select the TEMPLATE MAINTENANCE link on the right-hand side of the screen, above the COMPONENTS WHOSE WORK MODES ARE MANAGED area. A tabular overview of all work modes that were defined previously opens. When creating a new work mode, you must decide whether you want it to be a one-time work mode or a repeatable work mode. You therefore choose CREATE SINGLE TEMPLATE or CREATE RECURRING TEMPLATE accordingly. Then in the window that opens, select the work mode you require.

The following work modes are available:

- PLANNED DOWNTIME
- MAINTENANCE
- PEAK BUSINESS HOURS
- NON-PEAK BUSINESS HOURS
- NON-BUSINESS HOURS

Standardizing the work mode types provides you with an evaluation criterion to which properties are also assigned. Some of this occurs automatically when the type is assigned. You can then assign other properties in the window that opens.

For each work mode, you must also enter a title of your choice for the type selected. In the CATEGORY area, you can make a further restriction based on the type of work mode (for example, whether it concerns hardware or software maintenance). In the DESCRIPTION area, you can document the work mode or add documents or hyperlinks to documents directly.

If the work mode restricts system availability (PLANNED DOWNTIME or MAINTENANCE types), you can maintain and schedule email notifications to users on the INCIDENTS tab page. Such email is then sent at a time that you have chosen, prior to the work mode's coming into effect.

> **Warning**
>
> Notifications can be sent only to users who were previously maintained in notification management within SAP Solution Manager.

During this time, if you are still using CCMS monitoring, you can restrict monitoring in the CCMS area for the two work modes that restrict system availability, namely PLANNED DOWNTIME and MAINTENANCE. The following options are also possible here: alert notification deactivation (alert suppression), complete suspension (a pause in monitoring), or continued monitoring without restriction (full monitoring). These options help to avoid possible distortions in relation to system availability, for example, or to avoid unwanted alerts.

If a repeatable template is created, you can use the SCHEDULING tab page to specify the repetition period.

You can also add work modes to monitoring templates. Work modes are assigned to a template in the TECHNICAL MONITORING work center. Here, choose CONFIGURATION under RELATED LINKS on the left-hand side of the screen. Then, select TECHNICAL MONITORING from the navigation area. You then branch to a menu-supported, step-by-step configuration of technical monitoring, as described in Chapter 5 and Chapter 6 (see Figure 7.22).

Figure 7.22 Menu-Supported Configuration of Monitoring

441

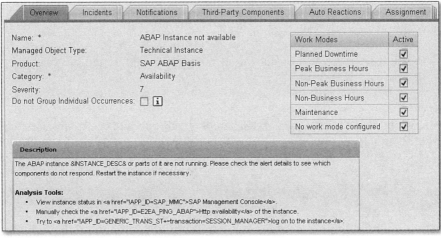

Figure 7.23 Activating a Template for Certain Work Modes

In the fourth step, TEMPLATE MAINTENANCE, you can decide for which type of operating mode each template is active. To do this, select the relevant template from the tree on the left-hand side of the screen, which contains all templates. Then, choose EDIT and EXPERT MODE to navigate to the advanced template configuration. Then, switch to the METRICS, EVENTS, ALERTS HIERARCHY tab page. The overview contains the selection options available for the work modes. Here, set the corresponding checkmark for the work modes in which the monitoring template is to be active. Figure 7.23 shows a template that is active in every work mode.

7.7   IT Calendar

The purpose of the IT calendar is to support IT-relevant activities and make them easier to manage. In the calendar, you can schedule all key IT events in the categories DEVELOPMENT, MAINTENANCE, GENERIC, or BUSINESS, as well as associated work modes for each instance or system. In this way, the IT calendar gives you a landscape-wide overview of all connected systems, as well as scheduled key events.

The IT calendar is available in the TECHNICAL ADMINISTRATION work center. To access it, select the IT CALENDAR entry from the overview or menu. In the next step, select, from the list of technical systems, the system whose calendar you want to maintain. Then choose CALENDAR. Figure 7.24 shows the IT calendar maintained for the system OTO and SAP NetWeaver Application Server Java (AS Java).

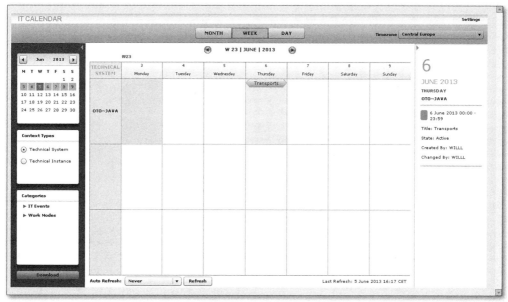

Figure 7.24 IT Calendar for the System "OTO Web AS Java"

If this system had further instances, they would be displayed in the calendar as additional rows. The IT event TRANSPORTS FROM DEVELOPMENT was created for Thursday, June 6. For more information, select the relevant day. The data recorded for the event or work mode is then displayed on the far right-hand side of the screen. If a large number of events or work modes were maintained for an instance, you can use the selection criteria in the lower-left area of the screen to restrict the display screen to certain categories.

If you want to record a new event, for example, select the relevant day by selecting the relevant field in the calendar. In the upper screen area, you can select the units in which the calendar is displayed (DAY, WEEK, or MONTH buttons). You can use the arrow buttons to scroll back and forth within the calendar. Once you have selected the relevant date, right-click. A selection menu is displayed in which you schedule a work mode or IT event (see Figure 7.25). You can also adjust the Adobe Flash Player settings for the display screen.

Figure 7.25 Maintaining an IT Event

For each event, you assign a title and define the duration. In the Is RECURRENT field, you also specify whether this is a regular, recurring event. If you maintain additional descriptions, you will help other colleagues to appreciate the significance and impact of the event and adapt accordingly. Once you have entered all the necessary data, choose SAVE and then CLOSE to return to the IT calendar.

> **Warning**
>
> The IT calendar is not refreshed automatically. For this to happen, you must explicitly choose REFRESH, as shown in Figure 7.24. If you want the IT calendar to be refreshed on a regular basis, you can select the relevant period in the AUTO REFRESH field.

If you want to assign a particular work mode, right-click the relevant date in the SCHEDULE WORK MODE from calendar field. You then branch to work mode management, as described in Section 7.6.

7.8   Central Tool Access

Since SAP Solution Manager supports all centralized operations in the SAP system landscape, it also provides support for administrative actions executed in the systems connected to it. The CENTRAL TOOL ACCESS menu option is located in the TECHNICAL ADMINISTRATION work center. The first step is to select the relevant system or instance from the list of managed systems and instances displayed. Then, choose CENTRAL TOOL ACCESS to navigate to a list of available transactions that you can execute remotely. You can use quick criteria maintenance and the relevant tab pages to restrict the list of possible actions to the area you require.

To prevent unauthorized use, you must log on to the relevant system when you call a transaction. If you want to add further tools, choose the button ADD TOOL. You can also remove tools (REMOVE TOOL button) or adjust properties (EDIT TOOL button). Figure 7.26 shows which properties need to be maintained in order to facilitate central tool access. Make sure to always choose suitable selection criteria, especially when you record new actions.

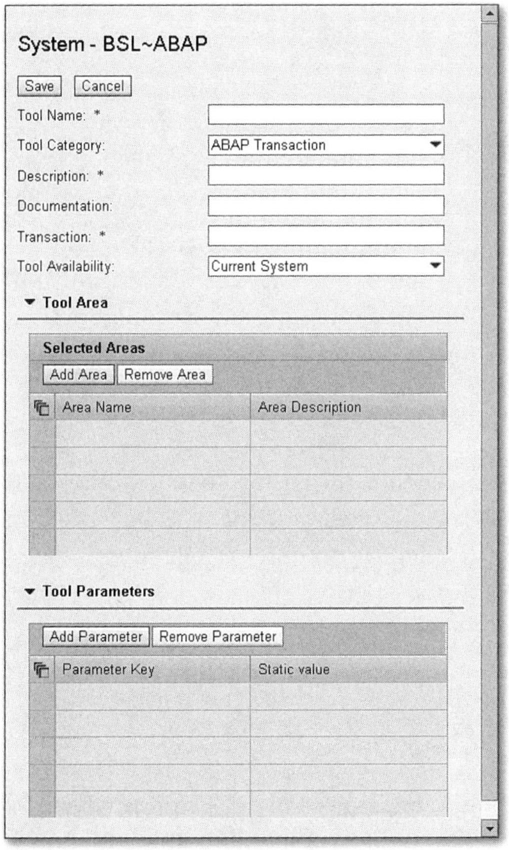

Figure 7.26 Maintaining Tools for Central Access from Within SAP Solution Manager

Using the actions available within central tool access is not discussed further in this book. However, their operation and use are covered within the basic principles of SAP NetWeaver Administration, which are described in *SAP NetWeaver AS ABAP: System Administration* by Frank Föse, Sigrid Hagemann, and Liane Will (4th edition, SAP PRESS 2011).

The DBA Cockpit plays a special role in actions that can be executed centrally. It comprises all the administrative actions necessary for database management, as well as a statistical analysis of database actions. You can use Transaction DBACOCKPIT to call the DBA Cockpit directly in SAP Solution Manager, which already supports remote management of all database systems in SAP solutions connected to it. However, you can also navigate away from central tool access and call the DBA Cockpit locally in the system connected to SAP Solution Manager.

Some thought must be given to these two execution options. If necessary, you must restrict them when assigning authorizations to SAP Solution Manager users.

7.9 Using Guided Procedures at Toys Inc.

Despite having implemented technical monitoring and endeavoring to achieve the greatest possible degree of automation for monitoring and automatic alert notifications, Toys Inc. has identified some activities that are very difficult to automate. Until now, the company had maintained instructions for typical and occasional actions in a table and defined them in the documentation area. Toys Inc. now plans to use the highly promising framework of guided procedures to replace these documents with interactive user guidance for guided procedures.

For Toys Inc., the benefits of guided procedures lie in the central storage and availability of these procedures and the fact that their execution can be logged. In particular, there are three areas in which guided procedures can be used:

▶ **Configuration tasks**
At Toys Inc., configuration tasks include instructions for checking or implementing configurations, even in non-SAP systems that were not previously connected to SAP Solution Manager.

▶ **SAP Notes implementation**
Guided procedures are also used when implementing SAP Notes, which, as

central notes, are subject to changes every so often and therefore must be checked and implemented on a regular basis.

▶ **Problem management**

In the past, action plans were maintained for typical user requests or problem messages. Table 7.2 shows how to handle vague problem messages concerning performance issues.

Step	Description of Activities	Tool
1	Clarify with the user which action is causing performance problems. System? Server? Runtime error? Who is affected?	Telephone
2	Check incoming email.	Outlook
3	Log on to the affected system.	SAP GUI
4	Check the processes. Do the work processes have the status PRIV or HOLD? Note: if there are a large number of work processes in this mode and possibly all of them are still working in the same table, this causes performance problems. Are work processes from all classes still available (update, background, and dialog)? Is only one server affected, or are all servers affected?	Transaction SM66
5	Check the system log.	Transaction SM21
6	Check the type, time, and quantity.	Transaction ST22
7	Check the hardware resources used.	Transaction ST02
8	Check the fill level of the database files and archive files.	Transaction ST06 and DB02
9	Use LAN Check Ping to check the network.	Transaction OS01
10	Further information in the documentation for handling common problems.	Document server

Table 7.2 Sample Instructions

Guided procedures are ideal for such instructions because they can be mapped directly to the corresponding guided procedures. Each step in the table is a step in a guided procedure. The description of activities becomes an explanation of the activity in the associated step in the guided procedure. The tool that needs to be called can be implemented directly as an activity, thus reducing the manual effort.

Toys Inc. assumes that SAP Solution Manager will establish itself as a central module in system operations and replace the manual maintenance and processing previously associated with such documented action lists. Unlike previous typical documentation, the activity lists can be converted into guided procedures, which means that they can be used immediately and will always remain up to date.

7.10   Additional Documentation

Links

▶ Wiki for technical information:
   http//wiki.sdn.sap.com/wiki/display/TechOps/techAdm_Home

▶ SAP Service Marketplace, alias *performance*

SAP Notes

Table 7.3 provides an overview of important SAP Notes for technical administration.

Contents	SAP Note
Maintaining guided procedures	1697805
Central note for CSA	1686849

Table 7.3   SAP Notes for Technical Administration

Technical analysis identifies medium- to long-term technical developments in the system landscape, thus enabling you to take timely corrective action in the event of erroneous developments.

8   Technical Analysis and Reporting

Technical analysis involves collecting system-specific, technical data from a system landscape for the purpose of medium- to long-term reporting. Automated data collection should occur on a regular basis, and ultimately this data should be analyzed by those persons involved in the process. This structured approach enables you to identify erroneous developments early on and take appropriate corrective action. For example, you should keep an eye on medium- to long-term database growth so that you can provide sufficient storage space on the hard disk at all times.

Another important aspect that requires medium- to long-term analysis is the average system response time or the performance of key business transactions. Technical analysis or its related functions in SAP Solution Manager are integral to ensuring incident-free technical operations within the entire system landscape.

In this chapter, we will first introduce you to the organizational background for technical analysis and reporting in the form of service level management. We'll then discuss the possibilities for implementing different reporting options for technical details within the system landscape in SAP Solution Manager. These include generated documents, such as SAP EarlyWatch Alert, SAP EarlyWatch Alert for Solutions, and Service Level Reporting (SLR), as well as interactive reports. Finally, we will discuss additional reporting options available in SAP NetWeaver Business Warehouse and introduce you to the concept of management dashboards.

8.1   Prerequisites and Motivation

To use the various functions within technical analysis, SAP Solution Manager must be set up, and the relevant systems must be properly connected to SAP Solution

Manager. It's also useful if SAP Solution Manager is already being used for technical monitoring of the system landscape because the data collected in this way can also become part of the analysis.

In addition to these purely technical prerequisites, you must also fulfill organizational and process-specific prerequisites. For example, while using SAP Solution Manager, you should have already identified critical key performance indicators (KPIs) for the system. You should have also ensured that technical analyses are evaluated on a regular basis—in other words, that a corresponding process for monitoring or improving key performance indicators has been or is being established.

A KPI is suitable for analysis if it can be measured immediately. Soft criteria, on the other hand, cannot be measured in practice and therefore are not very helpful. When defining key performance indicators, you should first ask yourself which measurable criteria are available. The measurement methods, data collection methods, and analysis tools available are extremely important in this regard.

When defining KPIs, there is a fundamental difficulty in using technical key performance indicators to express business process requirements or translating such requirements into technical key performance indicators. For example, depending on your business needs, you could define minimum requirements for the technical response times of certain transactions or background processes. For those KPIs actually associated with the business process, which then analyze the number of documents processed, for example, you can also use business process monitoring or the related analysis options.

You should also take the target groups associated with reporting into account. While detailed reports on system-specific measurements appeal to technical personnel, aggregated reporting, including forecasts regarding the development of KPIs, is of greater interest to management.

When creating reports, you need to differentiate between the current measurement readings for monitoring and the aggregated values associated with medium- to long-term reporting. You should therefore differentiate between KPIs used for alert monitoring and those used for medium- to long-term analysis, if required. All data collected can then be regularly evaluated within a service level management process.

8.2   Service Level Management

Service level management (SLM) is a business process that can be used to successfully manage all types of services from a quality and cost transparency perspective. IT services comprise operator services that are provided throughout the entire life cycle of a technical solution. They range from fulfilling individual, special requirements to end-to-end management of the entire solution.

Enterprises that use business software to support and conduct their key business processes rely heavily on smooth system operations. To ensure smooth operation, we recommend that you set down in writing which services are to be rendered by the operator, irrespective of whether the operator is your own IT department or an external service provider. This document and any related agreements are generally known as a *service level agreement* (SLA). Such SLAs not only define the scope of the services to be rendered, but also ensure that high-quality services will be rendered in the long term. To this end, the SLA comprises agreements on technical key performance indicators associated with the system, as well as KPIs relating to those organizational processes needed to support system operations. The goal is to ensure system availability, performance, and security, and thus ensure that the business processes run without incident.

Since the SLA needs to be checked on a regular basis, it has proven helpful to set up *service level reporting* (SLR), which can be used to report essential technical or organizational KPIs for system operations and their medium- to long-term development to the parties involved. For this reason, SLA and SLR are the most important tools within SLM. In the next section, we will discuss the importance of SLM, as well as the pros and cons of using SLM. We will then use SAP Solution Manager to show you how to support the SLM process.

8.2.1   Growing Importance of Service Level Management

As a result of the ongoing internationalization of companies, organizations, and service providers, SLM is becoming increasingly important in IT. To ensure proper collaboration among these increasingly global organizations, it is extremely important to accurately define all associated procedures and processes. This need gives rise to a greater standardization of processes, which is expressed in a growing number of best practices, such as the IT Infrastructure Library (ITIL) (see, for example, the handbook *ITIL Pocket Guide* (Van Haren Publishing 2011). In version 3, these best practices focus on providing ongoing support throughout the entire life cycle of the IT solution. SLM, which is regarded as a process within IT processes, uses appropriate, measurable key performance indicators to determine the effectiveness of IT processes, with a particular focus on their results. It therefore forms the basis for an optimization process known in the ITIL as *continual service improvement*.

The importance of SLM is further reinforced by the decentralization of the IT infrastructure. More and more technical components are needed to safeguard a business process, each of which covers only one small aspect of the entire business process. Current and future developments, such as the service-oriented architecture, which comprises small technical and organizational units that make services available, reinforce this trend even further. End users, all of whom have a growing number of mobile devices at their disposal, frequently need numerous IT services to interact with each other in order to complete their daily work.

Scenarios in which business processes rely on services from various providers, vendors or service providers are increasingly mapped using such service-oriented architectures. Consequently, different companies are increasingly growing together in terms of their information technology and therefore becoming more and more interconnected and mutually dependent on each other, all of which, from the perspective of the individual company, needs to be safeguarded by means of SLAs.

Nowadays, enterprises are adopting more and more quality-oriented approaches, all of which pursue more or less similar goals. Standards or legal requirements (for example, ISO 9000 or the Sarbanes-Oxley Act) contribute significantly to an all-encompassing level of quality awareness that does not stop short of IT management. Consequently, a quality-conscious IT department cannot avoid establishing qualified SLM.

8.2.2 Scope of Service Level Management

It goes without saying that the money, time, and effort you should invest in SLM depends on several factors. Elaborate SLM is worthwhile only if a large number of systems (including highly complex systems) or indispensable business processes need to be supported within your company. Therefore, SLM is a clear trade-off between the potential risk of failure associated with IT services or the consequences of such a failure for the company and the costs that undoubtedly exist with SLM itself, which are personnel costs, on one hand, and the setup and maintenance costs associated with the corresponding tools, on the other hand.

In small and medium-sized enterprises, the costs associated with the SLM process outlined here can, in many cases, be kept to a minimum. Large enterprises, which often deploy a large number of systems, on the other hand, may require several SLAs, each of which takes the various requirements of different business areas into consideration. If agreements are too general, there is a danger that they will not take account of the different roles and characteristics associated with the different systems. Therefore, in such environments it's worthwhile to detail the special requirements of the relevant solution or refine these requirements over the course of the IT service life cycle. For example, you can define different requirements for the average response time in different systems.

Ultimately, the content and scope of the SLA essentially depend on the degree of outsourcing (in other words, which tasks are actually outsourced to external organizations). Outsourcing models can range from *outtasking* to *application service providing* and *business process outsourcing*:

▶ In the case of outtasking, only individual tasks or the operation of individual applications are handed over to external service providers.

▶ Application service providing, on the other hand, involves outsourcing the entire data center.

▶ Lastly, business process outsourcing involves handing over entire business processes to external service providers.

The strategy most suitable for you depends largely on the type and scope of the business processes that need to be supported, as well as the technical implementation, which cannot be discussed in greater detail here. Therefore, in our continued discussion of SLM, we will assume that you have defined your strategy and will therefore focus on the practical implementation of SLM.

8.2.3 Pros and Cons of Using Service Level Management

Before you decide to introduce SLM to your system operations or decide how much you want to spend on SLM, you should take another look at the pros and cons associated with adopting such an approach.

All in all, the standardization achieved in SLM will result in better structured tasks. If you factor in the cost of the services, you can also achieve better cost controlling. For example, you could include the costs associated with a certain performance improvement measure in your deliberations. Better planning also reduces the likelihood of unforeseen costs. If services are defined accurately, this generally improves the actual scope of the services rendered. Both the customer and service provider are visibly disciplined by each other's increased visibility and transparency. Furthermore, it is possible to measure the customer's level of satisfaction with the service rendered.

Implementing SLM requires a great deal of time, effort, and money, all of which can be justified only if they will greatly improve the quality of system operations. There is always a risk that a great deal of time and money will be spent on negotiating unimportant goals. To prevent this, and because SLAs can be highly technical, both parties must have a certain technical understanding of the specific software solution. The operator should have an understanding of not only the importance of the business processes, but also their design. At the same time, the company that contracts out its IT services to an external service provider should take care not to dispense with all its in-house technical expertise in the relevant area.

If each party has a very different level of expertise and experience, there is a real danger that the SLA could be exploited by one party or another. This can happen when one of the parties retreats behind the written agreements even though they may not describe the actual requirements. In each case, a trustworthy and flexible working relationship is necessary so that problems that could not have been foreseen when defining the SLA can be solved jointly. In order to reduce the risk of parties' having different points of view and to be able to respond to unforeseen changes, regular knowledge transfers among all organizations involved can be established within SLM.

In the following sections, we will assume that you have found a suitable strategy for your operations and that you have agreed on suitable contractual provisions. We will now show you how you can use SAP Solution Manager to implement the technical analyses you require.

8.3   Technical Analysis in SAP Solution Manager

In SAP Solution Manager 7.1, the following two areas are available for technical analysis within the TECHNICAL MONITORING work center: GENERATED DOCUMENTS and INTERACTIVE REPORTING.

Generated documents comprise three different document types: SAP EarlyWatch Alert, SAP EarlyWatch Alert for Solutions, and SLR. Each of these reports uses the *service data download* as its main data collection method.

> **Warning**
>
> There is a fundamental difference between the methods used to collect data in ABAP instances and those used to collect data in Java instances. While the aforementioned service data download is used to collect AS ABAP data for statistical reports, root cause analysis tools are used to determine comparable AS Java data directly.

In SLR, you also have the option of including data from the Computer Center Management System (CCMS) infrastructure and SAP NetWeaver Business Warehouse (BW). When setting up SLR, the relevant configuration steps are described in detail so that a suitable data selection can be made for reporting purposes.

In contrast, interactive reporting is based on data collected using the Monitoring and Alerting Infrastructure (MAI) within the business warehouse in SAP Solution Manager. In the SAP SOLUTION MANAGER CONFIGURATION work center, the setup for technical monitoring in step 7 (Reporting) is used to configure interactive reporting so that it can be activated with the standard settings when the Monitoring and Alerting Infrastructure is activated. Note that a large volume of data can be generated, depending on the number of systems connected. However, this volume is capped because, when interactive reporting is activated, automatic data reorganization is also scheduled on a regular basis. To estimate the expected volume of data, you should use SAP Quick Sizer, which is available on SAP Service Marketplace (*http:// service.sap.com/quicksizer*).

Generated documents and interactive reporting also differ in terms of their use. While generated documents refer to a fixed period (for example, a week or a month) and evaluate the data according to certain criteria, interactive reporting is a loose collection of data whereby the user selects the relevant analysis period and filters the data according to suitable criteria. In IT management, such data analysis activities are normally integrated into an SLM process in order to evaluate the data systematically.

In addition to the aforementioned concepts of generated documents and interactive reporting, SAP Solution Manager 7.1 has a dashboard framework for displaying aggregated data. Management dashboards can be integrated into this dashboard framework (see Section 8.8). In addition to SLM, they can be used for appropriate communication with management and stakeholders.

In the following sections, we will discuss which data collection methods can be used for generated documents.

8.3.1 Generated Documents and Service Data Download

In SAP Solution Manager, the service data download is usually used to provide SAP Support Services (for example, SAP EarlyWatch, GoingLive, and so on) with data from managed systems. In the managed system, these downloads are controlled in Transaction SDCCN. This data collection method is also used for generated documents in the Technical Monitoring work center. SAP EarlyWatch Alert, which can be set up for every SAP system, is the basis for many analyses. Originally, only the ABAP part of the SAP system was considered. Now, however, the Solution Manager Diagnostics infrastructure makes it possible to include Java-based performance data in a report.

SAP EarlyWatch Alert is relatively easy to set up and facilitates initial reporting, irrespective of the KPIs defined in SLM. The global standardization of the report allows not only SAP Support but also all other parties involved to quickly assess the technical status and use of a special SAP system. Building on this, SAP EarlyWatch Alert for Solutions and SLR can also be set up, thus enabling data from several systems to be grouped together in one report.

8.3.2 SAP EarlyWatch Alert

SAP EarlyWatch Alert (EWA) (see also *http://service.sap.com/ewa*) is an automatic service that reflects the status of a system on a weekly basis and can therefore be regarded as the first step toward standardized SLR. SAP EarlyWatch Alert should not be confused with *EarlyWatch Check*. EarlyWatch Check, which is based on manual yet standardized checks and reports that contain measurement readings, is usually compiled by support staff at SAP.

SAP EarlyWatch Alert, on the other hand, examines different areas of technical KPIs depending on the system type. These include the SAP EarlyWatch Alert areas listed here:

▶ LANDSCAPE OVERVIEW
This area contains key system identifiers (for example, name, type and version, customer number and name, or installation number).

▶ SYSTEM CONFIGURATION
The SAP-specific software parameters are compared against system usage and examined in terms of optimization potential.

▶ HARDWARE CONFIGURATION
An overview of the hardware used and its usage is provided in this area.

▶ SOFTWARE CONFIGURATION
The Support Packages, SAP kernel versions, and database software used are analyzed here. Particular emphasis is placed on outdated software versions.

▶ SAP SOLUTION MANAGER SERVICE READINESS
Here, a check is performed to determine whether the system is connected to SAP Solution Manager, and therefore whether services within SAP Solution Manager can be executed for this system.

▶ SYSTEM PERFORMANCE
Of particular interest are the average system and application server response times measured in the past week, as well as any related historical data.

▶ WORKLOAD DISTRIBUTION AND WORKLOAD BY APPLICATION MODULE
Workload statistics help to identify how the load is distributed across systems, application servers, and components and help to achieve equal distribution, if necessary. It is also helpful to show the load distribution over the course of a day.

▶ DB LOAD PROFILE
As with the system load, the database load is also prepared and evaluated.

▶ SAP SYSTEM OPERATING
In this area, the settings for operating system-specific parameters are analyzed in comparison to system usage, and optimization proposals are made, if necessary.

▶ AVAILABILITY BASED ON COLLECTOR PROTOCOLS
System availability is determined on the basis of the information delivered by the operating system collector SAPOSCOL.

▶ PROGRAM ERRORS (ABAP DUMPS) AND UPDATE ERRORS
Statistics concerning program errors (in general) and update errors (in particular) are returned here.

▶ TABLE REORGANIZATION
The relevant tables are analyzed and evaluated on databases that need to be reorganized.

▶ HARDWARE CAPACITY
This area serves to assess the use of existing hardware resources. In particular, it allows conclusions to be drawn in relation to CPU and main memory utilization.

▶ DATABASE
The database itself and the database administration software used are of central importance to an SAP system. For this reason, each area in SAP EarlyWatch Alert is dedicated to a different aspect of the database (for example, data volume growth, largest tables, performance, administration, and missing indexes). Other areas refer to tables with special lock settings or to database interface libraries used.

▶ WAIT STATISTICS AND I/O PERFORMANCE
The performance considerations are completed with the analysis of wait situations that have occurred on the instances and the analysis of I/O activities.

▶ SECURITY AND SECURITY-RELATED SAP NOTES
Security also plays a role for SAP EarlyWatch Alert. Basic security settings are checked here and assigned an alert, if necessary.

▶ USERS WITH CRITICAL AUTHORIZATIONS
Here, a check is performed to determine whether critical authorizations, such as SAP_ALL or debugging authorizations in production systems, have been assigned to users.

▶ SOFTWARE CHANGE MANAGEMENT
The CHANGE MANAGEMENT area provides information about the number of objects transported in the period under analysis (in other words, the number of changed objects). Frequently, such changes also result in a change to the system status. For example, they may affect performance or influence the number of program terminations. If you can establish a link here, conclusions can be drawn in relation to the quality of the change process.

▶ JAVA PERFORMANCE DATA AND AVAILABILITY OF JAVA PERFORMANCE DATA
Separate areas are dedicated to Java instances, their performance, and their availability. Having fully configured root cause analysis tools for these instances is a prerequisite for the availability of the required data.

In the current version of SAP EarlyWatch Alert, the content is predefined, along with the thresholds that determine how critical a measurement is. It is anticipated that, in the future, it will be possible to adjust both the content and thresholds for a specific customer within a certain predefined framework.

SAP Solution Manager and the service data download from the managed system enable you to generate the SAP EarlyWatch Alert report within the system landscape of SAP Solution Manager and store it there. Previously, the reports were made available only on SAP Service Marketplace or the service channel located there. This new strategy of storing all service reports in SAP Solution Manager gives you easy access to your system's entire service history. Employees or external partners can access and obtain key system information on-site. Figure 8.1 compares the processes both with and without SAP Solution Manager.

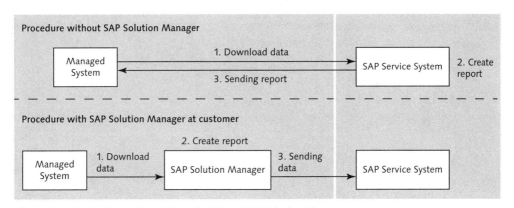

Figure 8.1 Service Procedure with and without SAP Solution Manager

Furthermore, the service data is regularly sent from SAP Solution Manager to the SAP service system so that SAP Support has a constant overview of the status of all customer systems and can, therefore, use this information to provide support when required. When used in conjunction with SAP Solution Manager Diagnostics and, in particular, the root cause analysis tools, it is possible to enhance SAP EarlyWatch Alert to include SAP Java components.

The SAP EarlyWatch Alert service is automatically scheduled for each system within a system landscape. Further SAP EarlyWatch Alert settings are available in the SYSTEM MONITORING work center under SETUP • EARLYWATCH ALERT AND SERVICES CONFIGURATION. Here, you can choose whether you want to see the settings for just one solution or for all solutions (see Figure 8.2).

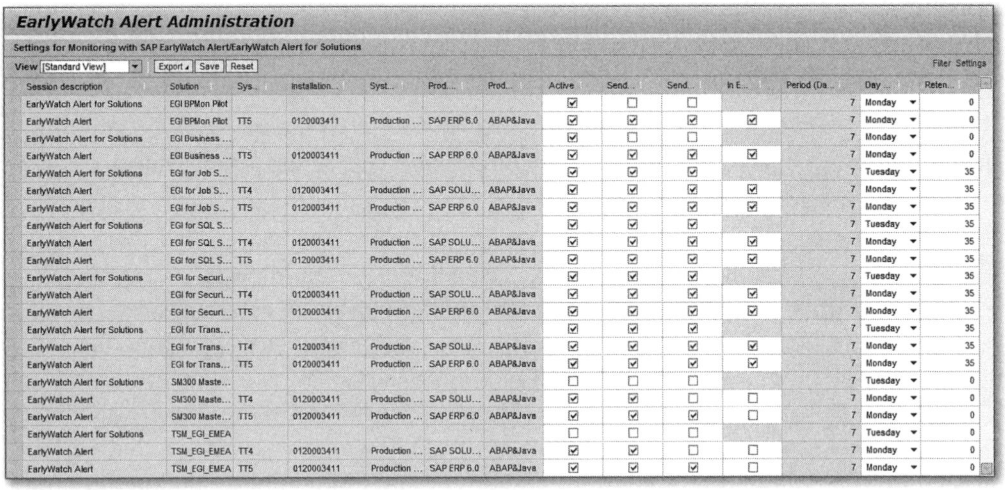

Session description	Solution	Sys...	Installation...	Syst...	Prod....	Prod...	Active	Send...	Send...	In E...	Period (Da...	Day ...	Reten...
EarlyWatch Alert for Solutions	EGI BPMon Pilot						☑	☐	☐		7	Monday	0
EarlyWatch Alert	EGI BPMon Pilot	TT5	0120003411	Production ...	SAP ERP 6.0	ABAP&Java	☑	☑	☑	☑	7	Monday	0
EarlyWatch Alert for Solutions	EGI Business ...						☑	☐	☐		7	Monday	0
EarlyWatch Alert	EGI Business ...	TT5	0120003411	Production ...	SAP ERP 6.0	ABAP&Java	☑	☑	☑	☑	7	Monday	0
EarlyWatch Alert for Solutions	EGI for Job S...						☑	☑	☑		7	Tuesday	35
EarlyWatch Alert	EGI for Job S...	TT4	0120003411	Production ...	SAP SOLU...	ABAP&Java	☑	☑	☑	☑	7	Monday	35
EarlyWatch Alert	EGI for Job S...	TT5	0120003411	Production ...	SAP ERP 6.0	ABAP&Java	☑	☑	☑	☑	7	Monday	35
EarlyWatch Alert for Solutions	EGI for SQL S...						☑	☑	☑		7	Tuesday	35
EarlyWatch Alert	EGI for SQL S...	TT4	0120003411	Production ...	SAP SOLU...	ABAP&Java	☑	☑	☑	☑	7	Monday	35
EarlyWatch Alert	EGI for SQL S...	TT5	0120003411	Production ...	SAP ERP 6.0	ABAP&Java	☑	☑	☑	☑	7	Monday	35
EarlyWatch Alert for Solutions	EGI for Securi...						☑	☑	☑		7	Tuesday	35
EarlyWatch Alert	EGI for Securi...	TT4	0120003411	Production ...	SAP SOLU...	ABAP&Java	☑	☑	☑	☑	7	Monday	35
EarlyWatch Alert	EGI for Securi...	TT5	0120003411	Production ...	SAP ERP 6.0	ABAP&Java	☑	☑	☑	☑	7	Monday	35
EarlyWatch Alert for Solutions	EGI for Trans...						☑	☑	☑		7	Tuesday	35
EarlyWatch Alert	EGI for Trans...	TT4	0120003411	Production ...	SAP SOLU...	ABAP&Java	☑	☑	☑	☑	7	Monday	35
EarlyWatch Alert	EGI for Trans...	TT5	0120003411	Production ...	SAP ERP 6.0	ABAP&Java	☑	☑	☑	☑	7	Monday	35
EarlyWatch Alert for Solutions	SM300 Maste...						☐	☐	☐		7	Tuesday	0
EarlyWatch Alert	SM300 Maste...	TT4	0120003411	Production ...	SAP SOLU...	ABAP&Java	☑	☑	☐	☐	7	Monday	0
EarlyWatch Alert	SM300 Maste...	TT5	0120003411	Production ...	SAP ERP 6.0	ABAP&Java	☑	☑	☑	☐	7	Monday	0
EarlyWatch Alert for Solutions	TSM_EGI_EMEA						☐	☐	☐		7	Tuesday	0
EarlyWatch Alert	TSM_EGI_EMEA	TT4	0120003411	Production ...	SAP SOLU...	ABAP&Java	☑	☑	☐	☐	7	Monday	0
EarlyWatch Alert	TSM_EGI_EMEA	TT5	0120003411	Production ...	SAP ERP 6.0	ABAP&Java	☑	☑	☑	☐	7	Monday	0

Figure 8.2 Settings for SAP EarlyWatch Alert

For each system landscape, you can determine the following settings:

- Whether SAP EarlyWatch Alert is to be active
- Whether the data is to be sent to SAP
- Whether notifications relating to SAP EarlyWatch Alert results are to be sent to SAP
- Whether SAP EarlyWatch Alert for Solutions (see Section 8.3.3) is to be set up
- On which weekday the report is to be executed
- How long the reports are to be retained in the solution before they are archived

SAP EarlyWatch Alert within SAP Solution Manager has some advantages over an SAP Early Watch Alert version set up on the SAP service system. These include the following:

- All SAP EarlyWatch Alerts within SAP Solution Manager are managed centrally.

- The data can be checked directly within the service session. In other words, there is no direct access to the download data.

- The Solution Manager Diagnostics tool can also be used as a data source, thus adding, for example, Java data to the report.

- The service session includes task management, which makes it possible to store additional information.

- Microsoft Word and HTML versions of the service report are available.

- The HTML version can be automatically sent to certain persons by email.

Considering these advantages, it is advisable to use SAP EarlyWatch Alert within SAP Solution Manager. The EarlyWatch Alert reports are available in the TECHNICAL MONITORING work center under the menu option GENERATED DOCUMENTS • EAR-LYWATCH ALERT. The Microsoft Word or HTML report can also be generated here.

8.3.3 SAP EarlyWatch Alert for Solutions

SAP EarlyWatch Alert for Solutions is an automatic service based on SAP Early-Watch Alert, which groups together data from several systems within a solution into one report. In order to use as up-to-date data as possible, SAP EarlyWatch Alert for Solutions is scheduled to run in the standard delivery on Tuesdays—one day after SAP EarlyWatch Alert, which is scheduled to run in the standard delivery on Mondays. No further configuration is required in order to create the report.

SAP EarlyWatch Alerts for Solutions is particularly suitable if Solution Manager Diagnostics was set up on the systems within the solution, because different reports are based on such diagnostics data. For example, data concerning the number of changes for the various product instances can be taken from end-to-end change analysis (see Figure 8.3).

Furthermore, SAP EarlyWatch Alert for Solutions contains statistics concerning the response times of key business processes if such business processes have been maintained within the solution. SAP EarlyWatch Alert for Solutions provides you with a compact overview of the status of all systems within a solution.

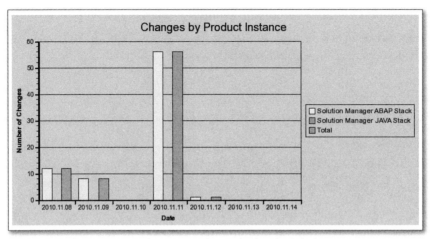

Figure 8.3 Change Statistics from SAP EarlyWatch Alert for Solutions

These documents are also available in the TECHNICAL MONITORING work center under the menu option GENERATED DOCUMENTS • EARLYWATCH ALERT FOR SOLUTIONS. The Microsoft Word or HTML report can also be generated here.

8.4 Service Level Reporting

SAP Solution Manager enables you to set up standardized SLR, which is based on data from the service data download as well as data from the Computer Center Management System (CCMS). A service session is used to set up SLR in a special system landscape. Here, you choose the systems and data that you want to include in the report.

SLR also combines information from several SAP EarlyWatch Alerts within a solution landscape. In *trend analysis*, specific data is shown over a period of three months. Furthermore, in standard Service Level Reporting, you can also include the average response times of certain CCMS transactions in the reports. The business process definitions provided in the Solution Directory are needed for this purpose.

Finally, you can include a limited amount of data from the *Central Performance History* (CPH) in SLR. This delivery route makes it possible to transfer some CCMS data to SLR. You can also include additional data relating to business process monitoring. With SLR, you can also extract a limited amount of data from SAP NetWeaver BW.

If Solution Manager Diagnostics is already configured, you can also include data acquired from this tool in SLR.

Another advantage of SLR within the solution landscape is that you can generate monthly reports from various weekly reports. In the most recent versions of SLR, you can set thresholds for certain KPIs, which are assigned a red rating in the report and therefore warrant special attention.

Figure 8.4 shows the basic data flows within SAP Solution Manager. The service data download from Transaction SDCCN and the CCMS are two such data sources within the managed system. The service download data is transferred via SAP EarlyWatch Alert to SLR, while the CCMS data is transferred via the CPH to the report. Finally, business warehouse data can be included in SLR. We will explain each of these options in greater detail in the next section.

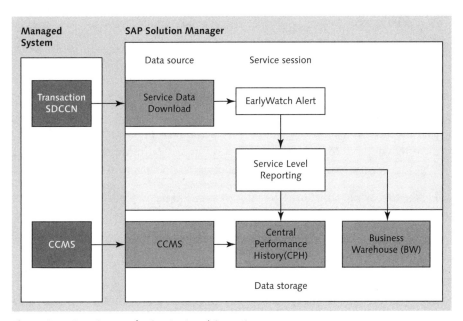

Figure 8.4 Data Sources for Service Level Reporting

8.4.1 CCMS Monitoring Infrastructure

In addition to the service data download, which accesses data that was predefined within the services, the CCMS monitoring infrastructure is available as a data collection method within SLR. You can use the CPH to collect values for certain key performance indicators and aggregate them according to freely definable time schemata. This enables you to collect real-time monitoring data on a persistent basis. Such data can then be used later in SLR. Note, however, that only particular time schemata can be used for SLR.

8.4.2 CCMS Enhancement Options

Within CCMS, a wide range of preconfigured monitoring options are available for each SAP system. You can usually make a useful selection from the available monitoring objects. However, depending on the business process and the interfaces or external software and hardware components used, you generally need to activate additional monitoring objects. A large number of CCMS enhancement options are available for this purpose.

For SLR, the most important enhancement options are the CCMSPING agent and the Generic Request and Message Generator (GRMG) infrastructure for continuous monitoring of the availability of SAP application services or web applications.

8.5 Setting Up Service Level Reporting

Now that we have provided some general explanations on collecting data in SLR, we will show you how to activate this function in SAP Solution Manager. You set up SLR in the SYSTEM MONITORING work center. To do this, proceed as follows:

1. Select the following path: SETUP • SERVICE LEVEL REPORTING • CONFIGURE SERVICE LEVEL REPORTING.

2. After you have selected the relevant menu option, select the system landscape for which you want to set up SLR.

3. This brings you to a session in which you can set up SLR. First, specify the name of the report in the VARIANTS ADMINISTRATION configuration step. You can also create different variants of the service level report here.

4. For each variant, you can specify whether the report will be executed on a weekly or monthly basis. You can also specify the day on which the report will be executed. Finally, you can activate the variant here (see also Figure 8.5).

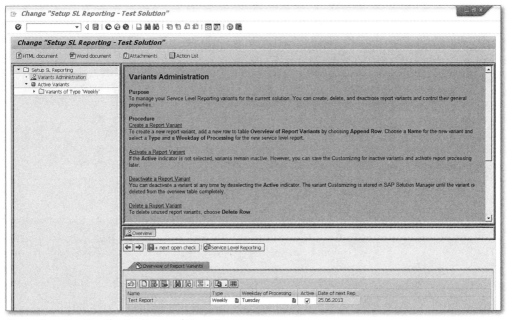

Figure 8.5 Creating the Service Level Report

When specifying the day of the week, you should bear in mind that SLR uses SAP EarlyWatch Alert as the basis for preparing its data. Consequently, SLR should not take place at shorter intervals than SAP EarlyWatch Alert. Since SAP EarlyWatch Alert runs on Monday in the default setting, the recommended default setting for SLR is Tuesday, which is also the case for SAP EarlyWatch Alert for Solutions. Consequently, the most recent data can be used in each case.

There is also a new VARIANT configuration step for each variant. Here, you can make some basic settings for how subsequent reports will look. For example, you can design the title page or decide which content will appear in the header and footer of your next report.

In the configuration step that bears the same name as the report, select those systems from the system landscape that you want to include in reporting (see Figure 8.6). To do this, select the relevant checkboxes in the SELECT FOR REPORTING? column. If business processes are already maintained in your solution, you can select them on the BUSINESS PROCESSES tab page. Depending on your selection in this configuration step, additional steps will appear in the overview on the left-hand side (see Figure 8.5).

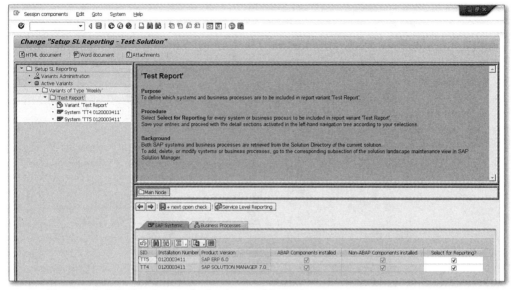

Figure 8.6 Selecting Systems for Service Level Reporting

8.5.1 Selection Options in the Service Level Report

For each system you have selected, there is a configuration step in which you can select the data sources for the service level report. Systems TT4 and TT5 were selected in Figure 8.6, and the corresponding configuration steps were automatically generated for these systems. For the next service level report, you can choose from the following data sources for each system:

▶ Content from SAP Solution Manager

▶ Content from EWA

▶ Content from CCMS

▶ Content from BI

In the case of the CONTENT FROM SOLUTION MANAGER data source, you can decide whether you want to add configuration information for the relevant system to the service level report.

Data from SAP EarlyWatch Alert

On the CONTENT FROM EWA tab page, you can decide which sections of the SAP EarlyWatch Alert report you want to include in SLR (see Figure 8.7).

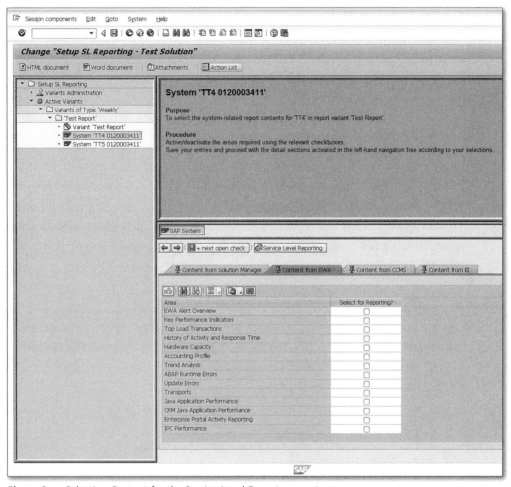

Figure 8.7 Selecting Content for the Service Level Report

A list of all available areas is displayed. By selecting the relevant checkboxes in the SELECT FOR REPORTING? column, you can select content from the following areas:

▶ EARLYWATCH ALERT OVERVIEW

▶ KEY PERFORMANCE INDICATORS

▶ TOP LOAD TRANSACTIONS

▶ HISTORY OF ACTIVITY AND RESPONSE TIME

▶ HARDWARE CAPACITY

- ► Accounting Profile*

- ► Trend Analysis

- ► ABAP Runtime Errors

- ► Update Errors

- ► Transports*

- ► Java Application Performance

- ► CRM Java Application Performance**

- ► Enterprise Portal Activity Reporting**

The areas marked with (*) are possible only in SLR and are not part of the standard SAP EarlyWatch Alert delivery, while those areas marked with (**) are product-specific areas and should be selected only if the selected system contains the corresponding product.

Each area has an additional configuration step in which you can specify whether you want to display the statistics in a table, graphic, or both variants. For the KPIs, you can also specify thresholds, which are marked separately in the table when exceeded. In the monthly version of SLR, a long-term history is output for all KPIs. The following KPIs are available:

- ► System Performance

- ► Max. Active Users

- ► Avg. Availability

- ► Avg. Response Time in Dialog Task

- ► Avg. Response Time at Peak Dialog Hour

- ► Max. Dialog Steps per Hour

- ► Database Space Management

- ► DB Size

- ► DB Growth

- ► Hardware Capacity

- ► Max. CPU Utilization on DB Server

- ► Max. CPU Utilization on Appl. Server

Apart from the accounting profile, there are no further technical prerequisites for most of the KPIs. The accounting profile enables you to create statistics for specific user groups. To this end, each user must be assigned an accounting number. To do this, proceed as follows:

1. Call Transaction SU01. In the OTHER DATA area on the LOGON DATA tab page, you can assign any accounting number to the user. Users with the same ACCOUNT-ING NUMBER are grouped together.

2. Once the assignments have been made, the corresponding settlement statistics are displayed in Transaction ST03N (System Load Monitor). To view the settlement statistics, switch to expert mode and select the relevant analysis period.

3. On the left-hand side of the screen, navigate to ANALYSIS VIEWS • USER AND SETTLEMENT STATISTICS • SETTLEMENT STATISTICS. On the SETTLEMENT NUMBER tab page, a detailed assignment of the dialog steps and other KPIs performed under the respective settlement number is displayed (see Figure 8.8).

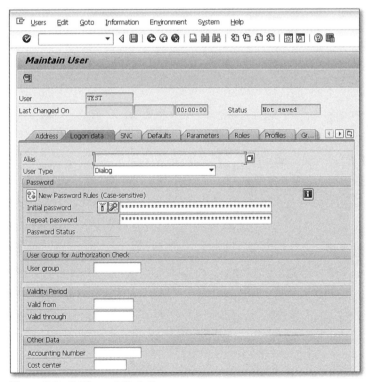

Figure 8.8 Settlement Statistics

CCMS Data

On the CONTENT FROM CCMS tab page, you can choose whether system availability data (in other words, CCMSPING agent data) is transferred to reporting and whether to include additional monitoring objects from CCMS. A prerequisite for this is that the system availability data or the other CCMS data is stored in the CPH.

Business Intelligence Data

Finally, on the CONTENT FROM BI tab page, you can choose whether to include values from SAP NetWeaver BW in SLR. Note that the data must be already available there.

8.5.2 Central Performance History

Normally, the individual values from the CCMS monitoring infrastructure are held for only a limited time. The CPH enables you to save the individual monitoring objects permanently (in accordance with a defined time period or aggregation level) and therefore keep them readily available for medium- to long-term SLR.

Here, you can freely define the time or time intervals between measurements, as well as the length of time for which the values are saved. However, such time intervals must be predefined for SLR. You can use Transaction RZ23N (Central Performance History) to make the relevant CPH settings (see Figure 8.9).

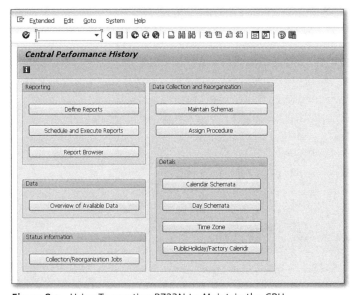

Figure 8.9 Using Transaction RZ23N to Maintain the CPH

To do this, proceed as follows:

1. Generally, the first step is to define the length of time for which you want the data to be stored in the CPH (including the relevant time interval). You can also specify how you want the collected data to be aggregated and when you want it to be deleted. Some of these schemata are already delivered with the system (Maintain Schemas button). Use the day or calendar schemata or the collection and reorganization schemata here. These options can be used to implement specific schemata that take, for example, the factory calendar and public holidays or certain maintenance windows into account (Details area).

> **Example: Aggregation Options**
>
> The aggregation options enable you to, for example, save values from a specific monitoring object known as a monitoring tree element (MTE) on an hourly basis and group these together on a daily basis before they can be evaluated.

2. The second step is to specify which MTEs are to be collected and which previously defined schemata (Assign Procedure button) are to be used for this purpose. Here, you can assign another schema to each MTE or the same schema to several MTEs.

3. In a final step, specify which pieces of collected information you want to display (Reporting area) in the CPH report definition. Here, you can group individual values together and then aggregate them. For example, you can group values from different systems together.

As soon as the data you have collected becomes available in the CPH, you should prepare it. You can use various methods here. For example, you can import the data into a spreadsheet program and then present it in a graphic.

8.5.3 Central Performance History and Service Level Reporting

In the SLR session within SAP Solution Manager, you can import data from the CPH and display it in a graphic or table. Note that the values for the KPIs in the CPH must be assigned to specific collection schemata. First, you must create the predefined collection schemata for system availability and the additional monitoring objects. To do this, proceed as follows:

1. Call Transaction RZ23N and choose MAINTAIN SCHEMAS.

2. In the SELECTED SCHEMA area, enter a name for the schema (for example, Z_SLR_AVAILABILITY for availability values or Z_SLR_CCMS for all other values from CCMS) and choose SAVE.

3. Then, on the left-hand side of the screen, select the collection schema you have just created.

4. Select the menu option EDIT • ADVANCED CONFIGURATION SCREEN.

5. For the collection schema Z_SLR_Availability, make the settings shown in Figure 8.10 and, for the collection schema Z_SLR_CCMS, make the settings shown in Figure 8.11. As you can see, the manner in which you make the settings is similar for both schemata.

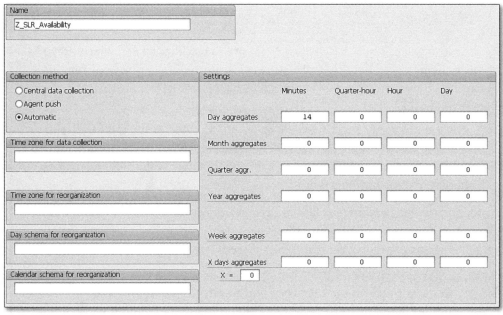

Figure 8.10   Collection Schema for Availability Data

You have now fulfilled the prerequisites for incorporating the relevant KPIs from the CCMS into SLR.

Finally, in the SETUP SERVICE LEVEL REPORTING session, you must activate the SYSTEM AVAILABILITY or MONITORING OBJECTS FROM CCMS option in the system-related configuration step on the CONTENT FROM CCMS tab page. In the other configuration steps, you can select which of the previously defined KPIs from the CPH you want to display. Here, you should take care to ensure that you use the same monitoring objects in the CPH and in the session because this will not be checked automatically.

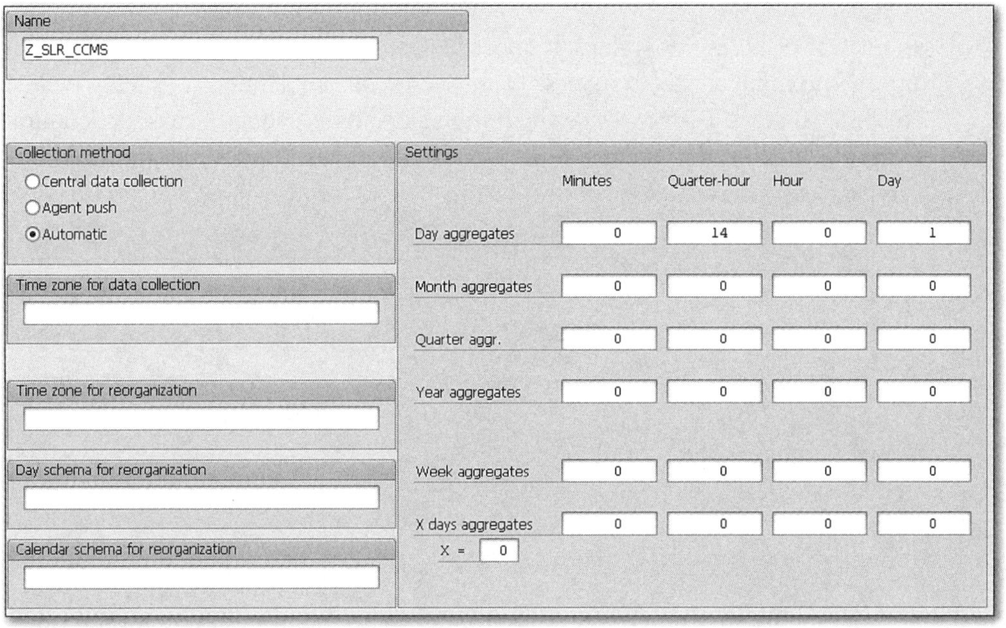

Figure 8.11 Collection Schema for Additional CCMS Data

In the SYSTEM AVAILABILITY configuration step, you can choose from the following variants for measuring availability:

► Instance Availability

► Instance Logon Availability

► Logon Group Availability

► System Availability ABAP Stack

► System Availability Java Stack

In the MONITORING OBJECTS FROM CCMS configuration step, you can select which MTEs you want to include in reporting. To do this, specify the monitoring segment, monitoring context, and monitoring object. A new configuration step is now displayed for every monitoring object. You can enter a description and define thresholds here. You can also specify whether all values are to be displayed in a table, graphic, or both variants. The SHOW 3-MONTH HISTORY option enables you to extend the display period in SLR to three months.

8.5.4 Planned Downtimes and Critical Uptimes

In the case of availability values, it's possible to use planned downtimes and critical uptimes to influence the statistics. To this end, you can define a detailed schedule in the TIMETABLE TEMPLATES configuration step. When you select this configuration step, a table of calendar weeks is displayed on the TIME WINDOW OVERVIEW tab page (see Figure 8.12).

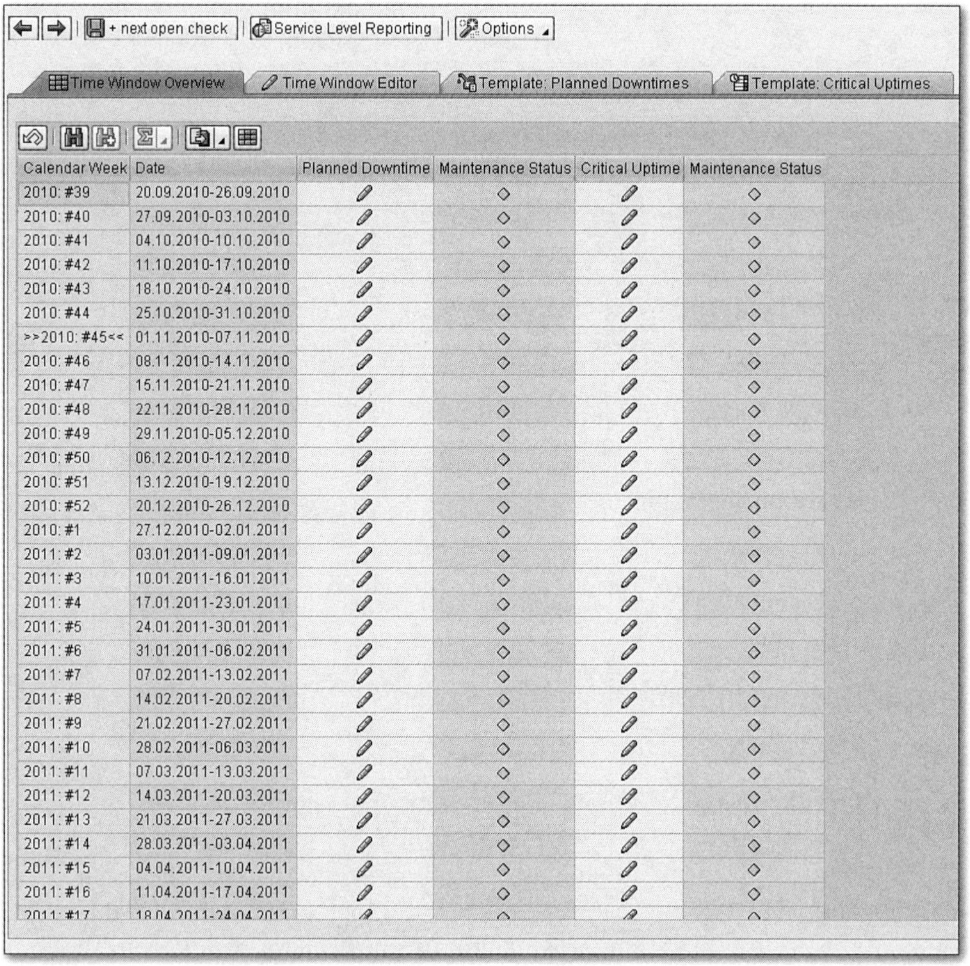

Calendar Week	Date	Planned Downtime	Maintenance Status	Critical Uptime	Maintenance Status
2010: #39	20.09.2010-26.09.2010				
2010: #40	27.09.2010-03.10.2010				
2010: #41	04.10.2010-10.10.2010				
2010: #42	11.10.2010-17.10.2010				
2010: #43	18.10.2010-24.10.2010				
2010: #44	25.10.2010-31.10.2010				
>>2010: #45<<	01.11.2010-07.11.2010				
2010: #46	08.11.2010-14.11.2010				
2010: #47	15.11.2010-21.11.2010				
2010: #48	22.11.2010-28.11.2010				
2010: #49	29.11.2010-05.12.2010				
2010: #50	06.12.2010-12.12.2010				
2010: #51	13.12.2010-19.12.2010				
2010: #52	20.12.2010-26.12.2010				
2010: #1	27.12.2010-02.01.2011				
2011: #2	03.01.2011-09.01.2011				
2011: #3	10.01.2011-16.01.2011				
2011: #4	17.01.2011-23.01.2011				
2011: #5	24.01.2011-30.01.2011				
2011: #6	31.01.2011-06.02.2011				
2011: #7	07.02.2011-13.02.2011				
2011: #8	14.02.2011-20.02.2011				
2011: #9	21.02.2011-27.02.2011				
2011: #10	28.02.2011-06.03.2011				
2011: #11	07.03.2011-13.03.2011				
2011: #12	14.03.2011-20.03.2011				
2011: #13	21.03.2011-27.03.2011				
2011: #14	28.03.2011-03.04.2011				
2011: #15	04.04.2011-10.04.2011				
2011: #16	11.04.2011-17.04.2011				
2011: #17	18.04.2011-24.04.2011				

Figure 8.12 Timetable Templates

You can schedule the planned downtimes and critical uptimes on the TIME WINDOW OVERVIEW tab page as follows:

1. Specify the time intervals for the corresponding week days on the TEMPLATE: PLANNED DOWNTIMES or TEMPLATE: CRITICAL UPTIMES tab page.

2. Select the TIME WINDOW OVERVIEW tab page and choose the calendar week for which you want to maintain such times. In the row that contains the calendar week, double-click the pencil icon in the PLANNED DOWNTIME or CRITICAL UPTIME column.

3. Switch to the TIME WINDOW EDITOR tab page and choose COPY TEMPLATE TO EDITOR or enter the relevant times manually.

4. Choose SAVE EDITOR to save your settings.

A colored icon should now appear in the MAINTENANCE STATUS column for the row you have selected. This shows whether times have been maintained for the relevant entry.

8.5.5 Service Level Reporting and Business Warehouse Systems

SLR in SAP Solution Manager also enables you to transfer data from SAP NetWeaver BW to the report. This transfer option exists irrespective of whether you want to use the BW system in SAP Solution Manager or an external SAP NetWeaver Business Warehouse. Normally, however, the BW system in SAP Solution Manager should be used.

This type of data procurement is worth considering if Solution Manager Diagnostics and the Monitoring and Alerting Infrastructure (MAI) are already set up because you can use predefined standard queries in both. In certain cases, it is also possible, in principle, to use user-defined queries, which can also be based on user-defined InfoCubes. You use the MONITORING OBJECTS FROM BI configuration step to define which queries you want to use. Please note its detailed instructions for the descriptive text.

8.5.6 Interpreting the Results from SAP EarlyWatch Alert and Service Level Reporting

Often, the SAP EarlyWatch Alert reports or the service level reports based on the SAP EarlyWatch Alert reports contain relatively technical information. With practice, however, it is possible to glean valuable information from this data. Such information is not only relevant for technicians, but can also be useful for user departments. We therefore strongly recommend that the data be analyzed together and, if necessary, prepared for different target groups.

In the next subsection, we've singled out some statistics or graphics, which we will use to clarify our interpretation of the results.

System Configuration and Hardware Usage

First of all, every service level report contains an overview of the system configuration (see Figure 8.13), which is divided into three components, as follows:

1.1.2 System Configuration

Hardware Configuration

Hardware Configuration

Server Type	Server	OS	OS Version	Number of CPUs	Memory [MB]
Database Server	bsl1041		SuSE Linux Enterprise Server 11 (x86_64)	4	32244

Database System

Database Server		Database System		Current Version
bsl1041		MaxDB		7.8.0

Software Configuration

Component Patch Levels

SAP Component	SAP Component Version	Patch Level
BBPCRM	701	8
BI_CONT	706	4
CPRXRPM	500_702	8
CTS_PLUG	200	2
GW_CORE	200	4
IW_BEP	200	4
IW_FND	250	4
IW_GIL	100	0
PI_BASIS	702	11
RTCISM	100	0
SAP_ABA	702	11
SAP_AP	700	27
SAP_BASIS	702	11
SAP_BS_FND	702	9
SAP_BW	702	11
SOCO	101	2
ST	710	6
ST-A/PI	01P_700	0
ST-BCO	710	4
ST-ICO	150_700	34
ST-PI	2008_1_700	6
ST-SER	701_2010_1	14
WEBCUIF	701	8

SAP Kernel Release

Kernel Patch Level

Instance	SAP Kernel Release	Patch Level
bsl1041 00	720_EXT_REL	300

Figure 8.13 System Configuration in the Service Level Report

► Hardware configuration (server and database)

► Software configuration (version of each individual software component installed)

► SAP kernel release

Apart from a few exceptions, the information concerning the versions, Support Packages, and hardware used is not evaluated. However, it provides important insights into the existing system configuration. For example, this information is used in reports outlining how changes to the system configuration will affect other KPIs. It can also be an important first source of information for support employees who are not familiar with the system.

Hardware Capacity

The hardware capacity report contains key indicators for assessing the resources available on the servers, namely maximum CPU utilization and maximum memory usage. The rating is determined from thresholds based on the experiences of SAP Active Global Support (see Figure 8.14). For example, the maximum CPU utilization is assigned a yellow rating if the value rises above 70% and a red rating if it rises above 90%. The memory used is assigned a yellow rating if the value rises above 125% or a red rating if the value exceeds the 150% mark. The percentage refers to overall memory usage, including the operating system's swap space. Therefore, in terms of physical memory, this percentage can be represented by a value greater than 100%.

1.1.7 Hardware Capacity

Hardware Capacity

Server	Max. CPU Load [%]	Date	CPU Rating	RAM [MB]	Max. Paging [% of RAM]	Date	Paging Rating
bsl1041	60	30.03.2013	✔	32244	0		✔

Figure 8.14 Hardware Capacity

Top Load Transactions

Figure 8.15 lists those transactions that cause the highest system load, based on percentage. In our SAP Solution Manager example, it is clear that Transaction RM_IMPORT_RC (Migration Data from Roadmap Composer to SAP Solution Manager) generates most of the workload. Therefore, in order to be able to evaluate these statistics, you require a broad overview of the business processes running in the system, along with a certain level of technical expertise. It is here, at the very latest, that technical measurement readings cannot be interpreted using technical expertise alone, and it therefore becomes necessary to assign the technical transaction names to individual business process steps.

Ask yourself the following questions:

▶ Which transactions are most significant from a business process perspective?

▶ Which transactions are used most often?

▶ Do these transactions also generate the greatest system load?

1.1.5 Top Load Transactions

Top Load Transactions

Transaction	System Load [%]	Avg. Response Time [ms]
RM_IMPORT_RC	33,2	116147
<NUMBER	26,4	555
SOLAR02	10,4	20963
/SDF/CD_CCA	4,4	1357
AGS_WORK_LAUNCHER	4,1	2539
SOLAR01	4,0	1592
SAPMSEU0	2,9	449
SESSION_MANAGER	1,9	717
RMMAIN	1,8	1154
BP	1,5	1547
SOLAR_PROJECT_ADMIN	1,3	1145
CNV_CDMC	1,3	723
SM30	0,4	195
SE55	0,3	1652
SE13	0,3	17627

Figure 8.15 Top Load Transactions

Change Management

SAP EarlyWatch Alert in SAP Solution Manager is a relatively easy way to obtain an overview of the number of changes that the SAP system was exposed to during the period under analysis (see Figure 8.16).

The number of changes is divided into *Software Maintenance* (for example, Support Packages or Enhancement Packages), *Parameter* (based on the instance, database, or operating system), *Transport Requests*, *SAP Notes*, and *Miscellaneous* (for example, security settings). In our example, a transport request was imported into the system on March 25 and March 26. In this way, you obtain an overview of whether the system is subject to many changes. For example, it is very common to observe a certain degree of regularity when performing transports, rather than transports' being implemented in a system on a daily basis and possibly in an uncontrolled manner. These statistics would also help you to check compliance with such defined rules.

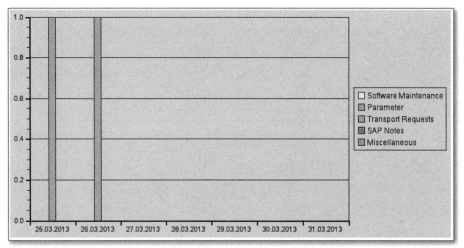

Figure 8.16 Number of Changes in EWA

Availability

In the SLR session, availability is calculated on the basis of the CCMS ping data and the timetable templates. In Figure 8.17, the data is displayed in a table and a graphic. In this example, we see the *Critical Uptime Availability (planned downtimes-adjusted)*. In other words, these statistics take account of the planned downtimes and critical uptimes from the timetable templates.

In principle, it would also be possible to create another graphic that shows real availability. For the sake of clarity, however, you should restrict yourself to only those graphics that you actually require in the case of availability.

It goes without saying that an availability measurement based on the CCMS ping has a limited information value. The technical availability of an instance, which can be checked using the CCMS ping, provides only an indication of availability from outside. However, this method cannot be used to determine the actual efficiency of an instance.

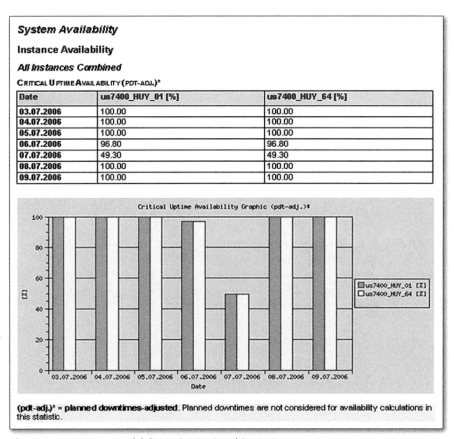

System Availability

Instance Availability

All Instances Combined

CRITICAL UPTIME AVAILABILITY (PDT-ADJ.)*

Date	us7400_HUY_01 [%]	us7400_HUY_64 [%]
03.07.2006	100.00	100.00
04.07.2006	100.00	100.00
05.07.2006	100.00	100.00
06.07.2006	96.80	96.80
07.07.2006	49.30	49.30
08.07.2006	100.00	100.00
09.07.2006	100.00	100.00

(pdt-adj.)* = **planned downtimes-adjusted**. Planned downtimes are not considered for availability calculations in this statistic.

Figure 8.17 Instance Availability in Service Level Reporting

Integrating Individual Monitoring Objects

Figure 8.18 shows an example of a monitoring object that is transferred from CCMS to SLR via the CPH. In this case, it concerns ALLOCATED BUFFER SPACE in the *single record buffer*, which you can identify from the CCMS object information (FULL CCMS PATH NAME entry in the INFORMATION column).

Here, the user decided to display the data in a table and a graphic. Furthermore, thresholds were defined for the value (LOWER LIMIT and UPPER LIMIT columns). These are also displayed in both display types (table and graphic). It is clearly evident that each value lies within the upper and lower thresholds. In the table, a green status was assigned to each value, while the value in the graphic lies within the thresholds for a red and yellow status.

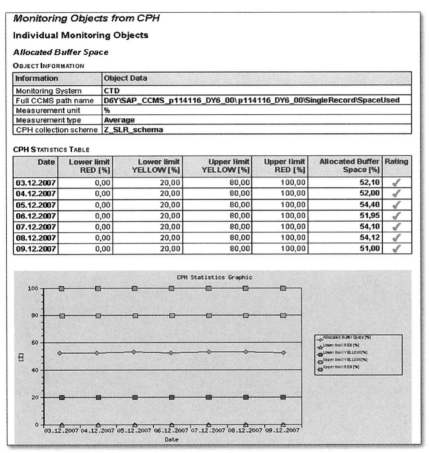

Monitoring Objects from CPH

Individual Monitoring Objects

Allocated Buffer Space

OBJECT INFORMATION

Information	Object Data
Monitoring System	CTD
Full CCMS path name	D6Y\SAP_CCMS_p114116_DY6_00\p114116_DY6_00\SingleRecord\SpaceUsed
Measurement unit	%
Measurement type	Average
CPH collection scheme	Z_SLR_schema

CPH STATISTICS TABLE

Date	Lower limit RED [%]	Lower limit YELLOW [%]	Upper limit YELLOW [%]	Upper limit RED [%]	Allocated Buffer Space [%]	Rating
03.12.2007	0,00	20,00	80,00	100,00	52,10	✓
04.12.2007	0,00	20,00	80,00	100,00	52,00	✓
05.12.2007	0,00	20,00	80,00	100,00	54,40	✓
06.12.2007	0,00	20,00	80,00	100,00	51,95	✓
07.12.2007	0,00	20,00	80,00	100,00	54,10	✓
08.12.2007	0,00	20,00	80,00	100,00	54,12	✓
09.12.2007	0,00	20,00	80,00	100,00	51,00	✓

Figure 8.18 CCMS Objects in the Service Level Report

8.5.7 Post-processing the Service Level Report

Once a service level report has been automatically executed in accordance with your specifications, the reports are available in the SYSTEM MONITORING work center under the menu option REPORTS • SERVICE LEVEL REPORTING. If you select the solution in question, an overview of all reports for all systems for which SLR has been defined is displayed in a separate window. You can use the icons in the ACTIVITIES column to post-process the service level report in a meaningful way.

The pencil icon brings you to the *post-processing session* (see Figure 8.19). Here, the display screen is divided into three areas. On the left-hand side of the screen, all possible actions are arranged in a tree structure. Then, you can make your entries in the area on the lower right-hand side of the screen for every action. Finally, the upper right-hand side of the screen contains explanatory notes for possible entries, actions, and so on.

In the post-processing session, each report result is displayed individually. In the STATUS AND ALERT OVERVIEW action on the SLR ALERT OVERVIEW tab page, all yellow and red alerts relating to the service level report are grouped together (see Figure 8.19). In the example for Toys Inc., the EWA ALERT OVERVIEW and KEY PERFORMANCE INDICATORS areas relating to the ERP system OTO are assigned a red rating. Further information on these ratings is available in the relevant actions within the system-specific sub-tree (see the left-hand side of the screen).

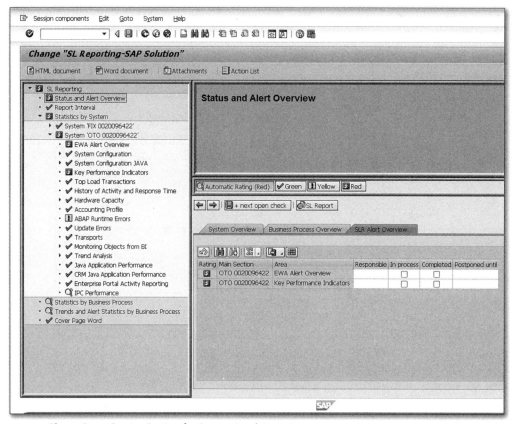

Figure 8.19 Service Session for Service Level Reporting

In the RESPONSIBLE column, you can specify a person who will be responsible for each alert. In particular, you can use this function to trigger follow-up activities to specific alerts and to specify a person who will be responsible for completing these activities. Furthermore, you can use the IN PROCESS and POSTPONED UNTIL columns to document the status of each stage of processing. If you define a person responsible and a processing status for each yellow or red rating, the rating for the overall report jumps to green, thus ensuring that a person responsible is always assigned to each problem category. Detailed information on each system is provided in the tree on the left-hand side of the screen, which lists the configuration steps under the STATISTICS BY SYSTEM group.

Here, you can use the Microsoft Word icon to generate a Microsoft Word report or the paperclip icon to view the report you have generated directly from the attachment list.

8.5.8 Publishing the Service Level Report

Once the reporting paths have been defined, the service level report can also be automatically sent from SAP Solution Manager by email. For this to happen, email sending must have been configured for SAP Solution Manager. This is usually done using SAPconnect in Transaction SCOT (SAPconnect: Administration) during the basic configuration of SAP Solution Manager (see Section 2.5.3). We will therefore assume that the email function is available within your version of SAP Solution Manager.

To configure automatic email, select the CONFIGURE AUTOMATIC REPORTS MAILING function in the SYSTEM MONITORING work center, and then select the relevant solution. You can then choose CREATE E-MAIL RECIPIENT to make the relevant assignment.

You can also send the report manually. To do this, complete the following three steps:

1. In the TECHNICAL MONITORING work center, select a report's session ID in order to access the relevant session.
2. Choose HTML DOCUMENT to generate an HTML version of the report.
3. An HTML link for sending the reports to an email address (entered manually) is displayed in the upper-left corner.

Furthermore, the documents are available in the TECHNICAL MONITORING work center under the menu option GENERATED DOCUMENTS • SERVICE LEVEL REPORTING, and the Microsoft Word or HTML report can be generated here.

8.6   Interactive Reporting

In the TECHNICAL MONITORING work center, interactive reporting comprises two parts: system reports and the metric monitor. The Monitoring and Alerting Infrastructure is used to transfer interactive reporting data to SAP NetWeaver BW, where it is centrally available to all systems in the system landscape for reporting purposes. The business warehouse system in SAP Solution Manager is generally used for this purpose. However, it is also possible to use an external BW in SAP NetWeaver BW.

Centralized data storage is one of the biggest advantages associated with SAP Solution Manager because you can now use the usual BW methods to evaluate the technical data in various systems and compare them with each other. It can therefore be assumed that reports on interactive data collected using the Monitoring and Alerting Infrastructure will become more important.

All in all, interactive reporting can also be used to determine, on the basis of the historical development of value ranges, useful thresholds for the relevant metrics. It can also be used to monitor compliance with defined SLAs.

In this section, we will describe both forms of interactive reporting—system reports and the metric monitor—in detail. We will also introduce you to the Extractor Framework (EFWK), which provides the technical background for collecting data for interactive reporting. Finally, we will show you how to use self-monitoring of BW-based reports to monitor the data collection process.

8.6.1   System Reports

System reports provide an overview of the most important utilization, availability, and performance metrics. System reports can be output for the following objects:

▶ Systems
▶ Scenarios

▸ Hosts

▸ Databases

If, for example, you want to analyze a system availability graphic for a system (see Figure 8.20), the first step is to open the work center under TECHNICAL MONITORING • INTERACTIVE REPORTING. Then, select the relevant system in the system list displayed and choose SYSTEM REPORTS to start the system reports. A table containing exact measurement readings is displayed below the graphic.

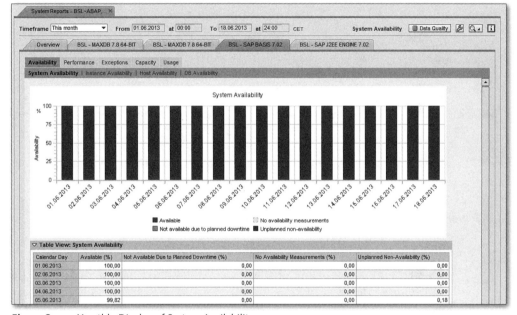

Figure 8.20 Monthly Display of System Availability

Figure 8.21 shows sample system reports for system availability that use a monthly display or summary, divided between ABAP and Java.

The upper-right corner of the reporting screen contains further options for assessing data quality, adjusting the reporting view, and accessing existing documentation for KPIs. In Figure 8.21, data quality was red (in other words, flagged as critical). Choose DATA QUALITY to navigate to BI status analysis. Here, you will find information about current data volumes, data integrity, and so on, which will help you to assess the reliability of the generated statistics.

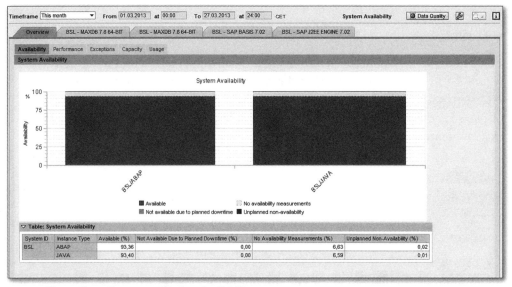

Figure 8.21 Summary of System Availability

In all system reports, you have the option of different time intervals at any time. You can use the Period field above the graphic to display the report for this period. Various predefined intervals are available for selection. However, you can also define your own period, if necessary. The KPIs listed next are currently available in standard system reports.

The following system reports are available for AS ABAP:

▶ Availability (system availability, instance availability, host availability, and database availability)

▶ Exceptions (ABAP exceptions: runtime errors, update errors, and aborted jobs)

▶ Capacity (CPU, database, main memory, file system, and paging rate)

▶ Usage (applications, transactions, and reports; RFC connections; web service consumers; RFC and web service providers; databases; and user activity)

▶ Performance (system performance, distribution of response times, compilation of response times, and database performance, see Figure 8.22)

The following system reports are available for AS Java:

▶ Availability (system availability, instance availability, host availability, and database availability)

- Capacity (CPU, main memory, file system, and paging rate)

- Usage (number of HTTP sessions)

- Performance (response times, distribution of response times, and Java Garbage Collection)

- Database

- Availability (database availability)

- Exceptions (deadlocks)

- Capacity (database and log usage)

For further information on the importance of each KPI, please refer to the book *SAP NetWeaver AS ABAP: System Administration* by Frank Föse, Sigrid Hagemann, and Liane Will (SAP PRESS 2011).

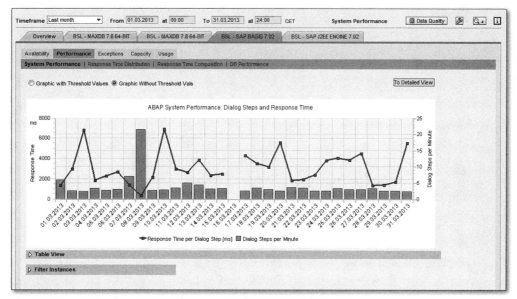

Figure 8.22 Graphic for System Performance, Dialog Steps, and Response Times

An example of a host report is shown in Figure 8.23, where CPU utilization is displayed along with the maximum and minimum values for the period under analysis. Here, you can show the thresholds that you defined in the template (see Section 5.4.4).

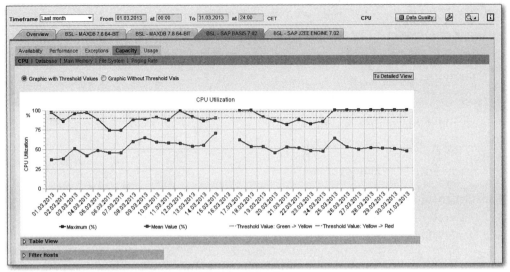

Figure 8.23 CPU Utilization in Interactive Reporting

8.6.2 Metric Monitor

The metric monitor makes all managed system metrics selected during the monitoring configuration process centrally available (see Figure 8.24). You can therefore display all selected metrics individually, along with their development over time (in other words, even those metrics not displayed in any interactive report). The metric monitor, therefore, supplements interactive reporting. In the metric monitor, you have the option to choose SHOW TREND to display linear trend lines that will also update the relevant metric into the future.

Figure 8.24 shows a sample graphic for R3DIALOGRESPONSETIME in the metric monitor. This graphic shows regularly occurring peaks that represent response times of 20 seconds or more for dialog processes. Such peaks indicate either configuration or load problems, the cause of which must be analyzed. The metric monitor, therefore, helps to identify such problems. Thanks to certain defined thresholds, future occurrences of such peaks can trigger automatic notifications to the relevant system administrators.

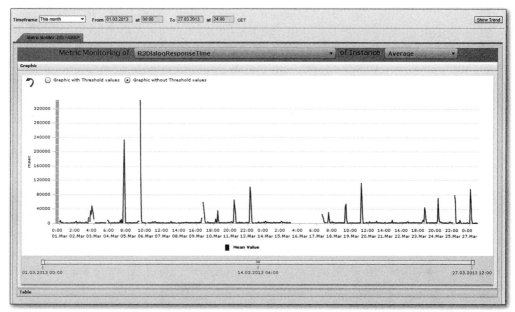

Figure 8.24 Graphic for R3DialogResponseTime in the Metric Monitor

8.6.3 Extractor Framework

The purpose of the Extractor Framework (EFWK) is to collect data in managed systems, prepare it, and then make it centrally available in SAP Solution Manager for reporting purposes.

Its main task is to manage the available system resources and schedule the extractors. Control settings ensure, among other things, that not too many extractors run at the same time, and therefore that the load generated on a managed system as a result of parallel data collection is not too high, thus avoiding performance problems.

The background job E2E_EFWK_RESOURCE_MGR takes care of all of these tasks. It is run by the system user SM_EFWK (or SOLMAN_BTC in SAP Solution Manager 7.1 SP4 and earlier) and starts every minute by default. This job activates the extractors asynchronously in dialog processes. Furthermore, the same user starts the background jobs E2E_EFWK_HOUSEKEEPER and E2E_HK_CONTROLLER once per day, thus ensuring that any old data or data no longer required in EFWK or business warehouse is aggregated or deleted.

To this end, the extractors access various types of data sources (for example, function modules, web services, or tables, to name but a few). Data is also extracted

489

from Introscope and direct database accesses in the same way. The EFWK then prepares the collected data, enriches it with the landscape information available in the Landscape Management Database (LMDB), and saves it in InfoCubes in the BW system in SAP Solution Manager or in its database tables.

Figure 8.25 shows a simplified depiction of the EFWK architecture. The data sources are located in the managed systems, and the data is transferred from these systems to SAP Solution Manager and prepared there. The data is stored in tables and in the BW system in SAP Solution Manager. The data can then be evaluated in different analysis areas. The EFWK is set up during the basic configuration. The background services are also scheduled at this time.

In the case of extractors, we differentiate among several setup types. Extractors of the setup type SOLMAN are responsible for collecting Solution Manager data. They are also scheduled during the basic configuration. Extractors of the setup type RCA are responsible for collecting data in the managed systems. They are scheduled during configuration of the managed systems. Extractors belonging to other setup types are scheduled de-centrally by the relevant applications while using the EFWK.

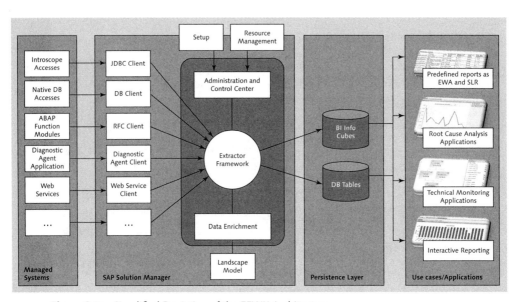

Figure 8.25 Simplified Depiction of the EFWK Architecture

You can use a new user interface integrated into the SOLUTION MANAGER ADMINISTRATION work center to manage the EFWK. The administration interface allows you to track these activities, including their status, start time, and duration, as well as to access the log information. On the administration interface, you can also activate and deactivate the extractors and release them for execution. In exceptional cases, you can delete extractors if you need to reschedule an extractor because errors have occurred.

The easiest way to call the administration interface is from the SOLUTION MANAGER ADMINISTRATION work center under the menu option INFRASTRUCTURE • FRAMEWORK • EXTRACTOR FRAMEWORK. If you suspect that only some data was collected from managed systems, you should start error analysis, which will check the status of the corresponding extractors. You will then see an overview of all extractors and their statuses, including, among other things, the active status ON, OFF, INCONSISTENT, or BANNED and the last status ERROR, WARNING, SUCCESSFUL, or UNKNOWN (see Figure 8.26).

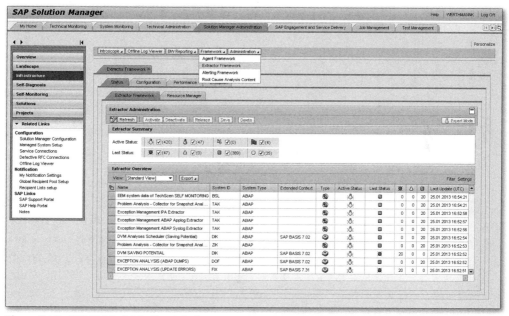

Figure 8.26 EFWK Administration Interface

Figure 8.27 shows the log for the selected extractor, WORKLOAD ANALYSIS (INTROSCOPE DATA), including its phases and their runtimes, as well as the number of data records collected.

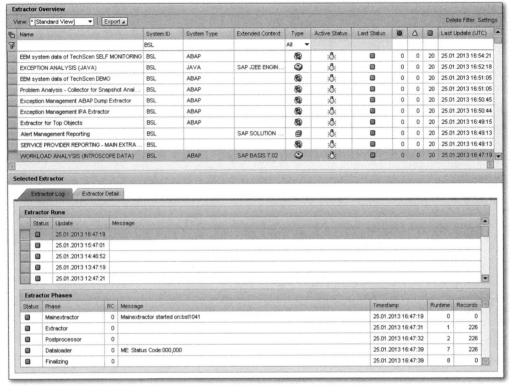

Figure 8.27 Extractor Status

By default, this data is available for the last 20 extractor runs. If you select one of these runs, you see the extractor's runtime and the number of data records collected by the extractor during this time. Furthermore, you can use the EXTRACTOR DETAIL tab page to retrieve further information about the managed system, extractor, RFC target destination, and the name of the SAP Netweaver BW InfoCube. This information will be helpful if you need to analyze potential problems with an extractor because you can use it to ascertain whether data was and/or will be collected from a managed system.

Figure 8.28 shows further information for the now-familiar WORKLOAD ANALY-SIS (INTROSCOPE DATA) extractor. The following two parameters are of particular interest here: PERIOD (time, in minutes, between extractor runs) and COLLECTION INTERVAL (not supported by all extractors; states that the extractor is to collect data for a maximum of 168 past hours).

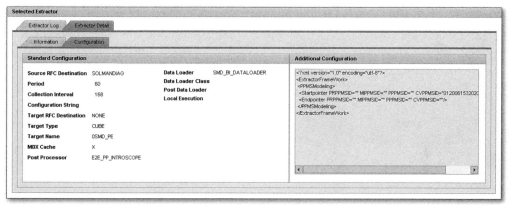

Figure 8.28 Extractor Configuration

8.6.4 Self-Monitoring of BW-Based Reports

BW-based reports in SAP Solution Manager collect a large amount of data from connected systems on a regular basis. Unlike normal BW-based reporting, the EFWK, which was introduced earlier, is used here as a data collection method. For monitoring the quality of the data collected by the EFWK, various pieces of information concerning the relevant data load process are available when you choose DATA QUALITY in interactive reporting. This data is also available in the SOLUTION MANAGER ADMINISTRATION work center under INFRASTRUCTURE • BW REPORTING (see Figure 8.29).

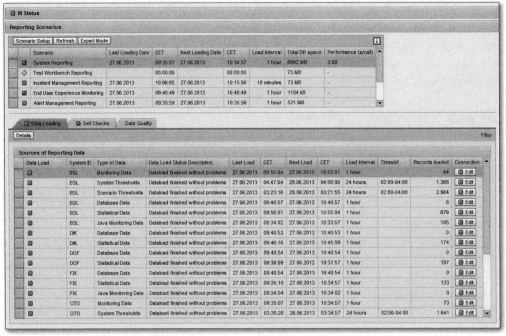

Figure 8.29 Self-Monitoring of BW-Based Reports

8.7 SAP NetWeaver Business Warehouse

The BI content installed on SAP NetWeaver BW delivers predefined web templates, which you can use to evaluate existing SAP NetWeaver BW data in terms of technical KPIs. For further analysis, you can go beyond the standard delivery and use two tools, BEx Query Designer and BEx Web Application Designer, to create your own queries and web templates for interactive reporting.

SAP Solution Manager is collecting data also from other IT management areas into SAP NetWeaver BW. Therefore, the data collected in SAP Solution Manager provides an excellent basis for devising your own reporting, with the help of some BW tools. If you connect other data sources, it is possible to add any amount of data to reporting, and therefore expand SAP NetWeaver BW in such a way that it becomes a central reporting platform for IT management.

SAP NetWeaver BW is a powerful tool for analyzing business data. Together with the IT Service Management (ITSM) data in SAP NetWeaver BW, it enables you to set up SLR in such a way that you have complete flexibility in terms of its content and how this content is displayed. The data within SAP NetWeaver BW is stored in *InfoCubes*, which permit fast access to the data stored there for all types of reports. The end user can view this data in various ways. For example, you can create your own web reports or use a separate front-end component, known as Business Explorer Analyzer (BEx Analyzer), to display them. However, you must take into consideration the fact that, in practice, implementing BW reporting can, in accordance with your own requirements, quickly develop into a separate project.

A more detailed description of using SAP NetWeaver BW is beyond the scope of this book. Therefore, for further documentation and reading material, please refer to the books *SAP NetWeaver BW 7.x Reporting–Practical Guide* by Jason Kraft (SAP PRESS 2011) and *Reporting and Analysis with SAP BusinessObjects* by Ingo Hilgefort (SAP PRESS 2012).

8.8   Management Dashboards

In addition to standard reporting options, SAP Solution Manager 7.1 also provides the management dashboard framework. The purpose of management dashboards is to prepare existing information in as compact manner as possible so that it is also suitable for management users. Management dashboards comprise dashboard apps that are based on Adobe Flash applications. Information from various applications can be summarized here or displayed in a highly aggregated form. Management dashboards can be preconfigured with different dashboard apps in order to take account of different user groups. Furthermore, users can compile their own management dashboards.

In the standard delivery, SAP provides different dashboard apps for specific applications in SAP Solution Manager. As a prerequisite for using these standard dashboard apps, you must have successfully completed the basic configuration of SAP Solution Manager and fully configured the underlying application in SAP Solution Manager.

> **Example**
>
> To display system performance, for example, you must have configured technical monitoring with the Monitoring and Alerting Infrastructure. As a result, the management dashboards can be used almost immediately and without too much effort as soon as monitoring is up and running. Active monitoring automatically guarantees actual data procurement.

Figure 8.30 shows a schematic diagram of the management dashboard architecture. The active applications in SAP Solution Manager send their data to the BW system in SAP Solution Manager, and the dashboard apps receive their data from SAP Solution Manager in turn.

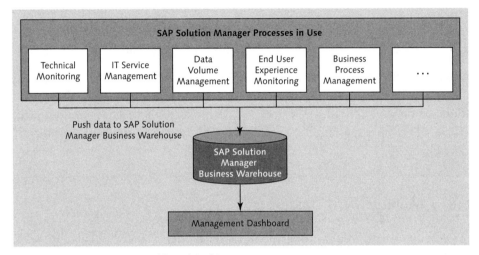

Figure 8.30 Management Dashboard Architecture

The following standard dashboard apps are available in Support Package 5:

- End-User Experience Monitoring
- System Availability
- System Performance
- ABAP Security
- Data Volume Management
- Custom Code Management
- Severity
- Quantity
- Quality
- Criticality
- IT Service Management
- Test Management

▶ Alert Reporting

▶ SAP Solution Manager Usage

For more information on management dashboards, see SAP Service Marketplace (quick link DASHBSOARDS).

8.8.1 Authorization Concept

Management dashboards have a detailed authorization concept that enables them to control end users' access to data in a flexible manner. The following three authorization roles are delivered for management dashboards by default:

▶ SAP_SM_DASHBOARD_DISP
This role grants the user authorization to view but not change existing management dashboards.

▶ SAP_SM_DASHBOARD_PROCESS
This role grants the user authorization to change existing management dashboards.

▶ SAP_SM_DASHBOARD_ADMIN
This role grants the user full administration rights. In other words, he or she can create or change management dashboards, register new dashboard apps in SAP Solution Manager, and so on.

The complete authorization concept is described in the Security Guide for SAP Solution Manager.

8.8.2 Calling and Managing the Management Dashboard

You can call the management dashboard with SAP GUI or directly via the URL provided in the dashboard management tool.

To call the management dashboard, you require administration authorizations from the role SAP_SM_DASHBOARD_ADMIN. To add the dashboard management tool to your favorites in SAP GUI, proceed as follows:

1. In the SAP Easy Access menu, call the FAVORITES entry and right-click it.

2. Select the ADD OTHER OBJECTS entry in the list of options provided. The system now displays a window with possible restrictions.

3. Select the WEB DYNPRO APPLICATION entry from the list. Another window, in which you can enter various parameters, opens.

4. In the WEB DYNPRO APPLICATION field, enter the name "dashboard_management."

5. Choose a suitable description (for example, "Dashboard Management Tool") (see Figure 8.31).

6. Finish creating the new entry. The entry you have just maintained is now displayed under FAVORITES.

7. Start the dashboard management tool by selecting the relevant entry under FAVORITES. You then automatically navigate to the defined HTTP address.

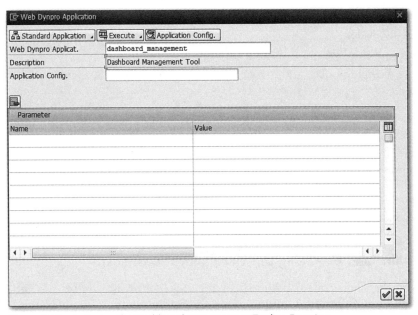

Figure 8.31 Assigning the Dashboard Management Tool to Favorites

On the initial screen of the dashboard management tool, you can create new management dashboards or edit or delete existing management dashboards. In your browser, you now see the URL generated by the system. If necessary, you can send specific dashboards (or the corresponding URLs) to other authorized users. To do this, select the relevant dashboard from the list of dashboards displayed (the dashboard ALM_REPORTING in Figure 8.32). In the DASHBOARD DETAILS area on the right-hand side of the screen, the corresponding URL is available under LINK TO DASHBOARD. You can now send the URL displayed on this screen by email to the intended users.

A dashboard app is an Adobe Flash application that reflects the status of an individual KPI (for example, the status of system performance). Dashboard apps can be developed in such a way that they can be configured by the user (for example, in terms of which systems or which period is to be displayed). The data source for standard dashboard apps is the BW system in SAP Solution Manager. In general, however, you can use any data source (for example, an external SAP NetWeaver BW or any database). You can select the relevant dashboard apps from the management dashboard repository and transfer them to a management dashboard.

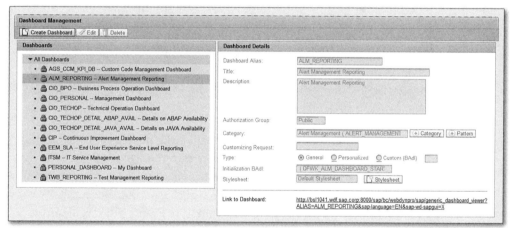

Figure 8.32 Technical Details for the "ALM_Reporting" Dashboard

To access the management dashboard repository, proceed as follows:

1. Open the management dashboard to which you want to add a dashboard app.

2. In the upper-right corner of the management dashboard, choose CONFIGURE to switch to configuration mode.

3. Then, choose ADD NEW APP. The management dashboard repository opens.

Figure 8.33 shows the design for the dashboard app repository and the dashboard apps available there, sorted by category.

Figure 8.33 Dashboard App Repository

You can also display several instances of a dashboard app in your management dashboard (for example, to compare KPIs over different periods). In configuration mode, you can also delete dashboard apps or change their configuration (for example, the period under analysis). You can also change the appearance of your management dashboard by using drag and drop to rearrange the dashboard apps.

Dashboard apps are developed with SAP BusinessObjects Dashboards. Since SAP delivers the source code for standard dashboard apps, you can further develop the dashboard apps in the standard delivery (in other words, to your own requirements). You can also use SAP BusinessObjects Dashboards and the framework to develop your own new dashboard apps from scratch. The activities necessary here are described in detail on SAP Help Portal. There are several exercises here, each of which shows how dashboard apps can be developed in varying degrees of difficulty. You require a license for SAP BusinessObjects Dashboards.

8.8.3   Typical Management Dashboard Views

Figure 8.34 uses the example of the dashboard app for End-User Experience Monitoring to show typical management dashboard views.

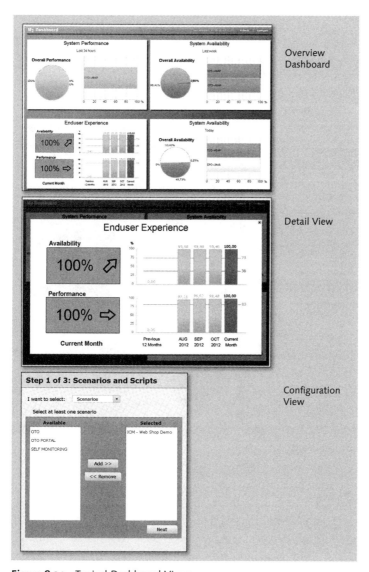

Overview Dashboard

Detail View

Configuration View

Figure 8.34   Typical Dashboard Views

First, you see the overview dashboard, in which several dashboard apps can be displayed. When you double-click one of these dashboard apps, the app is displayed in an enlarged detail view in the foreground so that you can take a closer look at it. Such dashboard apps can also have a configuration view in which the dashboard app can be adjusted by the user. Here, you can determine which systems or which period you want to display, for example.

Figure 8.35 shows a typical management dashboard in which several dashboard apps are displayed. In our example, they come from the following areas: SYSTEM PERFORMANCE, SYSTEM AVAILABILITY, and END-USER EXPERIENCE.

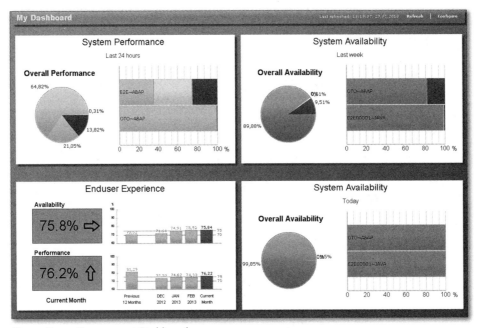

Figure 8.35 Management Dashboards

The previously available standard dashboards are only the starting point for further developments in this area. Nevertheless, the dashboard management tool extends the reporting options available for collected data, both in SAP Solution Manager and in other systems. In addition to its technical operation, the actual challenge lies in designing suitable dashboards and integrating existing support, analysis, and optimization processes into them.

Summary

Both SLR and interactive reporting provide powerful standard tools for technical analysis. These tools can be a starting point for establishing an SLM process. If certain service levels have already been agreed upon, you can cover these with existing KPIs or customize existing reports.

The main advantage associated with standardized SLR is the ease with which it can be set up and enhanced using values from the CCMS infrastructure. The fact that reports can be generated and sent automatically can also be a major advantage, depending on the purpose of SLR.

A further advantage associated with interactive reporting, on the other hand, is the ability to select data according to different periods at any time, thus providing a continuous insight into the development of the system landscape. Various BW-specific tools can be used to create customer-specific reports. (For more information, see SAP Help Portal.)

Finally, the management dashboards provide applications that permit a high level of transparency in terms of different pieces of information and KPIs from SAP Solution Manager, thus improving communication among all parties involved. In particular, this concerns management instances, such as stakeholders and sponsors.

8.9   Additional Documentation

Links

- SAP Service Marketplace, alias *quicksizer*
- SAP Service Marketplace, alias *ewa*
- SAP Service Marketplace, alias *slr*
- SAP Service Marketplace, alias *dashboards*

SAP Notes

Table 8.1 gives an overview of important SAP Notes on technical analysis and reporting.

Contents	SAP Note
Central Performance History and SL Reporting	872569
CCMS Ping and SL Reporting	944496
Parameters for ABAP statistics records extraction	1457010
How to display dashboards from SolMan 7.1 SP05	1831983

Table 8.1 Useful SAP Notes for Technical Analysis and Reporting

Although prices for permanent storage decrease continuously, data volume must be controlled and kept as low as possible. In this chapter, we show you how you can support an existing data volume management strategy. The core is increasing transparency throughout your organization.

9   Data Volume Management

The amount of information stored in an electronic system grows continuously. In addition, there are legally imposed requirements regarding data availability (for example, taxes and audits). The more data that's stored, the more important it is to find a solution to administer or manage increasing data volumes to handle the resulting effects on the system and to avoid, for example, performance problems. It is important to monitor, and possibly control, data volumes and their growth using appropriate tools.

Data Volume Management (DVM) provides a framework that helps you create an acceptable ratio of the need for business data availability, on one hand, and maintenance of databases and applications, on the other. This framework consists of best-practice documents, tools, SAP services, and self-services that can be used throughout the entire DVM lifecycle. Otherwise, it supports you in developing and operating a DVM strategy.

We show you how to ideally configure the tools available in SAP Solution Manager for your needs so that you can run the desired analyses and evaluate the results when you use these tools later on. The aim is to optimally adjust the existing range of tools to your specific needs. Due to the great number of options, configuring the tools forms the largest part of this chapter. Once the tools are configured, using them is almost self-explanatory. Therefore, properly configuring the tools is strategically significant.

First, however, our focus is on the motivation of a DVM project, and we'll deal with the questions that you should ask yourself beforehand.

9.1 Motivation and Key Questions

Uncontrolled data volume growth has many consequences: it leads to future costs due to data backup or, in an emergency, to database recovery, and also affects response times. The higher the data volume in a database, the larger the effort and expense required and the risk in administration.

To avoid this, it's important to develop a strategy in time for data volume management based on historical data and forecasts. This is the only way to make decisions regarding DVM project execution. In addition, you also want to avoid the creation of unnecessary data and consolidating data once it is generated. Otherwise, reports presenting the success of taken actions and tendencies are generated regularly.

To develop an appropriate strategy, you need to ask yourself the following questions:

- ▶ Where should the examinations start?
- ▶ Which data is essential for my daily business?
- ▶ Which business objects—for example, sales orders or delivery orders—need the most memory space?
- ▶ Which country or business area is not yet integrated in a general or globally defined DVM strategy?
- ▶ How old is the data in the entire system landscape?
- ▶ Which legal regulations must be complied with in regards to data storage? Do country-specific regulations play a role?
- ▶ Which applications have the largest growth rates? Is this growth equivalent to the increase in required storage in the database?
- ▶ Is there any data in the system that has never been used or is no longer used?
- ▶ Which data reduction possibilities are there in the system landscape?
- ▶ Where could I make improvements as fast as possible and at the least expense and effort, and are there any possible synergy effects?
- ▶ Which objects from which areas should be the first to analyze, optimize, and possibly archive?
- ▶ If you already archive: are expense/effort and savings in the desired relation?

To answer these questions and implement a resulting strategy, the DATA VOLUME MANAGEMENT work center was implemented within SAP Solution Manager. It is the central information and action platform for DVM topics in the SAP system landscape (ABAP systems). The work center is the central access point to get information fast and throughout the landscape, and it allows for DVM services, which can be both SAP services and services rendered by the customer.

Therefore, this chapter introduces the central DVM tools available in the DATA VOLUME management work center as part of SAP Solution Manager 7.1 SP06. The start screen of this work center is shown in Figure 9.1.

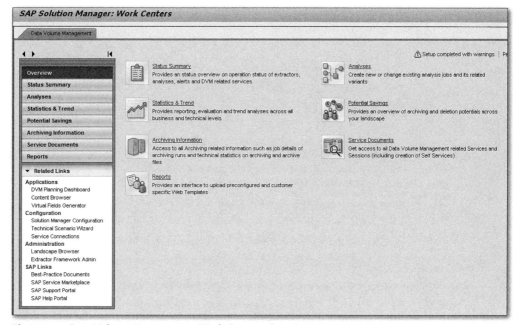

Figure 9.1 Data Volume Management Work Center—Overview

Here, the various activity areas are bundled. They are different in their functionalities, and their purpose is gathering information, configuration, or data volume management itself. In contrast to other work centers, requirements-oriented configuration, particularly for data acquisition, is essential for using the DATA VOLUME MANAGEMENT work center. Therefore, we first explain in detail how to activate the DVM infrastructure.

In this chapter, our descriptions are also based on the example of Toys Inc. Let's first take a close look at the prerequisites and how to set up DVM.

9.2 Prerequisites and Setup

Toys Inc. wants to optimize its data volume management. To find potential for optimization, more transparency of data allocation and growth in the SAP landscape must be reached. This particularly concerns the SAP ERP system, in which the key business processes are operated.

SAP Solution Manager is already integrated in the SAP system landscape, and all relevant SAP systems are connected (step CONFIGURATION OF MANAGED SYSTEMS). Therefore, activate the DATA VOLUME MANAGEMENT work center for data collection from the productive ERP system.

The IT team's job is to arrange for technical initialization. Using a setup user (Sol-man_Setup), they perform the required steps. For more information, see Chapter 2. Otherwise, an authorization concept is developed in which the future users receive the roles for their work in the DATA VOLUME MANAGEMENT work center.

9.2.1 Strategic Use/Benefit

Before you start activating the DVM infrastructure and implementing the DATA VOLUME MANAGEMENT work center, you should perfectly understand how to handle the data volume management and what support you can get using SAP Solution Manager. Always consider that using the DATA VOLUME MANAGEMENT work center supports you, but never automatically means that a DVM strategy is in place.

You need clearly defined goals to decide at the end of a project whether benefit is reasonably worth the effort. Defining clear goals is thus an essential prerequisite for a DVM project. The more systems are in focus, the easier it generally is to recognize and evaluate relationships across systems and business processes. Your goal should be obtaining an overview of the organization-wide landscape and, in particular, of the SAP systems. The more data you have available in your own business warehouse (BW) of SAP Solution Manager, the more precise an analysis you can run on specific details. This improves the possibilities of recognizing contexts across systems.

An important task of the DVM structure is transferring DVM-relevant information of the managed systems into the business warehouse of SAP Solution Manager. This includes both technical data and business information on the objects of the production applications. Before starting with the technical setup, you should know which systems to focus on from a DVM perspective. These are based on the goals you set at the beginning of the project.

Note

In order for you to detect tendencies in key figures, the information should be available, which means it should have been collected from the connected (managed) systems, for a period of four to six weeks.

9.2.2 Users and Authorizations

Users perform specific tasks in organizations. It must be ensured for data protection reasons as well, that the individual users can only perform the tasks assigned to them. A data growth analysis always enables you to draw conclusions to the type and scope of the used business processes and, thus, to the organization's business situation. In your preparation of DVM projects, you should therefore consider the topic of authorizations:

▶ **Users for technical start-up**
  The first focus is on technical initialization of the DVM infrastructure. For this, the user SMC_DVM_<SID> was automatically generated in the basic configuration of SAP Solution Manager. This user allows you to perform the initialization procedure, but no tasks beyond that. For configuration tasks to be performed after initialization, the user DVM_ADM_<SID> is generated in SAP Solution Manager. It is possible that the SAP Solution Manager application and internal business warehouse are installed in different clients. This means that you need a user with the appropriate authorizations in each client.

  Chapter 12 deals with the underlying concept and the details of roles and profiles in the user management of SAP Solution Manager.

▶ **DVM experts**
  The functionality of the DATA VOLUME MANAGEMENT work center was developed for DVM experts. This team of experts is generally responsible for all DVM activities. It is the interface to the business units for archiving, deleting, avoiding, or compressing data. Required changes are done in collaboration with the Change Management team. DVM experts work in SAP Solution Manager and in the managed systems. They use all or selected functions of the DATA VOLUME MANAGEMENT work center for data analysis, services, reporting, etc., and other functions required for performing DVM-relevant tasks (transactions, etc.).

This can be done in SAP Solution Manager using the user DVM_ADM_<SID>. In the managed systems, the user DVM_ADM_<SID> is also generated, but with different authorizations. This user is generated only during DVM infrastructure activation.

▶ **Users**
Finally, some users are only supposed to display reports or queries. For these, the user DVM_DIS_<SID> is generated during initialization of Data Volume Management.

> **Note**
>
> The specified template users are suggestions. You can use your own users and extend them as needed.

9.2.3 Technical Preparation

The key prerequisite for activating the DATA VOLUME MANAGEMENT work center is the successfully completed basic configuration of SAP Solution Manager using Transaction SOLMAN_SETUP (see Chapter 3). This ensures that, along with other basic aspects the BW system and the extractor framework (EFWK) are activated.

Also, to ensure that SAP Solution Manager can fulfill its role as the central management platform, all systems to be managed (production systems of the landscape) must be connected in the step CONFIGURATION OF MANAGED SYSTEMS.

To check the status of the connections, use Transaction SOLMAN_SETUP. If you choose CONFIGURATION OF MANAGED SYSTEMS from the menu, you receive an overview as shown in Figure 9.2. In the EXTENDED SYSTEM ID column, you can see that a filter has been applied for a system named OTO. The system is already connected. For the DATA VOLUME MANAGEMENT work center, only the APPLICATION SERVER ABAP system type (SYSTEM TYPE column) is relevant because all DVM-relevant data is stored in tables of the ABAP database schema.

The columns to the right of the SYSTEM TYPE column show different information about the configuration status of the individual systems. Statuses not marked green should be checked. To do this, follow the notes of the HELP area above or contact the experts in charge of basic configuration.

For initialization of the DATA VOLUME MANAGEMENT work center, the RFC STATUS, AUTO. CONF. STATUS, and PLUG-IN STATUS must be marked green (see Step 4 in Section 9.2.4).

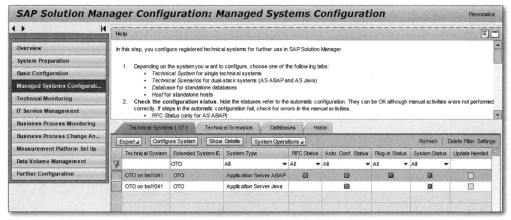

Figure 9.2 Checking the Status of Connected Systems

Note

The successful connection of all relevant systems to be managed is essential. If there are any errors at this point, it is possible that you will not successfully complete DVM extractor activation at a later point.

9.2.4 Guided Initialization

Based on perfect technical preparation, initialization is not particularly complex.

By performing the initialization, you check the software version of involved components of SAP Solution Manager and all relevant managed systems. You determine target systems for DVM, define template users and template configurations, and activate the appropriate extractors. The results of many actions you perform are logged—for example, creating users—but are not transportable objects.

Transporting the complete initialization of a development system or another system is not possible for particular reasons. Normally, you set up the DATA VOL-UME MANAGEMENT work center for the corresponding productive data volumes and structures. In the development and quality assurance system of SAP Solution Manager, this data is often not available and, therefore, cannot be evaluated. If it is available, the next challenge is to migrate the collected data into the business warehouse of the productive SAP Solution Manager system. Also, it is essential for you to go through the initialization steps described below and, for example, activate extractors in the provided user interface.

> **Note**
>
> Initializing the DATA VOLUME MANAGEMENT work center must be done directly in the productive SAP Solution Manager system.

However, to implement an SAP Note, you can use the normal test and transport procedures for the appropriate target system.

The guided initialization procedure for the DATA VOLUME MANAGEMENT work center can be done using the SMC_DVM_<SID> user, which you have already created in SAP Solution Manager.

Start Transaction SOLMAN_SETUP, and in the left-hand area call the DATA VOLUME MANAGEMENT menu item. In the right-hand work area, this launches the view shown in Figure 9.3.

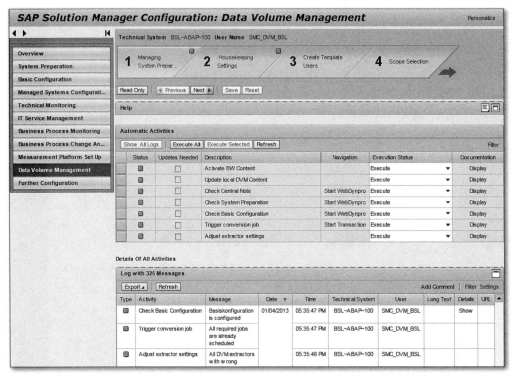

Figure 9.3 Guided Procedure for Data Volume Management Work Center Initialization

Activities can be performed only in the change mode. To do this, in the upper-left area, choose EDIT. The view now goes into change mode, and the button is replaced with READ ONLY. Press the button to get to the screen showing the initialization screen in change mode in Figure 9.3.

From now on, follow the guided procedure. It consists of several steps that must be completed sequentially. In each step, the HELP in the upper area provides background information. Please note you can expand and collapse most areas on the right-hand side by clicking the 🔲 button.

As you already know from basic configuration, the individual actions for each step are performed individually or in groups, depending on what was marked. The NEXT button allows you to go forward, whereas the PREVIOUS button takes you back step by step. First of all, you should always try to complete all activities in one step.

In the LOG area at the bottom, the results of all performed activities are logged automatically. Various message types are possible: information messages, success messages, warnings, and error messages.

For going through the initialization procedure, it is always recommendable to monitor the system information regarding the execution status and the messages in the upper area of the display. This provides information and indicates errors. Figure 9.4 shows an example.

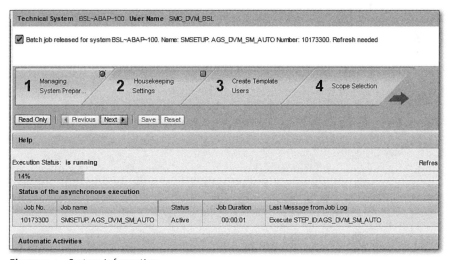

Figure 9.4 System Information

Figure 9.4 shows you that the SMSETUP: AGS_DVM_SM_AUTO job for the BSL ABAP system, client 100, has been started and is now being executed. In this case, SAP Solution Manager BSL also plays the managed system role.

After this introduction, we will now show you what you need to consider in the individual steps. Also, always make sure to note the help text in the upper area.

Step 1: Preparing the Managing System

In this step, you will prepare SAP Solution Manager as the managed system. Figure 9.5 shows this step and the individual activities for initialization of the DATA VOLUME MANAGEMENT work center. For each activity, you can display more background information by clicking DISPLAY in the DOCUMENTATION column.

Start the execution by clicking the EXECUTE ALL button. This automatically executes the steps listed in the table (DESCRIPTION column) and logs the results.

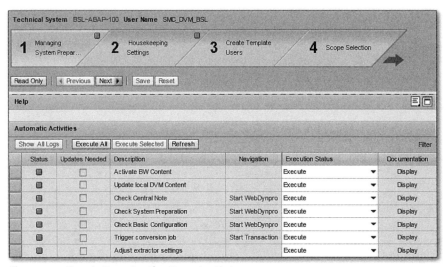

Figure 9.5 Step 1: Preparing the Managing System

The status (first column named STATUS) shows you the progress of initialization or whether it was successful. If there are any errors, they must be corrected, and the associated activity must be executed again. In this case, click EXECUTE ALL. Another window opens, prompting you to confirm the action (see Figure 9.6).

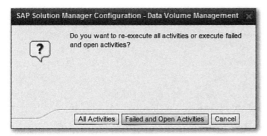

Figure 9.6 Possible Repetition of an Initialization Step

You do not need to re-execute successfully completed activities (marked green) at the same time, which means you can limit the activities to FAILED AND OPEN ACTIVITIES. Alternatively, you could have selected individual actions and started them separately using the EXECUTE SELECTED button. However, you are then responsible for the correct and complete execution of the selected actions.

There is nothing wrong with re-executing all activities, but this makes sense only once any technical requirements might have changed—for example, when a new software version of the ST-BCO component was imported, when there is a new version of the central SAP Note, or when there may have been changes in the system preparation or basic configuration.

When you do the activation for the first time, we recommend choosing EXECUTE ALL. In the following subsections, we are going to introduce the individual activities in detail and show you how you can check the results and where some extra work may be required.

Activity 1: Activate BI Content

With the first activity, ACTIVATE BI CONTENT, you activate the BW objects required for the DATA VOLUME MANAGEMENT work center in the BW client, which are InfoCubes, aggregates, web templates, and queries. The user needs special authorizations, which are mentioned in the activity description (see Figure 9.5, DOCUMENTATION column).

Activation is done by the background job SMSETUP: AGS_DVM_BI_CONTENT and may take a few minutes. You can check the job status and the activation using the job monitor (Transaction SM37). Note that the job is executed in the selected, possibly separate BW client, which might not be the one you are currently using.

In any case, we recommend that you subsequently check the result of the activation using Transaction RSA1. To do this, proceed as follows:

1. In the left-hand menu, select BI CONTENT.

2. Choose INFOPROVIDERS BY INFOAREAS.

3. In the central area, select SAP SOLUTION MANAGER (Technical Name: 0SM_DVM) and open it. The area below that in the hierarchy is opened.

4. Select SAP SOLUTION MANAGER — DATA VOLUME MANAGEMENT (Technical Name: 0SM_DVM).

5. Drag the InfoProvider SAP SOLUTION MANAGER — DATA VOLUME MANAGEMENT from the central area to the right-hand area. In the initial status, you will be asked for the source system where you selected the respective system. After that, the screen appears as shown in Figure 9.7.

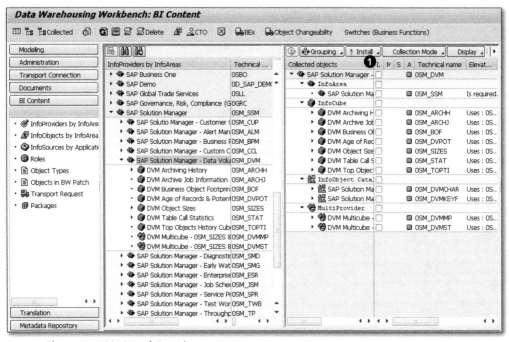

Figure 9.7 RSA1 — InfoProvider

If nothing has been selected in the INSTALL column (see ❶ in Figure 9.7) — in other words, if there is no tick mark — activation was successful. Otherwise, perform the activation here: use the GROUPING button to change the grouping to DATA FLOW BEFORE AND AFTERWARDS and start the activation by clicking the INSTALL button.

The activation is completed when no object is selected in the mentioned INSTALL column. Normally, no further BW-specific knowledge is required.

> **Note**
>
> Please note that successful setup of the BW system in SAP Solution Manager is a prerequisite for activation of DVM-relevant objects.

Activity 2: Update Local DVM Content

To create DVM analyses, object definitions such as standard variants, application-specific configuration, and definitions for Transaction TAANA (table analysis) are required. This information basis is maintained on the SAP side. It is continuously fed with experience from DVM services and projects, which are available to all customers as best practices. To work with the latest information, you should generally make sure to re-download this content prior to creating new analyses.

By executing the second activity, UPDATE LOCAL DVM CONTENT, you load these required, current object definitions via the SAPOSS RFC connection directly from SAP Service Marketplace into your system, and thus update the local DVM content. Details are included in the log.

Activity 3: Check Central Note

With the third activity, CHECK CENTRAL NOTE, you check whether the central collective note for SAP Solution Manager is implemented in the respective SP version. This composite note, which is associated with other notes, is extended and updated regularly. In the subsection "Step 3: Implement SAP Note" in Section 2.5.2, we elaborate on this point. We strongly recommend keeping this composite SAP Note up to date, also in respect to data volume management. Using Transaction SOLMAN_SETUP, the appropriate SAP Note is automatically determined, and the current implementation is aligned with the content.

If an error message was logged as a result of this activity, you will need to do some re-editing in the SYSTEM PREPARATION, step IMPLEMENT SAP NOTE. For access, use the START WEBDYNPRO link in the NAVIGATION column of the AUTOMATIC ACTIVITIES table (see Figure 9.5).

Activity 4: Check System Preparation

With the fourth activity, CHECK SYSTEM PREPARATION, you check the system preparation step for completeness based on the logged results in Transaction SOLMAN_SETUP. Details on the executed tests are in the log, which you can access via SHOW in the DETAILS column.

Again, if any messages are displayed here, re-editing is required; use the link START WEBDYNPRO in the NAVIGATION for that.

Activity 5: Check Basic Configuration

With the fifth activity, CHECK BASIC CONFIGURATION, you check the *Basic Configuration* step for completeness based on the logged results in Transaction SOLMAN_SETUP. Details on the executed tests are in the log, which you can access via SHOW in the DETAILS column.

Again, if any messages occur in the basic configuration, re-editing is required; use the link START WEBDYNPRO in the NAVIGATION column for that.

Activity 6: Trigger Conversion Job

With the sixth activity, TRIGGER CONVERSION JOB, you schedule a conversion job for migrating data into new infrastructures (tables, InfoCubes, attributes, etc.), which were collected in older SAP Solution Manager releases.

You can check the job execution in a parallel window using Transaction SM37. This is job `SMSETUP: AGS_DVM_BCK_JOB`.

It is possible to manually start the underlying report `RAGS_SISE_ACTIVITY_JOB`. For access, click START TRANSACTION in the NAVIGATION, which automatically starts Transaction SE38.

Activity 7: Adjust Extractor Settings

With the seventh activity, ADJUST EXTRACTOR SETTINGS, you adjust extractors that were activated in previous SAP Solution Manager releases or support packages (tables `E2E_ACTIVE_WLI` and `E2E_TEMPL`). Older extractors are deleted.

You can check the job execution using Transaction SM37 (`SMSETUP: AGS_DVM_SM_AUTO`).

Once you have completed all activities successfully, you can move on to Step 2. To do this, click the NEXT button. Transaction SOLMAN_SETUP also allows this even if not all activities have a green status. Still, make sure that all activities were completed successfully.

Step 2: Housekeeping Settings

This step allows you to define so-called *residence times* for each InfoCube that is related to data volume management. An InfoCube is an SAP NetWeaver BW object (data container) for a closed data volume. Figure 9.8 shows you which InfoCubes these are.

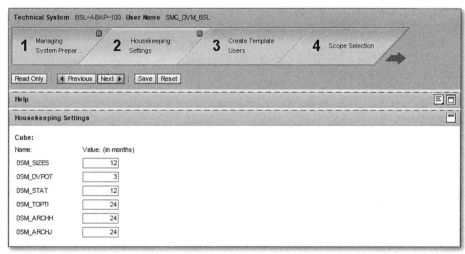

Figure 9.8 Step 2: Define Residence Times for DVM InfoCubes

With the residence time, you define for how long data is available in a cube before the data is deleted. Figure 9.8 shows the SAP default values that have proved to be useful in practice. You can accept these values or adjust them to your needs at a later time.

If you click NEXT, the default values or changed values are applied, and you are taken to the next step.

Step 3: Create Template Users

This step is optional. You can create template users in SAP Solution Manager, and thus prepare the future work center for use. By default, certain user roles are already defined, as shown in Figure 9.9.

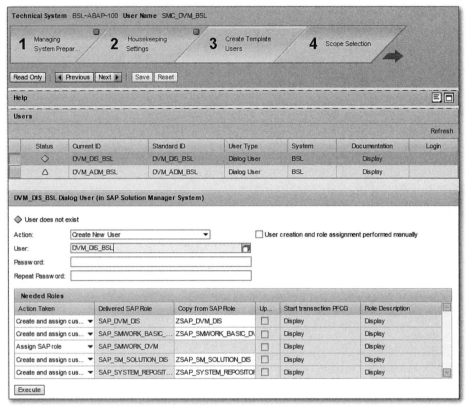

Figure 9.9 Optional Step 3: Create Template Users

In the upper area, you can see the standard users already mentioned in Section 9.2.2. They are suggested for potential adjustments. In the lower area, you can see which roles are available. Table 9.1 lists the assignments for roles for the two standard users.

User ID	Role Assignment
DVM_DIS_<SID>	▸ SAP_DVM_DIS ▸ SAP_SMWORK_BASIC_DVM ▸ SAP_SMWORK_DVM ▸ SAP_SM_SOLUTION_DIS ▸ SAP_SYSTEM_REPOSITORY_DIS

Table 9.1 Standard Dialog Users for Using the Data Volume Management Work Center

User ID	Role Assignment
DVM_ADM_<SID>	▸ SAP_DVM_ALL ▸ SAP_SMWORK_BASIC_DVM ▸ SAP_SMWORK_DVM ▸ SAP_SM_SOLUTION_ALL ▸ SAP_SYSTEM_REPOSITORY_DIS

Table 9.1 Standard Dialog Users for Using the Data Volume Management Work Center (Cont.)

You can accept this suggestion or change existing users. All activities are executed based on users, which means the respective user must be marked. You also must define roles in which the SAP standard roles are copied. To perform these definitions, click the EXECUTE button.

Authorizations should be assigned based on an authorization concept. Please also note the help text in the HELP area (in Figure 9.9, this area is still hidden). Chapter 12 has more information on creating an authorization concept in SAP Solution Manager.

Click NEXT to proceed to the next step, even if you have not performed any activity in this step.

Step 4: Scope Selection

In this step, the individual target systems, meaning the managed systems, are selected. These should have been connected previously with SAP Solution Manager (see Section 2.5.4).

This defines the actual focus of the DATA VOLUME MANAGEMENT work center. Only data from these systems is displayed in the DATA VOLUME MANAGEMENT work center after initialization.

Figure 9.10 shows the initial screen. All connected systems are automatically filtered by ABAP system type and green RFC status (success). You can change the default filter at any time or entirely remove the filter by clicking DELETE FILTER.

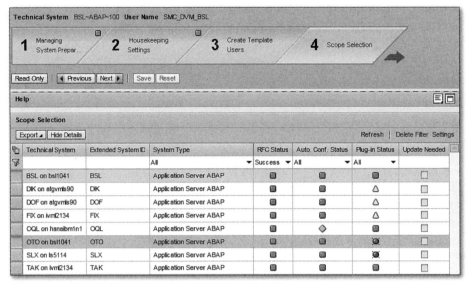

Figure 9.10 Step 4: System Overview in the Scope Selection

You need to select at least one system to get to the next step. You can also select more systems depending on your requirements. Mark the individual lines using the [Ctrl] or [Shift] keys and clicking your mouse. You can add new systems at any time at a later point (see Section 9.3.2).

Click the NEXT button to proceed to the next step.

Warning

Do not proceed to the next step for systems where warnings or errors are displayed for the RFC STATUS and AUTO. CONF. STATUS. In this case, first correct the errors in the CONFIGURATION OF MANAGED SYSTEMS.

Step 5: Technical Preparation

With this step, you prepare the previously selected managed systems for activation of the DVM infrastructure. This comprises checking the implementation of relevant SAP Notes and updating the DVM content in each of these systems. Similar activities were already performed in the first step for SAP Solution Manager.

Figure 9.11 shows the two activities performed in this step. Click the EXECUTE ALL button to start the activities for the selected systems. If another window opens to prompt you, as shown in Figure 9.6, you can click ALL ACTIVITIES again. The results are logged in the lower area.

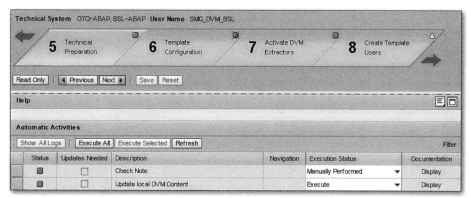

Figure 9.11 Step 5: Preparing the Managed System

In the first activity, CHECK NOTE, the system checks whether all required SAP Notes are available. If any notes are missing, details on the executed tests are in the log, which you can access via SHOW in the DETAILS column. Missing notes must first be implemented in the development system in accordance with the definitions of the change management, tested in the quality assurance system (if applicable), and, finally, transported into the production systems. Ideally, they should be implemented before you continue initializing the DVM infrastructure for this system.

The status of the DVM-relevant notes to be implemented can also be checked using the program RTCCTOOL. Run it in the managed system. Use the PREPARE FOR DVM (DATA VOLUME MGMT) SERVICE? option, which you access by clicking the SETTINGS button.

The second activity, UPDATE LOCAL DVM CONTENT, automatically checks and updates the DVM content in the systems. In the case of a failed update of the DVM content, you can find the note on the relevant system and a potential error cause in the log.

This concludes step 5. In the guided procedure, click the NEXT button to proceed to the next step.

Step 6: Template Configuration

This step is for initial configuration of a part of the DVM infrastructure and is optional. This is a pre-configuration of analyses for specific tables. If you are not sure how to use analyses, you can skip this step and configure the analyses later. For more information on the use of analyses, see Section 9.5. Figure 9.12 shows the initial screen for this step.

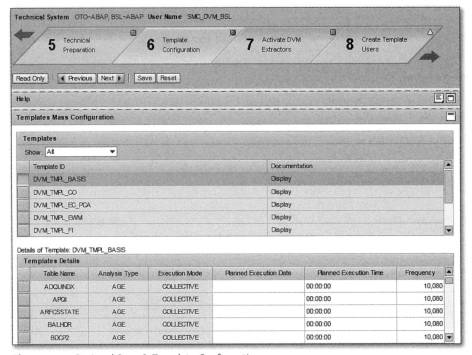

Figure 9.12 Optional Step 6: Template Configuration

SAP provides various standard templates for application-specific reports. Each SAP standard template includes a collection of typical tables for this application. For each table, the analysis type (ANALYSIS TYPE column; AGE stands for analysis of time-based data distribution), execution mode (EXECUTION MODE column; COLLECTIVE means collective execution in the managed system), and the execution frequency (FREQUENCY column, in minutes; 10.080 means weekly) are preset. The DOCUMENTATION column, which is available for each template, provides essential information on the use and background of every template. Table 9.2 lists all eight SAP standard templates.

The upper area of Figure 9.12 shows five of eight available templates (see TEMPLATE ID column). Clicking DISPLAY allows you to toggle SAP standard templates and customer templates, if available. If you define your own analyses at a later point, you can collect these in separate templates. The lower area of the TEMPLATES DETAILS table shows you an overview of pre-configured tables, analysis types, etc., for a selected template. Figure 9.12 shows this on the example of the template DVM_TMPL_BASIS. As you can see, no changes have been made for the template.

Template ID	Use
DVM_TMPL_BASIS	Analyze the data (that can be deleted regularly) in basis-related tables of the system landscape
DVM_TMPL_CO	Analyze the data (that can be deleted regularly) in CO-related tables of the system landscape
DVM_TMPL_EC_PCA	Analyze the data (that can be deleted regularly) in EC-PCA-related tables of the system landscape
DVM_TMPL_EWM	Analyze the data (that can be deleted regularly) in EWM-related tables of the system landscape
DVM_TMPL_FI	Analyze the data (that can be deleted regularly) in FI-related tables of the system landscape
DVM_TMPL_FI_CA	Analyze the data (that can be deleted regularly) in FI-CA-related tables of the system landscape
DVM_TMPL_IS_U	Analyze the data (that can be deleted regularly) in IS-U-related tables of the system landscape
DVM_TMPL_SUGEN	Measuring the business volume in the system landscape based on predefined SAP standard tables

Table 9.2 SAP Standard Templates

If you wish to configure analyses, you need to store data in the PLANNED EXECUTION DATE or PLANNED EXECUTION TIME column and in the FREQUENCY column. In doing so, always ask yourself whether you really need the analysis results more often than suggested by the best-practice values. The frequency is indicated in minutes. If you make the changes, make sure not to disturb the access to productive tables. To save, click SAVE.

This step thus allows you to define the execution and execution frequency of the prepared analyses. If you want to do this at a later point, you can proceed to the next step. You can repeat step 6 at any time.

Click NEXT to proceed to the next step, even if you have not performed any activity in this step.

Step 7: Activate DVM Extractors

Here, you activate the DVM extractors. Extractors are not responsible for the data transport from the managed systems to the BW system of SAP Solution Manager. Thus, extractors are the essential element within the DVM infrastructure because without data, no reports are possible.

> **Warning**
>
> Do not activate extractors as long as not all SAP notes were implemented in the managed system in step 5.

The extractors are activated per system and client, as shown in Figure 9.13. For each system, you need to select the corresponding target client via the HELP function. To do this, click the small black triangle at the right margin. In the example, the RFC CONFIGURED CLIENTS column shows you that for the OTO system of Toys Inc., client 800 is relevant, and for another system, BSL, client 100 is relevant.

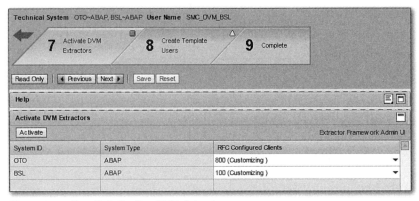

Figure 9.13 Step 7: Activating DVM Extractors

Click the ACTIVATE button above the list with the systems. If you want to activate the extractors for multiple clients in a system, you need to repeat this step for all relevant clients.

For performance reasons, the extractors are listed sequentially in the managed system. The first complete run can therefore take a while; this depends on the size of the database and can take 45 minutes or longer. The sequential execution of extractors in the managed system also means that it can take just as long for data in the DATA VOLUME MANAGEMENT work center to become visible. A green message in the log of this step (Transaction SOLMAN_SETUP) does not mean that all extractors started immediately. It just means that no errors have occurred yet. Therefore, it must always be checked simultaneously whether the extractors have already been executed completely.

We recommend that you check the activation in the EFWK using the link Extrac- tor Framework Admin UI above the system overview in Figure 9.13. Figure 9.14 shows a part of the start screen of the EFWK user interface.

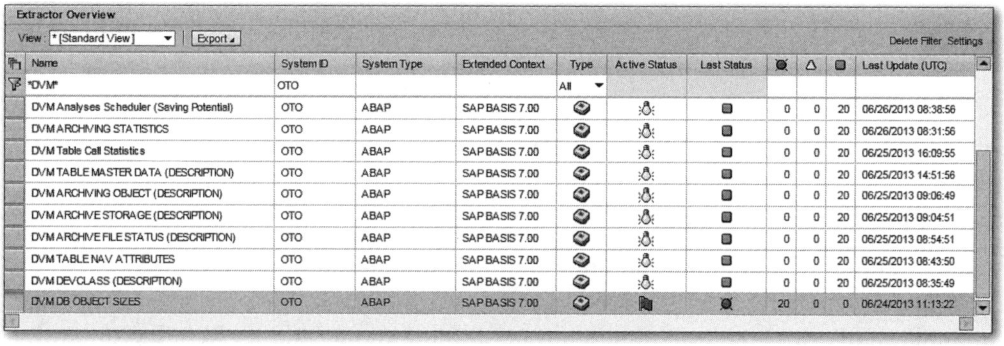

Name	System ID	System Type	Extended Context	Type	Active Status	Last Status	☼	△	▣	Last Update (UTC)
DVM	OTO			All						
DVM Analyses Scheduler (Saving Potential)	OTO	ABAP	SAP BASIS 7.00	⬡	☼	▣	0	0	20	06/26/2013 08:38:56
DVM ARCHIVING STATISTICS	OTO	ABAP	SAP BASIS 7.00	⬡	☼	▣	0	0	20	06/26/2013 08:31:56
DVM Table Call Statistics	OTO	ABAP	SAP BASIS 7.00	⬡	☼	▣	0	0	20	06/25/2013 16:09:55
DVM TABLE MASTER DATA (DESCRIPTION)	OTO	ABAP	SAP BASIS 7.00	⬡	☼	▣	0	0	20	06/25/2013 14:51:56
DVM ARCHIVING OBJECT (DESCRIPTION)	OTO	ABAP	SAP BASIS 7.00	⬡	☼	▣	0	0	20	06/25/2013 09:06:49
DVM ARCHIVE STORAGE (DESCRIPTION)	OTO	ABAP	SAP BASIS 7.00	⬡	☼	▣	0	0	20	06/25/2013 09:04:51
DVM ARCHIVE FILE STATUS (DESCRIPTION)	OTO	ABAP	SAP BASIS 7.00	⬡	☼	▣	0	0	20	06/25/2013 08:54:51
DVM TABLE NAV ATTRIBUTES	OTO	ABAP	SAP BASIS 7.00	⬡	☼	▣	0	0	20	06/25/2013 08:43:50
DVM DEVCLASS (DESCRIPTION)	OTO	ABAP	SAP BASIS 7.00	⬡	☼	▣	0	0	20	06/25/2013 08:35:49
DVM DB OBJECT SIZES	OTO	ABAP	SAP BASIS 7.00	⬡	📖	⬙	20	0	0	06/24/2013 11:13:22

Figure 9.14 User Interface of the Extractor Framework after Initialization

Use the filter function by clicking Filter. Limit the view of the DVM-relevant extrac- tors using the newly inserted selection line below the table header. If applicable, filter for more details—for example, systems. In Figure 9.14, the limitation was made for *DVM* and the OTO system. Check the time stamps in the Last Update column. When you activate the DVM extractors for a system for the first time, it is possible that a few extractors have not been executed yet and that zero values are found in the Last Update column.

Red status messages in the Extractor Framework Admin UI (Last Status column) are normal for extractors whose ID contains DVM SAVING POTENTIAL. These extractors do not generate a green status until the analysis results have been transported by the corresponding system. For more information on analyses, see Section 9.5. For all other extractors, red statuses must be examined if you wish to perform reliable analyses later.

Extractors with a red status should always be examined. If you mark an extractor, its line will be highlighted in orange. Below the Extractor Overview, you then receive execution information on runtime, result, and configuration details. You can start your error analysis based on this information.

To complete configuration step 7, you do not need to wait until each extractor has finished. Click the NEXT button to proceed to the next step.

For general background information on EFWK, see Chapter 8.

Step 8: Create Template Users

In this optional step, you can create template users in the managed systems. As you can see in Figure 9.15, this step is similar to the third step, CREATE TEMPLATE USERS.

This step summarizes the results of all configuration steps and the status of the executed actions. Figure 9.16 shows the general overview.

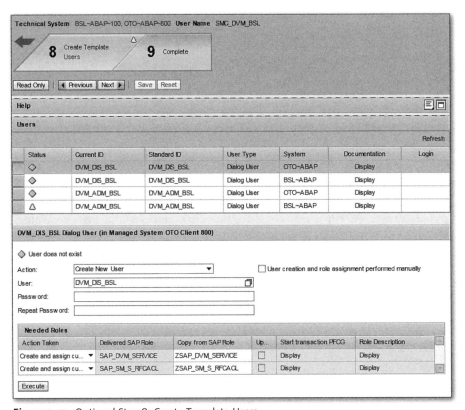

Figure 9.15 Optional Step 8: Create Template Users

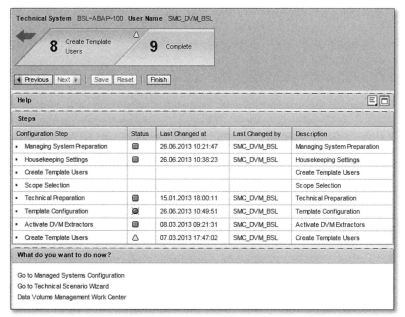

Figure 9.16 Step 9: General Overview

The main difference is that the two already described standardized users for display and administration can now be created for all systems of the DVM infrastructure. If you want to use DVM-specific tools in the systems, you should create the respective users in this step. Otherwise, skip the configuration and click NEXT to proceed to the next step.

Step 9: Complete

In the example of Figure 9.16, all steps except TEMPLATE CONFIGURATION were completed successfully. In this case, you would need to re-examine, correct, and re-execute this step. In the CONFIGURATION STEP column, you find the associated links to go back to previous steps, if required.

The lower area has links to tasks that are directly associated with the DATA VOLUME MANAGEMENT work center or that call up the DATA VOLUME MANAGEMENT work center.

9.2.5 Initialization at Toys Inc.

The IT team of Toys Inc. has now initialized the Data Volume Management work center and connected all relevant production systems (that correspond to step Configuration of Managed Systems in Transaction SOLMAN_SETUP). The check of the EFWK user interface has shown that the data transfer works. The initial activation of the DVM infrastructure is therefore complete.

All persons involved know that certain areas dealing with growth tendencies require four to six weeks for data collection. Analyses on the largest and/or fastest growing objects should be configured at a later point when the DVM general situation is transparent.

The next step is the preparation of the data view by defining a technical scenario. We will now show you how to define such a technical scenario in SAP Solution Manager.

9.3 DVM Landscape

The basic approach of a DVM strategy is to focus on all systems in the SAP system landscape that are important for running a business operation. In this context, it can be useful to structure the view of this DVM landscape; for example, due to different responsibilities. Another reason would be that business areas basically operate independently from each other.

With the so-called *technical scenarios*, SAP Solution Manager allows you to do such structuring. This term should not be confused with application scenarios in SAP Solution Manager. Technical scenarios should include all essential systems that are involved in a core business process. These highlight business processes and correlations between business operations and the involved business objects, as well as the technical data storage objects, such as tables and indexes. Only in this manner can you be sure that DVM scenarios provide a complete representation of correlations.

9.3.1 Technical Scenarios for Data Volume Management

Since information queries in the Data Volume Management work center are always based on technical scenarios, the latter must be generated first.

The technical scenarios are maintained using a wizard, which can be launched via Technical Scenario Wizard in the menu of the Data Volume Management work center under Configuration. The start screen lists all configured scenarios. The buttons above the table allow you to create, maintain, or delete technical scenarios (see Figure 9.17).

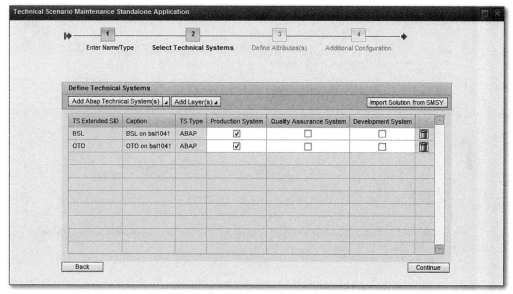

Figure 9.17 Technical Scenarios Wizard—Start Screen

Start creating new scenarios using the Create button; if you wish to maintain (modify) a scenario, click the Maintain button. You see a guided procedure, which guides you through the following steps:

1. First, select the Data Volume Management scenario type and enter a name and brief description. Of course, you can change an existing scenario, but you can also change the description this step.

2. In the second step, choose the relevant ABAP systems, i.e., the ABAP systems that have previously been initialized for Data Volume Management. To do this, first click the Add ABAP Technical System(s) button (see Figure 9.18). Multiple selections are possible. Please note that you need to select one of the three options: Production System, Quality Assurance System, or Development System. If you don't select any of the three options, no system will be assigned

to the change procedure at the end, and you will not see any data in the DATA VOLUME MANAGEMENT work center for the intended systems.

3. Finally, save your settings and check the result in the overview (see Figure 9.17). All specified ABAP systems should be visible in the INVOLVED TECH. ELEMENTS column.

Technical Scenario Maintenance

Name	Type	Description	Involved Tech. Elements
BSL System Monitoring	System Monitoring	System Monitoring for BSL	BSL~ABAP,BSL~JAVA
BSL SystemHome.bsl1041	Dual Stack	Dual Stack BSL on bsl1041	BSL~ABAP,BSL,BSL~JAVA
DEMO	End-user Exp. Monitoring	Demo Scenario	OTO~ABAP,OTO~JAVA
FIX.SystemHome.ivm2134	Dual Stack	Dual Stack FIX on ivm2134	FIX,FIX~JAVA,FIX~ABAP
Fokus: BSL und OTO	Data Volume Management	Fokus: BSL und OTO	OTO~ABAP,BSL~ABAP
Fokus: nur BSL	Data Volume Management	Fokus: nur BSL	BSL~ABAP
OTO System Monitoring	System Monitoring	System Monitoring for OTO	OTO~ABAP,OTO~JAVA,OTO
OTO.SystemHome.bsl1041	Dual Stack	Dual Stack OTO on bsl1041	OTO~ABAP,OTO~JAVA,OTO
SELF MONITORING	End-user Exp. Monitoring	Scenario for Self Monitoring	BSL~ABAP,BSL~JAVA
SELF-MONITORING	Self-Monitoring	Self-Monitoring Scenario	BSL~ABAP,WLY~IS_EM,BSL~JAVA
Toys Inc	BI Monitoring	Demo Scenario	BSL~ABAP,BSL~JAVA,OTO~ABAP,DIK~ABAP
Toys Inc	Connection Monitoring	Toys Inc	OTO~ABAP,BSL~ABAP,FIX~ABAP,ZIK~ABAP,DOF~ABAP,DIK~ABAP
Toys Inc	Data Volume Management	DVM Szenario	OTO~ABAP,BSL~ABAP,DIK~ABAP
Web Shop Spielzeug AG	Interface Monitoring	Schnittstellenkanalüberwachung	OTO~ABAP,FIX~JAVA,TAK~LIVE_CACHE,FIX~ABAP,ZAK~LIVE_CACHE

Figure 9.18 Setting Up Technical Scenarios

After you refresh the DATA VOLUME MANAGEMENT work center view, the new scenario or changes to an existing scenario are visible in the STATISTICS AND TREND, POTENTIAL SAVINGS, or ARCHIVING INFORMATION activity areas. Hence, you can now perform the queries there against an SAP system landscape defined in the scenario.

After all required systems were integrated in a technical scenario of the Data Volume Management type, the future DVM experts of Toys Inc. can basically work with the predefined dashboards in the DATA VOLUME MANAGEMENT work center.

The queries in the STATISTICS AND TREND activity area already provide data. They allow for a general overview of DVM objects of the focused DVM landscape.

However, before we go into more detail, we will show you in the following sections how you can integrate more ABAP systems into the DVM infrastructure and which typical maintenance tasks must be completed.

9.3.2 Integrating More Systems

If you find out that you need to integrate more systems into the analyses during your development of DVM scenarios, you can add them at any time after the initial configuration of the DVM infrastructure. The DATA VOLUME MANAGEMENT work center can be extended by new systems at any time. A general prerequisite is the successful connection to SAP Solution Manager, which means the configuration of the managed systems must be successfully completed.

Basically, follow the steps for initial configuration (see Section 9.2.4). For clarity, let's summarize a few facts.

Systems that are currently integrated can be checked at various locations. For example, in the STATUS SUMMARY in the EXTRACTORS area, you can call the EFWK and check for which systems DVM-relevant extractors are activated (see Section 9.4.1). Or, you can consider which systems are already integrated in which technical scenarios (see Section 9.3.1).

You can connect new systems by re-executing the DATA VOLUME MANAGEMENT guided procedure in Transaction SOLMAN_SETUP. You do not need to complete all steps; just the required activities are described next. For a detailed description of the individual steps, refer to Section 9.2.4. Make sure that you are in change mode before you start initialization.

1. **Preparing the managing system**
   With this step, you check the prerequisites in SAP Solution Manager. If the last execution was not too long ago or no changes have occurred in the system, this execution is optional. Of course, it is always recommendable to check the basic configuration or update the so-called Central SAP Note. The same applies to the BI Content that is shipped with the ST-BCO component (see SAP Note 1233709).

2. **Housekeeping settings**
   This step allows you to change the settings that define the residence times of the information in the DVM-relevant InfoCubes. If you do not want to change the preset values, click the NEXT button.

3. **Create template users**
   This step allows you to check which of the suggested standard users already exist in SAP Solution Manager and which roles are assigned to them. If you do not wish to create a new user or change an existing one, this step is also optional. Click the NEXT button to proceed to the next step.

4. **Scope selection**

   This is the decisive step for extending the DVM infrastructure. Select all systems that are now also moving into the DVM focus. You do not need to reselect the already integrated systems unless you wish to configure analyses for this system by using templates in step 6.

   > **Note**
   >
   > Do not proceed to the next step for systems for which the RFC STATUS or AUTO. CONF. STATUS displays warnings or errors. In this case, first correct the errors in the MANAGED SYSTEMS CONFIGURATION.

5. **Technical preparation**

   In this step, you check the prerequisites in the managed system(s) with regard to the DVM-relevant SAP notes and whether the DVM content is up to date.

6. **Template configuration**

   This step allows you to easily configure analyses for the new system, based on pre-configured templates. This step is optional. If you aren't yet sure whether you want to perform the suggested analyses, you can skip this step by clicking the NEXT button and configure analyses at a later point (see Section 9.5).

7. **Activate DVM extractors**

   In this step, you activate DVM-relevant extractors for the new system by clicking the ACTIVATE button. The extractors are activated per system-client combination. If you wish to activate the extractors for multiple clients in a system, you need to repeat this step for all relevant clients.

8. **Create template users**

   This step is basically identical to the third step. The difference is that that you now check which of the suggested standard users exist in the managed system and which roles were potentially assigned to them. If you do not wish to create a new user or change an existing one, this step is optional. Click the NEXT button to proceed to the next step.

9. **Complete**

   This step shows the status for most of the configuration steps and tells you when which user performed which step.

To complete the integration of the additional system, you can click the link TECH-NICAL SCENARIO WIZARD to then group the new system(s) in an existing or new technical scenario. For information on how to proceed, see Section 9.3.1.

Now that we have described how to integrate more systems in the DVM infrastructure, the next two sections will show you which typical maintenance tasks must be completed. First, we are taking a look at technical operations, and we will then show you how to configure tasks.

9.4   Maintenance of DVM Infrastructure

The typical maintenance measures for DVM infrastructure include checking its functions. Start this check in the DATA VOLUME MANAGEMENT work center. As mentioned previously, call it up using Transaction SOLMAN_WORKCENTER (or SM_WORKCENTER).

Data retrieval from connected managed systems is done automatically via the EFWK. Regular and error-free execution of extractors and, thus, of data retrieval is particularly important. You also need to check whether the configured analyses are running precisely and provide results as expected.

As soon as all DVM-relevant extractors have been executed at least once, data is available in the DATA VOLUME MANAGEMENT work center. You can check this, for example, by performing a query in the STATISTICS AND TREND activity area and plausibility-check the displayed result. However, this test provides only a first impression.

> **Note**
>
> For the check, proceed as described in Section 9.6.5. It is best to use a query from the DATA ALLOCATION STATISTICS area. In the SYSTEMS area, select the SUMMARY. This way, you can determine precisely whether the most important extractor, DVM DB OBJECT SIZES, has collected data, for example. It should be running for each system of the DVM infrastructure.

Before you execute more in-depth analysis and draw conclusions from the results, you should check the DVM infrastructure closely for errors.

9.4.1 Status Summary for the Data Volume Management Work Center

Checking the DVM infrastructure is one of the regular tasks of the DVM administrator. The STATUS SUMMARY activity area provides a general overview (see Figure 9.19). Here, the EFWK user interface in the EXTRACTORS area, execution information of the analyses in the ANALYSIS area, and solutions and services in the SOLUTIONS AND SERVICES are linked. When you click a link the next view always opens in a view pre-filtered for DATA VOLUME MANAGEMENT.

Focus on the links marked red. The errors in the EXTRACTORS area (link text ERROR) definitely must be examined for relevance and cause. Also, cancelled jobs in the ANALYSIS area (link text CANCELLED) are problematic.

To analyze the individual errors more closely, you can click ERROR. In some cases, you just need to decide for a specific technical scenario before you see the EXTRACTOR FRAMEWORK ADMIN UI in the respective view.

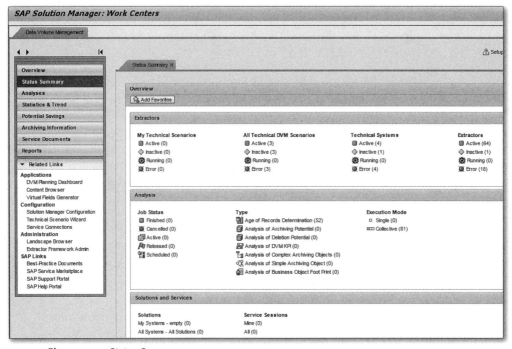

Figure 9.19 Status Summary

9.4.2 Treating Technical Problems

It's possible that messages are displayed above the actual work center when you call it. Figure 9.20 shows this for the example of green information.

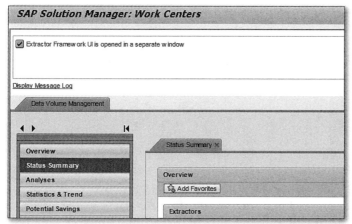

Figure 9.20 Messages in the Work Center

Messages indicate general problems—for example, regarding the infrastructure, which must be resolved. More detailed information is available in the message log.

To give you an idea of the meaning of the messages, we will now introduce a few typical and relatively frequent messages.

The DVM extractors with issues detected; reporting may be affected warning (yellow status) indicates malfunctions related to DVM extractors. This inevitably results in problems within the process of data collection and data transfer to the business warehouse. Because not all DVM-relevant data is available in this case, incomplete and erroneous reports must be expected. This situation is evaluated with a yellow status because at least some amount of data could be collected. However, the situation is basically critical and should be examined.

In concrete cases, a more in-depth error analysis should be performed in the EFWK user interface. Part of the EFWK user interface is shown in Figure 9.14. In that example, the DVM DB OBJECT SIZES is marked. A table further down, which is not shown in the figure, shows all important information on the individual extractor executions.

Please note that specific extractors do not immediately provide data after their initialization and, therefore, have a red status. This is typical of extractors whose name includes `DVM SAVING POTENTIAL`, for example. In this case, the simple reason is that no analyses have been configured yet.

Other errors (red status), which prevent communication and thus the execution of data extraction in early on, can be the following:

▸ <SID> RFC System Failure/Select one of the installed languages

▸ <SID> RFC System Failure/partner "FQDN" not reached/Select

▸ <SID> RFC Communication Failure/Error opening an RFC connection (CPIC-CALL:

In these cases, there are issues with the connection of the managed system. The error messages indicate that the access to the managed system already caused problems, which suggests that no data has been extracted at all. Hence, an analysis of the data is not possible, either. In this case, start your error analysis in Transaction SOLMAN_SETUP, in the MANAGED SYSTEMS CONFIGURATION activity area.

Another typical warning (yellow status) is *Query 'xyz' is already open in another mode*. In this case, the work center view was already opened in another mode. This resulted in a lock conflict. Check the windows you have opened. You can also use Transaction SM12 to check the available lock entries and clean them where applicable.

9.4.3 Data Volume Management at Toys Inc.

The activation of DVM extractors periodically loads DVM-relevant data into the SAP Solution Manager business warehouse. There, it is available for use and reporting.

The IT team at Toys Inc. has now operated the DATA VOLUME MANAGEMENT work center for several weeks, so it is able to quickly provide DVM-relevant information upon request of various competencies. Apart from the size statistics periodically collected by the managed systems, trend statements are now available, too. This has the important advantage that it is not just technical information, but conclusions can also be drawn about business organizations, products, document types, etc. The IT team now has an effective tool that allows them to support a DVM corporate strategy.

Now, it needs to be clarified whether it is possible to examine individual objects based on the type of data and its time-related distribution in more detail. The following section describes these possibilities.

9.5 Configuring Analyses

If you require information on the age of data and thus its time-based distribution, you need to configure appropriate analyses in SAP Solution Manager, specifically to clients and for the respective managed SAP system. It can be helpful, for example, to find saving potentials for archiving or deleting data, or if you want to obtain or increase transparency of the structure of your data in the SAP system landscape.

Analyses deepen general information of the DVM landscape by shedding more light on specific objects. Therefore, based on findings, analyses are object-specifically configured during the DVM process.

Analyses are performed in the managed systems based on background jobs. SAP Solution Manager enables you to combine the execution of multiple analyses in one background job. The analysis results are stored in the BW system of SAP Solution Manager.

Analyses are configured in the ANALYSES activity area. All configured analyses are table-specifically displayed in a tabular overview, including further execution information. If, during initialization of the infrastructure of the DATA VOLUME MANAGEMENT work center, you already made use of the possibility of mass configuration (see the subsection "Step 6: Template Configuration" in Section 9.2.4) using Transaction SOLMAN_SETUP, you can see these analyses here, too. You can add more analyses to this object amount.

> **Note**
>
> The ANALYSES activity area provides an overview of configured analyses and information about their execution. The results of the analyses can be found in the STATISTICS AND TREND and POTENTIAL SAVINGS activity areas.
>
> Analyses can also be deleted in the change mode. The data collected in the business warehouse are kept.

9.5.1 Defining the Analysis Scope

The configuration of new analyses is based on a procedure that you can start in the ANALYSES activity area using the CREATE button. After selecting the respective target system (or managed system), you define the scope of the analysis in the second step. This step is shown in Figure 9.21.

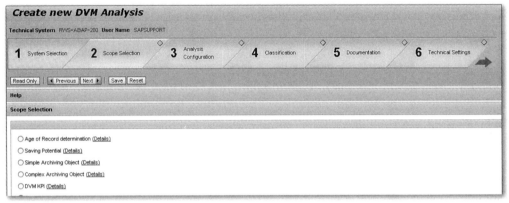

Figure 9.21 Procedure for Configuring Analyses

There are various options to define the scope of an analysis. These are described in more detail in the following subsections. During the configuration, note the help text that is offered in the individual steps. After defining the analysis, you can take the definition up into the template maintenance.

Scope Selection: Age of Record Determination

The AGE OF RECORD DETERMINATION analysis is based on the scheduling of jobs in the managed system that examine the distribution of records. Based on a specified time criterion—for example, the creation date, change date, or posting date—the number of records is calculated.

This type of analysis creates transparency in the age structure of objects or document types of a specific system landscape. It provides useful information, such as on the determination of savings potential, and is thus a preparing step toward making a decision. In addition, you can manage work priorities for all objects that must be considered in a DVM project.

For each new analysis, you can determine the analysis scope as follows:

- Top 30 analysis: Objects
- Top 30 analysis: Document types
- Top 30 analysis: Growing objects
- Top 30 analysis: Growing document types
- Analysis of tables with the greatest database activity
- Analysis of objects to be entered manually (table with or without specified document type)

The configuration is based on the use of virtual fields. Virtual fields are artificially created fields and contain only year and month data, no composite time information. They are important for the presentation of data.

You can also check or assign classifying information, such as area of use, organizational unit, or business area, and store your own text for documentation of the configuration. You always need to set technical parameters concerning the job execution in the managed system. The result of these analyses is shown in the STATISTICS AND TREND dashboards. You can retrieve them by clicking the TIME-BASED DATA DISTRIBUTION button.

Scope Selection: Saving Potential

The SAVING POTENTIAL analysis detects savings potential based on a configured residence time. The residence time indicates how long data must be kept in the database for various reasons. SAP best-practice values are stored for selected archiving objects.

You can work with various residence times simultaneously — in other words, create multiple analyses — and thus simulate various savings potentials. At the end of the day, however, as part of your DVM project work, you and the respective interest groups from business operations should agree on a specific residence time.

The definition of the analysis scope and the configuration itself correspond to the explanations on the AGE OF RECORD DETERMINATION analysis type. This analysis can also be used for an automated quality check for the objects of your DVM landscape, which are covered by a global data volume strategy. Data quality problems can be detected easily that, for example, can result in records' not being archived.

The output of this analysis can be seen in the dashboards in the POTENTIAL SAV-INGS activity area.

Scope Selection: Simple Archiving Object

The SIMPLE ARCHIVING OBJECT analysis can be scheduled once per system. It provides transparency of the size of the archiving object in an SAP system. In other words, you receive a statement on how many records you can transfer from the database, based on pre-defined analysis criteria, and which storage volume that corresponds to. It detects connections between tables and archiving objects if they represent a 1:1 relationship.

For all other objects use the COMPLEX ARCHIVING OBJECT analysis, particularly the so-called *cross-objects*, which contain multiple archiving objects.

The dashboards of these analyses can be found in the STATISTICS AND TREND activity area. Click the DATA ASSIGNMENT STATISTICS button and select the ARCHIVING OBJECT tab.

Scope Selection: Complex Archiving Object

The COMPLEX ARCHIVING OBJECT analysis provides transparency of the size of archiving objects that extend across multiple systems in an SAP system landscape. This is particularly interesting for tables that can be archived with multiple archiving objects. In contrast to the analysis of simple archiving objects, this analysis can be scheduled independently for each object. If this type has been selected, you receive a list of objects that are currently supported by this analysis type.

The number of available tables or archiving objects supported by this function varies depending on which ST-A/PI plug-in is implemented in the managed system. Currently, not all complex archiving objects are supported, but the content increases with each larger ST-A/PI release.

The dashboards of these analyses can be found in the STATISTICS AND TREND activity area. Click the DATA ASSIGNMENT STATISTICS button and select the ARCHIVING OBJECT tab.

Scope Selection: DVM KPI

The purpose of the DVM KPI is to measure the business growth of a system landscape and compare it with the technical growth of this system landscape. The aim is to detect disharmonies between the business growth and technical growth to allow for appropriate measures. It also provides an overview of the benefits of DVM measures already performed.

This analysis is directly linked to the group of dashboard applications made available for use by members of the project management or DVM experts. The dashboards of these analyses can be found in the STATISTICS AND TREND activity area. Click the DATA ASSIGNMENT STATISTICS button and select the MANAGEMENT tab.

Scope Selection: Business Object Footprint

The BUSINESS OBJECT FOOTPRINT analysis is a very powerful analysis of the selected managed system when it comes to business objects, such as company code, sales organization, plant, etc. Choose a business object during configuration. The system then identifies all tables that are linked with the selected object. The resulting set of tables can be changed after the identification process, so you can reduce the number of tables to be analyzed. As soon as the table set has been defined, an analysis is triggered in the backend system, which performs a breakdown on the assigned tables for each value of the selected business object. This analysis may take some time. At the end, you receive an overview of how many records or what percentage of the data have been generated by company code 1, 2, 3, etc. Based on these results, you can easily find out how much data has been generated by which business area, organizational unit, or country.

You can find the dashboards of this analysis in the STATISTICS AND TREND activity area by clicking the BUSINESS OBJECT FOOTPRINT button.

Scope Selection: Template Selection

The TEMPLATE SELECTION analysis is for the use of already-run and stored analyses that can be assigned to a customer-specific template. The main advantage is that systems in which similar objects must be processed using one of the analysis options can be easily configured based on a customer-related template.

A template contains the complete configuration of objects, including all associated technical parameters. Only a few of them, such as the next start date, frequency, etc., must be edited before they are activated.

> **Note**
>
> Generally, certain dashboards in the STATISTICS AND TREND and POTENTIAL SAVINGS activity areas can display data only if appropriate analyses have been configured. Which dashboards these are has been mentioned in the previous explanations of the various analyses.

9.5.2 Definition of Analyses at Toys Inc.

Since Toys Inc. has not performed any larger DVM projects so far, it can be assumed that a large amount of outdated data is stored in the database. However, no details are known so far. For a start into Data Volume Management, the current primary interest is an Age of Record Determination analysis. While using a service rendered by SAP, however, Toys Inc. receives the advice to also use the other analyses in order to view the data volume in the largest objects from several perspectives, not just one.

To increase the validity of the information, the decision is made to start discussing and deriving DVM measures after a few weeks—in other words, to effectively use the DATA VOLUME MANAGEMENT work center as part of a DVM strategy. The following section describes how this is done.

9.6 Reporting Using the Data Volume Management Work Center

Now that you have completely configured the DVM infrastructure, we are going to show you how to run analyses and reports in the DATA VOLUME MANAGEMENT work center.

Table 9.3 shows another overview of which individual activity areas can be seen in the initial screen of the DATA VOLUME MANAGEMENT work center.

Activity Area	Function
Overview	Initial screen for access to the following activity areas
Status Summary	Operation status information on extractors, analyses, solutions, and DVM services that are relevant to the DVM infrastructure

Table 9.3 Activity Areas and Functions of the Data Volume Management Work Center

Activity Area	Function
Analyses	Configuration overview and analysis management
Statistics and Trend	Gathering information based on scenarios
Potential Saving	Gathering information based on scenarios
Archiving Information	Gathering information based on scenarios; available if archiving is done using SAP tools
Service Documents	DVM, gathering information
Reporting	DVM, gathering information

Table 9.3 Activity Areas and Functions of the Data Volume Management Work Center (Cont.)

When you call up the work center, the OVERVIEW is displayed. From here, you can start the individual activity areas via the links in the right-hand area. Generally, it is always possible to use one of the menu buttons on the left-hand side.

The STATISTICS AND TREND and POTENTIAL SAVING activity areas are of particular significance for analyzing and reporting, as follows:

▶ The STATISTICS AND TREND area contains statistical information about the size and growth of various objects. Please note that the collected technical information is always enriched with additional business information, such as organizational units, document types, etc. Section 9.6.1 explains this area in more detail.

▶ The POTENTIAL SAVINGS area includes analyses from which you can derive saving potentials. These analyses are based on specific parameters. For background information on this, please see Section 9.5.

> **Note**
>
> For the availability of weekly or monthly trend information, you need to ensure that DVM-specific data was collected for a minimum of four to six weeks. For shorter analysis periods, the reliability of conclusions is limited, or conclusions are not possible.

The following section presents the key activity areas in more detail and shows you, using the example of Toys Inc., how to create a query in the DATA VOLUME MANAGEMENT work center.

9.6.1 Statistics and Trend

An important activity area in the DATA VOLUME MANAGEMENT work center is STATISTICS & TREND. Figure 9.22 shows the activity area.

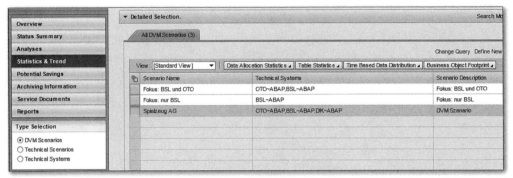

Figure 9.22 Data Volume Management Work Center—Statistics and Trend Activity Area

This activity area contains various groups, including pre-configured dashboards. They provide information on business-related and technical reporting. As you can see in Figure 9.22, four groups are available, which you can access via the following buttons: DATA ALLOCATION STATISTICS, TABLE STATISTICS, TIME BASED DATA DISTRIBUTION, and BUSINESS OBJECT FOOTPRINT. Next, we will introduce the individual groups in more detail.

Data Allocation Statisticss

The information you receive in the DATA ALLOCATION STATISTICS group from pre-defined BW queries supports your decision-making process. The dashboards provide various views of your data, from a product-oriented approach and an application-specific approach to a technical view of your table information. In other words, from various perspectives, they give you insight into the storage requirement and growth rates of individual or complex objects of your SAP landscape and allow for the following:

▶ Extensive analyses for finding complex DVM matters

▶ Simple analyses for identifying of trends and unusual growth rates

▶ Historic analyses on highly compressed and very detailed levels

The evaluation on data allocation statistics supports you in the following:

- Defining priorities in planned DVM projects

- Identifying the largest storage users in your landscape and per product

- Finding reduction options for various systems

After you have clicked the DATA ALLOCATION STATISTICS, apart from MANAGEMENT, the following access options are displayed: PRODUCTS, SYSTEMS, APPLICATION AREA, DOCUMENT TYPE, ARCHIVING OBJECT, and TABLES. Each of these areas contains various key figures, which are always assigned a dashboard. The key figures in most areas are similar. They provide information on the current size, history, largest growth or reduction, largest deviation, etc.

> **Note**
>
> Please note that the dashboards in the MANAGEMENT area (DVM KPI, Business Growth, Achievements) work slightly differently. These dashboards provide general DVM status information. Based on the number of business documents, the DVM key figure compares the business growth with the growth of the technical landscape. You can detect any situation where the two do not match.

A valuable key figure is behind the ARCHIVING OBJECT area. Here, you find information when you have configured analyses with the COMPLEX ARCHIVING OBJECT scope (see the subsection "Scope Selection: Complex Archiving Object" in Section 9.5.1). The dashboard then shows the storage allocation of an archiving object in the entire SAP landscape. This gives you information you would normally have to put together using various individual analyses.

Table Statistics

The defined BW queries of the TABLE STATISTICS group provide you with statements on the table statistics, i.e., which tables are used most or which are not used at all. That way, you increase the transparency of your individual business processes by doing the following:

- Extracting all database-relevant activities (reads, inserts, updates, deletes)

- Visualizing objects with the highest execution frequency

- Simply identifying objects of the business part that is most important for a DVM strategy

However, queries in this area also increase the transparency of unused data by doing the following:

▸ Evaluating objects long term that provide no clues for their use

▸ Discovering old, unrequired data (i.e., migrated data, obsolete business functions, etc.)

After you have clicked the TABLE STATISTICS button, the following areas are displayed: PRODUCT, SYSTEM, APPLICATION AREA, DOCUMENT TYPE, and TABLE. The dashboards of these areas provide information on the following indicators (key figures): current size, history, most accesses, and no accesses.

Time-Based Data Distribution

The defined BW queries in the TIME-BASED DATA DISTRIBUTION group provide you with detailed statements on the time-based distribution of records in the DVM landscape. They allow you to understand the "age structure" of your landscape and identify areas of "old" data. The gathered information can provide clues on archiving options or deletion projects in your system landscape and support you in your decision making process. Otherwise, they can reveal deficiencies in regards to data quality, such as data that is old enough for archiving but is not in the system yet.

When you click the TIME-BASED DATA DISTRIBUTION button, the following areas are displayed: SYSTEM, ORGANIZATION UNIT, APPLICATION AREA, DOCUMENT TYPE, and TABLE. Each of them provides two different dashboards: either an annual overview or an overview that presents the time-based distribution of data by month and year from the start. Here, only data for objects for which you have configured an analysis is displayed.

Business Object Footprint

The defined BW queries of the BUSINESS OBJECT FOOTPRINT allow you to receive reports of data used by the individual business object instances, such as company code, sales organization, or ledger.

After you click the BUSINESS OBJECT FOOTPRINT button, two dashboards for an object analysis are displayed. The two differ in the way they present information—in other words, whether the object analysis is sorted by ID or text.

9.6.2   Potential Savings

Another activity area in the DATA VOLUME MANAGEMENT work center is POTENTIAL SAVINGS (see Figure 9.23).

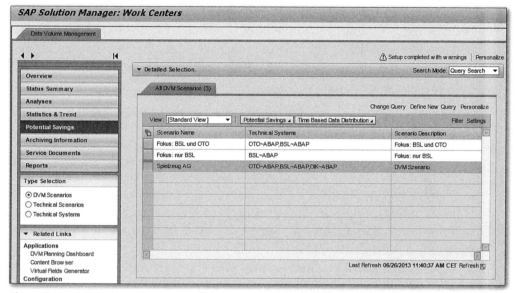

Figure 9.23   Data Volume Management Work Center—Potential Savings Activity Area

This activity area contains various groups of pre-configured dashboards. They provide detailed information on the optimization potential; in other words, you receive information on which data in which tables you can archive or delete. If you perform analysis for the same objects but using different parameters, you can simulate various options.

As you can see in Figure 9.23, two groups are available, and you can access them by clicking a button: POTENTIAL SAVINGS and TIME-BASED DATA DISTRIBUTION. Next, we will introduce the two groups in more detail. Here, only data for objects for which you have configured an analysis is displayed.

Potential Savings

Queries in the POTENTIAL SAVINGS activity area are based on the automatic execution of configured table analyses in the managed systems (Scope Selection: Savings Potential, Simple Archiving Object, and Complex Archiving Object). The results answer the question for possible savings potentials and provide support in your decision-making process.

The analyses are performed for the most important archiving objects. They always provide information on the time-based distribution of data (displayed under TIME-BASED DATA DISTRIBUTION). Moreover, depending on your configuration of criteria such as residence time or document type, you can highlight savings potential. Using the same analyses but different residence times, you can simulate various reduction approaches (aggressive, moderate, etc.). Finally, you can visualize the effect of archiving activities.

After you click the POTENTIAL SAVINGS button, you can choose from the following dashboards: SCENARIOS, PRODUCT, SYSTEM, ORGANIZATIONAL UNIT, APPLICATION AREA, DOCUMENT TYPE, ARCHIVING OBJECT, AND TABLE.

Time-Based Data Distribution

Queries in this area also support your decision making process. The defined BW queries in the TIME-BASED DATA DISTRIBUTION area allow for detailed conclusions about the time-based distribution of records in the DVM landscape. Data is displayed here only if you have configured an analysis and only for the objects configured in the analysis.

In other words, you use the distribution of records independently of whether you have configured analyses in regards of other criteria. Compare the explanations about time-based data distribution in Section 9.6.1.

9.6.3 Archiving Information

If there are any archiving activities in the DVM landscape, the corresponding statistics are also displayed in the pre-configured dashboards of the ARCHIVING INFORMATION activity area. This information is thus available for landscape-wide technical reporting.

The following areas are available in the ARCHIVING INFORMATION activity area: ARCHIVING JOBS, ARCHIVING STATISTICS, and ARCHIVE FILE STATISTICS. They all provide information on involved systems and archiving objects.

9.6.4   Service Documents

The analysis options offered by the DATA VOLUME MANAGEMENT work center provide a variety of information on the DVM landscape. This approach has allowed you to gain or increase transparency of the structure of your data.

Logically, it would now be interesting to find answers to the following questions:

▸ What is the data used for?

▸ Which options are there to clean up the data?

This DVM process step is supported by SAP Solution Manager as well. The SERVICE DOCUMENTS activity area in the DATA VOLUME MANAGEMENT work center provides functionality that helps you answer these questions. Here, you can easily gather information on selected DVM objects without any profound background knowledge.

This task is executed with a so-called self-service. It comprises the automatic determination of the key archiving or deletion objects and, if possible, the calculation of saving potential for selected objects, based on available SAP best-practice residence times. The result is a best-practice document that includes all relevant background information on the selected objects, such as application/process assignment, business background, or involved tables. The relationship between the selected objects and involved and dependent tables is identified. All possible data reduction options (for avoiding, summarizing, archiving, or deleting) are shown.

Execution of a self-service is thus the logical step after a phase of gathering information and reporting. The two phases require close cooperation of those responsible in business operations and technical operations.

Now that we have introduced the possibilities of the individual activity areas, the next section shows you how Toys Inc. executes queries.

9.6.5   Query Execution at Toys Inc.

All queries in the STATISTICS AND TREND, POTENTIAL SAVINGS, and ARCHIVING INFORMATION activity areas (see also Figure 9.1) query the data collected in the business warehouse.

Queries can be executed only based on a technical scenario. In a technical scenario, one or multiple system(s) were grouped for data retrieval. That way, various perspectives on data can be developed. The IT team of Toys Inc. has already implemented this configuration requirement.

Select Technical Scenario

Prior to each query start, the IT expert decides from which perspective they want to view DVM-relevant data. The expert must therefore decide on a scenario type. The TYPE SELECTION in the left-hand menu helps them select one of the following scenarios.

Type Selection	Explanation
DVM scenarios	Pre-defined collection of (ABAP) systems
Technical scenarios	Free choice of systems
Technical systems	Free choice of systems

Table 9.4 Type Selection

After the expert has chosen a scenario, they can execute the query by specifying a query period and granularity of the data display.

Executing a Query

This is generally started via the DETAILED SELECTION area (see Figure 9.24).

All queries are based on BW tools and are handled similarly. In this book, the handling principle is explained with one example. For example, to start a query regarding the data volume, do the following:

1. In the DATA VOLUME MANAGEMENT work center, select the STATISTICS AND TREND area.

2. In the left-hand menu, under TYPE SELECTION, select the appropriate scenario type. Select DVM SCENARIOS.

   Based on this selection, available scenarios are displayed in the DETAILED SELECTION area (see Figure 9.24). Select an appropriate scenario. Check whether all your target systems are mentioned in the selected scenario (see Section 9.3.1). Make sure that the relevant line is marked before you continue.

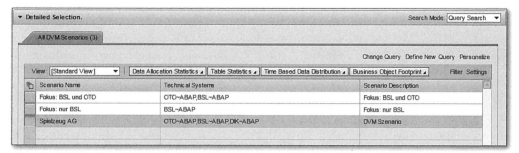

Figure 9.24 Scenario Selection in the Detailed Selection Area

3. Use the buttons above the table to perform the actual queries. All four options in Figure 9.24 were already described in the previous sections. For example, click the DATA ALLOCATION STATISTICS button. Decide how to open the next window. For each new query, you always need to decide whether the dashboards are to be displayed in the current window, i.e., imbedded in the work center, or in a new web browser window. This method should already be known from the other work centers.

4. Check and change the TIMEFRAME and the GRANULARITY of the report. Using the input help for the timeframe you can select, whether you wish to view the current or the previous week, month, or year. However, you can also define your own selection of time frames.

The display granularity can be defined using the WEEK, MONTH, and YEAR options.

5. Below the timeframe definition there are two selection levels:

▶ VIEW CLASSIFICATION
The view classification provides multiple possibilities of starting a query from a specific perspective.

▶ KEY FIGURES
Here, the dashboards are linked.

When the timeframe and granularity have been defined and the view classification and key figures are chosen, click the link CLICK HERE TO LOAD DATA FROM BUSINESS WAREHOUSE below the key figures in the (still) empty area.

Usually, however, you first need to select the access you consider useful from the upper tabs. Decide in which view you want the data to be displayed first.

Then specify the desired key figure in the tab row below, which is the actual dashboard.

In Figure 9.25, you can see that the BW data query was started from the SUM-MARY dashboard from PRODUCTS.

6. For almost every key figure, you can limit the result via a variable entry mask even before the actual BW query. Figure 9.25 shows this mask. Here, you can specify product names as query criteria, change the queried systems, or define the object size, for example. If you change the defined data in the variable fields, you should consider that the selection range is always based on the used scenario. It is not possible to enlarge the focus here.

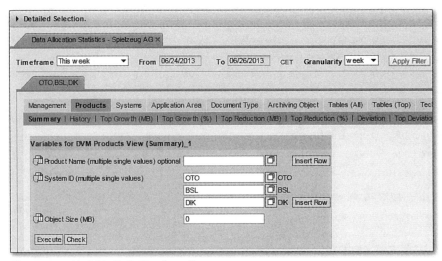

Figure 9.25 Variable Definition for a Query

7. Click the EXECUTE button to start the query or data retrieval from the business warehouse.

Note

Loading data from the business warehouse is a complex operation. Unclear specifications can result in time-consuming and performance-critical selections. In your queries, you should therefore make appropriate limitations!

All queries basically refer to the previously selected scenario, selected timeframe, and criteria stored in the variable definition. If you change the view timeframe and display granularity within a query, you need to set this filter again by clicking the top-right APPLY FILTER button.

You can execute multiple queries simultaneously and display them in corresponding windows. In order to open a new query next to an existing one, you need to open the DETAILED SELECTION, which is located above the queries.

Retrieving Query Results

When the runtime of the BW query is finished, a dashboard similar to that in Figure 9.26 is displayed. Which function blocks are displayed and how they are structured is pre-defined and varies from key figure to key figure. You can un-hide the individual function blocks by clicking the triangle to the left of the function blocks.

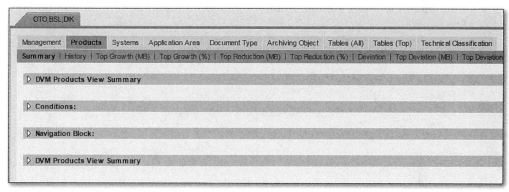

Figure 9.26 Handling a Dashboard (Web Template)

Usually, there are views that present the query data in a graphical and tabular way. Figure 9.27, for example, shows you the first block with the name DVM PRODUCTS VIEW SUMMARY. In this block, the database size of two systems is graphically presented in the form of a pie chart.

You could also have retrieved this information via the SUMMARY dashboard under SYSTEMS. However, because we left from PRODUCTS IN THIS EXAMPLE, we see the relevant product names.

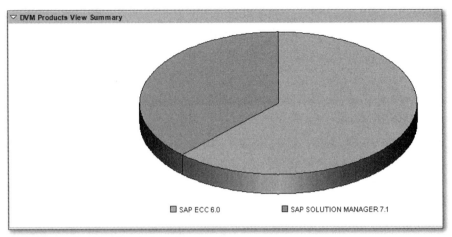

Figure 9.27 Graphical Result Overview

Figure 9.28 shows the lowest block named DVM PRODUCTS VIEW SUMMARY. This block displays the associated values in tabular form.

Product Name	Size (MB)
SAP ECC 6.0	279,292.125
SAP SOLUTION MANAGER 7.1	169,758.746
Overall Result	449,050.871

▽ DVM Products View Summary

Figure 9.28 Tabular Overview

The tabular view allows you to drill down to more data levels. This is a very important BW-typical basic function. Right-click a column. The range of options of the menu you see is determined by the pre-defined BW query (see Figure 9.29).

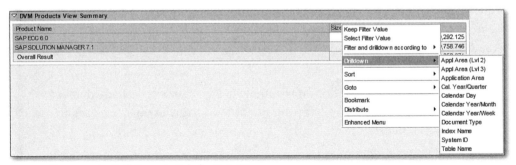

Figure 9.29 Drill Down in Tabular Data View

In the example, you could extend the display of product information by document types, times, table or index names, system IDs, etc.

To quickly change the view, each dashboard provides further BW-typical areas, such as the conditions or navigation block, which we cannot elaborate on at this point.

More Measures at Toys Inc.

During data analysis, it is determined that the BSEG table in the ERP system has grown significantly. The DATA VOLUME MANAGEMENT work center is used to collect information.

The data collected so far does not provide any clues about a time-based distribution of data in the table. Therefore, the decision is made to configure a table-specific analysis (TAANA).

The IT team receives the task to perform this analysis. The analysis is to be performed in the night, after any work day.

After the table analysis has been run once, data is available in the DATA VOLUME MANAGEMENT work center. Based on this data, conclusions can be drawn regarding reduction potential. The overall picture is completed by further, slightly changed table analysis (residence times) of the same table.

This forms the starting point for an archiving project. A self-service can be performed.

9.7   Additional Documentation

Links

▶ Recommendations for users of the DATA VOLUME MANAGEMENT work center:
http://wiki.sdn.sap.com/wiki/display/TechOps/DVM+Champion

▶ SAP Operation Support Standard SCN Wiki:
http://wiki.sdn.sap.com/wiki/display/TechOps/DVM_Home

SAP Notes

In connection with Data Volume Management, SAP Note 1233709 (DVM Cockpit—Central Preparation Note) may be useful.

The term "job management" stands for a wide range of requirements. In this chapter, we introduce the most important elements of job scheduling management and show you how to create your own concept.

10 Job Scheduling Management

Effective Job Scheduling Management (JSM) requires more than just performing jobs and waiting for them to stop. JSM is a key component of technical operations, and in the Run SAP like a Factory concept, it plays an important part. Furthermore, it is also part of introduction and start-up of business processes within Application Lifecycle Management (ALM). In this case, the introduction and starting-up of business processes is focused on. It can make sense, even in the blueprint and configuration phase of a project, to document planned jobs—i.e., collating relevant information and filing it in a reusable manner.

In this chapter, we'll stick to operational issues that are linked to JSM. First, we provide a summary of the individual components provided with SAP Solution Manager for JSM. Then, we will explain how to enter into the JSM scenario. The most comprehensive section focuses on the technical implementation of the individual functions, as well as their use. In this case, we will explain the Job Management work center and the management of job requests in greater detail.

10.1 Overview and Motivation

Experience in technical operations shows that high level of transparency in job management reduces expenditure for job management itself. Job management contains controlled scheduling and descheduling, automatic and landscape-wide job controlling, and monitoring and comprehensive documentation of jobs, among other things. It's essential that these functions are implemented for as many systems in the landscape and as centrally as possible. This means that there is a requirement for a central information and controlling platform, such as SAP Solution Manager. This is the technical platform for managing IT processes, especially for managing

JSM processes. Relevant fields of the application include scheduling and descheduling, documentation, and monitoring. A key advantage is that these functions can be implemented by means of an authorization concept.

The effectiveness of SAP Solution Manager as a central solution can be enhanced further by coupling the JSM scenario with an external scheduler. You can activate the software integrated in SAP NetWeaver called *SAP Central Process Scheduling by Redwood* (SAP CPS by Redwood) and link it with SAP Solution Manager (see Section 10.3.7). In principle, SAP Solution Manager can also be linked with other automation platforms; these must, however, be certified for use with the *SAP Solution Manager-Scheduling-Enabler* interface (SMSE).

As an application environment for JSM within SAP Solution Manager, *JSM-Suite* has become established. It supports the management requirements listed in Table 10.1 with tools (software) and functions that are provided within.

Challenges	Tools
Visibility/information store	Job documentation
Efficiency	SAP CPS by Redwood
Effectiveness	Monitoring/business process monitoring
Controlling/governance	Job request, redirection of job request (usually Re-direct or Job Control), interception of jobs (Job Interception)
Settling/clean-up	JSM Situation Check (usually JSM Health Check)

Table 10.1 Selected Elements of the JSM Suite

SAP Solution Manager ensures that the JSM scenario is properly integrated with other scenarios. Of particular importance is the possibility of integrating into IT Service Management (ITSM). This means that a link can be made to IT processes that are already established within your company and, for example, a job request process can be set up as a standardized process.

SAP has described the requirements for JSM in a document. Within this document, which can be found in the SAP Service Marketplace under the alias *supportstandards* and downloaded from the media library, you can find proven practical methods, tool descriptions, and notes on how to adapt the elements of JSM Suite to your own conditions.

This general explanation shows that the JSM should not be readily activated. In order to decide where processes can be optimized, the current situation should be thoroughly analyzed. As several people are involved in this process, analysis should be carried out as part of a project. In the following section, we will show you what should be taken into account during analysis.

10.2 Requirements for Job Scheduling Management

Before you start to implement the JSM scenario, an initial analysis should be carried out to ensure transparency. This enables to identify performance bottlenecks, peak loads, and disparities of load distribution, as well as other critical events. With this collated information, it is possible to assess the importance of these situations. Decisions can then be made on this basis.

10.2.1 Initial Analysis

The following questions should be answered in the course of initial analysis:

▶ Through whom or which users can jobs be scheduled, and in what manner? Is this an automatic or manual process?

▶ How many new jobs or changes are caused by whom on a daily or weekly basis?

▶ How many regular or irregular periodic jobs exist?

▶ Are there job chains—i.e., jobs that are dependent on each other?

▶ Where and when is there parallel processing?

▶ Which loads are generated by jobs that have become superfluous in the meantime? How many of these jobs exist? How can I find them?

▶ How do I clear up jobs from members of staff who have left the company?

▶ Which jobs generate errors? What are errors? How and how quickly are these errors recognized?

▶ Where is information regarding jobs available?

▶ Are there time frames, such as a period-end closing, planned maintenance, etc., that must be treated separately?

▶ Who is responsible for JSM?

These questions must be answered by those who are responsible for operations. When this analysis is carried out, the *JSM Health Check* is a very useful support tool, and it will be introduced in greater detail in Section 10.3.4. As the purpose of a job cannot always determined at an operative level, those responsible at application level (for example, business processes owners), must also be included in the analysis process. It is especially important to determine the importance of a job for business operations and to subsequently determine how much attention should be paid to the respective job, or whether it is necessary to make operating instructions available or to develop them in a document, for instance.

10.2.2 Analysis of Occurred Problems

Analyzing problems that have arisen is always an important aspect of JSM so that potential for improvements can be found. The analysis must be carried out from a technical point of view, as well as from a business point of view.

When an error occurs, it's important to estimate its relevance to the business process. For this reason, everyone responsible for business processes within the company and within IT should be fully aware of all processes within. Otherwise, monitoring is pointless if reaction is not in good time or not optimal in the case of an error. The better the process is organized, the more efficient the error analysis becomes.

The following questions help when carrying out error analysis:

▶ Was the monitoring concept complete, or were there potential gaps?

▶ Was the job sufficiently documented, as well as all relevant operating procedures? What scope and content should be included in suitable job documentation?

▶ Which calendars were used? Were they all synchronized?

▶ Was the error management sufficiently defined?

▶ Could naming conventions for jobs have prevented the problem?

10.2.3 Creating User Types and Assigning Roles

Within JSM, keep in mind that tasks are carried out by different people and teams with differing responsibilities. Applications should therefore offer the corresponding support. Users should have access to only the tools they require for their work. For this reason, you should deliberate over an authorization concept in good time.

Define template users for various tasks or responsibilities in accordance with your requirements, such as requester, process owners, technical administrators (responsible for scheduling and monitoring), and staff responsible for reporting. More information on user administration can be found in Chapter 12.

When introducing or enhancing an authorization concept, be sure to read the explanations in *Security Guide for SAP Solution Manager 7.1*. This document can be downloaded from the SAP Service Marketplace using the alias *instguides*. All important information for the JSM scenario can be found in the JOB MANAGEMENT and EXTERNAL INTEGRATION sections.

Within the JSM scenario, there are three basic types of users, which have certain authorizations, i.e., roles, which are assigned to them:

- **Technical users**
  Technical users are users who are in RFC connections within SAP systems or stored in objects in SAP CPS by Redwood.

- **Configuration users**
  For complete activation of all options, a configuration user in different systems and applications or clients is required. Extensive authorizations have the effect of simplifying matters; they often save time-consuming authorization analyses during the configuration process.
  Also note that, depending on the project situation, it may be necessary to carry out activities in SAP CPS by Redwood (see Section 10.3), such as authorization assignments within the user administration (SAP User Management Engine [UME]) of SAP Solution Manager.

- **Scenario users (scheduling user)**
  Scenario users are the actual end users or members of the central JSM team who, for example, would like to use SAP Solution Manager to schedule jobs.

For scenario users, three types of users are defined in the Security Guide for SAP Solution Manager 7.1, namely the *administrator*, who is allowed to carry out corresponding configuration tasks alongside JSM-relevant activities; the *operational user*, who carries out all JSM-related tasks; and the *viewer*, who has only display authorizations in the JSM scenario. Prepared composite roles are used for the assignment of authorizations (see Table 10.2).

Scenario Users	Composite Roles Used
Administrator	SAP_JOBMAN_ALL_COMP (contains SAP_SM_SCHEDULER_ADMIN)
Operational user	SAP_JOBMAN_EXE_COMP (contains SAP_SM_SCHEDULER_EXE)
Viewer	SAP_JOBMAN_DIS_COMP (contains SAP_SM_SCHEDULER_DIS)

Table 10.2 Standard Scenario Users According to the Security Guide

Also note the explanations regarding the work center headings TYPICAL TASKS and RELATED LINKS. Also, follow our recommendations in Section 12.3.3 and copy roles into individual name spaces before changing them.

A few functions within the JSM scenario, such as requesting a job, require the assigning of a *business partner* to the scenario users. This is necessary because several functions based on SAP Customer Relationship Management (CRM) objects are implemented within SAP Solution Manager. An example of this is the job request form, which is explained in greater detail in Section 10.3.8.

You maintain business partners in SAP Solution Manager using Transaction BP. You can search for business partners based on different information (e.g., addresses, names, etc.). You select the business partner you are looking for from a list by double-clicking it. It is sufficient for the JSM scenario when, in the two roles for the business partner, GENERAL BUSINESS PARTNER and EMPLOYEE, the respective IDENTIFICATION tab has been configured, as shown in Figure 10.1 and Figure 10.2.

Each entry in the IDENTIFICATION NUMBER column is composed of a system ID (in the example, BSL), the associated installation number, a client entry, and a user present in this client. Further entries can be manually added in this view, if required. To do so, you must be in change mode. Using the help function in the IDTYPE column, choose the value CRM001. Then, enter a term into the IDENTIFICATION NUMBER column with the same syntax as described and save it.

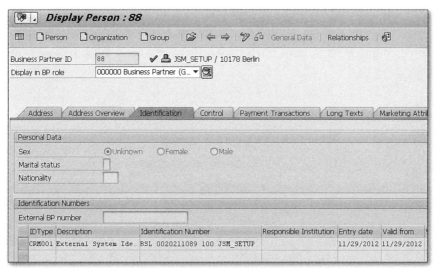

Figure 10.1 Business Partners—General Role for Business Partners

Figure 10.2 shows the definition that must be set for the role EMPLOYEE.

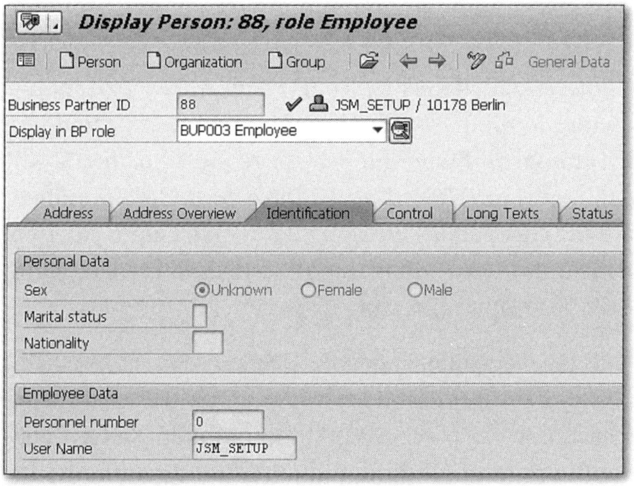

Figure 10.2 Business Partners—Employee Role

The only important thing here is the entry in the USER NAME field. In this example, you can see that business partner 88 is assigned to the user JSM_SETUP.

Both role settings allow the scenario user JSM_SETUP in SAP Solution Manager to generate job requests for the BSL system. The sphere of action for the JSM_SETUP user can be complemented with further identification numbers in the GENERAL BUSINESS PARTNER role, as described.

10.2.4 Technical Requirements

Activation of the JSM scenario in SAP Solution Manager requires that several preparatory be successfully carried out beforehand.

Ensure that the SYSTEM PREPARATION and BASIC CONFIGURATION steps have been successfully carried out via Transaction SOLMAN_SETUP. Furthermore, within the MANAGED SYSTEMS CONFIGURATION stage, all SAP systems that play a part in terms of JSM—for example, if jobs within these systems are requested by means of a central procedure—should be linked.

ITSM must be integrated in at least one of the two versions, as follows, so that the JSM scenario can be integrated with ITSM:

▶ Incident, problem, and request management

▶ Change Request Management

What's selected here depends on your ITSM concept. From a JSM standpoint, it's important to clarify whether job requests in the SAP Service Desk should be handled based on the SMIN transaction type (for service requests) or the SMCR transaction type (for change requests). Naturally, it is also possible to combine both variants. This means that a concept must be thought out first, before you start with the technical setup. Initialization and configuration of ITSM is carried out by Transaction SOLMAN_SETUP in a step of the same name.

For some functions, such as task management and template management, you need to activate JSM-relevant services in SAP Solution Manager. This is best done using Transaction SPRO. In this case, follow the path SAP SOLUTION MANAGER • CAPABILITIES (OPTIONAL) • JOB SCHEDULING MANAGEMENT • STANDARD CONFIGURATION • ACTIVATE SOLUTION MANAGER SERVICES.

10.2.5 Roadmap as an Integration Guide

A project for integrating JSM does not only require technical implementation, but also makes demands of those in management. For example, think of adjusting job scheduling from an individual user approach to a central JSM team approach. For such a change, it is necessary to convince the users affected to follow altered processes and make the required technical tools available to them. At the same time, the JSM team must be able to deal with job requests, use new tools, and schedule jobs within the framework of a concept. SAP Solution Manager supports you on the way from defining objectives through implementation up to starting up with the JSM scenario with the roadmap *ESRV RSLaF Business Proc. Oper. (V2.0)*.

Roadmaps can assign you to a project and work with its content. Also consider the explanations in Chapter 3. With Transaction RMMAIN, you can also look at roadmaps without being assigned to the project. Some of the documents contained in the roadmap can be found in SAP Service Marketplace under the alias *jsm* • Roadmap Documents • Realization/Implementation.

10.3 Setting Up and Using Components of the JSM Suite

The JSM suite comprises several applications in order to fulfill all requirements in a modern JSM environment. Several of these applications can be used independently, and others can be used only in conjunction with other applications.

Depending on which applications are required, there are different entry points into implementation. In a simple case, just the assignment of roles suffices to activate functions. Other applications require a greater expenditure of time and effort to implement and may require implementation via a project. In order to decide which applications are required, you must first find out where the need for action is greatest. The questions in Section 10.2.1 and Section 10.2.2 help during analysis.

Table 10.3 gives a summary of the components of the JSM suite. Furthermore, it states whether applications require much implementation effort and whether certain requirements need to be satisfied for implementation to take place. The entries in the Estimated Integration Time column are based on experience. They should serve as a guide to plan how much time should be calculated for implementing individual applications and how much the typical cost of integration of the respective application with other scenarios in SAP Solution Manager can be. The costs for the purely technical aspects of integration are also included in the entry. However, it is assumed that the necessary preparations have been carried out from a procedural viewpoint—for example, that ITSM is already used with SAP Solution Manager.

When you wish to get started within the field of JSM but have not yet defined individual integration steps, we recommend that you adhere to the sequence shown for the implementation of the JSM scenario (from top to bottom in Table 10.3). This way, some degree of optimization for JSM can be achieved quickly.

Because the individual applications can be implemented in almost any order, you may proceed in other ways. Depending on the results of the initial analysis (see Section 10.2.1), you could, for example, first use the JSM Health Check to improve transparency or optimize the job request process.

Application	Implementation Necessary?/Requirements	Estimated Integration Time
Job overview (Transaction SM37)	No, it is in the SAP system as standard.	–
Report BACKGROUND_JOB_ANALYSIS in Transaction ST13	No, it is in the SAP system as standard.	–
JOB MANAGEMENT work center including the central job overview	Yes	< 1 day
JSM Situation Check (usually JSM Health Check)	Yes/ JOB MANAGEMENT work center must be implemented.	~ 1 day
Job documentation, with a job template as an option	Yes	< 1 day
Business process monitoring	Yes	~ 1 week
BPMon Alert Reporting Analysis	Yes/Business process monitoring must be implemented.	~ 1 day
SAP CPS by Redwood	Yes	> 1 month
Job request/redirection of job request (usually re-direct or job control)	Yes	> 1 month
ITSM integration	Yes	> 1 month
Intercepting jobs (Job Interception)	Yes/External scheduler is required.	~ 1 week

Table 10.3 Overview of the Components in the JSM Suite

The individual components will now be illustrated in detail, and what must be taken into consideration during implementation will also be clarified at this point. Please note that a configuration user is required for implementing individual applications (see Section 10.2.3).

Integration of the JSM scenario should certainly be considered as a project. In this case, you can use the *ESRV RSLaF Business Proc. Oper. (V2.0)* roadmap as a guide.

Before you start off with the first integration steps, it is necessary to clearly define the functional scope of the planned JSM scenario. For this reason, it is important to know the current situation and establish corresponding targets. Depending on the circumstances, there are different entry points into integration. Alongside the questions from Section 10.2.1, the following questions may also be helpful when planning:

▶ Which processes should be supported (for example, the job request process, ITSM, job monitoring, or error management)?

▶ Which other challenges remain? (For example, should the job documentation be supplemented and centralized?)

▶ How should the responsibilities be distributed?

▶ Which team or users are involved, and what expectations do they have?

It is possible to begin with the integration of the JSM scenario in several different ways. Configurations must be carried out in the following areas, depending on the project situation:

▶ SAP Solution Manager: ABAP client, SAP NetWeaver BW client, UME, and SAP CRM user interface

▶ SAP CPS by Redwood

▶ Managed system(s)

In order for you to carry out the activation steps, a configuration user is required (see Section 10.2.3).

10.3.1 Job Overview

The job overview can be called up in every SAP system via Transaction SM37. The job overview provides a summary of job executions and relevant data, such as the status, user, and job log. Normally, such data is available only for a limited period of time before it is deleted by a reorganization job.

When the data is required for longer for reporting purposes or evaluations, the JSM Health Check can be used. Initialization of the JSM Health Check is explained in Section 10.3.4.

10.3.2 Report BACKGROUND_JOB_ANALYSIS

The BACKGROUND_JOB_ANALYSIS report can be called up in every SAP system via Transaction ST13. It links job execution data (Transaction SM37) with performance data from the SAP system (Transaction ST06). The maximum observation period is 24 hours.

This application is helpful in decision making. For example, the report can help you decide whether it makes sense from a performance perspective to schedule a new job in an advised time frame or whether the anticipated load has reached the possible load limit in this time frame.

10.3.3 Job Management Work Center

The central element in the JSM suite is the JOB MANAGEMENT work center. It makes all components available for job management in SAP Solution Manager. From here, you can navigate to the managed systems. Therefore, it makes the ideal work area for the technical administrator responsible for the scheduling and monitoring of jobs.

The availability of job-relevant information is a key advantage during the implementation phase, as well as in subsequent day-to-day operations. We therefore recommend that the JOB MANAGEMENT work center is activated first. The job documentation is made available in this manner at the same time.

Activating the Job Management Work Center

Each work center is made visible for individual users by means of the assignment of roles. JSM-relevant roles can be found using Transaction PFCG and the following search terms:

▶ *SAP_SMWORK_BASIC*

▶ *SAP_SMWORK_JOB*

▶ *JOBMAN*

Table 10.4 shows which roles are available in SAP Solution Manager and the authorizations that are linked to it.

Role	Authorizations
SAP_SMWORK_ BASIC_JSCHED (Single role)	The user can display the menu of the work center and has access to TYPICAL TASKS and RELATED LINKS. For this purpose, the role must be issued in conjunction with the SAP_SMWORK_JOB_MAN role.
SAP_SMWORK_JOB_MAN (Single role)	The user can display the menu of the work center and has access to TYPICAL TASKS and RELATED LINKS. For this purpose, the role must be issued in conjunction with the SAP_SMWORK_BASIC_JSCHED role.
SAP_SMWORK_JOBMAN_COMP (Composite role)	Example role for the job manager (full authorization)
SAP_JOBMAN_ALL_COMP (Composite role)	▶ Access to the JOB MANAGEMENT work center ▶ Carrying out all functions for job management ▶ Carrying out all applications relevant for BW ▶ Working in the administration view
SAP_JOBMAN_EXE_COMP (Composite role)	▶ Access to the JOB MANAGEMENT work center ▶ Carrying out all functions for job management ▶ Carrying out all applications relevant for BW
SAP_JOBMAN_DIS_COMP (Composite role)	▶ Access to the JOB MANAGEMENT work center ▶ View of all functions for job management

Table 10.4 Roles for Job Management

For the activation of the JOB MANAGEMENT work center, both the SAP_SMWORK_ BASIC_JSCHED and SAP_SMWORK_JOB_MAN single roles are of key importance. These are contained—alongside others—in the named composite roles. Detailed explanations of these roles can be found in the security guide of SAP Solution Manager under SAP HELP PORTAL • APPLICATION LIFECYCLE MANAGEMENT • SAP SOLUTION MANAGER • SAP SOLUTION MANAGER 7.1 • SECURITY INFORMATION.

> **Note**
>
> Assignment of these roles automatically provides other applications, such as job documentation with the ability to use templates the central job overview, and job request, accessible.
>
> For use of the central job overview, the user must also be assigned to a business partner. You can find out how to do this in Section 10.2.3.

Construction and Use of the Job Management Work Center

The JOB MANAGEMENT work center follows the typical design of a work center. Several activity areas, including JOB REQUESTS, JOB DOCUMENTATION, and JOB MONITORING (see Figure 10.3), can be found in the left-hand menu.

The area of JOB DOCUMENTATION is especially important. All job documentation can be found in a tabular overview, and individual documentation can be called up from there. This area thus serves as the central information basis. More information regarding job documentation can be found in Section 10.3.5.

Furthermore, you can find a collection of links that can be used to start or complete JSM-relevant tasks in the menu, under TYPICAL TASKS and RELATED LINKS. This also applies to generating new job requests or job documentations, which will also be described in the course of this chapter. In addition, you can find tools for the following:

▶ Carrying out evaluations of job requests and the assigned SAP CRM documents, as well as job documentations

  ▶ In this case, filter masks are used in which, for example, information regarding solutions, process data, logical components, organization data, times, etc., can be used for the search.

  ▶ With these, it is possible to find duplicate objects and ensure that it does not happen again within your JSM process, for example.

▶ The technical analysis (for example, the `BACKGROUND_JOB_ANALYSIS` report, the ABAP runtime error monitor [Transaction ST22], etc.)

▶ Importing jobs, so that job documentation can be generated

  ▶ This tool is based on Guided Procedures technology. As a result, it is relatively simple to transfer information about jobs or groups of jobs to SAP Solution Manager, especially job documentation.

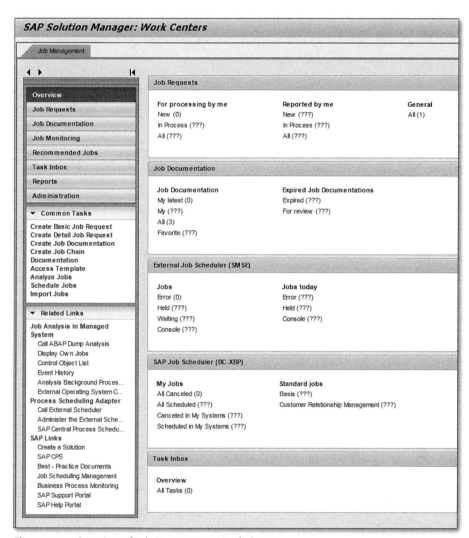

Figure 10.3 Overview of Job Management Work Center

▶ Generally, you can import from two sources: the managed system and SAP CPS by Redwood.

▶ Creating and changing solutions, including the configuration and starting operation of business process monitoring

Depending on the activity type, execution takes place in SAP Solution Manager or in the respective system that is being administered. These components are Web

Dynpro objects and can be called up via a URL. This URL can also be used outside SAP Solution Manager, so it is possible to integrate these applications into your own web interface, such as an intranet and a portal.

Queries and categories can be individually configured in the individual areas of each work center. This means that the work center is extremely flexible and can be configured to display precisely the information you really need.

Before touching upon the individual components within the JSM suite, we wish to point out another important aspect you can usually work within every work center.

Set Up a New Personal Object Worklist Request in the Work Center

With the aid of Personal Object Worklists (POWL), a selected amount of information can be displayed at an appropriate point within the work center.

When drawing up new queries, the work center offers support with the use of Guided Procedures. You start via the DEFINE NEW REQUEST link in the top right-hand corner. Proceed as follows:

1. Decide whether you wish to define the query anew or to base it on an existing query.

2. Define the query criteria (see Figure 10.4 as an example for setting up a query within the area of JOB MONITORING). In this case, for example, it deals with selection criteria, such as the job name, project, or job number (job count).

   In this example, the SYSTEM CATEGORY is an important criterion. The type of system from which information should be displayed is established in this field. You can choose from the options MANUAL, PROJECT, SOLUTION, and IBASE.

3. Before saving the query, it should be tested. Click the PREVIEW button underneath the input fields.

4. When the expected result is visible, add a name in the ENTER QUERY DESCRIPTION field for the query and assign the query to a present category or to a category that is yet to be defined.

Please note that the loading process may take some time. The vaguer the request is, the more data has to be read, which means that the results will take longer to find.

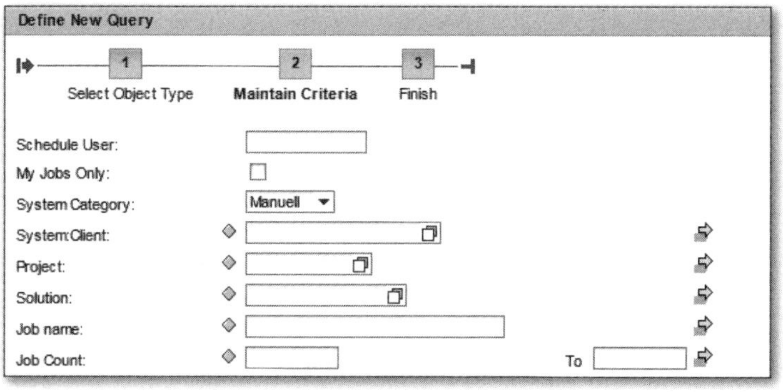

Figure 10.4 Definition of POWL Requests

Central Job Overview

One interesting function is the central job overview. When you are in the JOB MONITORING activity area under JOB MONITORING VIEWS, selecting the SAP JOB SCHEDULER (BC-XBP) OPTION makes the job execution information from the managed systems available in the JOB MANAGEMENT work center (see Figure 10.5). The same data is seen here as would be seen in the related managed system with the job overview (Transaction SM37). The advantage of a central job overview is that there is no need to log on to each individual machine to obtain the necessary data, but everything can be monitored centrally from the work center.

Various pre-configured queries in various categories are available depending on the authorizations that have been assigned. In Figure 10.5 you can see the two categories MY JOBS and STANDARD JOBS within the area of ACTIVE QUERIES.

The result of the specially configured query SLCA_LCK - Jobs is displayed here, and the SLCA_LCK_SYNCHOWNERS job, which was scheduled by user DIETZELE in the BSL system, is continuously interrupted. All information regarding the job execution that is highlighted can be found in the lower area, DETAILED SCHEDULE OF JOB. Now, you can select the JOB LOG tab to obtain information about the cause of the error.

Along with SAP JOB SCHEDULER (BC-XBP), there are two further JOB MONITORING VIEWS available:

▶ ALERT INBOX
In the ALERT INBOX view, you can find all alerts from the configured job monitoring. More information about this function can be found in Section 10.3.6.

▶ EXTERNAL JOB SCHEDULER (SMSE)
In the EXTERNAL JOB SCHEDULER (SMSE) view, alerts sent by SAP CPS by Red-wood to SAP Solution Manager are displayed, provided that this is configured.

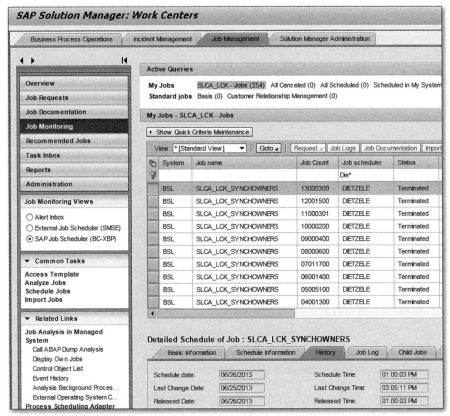

Figure 10.5 Central Job Overview in the Job Management Work Center

10.3.4 JSM Health Check

The JSM Health Check is an important instrument in ensuring transparency. The present and historic job execution situation can be evaluated with the JSM Health Check. Next, we will show you how to initialize the JSM Health Check.

Initialization of the JSM Health Check

In general, the following activities need to be carried out so that the JSM Health Check function can be initialized:

▶ **Activating BI objects**
In this step, the necessary queries and InfoCubes are activated.

▶ **Activating extractors**
In this step, the extractors in the extractor framework (EFWK), which are required for the JSM Health Check, are activated.

▶ **Maintenance of settings for data aggregation in the SAP NetWeaver BW system**
Data aggregation is a mechanism for controlling the growth of data, and it is used to compress detailed information about daily job executions into a weekly or monthly view. The corresponding time frames can be freely chosen.

▶ **Managing the reports in the Job Management work center**
For each of the three report groups—*Daily Jobs*, *Weekly Jobs,* and *Monthly Jobs*— it is defined whether information should be shown on a job or on a job-step level.

Note that after initialization, it is only possible to check in the daily overview whether data is displayed in the reports. Data is visible in the other two reports (weekly and monthly overview) only after data aggregation process within SAP NetWeaver BW has taken place.

▶ **Checking the settings for clients and user authorizations**
Without these settings, activation cannot take place.

▶ **Checking the activation of relevant services**
During this stage, the system checks whether all services required to use reports are activated.

The necessary steps can be carried out in a relatively straightforward manner with the help of the *Setup Guide: Job Scheduling Management Health Check* document. The document is available in the SAP Service Marketplace under the alias *jsm* in the Media Library.

Use of JSM Health Checks

The JSM Health Check is an independent BW-based application that, exactly like the central job overview and Transaction SM37, displays job execution data. This data was transferred over to the SAP NetWeaver BW system previously and is thus available for a long period of time. Therefore, it is possible to use typical BW means to analyze the data. On this basis, the JSM Health Check is especially useful for ad-hoc trend analysis. Jobs can be identified by means of pre-configured BW reports as follows:

- With the longest runtime
- That is carried out and/or are cut off frequently
- With the longest start delays

In addition, information is also given about the application server on which the jobs are carried out and users that scheduled and carry out the jobs.

Based on this information, it is simple to find problems and introduce measures for optimization. The JSM Health Check is therefore a good method to increase transparency regarding job execution in the considered SAP system landscape.

For the three different views of SAP NetWeaver BW reports (daily, weekly, and monthly summary), you can define whether you want only information relevant to the job, or also information about the job steps. This decision should be made during activation of the JSM Health Check component.

The reports can be found, as described in Figure 10.6, in the JOB MANAGEMENT work center within the REPORTS activity area. Select the option BW REPORTS in the radio button field and you will see all available reports on the right-hand side.

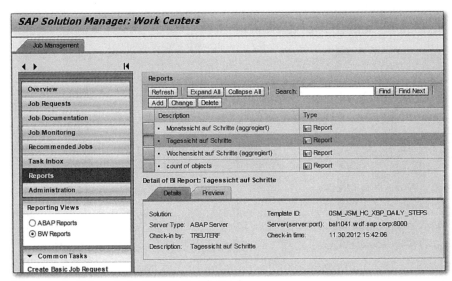

Figure 10.6 BI Reports for the JSM Health Check

To call up a report, click one of the links on the right-hand side, next to the description. In the following input mask, a system must be chosen, and a time frame must be established.

Toys Inc.

Toys Inc. is active worldwide, with many branches scattered all over the world. The business processes are carried out on several SAP systems.

The job scheduling team, which is split over different time zones, has established that frequently, but not regularly, problems appear during job execution, which has a significant effect on business operations. The situation check revealed that especially the jobs scheduled for close of business in Asia have a strong effect on resources in Germany.

As JSM is of great importance to business, the virtual JSM team decided to get an overview of the whole situation and centralize the documentation of jobs. Also the possibilities for centrally manage requesting of new jobs should be checked to increase the efficiency of JSM. The JSM team at Toys Inc. also gives great importance on a central application for job control, i.e., an external scheduler.

It is decided that transparency of the job execution situation should be improved at first by using the JSM Health Check. Above all, JSM Health Check also provides data about the users who schedule such jobs.

In addition, the JSM team has realized that in the case of a few jobs, there is no information available on how to react to errors. For this reason, the documentation of jobs in general should be optimized. To make such information generally available to all, all information should be stored in SAP Solution Manager.

10.3.5 Create Job Documentation

Job documentation can be found in the JOB MANAGEMENT work center in an activity area of the same name. This activity area is the central information basis and, hence, an extremely important central function. Access to all job documentation is available here (see Figure 10.7).

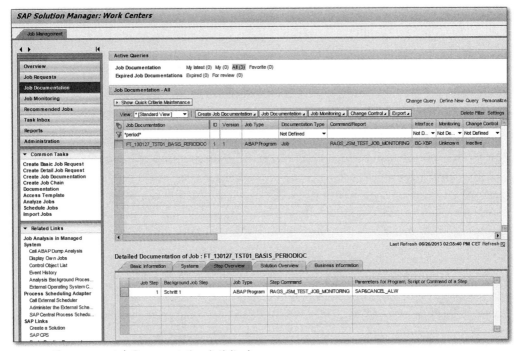

Figure 10.7 Job Documentation Activity Area

The JOB DOCUMENTATION activity area is constructed in a tabular format. The work center offers many options for structuring the data view, such as queries, views, and filters.

Job documentation can be drawn up in several different ways:

▶ Manually, in the JOB MANAGEMENT work center

▶ Via the SAP CRM user interface

▶ By importing a job

▶ By assigning to a business process as an object in the blueprint project phase

▶ By using a template (see the subsection "Create Job Documentation based on a Template")

▶ By copying existing job documentation

Job documentation contains several tabs, on which available information relevant to a job can be stored and organized (see Figure 10.8).

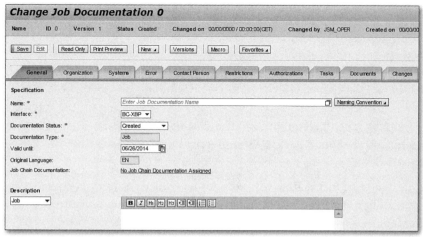

Figure 10.8 Job Documentation

Create Job Documentation Manually

When you manually create a job documentation, the initial state is displayed as CHANGE JOB DOCUMENTATION 0. As soon as you save the documentation by clicking on the SAVE BUTTON for the first time, the first currently free ID is assigned to it and displayed.

Along with (simple) job documentation shown in Figure 10.8, there is also job chain documentation. The difference is the additional JOB CHAIN STRUCTURE tab, which is for documentation of a job chain structure.

In the following section, we will provide you with a brief overview of the different tabs of job documentation:

▶ GENERAL
This defines the name under which the job documentation is kept, as well as further general aspects such as the interface, status, and job step information, which can be displayed as detailed information underneath the overview in the work center. The interface determines whether jobs were scheduled directly into SAP system or via SAP CPS by Redwood (see Section 10.3.7).

▶ JOB CHAIN STRUCTURE
This tab is available only when job chain documentation has been created. The sequence of consecutive and parallel steps in a job chain can be documented here.

▶ ORGANIZATION
Organizational assignments and business information is stored here.

▶ SYSTEMS
The assignment of jobs to systems, as well as solutions and processes, are defined here. Jobs and job chains, which can be carried out on SAP CPS by Redwood or directly in the SAP system via Transaction SM36, depending on the interface chosen, can be scheduled on this tab. The starting point for activating job monitoring can also be found here. This is covered in Section 10.3.6.

▶ ERROR
Store the operating instructions for execution activities—restart, abort, continue, and repeat—here. You can also document contact partners with relevant contact information.

▶ CONTACT PARTNERS
Contact partners from the business area are defined here.

▶ LIMITATIONS
Define constraints here.

▶ AUTHORIZATIONS
Authorization objects necessary for execute a job should be noted here.

▶ TASKS
Define tasks that are linked to job execution.

▶ DOCUMENTS
External documents can be uploaded, and links can be defined here.

▶ CHANGES
This tab lists all SAP CRM documents relevant for job documentation and also states their link to ITSM.

As you can see, job documentation can be used to store technical information, as well as information relevant to business operations. Job documentation should be filled out as completely as possible so that, in case of error, all required information is available at a central site.

> **Note**
>
> When you schedule jobs from the job documentation, the respective job executions are automatically linked to that job documentation in Transaction SM37 or SAP CPS by Redwood (full version) so that all information is available right away in the current version.

Create Job Documentation based on a Template

It is also possible to generate job documentation based on a template. Templates are used when it is necessary to generate job documentation relatively quickly. SAP Solution Manager comes with a range of templates. These refer to SAP standard jobs, and some technical information is pre-defined within them. Such information includes the report name, the recommended execution period, and a calendar reference. It is also possible to create your own templates so that it becomes even easier to create job documentation in the future.

If you would like to use a template to create job documentation, access the JOB DOCUMENTATION activity area and click the CREATE JOB DOCUMENTATION button, and then select the TEMPLATE option (see Figure 10.7). This initiates a guided procedure in which the procedure for further steps must first be set, and then a template is chosen. Figure 10.9 shows the entry screen of this process.

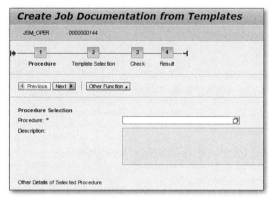

Figure 10.9 Creating Job Documentation based on a Template

In the PROCEDURE field, it is defined which actions can be carried out in conjunction with drawing up the job documentation. For example, it may be possible to assign *logical components* or business process steps, or the immediate scheduling of the job concerned.

If you would like to work on a template, click the ACCESS TEMPLATE link in the left-hand side menu in JOB MANAGEMENT work center (Figure 10.7). This opens the TEMPLATE DIRECTORY, which you can see in Figure 10.10.

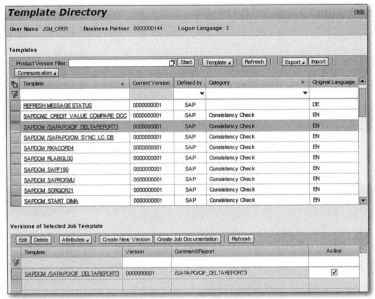

Figure 10.10 Template Directory for Template Management

To limit the list of desired templates, use the PRODUCT VERSION FILTER. This option is especially useful in larger production environments because they prevent templates that are irrelevant to your target product from being shown.

10.3.6 Business Process Monitoring Alert Reporting Analysis

With the business process monitoring function, it is possible to implement a company-wide concept to promptly recognize and resolve errors and critical situations in business processes. BPMon Alert Reporting Analysis is an SAP NetWeaver BW-based tool for trend analysis regarding business process monitoring.

Business process monitoring in SAP Solution Manager is a function for monitoring extremely diverse indicators that are directly linked to business processes. In addition to monitoring, the aim of this function is to implement a concept that deals with error handling and notifications. There are several monitors that can monitor business processes in SAP and non-SAP systems.

Monitors that can be used across applications or are application-specific are available. Application-specific monitors monitor business indicators, such as the throughput or *backlog* (accumulation due to no processing) of certain business process objects.

Cross-application monitors generally monitor technical indicators that (could) affect all business processes, such as ABAP errors and errors in RFC connections. The background job monitor also belongs to this group of monitors. An overview of monitors that are currently available can be found in the SAP Service Marketplace under the alias *bpm*.

Generally, business process monitoring with SAP Solution Manager requires a definition of *solutions*. On one hand, solutions contain business process definitions as a reflection of operational activities. On the other hand, they also contain *logical components*, which establish the technical systems on which the execution of business processes is based.

As a purely pragmatic approach, a process with one step per system, for example, could be used so that monitors can be used from a wide range of business process monitoring options. This does mean that direct assignment of indicators to operational processes is lost.

The relevant work center for business process monitoring is principally the Business Process Operations work center. All necessary configuration work can be started here. Only the set up of solutions must be carried out in the Solution Manager Administration work center.

Also, the alerts are principally displayed in the Business Process Operations work center. Specific alerts regarding job monitoring can also be seen in the Job Management work center. For this purpose, in the Job Monitoring activity area, select the Alert Inbox option in the Job Monitoring Views radio button (see Figure 10.11).

These alerts can be transferred to the BW system of SAP Solution Manager (BPMon Alert Reporting Analysis function). They are therefore available for ad-hoc trend analysis and reporting, and also for service level reporting.

> **Note**
>
> To use the monitoring opportunities within SAP Solution Manager for a job as fully as possible, a job documentation from which monitoring can be activated is required in SAP Solution Manager. You can find out how to create job documentation in Section 10.3.5.

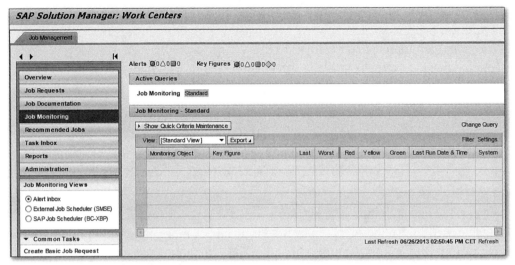

Figure 10.11 Alert Inbox Job Monitoring View

The implementation of business process monitoring—and, if you require alert information for longer periods of time, also from BPMon alert reporting analysis—is a complex topic only indirectly linked with technical operations. In this book, we can give only a rough summary in Section 11.1.4.

You can find more information in SAP Service Marketplace under the alias *bpm*. Instructions for implementation can be found in the Media Library under TECHNICAL INFORMATION. Also, consider SAP Note 521820, regarding potentially necessary software corrections, and SAP Note 784752, regarding the necessary infrastructure.

10.3.7 SAP CPS by Redwood

One important objective of JSM is the centralization of job scheduling, job execution, and job monitoring. For this reason, JSM should be implemented across the entire company and on all technical platforms.

The direct job control function is not directly covered by SAP Solution Manager. For this purpose, the *Cronacle* software from Redwood is integrated in SAP NetWeaver. It is delivered with this as SAP CPS by Redwood. The following outlines why it makes sense to use an external scheduler. Afterward, we will show you how to set up SAP CPS by Redwood.

Using SAP CPS by Redwood

SAP CPS by Redwood is a solution for central, group-wide job scheduling, execution, and monitoring. The term *job* can mean individual jobs, as well as extremely complex job chains; so, within the industry, it is referred to as *process automation*. SAP CPS by Redwood is integrated as software in SAP NetWeaver and requires a license before you can start operations. There are two licensed versions, and full functionality is available in only the fully-licensed version.

The connection between SAP CPS by Redwood and the SAP Solution Manager is an essential enhancement and offers the following advantages:

▶ Scheduling jobs is possible from SAP Solution Manager centrally for all systems. Monitoring and controlling these jobs is taken over by SAP CPS by Redwood.

▶ Monitoring information (alerts) can be sent to the SAP Solution Manager by SAP CPS by Redwood, provided that different monitoring information (central job overview and job monitoring with business process monitoring) is available centrally at a location in the JOB MANAGEMENT work center.

▶ Cross-application functions and applications, such as the interception of jobs (Job Interception) and the *SAP Financial Closing Cockpit*, which is an application for the automation of period-end closings, are supported.

▶ The scheduling of jobs in heterogeneous (SAP and non-SAP) system landscapes is possible.

Setting Up SAP CPS by Redwood

SAP CPS by Redwood is a piece of Java software. It is recommended that the current version be used with the most recent patches. At the time of printing this book, the current version is version 8.0 SP33. The newest version can be found in SAP Service Marketplace under the alias *swdc*. Follow the path SUPPORT PACKAGES AND PATCHES • BROWSE OUR DOWNLOAD CATALOG • SAP TECHNOLOGY COMPONENTS • SAP SOLUTION MANAGER • SAP SOLUTION MANAGER 7.1 • ENTRY BY COMPONENT • SOLUTION MANAGER JAVA STACK • SAP CPS BY REDWOOD 8.0.

For operations, it is generally recommended that you run SAP CPS by Redwood on a dedicated server. In the context of constructing a test landscape, it can also be run on the same system as SAP Solution Manager.

A license is required for initialization. Two license versions are available: basic or full license. The license determines the usable range of functions, which is limited in the basic version. You can apply for the required license key via the SAP CPS by Redwood license manager. Call up the URL *http://<server>:<port>/scheduler/ui* and try to register. On the first call-up, (if no license is available), a window with two buttons that can be used to activate either the basic license (ACTIVATE FREE OF CHARGE LICENSE button) or a full license (REQUEST KEY FOR ENTERPRISE LICENSE button) opens.

If you still have not decided whether to use SAP CPS by Redwood for your JSM project but wish merely to test it, it is sufficient to activate the free, basic license. Click the button ACTIVATE FREE OF CHARGE LICENSE. A message appears that the system now has a valid license, and you are now logged on to SAP CPS by Redwood.

> **Note**
>
> For a complete connection between SAP CPS by Redwood and SAP Solution Manager, a second part of the license is necessary. This part of the license is also known as a BAE license. *BAE* stands for Business Automation Enabler and refers to an application interface in SAP Solution Manager via which the scheduler communicates.

For connecting SAP Solution Manager and SAP CPS by Redwood, it is best to follow the instructions in SAP Note 1729766. How to obtain a BAE license is also clarified in this part.

After activation and subsequent creation of the link between SAP Solution Manager and SAP CPS by Redwood, further measures need to be taken before you use the scheduler. The following steps are required on a technical level:

▶ Connect further systems from the system landscape. These may include SAP, non-SAP, ABAP, and Java systems. Note that there are license dependencies here. With the basic license, it is possible to schedule jobs or job chains in just *one* SAP system, but not beyond system boundaries. Scheduling is also not possible in non-SAP systems.

▶ Generate the required SAP CPS objects, such as partitions (tantamount to isolation groups), job definitions, repetition patterns, etc. It is also necessary in this case to take note of the limitations of the basic license that have already been mentioned here. For example, each SAP system needs to be drawn up in its own isolation group.

▶ Import jobs so that SAP CPS by Redwood can take over operational control of these.

- Set up further ABAP, UME, and SAP CPS users in the framework of your utilization and authorization concepts.

Be aware that the use of an external scheduler means that a separate software solution has to be operated alongside SAP Solution Manager. Integration of an external scheduler into the IT infrastructure requires a certain degree of preparation: objects must be set up, job information must be transferred, and much more. All of these measures can take up considerable time and know-how. Along with initialization, you will also come across challenges when dealing with enhancements, for example when implementing complex execution structures (job chains).

Implementation of individual tasks can become very complex, and this is beyond the scope of this book. Always bear in mind that JSM processes are being influenced here. As a consequence, you should carry out the integration of SAP CPS by Redwood as a project, so inform those responsible and train those affected in good time.

10.3.8 Job Request, Job Redirect of a Job Request Shortcut, and Job Interception

The more complex the business processes that are settled within a system landscape are, the greater the importance attached to the optimization of the job application process is. The components in the JSM suite offer compatible options.

The objective of such optimization is to put control of user activities in the hands of a central JSM team. The independent and, hence, largely uncontrolled scheduling of jobs by individual users should be prevented. In this case, as much information as possible must be put together as quickly as possible and stored in such a way that it is centrally available. Information losses (e.g., through manual copying from one application to the next), should be avoided as much as possible during the application process.

The general approach in JSM is that claiming a new job, adaptations of current jobs, or deleting jobs is usually considered to be an ECR. This promotes integration with the ITSM. The central JSM team is then responsible for the actual scheduling, execution, and monitoring of jobs and has full transparency over the situation.

The JSM suite offers the following components in SAP Solution Manager for supporting a standard job application process:

- **Job request**
  The user usually generates a job request by means of a form that is saved in SAP Solution Manager.

- **Job allocation shortcut (usually Re-direct or Job Control)**
  The user, who wishes to schedule a job in the system that is being managed, is redirected to a guided procedure and fills in a job request, which is saved in SAP Solution Manager.

- **Intercepting jobs (Job Interception)**
  If you are unable to use a job request or to re-direct a user, then the job interception function offers the option of influencing the execution of jobs.

In the next section, we will introduce you to the three components in detail.

Job Request

The first basic step on the path to centralized job management is to (when possible) revoke user authorization for scheduling jobs. Instead of scheduling and executing jobs themselves, the user can fill out a job request form, which is subsequently sent to the JSM team, in the future. For this purpose SAP Solution Manager has two standardized, but different, forms available:

- Simple job request form (see Figure 10.12)
- Detailed job request form

With a simple job request form, the main information necessary for scheduling a job can be requested. It's meant to be used by end users because of its simple structure.

The detailed job request form allows a greater quantity of information to be stored. In structural terms, the detailed job request is very similar to the content of job documentation, and therefore suitable for use by process managers, IT managers, etc. The job request approach is also recommended for changing jobs or stopping jobs from being executed. Along with the job documentation, it is an excellent option for implementing a company-wide, standardized naming convention.

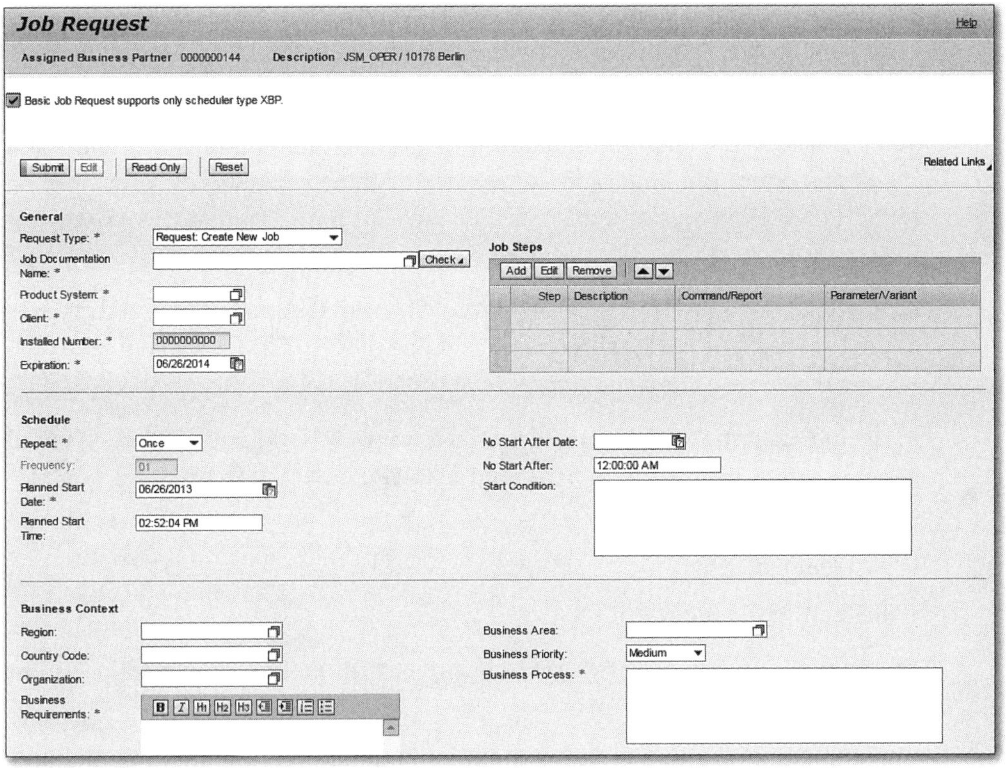

Figure 10.12 Form for a Simple Job Request

Note

If end users are allowed to generate jobs, and no specifications have been stipulated for standardized naming, then job names are randomly generated from different schedulers. Other participants (e.g., a central monitoring team), can only partly interpret these. In case of an error, it is then difficult to quickly take suitable corrective steps.

For this reason, we recommend setting up rules for the use of job names so that names give a hint regarding the purpose, creator, or person responsible for a job. With the use of job request forms, it's possible to introduce a standardized naming convention that is readily understood by all participants. By creating a job request form, you can ensure that the applicant adheres to conventions.

Naming conventions can also be used in the same manner as manually drawing up job documentation.

So that a user has access to the job request forms, the JOB MANAGEMENT work center and a business partner must be assigned (see Section 10.2.3).

Both the simple and detailed job request forms can be configured and tailored to your own requirements. Information on adjusting the request forms and shaping design access can be picked up from the roadmap documents, which can be found in SAP Service Marketplace under the alias *jsm* • ROADMAP DOCUMENTS • REALIZATION/IMPLEMENTATION.

All saved job requests can be seen by the JSM team in the JOB REQUEST activity area of the JOB MANAGEMENT work center, including the SAP CRM document numbers, which are generated when saving.

In the job request, it is determined with the *transaction type* which process is used in ITSM to process the job request. The following transaction types are available as standard:

▶ Incident (SMIN)

▶ Request for Change (SMCR)

At this point, integration with ITSM begins, which will be explained in greater detail in Section 10.3.9.

Job request forms can be integrated into web interfaces so that they can be called up via a URL (e.g., in an intranet or a portal). If you wish to ensure that your users do not need to log on to SAP Solution Manager, then a job request alias that uses a copy of the request form is required. Further information about this can be found in the roadmap documentation in SAP Service Marketplace.

Job Application Shortcut

If you cannot revoke authorizations for end users in the respective SAP systems for scheduling jobs, then in some cases it's possible to redirect scheduling activities. In the following cases, you can redirect the job request:

▶ A user would like to set up a job with Transaction SM36.

▶ A user attempts to change a job with the status SCHEDULED in Transaction SM37.

▶ A user would like to execute a program as a job in Transaction SA38.

In such situations, the end user is redirected to a standard procedure based on a guided procedure in SAP Solution Manager. The end user can then fill in the form, which is similar to the job request form in the work center. Depending on whether the job execution is scheduled to take place periodically or on only one occasion, the user generates a job request in SAP Solution Manager or schedules the one-off job directly into the system that is being administered.

Configuring such a redirection can be started in the JOB MANAGEMENT work center in the ADMINISTRATION activity area. Figure 10.13 shows this area.

First, click the CHECK BACK DESTINATION link in the BACK DESTINATION area to check that for every managed system that is relevant to JSM, there is a so-called *back destination* specified. A back destination is an RFC connection generated in each managed system during its connection to SAP Solution Manager and reverts to the SAP Solution Manager system. It is required for exchanging information for various technical functions and should already be available.

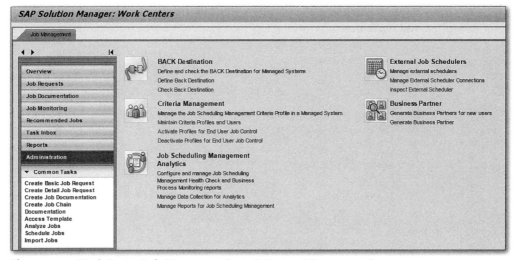

Figure 10.13 Work Center "Job Management"—Activity Area "Management"

Look for a name that corresponds to the following convention: *SM_<SolmanID>CL NT<SolmanMandant>_BACK*. Check whether a technical user has been entered with the following name: *SMB_<SolmanID>*.

As long as such a back destination is already available, it can be used for a job redirect. Click the DEFINE BACK DESTINATION link in the BACK DESTINATION area. In the PRODUCT SYSTEM field, you must select the system being managed, and in the CLIENT field, select in which the respective application is running. In the DESTINATION field, enter the name of the back destination.

> **Note**
>
> No new RFC connection is defined with this action. You simply choose one that is appropriate.

Corresponding criteria must also be defined. That means it is necessary to determine the users and in which systems this function will apply.

Start defining the criteria profiles with the MAINTAIN CRITERIA PROFILES AND USERS link in the CRITERIA MANAGEMENT area. Choose the administered system, as well as the client in which the user is working, that you would like to set up the job application shortcut for. Then, the criteria manager program, called CRITERIA_MANAGER, is called up in this system. When starting program execution, you see a similar screen to that in Figure 10.14. The job application shortcut can be configured for selected end users here.

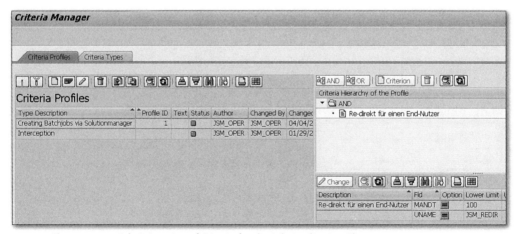

Figure 10.14 Administration of Criteria for the Job Application Shortcut

To do this, proceed as follows:

1. Within the left-hand area, define a criteria profile with the ☐ button by using the CREATING BATCH JOBS VIA SOLUTIONMANAGER criteria type. As an option, the profile can be given a description that is displayed in the TEXT column after saving.

2. Within the right-hand area, a structure is generated for the profile with the AND or OR buttons (the criteria hierarchy), to which individual criteria can be assigned by means of the CRITERION button.

3. For each individual criterion, a value combination can be established from the client (Field: MANDT) and user (Field: UNAME), and a text description can be stored.

4. The criteria profile works only when it is activated. Within the left-hand area, don't forget to use the ☐ button to activate it. As a result, a green status appears in the STATUS column.

You can easily activate and deactivate criteria profiles by going to the CRITERIA MANAGEMENT area and clicking on the ACTIVATE PROFILES FOR END USER JOB CONTROL link or the DEACTIVATE PROFILES FOR END USER JOB CONTROL link (see Figure 10.13).

> **Note**
>
> Criteria profiles can be changed only when they are deactivated. Before changing a profile, make sure that no green status can be seen in the STATUS column (see Figure 10.14).

Intercepting Jobs (Job Interception)

If it is not possible to revoke end-user authorizations for scheduling jobs, then central job management will take place. This means the following:

▶ Execution of these jobs is not monitored depending on the situation within the landscape. Overload situations may occur, which prevent the execution of important jobs. For example, this can be critical in period-end closing phases.

▶ Jobs from this user are not integrated in monitoring procedures within the framework of a Service Level Agreement (SLA) concept, which means that these jobs are not subject to central monitoring and, as a result, also not subject to agreed processes in case of error.

In this case, and for all jobs generated with other methods, the *job interception* function can be used. Job interception means the target-oriented interception of a planned job execution in accordance with the rules set out in order to execute the job at a later stage with corresponding resources. The function is implemented in SAP Solution Manager together with an external scheduler.

Thus, it is possible to influence the execution of jobs in your system landscape from a central entity. Job interception is, therefore, the logical extension of the principle behind job applications, which have already been described in this chapter. This function can be configured for users, as well as for job groups.

In order to activate this function, adjustments must be carried out in the relevant system that is being administered. In the second step, the changes are carried out in the scheduler. In this book, the process is explained using SAP CPS by Redwood as an example.

In SAP Solution Manager, configuration is started in the ADMINISTRATION activity area of the JOB MANAGEMENT work center (see Figure 10.13).

Start defining the criteria profiles by clicking the MAINTAIN CRITERIA PROFILES AND USERS link in the CRITERIA MANAGEMENT area. Choose the system administered, as well as the client for which job interception should be set up. Then, the criteria management program, also called CRITERIA_MANAGER, is called up in this system (see Figure 10.15). The first part of the job interception function is configured here. This means that you specify which jobs should be intercepted with the following parameters, which will now be described in greater detail.

The procedure here resembles the one for the job redirect:

1. Define a criteria profile in the left-hand area using the INTERCEPTION criteria type.
2. In the right-hand area, generate a structure for the profile using the AND or OR buttons and assign criteria with the CRITERION button.
3. For each individual criterion, a value combination can be established from the client (Field: AUTHCKMAN), job class (Field: JOBCLASS), job name (Field: JOB-NAME), and job creator (Field: SDLUNAME). Furthermore, it is also possible to save a descriptive text.

4. As already mentioned, criteria profiles work only when they are showing as active in the STATUS column.

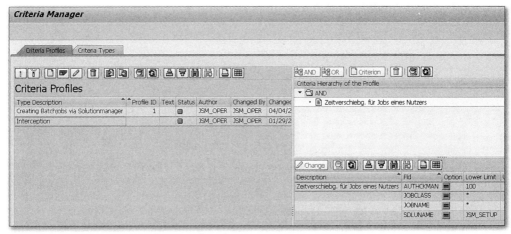

Figure 10.15 Administration of Criteria for Job Interception

You can easily activate and deactivate criteria profiles in SAP Solution Manager by going to the CRITERIA MANAGEMENT area and clicking the ACTIVATE PROFILES FOR END USER JOB CONTROL link or the DEACTIVATE PROFILES FOR END USER JOB CONTROL link.

The definitions established in the Criteria Manager have the effect that the corresponding jobs are not executed, but merely transferred over to INTERCEPTED status. This state can be checked with Transaction SM37.

So that the jobs do not remain in the INTERCEPTED status, it must be ensured that they are processed in the external scheduler. As a next step, the external scheduler has to be configured. Next, we will show you using SAP CPS by Redwood as an example of what such a configuration looks like.

Figure 10.16 shows the XBP JOB CONTROL RULES tab. All tabs displayed are accessible via the menu, which you can display by right-clicking within the system. Select the EDIT option.

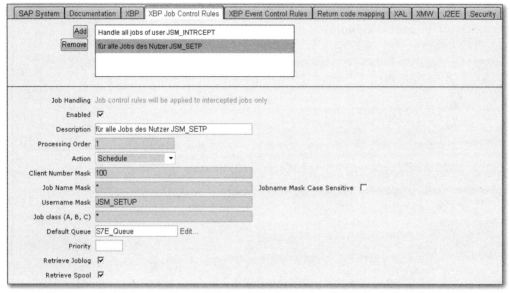

Figure 10.16 Job Interception in SAP System Definition in SAP CPS by Redwood

Enter the values of the criteria that were established in the Criteria Manager earlier. Table 10.5 shows you which criteria manager values must be taken over in which field by SAP CPS by Redwood. Furthermore, you can see what values are used in the example.

Criteria Field in the Criteria Manager	Field Name	Field in SAP CPS by Redwood	Value in Example
Client	AUTHCKMAN	CLIENT NUMBER MASK	100
Job class	JOBCLASS	JOB CLASS (A, B, C)	*
Job name	JOBNAME	JOB NAME MASK	*
Job creator	SDLUNAME	USER NAME MASK	JSM_SETUP

Table 10.5 Equivalence of the Criteria Values in SAP CPS by Redwood

Furthermore, establish in the ACTION field (possible options: HOLD, IGNORE, MONITOR, SCHEDULE, SCHEDULE INTERCEPTED, START IMMEDIATELY) how intercepted jobs should be handled by SAP CPS by Redwood. SCHEDULE means, for example, that the intercepted job in the SAP system will be executed by the scheduler at the time for which it was planned in the SAP system. However, if you choose SCHEDULE INTERCEPTED instead, then the scheduler tries to execute the intercepted job as soon as possible, that is as the defined XBP job control roles allow.

With the DEFAULT QUEUE field, you determine in which systems and when the jobs are executed. It is also possible, via the queue definition, to permit jobs to be carried out in specified time frames (e.g., during the night or on weekends).

To complete the configuration in SAP CPS by Redwood, you must set and save the JOB HANDLING option to INTERCEPTED on the SAP system.

10.3.9 ITSM Integration

When integrating the JSM scenario with ITSM, a strictly process-oriented approach is followed in JSM. From an ITSM viewpoint, each job request and each request regarding changing or stopping a job execution is regarded as a change event in the system. Changes to the system should be carried out by means of a standardized process. For this reason, a CRM document is always drawn up alongside the job request document. In the following sections, we illustrate three options for how to deal with such events in principle.

Incident Management Integration

In case of Incident Management integration, changes to jobs are seen as an event or incident and should be handled according to a standardized process. Therefore, when end users fill in a job request, a CRM document assigned to a defined handling routine (transaction type) is created at the same time. In this case, the SMIN transaction type is for Incident Management with SAP Solution Manager. The CRM document is used to manage the event in accordance with the defined process and document communication among all participants.

Integration with Incident Management within SAP Solution Manager is ensured by means of this CRM document. It is also used by the JSM team responsible for generating or changing job documentation as the central element for documentation, scheduling, and monitoring of jobs.

Change Request Management Integration

In the case of Change Request Management integration, changes to jobs are regarded as technical changes to the system. This should also be handled according to a standardized process and subsequently implemented. With the job request, the end user also generates an ECR at the same time. The CRM document generated in this case is based on the SMCR transaction type for Change Request Management with SAP Solution Manager.

The ECR is processed according to the defined change management process. This means that it is ensured that it undergoes an approval process.

If the request is approved, a SMAD document is generated from the SMCR document by means of which the desired change is implemented on a technical level. A job documentation is created or modified from this document.

Combined Integration

Combined integration means that job requests are handled first according to Incident Management (transaction type SMIN) and subsequently as an ECR in accordance with Change Request Management (transaction type SMCR).

CRM documents document the actions undertaken, as well as communication with those responsible. The ITSM user interface is used for processing (see Figure 10.17).

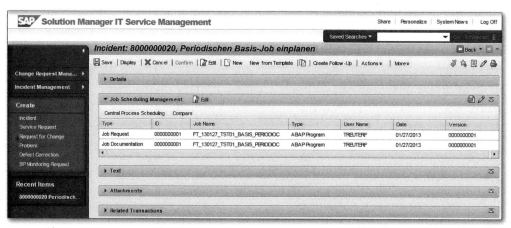

Figure 10.17 User Interface for ITSM

Here, the job documentation is generated from the job request after it has been checked by the responsible party assigned to it. In Figure 10.17, you can see in the JOB SCHEDULING MANAGEMENT area that this step for the FT_130127_TST01_BASIS_ PERODOC job has already taken place.

When you wish to use one of these options or a combination thereof, then the SAP Solution Manager system must be prepared accordingly. For this reason, carry out the IT SERVICE MANAGEMENT step in Transaction SOLMAN_SETUP.

It is possible to adjust the mentioned ITSM processes to your requirements. Integration into ITSM processes is a complex topic and cannot be comprehensively covered within this book. In the following section, we want to briefly touch upon another important function: notifications.

10.3.10 Notification

As already explained, the JSM scenario can be integrated into ITSM processes. Alongside this, it is also possible to use business process monitoring within SAP Solution Manager for job monitoring. When you also use SAP CPS by Redwood, you have the following options to implement a notification concept available to you:

▸ Email from ITSM integration—in other words, out of local processes with the Post Processing Framework (PPF)

▸ Email from BPMon, as this is used in the job monitoring function that is integrated in business process monitoring

▸ The options within SAP CPS for sending notifications

10.4   Toys Inc.

The JSM team at Toys Inc. established that a relatively large proportion of periodic jobs were manually scheduled by end users. These jobs were not subject to a standardized job request process, so it was not tested whether or not the expected results were already provided by other job executions. It also shows that no monitoring is carried out for manually scheduled jobs. Problems with jobs are therefore usually noticed by end users, so the JSM team finds out only some time later and, hence, can only react late.

This is the reason for the decision to intervene in the job request process when necessary. End users generate job requests, the testing and scheduling of which are carried out according to agreed ITSM processes.

Job scheduling that cannot be controlled in such a manner should be intercepted with SAP CPS by Redwood and be scheduled accordingly. For this reason, SAP CPS by Redwood is set as the central scheduler for job monitoring across the landscape. SAP CPS by Redwood is connected to the SAP Solution Manager, and the most important jobs are scheduled from the job documentation.

The illustrated measures have two advantages for Toys Inc.: job documentation exists within a central location for all jobs, and job monitoring is centralized across the entire landscape. The measures lead to noticeable easing during critical period-end closing times. Ultimately, the troubleshooting process can be improved due to enhanced transparency.

10.5 Additional Documentation

Links

- ▶ SAP Service Marketplace, alias *jsm*
- ▶ SAP Service Marketplace, alias *bpm*
- ▶ SAP Service Marketplace, alias *supportstandards*
- ▶ SAP Service Marketplace, alias *instguides*
- ▶ The *Security Guide for SAP Solution Manager 7.1* can be found at the URL *http://service.sap.com* and the path SAP HELP PORTAL • APPLICATION LIFECYCLE MANAGEMENT • SAP SOLUTION MANAGER • SAP SOLUTION MANAGER 7.1 • SECURITY INFORMATION.
- ▶ Information on technical details for JSM, as well as general overviews, can be found in the SAP Community Network (SCN) at *http://scn.sap.com*.

SAP Notess

Table 10.6 provides an overview of important SAP Notes in relation to the update system.

Contents	Note
FAQ: Job Scheduling Management with SAP Solution Manager	1054005
Job Scheduling Management Work Center	1117355
CPS—Solution Manager integration setup	1729766
Availability of business process monitoring	521820
BPMon in SAP Solution Manager—Requirements	784752

Table 10.6 Notes Regarding Job Scheduling Management

Monitoring and controlling complex system landscapes and the corresponding business processes is an important prerequisite for failure-free business operations in your organization. This chapter discusses monitoring business processes.

11   Business Process Operations

The previous chapters explained the possibilities of technical monitoring of the SAP system landscape. This chapter now describes the tools and functions you'll find available for monitoring and analyzing your business processes.

You may ask yourself what relevance this chapter has to your daily work. The challenges or problems to be solved in today's IT world cannot be considered only on a technical level or the applications level. Instead, the interaction of these two areas and their collaboration are becoming increasingly important in a company.

Technical operations and application operations basically have one common goal: smooth operations of IT-based business processes within the company. In technical operations, the main focus is on the underlying system, wheras in application operations, the focus is on the application layer itself. As a technical expert, you should also have an overview of the functions and business process operations in SAP Solution Manager to learn about other application-related monitoring options.

With the example of Toys Inc.'s procurement processes, this chapter explains the possibilities of business process operations and clarifies the differences to technical operations.

11.1   Business Process Monitoring Tools

SAP Solution Manager provides a multitide of tools to monitor and control IT-based business processes during the project phase and after the go-live phase in operations.

In Chapter 3, we explained that business processes themselves are the basis of many scenarios used in SAP Solution Manager. This means that after completion of a project, all relevant business processes are hand over to the solution. This solution is implemented in SAP Solution Manager and represents the operations part. It contains all critical core business processes that must be monitored and controlled.

11.1.1 Methods: Stabilization and Improvement

There are two methods for business process operations: *stabilization* and *improvement*.

Let's first take a look at the aspect of improvement: as shown in Figure 11.1, the quality of existing processes can be improved using analysis tools. Collected data serves as a basis to identify overdue or open receipts or documents—for example, open orders or overdue deliveries. These are documents that, due to their age, are no longer relevant and cannot be archived, or a work backlog of current documents.

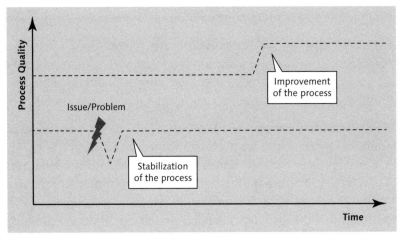

Figure 11.1 Improvement and Stablization

You should not perform any monitoring until these open documents have been processed and archived to ensure that an improvement of the process can be determined.

This is where the aspect of stabilization comes into play: in business process monitoring, these business process–relevant documents and technical key performance indicators can be monitored. Technical KPIs comprise monitoring jobs, interfaces, and errors to ensure early error recognition and keep the business process stable in its flow.

The following sections describe the measures that can be used to achieve an improvement or stabilization. This includes the following steps:

▶ Business process analysis (see Section 11.1.2)

▶ Business Process Analytics (see Section 11.1.3)

▶ Business process monitoring (see Section 11.1.4)

▶ Dashboards (see Section 11.1.5)

Figure 11.2 shows the procurement of new material for the production of toys.

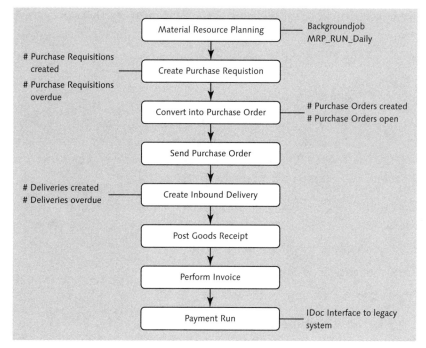

Figure 11.2 Procurement Process

A potential material requirement is determined by Material Requirements Planning, and the new material is ordered. The latter is done using the following basic documents:

▶ Purchase requisition

▶ Purchase order

▶ Inbound delivery

To secure the process, the following business indicators are monitored:

- Created purchase requisitions/overdue purchase requisitions
- Created purchase orders/overdue purchase orders
- Created deliveries/open deliveries

In addition to the pure business indicators, the execution of the material requirement planning (MRP) run and transmission of payment information to a foreign system via IDoc are to be managed. Apart from these indicators, other markers can be used; a list of other possible indicators can be found in Section 11.1.4.

With the example of Toys Inc., we will now present the measures that can be used for improvement and stabilization. To detect problems and potential for improvement, the first step is a business process analysis.

11.1.2 Business Process Analysis

In the standard business process analysis, which is available as an SAP service or as a self-service in SAP Solution Manager, standard busines processes of a system are analyzed. Contact your SAP representative for a service delivery, or perform a self-service in your SAP Solution Manager system as follows:

1. In the SAP ENGAGEMENT AND SERVICE DELIVERY work center, you can create new self-services.
2. Choose the CREATE option in the SERVICES area.
3. In the list that opens, select SAP BUSINESS PROCESS ANALYSIS.
4. Follow the further instructions of the wizard.

Various service variants are available for SAP ERP, SAP CRM, and SAP SRM systems. During a business process analysis, data is directly collected from the respective managed system. Let's take a look at the example of the created and open deliveries. Apart from the created deliveries per day, which are set in relation to the open deliveries, delivery categories and shipping points serve as initial clues for optimizing the example process.

Toys Inc. creates approximately 100 deliveries per day, 70 of those are pure deliveries, and 30 are returns. The number of created deliveries is a *throughput figure*. It tells you the extent to which the systems and individual organizational units, such as plants or documents, are involved in this process. Throughput figures are necessary to make reliable statements on possible improvement potential.

Apart from that, Toys Inc. has 1,575 open deliveries; the number of open deliveries is a *backlog figure*. As the excerpt in the business process analysis report in Figure 11.3 shows, almost 95% of the open receipts have the delivery type *Delivery*. The reason these deliveries are still open should be analyzed. A process gap or system operation error may be the root cause.

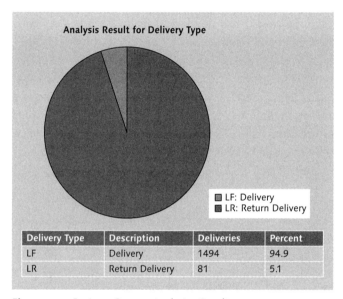

Analysis Result for Delivery Type

- LF: Delivery
- LR: Return Delivery

Delivery Type	Description	Deliveries	Percent
LF	Delivery	1494	94.9
LR	Return Delivery	81	5.1

Figure 11.3 Business Process Analysis—Results

To evaluate a problematic situation, throughput figures and backlog figures (the latter being open or overdue receipts) should always be compared for the corresponding organizational units and document types. In the case of Toys Inc., the backlog is twice as high as the weekly throughput. Although there is definitely room for improvement, it cannot be considered as critical.

This information can serve as a basis for monitoring the process because process issues have been revealed and corrected. Based on this data, indicators (figures) and their thresholds can be defined more easily.

Business process analysis, however, is just an initial analysis. If this type of information is necessary and needs to be checked for a longer period of time, we recommend to use Business Process Analytics.

11.1.3 Business Process Analytics

Using the Business Process Analytics tool, you can collect data from managed systems on a daily or weekly basis to store it in the business warehouse of SAP Solution Manager. In the long term, this data can be used for further analysis. In contrast to business process analysis, it is possible to generate trends, and thus evaluate the development of open and overdue documents for a longer period of time. Apart from this trend analysis, the data can be examined in regard to its age structure and used for comparisons. The selection can be adjusted dynamically and does not require a new data collection each time. In the selection, the axes can be assigned various values, such as document type, organizational unit, or plant. Apart from that, you can select individual values. If an optimization potential has been detected, you can go directly to a detail list in the managed system.

Figure 11.4 shows a benchmark for open deliveries. From here, you can call up all functions, such as age structure, trends, and the detail list for the corresponding buttons.

11.1.4 Business Process Monitoring

After the business process–relevant indicators have been checked with a Business Process Analysis and/or Business Process Analytics and the system has been cleaned up, these indicators (figures) can be monitored using business process monitoring. In addition, you can use technical indicators to secure the process flow. The following indicators are available:

- Application-specific indicators on the following:
  - SAP ERP (SD, MM, PP, LE, WM, QM, and FI)
  - SAP CRM (Sales, Services, Customer Interaction Center, and Marketing)
  - SAP APO and SAP SRM
- Monitoring of the following interfaces: IDoc, BDoc, tRFC, qRFC, bgRFC, Batch-Input, Flat Files, and SAP NetWeaver PI

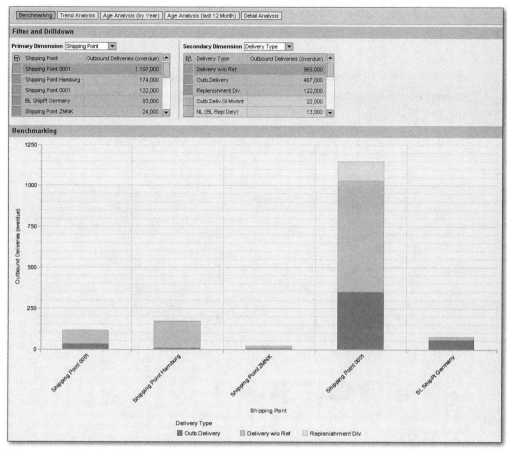

Figure 11.4 Example—Business Process Analytics

- ▶ Cross-application indicators on background jobs, ABAP dumps, update errors, the application log, and performance monitoring
- ▶ Industry-specific indicators on apparel and footwear, automotive, retail, and utilities

A detailed list of available indicators can be found at *service.sap.com/bpm* and via MEDIA LIBRARY • OVERVIEW AND DEMOS • BUSINESS PROCESS OPERATIONS KEY FIGURES • OVERVIEW.

For Toys Inc.'s procurement process, the MRP run and transmission of IDocs are to be monitored. To monitor the MRP run, a job monitor is added, which examines the job in regards to successful completion, errors, and a specific time window.

Only after successful completion of this job can it be ensured that the required materials are known.

As another indicator, all IDocs going out of the system are checked. Thus, both the throughput and errors within an IDoc can be checked. Only after successful transmission of the data to an external system the payment process can be completed successfully.

Figure 11.5 shows all relevant parts of business process monitoring.

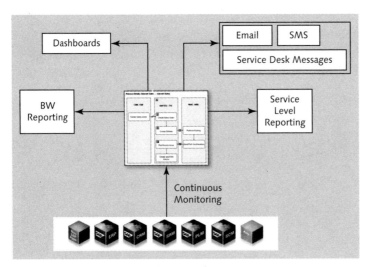

Figure 11.5 Business Process Monitoring—Overview

The data is collected by all managed systems and stored centrally in SAP Solution Manager. It includes alerts and business data stored in the business warehouse of SAP Solution Manager. Based on this data, it is possible to display alerts in the work center and check them; the information can be forwarded by email or, if available, the Service Desk. This way, tickets can be automatically created for IT Support, which ensures quick initiation of incident processing. Otherwise, the information can also be prepared and presented in dashboards.

11.1.5 Dashboards

A central access from the BUSINESS PROCESS OPERATIONS work center allows you to create individual reports of collected data. In these dashboards, all available sources (alert tables and BW InfoCubes) can be used. Overviews of all alerts can be presented in tables, and document data from the business warehouse of SAP Solution Manager (for example, from Business Process Analytics) can be used and presented in the form of pie, bar, and trend charts. A combination of various information sources is also possible to give area managers, team leads, and management an overview of the current system and process situation.

Figure 11.6 shows four different panels with different information on overdue deliveries. Each panel includes details from an associated information source (table or BW InfoCube).

Only the combination of throughput figures (see panel 1, top-left in Figure 11.6) and overdue deliveries (see panel 2, bottom-left) allow for a precise statement on the process situation.

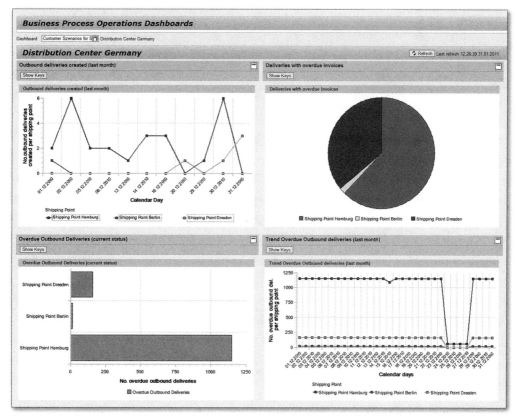

Figure 11.6   Example — Dashboard

11.2 Monitoring Concept and Standard Processes

To achieve a comprehensive monitoring, you should not only be able to handle the tools themselves, but also define your own processes to support monitoring. This section deals with concepts and possible standard processes.

11.2.1 Concepts and Roles in Business Process Monitoring

In addition to the technical provision of SAP Solution Manager for business process monitoring, an organizational structure all around monitoring should be developed, similar to technical monitoring (see Chapter 5).

A possibility of developing this organizational structure is to start creating a monitoring concept during the design of the processes. A lot of information necessary for monitoring can be derived from the technical integration and implementation. Apart from monitoring projects, you need to define threshold values, selection criteria, contact persons, escalation paths, action items, etc., as part of the concept. After completion of the concept, monitoring will be implemented, as shown in Figure 11.7, in accordance with the general project plan. This way, monitoring can be activated as the solution goes live. This simultaneous implementation is the ideal case. In most cases, monitoring is implemented when a solution is already in place. Make sure the information for threshold values, indicators, etc., is gathered completely.

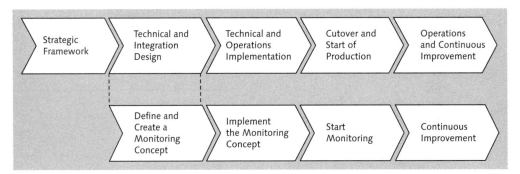

Figure 11.7 Monitoring Concept—Ideal Time

After the handover to production operations, the ongoing improvement phase starts. Business processes continuously change. Therefore, the indicators must be checked and possibly adjusted in regular intervals. You should pay special attention to the threshold values that trigger the yellow or red alert.

> **Example**
>
> If these threshold values are too low, this can lead to a "flood of alerts." The consequence of this might be that persons receiving the alerts are unable to process them all and generally question the purpose of the alerts. If the threshold values are too high, potential problem situations may not be detected.

Regularly check your identifiers (key figures) to maintain consistent acceptance and effectiveness of your monitoring.

As already mentioned, the choice of the right contact persons, responsibilities, and sponsors is important for monitoring (see Figure 11.8):

- ▶ **Sponsor**
  To secure the monitoring, sponsors are needed to support the project. Among other things, they are responsible for the provision of necessary resources. Ideally, they are involved in technical operations and are from one or multiple areas.

- ▶ **Overall responsibility**
  A person responsible for the entire monitoring project should be defined. That person should manage the available resources and coordinate the monitoring architecture.

- ▶ **Monitoring architects**
  Monitoring architects are responsible for the actual adaptation of business process monitoring. They receive information on threshold values and selection criteria from consumers/end users in IT and departments. Therefore, monitoring architects must be able to understand the business process, implement it in the system, and decide which indicators are useful for the individual purposes. Then, it must be clarified how to react to an alert. Apart from the method to be used (email, SMS, or Service Desk message), it must be decided who should be informed. Whether end users or a particular support organization are to be informed depends on the indicator and the organization of your company. For example, a support organization helps you resolve known problems faster and create a central solution database. A possible example of a distribution of roles can be found in Figure 11.8.

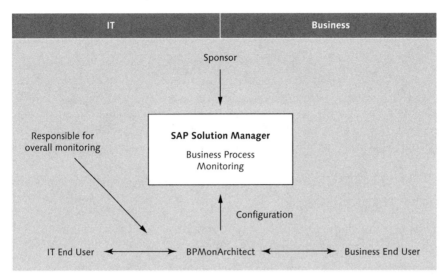

Figure 11.8 Distribution of Roles in Business Process Monitoring

Without such organizational structures, it cannot be ensured that the implemented monitoring is efficient and correct. Therefore, all relevant information and responsibilities should be documented prior to monitoring.

Even if monitoring isn't developed until a system and process environment already exists, you shouldn't create a monitoring procedure without a detailed concept. Building a monitoring system at a later time is not a problem as long as you make sure to consider and go through the phases shown in Figure 11.7. A defined process of treating alerts is part of the concept, as well. A possible standard procedure is described in the next section.

11.2.2 Standard Procedure for Alert Handling

For each indicator (key figure), you need to clearly define who should react when and how. In this context, the effect on the business process and the urgency play an important role. Generally, however, all reactions should follow a standardized procedure. Figure 11.9 shows an example of a monitoring process for business processes and interfaces.

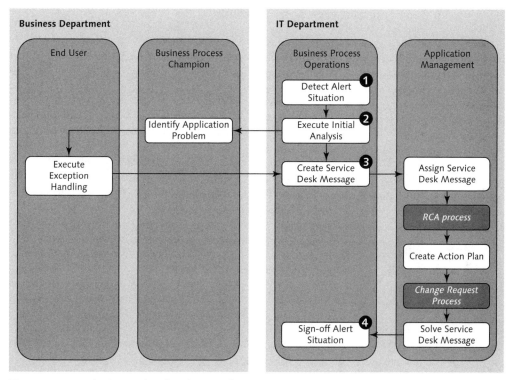

Figure 11.9 Standard Procedure for Alert Handling

Let's take a look at the individual steps in the alert handling process:

❶ The first step in the monitoring process is recognizing critical situations (exceeding the threshold value). This is done by email, SMS, or a Service Desk message or by checking the alert inbox in SAP Solution Manager (Business Process Management work center).

❷ After the incident is recognized, an initial analysis of the data in the connected system can be done. Depending on the indicator type (technical or business administrational indicator from a department), persons in charge of business processes, key users, or system administrators must be involved.

❸ If the incident is not known and a solution cannot be found, a Service Desk message should be created, and all relevant information should be passed on to IT Support. Once you have created a Service Desk message, root cause analysis is performed in Support. Then an action plan is created, and you will need to go through a change process—for example, changes in the program code. You can trigger this change process directly from the ticket that you receive from Support.

❹ After successful correction of the malfunction (incident), the alert must be acknowledged in SAP Solution Manager to indicate that the process has been restabilized. This is also done in the BUSINESS PROCESS MONITORING work center. In the left-hand menu bar under TYPICAL TASKS, you can find all access points for implementing monitoring, Business Analytics, and the dashboards.

This brief overview of business process monitoring is designed to make you aware that, apart from technical monitoring, you also need to monitor your business processes to ensure smooth operations in your company. In addition, by default, the tools business process analysis, Business Process Analytics, and dashboards provide a multitude of reporting options for your business processes and the documents included in them.

11.2.3 Additional Documentation

Links

For more information and material, please go to *service.sap.com/bpm*. The following documents are available in the MEDIA LIBRARY:

▸ Setup guides/roadmaps for all monitoring functions

▸ Overviews of available indicators (key figures)

▸ Best practices and customer examples

SAP Notes

Table 11.1 provides an overview of important SAP notes concerning business process operations.

Contents	SAP Note
Availability of business process monitoring	521820
BPMon in SAP Solution Manager—prerequisites	784752

Table 11.1 SAP Notes on Business Process Operations

A functional authorization concept is an important foundation for working with SAP Solution Manager. In this chapter, we will show you how to develop an authorization concept that meets your needs.

12 Authorizations in the SAP Solution Manager System

After discussing the topic of authorizations in each previous chapter, we will introduce you to the basic authorization concept of SAP Solution Manager and help you develop a suitable concept for your needs. We will present the roles of the SAP Solution Manager and the administered systems and show you how to plan, implement, and document a comprehensive authorization concept.

It pays to have a carefully planned authorization concept: it will not only help you to maintain information security in your company, but also facilitate organization of authorization granting and save you valuable time in rolling out the authorizations.

In the following section, we will first show you what options the SAP Solution Manager systems provides you with for servicing a system's various users.

12.1 Maintaining the User Master Record

As in other SAP systems based on SAP NetWeaver AS ABAP, the user master record is the foundation for assigning authorizations that allow users to perform actions. In this section, you will get to know the typical tools for user data maintenance and the different setting options.

A user can be created and maintained in user maintenance (Transaction SU01). The index card tabs you are familiar with from AS ABAP system administration are also used in user maintenance (for more information, refer to the book *SAP NetWeaver AS ABAP: System Administration* by Frank Föse, Sigrid Hagemann, and Liane Will (SAP PRESS 2011):

- ▶ ADDRESS

- ▶ LOGIN DATA

- ▶ SNC (SECURE NETWORK COMMUNICATION)

- ▶ FIXED VALUES

- ▶ PARAMETERS

- ▶ ROLES

- ▶ PROFILES

- ▶ GROUPS

- ▶ PERSONALIZATION

- ▶ LICENSE DATA

The PROFILES and ROLES tabs are the ones that are important for user administration. Here, you can assign authorizations to a user for precisely defined actions in the form of roles. A *role* should correspond as closely as possible to the tasks and activities of a user. A role is formed through the assignment of *profiles*. These roles can, in turn, be combined into *composite roles*. Figure 12.1 shows the structure of a user master record with composite roles, roles, and profiles.

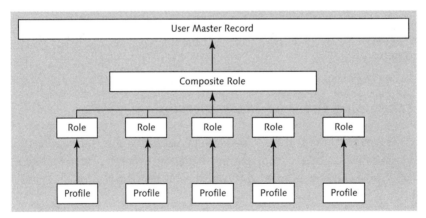

Figure 12.1 Structure of a User Master Record

In principle, you can also assign a user profiles directly. However, because it is generally necessary to assign several authorizations and profiles to a user, there is a risk of quickly losing one's overview. Authorizations are assigned to a user using the PROFILES and ROLES tabs. *Groups* are for grouping users with similar work tasks. This simplifies the identification and administration of users and has direct effects on their authorizations.

In order to assign authorizations to all users of a user group, mass user maintenance (Transaction SU10) is used.

In mass user maintenance, the USERS tab gives you the option of first, manually creating a list of users and second, selecting a user group by restricting a value range ([F4] button in a row of the USERS column).

In the context of SAP Solution Manager, a distinction is made between *end users*, who are users who work in dialog with the system, and *technical users*. A technical user is responsible for the implementation of technical processes and cannot work in dialog with the system.

Several technical users are created automatically during configuration of the SAP Solution Manager. If possible, these users should not be changed and should use the standard roles supplied by SAP. This facilitates support and any analyses that must be performed by SAP.

In addition to the technical users, end users that you can create manually in the system based on the application used are also required. To create a user, you must fill out at least the following tabs with data: ADDRESS, LOGIN DATA, and ROLES or PROFILES. The user type, which you must define under the LOGIN DATA tab, determines the security concept that is applied for the user. The following user types are possible here:

▶ **Dialog**
Each user who logs into the system requires a user of the *Dialog* type. During the dialog login, the system checks whether the password is expired or initial. The user can change his password himself. Multiple dialog logins are checked and logged, if necessary.

▶ **System**
The *System* user type is used for background processing and communication within a system. A dialog login is not possible. The passwords are not subject to the password change requirement and, therefore, cannot be initial or expired. Only a user administrator can change the password. Multiple logins are permitted.

▶ **Communication**

The *Communication* user type is used for dialog-free communication between systems. This is the case for the user CUA_<SID>, who is used for transporting user information to a central user administration system. A dialog login is not possible.

▶ **Service**

The *Service* user type is a dialog user who is available to an anonymous, larger circle of users. Such a user is used when a service such as an SAP EarlyWatch alert evaluation is to be performed by several SAP experts, for example. During the dialog login, the system checks whether the password is expired or initial. Multiple logins are permitted.

▶ **Reference**

The *Reference* user type represents a persons-related user that serves for the assignment of additional, identical authorizations. That is, this user serves solely as a template. If, for example, a dialog user is to be created from a reference user, it must be copied and the user type changed to Dialog. One cannot log on to the system with a reference user. To assign a reference user to a dialog user, specify it under the ROLES tab when maintaining the dialog user.

The Dialog and System user types have an especially important place in SAP Solution Manager because they are used for the majority of the functions provided. Both user types are therefore encountered especially frequently in the system.

You have now obtained a bit of insight into maintaining user master records and the various user types. Before we show you how to assign authorizations in Section 12.3, we will inform you of the options for password management in the following section.

12.2 Password Management

You specify the initial password for the user under the LOGIN DATA tab. Depending on the user type, this password may have to be changed after the initial login (see Section 12.1). Table 12.1 contains the profile parameters you can use to specify the initial password and the subsequently selected password.

Parameters	Description
login/min_password_lng	Definition of the minimum length of a password in number of characters.
login/password_history_size	Stipulation of the number of most recent passwords that the new password may not be equivalent with.
login/password_change_waittime	Stipulation of the time, in seconds, after which the user can again change his password. When the user administrator changes the user password, the user must change this initial password when logging in for the first time, regardless of when he last changed his password.
login/min_password_lowercase	Minimum number of lowercase letters a password must contain.
login/min_password_uppercase	Minimum number of uppercase letters a password must contain.
login/min_password_diff	The new password must differ from the old password by this number of characters.
login/password_max_idle_productive	Specification of the number of days after which a productive (selected by the user) password expires when it is not used.
login/password_max_idle_initial	Specification of the number of days after which an initial password (selected by the user administrator) expires when it is not used. After this period has expired, the password may no longer be used for authentication. Password login can be reactivated by the user administrator through assignment of a new initial password.

Table 12.1 Profile Parameters for Password and Login Rules

The parameters shown in the table are the parameters used frequently in general system administration for controlling password management. You can also use them for SAP Solution Manager. Because SAP Solution Manager holds a central position in your system, and because system and business process information is collected centrally in it, we recommend that you use the password concept that is generally valid within your IT system for SAP Solution Manager, as well.

12.3 Maintaining Roles and Authorizations Using the PFCG Transaction

As with other SAP systems, role maintenance (Transaction PFCG) is also used to assign authorizations in SAP Solution Manager. These authorizations and roles are also referred to as *PFCG authorizations* and *PFCG roles*.

As part of this, the design of the various authorizations based on authorization objects, and the definition of the field values contained in them is performed in roles. These roles are subsequently used to generate profiles via which the users receive their actual rights.

Other information can be linked to the role in addition to the authorization contained in it. For example, you can change entries in a user menu, add a description of the role, or set up an inheritance of the transactions from another role.

Two different types of roles exist:

▶ Single roles

▶ Composite roles

Composite roles consist of a collection of single roles that are combined for ease of administration. Composite roles themselves contain no authorizations, but rather only allow the rights that exist in the single roles.

You can create each of the two role types in role maintenance (Transaction PCFG). Various tabs based on the role type that allow you to individually adapt the roles are available within the role type. See Figure 12.2 for an overview of the user interface of Transaction PFCG.

Under the first tab, DESCRIPTION, you can add an explanatory LONG TEXT to the role. In the long text, it is advisable to list the customer-specific changes/adaptions for authorizations under the MENU tab or in the authorizations of the role. In addition, you should name a time stamp, the authorizing person, and the reason for the change. It is also sensible to indicate the changed authorization fields and objects. Because such a detailed representation could impair the readability of the text, this information should be recorded in a separate document for the authorization concept.

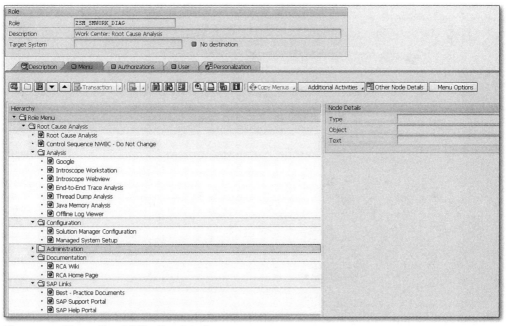

Figure 12.2 Transaction PCFG—User Interface

In addition to the description, you have the option of creating an inheritance for the transactions. Here, the transactions entered on the MENU tab are inherited by the child role from the parent role. To do this, a role from which the inheritance is to be taken must be specified in the DERIVE FROM ROLE field. When you specify a role here, all menu and personalization entries are transferred from the parent role and assigned to the child role. This automated reconciliation allows direct and seamless transfer of changes to the child role. Note that previously existing menu entries may exist, will be overwritten by the setting of the parent role, and are not restorable. Changes to the provided transactions must therefore be made in the parent role. You cannot edit the menu of the child role until the inheritance relationship has been dissolved. The relationship is dissolved using the DISSOLVE INHERITANCE RELATIONSHIP button, which is located in the DERIVE FROM ROLE field.

To recognize the existing inheritance hierarchy, the sub-item USAGE CERTIFICATION must be selected in the ROLE menu. There, you can see the inheritances for all PFCG roles in the system and jump to the corresponding PFCG roles. For a depiction of an example inheritance hierarchy, see Figure 12.3.

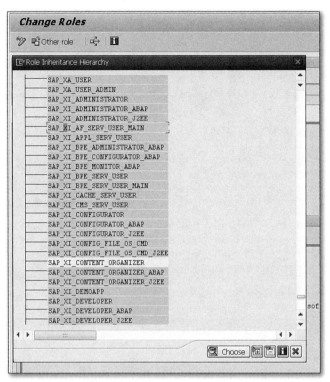

Figure 12.3 Display of the Inheritance Hierarchy of PFCG Roles

An existing inheritance can only be dissolved starting from the child role. When you dissolve the inheritance, all transactions are removed from the menu of the child role.

You can create and change the role menus on the MENU tab. You can use these role menus to create the contents of the user menu in the Session Manager or SAP Easy Access. If a user is assigned a role with an existing menu, he will be able to see and use it in the user menu. The usual content for the menu is transaction codes and web addresses, which are maintained in a tree structure. Once you have activated the inheritance of transactions, you can no longer make changes to the role menu. Another special feature concerns the menu of composite roles. For these, you can only adapt the structure of the menu tree; adding or changing new transactions, on the other hand, must be performed in the single roles.

The Authorizations tab is a central point in role distribution. The assignment of the role to an authorization profile, among other things, is performed here. This means that the authorization conception is performed in the role, which is later used to generate an authorization profile. This contains the authorizations consisting of authorization fields and authorization values. This assignment takes place automatically when you generate the profile on this tab.

You generate the profile by clicking the green checkmark icon. Next, click the ⊕ icon. If no profile is generated for the role, it is necessary to assign a profile name in the following window. Here, an automatically generated profile name is assigned, but you can change it. In this case, confirm the profile name by clicking the green checkmark icon and exit the transaction by clicking the ⊕ icon.

You can change the assignment of a profile to a role only by deleting the profile. If a green status is indicated on the Authorizations tab, an authorization file exists, and the authorizations of the role have not changed since the last profile generation. The authorization profile can therefore be used.

To create or change the authorization data of an authorization profile, click the Change Authorization Data button. This opens the profile generator. Here, click on the Expert Mode button in order to specify how the profile is to be maintained. The following maintenance types are available for selection:

▶ Delete Profile and Authorizations and Create New Ones
When you select Delete Profile and Authorizations and Create New Ones, all authorizations assigned to the role are deleted, and the profile is removed. All manually entered values are lost in this process. You should use this option if you wish to rebuild the authorizations of a role. When this option is selected, the authorization proposal values on the Menu tab are followed and loaded into the profile.

▶ Edit Old Status
Edit Old Status means that you edit the previously entered authorization profile, and no changes due to transaction assignments are updated in the menu. You should use this selection if you are not using the Menu tab of the role or do not wish to use the suggested value.

▶ Read Old Version and Reconcile with New Data
If you have made prior changes in the menu of the role, Read Old Version and Reconcile with the New Data is selected automatically.

This selection has the effect that the proposal values of a transaction added on the MENU tab are loaded into the profile without the old version's being overwritten.

These proposal values concern the authorization object, authorization fields, and values contained in the fields.

Note that the proposal values for the function in SAP Solution Manager provided by SAP are not sufficiently maintained and do not contain all necessary authorizations. You should give this particular consideration when you select the first or third option of the maintenance type. This allows you to overwrite or delete authorizations that are contained in the standard roles of SAP. We therefore recommend selecting the EDIT OLD VERSION option for these changes in order to avoid changing the authorizations of the roles with incorrectly maintained proposal values and thereby impairing the functioning of the role.

12.3.1 Editing the Proposal Values of the PFCG Roles

The proposal values for PFCG roles are the basis for the field values of the authorization fields provided in the profile generator.

You can use Transaction SU24 (maintenance of assignments of authorization objects) to change the proposed values for transactions you have entered in the menu of a role. You should always use this transaction when the proposal values provided by SAP do not meet your requirements but you wish to use them in creating a profile.

Proceed as follows in order to change the proposal values of the PFCG transaction:

1. Open Transaction SU24.
2. To do this, select TRANSACTION for APPLICATION TYPES and enter the PFCG transaction code.
3. Confirm your selection by clicking the ⊕ icon.
4. You are shown an overview of the authorizations entered so far, which you can also recognize in Figure 12.4.
5. Switch to change mode by clicking the 🖉 icon.
6. Select the rows in the AUTHORIZATION OBJECTS table in which the authorization object is located and for which the proposal value is to be changed.
7. Click the FIELD VALUES button.

8. In the table of authorization objects, you can see the proposed authorization values for the selected authorization objects by clicking the EDIT icon.

Save the changes by clicking the SAVE button. If you are creating your own transactions, you can define proposal values yourself by assigning authorization objects.

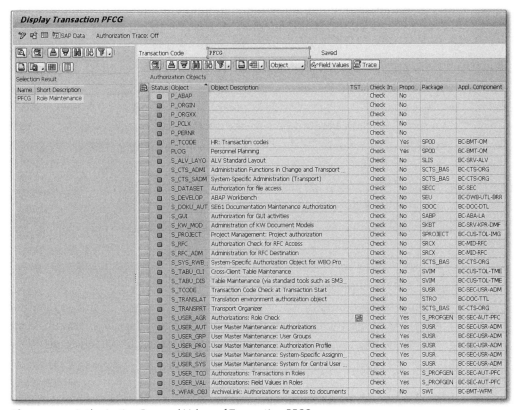

Display Transaction PFCG

Authorization Trace: Off

Transaction Code: `PFCG` Saved

Object | Field Values | Trace

Authorization Objects

Status	Object	Object Description	TST	Check In	Propo	Package	Appl. Component
	P_ABAP			Check	No		
	P_ORGIN			Check	No		
	P_ORGXX			Check	No		
	P_PCLX			Check	No		
	P_PERNR			Check	No		
	P_TCODE	HR: Transaction codes		Check	Yes	SP00	BC-BMT-OM
	PLOG	Personnel Planning		Check	Yes	SP00	BC-BMT-OM
	S_ALV_LAYO	ALV Standard Layout		Check	No	SLIS	BC-SRV-ALV
	S_CTS_ADMI	Administration Functions in Change and Transport		Check	No	SCTS_BAS	BC-CTS-ORG
	S_CTS_SADM	System-Specific Administration (Transport)		Check	No	SCTS_BAS	BC-CTS-ORG
	S_DATASET	Authorization for file access		Check	No	SECC	BC-SEC
	S_DEVELOP	ABAP Workbench		Check	No	SEU	BC-DWB-UTL-BRR
	S_DOKU_AUT	SE61 Documentation Maintenance Authorization		Check	No	SDOC	BC-DOC-DTL
	S_GUI	Authorization for GUI activities		Check	No	SABP	BC-ABA-LA
	S_KW_MOD	Administration of KW Document Models		Check	No	SKBT	BC-SRV-KPR-DMF
	S_PROJECT	Project Management: Project authorization		Check	No	SPROJECT	BC-CUS-TOL-IMG
	S_RFC	Authorization Check for RFC Access		Check	No	SRCX	BC-MID-RFC
	S_RFC_ADM	Administration for RFC Destination		Check	No	SRCX	BC-MID-RFC
	S_SYS_RWB	System-Specific Authorization Object for WBO Pro..		Check	No	SCTS_BAS	BC-CTS-ORG
	S_TABU_CLI	Cross-Client Table Maintenance		Check	No	SVIM	BC-CUS-TOL-TME
	S_TABU_DIS	Table Maintenance (via standard tools such as SM3..		Check	No	SVIM	BC-CUS-TOL-TME
	S_TCODE	Transaction Code Check at Transaction Start		Check	No	SUSR	BC-SEC-USR-ADM
	S_TRANSLAT	Translation environment authorization object		Check	No	STRO	BC-DOC-TTL
	S_TRANSPRT	Transport Organizer		Check	No	SCTS_BAS	BC-CTS-ORG
	S_USER_AGR	Authorizations: Role Check		Check	Yes	S_PROFGEN	BC-SEC-AUT-PFC
	S_USER_AUT	User Master Maintenance: Authorizations		Check	Yes	SUSR	BC-SEC-USR-ADM
	S_USER_GRP	User Master Maintenance: User Groups		Check	Yes	SUSR	BC-SEC-USR-ADM
	S_USER_PRO	User Master Maintenance: Authorization Profile		Check	Yes	SUSR	BC-SEC-USR-ADM
	S_USER_SAS	User Master Maintenance: System-Specific Assignm..		Check	Yes	SUSR	BC-SEC-USR-ADM
	S_USER_SYS	User Master Maintenance: System for Central User ..		Check	No	SUSR	BC-SEC-USR-ADM
	S_USER_TCD	Authorizations: Transactions in Roles		Check	Yes	S_PROFGEN	BC-SEC-AUT-PFC
	S_USER_VAL	Authorizations: Field Values in Roles		Check	Yes	S_PROFGEN	BC-SEC-AUT-PFC
	S_WFAR_OBJ	ArchiveLink: Authorizations for access to documents		Check	No	SWI	BC-BMT-WFM

Selection Result

Name	Short Description
PFCG	Role Maintenance

Figure 12.4 Authorization Proposal Values of Transaction PFCG

Next, you must transfer the SAP proposal values you changed in Transaction SU24 in the customer table of the profile generator. To do this, proceed as follows:

1. Open Transaction SU25.
2. If you have not yet used the profile generator of the SAP Solution Manager system, you must perform an initial fill-out of the customer table as a first step. This is the case for new installation of the SAP Solution Manager system. If this

applies to your system, first select INITIAL FILLING OF THE CUSTOMER TABLE and confirm the subsequent information by clicking the green checkmark icon.

> **Note**
>
> If values from old releases are already contained in the table, filling the table again is not necessary. Performing an initial filling of the customer table again would overwrite the already contained field values.

3. If your SAP Solution Manager system is not a new installation, proceed as follows:

  ▶ Click on Step 2A., PREPARATION: COMPARISON WITH SAP VALUES, in order to insert the delta changes between the current and previous releases in the customer tables. Here again, confirm the information by clicking the green checkmark icon.

  ▶ Then, click on Step 2B. COMPARISON OF TRANSACTIONS DECIDED ON, then confirm the following information with the green checkmark icon.

  ▶ Then, click on Point 2C., SELECT ROLES TO BE CHECKED. You are then shown an overview of all roles affected by the change of authorization proposal values. If you wish to update the already existing roles with the new proposal values, select the column in which the role is located.

  ▶ Then, click on Point 2D., DISPLAY CHANGED TRANSACTION CODES, to view an overview of the transaction codes that were changed in an existing role. If necessary, you can also replace the transaction codes in this selection.

The following steps are optional and should only be used in special cases:

▶ In the TRANSPORTING THE CUSTOMER TABLES step, you can transport the customer tables to other systems. This action is often advisable in multiple system landscapes in which a subdivision into; for example, development, quality assurance, and production systems can be performed.

▶ In the TEST CODE IN TRANSACTIONS (SU24) STEP, the test codes that were serviced in Transaction SU24 are reconciled. The authorization tests within a transaction can be adapted in Transaction SU24. It is also possible to specify the test codes.

▶ If the test code for an authorization proposal is set to TEST as the default, this is checked at start-up or during performance of the transaction. A change in the test code to `Do not Test` has the effect that this authorization object is not queried. You can thereby deactivate an authorization check. It is not possible to add an authorization check to a manually added authorization object because the check must be permanently anchored in the program code. If the value in the PROPOSAL column is set to YES, all existing transaction values are automatically recorded in the PFCG transaction during the creation of a role.

► In the SWITCH OFF AUTHORIZATION OBJECT GLOBALLY step, you have the option of switching off the authorization tests for an authorization object system wide.

► After this, in the TRANSFERRING DATA FROM ROLES step, you can transfer data from manually created profiles for PFCG role creation.

When this step is finished, you have successfully changed the proposal values for your roles.

In addition to PFCG authorizations, you must also be able to work with Java authorizations in an SAP Solution Manager system. These authorizations concern both SAP Solution Manager (because it can also include an AS Java as well as an AS ABAP) and the administered systems, which can also include an AS Java.

You can assign Java authorizations in two different ways. One option is assigning authorizations using PFCG roles, which are linked with Java authorizations. These contain no authorizations on the ABAP side, but rather serve only for authorization assignment for Java systems. One example is the SAP_J2EE_ADMIN role: if it is assigned to a user of the SAP Solution Manager system, that user can perform administrative activities on the AS Java. You can also adapt the authorizations directly on the AS Java. To do this, start SAP NetWeaver administration by going to the following address in a browser: *http://<hostname>:5<instancenumber>00*. Here, you can create new Java users, groups, and roles under the IDENTITY MANAGEMENT link.

Because Java authorizations are required in the SAP Solution Manager landscape primarily for technical users, you should not change Java authorizations and should use them with standard, delivered users and roles.

Now that you have become familiar with the general maintenance of authorizations and roles, we will go into the special role concepts in SAP Solution Manager.

12.3.2 The Role Concept in SAP Solution Manager

As already mentioned, authorizations in SAP Solution Manager are assigned through the assignment of roles. Authorizations are therefore created in roles first. Then, an authorization profile, which contains the authorization objects, fields, and field values, is generated. In the role concept of SAP Solution Manager, distinctions are made among three different types of roles:

► **Work center roles**
You can use these roles to control which work centers a user can access. Access to the ASSOCIATED LINKS area in the work centers is also controlled using work center roles. These roles are referred to as work center navigation roles. You can also adapt the appearance of the work center user—specifically using *work center basic roles*.

► **Functional roles**
Functional roles can be used to restrict a user's freedom of action within a work center.

► **Infrastructure roles**
With infrastructure roles, you can control the user's access to systems, projects, and solutions that are located in the system.

To give users the option of using a certain functionality in an SAP Solution Manager system, a combination of all three role types is necessary, as shown in Figure 12.5. If one of the role types is missing, the user will not be able to open the work center or use a function in the work center (or will be able to do so only to a limited extent), for example. Exceptions concern users who do not work in any of the work centers and therefore, require no work center roles. One example is the user administrator, who deals exclusively with authorization and user administration, and therefore does not need to access a work center.

Standard roles are supplied for all scenarios in SAP Solution Manager. This can be recognized by the prefix SAP_* (the *namespace*). In order to use standard and self-created roles effectively in your system, you must fulfill several requirements.

For example, roles must be generated before their use along with the underlying authorization profile. Due to the generation of the authorization profile, the proposal values existing in the role and the manually changed authorizations are accepted and can subsequently be used in the system.

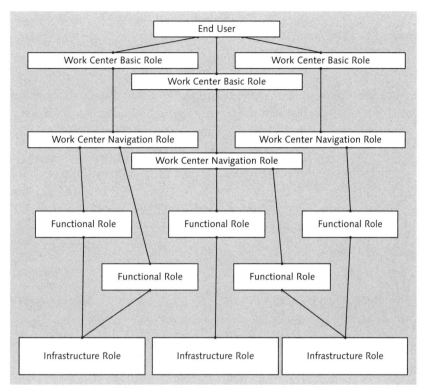

Figure 12.5 Interplay of the Various Roles in SAP Solution Manager

---

Tip

We recommend copying the standard roles in their own namespace before you generate and use them. This has several advantages: first of all you can revert to the delivered standard version at any time, and second, your individual adaptations to the role are not overwritten even in the event of an update.

Let's assume you would like to authorize the user to use the maintenance optimizer scenarios. To do this, proceed as follows:

1. Analyze the roles delivered in the SAP standard using *Security Guide for SAP Solution Manager 7.1*. Various role sets that are supplied by SAP are available for each scenario. Typically, a distinction is made in the role sets between an authorization for the display and administrative authorizations. In the system, the role

sets are generally represented by several composite roles, which contain the required individual roles.

For the Maintenance Optimizer, for example, you will find the composite roles SAP_MAINT_ADMIN_COMP and SAP_MAINT_DIS_COMP. On the DIS component, you can see that a user can open the Maintenance Optimizer in display mode using the SAP_MAINT_DIS_COMP role. In contrast to a user who has been assigned the SAP_MAINT_ADMIN_COMP role, this user can make no changes. In this example, we would like to create a user with administrative authorizations.

2. Thus, copy the corresponding composite role and the single roles contained in it to the customer-specific namespace. To do this, you need only to copy the composite role SAP_MAINT_ADMIN_COMP; the single roles are copied automatically. Now, the following roles should be located in the selected namespace:

   ▶ SAP_MAINT_OPT_ADMIN

   ▶ SAP_SM_SOLUTION_DIS

   ▶ SAP_SYSTEM_REPOSITORY_ALL

   ▶ SAP_SMWORK_BASIC_CHANGE_MAN

   ▶ SAP_SMWORK_CHANGE_MAN

3. The following describes the generation of the authorization profiles that must be carried out. This is necessary for all required single roles except the work center navigation role SAP_SMWORK_CHANGE_MAN. During this step, you can see the proposal values of the authorizations in the role. Looking at the role SAP_MAINT_OPT_ADMIN should show that proposal values are not included for all authorizations. Therefore, in this case, you must assign features to the authorization objects manually. For other roles, the proposal values are complete.

4. After you have generated the authorization profile of the roles, you can assign the composite role to a user. Then, that user can perform all administrative tasks of the scenario.

However, some standard roles also exist for which you create no copy, and no authorization profile must be generated. These include the work center navigation roles, CRM authorization roles, and roles with Java authorizations.

These roles have impacts on permissions in AS Java and contain no authorizations that can be adapted in role maintenance. When you copy the role and assign it to a user, this has no effects on the authorizations of the user. The following roles, therefore, must not be copied:

▶ SAP_J2EE_ADMIN

▶ SAP_J2EE_GUEST

▶ SAP_RCA_AGT_ADM

▶ SAP_RCA_AGT_ADM_VIA_SLD

All work center navigation roles which start with SAP_SMWORK_* except SAP_SMWORK_BASIC_*

12.3.3 The Role Concept in Administered Systems

SAP Solution Manager holds a central role in your system landscape. Therefore, you must not only take into consideration the authorizations for SAP Solution Manager itself, but also the authorizations for the administered systems.

Productive systems that are linked with SAP Solution Manager should, therefore, be given special consideration. Users who access the linked systems from the SAP Solution Manager system are largely technical users. These users, for the most part, must be created during configuration of the respective scenario or during configuration of SAP Solution Manager. The users are created automatically, but they can also be created manually. If you create the users manually, you should note that the technical users receive a specified name, which they must also indicate during the various configuration steps during changes to the system landscape. If the users are created using the corresponding guided procedure, they are automatically assigned the necessary roles and, simultaneously, the necessary authorizations. The roles of the users are thereby fully assigned with features and, therefore, do not need to be individually adapted. The tasks of this user differ from scenario to scenario and can consist of performing functions in the linked systems via RFC links.

The users relevant for a scenario and the necessary authorizations can be found in the *Security Guide for SAP Solution Manager 7.1*. This work offers a special chapter for each scenario in the scenario-specific section. A graphical representation of the communication links and technical users who use them precedes each scenario description.

In addition to these technical users, dialog users are necessary for some scenarios in order to perform special actions for the administered systems. These dialog users require roles for functional access. The following scenarios require authorizations for the administered systems to guarantee full functioning:

► Maintenance Optimizer

► Introduction and Upgrade

► Solution Documentation Assistant

► Test Management

► Business Process Change Analyzer

► Job Management

► Technical Administration

► Running business processes

► Administering change requests

► Quality Gate Management

The authorizations in the administered systems required in these cases can differ greatly and are therefore not contained in the documentation for authorizations in SAP Solution Manager. For example, for the scenario Maintenance Optimizer, you must assign authorizations to a user to be able to use Support Package Manager (Transaction SPAM). Only after this can you implement downloaded Support Package Stacks.

12.3.4 Work Center Roles in SAP Solution Manager

Work center roles in SAP Solution Manager are those roles that allow you access to the various work centers. A distinction can be made between work center basic roles and work center navigation roles.

This can be understood by viewing Figure 12.6. While access to the individual tabs of the work center and the ASSOCIATED LINKS is controlled in the work center navigation roles, which functions the user can access is controlled in the work center basic roles.

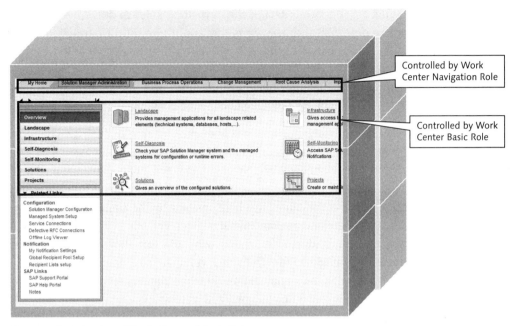

Figure 12.6 Interplay of Navigation and Basis Roles

Next, we will show you the two role types in detail and show you how to adapt the roles to your needs.

Work Center Navigation Roles

Work center navigation roles primarily allow access to the work area of the work center. Therefore, each work center of SAP Solution Manager has its own work center navigation role.

When you assign such a role to a user, the user sees the work area assigned to the role in the user interface when he opens Transaction SM_WORKCENTER or SOLMAN_WORKCENTER.

The names of the work center navigation roles consist of the SAP namespace, the prefix SMWORK, and an abbreviated form of the work center name. The name components are separated from one another by an underscore. Examples of work center navigation roles include SAP_SMWORK_DVM for Data Volume Management and SAP_SMWORK_SYS_MON for system monitoring.

If you look at the authorization data of the navigation roles in detail, you will see that they contain no ABAP authorizations that are important for a function. They contain only the authorization object S_TCODE with the value SOLMAN_WORKCENTER, which allows the user to call up Transaction SOLMAN_WORKCENTER. This authorization is also contained in the work center basic roles. Because the roles do not contain individual data, you do not have to copy them to the customer namespace.

You can specify the authorizations for a work center in role maintenance (Transaction PCFG) on the MENU tab. There, as the first point under the MENUS OF THE ROLE main node, you will find a Web Dynpro application of type AGS_WORKCENTER, which is started using the parameter WORKCENTER. Using the value of this parameter, you can specify which work center can be displayed by the user of the role. You can change the parameter manually. This also gives you the option of creating a special work center navigation role. In this way, you can allow end application users with one user to perform functions in several work centers. To do this, you must create a special work center navigation role that contains several Web Dynpro applications in your menu. To do this, proceed as follows:

1. Open role maintenance (Transaction PFCG) and create a new single role by entering a role name. This role name may not be located in the SAP namespace. Create the role using the SINGLE ROLE button.

2. Enter a more detailed explanation of the role in the DESCRIPTION field.

3. Switch to the MENU tab. Open the selection list of the TRANSACTIONS button by clicking the small black triangle. Then, select the WEB DYNPRO APPLICATION entry.

4. In the following window, enter AGS_WORKCENTER in the WEB DYNPRO APPLICATION field. In the PARAMETER table, enter the value of the desired work center in the NAME WORKCENTER column and the value of the desired work center in the VALUE column, for example AGS_WORK_DVM_NAV for the DATA VOLUME MANAGEMENT work center.

5. Save the role by clicking the diskette symbol and assign it to a user.

You will then have created a special navigation role for the entered work center.

The possible values for the WORKCENTER parameter can be taken from the work center navigation roles of the SAP standard. To do this, switch to the MENU tab of a standard role and right-click the upper menu node to display the DETAILS of the node. In the following window, you can take the VALUE for the WORKCENTER parameter from the PARAMETER table. This process can be repeated as often as desired until you have indicated all work centers relevant for the role in the menu using a Web Dynpro application.

The ASSOCIATED LINKS area in the work centers can also be influenced by navigation roles. In exactly the same way as for the authorizations for calling up work centers, the authorizations for the ASSOCIATED LINKS area can also be specified using the MENU tab in role maintenance:

1. Start role maintenance (Transaction PFCG) and enter the work center navigation role you would like to change in the ROLE field. Then, switch to change mode by clicking the pencil symbol or using the [F6] button. Note that you require the necessary authorizations in SAP Solution Manager to switch to change mode.

2. Select the MENU tab.

3. Open the selection list of the TRANSACTION button by clicking the small black triangle. Select WEB ADDRESS OR FILE.

4. Another window in which you can adapt already available web addresses or add new ones opens (see Figure 12.7).

5. Confirm your entries by clicking the green checkmark icon.

6. Save the role by clicking the SAVE icon.

These links are later shown to the users with the respective role in the ASSOCIATED LINKS area of the work center.

In addition to work center navigation roles, work center basic roles are provided in SAP Solution Manager.

Work Center Basic Roles

In contrast to the navigation roles, which allow the main access to the tabs of the work center, work center basic roles control the display of functions within the work center and thereby also influence the content and appearance. Exactly as with navigation roles, the basis roles in the standard are bound to a single work center. An exception is the role SAP_SM_BASIC, which represents a work center basis role for all available work centers.

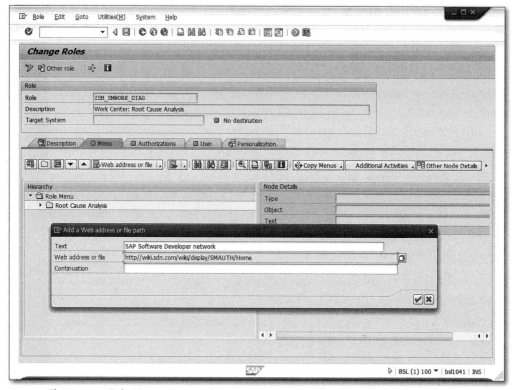

Figure 12.7 Role Maintenance with Transaction PFCG

The authorizations that are decisive for the function are assigned through authorizations rather than through use of the MENU tab in role maintenance. The authorizations of the basis roles do not directly stipulate which functions a user can call up, but rather only which elements of the user interface he or she can access.

The naming system of the basis roles is structured similarly to that of the navigation roles. They begin with the character string SAP for the SAP namespace, followed by the SMWORK_BASIC word master. For the navigation roles, the subsequent character string refers to the name of the respective work center. Examples of work center basic roles include SAP_SMWORK_BASIC_DVM for Data Volume Management and SAP_SMWORK_BASIC_SYSMON for system monitoring.

You can specify the authorizations of a role in role maintenance (Transaction PCFG) on the AUTHORIZATIONS tab. The authorization object that is decisive for the user interface of the work center basic roles is SM_WC_VIEW. You use this authorization object to control the visibility of navigation and of the TYPICAL TASKS area in a work center.

> **Note**
>
> Note that simply hiding a navigation button cannot prevent direct, manual call-up or execution of the corresponding web address. To prevent users from accessing functions, you must assign functional authorizations, which we will discuss in more detail in Section 12.3.5.

By adapting the authorization object SM_WC_VIEW, you can show and hide individual elements in the left-hand navigation bar and in the TYPICAL TASKS area. On the left-hand side of Figure 12.8, you can see how the navigation bar of the CHANGE MANAGEMENT work center looks when the authorization object has been fully assigned with features. In the representation on the right-hand side, on the other hand, only the authorization for displaying the OVERVIEW menu item has been assigned. Therefore, all other menu items have been hidden, and the ASSOCIATED LINKS are displayed at the very top.

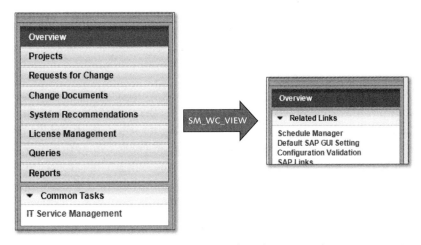

Figure 12.8 Maintaining the Navigation Bar with Authorization Object SM_WC_VIEW

All available functions in the menus and work center work areas are shown in the work center basic roles included by default in the SAP shipping package. However, if you do not wish to use individual functions of the work center and therefore wish to hide them, you can subsequently change this using the SM_WC_VIEW authorization object.

Let us assume you would like to authorize selection of the Maintenance Optimizers in the CHANGE MANAGEMENT work center only for one or more users. To do this, proceed as follows:

1. Start role maintenance (Transaction PFCG) and enter the role name of the copy that you made from the role SAP_SMWORK_BASIC_CHANGE_MAN in the ROLE field.

2. Switch to change mode by clicking the 🖉 icon.

3. Switch to the AUTHORIZATIONS tab and click the CHANGE AUTHORIZATION DATA button.

4. To display the technical names, select UTILITIES • TECHNICAL NAMES ON from the header menu.

5. Expand node SM in order to access the authorization object SM_WC_VIEW.

6. Double-click any authorization field to edit the authorization object.

7. In the following table, find the AGS_WORK_CHANGE_MAN entry in the WORKCENTER_ID column and select all entries of this value in which the value of the view is not MOPZ.

8. Confirm the selection of the table and generate the role.

9. Now, you can assign the role to one or more users. These users will then be shown only the MAINTENANCE OPTIMIZER entry in the CHANGE MANAGEMENT work center.

You have learned how to adapt the user interface of the work center for individual users and user groups using navigation and basis roles. Because the users can still access functions that are not displayed in the work center using direct links, you should also stipulate which functions individual users and user groups may access in order to protect the data security of your system. To do this, you can use functional roles, which we will describe in greater detail in the next section.

12.3.5 Functional Roles

Functional roles are the most important and frequently used roles in SAP Solution Manager systems. They allow you to specify which functions and actions a user may perform on a technical level. This takes place exclusively through the assignment of authorizations in role maintenance. Here, authorization fields in the role are inserted, changed, and deleted.

If you are already familiar with the authorization test of an AS ABAP system, you can naturally also transfer this concept to SAP Solution Manager. If a user executes an action (i.e., a program), in the widest sense, authorization checks arise in the individual step of program execution. These checks are contained statically in the program code and queried in the same way at every call-up. In such a test, the program checks whether the executing user has been assigned the necessary authorization object with the required feature assignment. Feature assignment is performed here using certain values in the *authorization fields*.

If the executing user has the authorization with the required feature assignment, he can use the program to the fullest extent (i.e., execute each individual function). If an authorization object fails, it can be due to a missing authorization object or insufficient feature assignment of the authorization object.

For example, it is possible to use a program to query whether the user has been assigned a role that contains the authorization object S_PROJECT with the feature assignment for changing all available projects in the system. One possible feedback message to this query is that the user does not possess this authorization object. He therefore cannot see, create, or change any of the projects in the overview the program generates. If the authorization test is positive—i.e., if the authorization object is present—a check is also performed for whether the feature assignment of the authorization fields meets the specified requirements. In our example, the authorization fields must contain two specifications. Both the project name and the CHANGE action type must be specified.

The authorization fields queried in this case are ACTVT with the feature assignment 02 for changing the project and PROJECT_ID with the name of the project for its visibility, as you can see in Figure 12.9.

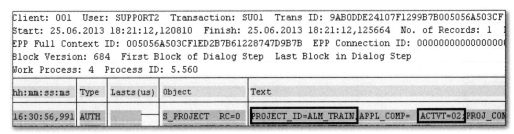

Figure 12.9 View of the Authorization Test in Debugging Mode of a Dialog Step

If the check is negative, the user either has no permission to change projects or cannot process the desired project.

To obtain an indication of the missing authorization object or incomplete feature assignment, you can analyze the authorization data. Two tools are available to you for this purpose. First, you can record the authorization test using System Trace (Transaction ST01). During the subsequent evaluation, you can identify the missing authorizations or authorization feature assignments. Second, you can display the last faulty authorization test using authorization error analysis (Transaction SU53).

The feature assignment of an object is determined through authorization fields and their values. Each authorization object contains at least one authorization field, as well as possible values for the authorization field. Generally, however, authorization objects contain a collection of authorization fields. The authorization field whose value determines the executable action is generally called ACTVT. Various possible actions and their values include displaying (03), changing (02), deleting (06), and creating (01). In addition to the activity, another authorization field is used to determine what focus the action should have.

For example, the visibility of solutions can be determined in the authorization object D_SOL_VSBL. The authorization object contains the authorization fields ACTVT and SOLUTION. With the ACTVT activation field, you determine the activity to be performed by the user of the role. In this case, the SOLUTION field contains the name of the solution for which the action is to be executable. For example, the user of the role for the feature assignment of authorization object D_SOL_VSBL shown in Figure 12.10 can view and change the solution SAP_SOLUTION. The name of the solution is shown through the object ID in the SOLUTION authorization field. You can view the associated name in the values help [F4].

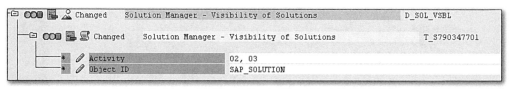

Figure 12.10 Feature Assignment of the Authorization Object D_SOL_VSBL

Proposal values for the fields are generally entered in the roles supplied by SAP so that, in many cases, you only have to generate the role to provide the user with the desired function. If no proposal values are provided for fields, you must enter the values manually later. This is the case for authorization objects that are checked for functions especially critical to security. These include, for example, the authorization object S_RFCACL. This checks the authorizations of RFC users, especially in trusted systems. If this authorization object is required for a function, you must assign features to it based on your system landscape.

Let's assume you would like to call up a function module on your administered system EP1 from your SAP Solution Manager system with the name SM1 and the client 100. In addition, the call-up of the function module on the administered system is to take place with the user ID RFCUSER1, which you also use in your SAP Solution Manager system SM1.

Based on these conditions, the authorization object S_RFCACL, as shown in Table 12.2, must be assigned features on the administered system.

You must then assign this authorization to user RFCUSER1 on the administered system. If you wish to use different user IDs on the two systems, you must fill authorization field RFC_USER with the user ID from system SM1 and change the value for the field RFC_EQUSER to No.

If the proposal values in the roles do not meet the requirements of your safety concept, you can change them manually. Before changing functional roles, you should copy them to a special namespace. This way, you can easily access the original status of the role at a later point.

Name of the Authorization Field	Value of the Authorization Field
RFC_SYSID	SM1
RFC_CLIENT	100
RFC_USER	(no value)
RFC_EQUSER	Yes
RFC_TCODE	*
RFC_INFO	*
ACTVT	16

Table 12.2 Variant of the Authorization Object S_RFCACL

12.3.6 Infrastructure Roles

In SAP Solution Manager, the term *Infrastructure* is used for all entities referring to systems, hosts, databases, solutions and projects. These units form the basis for the functionalities in all scenarios. *Infrastructure roles* are basically functional roles that, however, must be viewed separately because of their special functions. Like functional roles, infrastructure roles include authorizations you can maintain in role maintenance (Transaction PCFG).

Infrastructure roles determine for the entities whether and to what extent they can be used by a functionality.

Systems, databases, and hosts are combined in the *Systems* entity. The Systems entity is used in all scenarios in SAP Solution Manager. The *Solutions* and *Projects* entities, however, are used only in certain scenarios. Which of the two scenarios is used depends on the Application Lifecycle Management (ALM) phase in which the scenario is. For scenarios that are not used in production operations yet, the *Projects* entity is used. For scenarios that have already taken over in the production system, either the *Solutions* entity or the *Systems* entity is used.

Examples are the Business Process Operations and Test Management scenarios. Since both scenarios occur before go-live, the roles provided here include authorizations for the Projects entity. However, in scenarios such as root cause analysis, which play a role only after the go-live of a solution, this entity is no longer viewed. Instead, the *Systems* entity is used. However, this division of the infrastructure into a phase after and a phase before go-live is not always followed. There are exceptions to the individual scenarios, depending on their functioning.

Since the entities cover the entire lifecycle of a software, they are used in all scenarios provided by SAP Solution Manager. Users of SAP Solution Manager can make use of multiple scenarios in various phases of the lifecycle. Therefore, it must be ensured that the entities can be controlled centrally. Authorizations that have an impact on infrastructural entities are therefore managed in central roles. Table 12.3 shows the infrastructure roles used in SAP Solution Manager.

Role Name	Infrastructural Entities
SAP_SYSTEM_REPOSITORY_DIS	Display authorization for entries in the Landscape Management Database (LMDB) and access to Transaction SMSY

Table 12.3 Available Infrastructure Roles in SAP Solution Manager

Role Name	Infrastructural Entities
SAP_SYSTEM_REPOSITORY_ALL	Full authorization for entries in the LMDB and access to Transaction SMSY
SAP_SMSY_DIS	Display authorization for access to Transaction SMSY
SAP_SMSY_ALL	Full authorization for access to Transaction SMSY
SAP_SM_SOLUTION_DIS	Display authorization for solutions
SAP_SM_SOLUTION_ALL	Full authorizations for solutions
SAP_SOL_PROJ_ADMIN_DIS	Display authorizations for projects
SAP_SOL_PROJ_ADMIN_ALL	Full authorizations for projects

Table 12.3 Available Infrastructure Roles in SAP Solution Manager (Cont.)

12.3.7 CRM Authorization Roles

Another role type you can use in your SAP Solution Manager is CRM authorization roles. These are roles that can be used only in the ITSM scenario, and therefore do not necessarily have to be used in a system. CRM authorization roles are only used in SAP Solution Management systems. These roles cannot be found in managed systems.

12.3.8 Authorizations in SAP Service Marketplace

Since SAP Service Marketplace is not open to the public but to SAP customers only, authorizations are needed to control access.

These are required for access to SAP Service Marketplace via a web browser, as well as for accesses provided by functions within scenarios of SAP Solution Manager. The user needed for access to SAP Service Marketplace is named *S User*. It consists of a sequence of numbers preceded by an *S*. The following shows a few typical use cases where an S User is required.

▶ Exchanging problem reports using SAP

▶ Synchronizing system data of SAP Solution Manager and the managed systems using the Support Portal

▶ Creating service connections

▶ Exchanging information via messages exchanged with SAP

The following scenarios require a connection with SAP Service Marketplace and an S User:

- Maintenance Optimizer
- Incident Management
- SAP Engagement and Service Delivery

The authorizations of the S User can be viewed at *http://service.sap.com/user-admin/*. Apart from the authorizations of the user, you can also adjust person-related information of the S User here, change the password of the user, and create new S Users or delete them if you have the required authorization object. The following authorization objects are available for SAP Service Marketplace:

- Administration authorization
- Display all customer messages
- Maintain user data
- Send customer messages to SAP
- Create a customer message
- Register object and developer keys
- Security contact
- Download software

Information on the scope of the authorizations required to use a functionality in a scenario is available in the Security Guide for SAP Solution Manager. For more details on the Security Guide, see Section 12.4.1.

Since an S User is always bound to an individual user, you need to connect the S Users with an end user. This can be done in SAP SUPPORT PORTAL CONTACT PERSON ASSIGNMENT, which you can call using Transaction AISUSER. Here, you can enter a user in the USER column and then assign it an S User in the CONTACT PERSON column (see Figure 12.11). Please make sure not to enter the preceding S or zeros.

12.3.9 Access Administration in SAP Solution Manager

Access administration in SAP Solution Manager is structured in various levels (see Figure 12.12). The work center roles allow you to control the contents and looks of a work center. You can control the execution of activities using the so-called authorization roles or PFCG roles. Here, a distinction is made among functional roles, infrastructure roles, and Java roles.

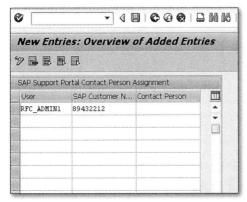

Figure 12.11 Assignment between Users and S Users

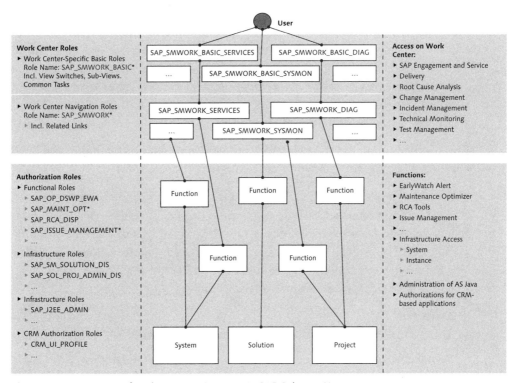

Figure 12.12 Structure of Authorization Concepts in SAP Solution Manager

It may happen that only the PFCG roles are used in your system because many of the scenarios just build upon these, and the other role types are used only on the technical side.

12.4 Information Sources for Authorization Assignments

Apart from the information on authorizations you can receive using SAP Solution Manager, there is external documentation available, which is provided by SAP and makes your work with authorizations easier. The two most important information sources are the following:

▸ Security Guide for SAP Solution Manager 7.1

▸ SAP Solution Manager—Security and Authorizations Wiki

12.4.1 Security Guide for SAP Solution Manager 7.1

The Security Guide is the central source of information on authorizations in SAP Solution Manager and authorizations required for functionalities on managed systems. Each SAP Solution Manager release has its own Security Guide, which can be found in SAP Service Marketplace, *http://service.sap.com/instguides*, at SAP COMPONENTS • SAP SOLUTION MANAGER • RELEASE <CURRENT RELEASE> • OPERATIONS • SECURITY GUIDE <CURRENT RELEASE>.

The Security Guide has the officially valid guidelines and recommendations and covers the installation, configuration, and operation phases.

The information on the individual phases is to ensure a medium security standard on SAP Solution Manager and the connected systems. Customer-specific requirements exceeding this scope of security cannot be considered due to the potential complexity of individual adjustment. The Security Guide has been designed to allow you to find all information required for planning authorization assignments in an authorization concept. The Security Guide is divided into two parts:

▸ **Main part**
This part includes information on universal authorizations.

▸ **Scenario-specific part**
This part provides information on specific authorizations in the individual ALM and Run SAP like a Factory processes.

The main part provides basic information on all authorization-relevant topics around SAP Solution Manager. For example, it shows you how to do authorization and role adjustments and explains the functions of the user administration. We recommend that you read the full main part before you start planning your authorizations because all information may be relevant for your SAP Solution Manager and managed systems.

The second part of the Security Guide is the scenario-specific part. It offers you information on the individual scenarios that you can use in your systems. The provided information includes the following:

▶ An overview of all technical connections to connected systems

▶ An overview and description of technical users and final users in the systems

▶ An overview and description of required roles and authorizations for user types

In contrast to the main part, you should refer to the scenario-specific part only if you wish to use the described scenario in your system landscape.

12.4.2 SAP Solution Manager—Security and Authorizations Wiki

The wiki SMAUTH in the SAP Software Developer Network is an additional information source that completes the SAP Security Guide. You can access it at *http://wiki.sdn.sap.com/wiki/display/SMAUTH/Home*. The wiki contains only information on SAP Solution Manager 7.1. Table 12.4 shows an overview of the covered topics.

Topic	Description
Authorization Objects	Overview and analysis of all authorization objects in SAP Solution Manager 7.1
Use Cases	Overview of the scenario-specific use of authorization objects
Best Practices	Recommendations on how to handle authorization objects
Technical Infrastructure	List of minimum requirements to the technical infrastructure for the scenarios used
Glossary	Definition of terms used in the authorization environment
FAQ	Frequently asked questions about SAP Solution Manager authorizations

Table 12.4 Overview of the Wiki SMAUTH Structure

The AUTHORIZATION OBJECTS area allows you to find information on authorization objects that are not entirely adjusted by SAP default. You can thus identify and adjust authorization objects that play a particularly important role in your system environment.

The overview also allows you to structure authorization objects based on their uses in the individual scenarios. That way, it is possible to identify multiple uses of authorization objects in the scenarios and transfer these authorizations (for example, into infrastructure roles), if you consider this useful.

The USE CASES subitem provides use cases for typical requirements that can be controlled by means of specific authorization assignments. The use cases are structured based on scenarios. Once you have selected a specific scenario, an overview of currently available use cases appears—for example, how to control the visibility of systems. The actual use cases are always structured based on the same pattern composed of the motivation, solution, and result.

General notes—for example, on how to copy standard SAP roles or what to consider when checking authorizations after an upgrade—can be found under BEST PRACTICES.

Detailed information on the basic applications and connections required for specific scenarios can be found in the TECHNICAL INFRASTRUCTURE subitem. That includes not only the names or ports of used connections, but also users needed for communication.

If you have any terminology-related questions on individual items, we recommend referring to the GLOSSARY or the FAQ area.

12.5   Creating an Authorization Concept

If you wish to use individual functions or all functions of SAP Solution Manager, it is necessary to create and document responsibilities and the resulting users and authorizations based on a defined scheme. This applies to both end users and technical users.

Apart from the resulting clarity and traceability of your decisions, an authorization concept implements the security standard you use.

The authorization concept not only comprises the users and connections that are available on SAP Solution Manager, but also deals with the connected systems, as you can see in Figure 12.13.

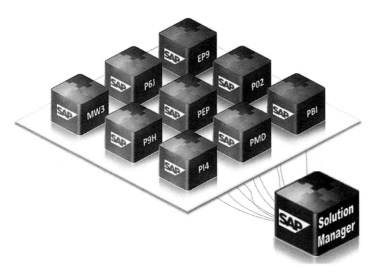

Figure 12.13 SAP Solution Manager—Connected Systems

This is necessary because some of the functions executed on the connected systems are security critical. The system risks are as follows:

▶ Damage to SAP Solution Manager due to unauthorized changes to stored data and unauthorized modifications of the configuration

▶ Damage to the connected systems by a user on SAP Solution Manager due to a missing authorization concept

It is the aim of an authorization concept to minimize these risks. To create an authorization concept, you should develop a systematic procedure. We recommend dividing the creation into individual steps. These steps form the process you should go through when a functionality is taken up into the concept or if the scope of an existing function changes. The authorization concept of SAP Solution Manager generally comprises the following components:

▶ Requirements analysis

▶ Basic concept

▶ Detailed concept

- Implementation and testing
- Handover to operations

Please note that these steps to create an authorization concept are merely a recommendation. They can be carried out in a different order with a different scope. The following provides more details on the individual steps.

12.5.1 Requirements Analysis

The requirements analysis is the basis and the first step to creating an authorization concept. In this step, you should first find the scope of your concept. It consists of the various systems and the scenarios and functions you can use. For example, the scope can consist of the following scenarios:

- Configuration validation
- Root cause analysis
- Maintenance Optimizer
- Service Level Reporting (SLR)
- Central system administration
- Change Request Management
- Development functions
- SAP Solution Manager administration

For your further planning, it is important to have a clear picture of the individual functions of the scenarios. This way, you can estimate which security-critical characteristics the individual scenarios have. For example, the administration of SAP Solution Manager bears a much greater risk potential than Maintenance Optimizer. The description of the functionalities of the scenarios in the SAP Solution Manager Security Guide (see Section 12.4.1) is a good reference for you to estimate the risk potential.

Otherwise, you should note the composite roles described in the SAP Solution Manager Security Guide. The composite roles and contained individual roles form the basis for the role concept. You should define the interest groups a scenario or functionality should use. For example, an interest group of the SAP Solution Manager administration can be the system administrator or the Basis team that maintains the system landscape.

Then, you should think about whether you want only end users or also technical users to be considered in the authorization concept. You also need to define the extent to which these users are to be considered. For example, you can add which roles are assigned to the technical users or just list the user names. Then, create a list of user groups. Examples of end-user groups are as follows:

▶ System administrators

▶ Authorization administrators

▶ Users—internal

▶ Users—external

▶ Developers

▶ System owner

Based on these details, you can create the so-called segregation of duties (SoD) matrix. This is an illustration indicating the relation between user groups and functions.

Table 12.5 shows an example of such an SoD matrix. The check marks in Table 12.5 indicate which scenarios or functions a user is allowed to use and whether the user is supposed to only receive display or also administrator permissions. In our example, we want the *System Administrator* to use the SAP Solution Manager Administration scenario with administrative authorizations. However, for configuration validation and the SLR, we want him to have only display permissions. Then, we want the *External User* to be able to use the SLR, central system administration, and change request management.

The aim of the requirements analysis is to name the user groups to be expected and assign them to various functions in the scenarios.

Scenario/Function	Authorization	System Administrator	Internal User	External User	Developer
Configuration validation	Administration		X		
	Display	X	X	X	X
Root cause analysis	Administration		X		

Table 12.5 Example of an SoD Matrix

Scenario/Function	Authorization	System Administrator	Internal User	External User	Developer
	Display			X	
Maintenance Optimizer	Administration		X		
	Display			X	
SLR	Administration		X	X	
	Display	X	X	X	X
Central system administration (CSA)	Administration		X	X	
Change Request Management	Administration		X	X	
Development functions	Administration				X
SAP Solution Manager administration	Administration	X			

Table 12.5 Example of an SoD Matrix (Cont.)

12.5.2 Basic Concept

Based on the information of the SoD matrix, the basic concept analyzes and documents which roles are already provided by SAP default and can thus be used in the concept. This information is available in the scenario-specific part of Security Guide for SAP Solution Manager 7.1 (see Section 12.4.1).

SAP Solution Manager offers one or multiple composite role(s) for each scenario. If there are multiple composite roles available for a scenario, they differ in the scope of granted authorizations. For example, for Maintenance Optimizer, there is a composite role with authorizations for an administrator and a composite role with display authorizations for end users.

After you have decided which roles you wish to apply, you should define which names the copies in your customer's namespace are to receive. For example, you can change the SAP* namespace to another namespace, such as ZSM_DEV*. That way, if you use a central user management, it is easier to define for which SAP system the role is intended. For example, the basic concept for Maintenance Optimizer includes that SAP has defined two composite roles that can cover the functions of an administrator and a display user.

The SAP_MAINT_ADMIN_COMP composite role is for the administrator and has the following individual roles:

- SAP_MAINT_OPT_ADMIN
- SAP_SM_SOLUTION_DIS
- SAP_SYSTEM_REPOSITORY_ALL
- SAP_SMWORK_BASIC_CHANGE_MAN
- SAP_SMWORK_CHANGE_MAN

The composite role for the display user is SAP_MAINT_DISP_COMP. It has the following individual roles:

- SAP_MAINT_OPT_DIS
- SAP_SM_SOLUTION_DIS
- SAP_SYSTEM_REPOSITORY_DIS
- SAP_SMWORK_BASIC_CHANGE_MAN
- SAP_SMWORK_CHANGE_MAN

The purpose of the basic concept is to name the composite and individual roles and to define the future namespace, and thus the role name.

12.5.3 Detail Concept

Since the authorizations of some roles that were determined in the basic concept are not entirely defined, you need to define and document them in the detailed concept.

Information on how to define authorizations or which authorizations are useful in a use case can be found in the mentioned information sources for authorizations (see Section 12.4). Make sure to always record a reason for your decisions so that you can comprehend them at future reviews.

It is also recommended to compile the roles defined in the basic concept to form composite roles in the detailed concept. In the above example (see Table 12.5), it is therefore useful to create a composite role for each of the System Administrators, Internal Users, External Users, and Developers user groups; that composite role should then include all individual roles of the scenarios that a user group requires. This helps you grant authorizations for the individual user groups.

12.5.4 Implementation and Testing

After creating a detailed concept, you can start implementing the authorizations. To do this, you need to copy the SAP default roles into the customer namespace based on the naming convention of the basic concept and define them in accordance with the specifications in the detailed concept. If you have designed roles of your own, you need to create them in SAP Solution Manager and, possibly, in the managed systems. If you wish to use these roles for other systems, as well, we recommend assigning the created roles in a transport request.

After that, you should create test users for each user group and, based on typical tasks of the individual user groups, thoroughly test whether your authorization concept is implemented properly.

12.5.5 Handover to Operations

After you have successfully completed all tests, you can hand over your authorization concept to operations. In doing so, you transfer a documentation, which contains the various aspects required for working with the roles for operations.

First, you should specify on which systems and clients you have created users. Depending on how detailed the structure of your authorization concept is, you can enter technical users and end users. Otherwise, the documentation should include which composite roles and individual roles in the various systems and clients have to be transferred to the individual users to enable operations. As far as your authorization concept includes infrastructure roles, you should enter these too, so that operations can track which infrastructure roles are used and in which case they must be assigned to a user. Also, it is recommended that you add a list of work processes that are executed in the individual scenarios. This way, it can be easily determined when a specific authorization is relevant for a user type. Finally, don't forget to document a transport request in which all transportable changes are listed.

12.6   Customer Example—Authorization Concept at Munich Re

After Mr. Carsten Bein gave us insight into his SAP Solution Manager upgrade project, he is now going to explain how Munich Re proceeded in creating an authorization concept.

Initial Situation and Challenges

The conception and maintenance of application-specific authorizations in an SAP system is very complex because very many organizational, process-related, and legal requirements need to be considered. This particularly applies to an SAP Solution Manager system because it is connected with all systems to be managed. In this view, the topic of authorizations within SAP Solution Manager systems is especially sensitive.

The standard roles included in the SAP shipping package are a very basis for the implementation of SAP Solution Manager. However, in our opinion, they include a few critical authorizations, which is why we normally created copies of standard roles to adapt them to our needs.

A special challenge in developing a sound authorization concept was to map the organizational structure and existing processes at Munich Re by adjusting the SAP standard roles. Munich Re's IT is structured based on so-called services. So, there are individual services that, for example, primarily handle basis administration, secure application operations, implement developments, or perform decided tests.

A perfect authorization concept always requires a good balance of individual role conception and taking over standard roles. In planning an authorization concept, it is always important to consider the pros and cons of the individual approaches.

Implementing the Authorization Concept

In our case, we updated and restructured our existing SAP Solution Manager authorization concept as part of our upgrade project to SAP Solution Manager 7.1. We are now following a modular approach, in which our technical IT service roles are assigned specific individual and composite roles. For visualization, we created an SoD matrix that conceptually clearly separates the individual responsibilities from one another.

The modularization allows us to administer scenario-specific roles of SAP Solution Manager beyond organizational borders and specifically react to necessary adjustments caused by changes to the software status. Moreover, the modular approach increases our flexibility and allows us to react more quickly to organizational changes in our authorization concept.

The roles are assigned using our own identity and access management (IAM) tool. In this connection, the required roles and associated approvers are registered in the IAM-related database. If a user requests a role via the IAM web frontend, the approval work flow is started. If the request is approved, the IAM tool assigns the user the requested role. For specific services, a so-called *business role* can be requested, which comprises all individual and composite roles required for the respective service.

Thanks to this workflow, the complex and time-consuming request process for individual roles is waived. Based on our experience in the SAP Solution Manager upgrade project, we strongly recommend that other SAP users use copies of the SAP standard roles and avoid any adjustments whenever possible.

12.7   Additional Documentation

Links

▶ Determining authorizations of S Users: *http://service.sap.com/user-admin/*

▶ Security Guide for SAP Solution Manager 7.1: *http://service.sap.com/instguides* under SAP COMPONENTS • SAP SOLUTION MANAGER • RELEASE <CURRENT RELEASE> • OPERATIONS • SECURITY GUIDE <CURRENT RELEASE>

▶ SAP Software Developer Network (SDN): Wiki SMAUTH *http://wiki.sdn.sap.com/wiki/display/SMAUTH/Home*

SAP Notes

In connection with authorizations in SAP Solution Manager, SAP Note 1572183 (Authorizations for SAP Solution Manager RFC Users) can be useful.

Appendices

A   Literature

Anderhub, Vital: *Service Level Management – der ITIL-Prozess mit dem SAP Solution Manager.* 2. aktual. u. erw. Aufl. Bonn: SAP PRESS 2011.*

Banner, Marcus; Klein, Heinzpeter; Riesener, Christian: *Mastering SAP NetWeaver PI – Administration.* 2nd edition, Boston, MA: SAP PRESS 2009.

Beims, Martin: *IT-Service Management in der Praxis mit ITIL3. Zielfindung, Methoden, Realisierung.* München: Hanser 2009.*

Bock, Wolfgang; Macek, Günter; Oberndorfer, Thomas; Pumsenberger, Robert: *ITIL. Zertifizierung nach BS 15000/ISO 20000.* Bonn: Galileo Press 2006.*

Föse, Frank; Hagemann, Sigrid; Will, Liane: *SAP NetWeaver AS ABAP – System Administration.* 4th edition, Boston, MA: SAP PRESS 2011.

Faustmann, André; Klein, Gunnar; Siegling, André; Zimmermann, Ronny: *SAP NetWeaver AS Java – Systemadministration.* Bonn: SAP PRESS 2009.*

Kasturi, Rajeev: *SAP R/3 ALE & EDI Technologies.* New York: McGraw Hill 1999.

Kessler, Torsten; Hügens, Torben; Drexler, Frank; Abdel Hadi, Mohamed: *Reporting mit SAP NetWeaver BW und SAP BusinessObjects. Das umfassende Handbuch.* Bonn: SAP PRESS 2012.*

Kösegi, Armin; Nerding, Rainer: *SAP Änderungs- und Transportmanagement.* 4. aktual. u. erw. Aufl. Bonn: SAP PRESS 2013.*

SAP AG: *Online Documentation Release SAP NetWeaver 7.3.* In: *http://help.sap.com.*

SAP AG: *Installation Guide for SAP NetWeaver 7.3.* In: *http://service.sap.com/instguides.*

SAP AG: *SAPinst Troubleshooting Guide V1.20.* In: *http://service.sap.com/sapinst.*

SAP AG: *Import Guide.* In: *http://service.sap.com/instguides.*

SAP AG: *Online Help Guide to Installation.* In: *http://service.sap.com/instguides.*

SAP AG: *Security Guides Bd. I-III.* In: *http://service.sap.com/securityguides.*

---

*Books marked with an asterisk are in German only.

Schäfer, Marc O.; Melich, Matthias: *SAP Solution Manager*. 3rd edition, Boston, MA: SAP PRESS 2011.

Schneider, Thomas: *SAP Performance Optimization Guide: Analysis and Tuning SAP Systems*. 7th edition, Boston, MA: SAP PRESS 2013.

Schreckenbach, Sebastian: *SAP Administration—Practical Guide*. Boston, MA: SAP PRESS 2011.

Stefani, Helmut: *Archiving your SAP Data*. 2nd edition, Boston, MA: SAP PRESS 2007.

B   Glossary

ABAP   Advanced Business Application Programming. SAP's programming language for the development of application programs.

ACID Principle   Describes the desired characteristics of the processing of information in a database management system (DBMS). In German, ACID stands for the following characteristics: atomic, consistent, isolated, durable; in German publications, the abbreviation AKID for the German terms is common.

Adaptive Computing Controller (ACC)   SAP Adaptive Computing Controller (ACC) is based on the J2EE Engine of SAP NetWeaver AS and enables administrators to control the entire landscape from one single location.

Applications Server (AS)   Computer on which at least one SAP instance is located.

Background Processing   Processing that is not done in dialogs. In this method, data is processed in the background while other functions are simultaneously executed on the screen. Although the background processes are performed invisibly to the user and without the user's direct influence (no dialog option), they have the same priority as online processes.

CA Wily Introscope Byte Code Adapter
The CA Wily Introscope Byte Code Adapter is used in connection with the Introscope Enterprise Manager to collect and store performance data.

CA Wily Introscope Enterprise Manager
Stand-alone server component for collecting application information of components without an ABAP basis. By complete integration into SAP Solution Manager, this information can be used for monitoring and reporting scenarios.

CCDB   → Configuration and Change Database

Client   In commercial, organizational, and technical terms, a self-contained unit in an SAP system with separate master records and its own set of tables.

Common Information Model (CIM)   Standard for the management of IT systems, which was developed and approved by the Distributed Management Task Force (DMTF). Its main purpose is to enable distributed applications to provide a unified management interface independent of a provider and platform.

Computing Center Management System (CCMS)   Tool that serves for the monitoring, control, and configuration of the SAP system. The Computing Center Management System supports 24-hour system management functions. They can analyze and distribute the system load and monitor the resource requirement of the various system components.

Configuration and Change Database (CCDB)   Collection of tables and interfaces to track changes in the technical configuration of managed systems. For that purpose, Solution Manager Diagnostics is used as the managed system.

Database A database comprises files required for permanent data storage on the hard drive and one or multiple database instance(s). Each SAP system has only one database.

Dialog Work Process SAP work process for processing user requests that work in dialog.

Dispatcher Coordinated process of the work processes of an instance.

Distributed Management Task Force (DMTF) The Distributed Management Task Force is a standardization organization consisting of IT company members. It is organized in work groups, made up of equal-size groups of manufacturers and users. Their aim is to coordinate the development, adaptation, and interoperability of standards for system management and initiatives for the coordination of system management in corporate and Internet environments (see also *www.dmtf. org*).

Data Provider Connector (DPC) The Data Provider Connector is responsible for transmitting monitoring data into the monitoring and alerting infrastructure (MAI). The required information can be transmitted via a push or pull mechanism; various data sources, such as the local CCMS, SAP NetWeaver management agents, or CA Wily Introscope are supported.

Extractor Framework (EFWK) The Extractor Framework in the data retrieval layer of SAP Solution Manager is used to actively collect (pull mechanism) or receive (push mechanism) data from connected systems and finally store it in the business warehouse of SAP Solution Manager.

End-to-End Methodology End-to-end methodology is a collection of multiple methods tuned to one another, where various tools from the SAP Solution Manager infrastructure are used to perform a root cause analysis, viewed from the end-user PC to the back end.

Feature Package (FP) For SAP Solution Manager, new functionalities are shipped using special Support Packages. They are called Feature Packages. Feature Packages are treated like Support Packages; they do, however, contain new functions that can have an impact on existing processes. Importing Feature Packages should therefore be carefully planned.

Graphical User Interface (GUI) Medium that enables the user to exchange information with the computer. The user interface allows you to select commands, start programs, display files, and perform other options by pressing function keys or clicking buttons, selecting menu options, and clicking icons using your mouse.

High Availability (HA) Service or system characteristic of remaining in production operations for the majority of time. High availability of an SAP system means that scheduled or unscheduled idle times are reduced to a minimum. A good system administration is decisive in this context. Unscheduled idle times can be reduced by using preventive hardware and software solutions aimed at reducing single points of failure in the services that support the SAP system. Scheduled idle times can be reduced by optimum planning of necessary maintenance activities.

HTML Hypertext Markup Language. Platform-independent language used for creating text and graphic pages on the Internet.

HTTP Hypertext Transfer Protocol. Protocol for data transmission between a web server and the web client.

IMG Implementation Guide. A tool for customer-specific adjustment of the SAP system. The Implementation Guide includes the following for each application component:

All steps for implementation of the SAP system:

▶ All default settings and all activities involved in configuring the SAP system

▶ The hierarchical structure of the IMG represents the structure of the SAP application components and lists all documentation relevant to the implementation of the SAP system.

Instance SAP instance. Administrative unit that combines the processes of an SAP system that provide one or more services.

The following services can be provided by an SAP instance:

▶ D: Dialog

▶ V: Update

▶ E: SAP Lock Management (Enqueue)

▶ B: Background Processing (Background)

▶ S: Print Processing (Spool)

▶ G: SAP Gateway

An SAP instance consists of a dispatcher and one or more work processes for every single service and a shared set of SAP buffers in the shared memory.

The dispatcher manages processing requests; work processes execute them. Every instance provides at least a dialog service and a gateway. Optionally, the dispatcher can also provide further services. However, there must be only one instance that provides the service of SAP lock management.

ITS Internet Transaction Server. Interface between the SAP system and a web server for the creation of dynamic HTML pages.

IT Service Management (ITSM) Framework for managing IT systems, which focuses on the quality of the services rendered to the customer.

Job Scheduling Management (JSM) A conceptual approach describing the entirety of methods, measures, tools, and responsibilities for optimal job management. Job Scheduling Management considers all aspects of a job execution: the job request (as a change to the system), job documentation and monitoring, and the automation and ongoing optimization of jobs.

Landscape Management Database (LMDB) Landscape database that has been implemented in SAP Solution Manager 7.1. It centrally represents all information of a system landscape.

Maintenance Optimizer (MOPZ) A scenario within SAP Solution Manager that guides you through planning, downloading, and implementing SAP Support Packages and patches and supports the installation and integration of Enhancement Packages in an upgrade for SAP products.

Manager of Managers (MoM) A CA Wily Introscope Enterprise Manager has limited capacities. Particularly in regards to large and complex landscapes, it is therefore common to use a MoM. Hence, already installed CA Wily Introscope Enterprise Managers can be added to the Manager of Managers as nodes.

Monitoring and Alerting Infrastructure (MAI) Infrastructure for technical monitoring and automated alerting of technical components in SAP Solution Manager.

Operating System (OS) Operating system of a server and computer unit. Management of resources and accesses to it.

Performance System performance, performance, or measurement of performance of an EDP system.

Plug-In Component Plug-in components are implemented as add-ons. They provide application-dependent functionality used by other components.

Pop-Up Window Screen window that is called up from a primary window and displayed in it.

Port Name for the channel via which the SAP system exchanges data with an external system.

POWL Generic design template that allows you to display a personal object work list (POWL) at runtime. POWL components are implemented using the `FPM_POWL_UIBB` Web Dynpro component (= POWL-UIBB).

Push Mechanism The remote components automatically send information to a central, processing instance. For this purpose, the Diagnostics Agent infrastructure exists in SAP Solution Manager. It transmits information to SAP Solution Manager in regular intervals.

Pull Mechanism In contrast to the push mechanism, information is requested by the processing instance and collected by the remote component.

RFC (Remote Function Call) RFC is an SAP interface protocol based on CPI-C. This significantly facilitates the programming of communication processes among systems. Using RFCs, it is possible to call and execute pre-defined functions on a remote system or within the same system. RFCs control the communication, pass on parameters, and do the troubleshooting.

SAP Central Process Scheduling (SAP CPS) by Redwood A software product integrated into SAP NetWeaver for job automation in heterogeneous landscapes. SAP CPS by Redwood maps and automatically executes complex job execution structures (job chains).

SAP GUI SAP Graphical User Interface. (→ Graphical User Interface).

SAProuter Software module that works as part of a firewall system and monitors and controls the network connection between your SAP network and the outside world (for example, SAP Net connection).

SAP Management Console (SAP MMC) Universal framework for centralized system management, monitoring, and control. The SAP Management Console is a Java applet that can be started from any web browser that supports Java. It can thus be used to manage remote systems without being locally installed beforehand.

SAP NetWeaver Business Client (NWBC) Desktop-based integration platform of SAP that can present a large diversity of applications.

SCS Instance SAP Central Services. AS Java instance of an SAP system that contains the Enqueue server and the message server. This instance exists in the Java cluster exactly once and can be made highly available (→ High Availability [HA]) as a single point of failure (SPOF).

Server The term *server* is ambiguous in an SAP environment and, therefore, should be used only when it is absolutely clear whether a logical unit (for example, an SAP instance) or a physical unit (for example, a computer) is meant.

SID SAP System Identifier. Placeholder for a three-digit name of an SAP system.

Simple Object Access Protocol (SOAP) Simple Object Access Protocol is an XML-based protocol for the exchange of information in a decentralized, distributed environment. The following elements are defined by a SOAP specification:

► A processing model for messages
► An envelope for exchanging XML documents
► Troubleshooting
► Using a transport protocol (for example, HTTP)
► An encryption schema for data types

Single Sign-On (SSO) Mechanism that allows users not to have to enter a password for each system they log on to. Single sign-on enables users to log on only once for all systems that are part of the SSO environment.

Support Package A collection of corrections for a defined release status of an SAP component.

System Landscape Concrete system constellation installed on the customer side. The system landscape describes the required systems, clients, their meaning, and transport paths for the implementation and maintenance process. Key methods and techniques are copying a client and the transport system. For example, the system landscape could consist of a development system, a testing system, a consolidation system, and a production system.

System Landscape Directory (SLD) Central infrastructure component collecting and managing the information on the applied systems and used versions, such as Support Package statuses, etc., and on the system landscape.

Transaction Code Sequence of alphanumeric characters that stands for a transaction in the SAP system.

Transaction Database transaction: operational unit on the database that meets the ACID principles.

URL Uniform Resource Locator. Address on the Internet.

XML eXtensible Markup Language. A specification of the W3C. XML is a light version of SGML specially designed for web documents. It allows for the generation of special tags to provide functions that cannot be implemented using HTML. For example, XML supports links to multiple documents, in contrast to HTML links, which can refer to only one document. XML has become the standard for data exchange. In an SAP environment, XML is used both for the data exchange with external systems and (since Basis Release 6.10) as the descriptive language in the configuration files for installation.

C   The Authors

Corina Weidmann has a degree in business informatics. After her studies, she joined SAP SI AG, Dresden as an SAP Service consultant in 2000. During this time, she gained extensive experience in analyzing and evaluating performance requests for SAP ERP and SAP SCM systems. She then specialized in technical monitoring in system operations, as well as business process monitoring using SAP Solution Manager in national and international projects on behalf of SAP AG. You can contact Corina Weidmann at *corina.weidmann@bautzen-it.de*.

Before **Liane Will** started dealing with SAP system administration and SAP Solution Manager, she worked in the areas of database consulting and support. Today, she is chief service architect in SAP AG's Active Global Support, where she heads a team for implementation and optimization of Application Lifecycle Management and technical operations based on SAP Solution Manager. She gathered the expertise required for this position in customer projects. Liane Will is also the author of the SAP PRESS book *SAP NetWeaver AS ABAP: System Administration* (2011). You can contact Liane Will at *liane.will@sap.com*.

Lars Teuber has been a consultant on SAP Basis topics at Bautzen IT. Group GmbH & Co. KG in Dresden since 2008. He has a degree in business informatics and data and information Technology. Since 2005, he has been supporting technical system monitoring projects and SAP Solution Manager implementation and upgrade projects. He gained his first experience with SAP Solution Manager's previous versions, 3.2 and 4.0. The main focus of his expertise is the worldwide consulting and optimization of Basis-side maintenance of SAP system landscapes. You can contact Lars Teuber at *Lars.Teuber@bautzen-it.de*.

Alexander Poplawski is a consultant at Bautzen IT.Group GmbH & Co. KG in Dresden. He completed his business informatics studies at the University of Applied Sciences Reutlingen with a Bachelor of Science degree. He gained his first experiences with SAP Solution Manager 7.0 and business process monitoring during his studies. Since 2010, he has been involved in numerous national and international projects as part of SAP Solution Manager implementations. Another key topic of his, apart from technical implementation of system monitoring and reporting tools, is the conceptual development of optimization approaches in technical operations of system landscapes.

Erik Dietzel works in SAP AG's Active Global Support. The emphasis of his expertise is on Basis-side operations of SAP system landscapes using SAP Solution Manager. After his studies, which he completed with a degree in business informatics, he gained valuable experience in the area of SAP performance analysis and optimization. Since 2006, he has been supporting SAP customers worldwide in implementation and upgrade projects of SAP Solution Manager. He also focuses on the SAP security authorization concepts, as well as technical system monitoring in SAP Solution Manager. He supports numerous customers in these areas.

Dr. Vital Anderhub studied Information Technology at Technische Universität Berlin. After his studies, he worked as a research associate at Humboldt-Universität in Berlin, where he received his PhD in economics. Since 2000, he has been Senior Support Consultant in SAP AG's Active Global Support. He has carried out system operations analyses for a number of notable SAP customers and designed the SAP training course "Systemadministration mit dem SAP Solution Manager" (system administration using SAP Solution Manager).

672

Max Dummer works at Bautzen IT.Group GmbH & Co. KG in Dresden and has a degree in business informatics. His main focus is on supporting customers in the areas of solution documentation, business process monitoring, and Application Lifecycle Management. He helps SAP customers worldwide with implementation and upgrade projects of SAP Solution Manager 7.0 and 7.1.

Axel Schulze has a degree in Business Informatics and is a consultant at Bautzen IT.Group GmbH & Co. KG. His main topics are solution documentation and implementation. In Template Management, he supports customers controlling global roll-out projects. He also provides worldwide consulting services to companies in creating documentation of their business processes and systems using SAP Solution Manager.

Dominique Noth works at SAP AG in Walldorf, Germany. He has a degree in business informatics. From 2006 to 2011, he was a consultant on various SAP Solution Manager projects. Since 2011, he has been responsible for the management dashboards of SAP Solution Manager. His responsibilities also include the ongoing development of management dashboards and the worldwide roll-out on our customers' sites.

Daniel Rudolph studied business informatics at Berufsakademie Dresden (University of Cooperative Education). Since 2011, he has been working as a consultant at Bautzen IT.Group GmbH & Co. KG. He supports national and international customers as a consultant and trainer for Basis work and authorization management using SAP Solution Manager. In this context, he supports customers particularly in planning and establishing authorization concepts.

Dr. Heinz-Ludwig Wolter received his PhD in physics at Technische Universität Hannover. Since 1989, he has been with SAP AG as a Senior Support Engineer in Active Global Support. Since 2001, he has been a consultant for SAP Solution Manager; SAP Education; and, on location, SAP Premium Engagement customers. His courses include the SAP courses "Ursachenanalyse mit dem SAP Solution Manager" (Root Cause Analysis using SAP Solution Manager) and "Change Control Management." He is responsible for the development and delivery of Expert Guides Implementation Services for the areas of Custom Code Management and Solution Manager Roadmap Design Service.

Florian Schmidt studied business informatics and has been working in the SAP environment since 2007. Since 2011, he has been a consultant for Bautzen IT.Group GmbH & Co. KG in Dresden. As such, he supports national and international customers in upgrade projects and implementing SAP Solution Manager. On the application level, his main topics are root cause analysis and system monitoring for various satellite systems.

Ferry Treuter has a degree in communication technology. Since 2005, he has been a consultant for SAP AG in various areas. He is experienced in integration and SAP system operations. In the first two years, he worked internationally in performance optimization for SAP ERP and SAP Enterprise Portal systems. Since 2008, his main areas of activity have been Application Lifecycle Management and consulting on integrating scenarios in SAP Solution Manager. His core topics are Job Scheduling Management, Data Volume Management, and business process monitoring. Apart from processes monitoring and the implementation of mentioned scenarios in international customers' system landscapes, Ferry Treuter works in Service Development and provides training.

Torsten Sternberg has degrees in economics and business and, in 2005, started his professional career at SAP Systems Integration AG in Dresden. There, he was responsible as a trainer and consultant on Service Desk and Change Request Management in national and international projects. Since 2008, Torsten Sternberg has been with Bautzen IT.Group GmbH & Co. KG, where his main topics are IT Service Management and Software Change Management. As a team lead, he is also responsible for organizing consulting services all around IT Service Management and Change Request Management. Otherwise, he is a project manager and trainer for these topics. You can contact Torsten Sternberg at *torsten.sternberg@bautzen-it.de*.

Thomas Hoefer works at Bautzen IT.Group GmbH & Co. KG in Dresden. He gained his first experiences with SAP Solution Manager during his activity at SAP Ltd. in Dublin, Ireland. Since 2012, he has been involved in numerous national and international projects as part of SAP Solution Manager implementations. Apart from technical implementation of system monitoring tools, his other key topic is the conceptual development of optimization approaches in technical operations of system landscapes.

Oliver Lutz has supported projects in the areas of SAP upgrades, Unicode conversions, and technical system monitoring, as well as various SAP Solution Manager monitoring projects, since 1997. Since 2002, he has been active as a freelancer in the SAP Basis environment. He already gained his first experience with SAP Solution Manager's previous versions 3.x and 4.0. His main fields of activity are worldwide analysis, consulting, and optimization of the SAP Basis system landscape. Otherwise, Oliver Lutz is a technical consultant developing Expert Guide Implementation training courses for SAP. You can contact Oliver Lutz at *ol@oliver-lutz.de*.

Erich Weirich has a degree in mathematics, and as a freelance technical consultant, he develops Expert Guide Implementation training courses for SAP. He has been active in the SAP Basis environment since 1994. He has been using SAP Solution Manager for technical monitoring of complex landscapes in a number of companies since release 3.2. Apart from the technical aspects, his main focus is on customized IT service management processes and project methodology. You can contact Erich Weirich at *erich.weirich@weirich-it-consulting.de*.

Index